THE BLOOMSBURY HANDBOOK TO J. M. COETZEE

THE BLOOMSBURY HANDBOOK TO J. M. COETZEE

Edited by Andrew van der Vlies and Lucy Valerie Graham

BLOOMSBURY ACADEMIC
LONDON • NEW YORK • OXFORD • NEW DELHI • SYDNEY

BLOOMSBURY ACADEMIC
Bloomsbury Publishing Plc
50 Bedford Square, London, WC1B 3DP, UK
1385 Broadway, New York, NY 10018, USA
29 Earlsfort Terrace, Dublin 2, Ireland

BLOOMSBURY, BLOOMSBURY ACADEMIC and the Diana logo are
trademarks of Bloomsbury Publishing Plc

First published in Great Britain 2023

Copyright © Andrew van der Vlies, Lucy Valerie Graham and contributors, 2023

The editors and contributors have asserted their right under the Copyright,
Designs and Patents Act, 1988, to be identified as Authors of this work.

For legal purposes the Acknowledgements in individual chapters throughout constitute an
extension of this copyright page.

Cover design: Rebecca Heselton
Cover image © Tim Robinson

All rights reserved. No part of this publication may be reproduced or transmitted in
any form or by any means, electronic or mechanical, including photocopying, recording, or
any information storage or retrieval system, without prior permission in writing from the publishers.

Bloomsbury Publishing Plc does not have any control over, or responsibility for, any third-party
websites referred to or in this book. All internet addresses given in this book were correct at the
time of going to press. The author and publisher regret any inconvenience caused if addresses have
changed or sites have ceased to exist, but can accept no responsibility for any such changes.

A catalogue record for this book is available from the British Library.

A catalog record for this book is available from the Library of Congress.

ISBN: HB: 978-1-3501-5204-5
       ePDF: 978-1-3501-5205-2
       eBook: 978-1-3501-5206-9

Series: Bloomsbury Handbooks

Typeset by Integra Software Services Pvt. Ltd.

To find out more about our authors and books visit www.bloomsbury.com
and sign up for our newsletters.

CONTENTS

Notes on Contributors … viii
Preface … xiii

PART ONE Life, institutions, reception

1 On the idea of a handbook to the works of J. M. Coetzee: 'Preposterous [?]' … 3
  Andrew van der Vlies and Lucy Valerie Graham

2 Life & times of J. M. Coetzee … 15
  Jane Poyner

3 Autobiographies/*autre*biographies/biographies … 29
  Alexandra Effe

4 J. M. Coetzee and his publishers … 43
  Andrea Thorpe

PART TWO Early Coetzee

5 Coetzee's poetry … 55
  Jarad Zimbler

6 *Dusklands* … 67
  Rita Barnard

7 *In the Heart of the Country* … 81
  Ian Glenn

8 *Waiting for the Barbarians* … 91
  Jennifer Wenzel

9 *Life & Times of Michael K* … 103
  Eckard Smuts

PART THREE Late and post-apartheid Coetzee

10 *Foe* … 115
   Patrick Flanery

11 *Age of Iron* Katherine Hallemeier	127
12 *The Master of Petersburg* Derek Attridge	137
13 *Disgrace* Chris Holmes	147
14 J. M. Coetzee's apartheid-era criticism Xiaoran Hu	159

PART FOUR Late-style Coetzee

15 The Costello project Andrew van der Vlies	169
16 *Diary of a Bad Year* Katarzyna Nowak-McNeice	181
17 The *Jesus* novels Timothy Bewes	191
18 Later criticism and correspondence Nick Mulgrew	207

PART FIVE Style, form, ideas

19 Coetzee's style Carrol Clarkson	221
20 Coetzee, religion and philosophy Alice Brittan	233
21 Coetzee, gender and sexuality Laura Wright	245
22 Coetzee and the nonhuman Daniel Williams	255
23 Coetzee, computers and binary thinking Rebecca Roach	267
24 Coetzee's humour Huw Marsh	275
25 Education and the novels of J. M. Coetzee Aparna Mishra Tarc	285

CONTENTS

PART SIX Contexts, intertexts, influence

26 Coetzee and the history of the novel 295
Andrew Dean

27 Coetzee's South Africans 305
Jan Steyn

28 Coetzee's modernists 317
Paul Sheehan

29 Coetzee's *Mitteleuropa* and Austro-Hungary 327
Russell Samolsky

30 Coetzee, Israel, Palestine 337
Louise Bethlehem, Dalia Abu-Sbitan and Shir Dannon

31 Coetzee's Russians 349
Jeanne-Marie Jackson

32 Coetzee's Latin America 359
Magalí Armillas-Tiseyra

33 Coetzee's Australians 373
Michelle Cahill

PART SEVEN Intermediation, adaptation, translation

34 Coetzee and photography 387
Hermann Wittenberg

35 Coetzee and the visual arts 397
Sean O'Toole

36 J. M. Coetzee and the work of music 407
Graham K. Riach

37 Adapting Coetzee for the stage and screen 415
Ed Charlton

38 Coetzee and translation 425
Jan Wilm

INDEX 435

CONTRIBUTORS

Dalia Abu-Sbitan is a PhD candidate at Université Sorbonne Nouvelle in Paris. She received her MA in English literature in 2022 from The Hebrew University of Jerusalem. Her doctoral research, funded by the French government (Campus France), investigates the genre of autofiction in contemporary French and American literature.

Magalí Armillas-Tiseyra is an Associate Professor in the Department of Comparative Literature at the Pennsylvania State University, specializing in Latin American and African literatures. She is the author of *The Dictator Novel: Writers and Politics in the Global South* (2019), as well as numerous essays and book chapters.

Derek Attridge has published books on South African literature, literary theory, poetic form and modern fiction. His publications on Coetzee include *J. M. Coetzee and the Ethics of Reading* (2004) and 'Reason and Its Others in Coetzee's "Jesus" Novels' (2021). He is Emeritus Professor at the University of York.

Rita Barnard is Professor of English at the University of Pennsylvania and Extraordinary Professor at the University of the Western Cape. Her recent publications include *South African Writing in Transition* (2019), *Trump, Zuma, and the Grounds of US-South African Comparison* (2021), and 'Reopening *Agaat*: Afrikaans, World Literature, and the Encyclopedic Novel' (2021).

Louise Bethlehem is Associate Professor in the Department of English and the Program in Cultural Studies at the Hebrew University of Jerusalem, and former PI of the European Research Council-funded project, APARTHEID-STOPS. She has written widely on South African literature, anti-apartheid expressive culture, African studies and cultural studies.

Timothy Bewes is Professor of English at Brown University. He is the author of several books including *Reification, or The Anxiety of Late Capitalism* (2002), *The Event of Postcolonial Shame* (2011), and most recently *Free Indirect: The Novel in a Postfictional Age* (2022).

Alice Brittan is Associate Professor of World Literature at Dalhousie University in Nova Scotia. She writes about contemporary fiction for both academic and general readers and is the author of a critical memoir titled *The Art of Astonishment: Reflections on Gifts and Grace* (2022).

Michelle Cahill is an Australian novelist and poet. Her short fiction *Letter to Pessoa* was awarded the NSW Premier's Literary Award for New Writing and shortlisted in the Steele Rudd Award. Her debut novel, *Daisy & Woolf,* is published by Hachette.

CONTRIBUTORS

Ed Charlton is Lecturer in Postcolonial Studies at Queen Mary University of London. He is the author of *Improvising Reconciliation: Confession after the Truth Commission* (2021) and is currently writing about visual, sonic and literary cultures in the global city.

Carrol Clarkson is Professor and Chair of the English Department at the University of the Western Cape. She has interdisciplinary research interests in language, literature, philosophy and the visual arts. Her books include *J. M. Coetzee: Countervoices* (2009) and *Drawing the Line: Toward an Aesthetics of Transitional Justice* (2014).

Shir Dannon holds an MA in Cultural Studies from the Hebrew University of Jerusalem and a BA in Hebrew Literature and Liberal Arts from Tel-Aviv University. Her research focuses on changes in media representations of femininity and masculinity over the twentieth century.

Andrew Dean is Lecturer in Writing and Literature at Deakin University, Victoria, Australia. His first academic book, *Metafiction and the Postwar Novel: Foes, Ghosts, and Faces in the Water*, was published in 2021.

Alexandra Effe is Postdoctoral Fellow at Oslo University, where she teaches anglophone and comparative literature. She is the author of *J. M. Coetzee and the Ethics of Narrative Transgression* (2017) and co-editor of *The Autofictional* (2022) and of a special issue of *Life Writing* on 'Autofiction, Emotions, and Humour'.

Patrick Flanery is Professor and Chair of Creative Writing at the University of Adelaide. A graduate of NYU and Oxford, he is the author of four novels, including *Absolution* (2012) and *I Am No One* (2016); a memoir, *The Ginger Child* (2019); and literary and film criticism.

Ian Glenn was Director of the Centre for Film and Media Studies at the University of Cape Town and is currently Research Fellow in Communications Sciences at the University of the Free State. His *Wildlife Documentaries in Southern Africa: From East to South* appeared in 2022.

Lucy Valerie Graham is Associate Professor in the English Department at the University of Johannesburg. She has a doctorate in English literature from the University of Oxford and is the author of numerous academic publications. She is co-editor of *The Bloomsbury Handbook to J. M. Coetzee*.

Katherine Hallemeier is Associate Professor of English at Oklahoma State University, where her research and teaching focus on anglophone postcolonial literatures. She is the author of *J. M. Coetzee and the Limits of Cosmopolitanism* (2013).

Chris Holmes is Associate Professor and Chair of Literatures in English at Ithaca College. His work has been published with *Novel, Modern Fiction Studies, Critique, Contemporary Literature, Literature Compass, Diaspora* and Oxford's *Research Encyclopedia*.

Xiaoran Hu is Associate Professor in British and World Literature in the School of Foreign Languages and Literature at Beijing Normal University. A graduate of Cambridge University and Queen Mary University of London, she has published on South African literatures in the *Journal of Commonwealth Literature*, *Textual Practice* and elsewhere.

Jeanne-Marie Jackson is Associate Professor at Johns Hopkins University. Author of *South African Literature's Russian Soul* (2015) and *The African Novel of Ideas* (2021), she works across Russian, Afrikaans, Shona and Anglo-Fante traditions, addressing questions of comparative method and interpretive scale in the framework of African literature and intellectual history.

Huw Marsh is Senior Lecturer in Twentieth and Twenty-First Century Literature at Queen Mary University of London. He is the author of *Beryl Bainbridge* (2014) and *The Comic Turn in Contemporary English Fiction: Who's Laughing Now?* (2020).

Nick Mulgrew was born in Durban in 1990. He writes novels, poetry and short fiction, and researches South African non-fiction and mining literature. Currently he is a PhD candidate at the University of Dundee, and the director of uHlanga, a poetry press. He lives in Edinburgh.

Katarzyna Nowak-McNeice is Adjunct Professor of English at the University of Wrocław, Poland. She is the editor and author of several monographs (most recently, *California and the Melancholic American Identity in Joan Didion's Novels*, 2020) as well as essays and chapters on American literature, critical posthumanities and gender studies.

Sean O'Toole is author of *Irma Stern: African in Europe – European in Africa* (2021) and *The Marquis of Mooikloof and Other Stories* (2006). He has edited three collections, including *The Journey: New Positions on African Photography* (2020). Recent curatorial projects include the exhibition *Photo book! Photo-book! Photobook!* (2022).

Jane Poyner is Associate Professor in English at the University of Exeter. Books include *J. M. Coetzee and the Paradox of Postcolonial Authorship* (2009), *The Worlding of the South African Novel: Spaces of Transition* (2020) and, as editor, *J. M. Coetzee and the Idea of the Public Intellectual* (2006).

Graham K. Riach is Lecturer in World Literature at Oxford University. While finishing one project – *The Short Story after Apartheid* – he is beginning another, called *Global Narratives of Ageing*. He has interests in South African Literature and the role of form and genre in postcolonial literature.

Rebecca Roach is Associate Professor in Contemporary Literature at the University of Birmingham. A scholar of contemporary literature and culture across the Anglophone world with an emphasis on the relationship between literature, media and book history, she is author of *Literature and the Rise of the Interview* (2018).

Russell Samolsky is Associate Professor of English at the University of California, Santa Barbara. He is the author of *Apocalyptic Futures: Marked Bodies and the Violence of the Text in Kafka, Conrad, and Coetzee* (2011), as well as a number of articles and book chapters on J. M. Coetzee.

CONTRIBUTORS

Paul Sheehan is Associate Professor in English at Macquarie University. Author of *Modernism, Narrative and Humanism* (2002) and *Modernism and the Aesthetics of Violence* (2013), he publishes and teaches in various areas of literature from the late nineteenth century to the present, particularly the changing cultures of modernism and postmodernism.

Eckard Smuts lectures in the Department of English at Stellenbosch University. After reading *Life & Times of Michael K* as an undergraduate student, he went on to write his PhD thesis on Coetzee. He has published numerous articles on the author, and more broadly in the field of the environmental humanities.

Jan Steyn is a scholar of contemporary world literatures in Afrikaans, English and French, with a particular focus on global literary circulation and translation theory. He is the current director of the MFA in Literary Translation at the University of Iowa.

Aparna Mishra Tarc is Associate Professor at the Faculty of Education, York University, Canada. She has published two monographs and several articles investigating the relation between person formation and literary education. Her recent book is entitled *Pedagogy in the Novels of J. M. Coetzee* (2020).

Andrea Thorpe is currently a postdoctoral research fellow at the University of Johannesburg. She holds a PhD from Queen Mary University of London and has published widely on South African literature. Her monograph, *South African London*, was published by Manchester University Press in 2021.

Andrew van der Vlies is Professor at the University of Adelaide and Extraordinary Professor at the University of the Western Cape. Books include *Present Imperfect: Contemporary South African Writing* (2017) and *South African Textual Cultures* (2007). He has contributed to or edited numerous volumes on South African writing and culture.

Jennifer Wenzel is a scholar of postcolonial theory and environmental humanities, jointly appointed in the Department of English and Comparative Literature and the Department of Middle Eastern, South Asian and African Studies at Columbia University. *The Disposition of Nature: Environmental Crisis and World Literature* was published in 2019.

Daniel Williams is Assistant Professor of Literature at Bard College. He has published on British and South African literature and the environmental humanities in venues including *ELH*, *Novel*, *Genre*, *Nineteenth-Century Literature* and *Safundi*. With Jeffrey Blevins, he co-edited 'Logic and Literary Form', a special issue of *Poetics Today* (2020).

Jan Wilm, PhD, is a writer and translator based in Germany. His books include *The Slow Philosophy of J. M. Coetzee* (2016), the novel *Winterjahrbuch* (2019), and the memoir *Ror.Wolf.Lesen.* (2022). With Patrick Hayes, he co-edited the collection *Beyond the Ancient Quarrel: Literature, Philosophy and J. M. Coetzee* (2017).

Hermann Wittenberg is Professor of English at the University of the Western Cape, South Africa. He is interested in the intersections of literature, film and photography, and co-curated the 'J. M. Coetzee: Photographs of Boyhood' exhibition, which was subsequently published as a book (2020). He previously edited Coetzee's *Two Screenplays* (2014).

Laura Wright is Professor of English at Western Carolina University. She specializes in postcolonial, ecocritical and animal studies; books include *Writing Out of All the Camps: J. M. Coetzee's Narratives of Displacement* (2006), *Wilderness into Civilized Shapes: Reading the Postcolonial Environment* (2010) and *The Vegan Studies Project* (2015).

Jarad Zimbler is Associate Professor of Modern English Literature at the University of Birmingham. He is author of *J. M. Coetzee and the Politics of Style* (2014) and editor of *The Cambridge Companion to J. M. Coetzee* (2020).

PREFACE

This project began in May 2017, when the editors were approached by David Avital to assemble a collection of essays on J. M. Coetzee. Originally planned as *A Companion to J. M. Coetzee*, it was decided in due course that it should appear in the Bloomsbury *Handbook* series, a new avenue for criticism in a range of fields. At thirty-eight chapters, *The Bloomsbury Handbook to J. M. Coetzee* is the most extensive collection of criticism yet on Coetzee, with the most diverse range of contributors, and from a wide range of locations – including Australia, Canada, China, Germany, Israel/Palestine, Norway, South Africa, the UK, the United States and Spain.

We are grateful to all our contributors for their professionalism in delivering such illuminating engagements with Coetzee's writing, contexts and influence, and especially for doing so despite the considerable disruptions caused to many of us by the Covid-19 pandemic. During the period in which we have worked on this collection, some contributors have moved institution or country, some have faced illness or bereavement. Indeed, both editors navigated significant translations themselves, one (Andrew van der Vlies) moving continents (from the UK to Australia), the other (Lucy Graham) from one side of South Africa to another (Cape Town to Johannesburg). That our *Bloomsbury Handbook to J. M. Coetzee* nonetheless rests in your hands, or appears on your screen, is in no small part due to the support offered by friends and colleagues, old and new, as well as the efforts of sterling research assistants Trisha May and Anna Douglass, who worked tirelessly to collate and format the manuscript for submission. The editors are grateful too to the University of Adelaide for its support, and to Ben Doyle, Laura Cope and their colleagues at Bloomsbury, for helping us see this project to completion.

Brief reference is made in two chapters in the collection to the most recent of Coetzee's works of fiction to be published, *The Pole*, which at this time has only appeared in Spanish translation. That this statement will very soon be outdated is testimony to the impossibility of any *Handbook* offering a complete picture of the work of a living writer, and especially one as suspicious of authority, as intellectually adventurous, as Coetzee. This volume is thus a provisional guide to the work to date, and will, we hope, provoke conversation, debate and elaboration.

Lucy Valerie Graham, Johannesburg, South Africa
Andrew van der Vlies, Adelaide, Australia

PART ONE

Life, institutions, reception

CHAPTER ONE

On the idea of a handbook to the works of J. M. Coetzee: 'Preposterous [?]'

ANDREW VAN DER VLIES AND LUCY VALERIE GRAHAM

If a prelude to a collection purporting to be a readers' companion to the work of *any* author is a difficult undertaking – *will it be up to date on publication? for how long afterwards? how comprehensive can one reasonably suggest the contents will be?* – initiating the reader into the idea of a *Handbook* to the work of J. M. Coetzee feels especially fraught. Indeed, it would be difficult to find another author whose writing warns the reader as repeatedly against searching for definitive interpretation or portrays so powerfully the fruitlessness of any search for a hermeneutic key. A reader might recall the scene in the opening pages of *The Childhood of Jesus* (2013), for example, in which there is some confusion about access to the room allocated to Simón and David, in a settlement for new arrivals in Novilla, a place where everyone appears to speak Spanish. 'Do you not have a – what do you call it? – a *llave universal* to open our room?', Simon asks. His interlocutor, Ana, responds that the term is '*Llave maestra*', master key. 'There is no such thing as a *llave universal*', she continues; '[i]f we had a *llave universal* all our troubles would be over'.[1] There are only ever local 'master' keys, and they are not always to hand.

Such admonitions to be wary of any desire for a universal explanation – or any position of final authority – recur throughout Coetzee's work. When the Magistrate in *Waiting for the Barbarians* (1980) is instructed by an agent of the state to interpret 'slips' found at an archaeological site, he offers various interpretations, noting that '[t]here is no agreement among scholars about how to interpret these relics of the ancient barbarians'.[2] In *Life & Times of Michael K*, a well-intentioned Medical Officer, seeking to understand the circumstances that have brought the eponymous protagonist into his orbit, can only interpolate his subject in terms that reflect his own desired answers. Similar processes of presumptuous speaking *for* recur in *Foe* (1986). Indeed, if the word 'guide' appears many times in the fiction, the promise of insight, direction or instruction promised is invariably disappointed, subverted or foreclosed upon. In *Disgrace* (1999), Lucy Lurie informs her father, David, dismissed from his position as a university lecturer for inappropriate conduct and seemingly unable to accommodate himself to his loss of authority, 'you are not the guide I need, not at this time'.[3] In *Age of Iron* (1990), the enigmatic Vercueil is an unreliable guide for the narrator, Mrs Curren, as she prepares to cross the threshold from life to death. Similarly, in *Diary of a Bad Year* (2007), a young Filipina named Anya becomes an unlikely chaperon for the man she calls Señor C, the distinguished author whose 'Strong Opinions' she is enlisted to prepare for publication and which she punctures with doses of irony, irreverence and common sense. In *Summertime* (2009), the authority of the author is rendered doubly ironic in an outrageously provocative – and entertaining – literalization of Roland Barthes's 'death of the author': we follow a biographer seeking in vain an edifying account of the life of the late 'J. M. Coetzee' from a series of bemused and disappointed acquaintances or lovers.

Coetzee's novels repeatedly suggest that *published* guides are *not* to be trusted either: the idea of a *handbook* is staged in *Disgrace*, via the novel's focalizer David Lurie, as instrumentalist to the point of being utterly ridiculous. Redeployed to teach a less academic subject than his training prepared him for, Lurie finds the accommodation frustrating: 'Although he devotes hours to his new discipline, he finds its premise, as enunciated in the Communications 101 handbook, preposterous'.[4]

*

The concept of a 'handbook' has, however, moved on in meaning since the late 1990s, when Coetzee was writing *Disgrace*. Rather than signifying a 'manual' on 'how to read', the Bloomsbury Handbooks series aims to offer 'state-of-the-art' research and 'cutting-edge perspectives',[5] presenting itself as a more adventurous – perhaps more avant-garde – complement to other collections of criticism on J. M. Coetzee, of which there are by now an impressive number. It is not contentious to describe this South African–born writer – novelist, academic, essayist and public intellectual – as one of the most celebrated living writers. Recipient of a host of awards and honours, not least the Nobel Prize for Literature in 2003, Coetzee has produced work that has attracted interest from scholars across a wide range of disciplines, from literary studies to philosophy, animal ethics and ecology to anthropology, gender studies and education.

Early readings of Coetzee's novels often cast them as allegorical, usually in the context of apartheid-era South Africa. Critics like Derek Attridge have argued 'against allegory' in approaching Coetzee's work, however, making the case that its meaning arises from engagements that are necessarily different with each reading. If allegory 'deals with the *already known*', Attridge argues, 'literature opens a space for the other' and 'Coetzee's novels and memoirs exemplify […] the value (but also the risk) of openness to the moment and to the future, of the perhaps and the wherever'.[6] Some critics argue that the oeuvre cannot be understood apart from the politics of the country in which Coetzee was born, while others cite the fiction as exemplary of 'World Literature' in the several understandings of that term developed over the past decades – writing that travels, appeals beyond context, or is born translated.[7] With the consolidation of Coetzee's expansive archive at the Harry Ransom Center at the University of Texas at Austin, in 2011, and in the wake of the publication of two biographies – the late J. C. Kannemeyer's authorized *J. M. Coetzee: A Life in Writing* (2013), and David's Attwell's account of influences and composition, *J. M. Coetzee and the Life of Writing: Face to Face with Time* (2015) – at least one branch of the field of Coetzee studies has taken yet another contextual and evidence-based turn.

In their introduction to the first significant multi-author companion to Coetzee's work, *Critical Perspectives on J. M. Coetzee* (1996), editors Graham Huggan and the poet Stephen Watson (then Coetzee's colleague at the University of Cape Town [UCT]) seem to confirm that there is no '*llave universal*' to understanding the work of Coetzee. Observing that Coetzee's 'international reputation' had at that time been consolidated 'by the many prestigious awards his novels have received' and that the study of his work was already a burgeoning field, they acknowledge that Coetzee's 'fictions seem almost deliberately constructed to escape any single framework of interpretation'.[8] Other early multi-author book collections that provided useful insights into Coetzee's contexts and hinted at the great range of critical responses to his work that would develop include a collection of essays edited by Jane Poyner, entitled *J. M. Coetzee and the Idea of the Public Intellectual* (2006), published in the wake of the Nobel Prize, and *J. M. Coetzee in Context and Theory*, edited by Elleke Boehmer, Robert Eaglestone and Katy Iddiols (2009), which grew from one of the many conferences on Coetzee's work that marked the first two decades of the new millennium. There have been a number of more focused edited book-length essay collections attending either to interdisciplinary concerns – for example Patrick Hayes and Jan Wilm's *Beyond the Ancient Quarrel: Literature, Philosophy, and J. M. Coetzee* (2017), or Sue Kossew and Melinda Harvey's *Reading Coetzee's Women* (2019) – or to the archive, which is the focus of Marc Farrant, Kai Easton, and Hermann Wittenberg's 2021 *J. M. Coetzee and the Archive: Fiction, Theory, and Autobiography*. As work on Coetzee has proliferated, so have collections become even more focused, as with the 2017 Bloomsbury collection of approaches to a single text, *The Childhood of Jesus*, edited by Anthony Uhlmann and Jennifer Rutherford.

There are to date two published self-declared 'companions' to Coetzee's oeuvre: *A Companion to the Works*, edited by Tim Mehigan (2011), and the *Cambridge Companion to J. M. Coetzee*, edited by Jarad Zimbler (2020). Mehigan's is a collection of fourteen chapters focused principally on Coetzee's novels (though there is a chapter on Coetzee's criticism), with limited attention to context and influence (except for a chapter on Coetzee and Beckett). The *Cambridge Companion*'s sixteen chapters are largely thematic in focus, and necessarily limited in scope. A volume on *Coetzee's Disgrace and Other Works*, edited by Laura Wright, Jane Poyner and Elleke Boehmer (2014) for the MLA's *Approaches to Teaching* series, might also be considered a companion volume: it contains an essay on materials and sources, along with twenty-three short essays, though as suggested by the title these reflect on approaches to *teaching*, and focus on a limited range of Coetzee texts, notably *Disgrace*, *The Lives of Animals*, *Foe*, *Age of Iron*, *Life & Times of Michael K* and *Waiting for the Barbarians*.

None of these volumes competes in amplitude or scope with the *Bloomsbury Handbook to J. M. Coetzee*, which follows in the footsteps of its antecedents but takes a syncretic approach that synthesizes the key insights of extant scholarship and seeks to pay attention to the whole range of Coetzee's life and works – as well as their afterlives – in a manner not attempted hitherto. Furthermore, while many of the same contributors appear in the three 'companion' volumes mentioned above, this *Handbook* draws together contributions from many more early- and mid-career scholars, from a wider range of disciplines, backgrounds and geographical locations.

The *Handbook* is arranged into seven parts: Part One collects engagements with the life, contexts and reception, while Two, Three and Four offer chapters on the published works (poetry, fiction, criticism) under the headings 'Early', 'Late- and Post-Apartheid' and 'Late-Style'. Parts Five, Six and Seven turn to questions of context, interpretation and mediation, under the headings 'Style, Form, Ideas', 'Contexts, Intertexts, Influence', and 'Intermediation, Adaptation, Translation'. Collectively, the thirty-eight chapters bring together insights by the most diverse cohort of scholars yet to be published in one collection on this author.

*

'If', Jane Poyner notes, 'Coetzee has successfully circumnavigated the celebrity status accorded twenty-first-century prize-winning novelists of his stature to ensure that his privacy remains protected, a surprising amount about his private life is available to those who care to look'.[9] In **Chapter 2**, 'Life & Times of J. M. Coetzee', Poyner offers an account of the outline of the author's life, addressing the apparent tensions between the prizewinning author-persona and the 'Autobiographical Self'. Attending, too, to the various contexts in which Coetzee has lived and worked – 'The Cape', 'London and the US', 'University of Cape Town' and 'Australia' – Poyner makes the argument that although Coetzee's work often 'deliberately unsettles borders between public and private spheres, his nonpositionality is not equivalent to sidestepping the political sphere, as some critics claim, but allows him to trouble orthodoxies of politics and power'.[10] Alexandra Effe's account, in **Chapter 3**, of autobiographical and biographical projects, adds to Poyner's analysis a close engagement with the three works of fictionalized memoir or *autre*biography Coetzee has published to date (*Boyhood*, *Youth* and *Summertime*, collectively *Scenes from Provincial Life*) to ask how this 'trilogy, as perhaps the most important and most intricate refraction of and source about Coetzee, enters into dialogue with other author personae – in novels, performances, critical essays, interviews, and archive – and with the work of Coetzee's biographers and critics'.[11] In **Chapter 4**, Andrea Thorpe looks outward to those publishers through whom Coetzee's work has reached its readers, using this as the basis for a complementary discussion of how three early works offer a useful critical lens through which to map the contours of Coetzee's later writing career.

The chapters of Part Two, 'Early Coetzee', contextualize Coetzee's early life as a writer and provide critical assessments of his first publications. They consider his experimental poetry, written in the 1960s and 1970s, and attend to each of the early novels, from *Dusklands* (1974) to *Life & Times of Michael K* (1983), which earned Coetzee his first Booker Prize. In **Chapter 5**, Jarad Zimbler offers the most complete account to date of Coetzee as poet, reminding us that even if he is 'not by reputation a poet. [….] his earliest writerly efforts were in verse. Indeed, until the appearance of *Dusklands* in 1974, [Coetzee's] body of published literary works consisted of twenty-four poems.'[12] Countering any impression (garnered, for example, from *Youth* or *Summertime*) that Coetzee *as poet* might have conformed to the stereotype of the 'sad, sober undergraduate, composing melancholy poems in isolation', Zimbler's research reveals a picture of 'a confident and promising young poet, a dedicated and sensitive critic of his peers, and an active participant in a localized but nonetheless vibrant print culture'.[13] Coetzee's first published prose fiction was a diptych of compelling and distressing narratives of depravity in very different temporal and regional locations. In **Chapter 6**, Rita Barnard offers a striking account of *Dusklands*' twin narratives, 'The Vietnam Project' and 'The Narrative of Jacobus Coetzee', that tests the assessment of Jonathan Crewe, critic and one of the book's first readers as Coetzee's university colleague, that *Dusklands* heralded the arrival of the modern novel in English in South Africa. Barnard discusses 'the usual modernist difficulties *Dusklands* entails – like fragmentation, an erudite range of allusions, and so forth', but pays particular and original attention to the ethical and aesthetic challenge of the book's 'relentless brutality'.[14] She concludes that *Dusklands* 'endures as the initial testing ground for some of the formal, ethical, and emotional difficulties that have rendered Coetzee one of the most challenging writers of our time'.[15]

Turning to *In the Heart of the Country* in **Chapter 7,** another of Coetzee's erstwhile UCT colleagues, Ian Glenn, reads 'Coetzee's literary and philosophical positioning *in* the novel' to argue that 'Coetzee made Magda a writer who acts as his alter ego and allows him to imagine a new beginning and new themes and concerns for South African writing.'[16] **Chapter 8** sees Jennifer Wenzel bring to bear her expertise as scholar of postcolonial millenarianism and the discontents of the Anthropocene to offer a new account of *Waiting for the Barbarians*, the novel that began to attract widespread attention to Coetzee's oeuvre in the United States and the UK, as a text that still 'resonates with the urgent challenges of the present, not least for its thematization of conflicting demands on our attention: an uneven contest between spectacular violence and more subtle processes that threaten the many worlds we know and love and do not want to leave'.[17] Finally, in **Chapter 9,** Eckard Smuts engages with Coetzee's dystopian representation of a (then) near-future South Africa during a civil war, *Life & Times of Michael K*, offering a survey of the novel's reception before proposing a novel way of approaching the text's particular challenges by 'rematerializing' its enigmatic central figure.[18]

The chapters in this volume's third part engage with Coetzee's career as an established writer, from the late-apartheid era through the early years of the post-apartheid settlement. In **Chapter 10,** novelist and critic Patrick Flanery assesses the intertextualities and possible allegories at the heart of *Foe*, placing Coetzee's fifth novel in conversation not only with Defoe's *Robinson Crusoe* and *Roxana*, as in extant criticism, but also lesser-known works by the eighteenth-century writer that offer ways of attending to *Foe*'s particular hauntological concerns, which are central – Flanery argues – to *Foe*'s exploration of 'the *limits* and *artifice* of realism, and the possibilities of a fiction that treats realism as a veil, a scrim of projections behind which the *real* action – of art's creation, the free-play of fiction in the field of its particular laws – occurs'.[19] In **Chapter 11,** Katherine Hallemeier offers a productively new way to read *Age of Iron*, testing the proposition that 'Coetzee's first realist novel is a gothic novel', or rather 'a meditation on how the self-centering metaphors of the gothic relentlessly delimit white perception, producing a reality that is stultified and stultifying', and following allusions to Nathaniel Hawthorne and Emily Dickinson, along with fascinating readings of the text's figuring of television.[20] In **Chapter 12,** one of the foremost contemporary critics and public intellectuals to have engaged with Coetzee's work, Derek Attridge (noted scholar too of Joyce, Derrida, and poetics) offers an illuminating account of Coetzee's 1994 fictional treatment of an episode from Dostoesvky's life, *The Master of Petersburg*. Teasing out a series of thematic threads (including mourning, guilt, falling, gambling and possession), and expanding on the novel's intertextual, biographical and historical contexts, Attridge makes the case for this being one of Coetzee's most subtle and sophisticated treatments of the relations among writing, ethics and betrayal.

Turning to what has perhaps been Coetzee's most controversial book, the 1999 novel *Disgrace* (the award to which of the Booker Prize made its author the first to win twice), Chris Holmes begins **Chapter 13** with a reminiscence of being berated by a colleague for teaching the text. 'Why, my colleague demanded, would anyone who cared about South Africa teach such a violently racist novel? What could possibly redeem a novel that planted a flag for afro-pessimism a mere five years after the transition to democracy in the country?'[21] Holmes attempts to answer the challenge in a thought-provoking analysis of *Disgrace* as 'a narrative machine for clearing intellectual space within the novel's South African imaginary'.[22] Finally, in **Chapter 14,** Xiaoran Hu offers an account of Coetzee's early criticism, from his collection *White Writing* (1988) to *Stranger Shores* (2001): this body of work, she writes, 'maps his global and comparative scope in thinking through the complex relationship between politics and literature during the apartheid era. It also directs readers to issues that will develop further after his departure from South Africa, both in his personal and intellectual life.'[23]

In the final part to address the breadth of the work in chronological fashion, Coetzee's 'Late-Style' is under discussion. Part Four begins with an account – in **Chapter 15**, by Andrew van der Vlies – of what one might call the author's 'Costello Project', constituted by all the texts featuring the fictitious Australian writer Elizabeth Costello, who appears in the fictions Coetzee began delivering in the mid-1990s in place of responding to invitations to speak by addressing audiences in his own voice; some appeared in various configurations as *The Lives of Animals* and *Elizabeth Costello*. Costello returned in the first of Coetzee's novels *set* in Australia, the Adelaide book *Slow Man* (2005). She is, Van der Vlies argues, 'a character whose outspoken forays into the realm of public-intellectual debate are [...] usefully regarded as Coetzee's working through, at arm's length, of a series of philosophical and aesthetic challenges' that include 'how to perform the barest modicum of realism without entirely breaking fiction's compact with the reader'.[24] The problem of realism, politics of voice and question of authority are explored repeatedly in all the late-style works, including *Diary of a Bad Year*, the subject of **Chapter 16** by Katarzyna Nowak-McNeice. As Nowak-McNeice argues, this novel's 'play with generic conventions corresponds to its rejection of a monolithic novelistic authority and enables an examination of the meaning and effects of various narrative modes, which suggests a re-evaluation of the nature of human subjectivity'.[25] The *Jesus* trilogy (*The Childhood of, The Schooldays of, The Death of*), which Tim Bewes discusses in **Chapter 17**, is another of the late-style works in which 'schemas of realist representation, allegory, figurative abstraction, exemplarity and (its complement) exceptionality – have been suspended'.[26] The writer and publisher Nick Mulgrew rounds off the section with an account of the later criticism, in **Chapter 18**.

Part Five presents the first set of essays that reflect on themes or questions of context relating to Coetzee's oeuvre as a whole. In this series of chapters, contributors offer a broad investigation of Coetzee's style, before considering a range of approaches to his work, and a canvassing of some of the most significant themes in relation to which it might be said to operate. In **Chapter 19**, Carrol Clarkson reads a selection of the author's critical essays alongside fiction to excavate 'the foundation for a philosophy of literary style'.[27] 'Through the conscious – and often metafictional – mobilization of the stylistic apparatus of a text', Clarkson argues, 'Coetzee raises ethical questions about the authority and answerability of the writer, troubles assumptions about the relation between fiction and autobiography, and [...] leads us to question received habits of thinking.'[28] Alice Brittan turns in **Chapter 20** to consider, with particular reference to *Life & Times of Michael K*, *Age of Iron*, *Disgrace*, *Slow Man*, and the *Jesus* novels, Coetzee's engagements with questions of belief, secular and otherwise. Addressing criticism's recent interest in postsecularism, Brittan demonstrates that Coetzee has long been interested in staging philosophically complex investigations of, *inter alia*, the limits of neighbourliness and the demands of alterity. In **Chapter 21**, Laura Wright considers how 'sex and sexuality', so often 'treated as problematic' in Coetzee's fictions, provide another lens through which to approach questions of reciprocity and alterity. Opening with *Disgrace*, Wright then turns to *Life & Times of Michael K* and *Foe*, 'narratives that are infused with scenes of disturbing, violent, and problematic sex'.[29]

Staying with Coetzee's treatment of concerns of ethical gravity, Daniel Williams, in **Chapter 22**, addresses how the 'nonhuman world has long constituted a fund of imaginative energy for J. M. Coetzee', by turns furnishing 'a repertoire of image and analogy', 'vehicle for philosophical rumination' and 'device[s] for decentring plot's human concerns'. Williams helpfully identifies four 'modes' through which Coetzee has treated the nonhuman across his career, and he insightfully labels these 'the Schreiner, Adorno, Rilke, and Dostoevsky modes', discussing them in turn in relation to select texts from the oeuvre.[30] Each mode presents a different set of strategies for challenging human-centred binary thinking, and in **Chapter 23**, Rebecca Roach looks back to Coetzee's early career as a computer programmer (treated in the fictionalized memoir *Youth*) to think about the long – and often unacknowledged – influence this has had on the writing. 'Across Coetzee's oeuvre', Roach contends, 'we find that literature – the vision of poets – promotes freedom from the troublesome binary thinking that computing fosters'.[31] Binary thinking is undone by humour, too, as any attentive reader of Coetzee's work will have noticed. For a writer so often represented in the media as dour, the fiction attests in fact to a writer – and man – for whom such characterization is likely a source of some (privately expressed) mirth. Huw Marsh considers Coetzee's treatment of humour in **Chapter 24**, invoking Beckett, Bergson, Freud and Sianne Ngai, to discuss the range of the comic in a selection of works including *Age of Iron, Youth, Boyhood*, and *The Childhood of Jesus*. The latter novel features prominently, too, in Aparna Mishra Tarc's discussion, in **Chapter 25**, of education in Coetzee's work. 'Numerous novels', Tarc writes, 'depict the historical and present pedagogical enactment of Western education that continues to take place in persistently colonial-style institutions'. Reading for the pedagogy reveals much, in other words, about the politics of the writing.[32]

Part Six turns to consider sources and influences, situating Coetzee's work in relation to the history of genre, as well as to literatures of particular regions that have been crucial to his work. In **Chapter 26**, Andrew Dean uses a series of moments in Coetzee's engagement with the novel to think about the author's particular experiments with the possibilities – and limitations – of the form. Dean takes, in turn, the history of the genre in South Africa (and in particular the model of the farm novel), 'the problem of endings' (negotiated in relation to the English novel of the eighteenth century, and Russian of the nineteenth) and the question of writing's materiality (considering Coetzee's relationship to Modernist progenitors) to structure an argument about what is 'at stake in each of these encounters': no less than 'issues central to literary thought', namely 'politics, aesthetics and value'.[33] In the chapters that follow, contributors take the measure of Coetzee's relationship with (and in some cases influence on) the writing of particular regions and/or periods (broadly construed[34]). Turning first to the literature of his native South Africa, Jan Steyn contends in **Chapter 27** that the writers from this canon with whom Coetzee has most conspicuously engaged (*inter alia* Olive Schreiner, Nadine Gordimer, Breyten Breytenbach) 'are not simply a national subset of Coetzee's literary influences' but instead 'often represent an obligation or constraint – they are those antecedents and peers to whom he *must* respond, and who are themselves responding to a shared history and landscape, albeit from varied perspectives and with diverse purposes'.[35] Paul Sheehan argues in **Chapter 28** that 'Coetzee's own writing practice has furthered the development of a robust and demanding late-modernist poetics within the canons of world literature', and assesses the influence on Coetzee's work of key Modernists Franz Kafka and Samuel Beckett, in particular, both with 'distinct transnational identities' that mirror Coetzee's own.[36] In **Chapter 29**, Russell Samolsky asks us to consider the fact that Kafka, along with other writers to whose work

Coetzee has not infrequently turned (Musil, Kleist, Hölderlin, Rilke, amongst others), hails from *Mitteleuropa* and often, with a striking frequency, from the territories at one time or another within the Austro-Hungarian Empire. '[I]it is only a slight exaggeration to playfully claim that all of Middle Europe went into the making of Coetzee's novels', Samolsky remarks, though this has been a process of 'creative inversion or revision or reimagining', rather than 'straightforward or literal carrying across'.[37]

No such straightforward carrying across is in evidence – literally and in the other direction – in the case of the translation of Coetzee's work in that complicated space that inherits some of the discontents of *Mitteleuropa*'s nineteenth- and twentieth-century politics, Israel-Palestine. **Chapter 30** features a groundbreaking collaboration between Louise Bethlehem (one of the key commentators on South Africa's literature of the late- and immediately post-apartheid period) and scholars Dalia Abu-Sbitan and Shir Dannon. On the basis of sources in English, Arabic and Hebrew, the three offer an assessment of Coetzee's engagements with the politics of this part of the Middle East (book-ended by his acceptance of the Jerusalem Prize in 1987, and his appearance at the Palestine Festival of Literature in Ramallah in 2016), and of the complex afterlives of his work in Hebrew translation. *In the Heart of the Country, Waiting for the Barbarians, Life & Times of Michael K, Foe,* and *Disgrace* have all been translated into Hebrew, and elicited considerable debate in Israel – not least in relation to the usefulness or otherwise of analogies for the occupation of Palestinian territories offered by apartheid South Africa. Analogies of a different kind are explored in Jeanne-Marie Jackson's discussion of Coetzee's long-term 'affinity for Russia's so-called "Golden Age" of nineteenth-century literature' – chiefly Turgenev, Tolstoy and Dostoevsky (the latter most famously developed in *The Master of Petersburg*) – in **Chapter 31**. If the condition of the serfs in pre-emancipation Russia offers an imperfect analogy for apartheid-era South Africa's treatment of its Black majority, the model of the writer of conscience's exploration of complicity proved productive. Jackson argues in conclusion that 'Coetzee turns to Russian writers to elaborate a vision of self-awareness as self-entrapment – and thereby also enforces a more controversial, continuous reading of Russian history, spanning its imperial and Soviet periods'.[38]

Turning to regions that have been enormously significant for Coetzee in later life, the final chapters of this section look to zones of the South that have come to structure the oeuvre in profound and critically under-examined ways. In **Chapter 32**, the comparative literature scholar Magalí Armillas-Tiseyra considers Coetzee's entanglement with Latin America, through his relationship with publishers in Argentina (for whom he has edited a series of texts collected as his 'Biblioteca personal' or Personal Library, and who have published some of his own work in Spanish translation *before* its publication in English), and through the imaginative spaces the continent has provided for the later work. Finally, in a creative-critical experiment (**Chapter 33**) that is by turns enlightening and profoundly moving, the Australian novelist, short-story writer and poet Michelle Cahill writes about her own fictionalized autobiographical persona's engagement with the work of Coetzee understood as an Australian writer. At one point, before a roadtrip,

> J. M. Coetzee's 'Australian' novels are carefully placed in a wide, shallow box about 4 inches high, with handles, two neat piles with *The Death of Jesus* at the top of one pile, and *Diary of A Bad Year* at the top of the other. The label on the box reads 'Fresh Australian Produce.'[39]

Tasked with writing on 'Coetzee's Australians', Cahill's writing self is keenly aware of her own positionality: 'Surely I must proceed carefully, as a woman author and poet, as a writer of colour, as an immigrant Australian, one who is scarcely herself representative of Australians.'[40] Moving in ways that would seem counter-intuitive within a white-dominated literary scene, she examines Coetzee's relationship, through his writing, to indigenous peoples, and to his support of refugees such as Behrouz Boochani, a Kurdish-Iranian journalist long detained in the notorious offshore Australian refugee camp on Manus Island, who 'kept a cell phone hidden in his mattress, typing his autobiographical account by text messages that were sent to a collaborator outside the gulag'.[41]

In the final section of this *Handbook*, contributors address aspects of the processes by which Coetzee's work draws on or engages with other arts, media and forms of expression, and has in turn been mediated – adapted, responded to, revisioned. In **Chapter 34**, Hermann Wittenberg, foremost scholar of Coetzee's engagement with photography and film (editor of two unproduced screenplays by Coetzee and author of a forthcoming monograph on Coetzee, photography and film), considers Coetzee's relationship to the still and moving photographic image. While scholars have attended to 'photographic moments in the fictions, as well as the influence of specific images on the genesis of particular novels', Wittenberg writes, 'images [...] also shape the style of narration'; 'significant moments in Coetzee's writing derive their force from the suggested presence of a camera lens where a photographic and cinematic visuality shapes narration and point of view'.[42] Many other 'optical devices, lens metaphors, light effects and camera analogies' are in evidence in the work.[43] Wittenberg draws out several in relation to two of the fictions of the middle period – *Michael K* and *Foe* – to suggest useful ways of approaching the oeuvre overall.

Noted South African art critic and writer Sean O'Toole offers a complementary account of Coetzee's career-long engagement with the visual arts more broadly in **Chapter 35**. Noting Coetzee's 'consistent interest in images and visuality, both in his fiction and nonfiction writing', O'Toole remarks on the 'silence around Coetzee's art writing' in extant scholarship, and offers the reader a way of engaging with a body of work he characterizes as sharing 'a hardness and durability that proposes a way of looking at images, of being in the world with them; also, of finding an adequate language and form to make images palpable, legible, intelligible, on the page, but also in the eye and ear of the mind'.[44] Graham Riach turns to consider the aural in greater detail in **Chapter 36**, describing in an accessible yet sophisticated analysis how Coetzee's writing engages with music. Frequently, Riach observes, descriptions of music are 'less concerned with describing features of particular pieces, and more with what happens to us when we hear music'; 'by describing aesthetic experience, while framing it in variously ironized narratives', he concludes, 'Coetzee creates an unstable state in which drastic proximity and gnostic distance become fused'.[45]

If Coetzee's fictions have not lent themselves to popular film adaptation in quite the same manner as (for instance) Cormac McCarthy, it is certainly not the case that they have not engendered multiple adaptations for screen *and* stage, from dance pieces to opera (most significantly, a setting of *Waiting for the Barbarians* by Philip Glass). In **Chapter 37**, Ed Charlton offers the reader a survey of film and television adaptations to date (including of *The Lives of Animals, Disgrace, In the Heart of the Country*, and *Barbarians*), before discussing a range of other interpretations and intermedial translations and offering an up-to-date assessment of the theoretical vocabularies with which we might understand them. Turning to textual translations in the final contribution to our volume, **Chapter 38**, the German scholar, writer, editor and translator Jan Wilm assesses the range and impact of the many translations of Coetzee's writing, as well as the 'various thematic and aesthetic engagements with translation' evident across the oeuvre. Indeed, Wilm argues, *translation* has been 'central' to Coetzee's career, 'to his hermeneutic interests, his international reputation and canonization, and to his narrative cosmos'.[46]

In the preface to the first significant multi-author companion to Coetzee's work mentioned above, *Critical Perspectives on J. M. Coetzee* (1996), edited by Huggan and Watson, the eminent South African novelist Nadine Gordimer (recent recipient of the Nobel Prize herself) sought to contest the label under which she had been invited to contribute to the volume. 'It might be better to call this an anti-preface rather than a preface', she wrote, noting that she was on the same side as Coetzee in relation to the critics, and suggesting that while writers might 'agree that for the health of literature' 'there must be a canon of criticism', on the question of 'how it functions I don't believe we are sure or don't care to enquire'.[47] Gordimer's comments, while doubtless somewhat tongue-in-cheek, are useful for us here in a preamble to a collection of essays by critics (with only few exceptions) on a writer of fiction (although also of criticism!). 'That a critique is firstly a dialogue between critic and critic is clear in this collection,' Gordimer continued, 'where the pollen of an insight garnered from Coetzee's work is blown through the pages of scholarly journals to fertilize a second generation of insights or mutations in contradiction'.[48] *The Bloomsbury Handbook to J. M. Coetzee* bears witness to long-term 'pollination' and the ongoing 'fertilization' of the critical field, but at the same time it aims to take seriously Gordimer's statements as *writer*:

> There is a space round a literary work that can't be filled by explication. Neither yours nor mine. It is a private space for the writer and the reader. The best thing about a collection of criticism is that it should send us, the readers, back to the works themselves.[49]

Her observations make it unlikely that *this* will be the *last* handbook, companion or collection of essays presuming to offer a guide to Coetzee's oeuvre. We also hope that *The Bloomsbury Handbook to J. M. Coetzee* sends readers back to the works themselves, as one hopes they will continue to accrete for years to come.

NOTES

1. Coetzee, *Childhood of Jesus*, 5.
2. Coetzee, *Waiting for the Barbarians*, 122.
3. Coetzee, *Disgrace*, 161.
4. Ibid., 3.
5. Bloomsbury, online.
6. See Attridge, *J. M. Coetzee and the Ethics of Reading*, 64.
7. See Damrosch, 'Introduction', 1–5; Moretti, 'Conjectures on World Literature'; Walkowitz, *Born Translated*, especially 'Introduction: Theory of World Literature Now', 1–48.
8. Huggan and Watson, 'Introduction', 1.
9. Poyner, Chapter 2 (this volume), 25.
10. Ibid.

11. Effe, Chapter 3 (this volume), 30.
12. Zimbler, Chapter 5 (this volume), 55.
13. Ibid., 57.
14. Barnard, Chapter 6 (this volume), 68.
15. Ibid., 77.
16. Glenn, Chapter 7 (this volume), 81.
17. Wenzel, Chapter 8 (this volume), 98.
18. Smuts, Chapter 9 (this volume), 104.
19. Flanery, Chapter 10 (this volume), 120.
20. Hallemeier, Chapter 11 (this volume), 127.
21. Holmes, Chapter 13 (this volume), 147.
22. Ibid., 150.
23. Hu, Chapter 14 (this volume), 165.
24. Van der Vlies, Chapter 15 (this volume), 169.
25. Nowak-McNeice, Chapter 16 (this volume), 181.
26. Bewes, Chapter 17 (this volume), 192.
27. Clarkson, Chapter 19 (this volume), 222.
28. Ibid.
29. Wright, Chapter 21 (this volume), 245.
30. Williams, Chapter 22 (this volume), 255.
31. Roach, Chapter 23 (this volume), 272.
32. Tarc, Chapter 25 (this volume), 285.
33. Dean, Chapter 26 (this volume), 295.
34. This is not the place to enter into a description of definitional debates about 'Modernism'.
35. Steyn, Chapter 27 (this volume), 305.
36. Sheehan, Chapter 28 (this volume), 323, 320.
37. Samolsky, Chapter 29 (this volume), 334.
38. Jackson, Chapter 31 (this volume), 350, 349.
39. Cahil, Chapter 33 (this volume), 378.
40. Ibid.
41. Ibid., 379.
42. Wittenberg, Chapter 34 (this volume), 387.
43. Ibid.
44. O'Toole, Chapter 35 (this volume), 397, 403.
45. Riach, Chapter 36 (this volume), 408.
46. Wilm, Chapter 38 (this volume), 425.
47. Gordimer, 'Preface', vii.
48. Ibid.
49. Ibid., xi.

WORKS CITED

Attridge, Derek. *J. M. Coetzee and the Ethics of Reading: Literature in the Event*. Chicago: University of Chicago Press, 2004.
Attwell, David. *J. M. Coetzee and the Life of Writing: Face to Face with Time*. Oxford: Oxford University Press, 2015.
Bloomsbury Academic. *Bloomsbury Handbooks*. https://www.bloomsbury.com/ca/series/bloomsbury-handbooks/?Page=2.
Boehmer, Elleke, Robert Eaglestone, and Katy Iddiols, eds. *J. M. Coetzee in Context and Theory*. London: Continuum, 2009.
Coetzee, J. M. *Age of Iron*. London: Secker & Warburg, 1990.
Coetzee, J. M. *The Childhood of Jesus*. 2013. London: Vintage, 2014.
Coetzee, J. M. *Diary of a Bad Year*. London: Harvill Secker, 2007.
Coetzee, J. M. *Disgrace*. London: Secker & Warburg, 1999.
Coetzee, J. M. *Foe: A Novel*. London: Secker & Warburg, 1986.
Coetzee, J. M. *Life & Times of Michael K*. London: Secker & Warburg, 1983.
Coetzee, J. M. *Summertime*. London: Harvill Secker, 2009.
Coetzee, J. M. *Waiting for the Barbarians*. London: Secker & Warburg, 1980.
Damrosch, David. 'Introduction'. In *World Literature in Theory*, edited by David Damrosch, 1–11. Chichester: John Wiley, 2014.
Farrant, Marc, Kai Easton, and Hermann Wittenberg, eds. *J. M. Coetzee and the Archive: Fiction, Theory, and Autobiography*. London: Bloomsbury Academic, 2021.
Gordimer, Nadine. 'Preface'. In *Critical Perspectives on J. M. Coetzee*, edited by Graham Huggan and Stephen Watson, vii–xii. Houndmills: Macmillan, 1996.
Hayes, Patrick and Jan Wilm, eds. *Beyond the Ancient Quarrel: Literature, Philosophy, and J. M. Coetzee*. Oxford: Oxford University Press, 2017.
Huggan, Graham, and Stephen Watson. 'Introduction'. In *Critical Perspectives on J. M. Coetzee*, edited by Graham Huggan, and Stephen Watson, 1–12. Houndmills: Macmillan, 1996.
Kannemeyer, J. C. *J. M. Coetzee: A Life in Writing*. Translated by Michiel Heyns. Johannesburg: Jonathan Ball, 2013.
Kossew, Sue, and Melinda Harvey, eds. *Reading Coetzee's Women*. Basel: Springer [Palgrave Macmillan], 2019.
Mehigan, Tim. 'Introduction'. In *A Companion to the Works of J. M. Coetzee*, edited by Tim Mehigan, 1–8. 2011. Rochester, NY: Camden House, 2013.
Moretti, Franco. 'Conjectures on World Literature'. *New Left Review* 1 (January–February 2000): 54–68.
Poyner, Jane, ed. *J. M. Coetzee and the Idea of the Public Intellectual*. Athens, OH: Ohio University Press, 2006.
Uhlmann, Anthony and Jennifer Rutherford, eds. *J. M. Coetzee's* The Childhood of Jesus: *The Ethics of Ideas and Things*. London: Bloomsbury Academic, 2017.
Walkowitz, Rebecca L. *Born Translated: The Contemporary Novel in an Age of World Literature*. New York: Columbia University Press, 2015.
Wright, Laura, Elleke Boehmer, and Jane Poyner, eds. *Approaches to Teaching Coetzee's* Disgrace *and Other Works*. New York: Modern Language Association of America, 2014.
Zimber, Jarad, ed. *The Cambridge Companion to J. M. Coetzee*. Cambridge: Cambridge University Press, 2020.

CHAPTER TWO

Life & times of J. M. Coetzee

JANE POYNER

THE NOBEL PRIZE AND THE AUTOBIOGRAPHICAL SELF

Picture the scene: the expectant hum as J. M. Coetzee stood marionette-like at the lectern, preparing to deliver his much-anticipated Nobel lecture. It was 7 December 2003, and in three days' time, he would be awarded the Nobel Prize in Literature – the pinnacle of any writer's career. No doubt the assembled guests were hoping for a real literary treat: nuggets about the distinguished literary life of a writer known to resist such outings and who notoriously did not show up to either of his two Booker Prize ceremonies, in 1983 for *Life & Times of Michael K* and in 1999 for *Disgrace*. Following the 1999 Booker announcement, Coetzee commented that '[c]elebrity status is something I have managed to dodge quite successfully all my life'.[1]

Instead of a lecture offered in his own voice, the Nobel lecture, entitled 'He and His Man', returned Coetzee to Daniel Defoe's *Robinson Crusoe* (1719), a narrative that has fascinated Coetzee from childhood and to which many of his fictions allude. *Foe* is explicitly a rewriting of Defoe's best-known work, yet the Robinsonade permeates his oeuvre. In Coetzee's second published book, the novel *In the Heart of the Country* (1977), for instance, the existentially isolated Magda reflects, '[w]e are castaways of God as we are castaways of history'.[2] In Coetzee's notebooks in the Harry Ransom Center (HRC) at the University of Texas in Austin, where Coetzee studied from 1965–9 for his PhD (a stylistic analysis of Samuel Beckett's fiction), he describes a period in the early 1970s when he felt 'unpolitical' and 'more detached'. He identified with Crusoe's sense of existential isolation when he confided his 'resigned bewilderment about [the] place one finds oneself in. Am I in the opening of [Beckett's] *Molloy*? Or on the other hand is this *Robinson Crusoe* I am in?'[3]

Aside from the sense of isolation and isolationism indexed by the Robinsonade motif, Coetzee has also been fascinated by its unsettling of the author function. In his introduction to the 1999 World Classics edition of *Robinson Crusoe*, Coetzee writes that Defoe's novels are 'fake autobiographies' bearing a 'personal and even confessional level of meaning'. He wonders what game Defoe is playing when he claims that Crusoe is a 'living person': 'what, beyond maintaining the by now *tired autobiographical charade*, might he mean?'[4] This question might be applied to Coetzee's work, too, not only to 'He and His Man', but also to *Scenes of Provincial Life*, the trilogy of *autre*biographies – *Boyhood* (1997), *Youth* (2002), *Summertime* (2009) – collected in a single volume in 2012. In his 1985 essay 'Confession and Double Thoughts', developed from his inaugural professorial lecture, 'Truth in Autobiography', given at the University of Cape Town (UCT) in 1984, Coetzee reflects on truth-telling in the confessional writing of Dostoevsky, Tolstoy and Rousseau.[5] His insights may resonate with a reader trying to make sense of a writer who famously has said that '[a]ll autobiography is storytelling, all writing is autobiography'.[6] In an interview with Joanna Scott, Coetzee distinguishes between lived experience and its retelling: *Boyhood* portrays 'the childhood *I have constructed for myself in retrospect*.'[7] This is the difference between autobiography and *autre*biography, which registers the plasticity of identity as it is shaped and reshaped in writing.[8]

The HRC archives, which David Attwell describes as 'remarkably complete,'[9] are fascinating terrain for the Coetzee scholar, giving insights into the life of a writer drawn apparently reluctantly into the public sphere. They include Coetzee's meticulously kept notebooks charting the genesis of the novels and memoirs, as well as the manuscripts from *Dusklands* to *Elizabeth Costello* (after that Coetzee worked with computer printouts), and private correspondence, for instance, with writer friends and colleagues, publishers, universities, visa offices. Yet rather than treat the archives as hard evidence, Jan Wilm argues, they might also constitute a 'counter-oeuvre' that will not readily 'provide answers to the novels', nor indeed to the writer's life.[10] Andrew Dean, too, probes the relationship between the archives and the oeuvre: 'the very excessiveness of Coetzee's self-archiving suggests that … they serve some independent function for him.'[11]

Coetzee has participated in only two biographies, neither authorized.[12] The more recent is Attwell's *J. M. Coetzee and the Life of Writing: Face-to-Face with Time* (2015), an account of five weeks spent in the HRC archives that proved 'both unsettling and illuminating' (xviii). Attwell also edited *Doubling the Point*, a collection of Coetzee's *Essays and Interviews* (1992), which Attwell describes as Coetzee's 'intellectual autobiography' and which includes a set of interviews (conducted in writing) in which Attwell probes Coetzee's critical thinking as a scholar and intellectual.[13] The heftier *J. M. Coetzee: A Life in Writing* (2012) by Afrikaans-language literary historian J. C. Kannemeyer, translated by Michiel Heyns, was completed after Kannemeyer's death in 2011, with Attwell's participation.[14] Elleke Boehmer notes its 'monumentalist' qualities, and Kannemeyer's endeavour to set Coetzee on a 'national pedestal', claiming him as an Afrikaner writer. Yet 'both [biographies] approach the question of how the *autre*fiction, or "everything [Coetzee] writes", has written him', Boehmer suggests.[15] Both volumes grapple to different degrees with the extent to which the memoirs correlate with Coetzee's life. It is to the story of that life that I turn now.

THE CAPE

John Maxwell Coetzee was born in Cape Town in 1940 to parents Jack (Zacharias) Coetzee, an attorney of Afrikaner heritage, and Vera, née Wehmeyer, a schoolteacher whose parents were from the Uniondale district of the Cape. Born in the United States, Coetzee's maternal grandmother Louisa was the daughter of German-speaking missionaries originating from an area of what is now Poland. She had nurtured 'a strong dislike of Afrikaners', gave her children English names and raised them speaking English.[16] Coetzee's maternal grandfather, Piet Wehmeyer, by contrast, was a founder of the National Party.[17] Coetzee and Vera lived an 'exceptionally nomadic existence' at this time, moving between Cape Town's suburbs, the Northern and Western Cape, and Johannesburg.[18] Family fortunes tracked the vicissitudes of Jack's career: he was struck off the roll of practising attorneys on two occasions for mishandling trust funds, which necessitated relocating the family and temporary career changes, and precipitated Jack's alcoholism.

Coetzee's birth came eight years before the National Party's 1948 election victory and the introduction of apartheid (Afrikaans for 'separateness'). But South Africa was already an egregiously unequal, racially divided society with a long, complex history of racial discrimination and segregation.[19] The archives, interviews and (increasingly fictionalized) memoirs reveal Coetzee's sense of liminality, positioned somewhere in the gap between two supposedly distinct white South African cultures, English and Afrikaner: between the mores, the language, the literatures and the mythologies pertaining to each. Dependent on boundary-making, as in all nationalist mythologies, such categories are far more porous and complex in terms of ethnicity, heritage and ideological loyalties than they are made to appear by those claiming a stake in them. Attwell writes about the greater flexibility, pre-apartheid, between Afrikaners identifying as culturally English and those as culturally Afrikaner, marked by differing allegiances to place, language and religious denomination.[20]

Often portrayed in the criticism as an outsider, Coetzee's relationship to the Afrikaans language and to (white) Afrikanerdom is a source of critical debate. He describes becoming part of that contingency of South Africans who 'have joined a pool of no recognizable ethnos whose language of exchange is English'.[21] As a child, he spoke mostly English at home, describing 'com[ing] from a mixed background; mixed in various ways', and, 'though we really only spoke English at home, very often we were speaking Afrikaans in our public life.'[22] His maternal grandmother, Louisa, 'favoured English' over Afrikaans,[23] and his father, an Afrikaans speaker whose parents were 'Afrikaans-speaking anglophiles',[24] was posted overseas during the Second World War, from 1942 to 1945, meaning Afrikaans was further displaced at home. Whilst 'Afrikaans', Coetzee comments, is a 'purely linguistic term' with 'linguistic and cultural overtones', 'Afrikaner' bears 'quite heavy political and ideological content'.[25] In *Doubling the Point*, Coetzee explains, the term has 'since the 1880s [...] been a word hijacked by a political movement, first primarily anti-British, later primarily antiblack, calling itself Afrikaner Nationalism'.[26] Rita Barnard argues that Coetzee quite deliberately 'translates' – or mistranslates – his Afrikaner identity through his writing. In *Boyhood*, she suggests, Coetzee turned his back on the Afrikaner man he could have become in order to self-fashion himself as 'cosmopolitan writer and intellectual'; this was a 'subject position *consciously* refused'.[27] Yet after the Nobel, when he was asked in an email by historian Hermann Giliomee if it was true, as the Afrikaans press was claiming, that he was an Afrikaner, Coetzee replied: 'If they want me, they can have me.'[28] This raises the question, why did Coetzee allow Kannemeyer, an Afrikaans-literature specialist, to write a biography, and one in Afrikaans? Reflecting on the influences on Coetzee of 'Afrikaans-language literature', Andrew van der Vlies notes that interest in Coetzee's oeuvre as world literature has tended to obscure this indebtedness to or conversations with Afrikaans literary traditions that have been inaccessible to wider audiences because of their 'minor' status.[29]

If language is central to Coetzee's cultural identity, so too was his early identification with the land. *Boyhood* grapples with John's conflicted attachment to the rugged landscape of the semi-desert Karoo, and to Voëlfontein, his paternal grandfather's farm, where John holidayed. In South Africa, this attachment is always already racialized, though in *Boyhood* this is largely implied, as the book only makes fleeting reference to the politics of which John is as yet dimly aware – the 1948 elections and the 'Nats' victory over the United Party; Black people being represented at the bottom of the racial hierarchy, which John readily assimilates as truth.[30] In *White Writing: On the Culture of Letters in South Africa* (1988), Coetzee addresses both European and Afrikaner mythologies of the land. Analysing the work of early European travellers to the Cape including nineteenth-century natural historian William Burchell, Coetzee notes that 'the European eye will be disappointed in Africa only as long as it seeks in African landscapes European tones and shades.'³¹ The Afrikaans-language *plaasroman*, or farm novel, props up the myth of the (white) Afrikaner founding fathers, reifying in the process the *volk*'s supposed natural right to the land. Such mythologizing, as Barnard shows, not only supports a 'history of settlement' but masks 'one of *displacement*' of South Africa's Black and indigenous peoples.³² In Coetzee's anti-farm novels, *In the Heart of the Country*, *Life & Times of Michael K* (1983) and *Disgrace* (1999), identity is refracted through a historically fraught relation to the land, figured in a tension between an imagined, longed-for pastoral idyll, and a landscape with which this idyll does not correspond and to which each protagonist must learn to accustom themselves in order to survive. Coetzee's rewritings thus expose the fraught relationship between the idea of land ownership and settler colonialism. His engagement with the politics of land reveals the gestation of an intellect ahead of its time, conscious of the ideological inflections of the farm; as he writes of the young John in *Boyhood*, '[t]he secret and sacred word that binds him to the farm is *belong*' (95–6), and yet '[t]he farm is not his home; he will never be more than a guest, an uneasy guest' (79).

Coetzee describes the formative role reading played in his development in a 2018 lecture entitled 'Growing Up with *The Children's Encyclopedia*', which he calls 'an essay in autobiography, specifically, an essay on [his] formation, between the ages of about 3 and 10, under the influence of reading and re-reading' this ten-volume series. He comes to the realization, 'aged about 10', that its editor, Arthur Mee, did not, when preparing the *Encyclopedia*, have children like him, those living on the cultural peripheries of Europe, in sub-Saharan Africa, in mind. In *Boyhood*, John turns to the *Encyclopaedia* as a kind of life manual, but it only serves to alienate him further. 'Childhood is a time of innocent joy, to be spent amongst the meadows amid buttercups and bunny-rabbits or at the hearthside absorbed in a storybook,' John reads. Yet this 'is a vision of childhood utterly alien to him[;]' in reality, childhood is nothing 'but a time of gritting the teeth and enduring' (14). John is not happy at school, which provides nothing more than 'a shrunken little world, a more or less benign prison' (139).

LONDON AND THE UNITED STATES

In the intervening years between his schooling and an interlude in London, Coetzee studied at UCT, receiving a Bachelor of Arts with Honours in English in 1960, and a Bachelor of Arts with Honours in Mathematics in 1961. 1955 had presented a formative moment in his intellectual development when he overheard Bach's *Wohltemperierte Klavier* issuing from his neighbour's house, an experience he describes in 'What is a Classic?', the title a nod to T. S. Eliot's essay, later anthologized in *Stranger Shores: Literary Essays, 1986–1999* (2001). Coetzee reflects on Eliot's essay as 'one of the most spectacular that occur to me of a writer attempting to make a new identity'.³³

In 1962, Coetzee moved to London. Back home in South Africa, this was the year of the arrest of Walter Sisulu, Nelson Mandela and other leaders of Umkhonto we Sizwe (isiZulu for 'Spear of the Nation'), the armed wing of the African National Congress (ANC). It was a mere two years after the Sharpeville massacre in which police had shot dead sixty-nine people peacefully protesting the notorious Pass Laws, seriously injuring a further 180. Whilst *Youth* does not explicitly mention the 1964 Rivonia trial at which Mandela and others were sentenced, John does comment on Sharpeville from London, and reflects on the tightening of the Pass Laws 'to which Africans and Africans alone are subjected': 'In the Transvaal the police fire shots into a crowd, then, in their mad way, go on firing into the backs of fleeing men, women and children' (37). It seems for John as if the move to London has ushered in a more mature consciousness, one less oblivious of the 'turmoil' of South Africa, yet he still seems determined to escape it. He tries his hand at writing a short story but is unsettled that 'he is still writing about South Africa': 'He would prefer to leave his South African self behind as he left South Africa itself behind' (62). Implicitly eliding language with ideology, John is conscious that, in the UK, '[s]peaking Afrikaans […] is like speaking Nazi', yet when his cousin visits him in London their use of Afrikaans feels like 'sliding into a warm bath' (127).

In London, Coetzee worked as a computer programmer for IBM and then ICT, its UK competitor from 1964. But he discovered that ICT, through the Cambridge Mathematical Laboratory, had links to the nuclear arms industry at Aldermaston. As this realization dawns on him in *Youth*, John believes 'he has lent himself to evil' (164). At ICT, John meets a fellow programmer from India, who sows the idea of relocating to the States, saying that '[w]e are all wasting our time' in the UK (151). *Youth* does not detail Coetzee's brief return to Cape Town in 1963 to finish his MA thesis, nor his re-acquaintance with student friend, Philippa Jubber, whom he would marry that year in Johannesburg. At this time, Coetzee began making enquiries about studying for a PhD at institutions in the United States, eventually settling upon the University of Texas at Austin, where he enrolled with a Fulbright Scholarship. Relocating to Austin with Philippa in 1966, they soon welcomed their first child, Nicholas, and, two years later, Gisela, yet neither Philippa nor the children appear in *Youth* or *Summertime*.

It was at Austin that Coetzee stumbled across Beckett's manuscripts, and this led to work on a stylistic analysis of Beckett's fiction for his PhD, finished in 1969. The same year, before completion, Coetzee took an assistant professorship in English at the State University of New York at Buffalo. There he began work on *Dusklands*, which he has described, as 'a product of the passionate politics of 1965–71'.[34] During the later 1960s, the United States was embroiled in the Vietnam War, with students at universities across the country protesting the conflict. *Dusklands*' two distinct narratives capture two forms of nationalist mythology: 'The Vietnam Project' portrays the propaganda machine of the US state during the war, whilst 'The Narrative of Jacobus Coetzee' depicts the partially fictionalized sojourns of Afrikaner Jacobus Coetzee in eighteenth-century South Africa. In 1969, with his visa due to expire, Coetzee enquired about gaining permanent residency in the United States and expressed being fearful about the effects on his children, who were US citizens, of exposure 'to the racial climate of the Republic of South Africa', including segregation in schools.[35] He also claimed that the South African government would categorize him a communist for his belief in universal suffrage, and that he was thus at risk of being banned (having restrictions placed on one's movement, association and speech). Coetzee's application and initial appeal were turned down.

Events took a dramatic turn when, on 15 March 1970, Coetzee and forty-four fellow academics were arrested for participating in a sit-in at the university, protesting the acting President's handling of campus protests. While all were found on appeal not guilty of criminal contempt and unlawful entry, the initial conviction was disastrous for Coetzee's family as it led to him being denied a re-entry visa to the US.[36] Coetzee returned reluctantly to South Africa in 1971, and, though he held numerous visiting professorships in the United States and made many overseas visits in the ensuing years, he did not leave South Africa on a permanent basis until his emigration to Australia in 2002.

UNIVERSITY OF CAPE TOWN

On his return to South Africa from the United States and after a brief period living in a remote farmhouse in the Karoo, Coetzee took up a position as a lecturer in English at UCT, from 1972. After several promotions, he was appointed Professor of General Literature in 1984. It was at UCT that he would write some of his best-known works, establishing a local and subsequently international reputation, both as a novelist and essayist. In 1980 he divorced Philippa, who moved to Johannesburg, while Coetzee raised their young children in Cape Town. Remaining on friendly terms with Philippa until her death from cancer in 1990, Coetzee would begin a relationship with Dorothy Driver, who subsequently taught in the English Department at UCT, becoming one of the country's leading authorities on women's literature and literary feminism in southern Africa. It was with Driver that Coetzee forged a new life in Australia from 2002.

Coetzee initially tried to get 'The Narrative of Jacobus Coetzee' published separately, but it was rejected by international publishers. In a 1994 lecture he explained that he presented it as a 'companion piece' because it did not really work on its own. The full manuscript of the book was also rejected by local and international publishers, until Ravan Press agreed to publish it.[37] Leading Afrikaans novelist André Brink praised it as 'an inescapable statement about South Africa and the world today',[38] but if *Dusklands* received mixed reviews and *In the Heart of the Country*, though greeted enthusiastically, reached only a small readership, *Waiting for the Barbarians* secured Coetzee's international reputation, winning three major awards: South Africa's CNA Prize, and, in the UK, both the James Tait Black and the Geoffrey Faber Memorial Prizes. Some South African critics were frustrated with the novel's apparently indeterminate, seemingly universalized setting, but it was quickly accepted for publication by Secker in the UK, with Tom Rosenthal describing it as 'a novel of quite devastating power'.[39]

Coetzee had returned to South Africa at a time when local protests and resistance to apartheid were gathering momentum. In the 1970s Black Consciousness was gaining traction under the leadership of student activist Steve Biko and an effective boycott movement against apartheid was underway internationally. In 1976 dissent mounted amongst school and college children in Soweto, a township complex south of Johannesburg, at Afrikaans being imposed as the language of instruction in schools, culminating in an uprising in June. Police opened fire on student protestors, killing more than 600, and precipitating a wave of departures of young leaders into exile as well as a new phase of violent resistance to apartheid inside South Africa. The archives reveal that the torture scenes in *Waiting for the Barbarians* were drawn from reports of the 1977 murder of Biko in police custody that emerged during a public inquest into his death, and in Coetzee's 1986 essay, 'Into the Dark Chamber: The Writer and the South African State', the author himself describes *Barbarians* as 'a novel about the impact of the torture chamber on the life of a man of conscience'.[40] Coetzee writes in notebooks from the period: 'I must make … the inspiration of the story by the Biko affair, clear. End it with a massive trial scene in which the accusers get put in the dock.'[41] The trial of Joll never takes place, but the Magistrate repeatedly invokes the law in his defence against Empire, a regime that, like late-apartheid South Africa's, is beginning to implode, hence the title's allusion to Constantine Cavafy's 1902 poem of the same name, which Coetzee possibly encountered via South African writer Mike Nichols's post-Soweto, 'After Cavafy', published in the late 1970s.

As with *In the Heart of the Country*, *Barbarians* was submitted to the Directorate of Publications, South Africa's censorship body, but eventually adjudged, in the Directorate's turn of phrase, 'not undesirable'. *Dusklands* had eluded the censors altogether.[42] Archival material reveals the circuitous lengths to which Coetzee and his publishers (Ravan Press in Johannesburg, and Secker & Warburg in the UK) went to have his work passed by the censors. As Van der Vlies describes, Coetzee wrote to Secker to ask if they would cede South African rights to Ravan to *In the Heart of the Country* (1976) if the British edition were to be banned in South Africa.[43] Coetzee suggested to Ravan's Randall blanking out three of the numbered passages in the novel most likely to give offence, including one in which the Black servant, Hendrik, apparently rapes Magda. Coetzee proposed that Ravan should publish a bilingual edition, with dialogue – as Coetzee had intended – in Afrikaans. *In the Heart of the Country*, *Waiting for the Barbarians* and *Life & Times of Michael K* were all assessed by the censors, and editions arriving in the country from abroad placed under embargo until this process was completed. But none received what Coetzee described in a 1990 interview as the 'badge of honour' censorship bestows. 'This honour,' Coetzee declared, 'I have never achieved nor, to be frank, merited.' The apartheid censors conceded there were elements in each book that could be deemed 'undesirable', especially references to inter-racial sex, which violated codes on 'indecent or obscene or offensive or harmful to public morals,' and critiqued the architecture of apartheid. All were passed either because they were not set in present-day South Africa, or were regarded as too universalizing to warrant concern.[44]

While *Dusklands* was in press, Coetzee was busy in 1973 with an 'unrealized' novel on censorship, 'The Burning of the Books'. He was unconvinced by the sense of place in the manuscript, however, feeling it lacked clear shape and plot.[45] In what might come as a shock to some contemporary readers, Coetzee's letters reveal that in 1974 he applied, unsuccessfully, to become a censor. In much later correspondence with Peter D. McDonald, Coetzee claimed he did so to play the censors at their own game, but Attwell is 'not entirely convince[d]' by this explanation, hypothesizing instead that working as a censor might get the unfinished novel off the ground. In 1981, Coetzee agreed to the Directorate's request to evaluate William Burroughs's novel *Cities of the Red Night* (1981), and recommended it as 'not undesirable'.[46]

The notebooks also record Coetzee's sense of personal hurt resulting from Gordimer's caustic 1984 review of *Life & Times of Michael K* that had received much scholarly attention. Whilst admiring of the novel's style, Gordimer was scathing of its failure to register Black agency in sustained, organized efforts to resist apartheid. Attwell records that 'two decades later Coetzee still felt the smart of this criticism, ... noting ... that Gordimer had accused him of lacking political courage.'[47] Coetzee commented that his 'fidelity is ultimately to [Mrs. Curren and Michael K] and for their unique plights, not to any grand historical trajectory they may be seen as belonging to'.[48] Then, in 1987, Coetzee delivered a talk, 'The Novel Today', at the *Weekly Mail* Book Week at the Baxter Theatre in Cape Town, in which he reflected on the ways fiction can engage critically with – the word he chooses is 'rivals' – the *discourse* of history, rather than simply append, or 'supplement', history.[49] Was this a riposte to Gordimer? The following year, in 1988, he and Gordimer were again apparently at loggerheads, this time over an invitation extended to Salman Rushdie to attend the same literary festival, organized by the *Weekly Mail* with the Congress of South African Writers (COSAW). Rushdie's controversial *The Satanic Verses* had appeared earlier that year, attracting protests from Muslim countries, organizations and communities for its representation of the

Prophet Mohammed and the Qur'an, which many regarded as blasphemous. Rushdie was to be the 'star' guest at the festival, again at UCT's Baxter Theatre, themed 'Censorship under the State of Emergency'. The programme invoked Heinrich Heine: 'Wherever they burn books, they will also in the end burn people.'[50]

COSAW decided to withdraw the invitation to Rushdie to protect him and avoid civil unrest, but also to avoid offending the local Muslim community. At the festival Coetzee declared his wish to 'register publicly my protest against the silencing of Mr Rushdie's voice', and condemned religious fundamentalism in all its forms.[51] A member of COSAW reported that Gordimer was looking 'shell-shocked'[52] by Coetzee's attack on the organization, of which she was a member.[53] Coetzee later conceded that Gordimer and COSAW had probably been right and there followed a friendly exchange between the two that contradicts accounts of a 'bitter' feud fanned by the local press.[54] As Van der Vlies records, the letters show that, in Gordimer's words, she 'resented very much' that the spat had been exaggerated. She goes on: 'It wasn't so. But what can one do with journalists when they want to invent a good story? … They're not going to make enemies out of us, believe me.' The letter is signed 'Affectionately', and Coetzee's response a few months letter closes 'with warmest affection', and the commendation that Gordimer, if ever she doubted herself for losing touch with fellow whites, has 'travelled so much farther down the [intellectual] road' than them. Shortly after the event, in 1989, Iran's Ayatollah Khomeini imposed a *fatwā* on Rushdie.[55]

Comments on writers' groups in a 2019 interview with McDonald prove revealing on Coetzee's politics. In the interview, he distances himself both from the largely white, liberal PEN South Africa, established in 1927, and the more radical COSAW, established in 1987. Whilst the former was 'too Anglo and too tame' – it presented itself as 'guardian of polite literature'[56] – 'COSAW conceived of itself as an arm of the Struggle', and, Coetzee said, 'I was not part of the Struggle.'[57] Yet from 2006 he served as Vice President of PEN International, an organization proactive in defending writers' freedom internationally. In 1996, the same year in which state censorship officially ended in South Africa, Coetzee published *Giving Offense: Essays on Censorship*, perhaps not surprisingly, given his own engagement with the censors, claiming that 'the polemics of writers against censors seldom do the profession credit'.[58] In an essay on Renaissance humanist Desiderius Erasmus, first published in 1992, Coetzee grapples with the role of the intellectual in the authoritarian state who risks becoming the state's rivalrous 'twin', being absorbed within the same imaginative economy. For Coetzee, as for Erasmus, carving a meticulous position of '*non*position' is the only effective means of standing outside the state's regime of terror.[59]

Whilst South Africa was progressing through a period of tumultuous political change, Coetzee's private life was riven by loss. Within a five-year period, from 1985 to 1990, his mother, father, son Nicholas and ex-wife Philippa all died. Nicholas' death at the age of twenty-three in 1989 was especially tragic: he had fallen eleven floors from his Johannesburg apartment in what appears to have been an accident. This personal tragedy is evoked in Coetzee's 1994 novel *The Master of Petersburg*, a book that raises issues of self-censorship by reimagining the suppressed 'At Tihons' chapter from Dostoevsky's *The Possessed*. In Coetzee's reworking, Dostoevsky's son Pavel falls to his death from a tower.

Bagging a second Booker Prize in 1999, his first post-apartheid novel *Disgrace* confirmed Coetzee's position as one of the world's most influential contemporary writers. *Disgrace* is set in Cape Town and the Eastern Cape in mid- to late 1997, in the immediate present of the 'new South Africa'. (The novel provides certain hints at the dating of the story, for example, that Lurie is fifty-two and was born in 1945.[60]) Texturing this novel are allusions to current affairs: the Truth and Reconciliation Commission (TRC), land reform and redistribution, South Africa's catastrophic levels of sexual violence, and, globally, the rationalization of higher education. Rewriting the *plaasroman*, it casts a backwards glance at the historico-ideological inflections of the land, whilst signalling a sense of resignation at the lack of substantial systemic change upon which the foundations of the fragile new democracy are laid.

The notebooks reveal that the TRC hearings provided the contextual canvas upon which the story of Lurie's sexual misconduct case was painted,[61] even though Coetzee had begun drafting *Disgrace* before the Commission was inaugurated. The notebooks dispel well-circulated myths, too, such as that Coetzee's move to Australia in 2002 was a consequence of the negative local reception of *Disgrace*.[62] Coetzee and his partner Driver made regular trips to the country in the 1990s, and in 1995 Coetzee contacted the immigration office in Canberra.[63] (He secured Australian citizenship in 2006.) In 2000, *Disgrace* featured in an ANC submission to the South African Human Rights Commission Inquiry into Racism in the Media, for illustrating the persistence of racism within South Africa. But there has been critical division on the ANC's use of *Disgrace* as a case study. Attwell argues that the ANC was treading a careful line between avoiding accusing Coetzee of racism, whilst showing how the book reflected prevailing attitudes amongst whites;[64] in the same issue of *Interventions*, McDonald suggests that ANC praised the novel (albeit ambivalently) for reflecting upon common racial stereotypes.[65]

Nonetheless, five years later, the ANC government paid tribute to Coetzee by awarding him the Order of Mapungubwe in Gold for 'putting South Africa on the world stage'.[66] By now he was holding regular visiting professorships in the United States, including with the Committee on Social Thought at the University of Chicago (1998–2003), with which he had built a close working relationship. He terminated this relationship in 2003, in his words in a 2004 letter to his Serbian translator, because of the 'political setup' in the United States under George W. Bush. Coetzee had previously voiced his concern at the infringement of human rights by the United States during this period when it was advancing its 'war on terror'. Bush, Tony Blair and Australia's John Howard would all be critiqued in the 'Strong Opinions' section of *Diary of a Bad Year* (2006), through another surrogate writer-persona referred to only as 'J.C.'

AUSTRALIA

One might have expected that a new life of semi-retirement in Adelaide, South Australia, from 2002, as a research fellow at the University of Adelaide, would usher in a quieter period for Coetzee. It has certainly provided opportunities for him to pursue his love of cycling and walking. Of Australia, he has described feeling 'a strong pull toward the land and the landscape' and found Adelaide in particular 'very attractive, very civilized, with a strong artistic community'. His commitment to animal rights led to an invitation to become President of the UK RSPCA, but he turned this request down.[67] Similarly, on occasion he turned down honorary positions and invitations to speak. But Coetzee continues to make regular appearances at conferences and seminars both in his new country of residence, and elsewhere. In his eightieth year, 2020, his work was celebrated formally at the University of Adelaide and Amazwi, the South African Museum of Literature in Makhanda, Eastern Cape.

A shift in style and location was signalled from the 1990s with the series of Elizabeth Costello lectures Coetzee first delivered at venues around the world. Some are fictions about Costello, a (fictional) aging and opinionated Australian novelist; others embed within fictional narratives the lectures Costello delivers – on animal rights, representing evil and so on. These were republished as 'lessons' in the novel *Elizabeth Costello* in 2003. Some reviewers were unforgiving about Coetzee's increasing literary abstruseness. Justin Cartwright describes the apparent use of Costello as a mouthpiece as 'something of a cop-out', while Hermione Lee wondered whether 'this difficult and unforgiving book' signalled Coetzee was on the brink of giving up fiction writing 'to focus on the philosophical essay instead'.[68] Adam Mars-Jones asks whether Coetzee was 'simply hamstrung by the hybrid status of his inventions'.[69]

Slow Man (2005) was Coetzee's first Antipodean novel proper and begins with the aftermath of a cycling accident – in Adelaide – in which the protagonist, Paul Rayment, is disabled. We follow his interactions with his carer, a Croatian migrant, and her son. Costello makes an unlikely appearance as an ironic guardian angel. *Diary of a Bad Year* (2007), highly self-referential and experimental, is set in Sydney. Rebecca Walkowitz argues this novel 'imitate[es] the visual format of interlineal and facing-page translation' by offsetting the 'Strong Opinions' of an elderly, South African–born writer referred to only as J. C., with his everyday thoughts, and with his amanuensis Anya's commentary, in distinct narrative strands arranged in bands across each page.[70]

In 2009, Coetzee published the third of his *autre*biographies, *Summertime*, which takes us up to the point in John's life at which the writing of *Dusklands* began.[71] The memoir's truth contract with the reader is stretched here to its limit because the noted novelist character John Coetzee dies before its present occasion of narrative begins. *Summertime* turns on the conceit of five transcribed and edited interviews, as Walkowitz argues, collected by a fictional biographer, Mr Vincent, 'of which at least two and possibly three have been translated into English'. The text is book-ended by extracts from the late author's notebooks, detailing events that dovetail very neatly with what is known about Coetzee's own life in this period.

The Jesus trilogy is Coetzee's latest series. *The Childhood of Jesus* (2013), *The Schooldays of Jesus* (2016) and *The Death of Jesus* (2020) present a Kafkaesque world curiously detached, not unlike *Waiting for the Barbarians*, from any identifiable geopolitical locale. Walkowitz reads the first of the series (though the analysis seems useful for all three) as a work that 'emphasize[s] Coetzee's focus on the novel's elasticity as a genre, its history as a medium of national collectivity, and its function, in translation, as a source of collectivities both smaller and larger than the nation'.[72]

It is clear from this brief account that Coetzee's life of writing, including his archives, is in part characterized by the ways in which he stretches genres, confirming that this life of writing and the story of his life and times do not neatly correspond. Certain questions, Barnard argues, drive the Nobel lecture, the memoirs and his essay on Dutch writer Achterberg: 'Is the distance [between author and character] constant? [I]s the notion of identity it embodies more complex and fluid?'[73] These underpin the later works too, probing in self-conscious ways the relationship between the author and (auto)biographical self, or character. In turn, under the guise of the *autre*biographical conceit, this has helped Coetzee to protect his private life and avoid being easily positioned politically, instead enabling his meticulously crafted nonposition. Yet Coetzee's reputation within South Africa (during the years of apartheid and then transition to democracy) of resisting being publicly known, one that relentlessly still clings to his public persona in media accounts today, does not ring true.

If his writing deliberately unsettles borders between public and private spheres, his nonpositionality is not equivalent to sidestepping the political sphere, as some critics claim, but allows him to trouble orthodoxies of politics and power. If Coetzee has successfully circumnavigated the celebrity status accorded twenty-first-century prize-winning novelists of his stature to ensure that his privacy remains protected, a surprising amount about his private life is available to those who care to look.

NOTES

1. *Irish Times*, 'Author Shuns Limelight'.
2. Coetzee, *In the Heart of the Country*, 134; 147.
3. Quoted with original formatting in Attwell, *J. M. Coetzee*, 82.
4. Emphasis added; Coetzee, 'Introduction', v–xi, vi.
5. This essay is collected in Coetzee, *Doubling the Point*, 251–93.
6. Coetzee, *Doubling the Point*, 391.
7. Emphasis added; Joanna Scott, 'Voice', 83.
8. Cf. Alexandra Effe in this volume.
9. Attwell, *J. M. Coetzee*, xix.
10. Wilm, 'J. M. Coetzee and the Archive,' 216.
11. Dean, 'Lives and Archives', 224.
12. Attwell suggests Coetzee would not authorize *any* biography (*J. M. Coetzee*, xxii), though he did collaborate in one way or another with the Kannemeyer and Attwell volumes. Another, by Lily Saint, is in progress.
13. Attwell, 'Editor's Introduction', 2.
14. Cf. Effe's chapter in this volume for a discussion of the biographies.
15. Boehmer, 'Reading Between Life and Work', 441–2; 447.
16. Attwell, *J. M. Coetzee*, 13.
17. Kannemeyer, *J. M. Coetzee*, 29. The National Party emerged as the leading white Afrikaner-nationalist entity in the 1930s, and came to power in the 1948 elections that foreshadowed the introduction of their formal *apartheid* legislative programme.
18. Kannemeyer, *J. M. Coetzee*, 34–6.
19. For an account of early racial segregation in South Africa, see Dubrow, *Racial Segregation and the Origins of Apartheid in South Africa, 1919–36*; for an account of the specificities of the South African apartheid, see Posel, 'The Apartheid Project, 1948–70.'
20. Attwell, *J. M. Coetzee*, 14.
21. Coetzee, *Doubling the Point*, 342.
22. Wachtel, 'J. M. Coetzee'.
23. Kannemeyer, *J. M. Coetzee*, 29.
24. Attwell, *J. M. Coetzee*, 12.
25. Wachtel, 'J. M. Coetzee'.
26. Coetzee, *Doubling the Point*, 342.
27. Barnard, 'Coetzee in/and Afrikaans,' 85–7, emphasis added.
28. Kannemeyer, *J. M. Coetzee*, 557.

29. Van der Vlies, 'World Literature', 4–5.
30. Coetzee, *Boyhood*, 65–6. Further references parenthetical.
31. Coetzee, *White Writing*, 39.
32. Barnard, *Apartheid and Beyond*, 32.
33. Coetzee, *Stranger Shores*, 7.
34. Qtd. in Attwell, *J. M. Coetzee*, 82.
35. Kannemeyer, *J. M. Coetzee*, 188–9.
36. Ibid., 195; 201.
37. Ibid., 235–7.
38. Ibid., 251.
39. Ibid., 344. On *Waiting*'s South African reception see Watson, 'Colonialism,' 376–7.
40. Coetzee, *Doubling*, 363.
41. Quoted in Attwell, *J. M. Coetzee*, 93.
42. For an account of Coetzee's work and the censors, see McDonald, *The Literature Police*, 303–20.
43. For a detailed account of the complex publishing history of *In the Heart of the Country*, including this discussion about the local and self-censored versions, see Van der Vlies, *South African Textual Cultures*, 135–8; cf. Van der Vlies, 'Publics', 241; Kannemeyer, *J. M. Coetzee*, 288.
44. McDonald, *The Literature Police*, 308; 310; 314–15.
45. Quoted in Attwell, *J. M. Coetzee*, 58; 60–1.
46. Attwell, *J. M. Coetzee*, 61; 73.
47. Ibid., 118.
48. Scott, 'Voice', 101.
49. Coetzee, 'The Novel Today', 3.
50. Harber, 'South Africa: Clash of Booker Titans.'
51. Kannemeyer, *J. M. Coetzee*, 418–20.
52. Harber, 'Clash'.
53. Kannemeyer, *J. M. Coetzee*, 418–20.
54. Attwell, *J. M. Coetzee*, 76.
55. Van der Vlies, 'Writing, Politics, Position', 64.
56. McDonald, *The Literature Police*, 168.
57. McDonald, 'Writers' Groups'.
58. Coetzee, *Doubling*, 299.
59. Coetzee, *Giving Offense*, 84.
60. Van der Vlies, *J. M. Coetzee's Disgrace*, 51.
61. Attwell, *J. M. Coetzee*, 196.
62. See, for instance, Donadio, 'Out of South Africa'; Kannemeyer and Attwell dispel these myths. Kannemeyer, *J. M. Coetzee*, 535; Attwell, *J.M. Coetzee*, 215.
63. Attwell, *J.M. Coetzee*, 215.
64. Attwell, 'Race in *Disgrace*', 334.
65. McDonald, '*Disgrace* Effects', 324.

66. As Van der Vlies suggests, Coetzee's international validation overseas, capped by the Nobel, made his oeuvre more amenable locally. See Van der Vlies, 'Publics and Personas,' 244.
67. Cartwright qtd. in Kannemeyer, *J. M. Coetzee*, 547; 578; 536; 591.
68. Lee, 'The Rest Is Silence.'
69. Mars-Jones, 'It's Very Novel.'
70. Walkowitz, *Born Translated*, 51.
71. Attwell, *J. M. Coetzee*, 154.
72. Walkowitz, *Born Translated*, 56.
73. Coetzee, *Doubling*, 69–70; quoted in Barnard, 'Coetzee', 86.

WORKS CITED

Attwell, David. 'Editor's Introduction'. In J. M. Coetzee. *Doubling the Point: Essays and Interviews*, edited by David Attwell, 1–13. Cambridge, MA and London: Harvard University Press, 1992.
Attwell, David. *J. M. Coetzee and the Life of Writing: Face-to-Face with Time*. New York: Viking, 2015.
Attwell, David. 'Race in *Disgrace*'. Special Topic: J. M. Coetzee's *Disgrace*. Edited by Derek Attridge and Peter D. McDonald. *Interventions: International Journal of Postcolonial Studies* 4, no. 3 (2002): 331–41.
Barnard, Rita. *Apartheid and Beyond: South African Writers and the Politics of Place*. Oxford: Oxford University Press, 2007.
Barnard, Rita. 'Coetzee in/and Afrikaans'. *Journal of Literary Studies* 25, no. 4 (2009): 84–105.
Boehmer, Elleke. 'Reading between Life and Work: Reflections on "J.M. Coetzee."' *Textual Practice* 30, no. 3 (2016): 435–50.
Coetzee, J. M. *Boyhood: A Memoir*. 1997. London: Vintage, 1998.
Coetzee, J. M. *Doubling the Point: Essays and Interviews*, edited by David Attwell. Cambridge Massachusetts; London: Harvard University Press, 1992.
Coetzee, J. M. *Giving Offense: Essays on Censorship*. Chicago: Chicago University Press, 1996.
Coetzee, J. M. 'Growing Up with *The Children's Encyclopaedia*'. Director's Lecture. Chicago Committee on Social Thought. University of Chicago, 9 October 2018. https://www.youtube.com/watch?v=Qo3ogEEbgfA.
Coetzee, J. M. 'The Novel Today'. *Upstream* 6 (1988): 1–5.
Coetzee, J. M. *Stranger Shores: Essays 1986–1999*. London: Secker & Warburg, 2001.
Coetzee, J. M. *White Writing: On the Culture of Letters in South Africa*. London and New Haven: Yale University Press, 1988.
Dean, Andrew. 'Lives and Archives'. In *The Cambridge Companion to J. M. Coetzee*, edited by Jarad Zimbler, 221–33. Cambridge: Cambridge University Press, 2020.
Donadio, Rachel. 'Out of South Africa'. *The New York Times*, 16 December 2007. https://www.nytimes.com/2007/12/16/books/review/Donadio-t.html.
Dubow, Saul. *Racial Segregation and the Origins of Apartheid in South Africa, 1919–36*. Basingstoke: Macmillan, 1989.
Effe, Alexandra. 'Autobiographies/*autre*biographies/biographies'. In *The Bloomsbury Handbook to J. M. Coetzee*, edited by Andrew van der Vlies and Lucy Valerie Graham, 29–42. London: Bloomsbury, 2023.
Harber, Anton. 'South Africa: Clash of Booker Titans'. *The Guardian*, 28 May 2013. https://www.theguardian.com/world/2013/may/23/salman-rushdie-nadine-gordimer-jm-coetzee.
Irish Times, The. 'Author Shuns Limelight'. *The Irish Times*. 2 October 2003. https://www.irishtimes.com/news/author-shuns-limelight-1.380629.
Kannemeyer, J. C. *J. M. Coetzee: A Life in Writing*. Translated by Michiel Heyns. Brunswick, Australia: Scribe, 2012.
Lee, Hermione. 'The Rest Is Silence'. *The Guardian*, 30 August 2003. https://www.theguardian.com/books/2003/aug/30/bookerprize2003.highereducation.

McDonald, Peter D. 'Disgrace Effects'. Special Topic: J. M. Coetzee's *Disgrace*. Edited by Derek Attridge and Peter McDonald. *Interventions* 4, no. 3 (2002): 321–30.

McDonald, Peter D. *The Literature Police: Apartheid Censorship and Its Cultural Consequences*. Oxford: Oxford University Press, 2009.

McDonald, Peter D. 'Writers' Groups: An Interview with J. M. Coetzee'. Writers and Free Expression Project, 7 January 2019. https://writersandfreeexpression.com/2019/01/07/writers-groups-an-interview-with-j-m-coetzee/.

Mars-Jones, Adam. 'It's Very Novel, but Is It Actually a Novel?' *The Observer*, 14 September 2003. https://www.theguardian.com/books/2003/sep/14/fiction.jmcoetzee.

Posel, Deborah. 'The Apartheid Project, 1948–70'. In *The Cambridge History of South Africa: 1885–1994*, 2, edited by Robert Ross et al., 319–68. Cambridge: Cambridge University Press, 2011.

Scott, Joanna. 'Voice and Trajectory: An Interview with J. M. Coetzee'. *Salmagundi* 114–15 (1997): 82–102.

Van der Vlies, Andrew. *J. M. Coetzee's* Disgrace: *A Reader's Guide*. Continuum Contemporaries. London: Continuum, 2010.

Van der Vlies, Andrew. 'Publics and Personas.' In *The Cambridge Companion to J. M. Coetzee*, edited by Jarad Zimbler, 234–48. Cambridge: Cambridge University Press, 2020.

Van der Vlies, Andrew. *South African Textual Cultures: Black, White, Read All Over*. Manchester: Manchester University Press, 2007.

Van der Vlies, Andrew. 'World Literature, the Opaque Archive, and the Untranslatable: J. M. Coetzee and Some Others'. *Journal of Commonwealth Literature* (February 2021): 1–18. https://doi.org/10.1177/0021989420988744.

Van der Vlies, Andrew. 'Writing, Politics, Position: Coetzee and Gordimer in the Archive'. In *J. M. Coetzee and the Archive: Fiction, Theory, and Autobiography*, edited by Marc Farrant, Kai Easton and Hermann Wittenberg, 59–76. London: Bloomsbury Academic, 2021. Bloomsbury Collections. http://dx.doi.org/10.5040/9781350165984.ch-004.

Wachtel, Eleanor. 'J. M. Coetzee on Language, Writing and the Pleasure of Reading: J. M. Coetzee in Conversation with Eleanor Wachtel' (2000). Writers & Company. CBC Radio, 13 July 2018. https://www.cbc.ca/radio/writersandcompany/j-m-coetzee-on-language-writing-and-the-pleasure-of-reading-1.4753607.

Walkowitz, Rebecca. *Born Translated: The Contemporary Novel in an Age of World Literature*. New York: Columbia University Press, 2015.

Watson, Stephen. 'Colonialism and the Novels of J. M. Coetzee'. Special Focus on Southern Africa. *Research in African Literatures* 17, no. 3 (1986): 370–92.

Wilm, Jan. 'The J. M. Coetzee Archive and the Archive in J. M. Coetzee'. In *Beyond the Ancient Quarrel: Literature, Philosophy, and J.M. Coetzee*, edited by Patrick Hayes and Jan Wilm, 216–32. Oxford: Oxford University Press, 2017.

CHAPTER THREE

Autobiographies/*autre*biographies/biographies

ALEXANDRA EFFE

J. M. Coetzee has to date written three books that are explicitly autobiographical, although not uncomplicatedly so: *Boyhood* (1997), *Youth* (2002) and *Summertime* (2009), together published as *Scenes from Provincial Life* (2011). They all feature a character named John Coetzee, who is a version of – but also clearly different from – his author. The former will henceforth be referred to as 'John' in order to distinguish him from 'Coetzee' as his creator. These texts have come to be called Coetzee's *autre*biography, taking up a term Coetzee himself has coined. In an interview coinciding with the first drafts of *Boyhood*, Coetzee speaks about his move from London to Texas, referring to himself in the third person, and notes that, at this point, '*he* [...] begins to feel closer to I: *autre*biography shades back into autobiography'.[1] The term acknowledges the inevitable distance between author and character, between life and its representation in narrative, and in particular between present and past self.

Scenes from Provincial Life is explicitly autobiographical and, at the same time, explicitly fictional. A link between author and protagonist is established through nominal reference and biographical details which largely map onto Coetzee's life. *Boyhood* and *Youth* are narrated continuously in the third person present tense, and focalized almost exclusively through the young John. *Summertime* makes use of the same *autre*biographical mode in notebook and diary entries allegedly written by John, but this volume is more experimental still.[2] It is built on the premise that the famous author is recently deceased, and largely consists of interviews that a fictional biographer, Mr. Vincent, conducts in view of compiling data for his book. All three pose challenges for publishers, critics and readers who wish to straightforwardly classify them as autobiography or novel.[3]

The complexity of his autobiographical practice, as well as Coetzee's own critical engagement with the subject, constitutes rich material for readers and critics interested in the relation between work and life. This same complexity also poses challenges in terms of how to approach Coetzee's generically shifty texts, and how to distinguish between biographical data about, and textual constructs of, Coetzee. The recent *Cambridge Companion to J. M. Coetzee* (2020) takes a largely thematic focus, and in consequence does not treat the *autre*biography separately. Individual volumes are discussed in a chapter on genre experiments by Derek Attridge, and under the heading of 'Scenes and Settings' by Meg Samuelson. Attentive to the fact that we only ever approach an author construct, 'the person of J. M. Coetzee, [...] refracted by his archive and writings, and by his public performances', the companion distinguishes between these refractions of Coetzee and 'the materials of his biography' outlined in an introductory chronology.[4] The kind of author construct we arrive at naturally depends on which refractions of the author we draw on and how we interpret them. This is attested to by the two existing biographical studies of Coetzee, by J. C. Kannemeyer and David Attwell. With different weighting and different aims, they draw on Coetzee's fictional, critical and autobiographical writing, conducting interviews and making use of unpublished archival material such as notebooks, manuscripts and letters. Kannemeyer offers a traditional, literary biography that attempts to offer details about Coetzee's life. Attwell, meanwhile, presents a critical biography that reads the works in relation to the context of their production.

This chapter considers how the *autre*biographical trilogy, as perhaps the most important and most intricate refraction of and source about Coetzee, enters into dialogue with other author personae – in novels, performances, critical essays, interviews and archive – and with the work of Coetzee's biographers and critics. Coetzee's own comments on truth in autobiographical writing do not make drawing distinctions between life and text any easier, but provide an insightful starting point for exploring his *autre*biographical project.

ON AUTOBIOGRAPHY, *AUTRE*BIOGRAPHY, TRUTH AND FICTION

The novelist Tim Parks observes that 'Coetzee does not do autobiography but, looked at another way, he doesn't do anything but.'[5] Attwell points out that the *autre*biographical trilogy ends with Coetzee's beginnings as a novelist and that '[t]hereafter, Coetzee's autobiography is the fiction itself'.[6] Coetzee's works are in fact full of author figures, some more and some less strongly linked to Coetzee: one thinks of Elizabeth Costello, JC and the different Coetzee figures in *Dusklands*, to name the most prominent, but also of characters such as Magda, Mrs. Curren, Susan Barton, Foe and Coetzee's version of Dostoevsky in *The Master of Petersburg*. Coetzee's reflections on the relation between truth, memory and autobiographical writing, on the writing process in general, and on the distinct potentialities of fictional modes, invite us to see the fiction as part of Coetzee's auto-, or rather *autre*biographical enterprise.

In his inaugural professorial lecture at the University of Cape Town (1984) and in an essay on Rousseau, Tolstoy and Dostoevsky (1985), Coetzee argues that it is impossible to arrive at truth about the self and discusses the implications for confessional writing. Rousseau's confessional mode, based on honest self-searching, Coetzee suggests, 'lands one in an endless regression'.[7] The self 'cannot tell the truth of itself to itself and come to rest without the possibility of self-deception'.[8] Coetzee revisits the issue of autobiographical truth and its relation to storytelling in several subsequent essays and interviews – most prominently in his conversations with Attwell in *Doubling the Point* (1992), and with psychotherapist Arabella Kurtz, published as *The Good Story* (2015). In the former, he asks whether the 'massive autobiographical writing-enterprise that fills a life, this enterprise of self-construction, [...] yield[s] only fictions', and whether 'among the fictions of the self, the versions of the self, that it yields', some 'are truer than others'.[9] Given this, he asks, 'How do I know *when* I have the truth about myself?'[10]

Coetzee's answer seems to be that writing constitutes or creates truth, although not *the* truth, which must be continuously deferred. Truth, he explains, cannot simply be told, but rather 'comes in the process of writing, or comes from the process of writing'; writing 'reveals (or asserts)' something potentially 'quite different from what you thought [...] you wanted to say in the first place'.[11] In this sense, as he puts it, 'writing writes us', a statement in line with his reflections on the verb *to write* as an instance of the middle voice, that is as simultaneously active and passive (writing and being written).[12] Coetzee's claim that 'in a larger sense all writing is autobiography', that 'everything that you write, including criticism and fiction, writes you as you write it', is the logical conclusion.[13]

Coetzee's 'enterprise of self-construction' – and, we might add, of self-questioning and searching – encompasses all of his writing, irrespective of genre or mode of discourse. It takes form in different degrees of fictionalization, impersonality and impersonation. The autobiographical dimension of the critical essays is most apparent in *Doubling the Point*. Attwell describes the volume as Coetzee's attempt at 'intellectual autobiography', worked out by drawing connections between his novels and scholarship in dialogue with Attwell, trying to remember what particular topics and pieces of writing meant to Coetzee at the time of composition and to understand how they shaped his thinking and his self.[14] Some of his essays include explicitly autobiographical anecdotes – this is the case, for example, in 'What Is a Classic?', collected in *Stranger Shores* (2001) – but all of Coetzee's critical writing invites autobiographical reading to an extent.[15] *Giving Offense* (1996), for instance, is easily read as a commentary on Coetzee as he was writing under censorship; *White Writing* (1988) as commentary on Coetzee's own relation to South African literary culture, and several of the reviews and essays on major authors across the globe as accounts of Coetzee's literary influences. Especially in collected form, the critical pieces appear to invite an autobiographical picture of Coetzee, presenting insights into the development of his literary, philosophical and socio-political thinking.

Derek Attridge introduces the collection *Inner Workings* by stating that here, in contrast to the fiction, Coetzee 'speaks in his own voice'.[16] In the criticism, we indeed seem to hear the author more directly than when Elizabeth Costello speaks, or JC, or Magda, or when Coetzee displaces himself as John in the *autre*biography. One should nonetheless keep in mind that the criticism, especially in volumes that involve selection and purposeful grouping together, is a form of autobiographical self-fashioning as much as self-expression. The same holds true for the archival material. Meticulously self-curated documents like correspondence and manuscript drafts may appear very personal and private, but in the case of an author as much part of, attentive to and knowledgeable about the culture of literary criticism and author celebrity as Coetzee, we must consider these documents composed and arranged for public self-presentation. His critical and literary engagement with issues of truth, autobiography and confession suggests that Coetzee himself is most aware of this, and most troubled by the awareness.

The truth Coetzee creates through his critical, fictional and autobiographical writing is purposefully unauthoritative and provisional. As there are always blind spots and self-interests of which one is unaware, all one can hope for, Coetzee writes, is 'a story that will not be the truth but may have some truth-value [...] – some historical truth, some poetic truth. A fiction of the truth in other words'.[17] Nonetheless, this 'fiction of the truth' is performative since it constitutes self-understanding and, as far as one puts it into writing and circulation, one's public image. Coetzee confirms in an interview that writing autobiographically, particularly in *Boyhood* and *Youth*, has changed his life, since it has 'changed the story of [his] life'.[18] Coetzee's doubts about the accessibility of an objective reality do not lead him to disregard truth. On the contrary, they lead him to what he refers to as a tragic double awareness: 'one believes sincerely in the truth of what one is writing at the same time that one knows it is not the truth'.[19] Coetzee's 'dogged concentration [...] on the ethical dimension of truth versus fiction' results in a continuous 'longing or nostalgia for the one and only truth'.[20] The *autre*biographical trilogy can be seen as a response to the recognition that he cannot tell the truth about himself with certainty, as a commitment to self-questioning, and as an attempt to forge new ways of thinking.

Coetzee is explicit about the ethical value of the capacity of fiction to be critical, destabilizing, experimental and creative. He criticizes a tendency to see the novel as subservient to historical discourse, stressing that storytelling should not be seen as a means for rendering messages more effective. He urges his audience to recognize that '[s]torytelling is another, an other mode of thinking'.[21] Coetzee gives an indication of what this mode enables when he explains that it is in his fiction that he does his 'liberating, [his] playing with possibilities'.[22] Coetzee sees what he terms 'storytelling' in this instance, and what we may also call fictional or literary writing, as allowing us to think in ways impossible without the text, and impossible in other modes of discourse. Such creative thinking is arguably what the *autre*biographical mode aims at.

The process of literary writing, perhaps especially in the *autre*biographies, constitutes for Coetzee a dialogic engagement with the fictions of the *I*. Likening the writing process to that of psychotherapy, Coetzee describes it as aimed at becoming aware of different aspects of oneself – aiming to 'hear all the voices in the room (in one's head), and sense all the ghostly presences', including those 'part of one's personal baggage', those 'that one is (according to one view) conjuring up or inventing or (according to another view) opening oneself up to as a channel'.[23] In conversation with Attwell, he describes such dialogic writing – the act of 'evok[ing]/invok[ing …] countervoices' in the self – as a sign of 'a writer's seriousness'.[24] Coetzee stresses that to pose such challenges to our thinking, to existing stories and to what at one moment appears to be the truth, is no less than an ethical imperative. He is concerned in particular that some members of settler societies – 'conquering group[s]', in his words – do not share his doubts about the often self-serving stories they tell themselves.[25] Truth, he argues, carries 'the threat of ending the enterprise of "*finding* the truth" or "*telling* the truth"', and is therefore a threat to 'the life of the discourse itself'.[26] This is a threat of particular significance for Coetzee, a white South African–born writer.

The *autre*biographical project forms part of a larger project of keeping the enterprise of finding and telling truth alive – of refusing authoritative assertions and truth claims, about the self but also more generally. Just as all of Coetzee's writing and all his performances can be seen as continuations of an autobiographical enterprise of self-construction, so are most of his self-performances forms of authorial displacement. Andrew van der Vlies shows how Coetzee, sceptical of external validation and authorship celebrity culture, has found diverse ways of skirting demands to provide straightforwardly autobiographical information about himself and to speak straightforwardly in his own voice.[27] Coetzee frequently responds to such demands by deflecting authority others bestow on him to fiction as 'an other mode of discourse'. The most prominent example is the figure of Elizabeth Costello, standing in for him on occasions where he is to appear in the role of the public intellectual. Coetzee's surrogate personae and the *autre*biographical project are linked, in that both attest to Coetzee's discomfort with positions of authority and to his doubts about what he holds to be true – especially about himself. Coetzee, in autobiography and in all other realms, searches for but rarely lays claim to truth. This serves to keep the discourse alive – successfully, if we take as indication how the *autre*biographical trilogy interacts with other forms of discourse by and about Coetzee. *Autre*biography, fiction, biography, criticism and archive form an ongoing dialogue – about Coetzee, about the relationship between life and writing, and about philosophical, ethical and political questions of importance for characters, readers and the author.

Scenes from Provincial Life

The bare 'facts' of *Scenes from Provincial Life* largely map onto Coetzee's biography. *Boyhood* is set in South Africa during the young John's childhood, roughly between the age of ten and thirteen (1940–3), when the Coetzee family had moved from Cape Town to Worcester after a business failure. During the period covered by *Youth* (1959–64), John moves, as did Coetzee, from Cape Town to London to live and work while completing his Master's degree. *Summertime* focuses again on a period Coetzee spent in South Africa, from 1972 to 1977, returned to Cape Town from several years in the United States university system because he was unable to renew his visa after an anti-Vietnam war protest. The three books give us snapshots of particular periods in Coetzee's life – particularly unhappy ones, it seems. *Youth* ends with John struggling to finish his MA thesis and *Summertime* picks up when he is on the search for work in Cape Town. Missing are the years in between, during which Coetzee completed his doctorate on Samuel Beckett at the University of Texas at Austin and worked as assistant professor at the State University of New York at Buffalo.

John's difficult interpersonal relations (with family, friends, colleagues, lovers), his ambivalent attitude to South Africa and to Afrikaans and English as languages and cultures, his feelings of historical complicity, and his unsatisfactory attempts to follow an artistic vocation are thematized to different degrees in each volume of the trilogy. All emphasize historical contexts and socio-political issues, most prominently the political climate of apartheid-era South Africa, but also other global and local developments, including the Cold War and immigration in London during the 1960s. The version of John we find in *Boyhood* struggles to find a place in the Coetzee family and in South Africa. He is conflicted between feelings of love and acts of betrayal towards his mother, is uncertain about the status of his father, and is torn between national, cultural, linguistic and religious affiliations that appear to him as binary choices: Roman Catholicism or Protestantism, English or Afrikaans, the Russians or the Americans. The young John's artistic and writerly inclinations are in evidence but more fully explored in the subsequent volumes. The alter-ego we encounter in *Youth* is employed as a computer programmer while seeking 'the sacred fire of art', '[t]he fire that burns in the artist',[28] by fleeing South Africa, imitating the diet of Ford Madox Ford (on whom he is writing a dissertation) and through sexual encounters – none of which delivers on its promise. He believes that to be a great writer, he needs to become part of the European tradition and free himself from his South African heritage, of which he is ashamed, yet he remains an outsider in London. *Summertime* offers a portrayal of John after his return to South Africa, in which he feels no less conflicted about his cultural, linguistic and historical place. He continues to struggle in his role as a son, in relationships with women, and with his identity as writer: he is ashamed of his poetry, interviews for a faculty position he does not actually want, and works as a teacher while writing his first novel.

John is presented very negatively, especially in *Youth* and *Summertime*, and this is one way in which the books alert us to the difference between self and self-portrayal. We are invited to read Coetzee's alter ego, inept in relations with his family and the opposite sex and unsuccessful as a writer, against any knowledge we might have of an internationally acclaimed author. For readers with more detailed knowledge of Coetzee's biography, the representation of John in *Youth* and *Summertime* as socially awkward bachelor, struggling professionally and derided by the Coetzee family for his poetry, is set against the knowledge that the author received his Master's degree and married Philippa Jubber during the period portrayed in *Youth*; and was, during the period covered by *Summertime*, living with his wife and two children, working at the University of Cape Town rather than relying on substitute work, and caring for his father, who in *Summertime* is widowed and falls sick with cancer several years earlier than in real life. *Summertime* matches the historical record in portraying John as working towards the publication of his first novels, *Dusklands* and *In the Heart of the Country*, but neglects to mention their success. Should we miss the more subtle hints at discrepancies between biographical and *autre*biographical record, Coetzee's depiction of John Coetzee as recently deceased definitely prohibits the equation of life and text.

Coetzee writes, and *Scenes from Provincial Life* shows, that '[a]ll autobiography is storytelling' and that '[a]ll versions of the *I* are fictions of the *I*'.[29] *Scenes from Provincial Life* constitutes an experiment with the genres of autobiography and fiction, with self, identity and truth, and most prominently, with narrative perspective. These dimensions are also the most frequent focus in the critical discussion of the *autre*biographical works. From Coetzee's notebooks, we know that the narrative mode of *Boyhood* and *Youth* emerged from the attempt to position himself as neither inside nor outside the action: neither a child immersed in events, nor an adult reflecting on them.[30] Attridge describes Coetzee's narrative mode in *Boyhood* and *Youth* as a response to an inevitable impasse encountered in confessional writing. The lack of retrospection and metanarrative perspective 'prevents the interminable spiralling of confession by short-circuiting it before it even gets going' and by extending responsibility for passing judgment to the reader.[31] While Coetzee's autobiographical texts are not explicitly retrospective, there is at times a dual perspective of experiencing and narrating consciousness, with the latter showing evidence of the advantages of hindsight. Carrol Clarkson refers to 'a tone of ironic double perspective' and 'the sensation of a *wrestling* [...] between self and other, present and past, self an self'.[32] If we believe Coetzee's own account, such wrestling with the self is a form of self-questioning that also aims to find or create truth, albeit of an uncertain kind. Elleke Boehmer gives an indication of the role that the third-person perspective plays in Coetzee's search for truth by explaining that, in autobiography, 'the other' or 'another objectified character' often functions 'to hold up various distorting and yet clarifying mirrors to the self'.[33] Truth has the potential to emerge from Coetzee's *autre*biographical mode, but this truth is not grounded in fact, and it cannot lay claim to certainty. Any glimpse of truth is, in consequence, only that – a momentary glimpse – as a scene at the end of *Boyhood* highlights. The young John can suddenly, for a fleeting moment, recognize family structures that he is not yet, or not usually, aware of: 'The sky opens, he sees the world as it is, then the sky closes and he is himself again, living the only story he will admit, the story of himself'.[34] The statement seems to refer to the author as much as to the protagonist. The position of higher vantage, the momentary vision of truth, does not last for either.

Boyhood, *Youth* and *Summertime* challenge their own claims to truth while continuing to work towards it. Through the double perspective of experiencing and narrating consciousness, and through explicit or implicit metanarrative comments, the texts repeatedly ask us to question whether they are self-revealing or self-serving. The emphasis on failings and deficiencies highlights that author and character are not to be equated, and may even have the effect of foregrounding Coetzee's achievements in contrast to John's failures. Hermione Lee describes *Youth* as 'self-parody' rather than 'inward exploration, or [...] ethical indictment of the author/subject'.[35] Attridge, by contrast, suggests that '[t]he urge to confess may itself distort the representation of the past, producing an exaggeration of one's failings'.[36] Coetzee's texts themselves indicate that both the impulse to hide negative dimensions of the self and the desire to reveal them may ultimately be self-interested. As

Sue Kossew notes, *Scenes from Provincial Life* addresses ethical implications of life-writing in that Coetzee draws attention to 'the double bind of self-interested confession that is an inevitable part of autobiography', to 'the constructed nature of any version of the self', and to 'the impossibility of representing "truth" in any genre'.[37] In so doing, *Scenes of Provincial Life* cautions readers to approach Coetzee's *autre*biography with at least as much doubt about the truth-value of self-narration as the Coetzee surrogates themselves showcase.

In *Boyhood*, the young John is uncertain about the truthfulness of what he presents as his first memory in competition with a classmate. He is certain that it is 'a magnificent first memory' that 'trump[s]' that of his friend, but wonders how much of it is merely the result of his imagination.[38] In *Youth*, John reflects on whether what he records in his diary is true or 'one of many possible fictions, true only in the sense that a work of art is true – true to itself, true to its own immanent aims'.[39] John also hopes that a shameful episode involving the opposite sex will remain secret, since he does not know 'how to fit it into the story of his life that he tells himself'.[40] The question is not so much what has happened, but what narrative about the self to choose. By revealing or inventing stories that John wants to keep silent, Coetzee makes us aware of the fact that the confessions in his *autre*biographies – and perhaps also those to be found in the archive – may ultimately be self-interested.

Summertime highlights the biases of each of the ostensible contributors to Mr. Vincent's biography and illustrates how stories and lives transform in acts of telling, retelling, transcription and editing. The first interviewee, for example, warns the biographer that 'as far as the dialogue is concerned, I am making it up as I go along' – a warning by implication addressed to readers of *Summertime*.[41] By providing different perspectives on John, *Summertime* foregrounds the fact that different stories bring the self – in this case, the autobiographical subject – into being in different versions, and that no single perspective holds authority. Each interviewee, along with John in his diary entries and Vincent through what he forms out of the interviews, contributes to the (self-)portrait of John Coetzee. Vincent believes that fact and subjective distortion or intentional deception can, and should, be held separate. He therefore dismisses John's notebooks, along with his letters and diaries, as part of 'the massive unitary self-projection comprised by his oeuvre' – 'fiction of himself for his correspondents', 'for his own eyes, or perhaps for posterity'.[42] Vincent's description echoes Coetzee in *Doubling the Point*, when he speaks of the 'massive autobiographical writing-enterprise', the 'enterprise of self-construction'.[43] The trilogy, and *Summertime* in particular, stresses that John's – and by implication, Coetzee's – diary entries and other texts in the archive are indeed acts of (self-)construction. So too are the interviewees' contributions in *Summertime*; along with Mr. Vincent's fictive biography, and, by implication, Attwell and Kannemeyer's real ones. As Vincent admits when prompted by one of his interviewees, 'we are all fictioneers'.[44] Our versions of self and other, Vincent recognizes, are always constructs. Unlike Vincent himself, *Summertime* accords value to all of these versions.

The trilogy holds out the promise of a fleeting, uncertain and performative kind of truth, arrived at through a mode of writing that is characterized by self-questioning, fictionalization and dialogue. John, in *Youth*, comes up with the concept of an 'aura of truth', which he believes can emerge from a kind of writing that involves forgetting rather than accumulating knowledge from history books.[45] Through its structural make-up, *Summertime* suggests that what holds most promise is the telling of multiple stories in diverse modes by different people. *Boyhood*, *Youth* and especially *Summertime* thus constitute unauthoritative autobiographical writing and invite negotiations of truth and self. I have argued elsewhere that for Coetzee to extend such invitations constitutes his ethics of writing: in *Summertime* and in his oeuvre in general, he opens up a conversation with readers, enlisting them to answer questions, to resolve moral dilemmas and to arrive at knowledge about self and world where the author and his surrogates fail.[46] Jan Wilm, too, sees Coetzee's self-reflexive mode as a way of engaging readers in the questions that are posed by and for Coetzee's characters, but also by and for the author himself. Wilm, noting the sheer number of questions present in the *autre*biographies, argues that the unanswered question as narrative device provokes reflection in the reader's mind.[47] This indicates a particularly strong uncertainty on Coetzee's part in the context of writing about the self. The fact that the questions in the trilogy are posed in present tense indicates an ongoing uncertainty, still present at the time of writing, and possibly also makes readers feel more directly responsible for attempting to find answers.

Boyhood, *Youth* and *Summertime* challenge their readers to reconsider what constitutes truth, especially in autobiographical and biographical writing, but this does not prevent the *autre*biographies from creating subjective and provisional truths for author and reader. For Attridge, *Boyhood* offers 'first and foremost [the truth] of testimony: a vivid account of what it was like to grow up as a white male in the 1950s in South Africa'.[48] Jonathan Crewe, too, finds in *Boyhood* 'generic experiences of South African boyhood', and feels that Coetzee has written a memoir for him as well as all other white, Anglo-South African contemporaries.[49] Crewe goes even further in arguing that the 'abstract condition of "boyhood"', especially in combination with the third-person perspective, 'can potentially accommodate any reader'.[50] As comments from the author and critics suggest, *Scenes from Provincial Life* allows both its writer and readers to glimpse different kinds of truth, none of which are final or authoritative. Because the truths that emerge from the *autre*biographical mode are provisional in nature, the discourse about Coetzee, as well as the theoretical and ethical questions his works ask us to consider, remains alive. We see this reflected in Kannemeyer and Attwell's biographies.

BIOGRAPHY

Kannemeyer's approach to *Scenes from Provincial Life* indicates that he found it challenging to find appropriate ways of drawing on, and determining the truth-value of, the different sources we have about Coetzee and his life. Kannemeyer has published acclaimed biographies of major Afrikaans writers such as Uys Krige, C. J. Langenhoven, Etienne Leroux, C. Louis Leipoldt, D. J. Opperman and Jan Rabie, as well as a two-volume *History of Afrikaans Literature* (*Geskiedenis van die Afrikaanse literatuur*). His background as a South African biographer and historian determines his approach to Coetzee's life and writing. Focusing on genealogy and historical records, he offers a picture of Coetzee as a major South African national author – paying less attention to Coetzee's complex and sometimes ambivalent attitude towards his heritage, or his complex understanding of fiction and the literary.[51] Kannemeyer primarily draws on archival sources and on the extensive interviews he conducted with Coetzee and people who knew him. Coetzee's creative output does not have as much weight for Kannemeyer, since he sees the biographer as someone who must 'search for true facts outside or beyond the novels'.[52] This is arguably what *Summertime* cautions us against; and Kannemeyer himself seems to have understood that, in the case of Coetzee, this approach is not entirely adequate. *Scenes from Provincial Life* clearly needs to form part of a biographical study of Coetzee, but Kannemeyer's use of it is selective and conflicted. He details where *Summertime* and *Youth* differ from the historical record and notes that any biographer would have to be wary of 'appropriating *Summertime*, in particular, to his project', but regards *Boyhood* 'as based for the most part on verifiable facts'.[53] Kannemeyer's self-professed aim was to 'make available facts that were not previously in the public domain',[54] and *A Life in Writing* is particularly valuable for providing a comprehensive historical record of many dimensions of Coetzee's public and private life that would otherwise be difficult for the average reader to access. Yet *A Life in Writing* fails to challenge the truth-value of the 'facts' it records in relation to Coetzee's fiction, or fails to do so to a degree that would be adequate for a writer with as complex an understanding of facts, truth and fiction as Coetzee. One might thus turn to Attwell's critical biography for an account of how Coetzee's life and fiction are linked in a process of self-formation.

The Life of Writing focuses on the genesis of Coetzee's published texts, and on how the self is woven into and then out of them in turn, 'leaving its imprint as a shadowy presence'.[55] In his approach to biography, Attwell remains first and foremost a literary critic and Coetzee specialist. He has published numerous essays on Coetzee, an early monograph on the rootedness of Coetzee's works in the South-African historical and political context (*J. M. Coetzee: South Africa and the Politics of Writing* [1993]) and worked for three years with Coetzee on *Doubling the Point*. His is essentially a work of genetic criticism, with an interest in how Coetzee's life has shaped his novels, and with an understanding of writing as shaping life in turn. On the basis of Coetzee's manuscripts and notebooks, Attwell gives an account of Coetzee's writing process – a lengthy procedure of researching, drafting and multiple stages of revision. Attwell provides archival evidence for what Coetzee's explicitly autobiographical texts intimate and thematize: namely, that acts of fictionalization form part of a self-questioning search for truth; and that acts of (autobiographical) writing are performative and transformative for the writer. Attwell, moreover, shows that this dynamic of life and writing is at play, behind the scenes, in most of Coetzee's works. *The Life of Writing* thus offers singular insight into Coetzee's creative process and evidence for the inseparability of art and life, at least in the case of Coetzee.

Despite their very different approaches, both Attwell and Kannemeyer's biographies subscribe to Coetzee's understanding of all writing as autobiography. In different ways, they both mine the writing for the writer, based on a belief that writing shapes and gives insight into the self that writes. That these studies also register autobiographical information about the biographers themselves confirms Coetzee's conceptualization of the link between writer and writing. In *A Life in Writing*, Kannemeyer presents himself as a highly systematic historian, much concerned with how Coetzee features in the context of South African national history. Attwell provides autobiographical information about himself in a preface – noting, for example, the sentimental element of working again in the library where he had studied other South African writers in the 1980s, and where Coetzee had worked on Beckett in the 1960s.[56] Drawing a parallel between Coetzee's reading of William Burchell's early European travel narratives to South Africa, and the connection to home that his own work on writers like Olive Schreiner and Alan Paton provided, Attwell speaks of 'the autobiography that seems to be embedded in the work of biography'.[57] *The Life of Writing* shows us Attwell as an expert critic of South African literature; an expert on Coetzee, as well as someone with strong admiration for his writing. We understand that Attwell has followed Coetzee's career for over forty years, and that his thinking has been fundamentally shaped by Coetzee as author and former teacher.

Because Coetzee's life and art are inextricably linked, *A Life in Writing* and *The Life of Writing* are ideally read together for an account of two different, but equally important, dimensions of Coetzee's life and work. The two biographical studies are equally valuable when read in dialogue with Coetzee's fiction, criticism and *autre*biographical writing. This is in fact how *A Life in Writing* and *The Life of Writing* came into being. Attwell was initially approached with the request for a short biography of Coetzee by Eva Cossee, Coetzee's Dutch publisher, who wanted a biography to appear alongside *Summertime*. He had to decline for time reasons; but after he learned about Kannemeyer's biographical project, Attwell developed the idea of a different kind of biographical study. This led to an exchange with Kannemeyer and to Attwell commenting on Kannemeyer's manuscript.[58] This dialogue was unfortunately cut short, since Kannemeyer passed away before he could in turn comment on Attwell's work, but its existence is very much in the spirit of Coetzee's understanding of the lack of authority of any discourse – be it autobiography, biography, criticism or fiction. Attwell's description of his study as 'mainly an account of [his] reading Coetzee's manuscripts' indicates a similar attitude.[59] Coetzee's collaboration with his biographers can also be seen in this light. Coetzee, as Kannemeyer reports, freely offered information through interviews and private material, merely asking 'that the biography should be factually correct' but not wanting to 'interfere with [Kannemeyer's] interpretation of the data'.[60] Each participant in the dialogue – Attwell, Kannemeyer and Coetzee – offers his perspective without claiming authority for it. Should one of these voices risk becoming too dominant, there is always the fiction and the *autre*biography to hold it in check.

CONCLUSION

An ongoing dialogue emerges from the different voices that speak for, through and about Coetzee. The dialogue is conducted across genre categories: Coetzee's fiction, his criticism and interviews, his archive and the *autre*biographical trilogy all form part of the conversation. The dialogue includes Coetzee's biographers, as well as readers and critics, and even other literary contributors. Crewe, a former colleague and friend of Coetzee's who we find to some degree represented in the figure of Martin in *Summertime*, joins with his own autobiographical account under the title *In the Middle of Nowhere: J. M. Coetzee in South Africa* (2016). This work focuses on the years between 1972 and 1974, when Crewe and Coetzee were colleagues at the University of Cape Town. Coetzee's *autre*biographies, his authorial personae, his notorious reserve but simultaneous laying open of sources in the archive, actively invite such dialogue. Crewe notes his hope to make a 'small contribution to the Coetzee archive', and his feeling that his perspective might 'contribut[e] to an understanding of the beginnings of Coetzee's work and the unfolding career'. These statements certainly indicate that he understands archive and *autre*biography as invitations to participate in a conversation.[61] None of the participants has the final authority to pronounce on the autobiographical subject or on the issues Coetzee's texts engage with. The authorial self remains elusive; ethical, political and philosophical questions are posed but not answered. In consequence, the (life of the) discourse must continue.

This it does, with new critical work contributing fresh perspectives on Coetzee and his writing, and with Coetzee himself continuing to revisit themes and questions of the autobiographical self. *The Childhood of Jesus*, the first instalment of Coetzee's second and latest trilogy, for example, reworks autobiographical elements from *Boyhood*. Julika Griem compares a scene in which the young John finds a photograph of his mother in white dress, with a tennis racket and next to an Alsatian, to one in which Simon and David see Ines – who also owns an Alsatian, is also on the tennis court, and is also dressed in white. For Griem, the parallel raises questions 'about the autobiographical contours' of the characters in Coetzee's novel and 'about generic boundaries between fiction and non-fiction'.[62] Such questions are raised even more prominently by Attwell's biography, by the author figures in Coetzee's novels, and of course by the *autre*biography.

These questions also have implications that extend beyond the discussion of Coetzee's life and work. His performance and commentary, especially in combination, provide insights into complex psychological processes of identity formation and memory. Coetzee's work contributes to autobiography theory, and to investigations in psychology and cognitive science into how the human mind projects into past, future and hypothetical scenarios – how it constructs stories and imagines in creative processes of meaning making. To detail what Coetzee has to offer for work on life writing and cognition is beyond the scope of this chapter, but one can hope that theorists from diverse disciplines will continue to engage with his fictional, critical and *autre*biographical writing. They might make productive use of his unanswered questions, and remember to pause and reconsider if they believe themselves to have come to a definitive understanding of his *autre*biographical project. Coetzee's work and life invite multiple perspectives and an ongoing conversation. It is in this spirit, I would assume, that Coetzee has allowed the public access to many of his private papers, cooperating with biographers and refusing to interpret his own texts. It is also in this spirit that this chapter is offered, presenting one more perspective in a continuous dialogue.

NOTES

1. Coetzee, *Doubling the Point*, 394. See also Attwell, '"A Life in Research" with J. M. Coetzee', 253.
2. Attwell, presumably based on a comparison with Coetzee's actual notebooks, describes the entries as 'lightly fictionalized extracts'. Attwell, *J. M. Coetzee and the Life of Writing*, 182.
3. In the initial publications, only *Boyhood*, *Summertime* and the US edition of *Youth* featured the subtitle, *Scenes from Provincial Life*, which led to additional confusion about how to class *Youth*. For a discussion of early reviews, some of which fail to take account of the autobiographical dimension, see Lenta, '*Autre*biography: J. M. Coetzee's *Boyhood* and *Youth*'.
4. Zimbler, 'Introduction', 3.
5. Parks, 'In Some Sense True', 28.
6. Attwell, *The Life of Writing*, 30.
7. Coetzee, 'Truth in Autobiography', 4.
8. Coetzee, 'Confession and Double Thoughts', 230.
9. Coetzee, *Doubling the Point*, 17.
10. Ibid., 17, emphasis added.
11. Ibid., 18.
12. Ibid., 18, 94–5. See also Clarkson, *Countervoices*, 42–5.
13. Coetzee, 17.
14. Attwell, 'A Life in Research', 253.
15. For discussions of Coetzee's critical writing, see Clarkson, 'Coetzee's Criticism'; Kossew, 'Criticism and Scholarship'; and Chapters 14 and 18 in this volume.

16. Attridge, 'Introduction', in J. M. Coetzee, *Inner Workings: Literary Essays*, ix.
17. Coetzee, 'Fictions of the Truth', 7.
18. Coetzee, 'All Autobiography Is *Autre*-Biography', 216.
19. Coetzee and Kurtz, *The Good Story*, 68.
20. Ibid.
21. Coetzee, 'The Novel Today', 4.
22. Coetzee, *Doubling the Point*, 246.
23. Coetzee and Kurtz, 'Nevertheless My Sympathies Are with the Karamazovs', 65.
24. Coetzee, *Doubling the Point*, 65.
25. Coetzee and Kurtz, *The Good Story*, 76–9.
26. Coetzee, 'Truth in Autobiography', 3, 6.
27. Van der Vlies, 'Publics and Personas', 234–48.
28. Coetzee, *Youth*, 66.
29. Coetzee, *Doubling the Point*, 391, 75.
30. Wilm, *The Slow Philosophy of J. M. Coetzee*, 74.
31. Attridge, *J. M. Coetzee and the Ethics of Reading*, 143.
32. Clarkson, *J. M. Coetzee*, 26–7, 39. For additional examples, see Lenta, '*Autre*biography', 164; and Attridge, *J. M. Coetzee*, 161 n24.
33. Boehmer, 'Reading between Life and Work: Reflections on "J. M. Coetzee"', 438.
34. Coetzee, *Boyhood*, 160–1.
35. Lee, 'Uneasy Guest', 15.
36. Attridge, *J. M. Coetzee*, 161.
37. Kossew, 'Writing Self as Other: J. M. Coetzee's "Life Writing" in *Scenes from Provincial Life*', 374.
38. Coetzee, *Boyhood*, 30.
39. Coetzee, *Youth*, 10.
40. Ibid., 130.
41. Coetzee, *Summertime: Scenes From Provincial Life*, 32.
42. Ibid., 226.
43. Coetzee, *Doubling the Point*, 17.
44. Coetzee, *Summertime*, 226.
45. Coetzee, *Youth*, 138–9.
46. Effe, *J. M. Coetzee and the Ethics of Narrative Transgression: A Reconsideration of Metalepsis*.
47. Wilm, *The Sow Philosophy*, 72, 75. Attridge, too, notes the high number of questions in *Boyhood* and *Youth*. See Attridge, *J. M. Coetzee*, 58.
48. Ibid., 155.
49. Crewe, 'Arrival: J. M. Coetzee in Cape Town', 12.
50. Crewe, *In the Middle of Nowhere: J. M. Coetzee in South Africa*, 69.
51. Clarkson notes that the original version of the biography in Afrikaans is in instances more attentive to Coetzee's literariness, offering 'a different and illuminating appreciation of Coetzee's own writing'; see Clarkson, 'J. M. Coetzee: 'n Geskryfde Lewe./J. M. Coetzee: A Life in Writing', 267–8. See Rita Barnard's 'Coetzee in/and Afrikaans' for an insightful account of Coetzee's complex attitude to national

identity and belonging, including his attitude towards English and Afrikaans. For a discussion of how different national and cultural dimensions of John's identity are negotiated between John's diary entries and the interviewees in *Summertime*, see Effe, *J. M. Coetzee and the Ethics of Narrative Transgression*, 122–3.
52. Kannemeyer, *J. M. Coetzee: A Life in Writing*, 10.
53. Ibid., 9–10.
54. Ibid., 14.
55. Attwell, *The Life of Writing*, 27.
56. Ibid., xviii.
57. Ibid., 18–19.
58. Attwell describes these origins of his study and his exchange with Kannemeyer in '"A Life in Research"' (257). When Kannemeyer's editor, Hannes van Zyl, faced the difficult task of editing the unfinished manuscript after Kannemeyer's death, Attwell provided suggestions on aspects of his editorial work, including the conclusion (private email correspondence, 4 November 2020).
59. Attwell, *The Life of Writing*, 17.
60. Kannemeyer, *A Life in Writing*, 7–8.
61. Crewe, *In the Middle of Nowhere*, 12–13; 'Arrival', 13.
62. Griem, '"Good paragraphing. Unusual content": On the Making and Unmaking of Novelistic Worlds', 86.

WORKS CITED

Attridge, Derek. *J. M. Coetzee and the Ethics of Reading: Literature in the Event*. Chicago: University of Chicago Press, 2004.

Attwell, David. *J. M. Coetzee and the Life of Writing: Face to Face with Time*. Melbourne: Text Publishing, 2015.

Attwell, David. *J. M. Coetzee: South Africa and the Politics of Writing*. Berkeley: University of California Press, 1993.

Attwell, David. '"A Life in Research" with J. M. Coetzee'. Interview with Michaela Borzaga. *Life Writing* 12, no. 3 (2015): 251–63.

Barnard, Rita. 'Coetzee in/and Afrikaans'. *Journal of Literary Studies* 25, no. 4 (2009): 84–105.

Boehmer, Elleke. 'Reading between Life and Work: Reflections on "J. M. Coetzee."' *Textual Practice* 30, no. 3 (2016): 435–50.

Clarkson, Carrol. 'Coetzee's Criticism.' In *A Companion to the Works of J. M. Coetzee*, edited by Tim Mehigan, 222–34. Rochester: Camden House, 2011.

Clarkson, Carrol. *J. M. Coetzee: Countervoices*. Basingstoke: Palgrave Macmillan, 2009.

Clarkson, Carrol. 'J. M. Coetzee: 'n Geskryfde Lewe./J. M. Coetzee: A Life in Writing'. *Life Writing* 11, no. 2 (2014): 263–70.

Coetzee, J. M. 'All Autobiography Is *Autre*-Biography: J. M. Coetzee Interviewed by David Attwell'. In *Selves in Question: Interviews on Southern African Auto/biography*, edited by Judith Lütge Coullie, Stephan Meyer, Thengani H. Ngwenya and Thomas Olver, 213–18. Honolulu: University of Hawai'i Press, 2006.

Coetzee, J. M. *Boyhood: Scenes from Provincial Life*. London: Secker & Warburg, 1997.

Coetzee, J. M. *The Childhood of Jesus*. London: Harvill Secker, 2013.

Coetzee, J. M. 'Confession and Double Thoughts: Tolstoy, Rousseau, Dostoevsky'. *Comparative Literature* 37, no. 3 (1985): 193–232.

Coetzee, J. M. *Doubling the Point: Essays and Interviews*. Edited by David Attwell. Cambridge: Harvard University Press, 1992.

Coetzee, J. M. 'Fictions of the Truth'. *Age Saturday Extra*, 13 May 2000: 7.
Coetzee, J. M. *Inner Workings: Literary Essays 2000–2005*. New York: Viking, 2007.
Coetzee, J. M. 'A Note on Writing'. In *Momentum: On Recent South African Writing*, edited by Margaret J. Daymond, Johan U. Jacobs, and Margaret Lenta. Pietermaritzburg: University of Natal Press, 1984. Reprinted in *Doubling the Point: Essays and Interviews*, edited by David Attwell, 94–5. Cambridge: Harvard University Press, 1992.
Coetzee, J. M. 'The Novel Today'. *Upstream* 6, no. 1 (1988): 2–5.
Coetzee, J. M. *Scenes from Provincial Life*. London: Harvill Secker, 2011.
Coetzee, J. M. *Summertime: Scenes from Provincial Life*. London: Harvill Secker, 2009.
Coetzee, J. M. 'The Sympathetic Imagination: A Conversation with J. M. Coetzee'. Interview with Eleanor Wachtel. *Brick* 56 (2001): 37–47.
Coetzee, J. M. *Truth in Autobiography*. Cape Town: University of Cape Town Press, 1984, 1–6.
Coetzee, J. M. *Youth*. London: Secker & Warburg, 2002.
Coetzee, J. M. and Arabella Kurtz. '"Nevertheless, My Sympathies Are with the Karamazovs": An Email Correspondence, May–December 2008'. *Salmagundi* 166/167 (2010): 39–72.
Coetzee, J. M. and Arabella Kurtz. *The Good Story: Exchanges on Truth, Fiction and Psychotherapy*. London: Harvill Secker, 2015.
Crewe, Jonathan. 'Arrival: J. M. Coetzee in Cape Town'. *English in Africa* 40, no. 1 (2013): 11–35.
Crewe, Jonathan. *In the Middle of Nowhere: J. M. Coetzee in South Africa*. Lanham: University Press of America, 2016.
Effe, Alexandra. *J. M. Coetzee and the Ethics of Narrative Transgression: A Reconsideration of Metalepsis*. Cham: Palgrave Macmillan, 2017.
Griem, Julika. '"Good Paragraphing. Unusual Content": On the Making and Unmaking of Novelistic Worlds'. In *Beyond the Ancient Quarrel: Literature, Philosophy, and J. M. Coetzee*, edited by Patrick Hayes and Jan Wilm, 70–88. Oxford: Oxford University Press, 2017.
Kannemeyer, J. C. *J. M. Coetzee: A Life in Writing*. Translated by Michiel Heyns. Melbourne: Scribe, 2012.
Kossew, Sue. 'Criticism and Scholarship'. In *The Cambridge Companion to J. M. Coetzee*, edited by Jarad Zimbler, 138–51. Cambridge: Cambridge University Press, 2020.
Kossew, Sue. 'Writing Self as Other: J. M. Coetzee's "life writing" in *Scenes from Provincial Life*'. *Forum for World Literature Studies* 2, no. 3 (2010): 363–75.
Lee, Hermione. 'Uneasy Guest'. *London Review of Books* 24, no. 31 (11 July 2002): 14–15.
Lenta, Margaret. '*Autre*biography: J. M. Coetzee's *Boyhood* and *Youth*'. *English in Africa* 30, no. 1 (2003): 157–69.
Parks, Tim. 'In Some Sense True'. *London Review of Books* 38, no. 2 (2016): 25–8.
Van der Vlies, Andrew. 'Publics and Personas.' In *The Cambridge Companion to J. M. Coetzee*, edited by Jarad Zimbler, 234–48. Cambridge: Cambridge University Press, 2020.
Wilm, Jan. 'The J. M. Coetzee Archive in J. M. Coetzee'. In *Beyond the Ancient Quarrel: Literature, Philosophy, and J. M. Coetzee*, edited by Patrick Hayes and Jan Wilm, 215–31. Oxford: Oxford University Press, 2017.
Wilm, Jan. *The Slow Philosophy of J. M. Coetzee*. London: Bloomsbury Academic, 2016.
Zimbler, Jarad, ed. *The Cambridge Companion to J. M. Coetzee*. Cambridge: Cambridge University Press, 2020.

CHAPTER FOUR

J. M. Coetzee and his publishers

ANDREA THORPE

In Coetzee's novel *Elizabeth Costello* (2003), the eponymous protagonist listens to a speech on 'The Novel in Africa' about the influence of the global publishing economy on African literature. The speaker, Emmanuel Egudu, a Nigerian academic, argues that to be financially prosperous as an African writer, 'you must put out books that will be prescribed for schools', meaning 'writers with serious ambitions ... must look elsewhere for their salvation'.[1] Egudu concludes that 'The Future of the Novel' (the title of Costello's talk on the cruise) is not in Africa, because there 'storytelling provides a livelihood neither for publishers nor for writers'.[2] Similarly, in an 1978 interview, Coetzee labelled publishing in South Africa a 'colonial' enterprise in which 'our literary products are flown to the centre and re-exported to us at a vastly increased price'.[3] Coetzee's novels frequently narrativize the processes by which books come to be available to their publics, highlighting not only the craft of writing and the nature of authorship, but the local and global structural conditions that shape how and where books are read. His awareness of publishing economies was deepened by his own experiences with Ravan Press, his first, South African publisher; by the effects of censorship when he was writing under apartheid; and by the fraught negotiations between his early local and global publishers.

Despite his damning overview of the African publishing industry, Egudu concedes the possibility of finding African publishers 'one here, one there, who will support local writers even if they will never make money'.[4] This description might accurately be applied to Ravan Press, which was both exceptional and embedded in a progressive English-language publishing milieu in 1970s South Africa. In this chapter, I focus chiefly on the publishing histories of Coetzee's first three books, published by Ravan: *Dusklands* (1974), *In the Heart of the Country* (1977), and *Foe* (1986). As Andrew van der Vlies has argued, Ravan offers 'a significant institutional context for Coetzee's writing, given its association ... with "black consciousness" ideology, a self-consciously Marxist dedication to engaged writing, and a scepticism about aesthetic validations and categories of literariness'.[5] The publication of these early works by a small, radical South African press during a tumultuous period in South African history meant Coetzee had perforce to evaluate and construct his designation as a 'South African' writer. Such choices and negotiations shaped the novelist he was to become. These early publishing relationships, particularly with Ravan, are thus intriguing and illuminating in comparison to the largely uneventful and enduring relationships he later experienced with his international publishers. The publishing histories of these three early works provide a useful critical lens through which to map the contours of Coetzee's later writing career.

DUSKLANDS: PUBLISHING A 'MODERN, SOUTH AFRICAN' NOVELIST

Ravan Press was certainly not the publisher Coetzee originally envisioned for his first book. Neither was he at first set on a South African publisher at all. He had failed to secure an agent in London or New York, making publication overseas out of reach.[6] In South Africa, he had experienced several rejections (including from progressive publishing house Ad Donker) before the manuscript was accepted by Ravan's editor, Peter Randall, in 1973.[7] For this reason, Ravan Press had a marked influence on Coetzee's career, since Randall's prescient appreciation of his talent and originality was key to Coetzee's early success. With David Philip and Ad Donker, Ravan was one of three new English-language South African publishers established in the early 1970s. All three, as Peter McDonald explains, 'developed substantial literary lists' alongside non-fiction titles, and 'transformed the literary marketplace'.[8] Their outputs over the 1970s represented notable growth in the South African publishing industry, and their licensing agreements with international publishers extended their reach and profitability.[9] These publishers' modest success in the face of ongoing censorship by the South African Publications Control Board (PCB) was impressive, especially as these imprints frequently published overtly anti-apartheid writing. McDonald points out that Ravan, in particular, 'always existed on the margins of the market economy'.[10] This was in part due to its origins in the Christian Institute, established by theologian Beyers Naudé, whose surname provided the 'N' of the portmanteau 'Ravan' – Peter *Ra*ndall and Danie *va*n Zyl were the imprint's co-founders.

Before Coetzee became their flagship author, Ravan had published works by other experimental and radical writers, including a collection of James Matthews' and Gladys Thomas's poems entitled *Cry Rage!* (1972), and Wopko Jensma's poetry and woodcut collection *Sing for Our Execution* (1973). Jensma's second Ravan title *where white is the colour where black is the number* (1974) would be banned, like many of the publisher's future books. Ravan also famously published *Staffrider* magazine from 1978 until 1993. Featuring poetry, short fiction, artworks and photographs from established and lesser-known contributors, *Staffrider* was defined by a self-editing ethos and explicitly radical, anti-apartheid agenda. Despite some similarities in approach, the leftist origins and impetus of Ravan's list set it apart from the other English, white-owned publishers, who were arguably more liberal-leaning. Even if Coetzee's original association with the publisher was more happy accident than strategy, he continued to forge an active relationship with this influential South African press for a decade, through several notable obstacles, even after winning international accolades like the Booker Prize, and often against the grain of his literary agents' and his British publisher's preferences.

Correspondence about *Dusklands* between Coetzee and his Ravan editor, Peter Randall, reveals the first signs of Coetzee straining against the designation of a respectable, white, liberal 'South African' writer. In a letter of 11 January 1974, Randall explained that they were proceeding with the publication of *Dusklands*, 'in between court cases, visits from police and other unsavoury matters', evoking the tension-ridden context in which *Dusklands* entered the public realm. Randall requested a photograph and some information about Coetzee's 'school education' or 'family background'.[11] Coetzee's response explains his anxiety about settling for a 'particular identity' that he would 'feel most uneasy in'. He continues:

> A few words about my schooling, for example, make me a player in the English-South African game of social typing and can even be read as a compliment to those monsters of sadism who

ruled over my life for eleven years. As for my family background, I am one of the 10,000 Coetzees, and what is there to be said about them except that Jacobus Coetzee begat them all?[12]

This is an important moment in Coetzee's long-term struggle to 'manage the terms under which work gathered by the function of the proper name "J.M. Coetzee" has entered the world', as Van der Vlies puts it.[13] As a 'compromise', Coetzee sent Randall a photograph and a list of his 'non-professional' interests: 'crowd sports; other people's ailments; apes and humanoid machines; and the politics of consent'.[14]

This sardonically proffered 'compromise' reflects Coetzee's refusal to play the role of the respectable, provincial scholar-author. Proofing a later version of the dust jacket, he suggested that 'the Dr Coetzee angle should be avoided'.[15] Included, however, were the list of 'interests' and the line about Jacobus Coetzee and the 10,000 Coetzees (to which Coetzee apparently objected). During production of the Ravan edition of *In the Heart of the Country* (1978), Coetzee told then-editor Mike Kirkwood that the *Dusklands* cover had been 'a mistake from every point of view',[16] later remarking that Randall had 'lifted' the note used for *Dusklands* 'without permission from a letter'.[17]

Coetzee's later criticism of the *Dusklands* jacket included the cover image. He had proposed a plate of a young Khoisan woman from a 1907 text by anthropologist Leonard Schulze; Wittenberg suggests Coetzee might have wanted the image to 'function ironically, in keeping with the anti-colonial critique of the Jacobus Coetzee narrative'.[18] Ravan, however, selected a watercolour landscape by nineteenth-century painter Thomas Baines. While J. C. Kannemeyer argues that the geographically specific image was at odds with *Dusklands*'s spatially bifurcated structure, since the first section is set in the United States and deals with the Vietnam War,[19] Wittenberg suggests that it 'served to strengthen the fictive historical framing of the Jacobus Coetzee narrative'.[20] The typically South African image both conflicted and chimed with the blurb's designation of *Dusklands* as '[p]robably the first truly major modern South African novel'.[21] While the 'South African' elements and provenance of the novel are, as in the watercolour image, emphasized, the appeal to modernity in this description promotes Ravan Press as a progressive publisher of experimental literature, challenging assumptions of supposed South African provincialism.

Given Coetzee's resistance to certain types of national inscription, an intriguing section of the correspondence concerning *Dusklands* deals with Coetzee and Randall's concerted efforts to have his debut book reviewed by the South African Broadcasting Corporation (SABC). Coetzee asked Randall in February 1974 about the possibility of having the book reviewed pre-publication on the SABC's cultural radio programmes.[22] Considering the SABC's nationalist, propagandistic agenda, one might imagine that a book published by the radical Ravan Press might not be warmly welcomed by the state broadcaster, and it was only after multiple requests from Peter Randall, some strongly worded,[23] that the SABC finally agreed to review *Dusklands* in a cultural radio show, 'Talking of Books'.[24] The SABC's September 1974 review was lukewarm, suggesting the publisher's claims of Coetzee's brilliance were overblown.[25] As the lengthy correspondence that led to this broadcast illuminates, it was not straightforward for more radical voices, ideas or cultural products to be given fair hearing in South African national media. Coetzee's efforts to publish and market experimental literary fiction in this unpropitious context, alongside his unwillingness to be co-opted into specific moulds of South African identity while remaining committed to local readers and publishers, were to shape his development as a writer. They would come to a head in even more dramatic ways during the production of *In the Heart of the Country*.

IN THE HEART OF THE COUNTRY: REACHING GLOBAL READERS, CONFRONTING LOCAL CHALLENGES

The publishing history of *In the Heart of the Country* has been more thoroughly researched than that of any of Coetzee's other works. There are two reasons for this: firstly, its potentially objectionable content in the view of the South African censors; and secondly, the use of Afrikaans in the Ravan edition, which was published alongside the Secker & Warburg version.[26] The narrative of the novel's publication is worth retelling since it sheds light on Coetzee's relationships with his local and international publishers against the context of censorship in South Africa. It is at this point in his career that we witness Coetzee seriously evaluating the possibility of continuing to publish in South Africa, even as he insists on the ethical and political imperative of reaching a South African readership. Coetzee's involvement in the negotiations around the publication of the different versions of *In the Heart of the Country* thus constitutes an important moment in his development as a 'South African' and international novelist.

The plot of *In the Heart of the Country*, which includes 'interracial' sexual relationships between characters, immediately made the book a possible target for censorship or banning in South Africa. In his initial correspondence with Randall about the work while it was still being written, Coetzee envisioned how the novel might be banned on grounds of obscenity and impairing 'good race relations'.[27] Apart from Coetzee's desire to grow his global readership, the context of widespread censorship increased the urgency of securing an international publisher. On the very day that Coetzee first wrote to Randall about *In the Heart of the Country*, the PCB banned Wopko Jensma's second book, published by Ravan.

Fortunately, Secker & Warburg, one of the first major publishers approached by Coetzee's agent Murray Pollinger, enthusiastically accepted the manuscript. At first it seemed that this new agreement would exclude Ravan; Coetzee explained to Randall that as a writer of 'minority taste novels' he had to 'break out of the local market'.[28] Yet Coetzee perceived in Secker & Warburg's early reluctance to risk possible banning by the PCB an opportunity for Ravan to publish the original version of the novel with the dialogue in Afrikaans.[29] Coetzee had translated the Afrikaans text for the manuscript sent to international publishers, but expressed a preference for the bilingual version.[30] Secker & Warburg vacillated several times over whether to distribute the novel in South Africa before finally deciding to export a few hundred copies to South Africa.[31] This move, as both Coetzee and Randall foresaw, was tantamount to submitting the novel to the censors, since it was immediately impounded, embargoed and submitted to the PCB. The novel would eventually be passed by the censors,[32] but while awaiting their verdict, Randall and Coetzee mooted a Ravan edition, to which Secker & Warburg agreed. The fortunate existence of the bilingual text was an important factor in this negotiation, since the Ravan version thus differed considerably from its British counterpart. Among the many dramatic turns in the life of this novel was the banning of Peter Randall in October 1977, along with other supporters of Black Consciousness ideals in the wake of Steve Biko's murder. This meant that Randall was barred from preparing material for publication and had to turn the editorship of Ravan over to Mike Kirkwood.

In the United States, Coetzee's second novel was published in 1977 by Harper & Row, to whom Secker & Warburg had sold rights, with a slight change in the title: *From the Heart of the Country*. This was Coetzee's preferred amendment, given that Harper & Row had a similar sounding title on their list.[33] Unlike the abstract dust jackets of the South African and British editions, the US Harper & Row edition appeared, Van der Vlies suggests, 'consciously calculated to suggest the novel's geographical setting'.[34] The cover featured rock-art figures that suggest an 'iconically "African"' aesthetic, thus invoking 'South African politics without suggesting that the novel was a protest novel'.[35] That the British and Ravan versions steered away from this particularly African aesthetic – on Coetzee's advice, in Ravan's case – was notable, given Coetzee's criticism of *Dusklands*' overtly South African dust jacket.

Simultaneously, Coetzee was committed to making *In the Heart of the Country* available in South Africa in some form despite considerable obstacles. In a letter to his literary agent early in the publishing process, Coetzee explains that if the book cannot be read in South Africa, 'it loses much of its raison d'être'.[36] In later correspondence with Secker & Warburg editor Tom Rosenthal, he emphasizes the importance of making the book 'available in the only country in which it really attains its full significance'.[37] While awaiting the censors' decision, he even considered a version of the novel with certain offending passages blanked out.[38] South Africa was a small but important commercial market for Coetzee, but more broadly, he understood the urgency of local publication: publishing potentially objectionable literature constituted a valuable, if at times quixotic, statement against state suppression in the aftermath of the violent crackdown of the Soweto Uprising of 1976.

The eventual existence of the Ravan version was thus not simply a matter of loyalty to his first, local publisher. Rather, Coetzee made a strategic decision, knowing that non-commercial Ravan would be more likely to risk South African publication, and an aesthetic choice, in that he preferred the Afrikaans dialogue to the 'rather colourless colloquial English'.[39] The bilingual nature of the Ravan edition deepens and complicates certain aspects of the narrative, as both Andrew van der Vlies and Susan Fitzmaurice have argued. Fitzmaurice suggests that that the dual languages evoke 'two worlds', one fictional and one 'phenomenal',[40] while Van der Vlies draws attention to the effects of distance and familiarity conveyed by Afrikaans pronouns and qualifiers.[41] Imagining a bilingual reader who could appreciate complex meanings conveyed by the inclusion of Afrikaans dialogue amongst the English text, Coetzee was understandably committed to seeing this alternative edition published.

The negotiations about *In the Heart of the Country* between Ravan's Peter Randall and Secker & Warburg's Tom Rosenthal, with Coetzee frequently serving as mediator, evince the uneven power differential between the two parties – the 'colonial' publishing structure referred to by Coetzee. Yet Ravan was also better equipped to navigate the unique challenges of the South African publishing context. Secker & Warburg made several missteps, and a degree of metropolitan arrogance is evident in Rosenthal's rejection of Coetzee and Randall's advice about the inadvisability of importing the book without first submitting it before the PCB, or without allowing Ravan to first attempt to distribute their own version.[42] Another potential pitfall involved Seckers' distribution of pre-publication press releases, mentioning particular aspects which might draw the censors' attention.[43] On the other hand, Rosenthal's expressions of sympathy upon Randall's banning,[44] and his eventual agreement to the Ravan edition without any financial consideration between the two houses, based on his sympathies for the 'painful' nature of 'publishing and selling in South Africa', speak to the existence of strong anti-apartheid solidarities in the global liberal literary milieu of the 1970s.[45]

FOE: A FINAL LOCAL PARTNERSHIP

Coetzee's next two novels, *Waiting for the Barbarians* (1980) and *Life & Times of Michael K* (1983), were published once more by Secker & Warburg, and distributed and rejacketed under license in South Africa by Ravan. For his 1986 novel, *Foe*, however, Coetzee negotiated a separate South African edition to be published by Ravan. The discussions around this final Ravan edition once more reveal the sensitive power relations between metropolitan and South African publishers, and underscore Coetzee's continued commitment to developing a global and local audience, given the importance of the novel's themes to the South African situation in the 1980s. In his initial correspondence with Mike Kirkwood, Coetzee remarked that *Foe*, which he began writing in 1982, might be perceived as out-of-touch with the mid-eighties 'temper of the time'.[46] Yet critics have recognized its pertinence to 'the South African political situation' as an allegorical 'rendering of the conditions of apartheid'.[47] In particular, as Jarad Zimbler argues, Coetzee's insistence on a Ravan version of the text situates 'the novel as a subversive text associated with the struggle against South Africa's white nationalist regime'.[48] In the wake of a State of Emergency declared by Prime Minister P. W. Botha in July 1985, which authorized draconian restrictions on anti-apartheid protests and freedom of speech, Coetzee's commitment to having the novel published by a radical South African press that had been harangued by police and censors was politically resonant.

A South African version of *Foe* was originally suggested by Ravan's Mike Kirkwood in a conversation during the publication of *Life & Times of Michael K*.[49] Coetzee offered to show Kirkwood the manuscript, then untitled, before even sending it to his agent. Following Kirkwood's enthusiastic endorsement, Ravan set about negotiating the publication of a local edition with Murray Pollinger and Secker & Warburg.[50] Correspondence about this edition attests to tensions between the metropolitan publisher and agent and the small South African imprint. In these negotiations, Ravan's Jesse Duarte recalled difficulties around the publication of the *Life & Times of Michael K*, when Secker & Warburg decided at the last minute to market their own edition in South Africa – a decision vehemently vetoed by Coetzee.[51] Coetzee's belief in the importance of local distribution and marketing for his works emphasizes that he envisioned his early novels speaking to a South African readership in crucial ways. On the other hand, Secker & Warburg's desire to hold on to the South African market can be explained by Coetzee's rising popularity and eminence, following his Booker Prize win for *Life & Times of Michael K* in 1983.

Despite an agreement with Secker & Warburg, Ravan published its version of *Foe* some months later than the UK edition. Both Coetzee and Ravan were concerned by this delay, preferring simultaneous publication.[52] Coetzee wrote to the Secker & Warburg editor David Godwin, expressing his dismay and ascribing the fault to Secker & Warburg, who had not yet despatched the materials needed for Ravan to print their version. His most trenchant remarks in this letter make explicit his fealty to his local readership and to Ravan: '[Y]ou will understand that, for an author living in South Africa, the details of local publication come to seem just as important as details of UK publication'.[53] Coetzee and Kirkwood were anxious that Secker & Warburg wished to delay Ravan's publication of the novel, intending to market their own imported version.[54] In the end, Secker & Warburg apologized for the delay and the South African version was published.[55] Yet the nervy correspondence around the delayed local publication of *Foe* conveys both Coetzee's insistence on the novel's significance to a South African readership amidst the tense atmosphere of the 1980s, and the persistence of uneven power relations between local and international publishers.

Coetzee persisted in negotiating locally printed, Ravan editions for a full decade even as he gained international acclaim. This demonstrates how crucial his publishing origins with the small, radical, non-commercial South African press were to his self-identity as a writer. His pursuance of these allegiances in his early writing life suggests a critical perspective from which to view both his early and later works, offering a rich sense of his ideological alignments with radical, locally embedded protest movements and art. Equally, Coetzee's lengthy connection with Ravan speaks to his minor, even symbolic attempt to redress the 'colonial situation' of publishing in Africa – even if, like Emmanuel Egudu, he recognized that African writers 'must look elsewhere for their salvation'.[56]

AFTER RAVAN: COETZEE'S INTERNATIONAL PUBLISHERS

Though *Foe* was the last of Coetzee's novels to be published by Ravan, this should not necessarily be read as a failure of loyalty to the publisher. Rather, as J. C. Kannemeyer explains, to blame was the 'administrative chaos that befell Ravan Press after the departure of Mike Kirkwood'.[57] Harvill Secker, now owned by Penguin Random House, continues to publish Coetzee's books for the British market, while Viking (also part of Penguin Random House) publishes his works in the United States. In Australia, Coetzee's books from *Diary of a Bad Year* (2007) onwards have been published by Text Publishing in Melbourne. His publication in translation in numerous languages underscores global interest in Coetzee as much as the achievement of his desire, already incipient in the correspondence about the Ravan editions, to move beyond both the South African publishing market and 'the fate of being a "South African novelist"'.[58]

Just as most of Coetzee's novels probe the authority of the author and the act of novel-writing itself, so they draw attention to what Hermann Wittenberg calls the 'materiality of the book as an aretefact'.[59] In *Elizabeth Costello*, for instance, the dearth of publishing activity in Africa and Egudu's pragmatic understanding of this situation is contrasted with the chapter that precedes it on 'Realism', in which Costello recalls publishing her first book, significantly in London, which she calls 'the great cultural metropolis for Antipodeans',[60] mapping the northward flow of 'literary products'. She recounts her thrill at holding the 'real thing' in her hands, and how she would not rest until the deposit copies had gone out to libraries and museums.[61] Both the physical artefact of the book and its future lives in the world are what interests Costello, and arguably, Coetzee. The publishing history of *Elizabeth Costello* itself is particularly unusual, since the work includes six chapters that began their lives as public lectures delivered by Coetzee. These lectures were fictional accounts of a writer character, Elizabeth Costello, including her views on a range of subjects, often in the form of lectures Costello herself was invited to deliver. These 'lecture narratives' were eventually collected as the novel, *Elizabeth Costello: Eight Lessons*.[62] To complicate the history of these narratives further, two of the 'lessons', first delivered as public lectures at Princeton University, were initially published as *The Lives of Animals* (1999) by Princeton University Press. In the Princeton version, the lectures were introduced and edited by political philosopher Amy Gutmann, with accompanying responses by four experts. London-based publisher Profile Books published Coetzee's two Princeton essay-lectures separately in 2000. Derek Attridge has pointed out that the Princeton edition provides 'some of the trappings of an academic treatise', a genre-bending feat, considering that 'what looked like a scholarly production turned out to have, at its heart, two fictional stories'.[63] Coetzee's involvement in the different lives of these pieces, re-inserted in alternative contexts and re-published with different imprints, emphasizes once more his interest in the paratextual and generic framing (and reframing) of his writing. While the eventful Ravan years reveal particularly close encounters with the fraught economies of South African and global publishing, Coetzee has throughout his long career demonstrated a similar care and interest in how and where his books are produced, distributed and read.

NOTES

1. Coetzee, *Elizabeth Costello*, 41.
2. Ibid.
3. Watson, 'Speaking, J.M. Coetzee', 24.
4. Ibid., 41.
5. Van der Vlies, *South African Textual Cultures*, 137.
6. McDonald, *The Literature Police*, 137.
7. Ibid. Also see: Wittenberg, 'Towards an Archaeology of *Dusklands*', 78.
8. McDonald, *The Literature Police*, 132.
9. Ibid.
10. Ibid., 135.
11. Quoted in Wittenberg, 'Towards an Archaeology of *Dusklands*', 78.
12. Ibid., 79.
13. Van der Vlies, 'Publics and Personas', 239.
14. Quoted in Wittenberg, 'Towards an Archaeology', 79.
15. Ibid.
16. Ibid.
17. Ibid.
18. Wittenberg, 'Towards an Archaeology of *Dusklands*', 81.
19. Kannemeyer, *J.M. Coetzee: A Life in Writing*, 513.
20. Wittenberg, 'Towards an Archaeology of *Dusklands*', 81.
21. Coetzee, *Dusklands*, dust jacket blurb.
22. J.M. Coetzee to Peter Randall, 13 February 1974, 1998. 8.1.31. Ravan papers, Amazwi.
23. Peter Randall to Head of English Service, SABC, 25 June 1974, 1998. 8.1.61. Ravan papers, Amazwi.
24. Anthony Falkiner to Peter Randall, 26 July 1974, 1998. 8.1.66. Ravan papers, Amazwi.
25. Transcript of 'Talking of Books' programme, English Service, SABC, 27 September 1974, 1998. 8.1.73. Ravan papers, Amazwi.
26. See, for instance, Van der Vlies, '*In* (or *From*) *the Heart of the Country*'; Wittenberg, 'The Taint of the Censor'; McDonald, 'The Writer, the Critic and the Censor'.
27. Quoted in Wittenberg, 'The Taint of the Censor', 135.
28. Ibid.
29. J.M. Coetzee to Peter Randall, 14 June 1974, 1998. 8.1.108. Ravan papers, Amazwi.
30. J.M. Coetzee to Celia Catchpole, 31 May 1976, 2013. 71. 12. 15. 3. Kannemeyer papers, Amazwi.

31. J.M. Coetzee to Peter Randall, 5 July 1977, 1998. 8.1.114. Ravan papers, Amazwi.
32. See McDonald's detailed analyses of the censors' report on *In the Heart of the Country* in *The Literature Police* (2009) and 'The Writer, the Critic and the Censor' (2004).
33. J.M. Coetzee to Corona Machener, 29 October 1976, 2013. 71. 12. 15. 3. Kannemeyer papers, Amazwi.
34. Van der Vlies, *South African Textual Cultures*, 143–4.
35. Ibid.
36. J.M. Coetzee to Celia Catchpole, 31 May 1976, 2013. 71. 12. 15. 3. Kannemeyer papers, Amazwi.
37. Quoted in Attwell, *J.M. Coetzee and the Life of Writing*, 95.
38. J.M. Coetzee to Peter Randall, 5 July 1977, 1998. 8.1.114. Ravan papers, Amazwi.
39. Quoted in Attwell, *J.M. Coetzee and the Life of Writing*, 95.
40. Fitzmaurice, 'Aspects of Afrikaans', 179.
41. Van der Vlies, 'In (or From) the Heart of the Country', 234.
42. Peter Randall to Tom Rosenthal, 21 July 1977, 1998. 8.1.105; J.M. Coetzee to Tom Rosenthal, 8 June 1977, 2013. 71. 12. 15. 3, Kannemeyer papers.
43. Wittenberg, 'The Taint of the Censor', 142.
44. Quoted in Attwell, *J.M. Coetzee and the Life of Writing*, 96.
45. Tom Rosenthal to J.M. Coetzee, 28 June 1977, 2013. 71. 12. 15. 3. Kannemeyer papers, Amazwi.
46. J.M. Coetzee to Mike Kirkwood, 25 October 1985, 2013. 71. 12. 15. 3. Kannemeyer papers, Amazwi.
47. Zimbler, 'Under Local Eyes', 51.
48. Ibid.
49. J.M. Coetzee to Mike Kirkwood, 20 October 1985, 2013. 71. 12. 28. 1. Kannemeyer papers, Amazwi.
50. Mike Kirkwood to J.M. Coetzee, 18 December 1985, 2013. 71. 12. 28. 1. Kannemeyer papers, Amazwi.
51. Yasmin Duarte to Murray Pollinger, 21 January 1985, 2013. 71. 12. 28. 1. Kannemeyer papers, Amazwi. Mike Kirkwood reported how Coetzee, upon hearing of this decision about *Life & Times of Michael K* by Seckers, offered to 'phone Tom [Rosenthal] and throw some of his moral rhetoric back at him' (quoted in Van der Vlies, 'In (or From) the Heart of the Country', 245).
52. Yasmin Duarte to Peter Grose, undated; J.M. Coetzee to Mike Kirkwood, 4 August 1986, 2013. 71. 12. 28. Kannemeyer papers, Amazwi.
53. J.M. Coetzee to David Godwin, 15 August 1986, 2013. 71. 12. 28. 1. Kannemeyer papers, Amazwi.
54. J.M. Coetzee to Mike Kirkwood, 20 August 1986, 2013. 71. 12. 28. 1. Kannemeyer papers, Amazwi.
55. Robin Robertson to Mike Kirkwood, 19 August 1986, 2013. 71. 12. 28. 1. Kannemeyer papers, Amazwi.
56. Coetzee, *Elizabeth Costello*, 16.
57. Kannemeyer, *J. M. Coetzee: A Life in Writing*, 597.
58. Morphet, 'Two Interviews', 460.
59. Wittenberg, 'Towards an Archaeology of *Dusklands*', 73.
60. Coetzee, *Elizabeth Costello*, 16.
61. Ibid.
62. Cornwell, '*Elizabeth Costello* and the Inevitability of "Realism"', 348.
63. Attridge, 'Genres', 86.

WORKS CITED

Attwell, David. *J. M. Coetzee and the The Life of Writing: Face to Face with Time*. Oxford: Oxford University Press, 2015.

Attridge, Derek. 'Genres: *Elizabeth Costello, Diary of a Bad Year, Summertime*'. In *The Cambridge Companion to J.M. Coetzee*, edited by Jarad Zimbler, 84–100. Cambridge: Cambridge University Press, 2020.

Coetzee, J. M. *Elizabeth Costello*. London: Secker & Warburg, 2003.

Cornwell, Gareth. 'J.M. Coetzee, Elizabeth Costello, and the Inevitability of "Realism"', *Critique: Studies in Contemporary Fiction* 52, no. 3 (2011): 348–61.

Fitzmaurice, Susan. 'Aspects of Afrikaans in South African Literature in English'. In *Imagined Commonwealths: Cambridge Essays on Commonwealth and International Literature in English*, edited by J. J. Cribb, 166–90. Houndmills: Macmillan, 1999.

J. C. Kannemeyer papers, J. M. Coetzee, Room B11, Amazwi South African Museum of Literature, Makhanda, Eastern Cape, South Africa.

Kannemeyer, J. C. *J. M. Coetzee: A Life in Writing*. Brunswick: Australia: Scribe Publications, 2012.

McDonald, Peter D. *The Literature Police: Apartheid Censorship and its Cultural Consequences*. Oxford: Oxford University Press, 2009.

McDonald, Peter D. 'The Writer, the Critic and the Censor: J. M. Coetzee and the Question of Literature', *Book History* 7 (2004): 285–302.

Morphet, Tony. 'Two Interviews with J.M. Coetzee, 1983 and 1987'. In *From South Africa: New Writings, Photographs & Art*, edited by David Bunn and Jane Taylor, Special Issue, *TriQuarterly* 69 (1987): 454–64.

Ravan Press Correspondence. Ravan Press, Room B11, Amazwi South African Museum of Literature, Makhanda, Eastern Cape, South Africa.

Van der Vlies, Andrew. '*In* (or *From*) *the Heart of the Country*: Local and Global Lives of Coetzee's Anti-pastoral'. In *Print, Text and Book Cultures in South Africa*, edited by Andrew van der Vlies, 166–194. Wits University Press: Johannesburg, 2012.

Van der Vlies, Andrew. 'Publics and Personas'. In *The Cambridge Companion to J. M. Coetzee*, edited by Jarad Zimbler, 234–48. Cambridge: Cambridge University Press, 2020.

Van der Vlies, Andrew. *South African Textual Cultures*. Manchester: Manchester University Press, 2007.

Watson, Stephen 'Speaking, J.M. Coetzee'. *Speak* 1, no. 3 (1978): 21–4.

Wittenberg, Hermann. 'The Taint of the Censor: J. M. Coetzee and the Making of *In the Heart of the Country*', *English in Africa* 38, no. 2 (2008): 133–50.

Wittenberg, Hermann. 'Towards an Archaeology of *Dusklands*'. *English in Africa* 38, no. 3 (2011): 71–89.

Zimbler, Jarad, 'Under Local Eyes: The South African Publishing Context of J.M. Coetzee's *Foe*'. *English Studies in Africa* 47, no. 1: 47–59.

PART TWO

Early Coetzee

CHAPTER FIVE

Coetzee's poetry

JARAD ZIMBLER

J. M. Coetzee is not by reputation a poet. In its citation, the Nobel Prize committee identifies him simply as a writer, and its press release records only the novels and autobiographical fictions published prior to 2003. The huge edifice of criticism that has grown up around his oeuvre deals almost exclusively with these and later fictions, and otherwise with his volumes of scholarship, correspondence and translation. Yet his earliest writerly efforts were in verse. Indeed, until the appearance of *Dusklands* in 1974, his body of published literary works consisted of twenty-four poems.

Little has been written about these poems, which appeared in two literary periodicals, *A Literary Miscellany* and *Groote Schuur*, between 1958 and 1961, while Coetzee was a student at the University of Cape Town (UCT). Both publications were associated with UCT, and if we are seeking reasons for the neglect of Coetzee's poems beyond the difficulty of accessing them – they are available in only a few libraries – we might look to the presumed character of student writing (devoid of editorial standards, lacking in seriousness) and their dates of publication (more than a decade prior to *Dusklands*). On both grounds, Coetzee's poems might be regarded as juvenilia, the callow efforts of a young provincial whose real literary labours would not begin until 1970, an impression only strengthened by the fact that, in the years since, he has published only the one computer poem 'Hero and Bad Mother in Epic', which appeared in 1976.

On the other hand, Coetzee has made no bones about his interest in poets such as Ezra Pound, T. S. Eliot, Zbigniew Herbert and Pablo Neruda,[1] and he has devoted a good portion of his labour as translator and critic to verse.[2] Moreover, the concision, care and occasional lyricism of his prose invite questions about the enduring effects of his apprenticeship in poetry. If the language of his novels has a cold electricity, a restrained beauty, is this because it comes from a man who has been, from the outset, essentially a poet? Answering this question lies beyond the chapter's scope.[3] Instead, what it provides is an account of the earliest stages of Coetzee's career, focused on his published poems.[4]

*

Although critics have generally overlooked Coetzee's poetry, readers of *Youth* (2002) and *Summertime* (2009) may feel they have some sense of it. Both texts, but especially the former, frame Coetzee chiefly as a poet. Yet the impression these fictions create is of artistic failure. The poetry seems confected by a young man inured to solitude and desperate for romantic attachment but bewildered by others' needs. This impression serves to block any further exploration of Coetzee's earliest literary endeavours, although the story told by the poems themselves, and by the periodicals in which they appeared, is quite different.

Throughout his undergraduate years, Coetzee was in fact closely involved with a circle of students drawn together by UCT's Imaginative Writing Class, which his foreword to the 1959 issue of *A Literary Miscellany* describes as 'a group, limited to no one Department or Faculty, meeting once a week to read and discuss new writing'. This group, Coetzee continues,

> is notably without 'programme'; it was founded in 1956 by Professor R. G. Howarth, principally on the lines of the Creative Writing groups of American universities, but without their element of the professional. The intention was as much to display to students of literature the basic problems facing a writer as to encourage in young writers a self-critical sense. [...] The profit to both writers and critics has undoubtedly been great; in particular, the writers who form the nucleus of the group have gained the encouragement always needed by beginners unsure of themselves.[5]

A firm part of this 'nucleus' – along with the poets Geoffrey Haresnape, Martin Kok (also known as 'Coque') and C. J. Driver – Coetzee began in his third year to take a leading role. He helped to prepare the second *Miscellany* and served as an editor of *Groote Schuur* in 1960 and 1961.

This may indicate little more than a talent for organization, but Coetzee's associates also recognized him as a leading poet. In his editorial for *Groote Schuur* 1959, Haresnape noted: 'During the last eighteen months a small group of promising writers has been forming amid the somewhat heterogeneous collection of occasional writers [...] I recommend to your special attention C. J. Driver and John Coetzee'.[6] Two years later, describing an anthology of South African poetry he was then preparing, R. G. Howarth remarked:

> The best of the student poets at UCT, of whom Martin Kok, Geoffrey Haresnape, John Coetzee, C. J. Driver and Daniel Hutchinson may be named, in my opinion offer the new hope for South African poetry. They start with talent, have acquired a wide knowledge of poetry and its techniques, have received some training in expression, and assiduously practise writing. It is not too much to predict that if they continue as they have begun they will go a long way in authorship.[7]

Frequently mentioned amongst UCT's foremost poets, Coetzee felt it necessary to warn that 'the group is not in any sense a literary movement', and that its productions were 'remarkable for extreme variety of style and subject matter'.[8] He and his peers *were* aligned, however, in cleaving to the poetic masters of Anglo-American modernism. Uys Krige observed of the verse in *Groote Schuur*: 'Many modern influences are discernible [...]: those of T. S. Eliot, Ezra Pound, Dylan Thomas, W. H. Auden'. Krige attached Driver to Thomas and Coque to Eliot, before identifying 'more than an ounce of Pound' not only in Coetzee's 'Returning from Carthage' (which he found 'altogether charming') but also in the poems of Robin Malan and Anthony Lykiardopulos.[9] Far from being a lone Cape modernist, Coetzee was very much a young man of his moment.

He was also attentive to the work of his peers. In his foreword to the second *Miscellany*, Coetzee comments extensively on Kok and Driver, singling them out for their 'consistently high and original quality'. Driver's 'best', he opines, is 'characterized by a powerful, sustained period which grows out of a passionate concentration on a single point', even though his poetry remains that 'of a young man, its themes love and death, its manner grand'. Kok's poetry, in contrast, is 'at once more original and more uneven', with 'a subtlety not so much of meaning as of music'.[10] Several years later, Coetzee would develop these thoughts in an essay for *Groote Schuur*, where he writes that Coque's poetry 'approaches the condition of music, and too often approaches that condition so nearly that words become musical counters and cease to mean very much'. As for Driver, in terms that resonate with developments in his own practice, Coetzee praises a dedication to craft and a determination to work and rework every poem, 'each time condensing it, making it tighter and more compact'.[11]

So much then for the story of Coetzee as a sad, sober undergraduate, composing melancholy poems in isolation, generally misunderstood and disliked. From the pages of *A Literary Miscellany* and *Groote Schuur*, there emerges a story of a confident and promising young poet, a dedicated and sensitive critic of his peers and an active participant in a localized but nonetheless vibrant print culture. Of course, neither the story of failure nor the story of success captures the whole truth. Both are fictions of a kind, with their own characters and arcs, and there is nothing in the poems or periodicals to suggest that the Imaginative Writing Class was a source of deep companionship or sustained friendship. But if my brief account of this period need not be taken to dispute the veracity of the reports in *Youth* and *Summertime*, it might at least clear a space in which to consider Coetzee's poetry more attentively, and, as it were, from the ground up.

*

Identifying the distinctive qualities of UCT's promising poets, Guy Howarth describes Coetzee as a 'scholarly and finished artist'.[12] It is a remark unlikely to surprise readers familiar with the later fictions. A more striking feature of the early poems is their generic variety: Coetzee deploys closed and highly formalized genres – sonnet, ballad, epigram – as well as looser forms: there are several short lyrics, a few prosodically complex longer poems and a passage from a verse drama. This variety throws into relief another surprising feature, which is their thematic consistency: they are all poems of love, or of matters related to love – sensuality, desire, romantic feeling, erotic encounter.

In light of the hackneyed character of love poetry, and of his remark on Driver that love and death are the young man's themes, does this consistency speak simply to Coetzee's naivety? In fact, his poetry reveals that Coetzee was acutely conscious of the conventions on which he drew and of their banalization by over-use. This consciousness is nowhere clearer than in 'The Love Song', a fairly long poem (120 lines) which appeared in *A Literary Miscellany* in 1958.[13] Here are the first verse paragraphs:

>   Raphael made a century of sonnets,
> Made and wrote them in a certain volume
> Dinted with the silver-pointed pencil.
>
>   She cometh, clad in white and blue, in Mary's colour.
>   Hide behind a hedge and sing, canzoni, sing
>   Like crickets.

> She that cometh first is naméd Primavera,
> Which is to say, Spring,
> Being thus named because she walketh before Beatrice,
> Which is Love.
>
> >   And should I then presume?
> >   And how should I begin?
> >   Should I say:
>
> My love doth move with gentle tread;
> She bruiseth not the grass;
> The tallest tree bows low its head
> And sighs when she doth pass.
> >   If nature bend
> >   To her its knee,
> >   Can she refuse
> >   A lover's plea?
>
> >   Signifying nothing.
>
> (ll. 1–22)

Language, style, prosody and tone shift noticeably from paragraph to paragraph, and, in spite of some antiquated diction and syntax, the poem's shape on the page (and its title), mark it as assertively modern, even modernist, indebted specifically to T. S. Eliot. Nevertheless, once over the interpretive hurdle of the first paragraph (the meaning of which remains somewhat opaque), it is not difficult to follow the developing line of thought: a woman comes onto the scene, prompting excitement in the persona and a desire that his love be declared ('sing, canzoni, sing'), though this excitement is troubled by doubt ('how should I begin?'). In the lyrical effusion of the fifth paragraph, this doubt seems momentarily overcome, only to return with a jolt in the sixth, which dismisses the 'lover's plea' as meaningless.

If there is something oddly familiar about this shuttling between enthusiasm and doubt, it is because the pattern is well established in the English love lyric. It is also, more importantly, because several of the poem's phrases are lifted from elsewhere. 'Signifying nothing' – the words with which Shakespeare's Macbeth concludes his reflections on the brevity and absurdity of life. 'And should I then presume?/And how should I begin?' – questions posed by Eliot's Prufrock. In fact, as soon as we latch on to the more recognizable citations, it becomes apparent that, in order to sing its lover's lament (which is also a song about the difficulty of giving voice to passion), Coetzee's poem has cobbled together fragments from other poems, sometimes whole stanzas, sometimes phrases or conceits. Even in this brief extract there are citations of or allusions to Robert Browning (first paragraph), Ezra Pound (second) and Dante (third). In other parts of the poem we encounter words or lines from Samuel Coleridge, Emily Bronte, W. B. Yeats and the Song of Solomon, as well as further references to Shakespeare and Eliot.

'The Love Song' is a verse bricolage. This does not stop it working as the celebration of a particular love object, but over and beyond this the poem is a vehicle for charting the course of the European love lyric and reflecting on its gradually vacated project and attenuated condition. 'The Love Song' operates, in other words, both as ode and elegy, praising a loved other *and* lamenting the lyric of love. It also pokes fun at the high seriousness of much love poetry, including the author's own: the fifth verse paragraph is taken not from any canonical antecedent, but from Coetzee's unpublished 'Lamentation'. One might read this in a comic light, as Coetzee's self-mocking acknowledgement of his youthful pretensions. Or one might read it as a hint that the project of Coetzee's early poems was to perform particular postures or personae – none wholly sincere, each superseding the last. This would encourage us to treat all of these poems as finger exercises for developing technical proficiency. It would also explain their thematic consistency and generic diversity.

There may be something to this view, which is aligned with Howarth's assessment. Yet the poems, to my mind and despite the reservations of *Youth*'s narrator, are nonetheless capable of conveying the charge of certain affective predicaments. 'The Love Song', for instance, dramatizes quite powerfully a self-consciousness of exhausted personhood in the vein of Prufrock, but also of exhausted poetic potentiality. The final verse paragraph seems especially poignant:

> And I stand waiting for the past
> Waiting to say what has been said,
> To write what has been written
> With the silver-pointed pencil.
>
> (ll. 117–120)

The closing line's 'silver-pointed pencil' takes us back to the opening verse paragraph, which is lifted in its entirety from Robert Browning's 'One Word More', the final poem of his collection *Men and Women* (1855). Here, Browning appears to drop his many masks and to step forward in his own person (if only to lament the lack of a communicative means untainted by art and artifice). Incorporated in Coetzee's 'The Love Song', Browning's enactment of direct address is initially undercut – it becomes one more mask. It is then revived in the final paragraph, where the authorial persona of Coetzee's own poem seems to emerge, casting an eye back over his performance whilst recognizing that even this authenticating gesture belongs to the past.

The pathos and sometimes bathos of this predicament are close to the surface in other of Coetzee's early poems, including the two that appeared alongside 'The Love Song' in *A Literary Miscellany*, 'Procula to Pilate' and 'Attic'. These are likewise steeped in classicism, markedly citational, and concerned with masks (tragic as well as comic) and the death of poetic and erotic immediacy. But while the preoccupation with love continues, Coetzee finds alternative means of expressing his classicism and world-weariness. Turning from the longer-mixed forms of 'The Love Song' and 'Attic', he works towards greater compression and develops a different voice – wry, restrained, urbane – that is crystalized in twelve epigrams published in the second *Miscellany*.

Influenced by Catullus and Martial by way of Pound, Coetzee's epigrams vary in length between two and six lines (though most are three or four) and deploy a simpler diction and sudden reversals, often satirical or caustic, the force of which depends on the play of parallelism or syntactical inversion. These features are apparent in the first epigram of eleven included under the title 'Trivial Verses':

> Lady, thanks are due to you for your delicate conversation.
> Neoptolomos did not believe in the likes of you,

> But Neoptolomos is long since dead,
> While you remain to charm both Philolaus and me.[14]

There is no strict metre here and no pattern of beats either, but a propulsive movement is achieved through condensation and the interaction of syntactic poise and lineation. The poem consists of four finite clauses, each occupying a line. The first apostrophizes and compliments the unnamed 'Lady', a recurring figure in Coetzee's epigrams, and establishes the scenario of the poem. This scenario is then complicated across the second, third and fourth lines, with each subsequent clause unsettling the meaning of the one preceding it, so that every line-ending becomes a site of suspense: the second indirectly introduces a doubt about the lady's sincerity; the third seems to cancel that doubt by noting the obsolescence of its source (though being 'long since dead' has nothing to do with Neoptolomos's perspicacity); and the fourth reawakens it on different grounds: how good a judge of delicacy might the poet be, when he is so cavalier about the death of an acquaintance and so clearly subject to the lady's charms? And does this delicacy anyway lie merely in her ability to keep two suitors under her spell?

As well as the changes in form and style, this epigram has two further noteworthy features. First, it summons a social world that extends beyond the lover and beloved, a world of friends and rivals, conversation and competition. In subsequent epigrams, this world becomes one of marriage and infidelity, display and pursuit. Second, it continues to encode, though more subtly, an anxiety about the sincerity of the passions and of the words through which they are expressed. This is hinted at in the ambivalence of 'delicate conversation', but in later epigrams, such as the eighth, it becomes more explicit:

> If Philolaus' poem of praise is twice as long as mine,
> You must remember, lady, that poets are liars,
> And his lie therefore twice as great as mine.[15]

Here we have the same love triangle – persona, lady and Philolaus – but now the rivals are clearly identified as poets, with poetry their vehicle of seduction. The sting in the tail, however, is that poems are inherently dishonest, and all the more dishonest the longer, and by implication the more elaborate, they become. But if this seems merely a cynical restatement of the paradox of writing love poetry in an awareness that its possibilities have been liquidated, the sense of belatedness has dissipated, and the implicit association between concision and greater honesty suggests a route out of the quandary. Suddenly, epigrammatic compression is given a moral dimension, albeit that the poem's persuasiveness is shadowed by the artificiality of its rhetoric and by the ludic quality attributed to the epigrams by their title, 'Trivial Verses'.

The concern with compression is found again in two later poems, which appeared in *Groote Schuur* 1960 beneath the following epigraph:[16]

> 'Poems must be like glass, and round – but not absolutely round. They must be – *so!*'
> 'How – *so?*' said Wuss.
> 'So – just so.' He held his hands a little apart, cupped. 'Or so.' He made a circle of thumb and
>   forefinger.
>
> Mertens, Wiss and Wuss

The epigraph seems as if it comes from a novel not unlike Samuel Beckett's *Murphy* (1938), but there is no such book as *Wiss and Wuss* and no such writer as 'Mertens'. This is another citational game about literary authority, which also plays with ideas about a poetics of transparency: the proposition that poems should be 'like glass' is rather murky, and though the description of Wiss's gestures is wonderfully precise (one sees immediately what he is doing with hands and fingers), the meaning of these gestures remains opaque. But this confusing or at least ambivalent simplicity is in fact excellent preparation for encountering the poems that follow, which are, indeed, small and clear and perhaps even somewhat round (smooth, circular, but not perfectly regular). And yet, though their words couldn't be simpler, their meanings remain clouded.

Here is the first:

The wives of the rock lobster fishermen
Have grown accustomed to waking alone,
Their husbands having for centuries fished at dawn;
Nor is their sleep as troubled as mine.
If you have gone, go then to the Portuguese rock lobster fishermen.[17]

This is perhaps the best-known of Coetzee's early poems because it is included in *Youth*. Its peculiar charm has to do with the subtlety of its end-rhymes (every line ends /n/) and the way words and sounds echo across it (fishermen/ fished at dawn/ fishermen; rock/ lobster; grown/ alone; gone/ go then). In it, one finds many of the same features apparent in the epigrams: compression, lexical simplicity, alignment of syntax and lineation, a barbed final line. But there are also developments. To begin with, the classical scaffolding and its urbane world have been removed. Here we return to a relationship between lover and beloved, without rivals or jaundiced views of marriage and fidelity, and also without concerns about belatedness, artifice or the insincerity and exhaustion of love poetry. Instead, the poem invokes a world far closer to home, the coastal waters of the Western Cape summoned in its reference to rock lobster fishermen, but also in its movement (an undulation made of peaks and troughs of stress), and in its imperfect rhyme (which suggests a muffling produced by the ocean's roar). Against this background, the poem's scenario is a simple one: the persona, waking from disturbed sleep to an empty bed, imprecates the lover who has abandoned him. And yet there is something odd, some indigestible grit, which has to do with the inexact parallel: the persona is compared with the fishermen's wives, his lover with the fishermen, but it is to the fishermen that the lover is sent, not to their wives.

The trend towards compression as well as simplicity continues in the last of Coetzee's UCT poems, published in *Groote Schuur* 1961, as does the preoccupation with failed love. Indeed, much like 'The Love Song', 'Five Night-Thoughts of a Loving Sleepless', along with the two untitled poems appended to it as if they are afterthoughts, stage contrasting attitudes to love and the beloved. They do so, however, in an entirely different register and form. This is apparent if we consider the first and second stanzas of 'Five Night-Thoughts', which describe ecstatic sexual encounter and then a post-coital drift towards doubt:

Our mad pulse hurls the singing-birds of love
Into the drift of unregarding stars

And still the golden birds cry *More!*
And hurtle back across the tattered evening.

> Easily you are gone into the kingdom of the sea of sleep,
> And leave me in a half-state, drifting,
> In my ears the memory, the surge,
> The desperate breaking of the waves of our incontinence.[18]

This drift will terminate in now familiar despondency: 'Nothing so pure as the white of this dawn,/ Nothing so pure as this regret'.[19] Yet the predicament of 'The Love Song' as well as its literary colouring have been entirely stripped out. There are no obvious citations or allusions here, no conscious masking, no fears of belatedness, no doubts about poetic speech. Instead, we have a work that may not be earth-shatteringly original but is nonetheless evocative, even poignant. Indeed, though it retains an epigrammatic quality (each of its stanzas is self-enclosed, tracing a discrete experience with a gentle turn in the end-stopped final line), 'Five Night-Thoughts' seems considerably more lyrical than 'Trivial Verses'. This is because it comes closer to metre, its use of metaphor is intensified and it appears more serious and forthright. On the same grounds, 'Five Night-Thoughts' might be distinguished from 'The wives of the rock lobster fishermen', another poem of troubled sleep, though its action too unfolds in proximity to the ocean, the sound and motion of which shape the persona's sleepless 'half-state' as well as his memory of sexual experience.

*

The story I have told about Coetzee's early poetry is different from the one found in *Youth* and *Summertime*. It is a story of fruitful apprenticeship and growing confidence, in which the author hones his craft and moves away from Miltonic phrasing and ponderous intertextuality towards concision and a poetics of description increasingly alert to contexts and concrete locations. All the same, there are continuities, above all the thematics of love and sex.

A less prominent through-line, though one pertinent to Coetzee's later career, is a narrative sensibility that is latent but nonetheless detectable in many of the poems, especially in the episodic arrangement of their materials. In 'The Love Song', fragments are selected from an established repertoire and composed into a sequence that is rhythmically satisfying, and which, perhaps for this reason, possesses narrative thrust. The 'Trivial Verses' too are so arranged as to develop the story of a love triangle terminating in disappointment. And after the stanzas of 'Five Night-Thoughts' trace the emotional arc of several hours, from ecstasy to regret, the two additional poems, rather than being arbitrary appendages, seem to round out the account, describing the origin of the relationship ('At our first meeting we talked of fairy tales'), and its melancholy aftermath ('You are gone').

Of course, our own predilections for storytelling may prompt us to see continuity where there is only absence or dissipation. Yet the processes of selection, combination and composition that go into making 'The Love Song' seem remarkably similar to those at the heart of the computational experiments that Coetzee would conduct over the subsequent decade. Indeed, seeking to automate these processes would lead him eventually to 'Hero and Bad Mother in Epic', a poem very much concerned with how stories are put together, and with what happens when a personal consciousness is withdrawn from narrative.

Which brings me to my final point: *Youth* encourages us to view John's desire to become a poet as doomed from the outset by his naivety and narcissism. There is something arid in his soul, and, it is implied, in his writing. To some extent, Coetzee's early poems do attest to an experience of arid practices, of exhausted forms. Exhaustion and, indeed, aridity characterize other projects described in Coetzee's novels, such as Magda's stone words and Cruso's barren terraces, both of which involve assembling and re-assembling found objects. What is missing from these projects, and perhaps from Coetzee's early poems too, is an orientation beyond the limited configuration of the love song, in which only the lover and beloved occupy the stage. We might think of this absent orientation as social in character, meaning by this a gesture beyond the immediate community of rivals and lovers and towards the larger world of social relations and political conflicts.

In this light, we might dwell on Coetzee's withdrawal from poetry, or at least from the print community in which he had participated, which coincided, more or less, with his departure for England, but also with a literary debate sparked by student radicalization in the aftermath of the Sharpeville massacre. One of the direct consequences of this debate was the founding of a new UCT literary magazine, *The Lion and the Impala*. In its first editorial, those involved – chief amongst them C. J. Driver – noted that their aim was 'to make this a "committed" magazine'. Although they would not refuse to 'publish love-lyrics', their preference would be for 'lyrics about the difficulties of love in a hate-ridden country'.[20] Did this, too, have a chilling effect on Coetzee's further involvement with his peers? His later remarks make it difficult to be certain. Coetzee's essay of 1963 favours Driver's poetry over his 'more facile prose polemic', but it also concedes that 'writing poetry about South Africa implies writing political poetry' and praises the depth of Driver's 'awareness of the nature of the country'.[21]

As for 'Computer Poem', Coetzee's own contribution to *The Lion and the Impala*, this did not appear until March 1963, by which stage the magazine had abandoned its policy of commitment and 'devoted' itself 'simply to the arts'.[22] This does not make it easier to parse the intentions of the piece, which consists of two versions of a poem (one 'ex computer', the other 'edited'), and a commentary on the processes behind their composition.[23] These processes include the programme Coetzee had written and the vocabularies and structure he had provided. They also include the means by which this particular randomly generated sequence had been chosen and shaped: 'The editor now wades through what has been printed (in this case 2,100 poems at a rate of 75 poems per minute), makes his selection, reduces it to standard form, and sends it to the editor'.[24]

Across the piece as a whole, the tone is caustic, reminiscent of the early poetry's world-weariness and anxiety about meaning and originality. In an especially biting moment, Coetzee claims that, though the making of his computer poem had required 'elementary critical abilities [...] it should not be immensely difficult to write a computer programme that could be run by a hack'. Is this merely comic self-deprecation or a species of irony? Coetzee's remarks impute an automatism even to the procedures of the 'editor', but we might wonder at the self-revealing perspicacity of his choice of 'personal estrangement' as the 'area of life' out of which to build his vocabularies. We might wonder also at the decision to include 'Blackmen' amongst the 'random vocabulary of nature-words' to be 'inserted randomly' in the poem; and at the instinct which led Coetzee to select, in preference to the 2,099 alternatives, an output he was able to convert into the following:

You spend the nights away from me,
Terrified, rapt,
Among owls and black men,
Hoping for violence.[25]

Perhaps there really is no more to Coetzee's 'Computer Poem' than a laconic disenchantment with poetry and poets. Or perhaps the essay smuggles in a lyric that does indeed contend with the distortions of love and desire in a country saturated by Manichean violence – and thereby points the way to the achievements of Coetzee's early fictions.

ACKNOWLEDGEMENT

An early version of this chapter was presented in 2017 at the conference "Travelling with Coetzee: Other Arts, Other Languages", hosted by the Oxford Research Centre in the Humanities. I am grateful to the organizers, Michelle Kelly and Elleke Boehmer, for their invitation.

NOTES

1. Asked about influences in 1978, Coetzee identified Pound, Rilke, Herbert and Neruda as poets whom he'd 'read with more intensity' than 'any novelist'. See Coetzee, 'Speaking: J. M. Coetzee', 24.
2. Coetzee has translated six Dutch poets, collected in *Landscape with Rowers* (2004), as well as Ina Rousseau's 'Eden', *Poetry* 190.1 (2007): 10–11. Several essays in *White Writing* (1988) and *Doubling the Point* (1990) concern South African and Dutch poetry, and he has written about Paul Celan, Walt Whitman, Friedrich Hölderlin and Les Murray for the *New York Review of Books*.
3. I explore the poetic dimensions of Coetzee's style and the significance of 'Hero and Bad Mother in Epic' in Zimbler, *Politics of Style*, 87–119.
4. The Coetzee Papers include manuscript and typescript drafts of more than fifty unpublished poems, dated between 1956 and 1963.
5. Coetzee, 'Foreword', [iii].
6. Haresnape, 'Editorial', 1.
7. Howarth, 'Towards an Anthology', 8.
8. Coetzee, 'Foreword', [iii].
9. Krige, '*Groote Schuur*: A Few Notes', 9–10.
10. Coetzee, 'Foreword', [iii–iv].
11. Coetzee, 'Haresnape, Driver and Coque', 3–4.
12. Howarth, 'Towards an Anthology', 8.
13. Coetzee, 'The Love Song', 14–15.
14. Coetzee, 'Trivial Verses', 7.
15. Ibid., 30.
16. Coetzee, 'Poems must be like glass …', 15.
17. Ibid.
18. Coetzee, 'Five Night-Thoughts', 11 (ll. 1–8).
19. Ibid. (ll. 16–17).
20. 'Why and the Wherefore', *The Lion and the Impala*, 1.
21. Coetzee, 'Haresnape, Driver and Coque', 4.
22. 'Editorial', *The Lion and the Impala*, 1.
23. Coetzee, 'Computer Poem', 12–13. For background to this essay, as well as Coetzee's experiments with computer poetry, see Roach, 'Coetzee's Aesthetic Automatism', 320–4.

24. Coetzee, 'Computer Poem', 13.

25. Ibid., 12–13.

WORKS CITED

Coetzee, J. M. 'Computer Poem'. *The Lion and the Impala* 2, no. 1 (1963): 12–13.
Coetzee, J. M. 'Five Night-Thoughts of a Loving Sleepless; to which are Appended Two Poems'. *Groote Schuur* (1961): 11.
Coetzee, J. M. 'Foreword'. *A Literary Miscellany* 2 (1959): iii–iv.
Coetzee, J. M. 'Haresnape, Driver and Coque – Retrospect June 1962'. *Groote Schuur* (1962/63): 1–4.
Coetzee, J. M. 'Hero and Bad Mother in Epic, a Poem'. *Staffrider* 1, no. 1 (1978): 36–7.
Coetzee, J. M. 'The Love Song'. *A Literary Miscellany* (1958): 14–17.
Coetzee, J. M. 'Poems Must Be Like Glass …'. *Groote Schuur* (1960): 15.
Coetzee, J. M. 'Speaking: J. M. Coetzee'. With Stephen Watson. *Speak* 1, no. 3 (1978): 21–4.
Coetzee, J. M. 'Trivial Verses'. *A Literary Miscellany* 2 (1959): 7, 14, 16, 20, 22, 30, 40, 56.
'Editorial'. *The Lion and the Impala* 2, no. 1 (1963): 1.
Haresnape, Geoffrey. 'Editorial'. *Groote Schuur* (1959): 1–2.
Howarth, R. G. 'Towards an Anthology of Contemporary South African Poetry'. *Groote Schuur* (1961): 7–9.
Krige, Uys. 'Groote Schuur: A Few Notes'. *Groote Schuur* (1960): 8–11.
Roach, Rebecca. 'J. M. Coetzee's Aesthetic Automatism'. *Modern Fiction Studies* 65, no. 2 (2019): 308–37.
'The Why and the Wherefore'. *The Lion and the Impala* 1, no. 1 (1962): 1.
Zimbler, Jarad. *J. M. Coetzee and the Politics of Style*. Cambridge: Cambridge University Press, 2014.

CHAPTER SIX

Dusklands

RITA BARNARD

THE DIFFICULTY OF *DUSKLANDS*

The critical life of *Dusklands*, J. M. Coetzee's first published fiction, begins with Jonathan Crewe's review of the work in the South African journal *Contrast* in 1974. To start this chapter with Crewe's assessment makes practical sense and also honours his agency, as a perceptive early reader of the manuscript and a facilitator in the publication of this barbed diptych of novellas. These novellas are 'The Vietnam Project', set in California and dated 1972–3, and 'The Narrative of Jacobus Coetzee', set – insofar as it has a singular location or date – at the far frontiers of the Cape Colony around 1760. Crewe's review is bold in its praise. Noting the way in which the work is not only referential (it definitely had something to say about those two separate yet connected worlds) but also reflexive, Crewe hailed *Dusklands* as heralding the arrival of the modern novel in South Africa.[1] The second novella in particular, with its 'journey of the Western consciousness out of the polity and into the void' and the consequent 'orgy of horror, pain, cruelty, and exultation', is a work that 'deserves to be spoken of in the same breath as *Heart of Darkness*'.[2] Canonizing and prophetic words indeed.

The immediate impact of *Dusklands* in South African literary circles (it took some years for Coetzee to receive international notice) was mixed. The reception ranged from incomprehension and distress to disapprobation (especially from Marxist cultural activists) to excitement. This excitement I remember well. In 1977 the distinguished Afrikaans novelist Elsa Joubert brandished her copy of *Dusklands* at me, urging me to give up my master's thesis on Ted Hughes (yes, friends) and attend instead to works like this one: works that truly did something new and, even more importantly, addressed the turbulent decolonizing world in which I found myself. Eventually, whether consciously and unconsciously, I ended up following Joubert's advice.

But now I find myself in a perplexing position: after many years of teaching *Dusklands* in the United States, along with Conrad's *Heart of Darkness* or Werner Herzog's *Aguirre*, I find my students, a diverse and intelligent lot, balking at the text. In the wake of the Black Lives Matter protests, which (once again) laid bare the longue durée of settler colonialism, the gruelling engagement with 'the malady of the master's soul' that *Dusklands* demands of its readers was distinctly unwelcome.[3] So much so that several students declined to read Coetzee's *Waiting for the Barbarians* at the end of the course and refused to watch the new film version of the novel. Should they be faulted? After all, the revelations about colonial discourse that *Dusklands* stunned us with in the 1970s are no longer new; my students were already trained to look for silences, racist misrepresentations and epistemic violence in a text. So, is it worth their while to be subjected to *Duskland*'s merciless exposures of imperial pathologies? Or could their response perhaps encourage us to describe the work in a different way – one that includes their reaction, sidesteps some of the fine work that critics have done towards laying out the work's ironic pseudo-philosophy and tries to recapture something of its very real challenges and its enduring effects?

THE PROBLEM OF CRUELTY

Let me try. I would like to return to Crewe's annunciation of *Dusklands* as the first truly modern novel in South Africa. In later writing, Crewe doesn't double down on the choice of phrase (the word 'postmodernism', he notes, was not yet in wide circulation), but his original designation is to my mind felicitous.[4] Consider, for a moment, the applicability of Richard Poirier's provocation, 'The Difficulties of Modernism and the Modernism of Difficulty,' written just a few years after Crewe's review. Modernism, Poirier argues here, is not so much a style or set of ideas, but a situation: a situation of grim reading.[5] There is something about the modern text that makes it impossible to read it in any way other than seriously – perhaps even solemnly. Poirier's description, though based on writers like Joyce and Eliot, captures some of the defining features of Coetzee's writing – not least the way in which it hovers between literature and (self)criticism and the way in which it often feels intimidating.[6] The difficulty of modernism, Poirier notes, lies in the way it makes us feel as though any interpretation we might put forward will be insufficiently critical, or will already be incorporated in the text.[7] (Coetzee critics know this feeling.) Grim reading is therefore a fraught, unfinishable and curiously intimate process: the modern text seeks – or creates – a reader willing to be complicit with the author, willing to match his intellectualism and seriousness, even if that willingness may not be rewarded by the text's yielding to any order the reader might impose. This is surely true with regard to *Dusklands*, which, as Crewe puts it, confronts the reader with 'the practically forced acquisition of a new sophistication'.[8]

In what follows, I will touch in passing on some of the usual modernist difficulties *Dusklands* entails – like fragmentation, an erudite range of allusions and so forth – but what I want to assert is that with *Dusklands* the fraught transaction goes beyond grim. The problem my students faced, after all, was not the complexity of the text, but rather its relentless brutality: the repulsive subject positions they were forced to inhabit. To require the reader to receive chummy advice on how to hunt, trap, and kill a bushman, gleefully share in plans for a devastating air war or witness a massacre from the point of view of the perpetrator is a heavy burden. The usual readerly complicity may feel tainted by a deeper form of complicity – by a degree of identification with the perpetrators and the repugnant narrators that readers have sensed in this work (and which goes far beyond the inscription of the name 'Coetzee' in both novellas).[9] We are dealing, I want to say, not only with difficult, but with cruel reading.

This is a situation that David Attwell already described in his pioneering chapter on *Dusklands* in 1993. He quotes at some length the ruthless, violent and vulgar execution scene at the end of the first part of 'The Narrative of Jacobus Coetzee,' one that spares no bodily detail. The justification the narrator offers for his deeds does nothing to mitigate their horror: the writing remains 'transgressive,' Attwell observes, and 'not in a theoretical manner that enables one to explain it away, but in an *aggressive* mode that is aimed at readers' sensibilities.'[10] Why this excess? Attwell offers, tentatively, a kind of political resolution, in line with his overall project of historicizing Coetzee's work in non-reductive ways. The relentless fierceness, he suggests, is a measure of the intensities of historical situation in which the author was operating: these may account for the assault, in the dark days of apartheid and Vietnam, on liberal humanist readers, who are given no wiggle room at all in this work, lest they distance themselves from the darkest aspects of (neo) colonialism. (We might mark here the striking distance from Conrad and his gentlemanly narrator Marlow, who circumnavigate and euphemize such horrors.) It is an unsatisfactory resolution, however, and I sense in the discussions about this matter in *Doubling the Point* that Attwell knows this. But we can keep his argument in mind as we probe further.

A different account, one that puts forward a psychological rather than political motivation, is offered by Coetzee himself in *Summertime*. The fictive situation here is that a would-be biographer of the deceased author interviews one of his previous lovers, a psychologist, who offers an intriguing take on the work:

> As a piece of writing I don't say *Dusklands* is lacking in passion, but the passion behind it is obscure. I read it as a book about cruelty, an exposé of the cruelty involved in various forms of conquest. But what was the actual source of that cruelty? Its locus, it now seems to me, lay within the author himself. The best interpretation I can give of the book is that writing it was a project in self-administered therapy.[11]

Of course, we need not agree with the view of this character. The work, after all, offers little possibility of healing or closure and 'The Vietnam Project,' as we will see, treats psychotherapy in a way that hardly gives it much credibility. Yet I would agree that there seems to be some strange personal dimension to the work (some Coetzee critics see it an exorcism of the danger of becoming someone like Dawn or his Coetzee ancestors).[12] So, this view is also worth keeping in mind – not least for the authorial admission of *Dusklands'* cruelty.

Two more literary and ethical perspectives arise for me out of the psychologist's assessment. Let us ponder for a moment an intriguing hypothesis in Fredric Jameson's early meditations on modernism. Modernist style, he argues, often involves a homeopathic strategy. Think, for example, of the insistent repetitions of Gertrude Stein's prose. Could we understand it as a formal response to the repetitions, copies and reiterations of mass production? If so, as Jameson puts it, 'the scandalous and intolerable external irritant is drawn into the aesthetic process itself and thereby systematically worked over, "acted out," and symbolically neutralized'.[13] Now, I would question that phrase 'symbolically neutralized' (which comes too close to the resolutions of 'therapy'), but the hypothesis is worth entertaining. Coetzee's observations about US life in the years of the Vietnam War, where a kind of rage and violence seemed to seep into the very fabric of quotidian existence, seem relevant. He describes his own 'voyage into the belly of the beast' along with complicated feelings of revulsion and, if not complicity, then burdensome knowledge. 'Why that revulsion?' he asks:

> I can only say that violence and death, my own death, are to me, intuitively the same things. Violence, as soon as I sense its presence within me, becomes introverted as violence against myself: I cannot project it outwards. ... Or to explain myself in another way: I understand the Crucifixion as a refusal and an introversion of retributive violence, a refusal so deliberate, so conscious, and so powerful that it overwhelms any reinterpretation, Freudian, Marxian, or whatever, that we can give to it.[14]

Do these revealing comments then suggest that the excessive cruelty readers sense in *Dusklands* has to do not with therapy as such, nor with assaulting the reader (at least in the first instance), but with the introjection of violent discourses and cruel subjectivities while also deriving a literary form – that of the monologue and parodic document – from the exercise? To permit oneself to be occupied by a repulsive sensibility like that of a Vietnam-era think-tank contributor (a neurotic version of the fat, callous and morally outrageous policy wonk, Herman Kahn) or of a self-important Hottentot-killer of the eighteenth-century Cape, to speak their own monologues, as it were, is to risk some psychic damage.[15] The strategy of introversion is different from the usual writerly process, which Coetzee describes in *Doubling the Point* as the calling up of other voices inside him, in order to engage with them in a dialogic exploration. What *Dusklands* presents is not dialogue, nor even satire, but rather an absorption and performance (perhaps in the spirit of a strange self-sacrifice) of the cruelty around the author's environment and the cruelty to which he is heir. There is a possible figure for this risky experiment in 'The Vietnam Project'. The speakers of the constituent monologues inhabit the writer – or at least the writing – as 'a hideous mongol boy who stretches his limbs inside my hollow bones, gnaws my liver with his smiling teeth, voids his bilious filth into my systems, and will not go' (49). This is closer to a kind of literary demon possession than therapy.

I will return to this suggestion eventually. But we should also ponder some of the ideas about cruel reading and writing that are actually articulated in the work itself (even though, again, these assertions are voiced through an untrustworthy narrator). I am thinking here of the strange account of the nature of print in 'The Vietnam Project'. Here Eugene Dawn, whose work entails recommendations for broadcast propaganda to the Vietnamese enemy, contrasts the 'pure authority' of radio information to the affective complexities of print:

> Print ... is sadism, and properly evokes terror. The message of the newspaper is: 'I can say anything and not be moved. Watch as I permute my 52 affectless signs.' Print is the hard master with the whip, print-reading a weeping search for signs of mercy. Writer is as much abased before him as reader.
>
> (20)

What seems to be evoked here, we might say, are the problems of cruel reading. And what is proposed as a break from this torturous relationship between writing and reading is, surprisingly, pornography:

> The pornographer is the doomed upstart hero who aspires to such delirium of ecstasy that the surface of the print will crack beneath his words. We write our violent novelties on the walls of lavatories to bring the walls down. This is the secret reason, the more hidden reason. Obscuring the hidden reason, unseen to us, is the true reason: that we write on lavatory walls to abase ourselves before them. Pornography is an abasement before the page, such abasement as to convulse the very page.
>
> (20)

This is not a passage that is easy to unpack, as is indeed the case with the entire monologue of this speaker, who is at one moment violent and megalomaniacal and at others abject and obsequious. Given these vacillations any interpretation must be tentative. But it is worth recalling here that the first draft of the novella was entitled 'Pornography', which suggests that the workings of pornography as outlined here may bear some relationship to the intended workings of the text itself.[16] The suggestion seems to be that affective excess – those 'deliriums' of ecstasy and shame – might break through the devious rigidities of the authorized script. Of course, in *Dusklands* we cannot but think of 'print' as the pseudo-manuscripts included in the work, the text of Dawn's policy proposal in 'The Vietnam Project' and the academic afterword to 'The Narrative of Jacobus Coetzee', documents that (until they descend into obvious craziness) lay out and normalize vicious and ecocidal views, and, in the latter case, whitewash, erase and even celebrate such murderous activities. One can then understand an impulse to bring down the walls of print, and perhaps even entertain the idea that 'violent novelties' may offer a way to do so.

I am not comfortable with this idea, but I explain the hypothesis to myself in the following way. It is perhaps a kind of anti-Brechtian strategy.[17] In both Coetzee and in Brecht, after all, there is the aim of ideological exposure; there is also a refusal of catharsis with its well-established management of affect – of pity and fear. (We could perhaps take the 'milking' of Jacobus Coetzee's anal carbuncle as a kind of horrific literalization of the very idea of purgation.) But whereas in Brecht there is a suspension of the audience's emotional response in order to foster ratiocination and critical revelation, what we have in *Dusklands* is the opposite: a galvanizing of excessive emotions – disgust, horror, anxiety – in order to dislodge a kind of authorized madness. Rationality is to no avail, for *Dusklands* entails, as many scholars have argued, a critique of reason, tainted as it is by imperial discourse. And no didactic message is possible here given that the very medium – language and print – is shown to be part of the problem. But perhaps print can be made to crack, as it were, even that staid archival document reproduced at the end of 'The Narrative of Jacobus Coetzee' (seen by some readers as finally providing the historical truth), so that its fifty-two signs can no longer be taken as 'affectless'.

Speculative, I know. But these are ways of thinking about the radical situation of reading and writing generated by the event of *Dusklands*: this is difficult reading – and more.

THE NECESSITY OF COMPARISON

If *Dusklands*, then, can be disturbing and perhaps damaging (also for the author), there is one respect in which the work's difficulty – a specific challenge that all readers have to ponder – has greatly enhanced the work's reputation and impact. I am thinking here of the work's diptych structure: the inclusion of 'The Vietnam Project' and 'The Narrative of Jacobus Coetzee' under a single evocative title. It is clear from J. C. Kannemeyer's biography that there was a degree of happenstance in the final shape of the text: the constituent novellas were too short to be marketed separately. But in terms of Coetzee's ambition, the combination – and the comparative reading it demands – is absolutely crucial. As Coetzee recalls in a recent interview, his desire was not only to get published, but to get published abroad: in London and especially in New York.[18] To do so, he needed not just the wordcount but the weighty historical implications that the dual frames of reference open up.

Critics have, of course, long understood that that to make sense of *Dusklands* one must offer some account of the relationship between the work's two parts. This requires some interpretative labour, for *Dusklands* is not, as Dominic Head has posited, 'a unified and single entity.'[19] To be sure, as Coetzee himself has observed, the 'two narratives have a relation at the level of ideas'.[20]

These include the ontological problems of the master-slave dialectic, the misogynistic nature of the colonial project and the solipsism of the Cartesian cogito. Both parts, moreover, include parodic documents and both meditate on matters that relate to Coetzee's earlier work in mathematics and linguistics: the fallacy of numbers and the quasi-grammatical idea of the copula, the camera in 'The Vietnam Project' and the gun in 'The Narrative of Jacobus Coetzee' respectively. But the two parts remain different and disjunct enough to make the tasks of relating them strenuous – not least because they are not chronological and are internally fragmented into stylistically very different parts. Each part, shall we say, is difficult.

Today the spheres of Dutch and American colonialism are perhaps no longer considered unrelated: witness the matching chapters on the violence in the Banda archipelago and in New Amsterdam in Amitav Ghosh's unflinching account of colonial ecocide in *The Nutmeg's Curse*. But at the time of *Dusklands*' publication, the inclusion of both the American and Dutch zones of reference was startlingly new. It constituted, in Crewe's retrospective assessment, nothing less than a daring 'undoing and reconfiguration of the category of South African literature'.[21] (After all, nothing could be further than *Dusklands* from the slightly moralistic anti-apartheid English novel as defined by Paton's *Cry, the Beloved Country*.) This is to say that *Dusklands* with its 'un-English cosmopolitanism' has a performative dimension: it created – by negation and refusal as much as creative invention – a 'speaking place' from which Coetzee could launch a career as a global, rather than merely a provincial writer.[22] No wonder then that *Dusklands* met with some resistance from South African readers schooled in the militantly Leavisite English departments of the sixties and seventies, where a narrow canon of English writers was the staple offering and American literature was barely afforded a glance.[23]

To say that this particular readership is treated cruelly by the text perhaps goes too far. But they are certainly baited, especially in the part of the work that contemporary international readers might think of as a familiar terrain for South Africans, 'The Narrative of Jacobus Coetzee'. In it the reader is constantly reminded of the problems of language in colonial situations; English is not assumed to be the transparent medium, as in the realist South African novel. Instead, we find a kind of refusal on Coetzee's part to be an 'English' author.[24] This may sound strange, but the claim makes all the more sense in retrospect, in light of his increasing distaste for English as a globally hegemonic language.[25] While he could not write in Afrikaans, for that would entail another set of political problems and an even more marginal reception, Coetzee masquerades, as the novella's title page would have it, as the translator of both the eighteenth-century narrative and its afterword, his putative father S. J. Coetzee's lecture on the ancestral explorer, dating from the 1930s. The narrative frequently marks a curious distance from – or a lack of comfortable habitation in – the language in which it appears: not just in passages where the 'original' grammar shines through (as in the utterances of Coetzee's Hottentots), but also in its frequent comments on tricky negotiations between speakers of Dutch and Nama.[26] These passages trouble the English reader's assumption of linguistic privilege and mastery. And there are even more calculated and uncomfortable moments in the afterword, which in its blithe way is fully as racist and callous as the murderous first-person chronicle that precedes it. English South African readers, prone to projecting the evils of racism and apartheid onto Afrikaners, find themselves at the receiving end of a nationalist hagiography of the same frontiersman whose genocidal adventures they have just witnessed. They are addressed in the first-person plural as descendants of this bloody-minded Coetzee, urged to accept him as a hero to 'our people', and advised that 'piety' towards him is the correct response (130). They must endure slights directed at Anglo explorers, like that 'supercilious English gentleman Barrow' (131), whose mission is dismissed as far from civilizing: 'We hunt in vain', the Afrikaans professor declares, 'for a British exporter of the virtues of humility, respect, and diligence' (133).

If *Dusklands*, then, interpellates the English South African reader into unfamiliar and awkward positions of complicity, it does not let the putative American reader off the hook too easily either. To be sure, such a readership was notional at the time of the work's publication, but 'The Vietnam Project' is even more deeply informed by Coetzee's readings in American literature and his take on the pathologies of quotidian life in the United States than has previously been articulated. Martin Woessner's excellent study of Coetzee and America has observed that *Dusklands* originates in the United States and then extends to Southern Africa, to find further subject matter, audiences, and publication.[27] But 'The Vietnam Project' can actually be read as a pretty brutal undoing and reconfiguration of contemporary American literature in and of itself.

Critics have sometimes noted allusions in Coetzee's work to Hawthorne, a writer whose sense of complicity in his ancestors' cruelty echoes Coetzee's own. The references to *The Scarlet Letter* in *Waiting for the Barbarians* and *Age of Iron* are obvious.[28] Less frequently remarked is reference in *Dusklands* to Hawthorne's idea of the 'neutral territory' (38): a fertile idea in his reimagining of genre from the famous Customs House sketch, which is evoked in 'The Narrative of Jacobus Coetzee' and reapplied to the rule-free territories of the African frontier, so alluring to the amoral, perhaps sadistic imagination.[29] The decimation of the Native American population is noted with approbation in the novella's academic afterword, and the idea of manifest destiny, of course, undergirds the nationalistic S. J. Coetzee's philosophy of history, and finds an apocalyptic twentieth-century elaboration in Eugene Dawn's megalomaniacal theorizing.

But 'The Vietnam Project' also elaborates a more idiosyncratic and acerbic view of certain tendencies in the American psyche and behaviour, especially in the narrator's preoccupation with inimical relationship between body and mind. The body is consistently imagined as revolting (not least in the sexual passages) and the speaker's alienation from it reaches a climax in the scene at the aptly named Loco Motel, where Dawn stabs his son:

> My mouth opens, I am aware, if that is awareness, of two cold parted slabs that must be lips, and of a hole that must be the mouth itself, and of a thing, the tongue, which I can push out of the hole, as I do now .... I kneel behind Martin and smile over his shoulder to show that everything is all right, though I am not sure in retrospect that it is the right smile I employ, there being too much tooth in it, and the light flashing too much on that tooth.
>
> (53)

The horrifying fragmentation here should remind us that one of the aims of the document Dawn produces is to induce a similar fragmentation of the Vietnamese psyche to sap their spirit of resistance. And fragmentation affects the textual body as well. At the end of his policy document Dawn confesses, 'What I say is in pieces,' and asks his supervisor to tear off his postscript – and perhaps he did, for all we know (30). Indeed, the entire domain of signification is affected. Dawn alerts us to the psychology of gesture (8) in which he takes a theoretical interest; but the possibility of any gesture as a bodily expression of meaning and affect is increasingly remote from what he can perform.[30] This disruption of a natural expressivity, of the organic language of gesture, is an exaggerated instance of what for Coetzee is an American condition:

> For in America the model of the self as a ghost inhabiting a machine goes almost unquestioned at a popular level. The body as conceived in America, the American body, is a complex machine comprising a vocal module, a sexual module, and several more, even a psychological module. Inside the body-machine the ghostly self checks readouts and taps keys, giving commands which the body obeys.[31]

This horrific mechanization, here figured as a condition of the individual subject, is yoked at the end of Dawn's position paper to a teleological understanding of history. Dawn proposes an apocalyptic air war and justifies it with assertion that 'the goddess of *techne*' is destined to override 'the symbiosis of heaven and earth' (34). Such a destructive imperial vision and its rationalization seem to arise from the fragmented subjectivity that is exposed throughout 'The Vietnam Project'. It is a cruel vision and one that, as Dawn confesses, triggers an unacknowledged shame on the part of Americans.

Now, this critique may seem excessively harsh and hyperbolic, but as Attwell has shown, Dawn's 'New Life for Vietnam' paper is a parody of actual work produced by Vietnam-era thinktanks.[32] Indeed, it hugs fairly closely to Herman Kahn's fluent but merciless and utterly inhumane contribution to the volume *Can We Win in Vietnam?* (It is surely telling that the historical Kahn and the fictional Dawn both stand accused of being 'avant-garde'.[33]) But the most sustained parodic habitation of 'The Vietnam Project' is not of a particular text but rather of what Richard Ohmann, in a comprehensive account of the canon of US fiction from 1960–75, has called 'The Illness Story'.[34] He applies this rubric to such famous novels from the period as *Franny and Zooey*, Updike's Rabbit series, *One Flew Over the Cuckoo's Nest*, *Portnoy's Complaint*, *The Bell Jar* and *Herzog*, the latter being – not coincidentally – one of the books that Eugene Dawn takes along with him in the Loco Motel, in the hope of learning from it how to write realistically. These works are characterized in Ohmann's account by the way in which profound socio-political contradictions, denied in a rosy notion of middle-class American life, are displaced onto images of personal illness or breakdown. Ohmann himself is critical of such texts' operations, especially of their failure to bring any kind of broader political perspective into play (and this is, after all, the period of the Vietnam War). While they register social problems – indeed, those are the reasons the protagonists suffer – the resolution of these novels offers no solution other than therapy or institutionalization or nostalgic forms of spiritual healing. These quiescent endings are often embarked on because of the intervention of characters Ohmann calls 'reality instructors':[35] shrinks, big brothers or catalyst figures like Murphy in *One Flew over the Cuckoo's Nest*.

I would like to suggest that 'The Vietnam Project' offers, yes, an avant-garde version of such narratives – to the point of operating as a kind of savage parody. It is striking how closely its plot, such as it is, maps onto these 'illness stories' (and I am essentially quoting Ohmann's generic summary here): a semi-functional suburbanite, successful or respectably employed, registers a tension between aspiration and quotidian social existence, suffers a breakdown or enters a period of 'disreputable experimentation' (and how!, readers of *Dusklands* might say) and finally, well, gets a little better.[36] Coetzee's narrator mocks such tales, even though his fate ends up conforming to them, with his breakdown, murder and final institutionalization. He disparages his wife's notion that his 'psychic brutalization will end with the end of the war and the Vietnam project' and that 'reinsertion into civilization will tame and eventually humanize' him (15). This is, he feels, a 'novelettish' version of his plight (15). I must admit I find it rather funny to consider Dawn's supervisor, the dreaded but affable 'Coetzee', as the work's 'reality instructor' – accommodation being the last thing that J. M. Coetzee's disruptive work would advocate. Indeed, the final section of 'The Vietnam Project' is a harshly comical send-up of the muted optimism with which Ohmann's canonical 'illness stories' conclude. Eugene Dawn is locked up in an all-male mental institution, where he behaves, he claims, as a 'model of friendly cooperation' with his puzzled, bespectacled doctors, dutifully obliging them with a 'neat condensation here, an odd displacement there' (62). But he is still the same: his obsequiousness is, after all, old news, as is his furtive arrogance: he remains proud of his 'definite contributions to the science of war' and stands ready, in fact, to rewrite his vile paper, each and every one of those sentences, 'erect with the power of truth' (59). Coetzee's critique of the institutions of therapy – to which so many canonical American novels of the time turn, as a kind of weary, default closure – could not be more cutting.

To summarize, then, Jonathan Crewe is absolutely correct when he says that the potential for being a global writer was inherent in Coetzee's work from the start. *Dusklands*, barbed and strange as it is, is an enormously ambitious work: it requires and, in a sense, works to create an audience that is 'cosmopolitan, contemporary, sophisticated'.[37] While it is possible to read the work as a liberal English-speaking South African or as a liberal middle-class American, those positions are rendered uncomfortable, if not untenable: allegiances to established middle-brow national canons on either side of the Atlantic (or, for that matter, in England) can only make the event of reading more disconcerting and grim. The aim for this work is performative, as avant-garde interventions often are: to show up the provincial character of South African literature, and, in the US case, to point to the quiescent deflection of literary attention in the most successful contemporaneous works from the burning, traumatic issues of the time. In each case a reproach is implicit: without global or comparative thinking, South African literary production dooms itself to operate in the shadow of a waning British hegemon, and American literature dooms itself to be confined to psychological and individual solutions at a time when American politics is destructively hegemonic – a symptom, perhaps, of that dangerous fragmentation and disconnection metaphorized so horrifically in 'The Vietnam Project'.

BEGINNINGS AND ENDINGS

I originally thought, in an anti-academic moment, that I might start this chapter by saying that *Dusklands* is basically about a guy who can't take criticism and a guy who can't take a joke.

My formulation, to be sure, is simplistic. Eugene Dawn and Jacobus Coetzee are not 'guys' and to call them that is to ignore one of the key operational difficulties presented by Coetzee's early fiction: that we must, as Tyrus Miller puts it in reference to Beckett, 'abandon much of our naturalized faith in the fictive persons we reify out of linguistic figures of action and voice'.[38] My quip, moreover, elides the fact that both novellas contain more than just the monologues of the two narrators: they are both composite texts that expose the processes and institutions of reception that tame and naturalize the outrages of the monologues. Such practices are obvious in 'Narrative of Jacobus Coetzee', in which the genocidal first-person chronicle gets an academic facelift in the obtuse nationalistic lecture that follows. But they are also evident in 'The Vietnam Project', where an outrageous proposal for military victory is, after all, institutionally supported with library access, carrells, salary, supervision and the like, and the criticism it receives is only to make it more palatable to the military.

Yet my non-serious summary is not out of line with Coetzee's own in the blurb for the first edition of the book – the only blurb he was ever to write for this own work:

> A specialist in psychological warfare is driven to breakdown and a murderous assault by the stress of his work on a cold-blooded RAND-type project to destroy Vietnam.
> A megalomaniac frontiersman wreaks vengeance on his Hottentot captors for daring to see him as a man, fallible and absurd, rather than as a white god. [....][39]

These comments – especially if we take the 'stress of work' in *The Vietnam Project* to lie not in the horror the narrator contemplates but in the rejection of his precious policy document – place an emphasis on the mental breakdown of the two narrators. The turning points in both of these novellas are moments of humiliation: the polite disapprobation of Dawn by his boss and the irreverent treatment of the self-important Jacobus by children enjoying a little prank. The brutalities that follow are thus the retribution for narcissistic woundings.

Read somewhat allegorically, then, *Dusklands* draws our attention to the retaliatory quality of (neo)colonial violence. This is an intriguing idea and historically resonant. After all, in the strategic thinking of Kahn and the RAND Corporation, the idea of retaliation is a prominent one: a problem that beset them is the forms a 'limited' war might take when (unthinkable) nuclear retaliation stands as the ultimate option.[40] Retaliation is also woven into the history of the South African frontier, where punitive strikes on indigenous people who impinged on white property are legion: all those *strafkommandos*[41] we learned about in high-school history classes. But Coetzee's most relevant and abiding interests are not historical so much as ethnophilosophical. When asked in a recent interview about his religious beliefs he turned to René Girard's meditations on retributive violence, specifically, the idea in Girard's *Violence and the Sacred* that endless retaliation and vendettas can only be brought to an end through sacrifice.[42] Thus, we are back again at Coetzee's understanding of the crucifixion and the idea I floated earlier that there is (dare we think this?) something sacrificial about the introversion of violence at stake in his adoption of the repugnant, racist narrative voices we hear in the monologues. Viewed in this light, *Dusklands* becomes legible as an experimental response – a formal ingesting, if you will – of the retaliatory violence of (neo)colonialism – perhaps in the hope of imagining or enacting some sort of end to it.

We may then contemplate the extent to which *Dusklands* marks both beginnings and endings in Coetzee's career. It is, as I have argued here, a career-defining first work, in so far as it opens up a speaking place that is global, rather than national, or even strictly monolingual or monogeneric. It introduces, furthermore, a slew of themes Coetzee was to explore in subsequent novels: an interest in the body, in torture (the 'masters of the interrogation chamber' [20] make their appearance), in reason and madness, in the relationship between fiction and history, and in complicity and confession. But perhaps the endings of *Dusklands* are as important. Several critics and even Coetzee himself have suggested that *Dusklands* is driven by a fierce satirical impulse that is not evident in subsequent work. And it is true that Coetzee never again produces anything like the savage prose of Swift's *A Modest Proposal* to which *Dusklands*'s parodic documents with their hateful pseudo-reasoning have been compared. (Defoe, not Swift, becomes the eighteenth-century master he alludes to again and again.) When he returns in *Waiting for the Barbarians* to the constitutive violence of the colonial project and the paranoia inherent in the temporality of imperial history (its penetrative 'thrust into the future' [144], as S. J. Coetzee would have it), it is through the eyes of a narrator who may be complicit, but is, unlike Dawn and Jacobus Coetzee, a 'man of conscience'.[43]

But it would not be like Coetzee to leave any endings definitive. To compare *Dusklands* to *A Modest Proposal* simplifies the difficulties the former poses for the reader. After all, Swift's satire works to elicit a simple protest in the reader: to produce the empathy that is so markedly absent in the pseudo-rationality of political arithmetic and, beyond that, in the treatment of the Irish poor. The affective workings of *Dusklands*, by contrast, are far murkier and more uncomfortable, precisely because they permit neither reader nor author a clean distance from the horrors the work exposes. And while it is true that Coetzee never again gives voice to such cruel narrators, the possibility of an authorial possession by evil does arise again, at the end of what I would risk calling his most personal novel: those closing moments in *The Master of Petersburg* when the Dostoyevsky character permits his writing to be open to the arrival of the utter evil that is Stavrogin, the child seducer, rapist and destroyer of *The Possessed*. So, yes, *Dusklands* initiates and attempts to foreclose; it endures as the initial testing ground for some of the formal, ethical and emotional difficulties that have rendered Coetzee one of the most challenging writers of our time.

NOTES

1. Crewe, 'Dusklands,' 91, 90.
2. Ibid., 92.
3. Coetzee, *Dusklands*, 97 (subsequent page references given parenthetically in the text).
4. Crewe, *In the Middle of Nowhere*, 41.
5. Poirier, 'The Difficulties of Modernism,' 272.
6. Ibid.
7. Ibid.
8. Crewe, *In the Middle of Nowhere*, 46.
9. See ibid., 44.
10. Attwell, *J. M. Coetzee*, 55.
11. Coetzee, *Summertime*, 58.
12. See for example Woessner, 'In the Heart of the Empire,' 114.
13. Jameson, 'Reification and Utopia in Mass Culture,' 136.
14. Coetzee, *Doubling the Point*, 337.
15. In an intriguing comment in a notebook he kept from around March 1974 to February 1976, Coetzee confesses that around the inception of *Dusklands* he was aroused by US political events 'in a way [he] feared to be aroused'. See Woessner, 'In the Heart of the Empire,' 120.
16. Woessner, 'In the Heart of the Empire,' 123 and fn. 62. For further comments on both this intriguing archival discovery and, more broadly, on pornography in Coetzee's oeuvre as a whole, see Lucy Valerie Graham's fascinating chapter, '"Writer Pornographer": Sex, Violence, and the Engagement with Radical Feminism,' in her forthcoming book, *J. M. Coetzee, Women's Voices, and Feminism*.
17. In my essay, '*Bitterkomix*: Notes from the Post-Apartheid Underground,' I make a somewhat similar argument about the workings of the graphic art of Anton Kannemeyer, which often flirts with

the pornographic. I never would have thought that Coetzee and underground comix should even momentarily be legible in the same light; and yet, there is a stylistic connection between outrageous narrative voicings in Dostoyevsky's *Notes from the Underground* and those in *Dusklands*.

18. See Coetzee's interview with Raquel Serur, 'Coetzee en la UMAM.'
19. Head, *Cambridge Introduction*, 38.
20. Scott, 'Voice and Trajectory,' 87. Coetzee adds, however, that 'the relation is loose' (ibid.).
21. Crewe, *In the Middle of Nowhere*, 4.
22. Ibid., 39. The idea of the 'speaking place' comes to me from the poetry and critical work of Jeremy Cronin (see Barnard, 'Speaking Places'), where it has a performative quality (in both senses of the word, as spoken before and audience and as an utterance that effects and transforms). I use it here intentionally to amplify my sense that Coetzee strives to bring about something new about with this first fiction.
23. Crewe sketches out this context beautifully in *In the Middle of Nowhere*, 20–2, as does Kannemeyer in his biography (see *J. M. Coetzee*, 224–34). These passages kindled my own recollection of the narrow and doctrinaire (if on the surface humanistic) critical persuasions that still reigned when I embarked on my graduate work in South Africa in the late seventies.
24. Crewe evokes something Coetzee's dogged refusal to be pinned down generically or even linguistically in a marvelous comment on *In the Heart of the Country*: 'Betraying just a trace of satanic pride, Magda prefers the "impossible" task of soliciting aliens to the easier one of becoming a "South African poet"' (*In the Middle of Nowhere*, 3). For more on Coetzee's relationship to Afrikaans, see my essay 'Coetzee in/and Afrikaans'.
25. See Coetzee's UNAM interview, 'Coetzee en la UMAM'.
26. See, for example, the typical Afrikaans avoidance of the third-person pronoun when speaking to superiors in the servant Plaatjie's dialogue: 'Master must lie down and get his strength back. Later, when we get up, we will send something to master. Master lives over there on the other side of the water, doesn't master?' (105).
27. Woessner, *In the Heart of the Empire*, 121.
28. See Coetzee, *Waiting for the Barbarians*, 79, and *Age of Iron*, 114. The essay 'Into the Dark Chamber' also opens with Hawthorne's evocation of prison as 'the black flower of civilization' (361).
29. See Hawthorne, 'The Custom House – Introductory,' in *The Scarlet Letter*, 38.
30. It is telling that this inability is overcome in a dream encounter with Vietnamese soldiers and prisoners: 'In euphoric gestures of liberation I stretch out my right hand. My fingers, expressive, full of meaning, full of love, close on their narrow shoulders, but close empty, as clutches have a way of doing in the empty dream-space of one's head' (34).
31. Coetzee, *Diary of a Bad Year*, 133.
32. Attwell, *J. M. Coetzee*, 33–40 (the section 'Parody: The American Context').
33. Menand, 'The Fat Man.'
34. Ohmann, 'The Shaping of a Canon,' 212–19.
35. Ibid., 218.
36. Ibid., 215.
37. Crewe, *In the Middle of Nowhere*, 41.
38. See 'What Is a "Disintegration"?' on Miller's blog, *Crosspollen*.
39. Quoted in Kannemeyer, *J. M. Coetzee*, 247.
40. See Menand, 'The Fat Man.'
41. Punitive expeditionary forces.
42. See Coetzee's UNAM interview, 'Coetzee en la UMAM'.
43. Coetzee, 'Into the Dark Chamber,' 363.

WORKS CITED

Attwell, David. *J. M. Coetzee: South Africa and the Politics of Writing*. Berkeley: University of California Press, 1993.
Barnard, Rita. 'Bitterkomix: Notes from the Post-Apartheid Underground'. *South Atlantic Quarterly* 103, no. 4 (2004): 719–54.
Barnard, Rita. 'Coetzee in/and Afrikaans'. *Journal of Literary Studies* 25, no. 4 (2009): 84–104.
Barnard, Rita. 'Speaking Places: Prison, Poetry, and the South African Nation'. *Research in African Literatures* 32, no. 3 (2001): 155–76.
Coetzee, J. M. *Age of Iron*. 1990. New York: Vintage, 1992.
Coetzee, J. M. 'Coetzee en la UMAM'. Interview with Raquel Serur. Seminario Universitario de la Modernidad, Universidad Nacional Autónoma de México. https://www.youtube.com/watch?v=KowFc34iqcs.
Coetzee, J. M. *Diary of a Bad Year*. 2007. New York: Penguin, 2008.
Coetzee, J. M. *Doubling the Point: Essays and Interviews*. Edited by David Attwell. Cambridge, MA: Harvard University Press, 1992.
Coetzee, J. M. *Dusklands*. 1974. New York: Penguin, 1984.
Coetzee, J. M. 'Into the Dark Chamber: The Writer and the South African State'. In *Doubling the Point: Essays and Interviews*, edited by David Attwell, 361–8. Cambridge, MA: Harvard University Press, 1992.
Coetzee, J. M. *The Master of Petersburg*. 1994. New York: Penguin, 1995.
Coetzee, J. M. *Summertime*. New York: Viking, 2009.
Coetzee, J. M. *Waiting for the Barbarians*. 1980. New York: Penguin, 2010.
Crewe, Jonathan. 'Dusklands'. *Contrast* 9, no. 2 (1974): 90–5.
Crewe, Jonathan. *In the Middle of Nowhere: J. M. Coetzee in South Africa*. Lanham, MD: University Press of America, 2016.
Ghosh, Amitav. *The Nutmeg's Curse: Parables for a Planet in Crisis*. Chicago: University of Chicago Press, 2021.
Girard, René. *Violence and the Sacred*. Baltimore: Johns Hopkins University Press, 1979.
Hawthorne, Nathaniel. *The Scarlet Letter*. 1850. New York: Vintage, 2014.
Head, Dominic, ed. *The Cambridge Introduction to J. M. Coetzee*. Cambridge: Cambridge University Press, 2009.
Jameson, Fredric. 'Reification and Utopia in Mass Culture'. *Social Text* 1, no. 1 (1979): 130–48.
Kannemeyer, J. C. *J. M. Coetzee: A Life in Writing*. Translated by Michiel Heyns. London: Scribe, 2013.
Mehigan, Tim and Christian Moser, eds. *The Intellectual Landscape in the Works of J. M. Coetzee*. Rochester: Camden House, 2018.
Menand, Louis. 'Fat Man'. *New Yorker* 81, no. 18 (2005). https://www.newyorker.com/magazine/2005/06/27/fat-man.
Miller, Tyrus (tyrus63). 'What Is a "Disintegration"? Monologue and Subjectivity in Samuel Beckett and Thomas Bernhard'. *Crosspollen*, 21 November 2013. https://crosspollenblog.wordpress.com/2013/11/21/what-is-a-disintegration-monologue-and-subjectivity-in-samuel-beckett-and-thomas-bernhard/?fbclid=IwAR0WEu198ZtyPl_oygL6qyt0X638eNs6erX_fjycqNyNOIZ9nANTkq8gNy0.
Ohmann, Richard. 'The Shaping of a Canon: U.S. Fiction, 1960–1975'. *Critical Inquiry* 10, no. 1 (1983): 199–223.
Poirier, Richard. 'The Difficulties of Modernism and the Modernism of Difficulty'. *Humanities in Society* 1 (1978): 271–82.
Scott, Joanna and J. M. Coetzee. 'Voice and Trajectory: An Interview with J. M. Coetzee'. *Salmagundi* 114/115 (1997): 82–102.
Woessner, Martin. 'In the Heart of the Empire: Coetzee and America'. In *The Intellectual Landscape in the Works of J. M. Coetzee*, edited by Tim Mehigan and Christian Moser, 109–31. Rochester, NY: Camden House, 2018.

CHAPTER SEVEN

In the Heart of the Country

IAN GLENN

I suspect I was the first mis-reader of any part of *In the Heart of the Country*. In 1975, in the Easter holidays or a long week-end close to it, I went on holiday with John and Philippa Coetzee and their children Nicolas and Gisela to a small cottage on the beach at Arniston, a seaside resort in the Southern Cape. In the communal living area, I saw on the table one of the University of Cape Town examination books that were discarded after exams and used for scrap paper. I opened it and saw John's hand-writing and a sentence starting 'My father'. I thought this was private, stopped reading, and asked John if he was writing a memoir. No, he said, it's a new novel. I had seen an early creative piece – perhaps of section 21 or section 63.

Coetzee's second novel turned out to be a dense, complex novel of ideas that plays formal games, not least with pronouns and what they refer to, and uses inter-textual references to plot a new way forward for South African literature. Magda, a lonely spinster living on an isolated Karoo farm in an era before motorized transport (yet in an era where planes fly overhead), is the I-figure who narrates, in 266 numbered sections, her complex relationship with her father and a number of 'coloured' farmworkers. In the opening sections, Magda's father brings a new bride back to the farm and Magda kills them both while they are in bed. The father, however, reappears (section 36) to enter into a new, more darkly colonial sexual relationship when he seduces Klein-Anna, the wife of Hendrik, a farm labourer. Magda kills her father (again) and then attempts to enter into a relationship with Hendrik and Klein-Anna and, when they leave the farm, she attempts to commune with machines flying overhead by forming words, apparently in Spanish, with rocks she has painted white, arranged on the ground. By the end of the novel, the father has re-appeared and it seems the events of the novel may have taken place in Magda's imagination.

There are many insightful and important readings of this novel dealing with such questions as the influence of Coetzee's reading in feminist theory, the importance of Beckett or the creative conditions of the novel's composition in an age of censorship.[1] My focus in this essay, however, will be on Coetzee's literary and philosophical positioning *in* the novel. My argument is that Coetzee made Magda a writer who acts as his alter ego and allows him to imagine a new beginning and new themes and concerns for South African writing.[2]

TEXTUAL DIFFERENCES

The novel was first published in the UK in 1977 and in the United States with the title *From the Heart of the Country* – apparently out of concern that the British title might lead to confusion with William H. Gass's 1968 collection of short stories titled *In the Heart of the Heart of the Country*. In the original English language editions, there was a puzzling note in the prefatory material reading

'English version prepared by the author'. This note, not found in later editions, continued the textual games of blurred authors in *Dusklands* by hinting at the colonial otherness of the original text – in this case, the later 1978 Ravan Press edition only published in South Africa. This version of the text included substantial sections of dialogue in Afrikaans and, intriguingly, in a mixture of Afrikaans and English between Magda and Klein-Anna in section #203. Work on the manuscript material by Kannemeyer and Attwell suggests that the switch to Afrikaans dialogue helped Coetzee creatively, so this aspect of the text deserves particular attention.[3]

Susan Fitzmaurice and Andrew van der Vlies have analysed the different versions, considering the importance of the Afrikaans sections and Coetzee's rendering of them into English.[4] Van der Vlies convincingly demonstrates what was lost in social nuance in the English-only version. Fitzmaurice argues that Coetzee intended the Afrikaans versions to reflect reality, while the English versions reflect Magda's made-up world. This seems unlikely, because it would mean that Coetzee had no way of maintaining this distinction in the English only versions. It also misses that the Afrikaans sections contain an important inter-textual reference to Alex la Guma – suggesting that, even there, writerly games are going on.

MAGDA AS WRITER

Coetzee's way of taking on and overcoming the postmodernist legacy was to make his central character a writer, but he scatters his clues so cleverly that several critics have missed this narrative trickery and argued that Magda does not write at all.[5] Where are the clues? Dick Penner reports that Coetzee himself prefaced a reading from the novel by saying that, 'In the course of the action people get killed or raped, but perhaps not really, perhaps only in the overactive imagination of the story teller.'[6]

Once one views Magda as an imaginative storyteller, literally hundreds of statements in the novel ('my story') change their force. She concludes her introduction to her father and new bride with the statement 'Those are the antagonists.' (#1) That phrase could come out of a creative writing class; when the new bride turns out to be a fiction (#36), it seems it has.

Why play this game of making Magda an exemplar of the novelist-creator? A first reason was to repeat the lesson of Klawer's double death in *Dusklands* that so puzzled South African readers when Coetzee's first novel was published.[7] Almost as though showing those critics that it was no misprint or error, Coetzee repeats the motif of one character dying multiple times. Magda pushes us to her literary, non-corporeal essence when she asks: 'A woman with red blood in her veins (what colour is mine? a watery pink? an inky violet?)' (#122). She even confronts the most basic creative question for the writer of detective fiction: 'I ask myself: What am I going to do with the bodies?' (#30).

A second benefit in making Magda the narrator was to undermine realism by repeatedly insisting that fiction can throw up different versions of a narrative. The first paragraph sets in motion a whole series of 'Or perhaps' scenarios that, by the end of the novel, have turned realism into a matter of research (bicycles or horseback? – #6) or probability. There are twenty-two incidents of the phrase 'Or perhaps' in the novel, repeatedly signalling its artifice and random relation to conventional truth.

A third benefit was to allow Coetzee to explore and expose various narrative options for the South African novel by turning reality into a series of algorithmic explorations of possibilities, as in the various scenarios for the seduction of Klein-Anna (#80) or rape of Magda by Hendrik (#205–212). Coetzee, the mathematician and computer programmer, turns social reality into a variety of scenarios whose probability might be explored, rather as mathematical modellers calculate the likely winners of elections or sports contests by running multiple simulations.

The fourth benefit of using Magda as writer is that it allowed Coetzee to re-imagine what South African literature could or should be. This was a question of his practice as a writer, but also of cultural direction at a time of disciplinary and institutional upheaval.[8] In 1974, a year or so before Coetzee started the novel, he and I co-taught, for the first time, a course in nineteenth-century American literature. This course was an innovation and a response to dissatisfaction with a narrowly British view of literatures in English in the University of Cape Town English department. It may also have helped Coetzee as writer to explore his own alternatives to an English-based realist tradition.

The American echoes in the novel are insistent. From Hester in Hawthorne's *The Scarlet Letter* (1850) we have Magda as the dark, sinister force doubled with the noble Angel, carer for the sick and frail (#13). In response to Whitman – who, in *Song of Myself* (1855), writes 'I am the man – I suffer'd – I was there' on witnessing historical horrors – we have Magda, who claims more immediate, urgent experience: 'I live, I suffer, I am here' (#10). From Melville, we have echoes of the crazy hornpipe that Flask dances in Chapter 34 of *Moby Dick* (1851) when Magda pursues her solitary asocial art in the 'crazy hornpipe I dance with myself' (#18). Her desire to burst through the 'screen of names' to reality (#38) surely evokes Ahab's monomaniacal quest. From Poe's 'Fall of the House of Usher' (1839) we have Magda imagining a castle falling into a tarn (#38). And if there is any model for the lonely female haunted by the Protestant notion of being (or rather, not being) one of the 'elect' (#88) and making poetry out of her isolation, surely it is Emily Dickinson?

In an 1872 letter, Henry James wrote that 'it's a complex fate, being an American, and one of the responsibilities it entails is fighting against a superstitious valuation of Europe.' This phrase provided the title of a book on American fiction by Marius Bewley, with commentary by F. R. Leavis, which we used in the 1974 course.[9] Early on in the novel (#12), Magda describes her 'complex fate'. This surely signals that, through her, Coetzee was using American writers as a way to explore what South African fiction could or should be – making Magda not only an exemplar of colonial politics or family dramas, but a writer questing for form, content and style in opposition to a dominant metropolitan mode.

What all these inter-textual references reveal is the predicament of the writer in English not in England, whose complex fate, as James noted, is to inherit but also to resist British tradition. When Coetzee describes this novel as 'Cervantean pastoral or antipastoral', he points out that the idea of a modern writer describing a limited, safe, imagined space or community was an anachronism.[10] For better or worse, the colonizers inherit the burden of world culture and a world language that separates them from the colonized – 'I spoke like them before I learned to speak like this' (#16) – without the benefit of insular isolation. There is no safe physical or intellectual space; or if there is, the end of the novel reminds us that Magda-Coetzee sees it as 'too easy'.

Finally, Magda allows Coetzee to explore, perhaps confess, his own artistic drive and focus. Through interrogating Magda, we confront Coetzee. Given Coetzee's frustration with literary interviewers,[11] the novel allows us to imagine the suggested questions of a good interviewer, and to divine Coetzee's answers through Magda's utterances. Though David Attwell's interviews with Coetzee are an indispensable resource, in their exchange on this novel Coetzee hints at a way of reading Magda that differs from Attwell's interpretation of her. Coetzee writes: 'The novel, on the other hand, allows the writer to *stage* his passion: Magda, in *In the Heart of the Country*, may be mad (if that is indeed your verdict), but I, behind her, am merely passionate.'[12] What are the 'merely passionate' motives being expressed and explored through Magda? Here are some ways an imaginary interview might help us to understand Coetzee's passions through Magda's utterances:

Why do you write? I fight against being one of the forgotten ones of history.

(#10)

Why do you find writing tough? I find none of that heady expansion into the as-if that marks the beginning of a true double life.

(#12)

What is the secret of narrative? Prolong yourself, prolong yourself, that is the whisper I hear in my inmost.

(#14)

Is writing liberating? Alone in my room, with my duties behind me and the lamp steadily burning, I creak into rhythms that are my own, stumble over the rocks of words that I have never heard on another tongue. I create myself in the words that create me …

(#18)

Why undertake the difficult task of writing? What keeps me going … is my determination, my iron intractable risible determination to burst through the screen of names into the goatseye view of Armoede and the stone desert …

(#38)

Are you ambivalent about the traditional novel? I want my story to have a beginning, a middle, and an end, not the yawning middle without end which threatens …

(#89)

Melville said that the future is the Bible of the free. Do you agree? My life is not past, my art cannot be the art of memory. What will happen to me has not yet happened. I am a blind spot hurtling with both eyes open into the maw of the future, my password 'And then?'

(#89)

I believe you used to write poetry? Why? My talent is all for immanence, for the fire or ice of identity at the heart of things. Lyric is my medium, not chronicle.

(#136)

That imaginary interview takes up Coetzee's hint on how to read Magda and complements Attwell's exchange with him.

A NOVEL OF IDEAS

If Magda is a writer burdened with the weight of world literature, she is also burdened with the intellectual weight of history. The novel is chiefly a novel of ideas – perhaps the only South African novel of ideas, though certainly not Coetzee's only novel of ideas. The display of erudition and denseness of intertextual reference has made some critics uneasy. In an early response, Cherry Wilhelm criticized the novel as 'showing off', while Stephen Watson argued that understanding the literary references made the novel easy to understand, suggesting that interpretation involved a mechanical tracing of borrowed ideas.[13] I want rather to argue that Coetzee found a way to embody the intellectual resolutions and discoveries in the plot of the novel, and that there are complex dialectics and resolutions.

What kind of reading does Magda do? Here there is an intriguing discrepancy between the British and South African editions. In the former, Magda is introduced in the first paragraph as 'reading a book' while in the local edition, it is 'reading in a book'. The book one reads in is, pre-eminently, the Bible. This suggests that Magda's reading is not for plot, narrative or escapism, but as a search for the truth, the Word, God, understanding.

This opens another way of understanding the use of numbered sections in the novel. (When I asked Coetzee why there were numbers, he replied, deadpan, that the numbers let him keep things in order.) While Coetzee has given an account of his interest in filmic innovations as a way of accounting for this structure,[14] the numbered sections also place Coetzee-Magda in another tradition: that of the philosophical or religious treatise. When the pieces of reading come to Magda as disembodied voices in sections 247–50 and in 258–9, we can observe that many of the authors cited (Calvin, Pascal, Rousseau, Blake, Nietzsche, Hegel) wrote texts with numbered paragraphs.

In Magda's case, the recourse to, say, Rousseau on the psychological effects of slavery, or Hegel on Master-Slave relationships, is a way of dramatizing and historicizing her social situation and plight. Ideas are not decorations, but discoveries and insights that may offer a way out of her colonial solitude and also heighten the stakes of the search. There seem to be four main intellectual concerns that come together in the climactic section 259: the legacy of class and racial difference; the mystery of the divine and predestination; the frustrations of desire; and the search for at-homeness in the world.

After Magda's attempts to communicate with the sky-gods in Spanish, voices come to her, first in 'tight little epigrams' (#247–50), and then in a Delphic logorrhea (#259) in which the italicized sections move from Rousseau on the social contract and the condition of slavery, to Spinoza's *Ethics* on God not feeling pleasure or pain and on man not expecting God to love him in return, to Pascal saying that *God is hidden, and every religion that does not affirm that God is hidden is not true*.[15] Magda interjects, but the 'flowing periods' continue via the Spanish poet Luis Cernuda's poem 'No decía palabras' on the inexplicability of desire, to a quotation from Octavio Paz's *Labyrinth of Solitude* on the longing for a place that most cultures see in their founding myths as '*the centre of the world, the navel of the universe*'.[16] The quotations end with two quotes from William Blake on desire, and two quotes from Calvin on the paradox of God's role in decisions about the elect.[17]

One could spend a long time teasing out the resonances and logic of those dizzying segues. The most revealing allusion is probably to Paz's *Labyrinth of Solitude* which has the sub-title: *Life and thought in Mexico*. Particularly in Chapter 9, 'The dialectics of solitude', from which the quotation comes, the themes of religious loss, of social and racial distancing in a post-colonial society, of the quest for love and its impossibility are woven together in ways which Coetzee addresses in fictional terms.

One way of linking Rousseau on slavery and the Calvinist notion of a pre-destined elect is to see that in South Africa, racial inferiority and religious notions of those pre-destined to not be among the elect were strongly connected. The South African edition carried a literary reference that is lost in English and that may make this connection clear. When Magda curses Hendrik (#180) for not helping her bury her father, she calls him, in the original, 'Jou verdomde hotnot' (translated in the English version as 'You damned *hotnot*'). Magda's language at that point shows colonial brutality in the term 'hotnot' – a term for indigenous Khoikhoi people which is more powerfully pejorative in Afrikaans than the English Hottentot – and religious bigotry speaking through her. *Verdomde* carries with it the notion of accursed and is heavy with Old Testament and self-serving colonial interpretations of Genesis 9:25 of Black people as the children of Ham, cursed never to be among the elect.

But, more than this, 'Verdomde hotnot' seems to be a reference to 'Lemon Orchard', a short story by South African author Alex La Guma, about whom Coetzee had written a few years earlier.[18] This story is told from the point of view of an unnamed English-speaking narrator of colour who says nothing, but seems to be destined for a lynching or beating at the hands of four white men, one of whom calls him a 'verdomde hotnot'. The echoing of the slightly archaic and literary insult makes Magda complicit – at that point – in white colonial violence and shows Coetzee, at least, as recognizing the position of the insulted man.

In the later section, however, Magda renounces any position as one of the racially superior and religious elect and confronts the problems Paz raised. Magda's irate retorts to the quotations in #259 in the next section, #260, move from the primly uncomprehending to the firmly resolute as she finds her voice and diagnoses how her colonial situation affects her response:

> There is no love from us toward God nor any wish that God should turn his mind to us. The flow has ceased. We are the castaways of God as we are the castaways of history. *That* is the origin of our feeling of solitude. I for one do not wish to be at the centre of the world, I wish only to be at home in the world as the merest beast is at home.
>
> (#260)

Like Paz, Magda accepts that the primitive belief that one comes from a divine centre is outmoded, and that solitude is the inevitable result. While Paz imagines a possible re-integration of the solitary individual into society or a temporary end to solitude in love, Magda remains apart:

> Are not all these dicta from above blind to the source of our disease, which is that we have no-one to speak with, that our desires stream out of us chaotically, without aim, without response, like our words ....
>
> (#260)

Paz might see that state of mind as typically adolescent. The response from Coetzee-Magda might be that Mexico was in a healthier state of social integration than South Africa; that it was easier for a man to articulate desire than a woman (something Paz addresses admirably); and perhaps that 'our words' from Magda and Coetzee fall into an uncertain literary space of reception, whereas Paz knew he was writing for a local and European audience who were receptive.

SEX AND RACE IN THE SOUTH AFRICAN NOVEL

In writing about La Guma, Coetzee offered a suspicious Barthesian analysis of the 'tragedy of inter-racial love' in South African English fiction in which the transgressing lovers are destroyed or driven into exile. Coetzee concludes: 'The overt content of the fable here is that love conquers evil through tragic suffering when such suffering is borne witness to in art; its covert content is the apolitical doctrine that defeat can turn itself, by the twist of tragedy, into victory'.[19] Coetzee goes further than previous writers on this theme by combining two common plots. In most novels on the inter-racial love theme that he was analysing, perhaps best typified in Gordimer's work, the protagonists are a Black man and a white woman whose relationship challenges social prejudices. In an older racist genre of writing about race and sex in South African literature, white women writers decry the predilection of older white men for young attractive women of colour and the social and political upheaval this causes.[20] What Coetzee does in this novel is link these two plots together causally, seeing white male exploitation of women of colour leading to psychic reaction and retaliation. (This structure recurs, of course, in *Disgrace*.)

Magda's quest to allow Hendrik to reach her through her sexual submission, perhaps something like an act of Fanonian liberation for the Black man through sexual violence, also fails, notably where Magda's sexual intercourse with Hendrik fails to move them to reciprocity, leaving him as the external third person and her as the isolated first person: 'I am pressed but not possessed, I am pierced but my core is not touched. At heart I am still the fierce mantis virgin of yore. Hendrik may take me, but it is I holding him holding I' (#227).

Why can Magda and Hendrik not reach a relationship of 'I-thou' reciprocity any more than her father could with Klein-Anna or she does with Klein-Anna? Here, I suggest, Coetzee takes a pessimistic, perhaps conservative view of the weight of colonial history and familial structures on colonizers and the colonized. Drawing on Freud and structuralist writers like Levi-Strauss, he sees linguistic, sexual and social issues as interlinked, with Magda caught in the prison-house of her father and language. Confronting the social and political situation in South Africa left Coetzee and his protagonists confronting their historical position. If we 'have no-one to speak with' (#260), that seems to be a failure to settle properly, to allow kinship exchanges with those around us, to make a new place or a place new. The protagonists of his next novels would take up those challenges – though, as in the case of *Disgrace,* the pessimistic sense of failed reciprocity remains.

CONCLUSION

Coetzee's second novel is an intriguing mix of self-reflexive mischief, narrative invention, intertextual allusion and cultural diagnosis and prescription. This essay has focused on the novel as cultural intervention and as commentary on the problems and possibilities of the modern writer in South Africa. In pushing the post-modernist play with the author to a *nec plus ultra*, Coetzee put these concerns behind him, freeing himself to turn more directly to political and social divides in *Waiting for the Barbarians* and the later novels.

NOTES

1. Graham, 'The Use of the Female Voice'; Roberts, 'Cinderella's Mothers'; Wright, 'Displacing the Voice'; Wittenberg, 'The Taint of the Censor'; Cantor, 'Happy Days'; Attridge, 'Sex, Comedy and Influence'.
2. This essay draws on an earlier article on the novel – see Glenn, 'Game Hunting'.
3. Kannemeyer and Heyns, *J.M. Coetzee*; Attwell, *J.M. Coetzee and the Life of Writing*.
4. Fitzmaurice, 'Aspects of Afrikaans'; Van der Vlies, '*In* (or *From*) *the Heart of the Country*'.
5. Gallagher, *A Story of South Africa*; Briganti, 'A Bored Spinster'.
6. Penner, *Countries of the Mind*.
7. Kannemeyer and Heyns, *J. M. Coetzee*, 253–4.
8. Glenn, 'J M Coetzee and the English Department'.
9. Bewley, *The Complex Fate*.
10. Coetzee, *Doubling the Point*, 62.
11. Ibid., 64–5.
12. Ibid., 61.
13. Watson, 'Colonialism and the Novels of J. M. Coetzee'; Wilhelm, 'South African Writing'.
14. Coetzee, *Doubling the Point*, 60.
15. Rousseau, *The Social Contract*; Spinoza, *Ethics* 5: 17, 19; Pascal, *Pascal's Pensées*, paragraph 584.
16. Cernuda, *La Realidad*; Paz, *The Labyrinth of Solitude*, 208.
17. Calvin, *Institutes* 3: 23,1; Calvin, *Calvin's Commentaries* I XVIII, 4.
18. La Guma, *A Walk in the Night*; Coetzee, 'Man's Fate' – reprinted in *Doubling*, 344–60.
19. Coetzee, *Doubling the Point*, 346.
20. Glenn, 'Legislating Women'.

WORKS CITED

Attridge, Derek. 'Sex, Comedy and Influence: Coetzee's Beckett.' In *J M Coetzee in Context and Theory*, edited by Elleke Boehmer, Robert Eaglestone and Katy Iddiols, 71–90. London: Bloomsbury, 2009.

Attwell, David. *J.M. Coetzee & the Life of Writing: Face to Face with Time*. Oxford: Oxford University Press, 2015.

Bewley, Marius. *The Complex Fate: Hawthorne, Henry James, and Some Other American Writers*. London: Chatto & Windus, 1952.

Briganti, Chiara. 'A Bored Spinster with a Locked Diary: The Politics of Hysteria in *In the Heart of the Country*'. *Research in African Literatures* 25, no. 4 (1994): 33–49.

Calvin, Jean. *Institutes of the Christian Religion*. Peabody, MA: Hendrickson Publishers, 2008.

Calvin, John and John King. *Commentaries on the First Book of Moses, called Genesis*. Edinburgh: Calvin Translation Society, 1847.

Cantor, Paul A. 'Happy Days in the Veld: Beckett and Coetzee's *In the Heart of the Country*'. *South Atlantic Quarterly* 93, no. 1 (1994): 83–110.

Cernuda, Luis. *La Realidad Y El Deseo, 1924–1962*. Tezontle. 1. reimp. de la 4. ed. México: Tezontle, 1970.

Coetzee, J. M. 'Achterberg's "Ballade Van De Gasfitter": The Mystery of I and You'. *Publications of the Modern Language Association of America* 92 (1977): 285–96.

Coetzee, J. M. 'Man's Fate in the Novels of Alex La Guma'. *Studies in Black Literature* 5, no. 1 (1974): 16–23.

Coetzee, J. M. and David Attwell. *Doubling the Point: Essays and Interviews*. Cambridge, Massachusetts; London: Harvard University Press, 1992.

Fitzmaurice, Susan. 'Aspects of Afrikaans in South African Literature in English'. In *Imagined Commonwealths: Cambridge Essays on Commonwealth and International Literature in English,* edited by T. J. Cribb, 166–89. London: Palgrave Macmillan, 1999.

Gallagher, Susan VanZanten. *A Story of South Africa: J M Coetzee's Fiction in Context*. Cambridge, MA: Harvard University Press, 2013.

Glenn, Ian. 'Game Hunting in *In the Heart of the Country*'. In *Critical Perspectives on J. M. Coetzee,* edited by Graham Huggan and Stephen Watson, 120–37. London: Macmillan, 1996.

Glenn, Ian. 'J M Coetzee and the English Department at the University of Cape Town'. *Safundi* 20, no. 4 (2019): 414–29.

Glenn, Ian. 'Legislating Women'. *Journal of Literary Studies* 12, no. 1–2 (1996): 145–70.

Graham, Lucy Valerie. 'The Use of the Female Voice in Three Novels by J M Coetzee'. MA Dissertation, Rhodes University, 1997.

Kannemeyer, John Christoffel and Michiel Heyns. *J.M. Coetzee: A Life in Writing*. Melbourne; London: Scribe, 2012.

La Guma, Alex. *A Walk in the Night: And Other Stories*. Evanston: Northwestern University Press, 1967.

Pascal, Blaise, W. F. Trotter and T. S. Eliot. *Pascal's Pensées*. London; Toronto; New York: J.M. Dent and Sons; E.P. Dutton and Co., 1931.

Paz, Octavio. *The Labyrinth of Solitude: Life and Thought in Mexico*. New York and London: Grove Press and Evergreen Books, 1961.

Penner, Allen Richard. *Countries of the Mind: The Fiction of J M Coetzee*. New York: Greenwood Press, 1989.

Roberts, Sheila. 'Cinderella's Mothers: J M Coetzee's *In the Heart of the Country*'. *English in Africa* 19, no. 1 (1992): 21–33.

Rousseau, Jean-Jacques and Victor Gourevitch. *The Social Contract and Other Later Political Writings*. Cambridge: Cambridge University Press, 2019.

Spinoza, Benedictus de, Andrew Boyle and G. H. R. Parkinson. *Ethics*. Everyman Classics. London: Dent, 1989.

Van der Vlies, Andrew. '*In* (or *From*) *the Heart of the Country*: Local and Global Lives of Coetzee's Anti-Pastoral'. In *Print, Text and Book Cultures,* edited by Andrew van der Vlies, 166–94. Johannesburg: Wits University Press, 2012.

Watson, Stephen. 'Colonialism and the Novels of J M Coetzee'. *Research in African Literatures* 17, no. 3 (1986): 370–92.

Wilhelm, Cherry. 'South African Writing in English, 1977'. *Standpunte* 32, no. 3 (1979): 43.

Wittenberg, Hermann. 'The Taint of the Censor: J M Coetzee and the Making of *In the Heart of the Country*'. *English in Africa* 35, no. 2 (2008): 133–50.

Wright, Laura. 'Displacing the Voice: South African Feminism and J. M. Coetzee's Female Narrators'. *African Studies* 67, no. 1 (2008): 11–32.

CHAPTER EIGHT

Waiting for the Barbarians

JENNIFER WENZEL

AFTER ALLEGORY

For nearly thirty years, I have been reading the same Penguin paperback copy of *Waiting for the Barbarians* (1980), its yellowed pages now a palimpsest of inscriptions in thick gel blue and pink, circumspect graphite gray, or ballpoint red and green. Because I chose a used copy at a textbook store across the street from the University of Texas at Austin, there are also traces of a reader who came before me. No longer can I confidently differentiate between our underlines and brackets, but it is surely an alien hand that comments about the dream in which the Magistrate offers a coin to the blank-faced figure, 'He wants to buy her story – her identity – he wants the story of her scarring.'

One might find this readerly predicament described – even if obliquely, analogically, allegorically – in the pages of *Waiting for the Barbarians*. How does one read the already-read, or inscribe the already-inscribed? As the Magistrate asks himself, how can he (re)see the girl as she was before her encounter with Colonel Joll? This time, I resolve to abjure the harried professor's shortcut of re-reading *only* the marked-up bits, to come to the text with a mind fresh as new-fallen snow and to allow each word to fall into place, as the frontier settlement comes into view. Discs of glass, inn, ramparts, walnut trees, granary, communal land, irrigation dam. I'm surprised at my pleasure in watching this world emerge. And when my eye strays to the margins of the page, sometimes I cringe to read the record of my earlier thoughts.

Despite myself, despite my intention to leave allegory aside and to just read the book for once, I hear how the Magistrate's voice infects my own.[1] As a young doctoral student in the early 1990s, I became convinced that *Waiting for the Barbarians* was about torture.[2] To make my case, I drew on similar interpretations of Coetzee's novel by Susan van Zanten Gallagher and Barbara Eckstein.[3] I also had to grapple with the arguments of critics who understood this novel to be about something else – including, most notably, an endless Derridean deferral of meaning,[4] 'liberal humanist novelistic discourse' and the Lacanian emergence of the self,[5] or the contest between the time of Empire and the time of nature.[6] Regardless of the conflicting arguments that critics advanced in these readings, all of us were haunted by the same question: whether and how the novel was – or should be – about apartheid South Africa.

Fundamentally, *Waiting for the Barbarians* is about an unnamed Magistrate who administers a remote frontier outpost of an unnamed Empire and experiences a crisis of conscience (and desire) when Colonel Joll, a member of the security police, arrives from the unnamed capital to investigate rumours of barbarian restiveness along the frontier. Here my use of *about* veers away from the strong allegorical readings enumerated earlier and towards what Derek Attridge would call a '*literal*' (and 'literary') approach.[7] My recent endeavour to read the novel while leaving allegory in abeyance is compatible with Attridge's account of what is lost if readers turn away from the 'immersion in the text' that comes from 'follow[ing] the words one by one'.[8] According to Attridge, such readers miss out on the many 'rich and sometimes apparently quite contingent details' that fall by the wayside because they do not serve as fodder for allegory, which risks 'moving too quickly beyond the novel to find its significance elsewhere'.[9] In order to illustrate what it would mean to 'do justice' to this book – to read *Waiting for the Barbarians* as an 'event' or 'experience' rather than an allegorical statement of some other truth (which 'we can apprehend perfectly well without Coetzee's aid') – Attridge attends to the paragraph early in the novel where two boys play with a hoop in the wind.[10] (The passage falls between two encounters with the girl before the Magistrate brings her into his apartment.[11]) And indeed, *how crisp and finely observed an image!*, I had thought about these sentences during my recent re-reading; in my well-worn copy of the novel, this passage has never once been underlined or commented upon.

Published in 2004, Attridge's 'Against Allegory' is not the first time that critics have noted the tendency to read *Waiting for the Barbarians* through the lens of allegory. But it is a pivotal intervention in the novel's reception for several reasons. First, the sympathy with which Attridge accounts for the phenomenon, which he attributes to allegory's capacity 'to make sense of texts that, for one reason or another, are puzzling when taken at face value'.[12] (As Coetzee observed in a notebook late in the drafting process, 'This is a novel in which meaning is continually held back.'[13]) Second, Attridge makes a two-pronged argument about the limitations of allegorical approaches. Not only do readers hot on the trail of allegory miss out on what makes the novel *a novel* by following the spoor of a single idea; they also discount the complications posed by the fact that the Magistrate is himself a compulsive interpreter and frustrated allegorist.[14] A significant portion of the novel details the Magistrate's searching after signs, significances and correspondences, whether holding his ear to the ground at the excavated ruins of the ancient town, parsing the mysterious characters inscribed on the poplar slips he finds there, or reflecting repeatedly upon the disturbing similarities between himself and Joll in how they treat the barbarian girl.

One might say, conversely, that it is precisely the Magistrate's tendency towards allegory – his disposition towards an understanding of the world 'in which events are not themselves but stand for other things' (40) – that invites allegorical interpretations. To 'do justice' to this text, in Attridge's sense, requires confronting the diegetic *failures* of allegory and the Magistrate's reluctance to allow things to be themselves. To do justice to *Waiting for the Barbarians* (or to *Life & Times of Michael K* [1983], which Attridge discusses in the same chapter) would be to allow *it* to be itself rather than 'stand[ing] for other things'. As Attridge asks,

> [W]hat happens if we *resist* the allegorical reading that the novels seem half to solicit, half to problematize, and take them, as it were, at their word[?] Is it possible to read or discuss them without looking for allegorical meanings, and if one were to succeed in this enterprise would one have emptied them of whatever political or ethical significance they might possess?[15]

I want to suggest that this idea of 'doing justice' to the novel is historically contingent, that Attridge's advocacy for an ethics of reading makes a certain kind of sense in 2004, at the end of the first decade of the South African democratic experiment, that it might not have made previously. Shining a sceptical light on allegory, as Attridge does, might help to bring into focus some of the exigencies of the late 1970s and 1980s – in South Africa and abroad – that shaped the novel's composition and early reception. Readers coming to *Waiting for the Barbarians* for the first time now are, in a certain way, not reading the same novel as readers in the 1980s and early 1990s. In addition to teasing out these contradictory historical pressures that bear precisely upon ideas of justice, I will also consider the extent to which our understanding of *Waiting for the Barbarians* in its historical context has been transformed by the recent release of two kinds of previously unavailable documents from that moment: Coetzee's papers held by the Harry Ransom Humanities Research Center (HRC) at the University of Texas at Austin; and the records of the Publications Control Board, the apartheid-era state entity that determined whether texts were 'undesirable' enough to be censored, now held at the National Archive of South Africa. What new insights might these old documents facilitate?

The HRC papers indicate that Coetzee began sketching ideas for what would become *Waiting for the Barbarians* in July 1977, and started drafting a manuscript in Cape Town on 20 September 1977. After several major transformations in the narrative's premise and setting, he completed the typescript in Austin, Texas on 1 June 1979.[16] Secker & Warburg published *Waiting for the Barbarians* in London in October 1980, and worked with Ravan Press to release a South African edition in 1981. Penguin published an American edition in 1982, the first time that it debuted a novel in trade paperback.[17] *Waiting for the Barbarians* was pivotal in establishing Coetzee's international reputation: it attracted admiring reviews in the London *Times Literary Supplement* and *Sunday Times*, as well as *The New York Review* and the *New York Times Book Review*, and also won awards in three countries – the James Tait Black Memorial Prize in Scotland, the Geoffrey Faber Prize in England and the CNA Prize in South Africa (which Coetzee had also won for *In the Heart of the Country*).[18]

The early reception of *Waiting for the Barbarians* offers a stark example of Fredric Jameson's account of literary interpretation 'as an essentially allegorical act, which consists in rewriting a given text in terms of a particular master code'.[19] 'We never really confront a text immediately, in all its freshness as a thing-in-itself,' Jameson observed in *The Political Unconscious*; instead, texts 'come before us as the always-already-read; we apprehend them through sedimented layers of previous interpretations, or [...] through the sedimented reading habits and categories developed by those inherited interpretive conditions.'[20] These ideas resonate with those of Attridge and Coetzee's Magistrate, not least when the latter sifts through the sands that have sedimented over the ruins of the ancient town. Published in 1981, Jameson's landmark text indexes here the proliferation of interpretive 'master code[s]' that transformed metropolitan literary studies in the 1970s and 1980s. I have in mind the rise of literary 'theory' in the wake of the broader linguistic turn across the humanities and the humanistic social sciences, in which the implications of Ferdinand de Saussure's early-twentieth-century insights about the arbitrary relationship between signifier and signified were pursued in arguments about the instability of linguistic and literary meaning and about the social constructedness of ideas, ideologies and institutions. To call this phenomenon 'poststructuralist' underestimates how broadly these insights underwrote not only deconstruction, but also various emergent strands of feminist, ethnic, Marxist, psychoanalytic and postcolonial criticism. (Inspired by Michel Foucault's account of the workings of discourse and the relationship between power and knowledge and anticipating the Magistrate's reflections on his relationship to Empire, Edward W. Said's *Orientalism* appeared in 1978.) Each of these critical approaches, Jameson observed, 'rewrite[s]' texts according to its own 'master code'. Let a thousand allegories bloom.

Having spent significant time at American universities in the late 1960s and 1970s as a student and professor of literature and linguistics, Coetzee was no stranger to this semiotic ferment. His early novels instantiate, in a particularly salient way, Jameson's sense of texts having been 'always-already-read': they seem to anticipate (and thereby frustrate) the interpretive moves that readers in the era of high theory would bring to them. Notice the disturbing parallel between Coetzee staying one step ahead of his readers and Colonel Joll pre-empting the Magistrate's critiques by voicing them himself. In 'The Novel Today', a lecture delivered in Cape Town in 1987, Coetzee expressed scepticism about modes of reading-as-rewriting reminiscent of those described by Jameson: 'There is a game going on between the covers of the book, but it is not always the game you think it is. No matter what it may appear to be doing, the story is not really playing the game you call Class Conflict or the game called Male Domination or any of the other games in the games handbook.'[21]

Coetzee's rather dismissive figuration of literary interpretation as a 'game' whose rules one can find in the 'games handbook' resonates strangely with his more anguished account of the South African writer's predicament regarding the literary representation of torture. In 'Into the Dark Chamber', a 1986 essay in the *New York Times Book Review*, Coetzee reflects on how difficult it is for the writer to avoid

> allow[ing] himself to be impaled on the dilemma proposed by the state, namely, either to ignore its obscenities or else to produce representations of them. The true challenge is: *how not to play the game by the rules of the state*, how to establish one's own authority, how to imagine torture and death on one's own terms.[22]

Written in the wake of the international success of *Waiting for the Barbarians,* 'Into the Dark Chamber' has been a key text for making sense of how Coetzee stages the depiction and discussion of torture in this novel. What I want to register here are the overlaps and tensions between what Coetzee dubs the 'game' of literary interpretation and the 'game' of state violence, both of which shaped not only Coetzee's own writerly predicaments but also a broader debate in South Africa, following the explosion of writing, militant resistance and escalating repression in the wake of the 1976 Soweto Uprising. Amidst massacres, marches in the streets and a series of States of Emergency, this debate was about the role of culture in the anti-apartheid struggle and the modes of writing that were most politically efficacious or – in the language of the day – 'relevant' to the task of liberation.[23] It was not until *Disgrace* and after the democratic transition of the mid-1990s that Coetzee would write anything like a straightforwardly realist, ripped-from-the-headlines account of the South African present – the privileged mode of fictional narrative in late 1970s and 1980s South Africa.

All interpretation is allegorical, says Jameson, but Coetzee's fiction of this period was read as allegorical partly because of its vexed relationship to the South African context and these literary-political pressures of relevance and urgency. One can insist, as I do below, that the Empire is not 'really' (i.e. allegorically) reducible to South Africa, while also recognizing how the death-in-detention of Black Consciousness founder Steve Biko on 12 September 1977, as well as the scandalous denials and explanations offered by officials of the apartheid state, profoundly disturbed Coetzee, who kept a folder of press clippings on the November 1977 inquest.[24] Biko's killing was not the original impetus for *Waiting for the Barbarians*, whose manuscript Coetzee began writing in earnest several days afterward from notes made earlier in the year.[25] That event, however, would be inscribed into his geographically and historically indeterminate narrative: Joll's report on the prisoner who died during interrogation towards the beginning of the novel closely echoes language from the Biko inquest.[26]

If not late 1970s South Africa, what *is* the setting of *Waiting for the Barbarians?* The Magistrate serves the Empire at a historical moment when sunglasses seem to be a newfangled invention, when horses and horse-drawn carriages are the only available aids to human locomotion, and when heat and light come from wood, oil lamps and tallow candles. It is, in other words, a pre-petromodern Empire. Geographically, the situation is more complex. The narrative traces the cycle of the seasons over a year; since March brings the onset of spring, we're in the northern hemisphere, yet the landscape also features flora and fauna endemic to the southern hemisphere.[27] These details obviate any actually existing geographic location. In an interview with David Attwell, Coetzee describes the setting as a 'landscape I have never seen ... [which] represented a challenge to my power of *envisioning'*, as opposed to 'the tedium of reproduction' involved in faithfully representing a literarily over-described landscape like the southern African Karoo.[28] The literary 'classics' that occupy the Magistrate's leisure hours during periods of peace along the frontier are never named or cited, so they could just as easily be Chinese or Mughal as Greek or Roman. Indeed, Coetzee's notebooks and manuscripts shed light on how this invented landscape borrows features from both the Karoo semi-desert and the Mongolian steppe of Central Asia.[29]

This envisioning of landscape involves a paradoxical investment in detail. The novel describes the oasis and its surrounds with a realist particularity through which it becomes cognizable, but without the referentiality that would make it *recognizable* as an actual place. This paradox goes to the heart of the novel's reception, in which this absence of referentiality has been read as evidence of the novel's *universality* – an interpretive gesture epitomized in Bernard Levin's London *Sunday Times* review. Because the narrative is 'timeless, spaceless, nameless and universal', Levin claims, 'Coetzee sees the heart of darkness in all societies, and gradually it becomes clear that he is not dealing with politics at all, but inquiring into the nature of the beast that lurks within each of us ... waiting for the barbarians'.[30] Not only is this claim of universality ethnocentric (who *are* the barbarians everyone is waiting for?), it also vitiates questions of political responsibility for both Coetzee and his readers. If all of us are complicit in the way the Magistrate recognizes that he may be, then complicity (or refusal) ceases to count for much.[31]

In an astute corrective to this depoliticizing approach, Attwell insists on 'a difference between universalism ... and a strategic refusal of specificity, a refusal that is the result of being painfully conscious of one's immediate historical location'.[32] This cognizance of the South African situation also underwrites Stephen Watson's 1986 invocation of Albert Memmi's notion of the 'colonizer who refuses' to elucidate the force of Coetzee's pointed critique of colonialism – rather than, as readers like Levin would have it, an articulation of the 'universal' predicament of being human. Watson sees Coetzee and his 'dissenting colonizer' protagonists as trapped within a 'failed dialectic', caught between thought and (the impossibility of) action; they 'beat against the shackles of their historical position in vain'.[33] *Waiting for the Barbarians* examines 'the status of liberal values in a situation that simply has no room for them anymore'; while this observation by Attwell may feel familiar to readers in the twenty-first century, Watson's attention to the marginalization of the Anglophone intelligentsia after 1948 situates this predicament within the apartheid context.[34]

As with the tendency towards allegorizing interpretations discussed earlier, this debate about the universality or particularity of *Waiting for the Barbarians* has taken on additional historical poignancy in the twenty-first century. We now know that it was precisely the novel's '"obscure"' locale and its '"world-wide significance – not particularized"' to contemporary South Africa, that led Professor Reginald Lighton of the South African Directorate of Publications to find '"no convincing reason for declaring the book undesirable"' when he reviewed the embargoed Secker & Warburg edition in December 1980.[35] For Lighton and his fellow censors, not only this 'redeeming universality' (to borrow Peter McDonald's phrase), but also the fact that Coetzee's fiction had '"no popular appeal"', obviated its potential undesirability.[36] In his study of apartheid-era censorship, McDonald teases out the historical ironies regarding 'what could count as serious literature' in this moment, not all of which were fully evident at the time.[37] For the censors, the obvious literariness of Coetzee's fiction limited its potential political effect – a judgement shared, albeit from a diametrically opposed political position, by some progressive South African critics, whom McDonald strikingly dubs 'self-appointed literature police', no less involved than the censors in 'shaping the category of the literary in history'.[38]

From this consideration of Coetzee's novel within its time, I want to shift to the place of time and temporality within the novel. The Magistrate is occupied equally by history and futurity; thoughts of endings and new beginnings consume him, and, as I suggest elsewhere, he waits as much for the historians who will someday memorialize the outpost as for the barbarians rumoured to be set on destroying it.[39] (Another important intertext is C. P. Cavafy's poem 'Waiting for the Barbarians'; in the poem, the barbarians never appear, and the speaker wonders pointedly, 'Now what's going to happen to us without barbarians?/Those people were a kind of solution.'[40]) The Magistrate recognizes that temporality is among the realms of existence upon which Empire imposes its will. Towards the end of the novel, he remarks:

> What has made it impossible for us to live in time like fish in water, like birds in air, like children? It is the fault of Empire! Empire has created the time of history. Empire has located its existence not in the smooth recurrent spinning time of the cycle of the seasons but in the jagged time of rise and fall, of beginning and end, of catastrophe. Empire dooms itself to live in history and plot against history. One thought alone preoccupies the submerged mind of empire: how not to end, how not to die, how to prolong its era.
>
> (133)

Here and elsewhere, the Magistrate understands the time of Empire as antagonistic to his own desires and to the frontier settlement's broader rhythms, which he naturalizes into the immersive temporality of non-human creatures or the seasonal cycle whose constancy seems like stasis: the presence of the Third Bureau is for him an 'irruption of history into the static time of the oasis' (143).

But this distinction between the discordant temporalities of Empire's centre and periphery threatens to obscure the more fundamental coloniality of time in the novel. The annual rhythms of the nomadic pastoralist barbarians and the Empire's settler agriculturalists intersect uneasily, as the barbarians move their flocks up and down the mountain and the settlers watch for the right time to plant and harvest. One might say that *Waiting for the Barbarians* is as much about agriculture as it is about torture, since the Magistrate devotes a significant amount of narratorial attention to his responsibilities in supervising agricultural labour on the communal lands and maintaining the irrigation works; when the Third Bureau decamps, they take stores of grain with them. He notes the difference between the barbarians, their 'bodies clothed in wool and the hides of animals and nourished from infancy on meat and milk' and the linen- and cotton-clad settlers who know 'the virtues of the placid grains' planted in fields from which the nomads have been displaced 'by the spread of Empire' (72). For the Magistrate, as in European thought dating back to the Greeks, a fundamental distinction between barbarity and civilization is quite literally *cultivation*, and the Magistrate understands the taste of bread as a gateway drug that might 'seduce' both the aboriginal fisherfolk and the barbarians into the ways of Empire (19, 155). Even amidst the difficulties of the expedition to return the girl to the barbarians, the Magistrate has his men build a makeshift oven in the desert so they can bake bread.

One might say that the Magistrate's attention to these classical differences among so-called savage, barbarian and civilized modes of production complicates the deconstructive/postcolonial gesture of castigating reversal, in which the 'true' barbarians are actually the men of Empire. But just as the Magistrate recognizes that he is 'the lie that Empire tells itself when times are easy' (135) (while Joll is the Empire's harsher truth), the very notion of 'placid' or 'pacific grains' is implicitly shown to be a lie (155). How can agriculture be among the arts of peace when it requires stolen land and an army to defend it? (51). The Magistrate admits as much when he answers the newly arrived military officer's question about what the barbarians want: '"They want an end to the spread of settlements across their land. They want their land back, finally. They want to be free to move about with their flocks from pasture to pasture as they used to"' (72). Agriculture and torture are twinned faces of Empire: it is the settlement's *granary* that Joll commandeers for his dark chamber. Agriculture follows a cyclical rhythm, but so do the periodic irruptions of 'hysteria about the barbarians' that occur 'once in every generation, without fail', as the Magistrate observes near the end of his long career serving the Empire (8). As I argue elsewhere, his archaeological pursuits lead him to 'replot [...] imperial time as a cycle,' 'one of the gestures through which the Magistrate disavows complicity with the Empire's violence: there have been magistrates and barbarians before him, and will be afterward'.[41]

If the Empire and its subjects are waiting for the barbarians, then the barbarians are outwaiting the Empire, at least according to the Magistrate. He also knows that the barbarians have both time and nature on their side. As he explains to the military officer:

'Every year the lake-water grows a little more salty. There is a simple explanation – never mind what it is. The barbarians know this fact. At this very moment they are saying to themselves, "Be patient, one of these days their crops will start withering from the salt, they will not be able to feed themselves, they will have to go." That is what they are thinking. That they will outlast us.'
(51)

This key detail – half-obscured, even in the telling – has been largely overlooked in the novel's reception and in critical discussions of its visions of futurity.[42] Even the Magistrate seems perhaps to have forgotten it when he rails against the time of Empire in the passage cited earlier; he thinks those thoughts about Empire plotting against its end while wading in that same lake at sunset, full of 'love' for 'a world I know ... and do not want to leave' (132). The Magistrate's love for and knowledge of the land and its waters contrasts powerfully with the dismissively stark observation offered by a sentry guarding the outpost: '"You can't live on the fruit of the land out here, can you? I've never seen such dead country."' (99). And yet, this settlement's days *are* numbered, barbarians or no barbarians. The Magistrate's expedition across the dried-up ancient lakebed with its brackish water thus implicitly offers a glimpse of the future of the oasis, just as the Magistrate sees himself and the Empire prefigured in the ruins of the ancient town. (As Attwell observes, it was while standing amidst the ruins of ancient Rome that Edward Gibbon hatched the idea of narrating its decline and fall.[43]) Precisely because readers are not privy to the 'simple explanation' for the lake's gradual salinization, we can take it as given and reflect on the Magistrate's (and Coetzee's) recognition that the time of nature is not *only* cyclical: it is, like Empire, susceptible to linear changes (at least at the scale of human time) that can bring 'catastrophe'.[44] Empire is doomed to live in environmental history and plot against environmental history, wittingly or not.

For their part, the barbarians seem not entirely content to wait for nature to take its course, at least while Joll and his men are undertaking expeditions that round them up, string wires through their cheeks and torture them until they tell the 'truth'. Whether in drawing the expeditions further into the desert or in burning crops and sabotaging the irrigation works, the barbarians know that exposure to the elements is as effective a weapon against the Empire's soldiers as fire and water are against its wheat. (Depending on that never-disclosed 'simple explanation', the lake's salinization may or may not be an instance of what postcolonial ecocritic Rob Nixon calls 'slow violence'.) Attending to the pivotal role of the forbidding landscapes beyond the settlement, Tom Bradstreet argues that ecocritics have tended to ignore *Waiting for the Barbarians* in favour of the post-Costello, animal-focused *oeuvre*, despite 'substantial ecological concerns hiding in plain sight'.[45] While this observation is salutary, Bradstreet himself ignores the environmental situation *within* the settlement and thereby misses the Magistrate's multiple concerns with what Bradstreet terms 'ecological materiality'; Bradstreet imputes to the Empire a kind of nature-blindness without exception that he sees the novel's critics as having shared.[46] Bradstreet's broader point, however, resonates with Attridge's concern about allegory: aside from the animals, Coetzee critics have tended to transmute the materiality of environmental detail into 'metaphoric or metonymic' terms, 'thereby tacitly denying ... [their] value as entities in themselves'.[47]

After allegory, then what? Attridge urges a mode of reading that is 'inevitably ... colored by the reader's personal situation and history. Doing justice to a work of literature involves doing justice at the same time to who, where, and when we are'.[48] *Waiting for the Barbarians* is no more 'about' climate change and the Anthropocene than it is 'about' torture, and yet I have found its meditation on the violence of inscription useful for thinking about the ways that (some) humans have inscribed themselves upon the planet. For this reader, *Waiting for the Barbarians* resonates with the urgent challenges of the present, not least for its thematization of conflicting demands on our attention: an uneven contest between spectacular violence and more subtle processes that threaten the many worlds we know and love and do not want to leave. Both can stand in the way of justice.

NOTES

1. Compare Teresa Dovey's similar observation: 'Undertaking to resolve the enigma of these relationships [in Coetzee's novel], particularly the Magistrate's relation with the barbarian girl, one finds that one's interpretive activity inevitably repeats the structures of these relationships'. Dovey, *Novels*, 208.
2. Wenzel, 'Keys to the Labyrinth'.
3. Van Zanten Gallagher, 'Torture and the Novel'; Eckstein, 'The Body'.
4. Olsen, 'The Presence of Absence'.

5. Dovey, *Novels*, 210.
6. Attwell, *J. M. Coetzee: South Africa and the Politics of Writing*, 72.
7. Attridge, 'Against Allegory', 39.
8. Ibid., 48, 46.
9. Ibid., 43.
10. Ibid., 39, 40, 45–6.
11. Coetzee, *Waiting for the Barbarians*, 27. Further references cited parenthetically in text.
12. Attridge, 'Against Allegory', 39.
13. Coetzee qtd. in Attwell, *J. M. Coetzee and the Life of Writing*, 104.
14. Compare Sue Kossew's suggestion that 'the allegorical form is … used paradoxically: it invites interpretation only to subvert it'; she considers arguments by Stephen Slemon and Lois Parkinson Zamora about what Slemon calls the counter-discursive 'exposure' of allegory as a colonizing stratagem. See Kossew, *Pen and Power*, 87, 94. On postcolonial allegory, see Slemon, 'Monuments of Empire'.
15. Attridge, 'Against Allegory', 35; emphasis in original.
16. Attwell, *Life of Writing*, 83; Kannemeyer, *J. M. Coetzee*, 334, 345.
17. Kannemeyer, *J. M. Coetzee*, 347.
18. Ibid., 342–3, 348–9, 353.
19. Jameson, *The Political Unconscious*, x.
20. Ibid., ix–x.
21. Coetzee qtd. in McDonald, 'The Writer, The Critic, and the Censor', 294. McDonald offers a helpful account of the charged context of this event: see 300 n15.
22. Coetzee, 'Into the Dark Chamber', 364; emphasis added.
23. On these debates, see Gwala, 'Writing as a Cultural Weapon'; Ndebele, *Rediscovery of the Ordinary*; Bethlehem, 'A Primary Need as Strong as Hunger'.
24. Attwell, *Life of Writing*, 89–90. Coetzee was also disturbed by the deaths in detention of Ahmed Timol and Neil Aggett and the assassination of Rick Turner (Kannemeyer, *J. M. Coetzee*, 329; Wittenberg and Highman, 'Sven Hedin's "Vanished Country"', 4).
25. See Attwell, *Life of Writing*, 93.
26. Coetzee, *Waiting for the Barbarians*, 6. See Susan Van Zanten Gallagher, *A Story of South Africa*, 112–18.
27. Many of the species mentioned in the novel are European or Eurasian, but waterbuck (9) are found in sub-Saharan Africa and cananga (or *ylang-ylang*) (46) in tropical Asia.
28. Coetzee, *Doubling the Point*, 142.
29. Attwell, *Life of Writing*, 90–2. For an account of Coetzee's reading of Central Asian travelogues as part of the labour of this envisioning, see Wittenberg and Highman, 'Sven Hedin'.
30. Levin, 'On the Edge of the Empire', 44.
31. I find Levin's assessment misguided and troubling, as perhaps did Coetzee (see Kannemeyer, *J. M. Coetzee*, 350–1), but his interpretation is compatible with Abdul JanMohamed's judgment that *Waiting for the Barbarians* epitomizes the mystifications of liberal 'colonialist fiction', which refuses responsibility by suggesting 'that we are all somewhat equally guilty and that fascism is endemic to all societies'. JanMohamed, 'The Economy of Manichean Allegory', 73.
32. Attwell, *South Africa*, 73.
33. Watson, 'Colonialism and the Novels of J. M. Coetzee', 378, 382–3.
34. Attwell, *South Africa*, 84; Watson, 'Colonialism', 380–1.

35. McDonald, 'The Writer', 288, 290. For Lighton's report, see https://theliteraturepolice.files.wordpress.com/2018/07/censors-report-on-coetzees-barbarians-19802.pdf.
36. McDonald, 'The Writer', 291.
37. Ibid., 295.
38. Ibid., 299.
39. Wenzel, 'Stratigraphy and Empire', 180.
40. See Cavafy, 'Waiting' (also online: https://www.poetryfoundation.org/poems/51294/waiting-for-the-barbarians). On the significance of Cavafy in 1970s South Africa, see Field, 'Home'.
41. Wenzel, 'Stratigraphy', 171.
42. Coetzee includes a '"lake [that] is drying up"' in notes about the manuscript project from November 1977; see Wittenberg and Highman, 'Sven Hedin,' 6.
43. Attwell, *South Africa*, 75.
44. An alternative interpretation would be that the Magistrate 'reads' this 'fact' of the landscape for the military officer just as tendentiously as he 'reads' the slips later on.
45. Bradstreet, 'The Coming of the Storm', 3.
46. Ibid., 2, 6, 10.
47. Ibid., 3.
48. Attridge, 'Against Allegory', 45.

WORKS CITED

Attridge, Derek. 'Against Allegory: *Waiting for the Barbarians* and *Life & Times of Michael K*'. In *J. M. Coetzee and the Ethics of Reading*, 32–64. Chicago: University of Chicago Press, 2004.
Attwell, David. *J. M. Coetzee and the Life of Writing: Face to Face with Time*. Oxford: Oxford University Press, 2015.
Attwell, David. *J. M. Coetzee: South Africa and the Politics of Writing*. Berkeley: University of California Press, 1993.
Bethlehem, Louise. '"A Primary Need as Strong as Hunger": The Rhetoric of Urgency in South African Literary Culture under Apartheid'. *Poetics Today* 22, no. 2 (2001): 365–89.
Bradstreet, Tom Z. '"The Coming of the Storm": Imperial Empiricism and Ecological Indifference in *Waiting for the Barbarians*'. *Ariel* 48, no. 2 (2017): 1–23.
Cavafy, C. P. 'Waiting for the Barbarians'. In *The Collected Poems*, translated by Evangelos Schperoglou, 15–17. Oxford: Oxford University Press, 2007.
Coetzee, J. M. 'Into the Dark Chamber: The Writer and the South African State'. In *Doubling the Point: Essays and Interviews*, edited by David Attwell, 361–8. Cambridge, MA: Harvard University Press, 1992.
Coetzee, J. M. *Waiting for the Barbarians*. New York: Penguin Books, 1980.
Dovey, Teresa. *The Novels of J. M. Coetzee: Lacanian Allegories*. No. 86. Johannesburg: Ad. Donker, 1988.
Eckstein, Barbara. 'The Body, the Word, and the State: J. M. Coetzee's "Waiting for the Barbarians"'. *Novel: A Forum on Fiction* 22, no. 2 (1989): 175–98.
Field, Roger. 'Coming Home, Coming Out: Achmat Dangor's Journeys through Myth and Constantin Cavafy'. *English Studies in Africa* 54, no. 2 (2011): 103–17.
Gwala, Mafika. 'Writing as a Cultural Weapon'. In *Momentum: On Recent South African Writing*, edited by Margaret Daymond, Johan Jacobs and Margaret Lenta, 37–53. Pietermaritzburg: University of Natal Press, 1984.
Jameson, Fredric. *The Political Unconscious: Narrative as a Socially Symbolic Act*. Ithaca: Cornell University Press, 1981.

JanMohamed, Abdul R. 'The Economy of Manichean Allegory: The Function of Racial Difference in Colonialist Literature'. *Critical Inquiry* 12, no. 1 (1985): 59–87.

Kannemeyer, John Christoffel. *J. M Coetzee: A Life in Writing*. Melbourne: Scribe Publications, 2012.

Kossew, Sue. *Pen and Power: A Post-colonial Reading of J. M. Coetzee and André Brink*. Amsterdam: Rodopi, 1996.

Levin, Bernard. 'On the Edge of the Empire', *Sunday Times*, 23 November 1980, 44.

McDonald, Peter D. 'The Writer, the Critic, and the Censor: J. M. Coetzee and the Question of Literature'. *Book History* 7, no. 1 (2004): 285–302.

Ndebele, Njabulo S. *Rediscovery of the Ordinary: Essays in South African Literature and Culture*. Johannesburg: Congress of South African Writers, 1991.

Olsen, Lance. 'The Presence of Absence: Coetzee's *Waiting for the Barbarians*'. *Ariel: A Review of International English Literature* 16, no. 2 (1985): 47–56.

Slemon, Stephen. 'Monuments of Empire: Allegory/Counter-discourse/Post-colonial Writing'. *Kunapipi* 9, no. 3 (1987): 1–16.

Van Zanten Gallagher, Susan. *A Story of South Africa: J. M. Coetzee's Fiction in Context*. Cambridge: Harvard University Press, 1991.

Van Zanten Gallagher, Susan. 'Torture and the Novel: J. M. Coetzee's *Waiting for the Barbarians*'. *Contemporary Literature* 29, no. 2 (1988): 277–85.

Watson, Stephen. 'Colonialism and the Novels of J. M. Coetzee'. *Research in African Literatures* 17, no. 3 (1986): 370–92.

Wenzel, Jennifer. 'Keys to the Labyrinth: Writing, Torture, and Coetzee's Barbarian Girl'. *Tulsa Studies in Women's Literature* 15, no. 1 (1996): 61–71.

Wenzel, Jennifer. 'Stratigraphy and Empire: Waiting for the Barbarians, Reading under Duress'. *Anthropocene Reading: Literary History in Geologic Times* (2017), 167–83.

Wittenberg, Hermann and Kate Highman. 'Sven Hedin's "Vanished Country": Setting and History in J. M. Coetzee's *Waiting for the Barbarians*'. *Scrutiny2* 20, no. 1 (2015): 103–27.

CHAPTER NINE

Life & Times of Michael K

ECKARD SMUTS

One of the first things readers learn about Michael K, the eponymous protagonist of J. M. Coetzee's Booker-prize winning fourth book *Life & Times of Michael K* (1983), is that he has trouble eating. Born with a cleft lip, he 'could not suck from the breast and cried with hunger'; fed by his mother with a teaspoon, 'he coughed and spluttered and cried'.[1] The episode alludes to the life of hardship the country of his birth has in store for him and prefaces the crudely pragmatic approach to food and eating that accompanies him through childhood into adult life. Set in a dystopian, near-future version of South Africa in which the racial animosities of the 1980s have boiled over into civil strife, the narrative charts K's unlikely journey from Cape Town, where he quits his job as a lowly municipal gardener, to return his ailing mother to the landscape of her youth in the Karoo. He pushes her along in a handmade barrow, and when she passes away en route – in a hospital in Stellenbosch – continues the journey alone, planning to return her ashes to the farm outside Prince Albert where she spent a portion of her childhood. Traversing the arid hinterland of the country on foot, K subsists on whatever he can find, scrounging food as the occasion allows. Near Worcester, in an abandoned orchard, he eats rotten apples, 'taking bites of good flesh here and there, chewing as quickly as a rabbit, his eyes vacant' (39). When there is nothing to eat, he eats nothing. In due course he loses his taste for meat and discovers that the best of all foods, for him, is what he has cultivated from seed. The 'soft and juicy' flesh of the pumpkins he grows while in hiding from the war is 'the first time since he had arrived in the country' – if not the first time in the book – that he finds pleasure in eating (114).

Critics have generally viewed K's minimal eating habits as a symptom of his larger withdrawal from the dominating forces controlling the terms of life in a time of war, considering it as a part of the book's enactment of a powerful politics of absence. But an essay Coetzee published more than ten years later suggests a surprising provenance for K's unassuming diet, pointing to a way of reading his character in less negatively defined terms. In 'Meat Country', an appraisal of American food culture written while he was living in Texas, Coetzee strikes a curiously apologetic note for following a 'diet without flesh'.[2] Linking it to his 'dislike for cars', he frames it as a throwback to a species of 'crankhood' that emerged in England in the 1890s – a creed that involved 'brisk cold showers, sandals in all weathers, free love, bicycle locomotion and the avoidance of animal flesh'. His attachment to a similar regime in late-twentieth-century Texas, Coetzee writes, is 'eccentric and dated', even 'uninteresting', a 'way of life without a future'. Early adherents to the creed – people like George Bernard Shaw and Edward Carpenter – seem, from the perspective of a society powered by consumer capitalism, a 'comical lot', and he is well aware of the ridicule his obstinate clinging to these habits may attract.[3]

Coetzee's careful skirting of polemic and his refusal to occupy a position of authority in his role as a writer has been recognized by critics as an important condition for the disruptive potential of his work. An argument might be made that the framing of his vegetarianism in 'Meat Country' as an eccentric or outsider position interacts in meaningful ways with the critique of food culture that follows in the essay. But at present, when our understanding of food systems has begun to intersect more urgently with questions of social justice and planetary health, it seems unlikely that a critique of flesh consumption – or dietary habits more broadly – could in good faith be advanced in a similarly self-deprecating spirit, or framed quite so easily as an eccentricity.

Food – its production, distribution and consumption, its environmental impact, social, cultural and ethical meaning – has in the quarter century since the publication of 'Meat Country', and certainly since the publication of *Life & Times*, gained considerable traction as a subject of political contestation. In the aftermath of colonization and capitalist expansion, the realization that 'our collective ability to sustain ourselves and live in harmony with the cycles of nature is being destroyed', and that alternative ways of cultivating and preparing food can be seen as 'a creative act of resistance', has more firmly begun to take hold.[4] Coetzee's meat-refusing 'cranks', with their communitarian ideals and their mistrust of institutional power, might indeed be looked on with more sympathy by burgeoning food sovereignty movements today, even if in their own time they may not have been alive to their eating habits as a form of mobilization in the teeth of a disenfranchising and ecologically destructive global food industry. In brief, the politics of our time appears to have caught up with the early vegetarians, and Coetzee's refusal to eat meat in the heart of Texas, far from being an eccentricity, may have brought him to the front lines of a struggle that cannot but, in our shared present, be polemical. The same might be said, I propose, for Michael K's discovery of a preference for eating pumpkins he has grown from seed.

RE-MATERIALIZING MICHAEL K

Throughout his journey, which eventually leads back to Cape Town, K, with his cleft lip and his mind that is 'not quick' (4), proves himself as allergic to confrontation and polemic as his author professes to be ten years on in 'Meat Country'. Eluding the various institutional forces that would curtail his freedom by pressing him into one or another role in the war-torn society, K manages against the odds to slip through the cracks of the war and live life on his own terms, however meagre those terms might seem to others. It is partly for this reason that, in the critical orthodoxy that has established itself around the book, K has often been read (to borrow the words of the medical officer whose journal entries comprise part two of the book) as 'an allegory – speaking at the highest level – of how scandalously, how outrageously a meaning can take up residence in a system without becoming a term in it' (166).

Early reviewers found the elusive nature of the protagonist to be a source of exasperation. They were critical of K's apparent lack of interest in his social environment, seeing it as a betrayal of the prevailing opinion, among the left, that writers had a social duty to represent black agency in the face of apartheid.[5] One anonymous reviewer, for example, took exception to the novel's being awarded the Booker-McConnell Prize (1984), complaining in *The African Communist* that, in the figure of K, 'we are dealing not with a human spirit but an amoeba' from whom 'those interested in understanding or transforming South African society can learn little'.[6] David Attwell describes how progressive readers in South Africa in the 1980s required fictional protagonists to model, in social realist mode, 'certain forms of behavior or capacities for change'; they could not, as K appears to do, simply float untethered into a discursive system wholly defined by the social evil of apartheid, where 'every sign, no matter how innocent, becomes a signifier at another level, pointing to the larger conflict'.[7] An influential early review by Nadine Gordimer noted with disapproval Coetzee's failure, as she saw it, to harness the social energies of resistance to apartheid as integral to the development of his protagonist. Even though Gordimer was satisfied that the descriptive texture of the book evoked the hardships of social injustice in South Africa, she could not approve of K's seeming detachment from the reach of that historical reality. His capacity for living a life seemingly 'entirely outside political doctrine' was too much of a distortion of 'the integral relation between private and social destiny' that, for Gordimer, lay at the heart of writing.[8]

It is not surprising then that, subsequent to Gordimer's review, a great deal of scholarly energy went into redeeming *Life & Times*'s careful negotiation of the codes of narration, and in particular the forms of authority that govern those codes, as precisely the terms for its political intervention. Attwell argues, for example, that *Life & Times* dramatizes the 'historically constrained' freedom of textuality, and by doing so brings into focus 'the problem of authority within the fractured and unequal context of South African nationhood' (93). The book's singular narrative perspective, hovering 'somewhere between free indirect discourse and narratorial reporting' and keeping readers at a discrete distance from the interiority of K's consciousness,[9] supplied a stylistic point of entry for such readings. Critical opinion about *Life & Times* thus developed alongside the postmodern turn that took place in postcolonial criticism in the 1980s and 1990s. It was a time, as Neil Lazarus explains, in which postcolonial thought moved away from a politics of liberationism vested in an 'institutionally specific' experience of 'imperial dominance', to consolidate itself in a less materially bound 'politics of alterity' – one that concerned itself, in the words of Homi Bhabha, with 'the unequal and uneven forces of cultural representation involved in the contest for political and social authority in the modern world order'.[10] In its emphasis on the power dynamics linking representation with authority, such a politics views K's detachment from society – or more precisely, his evasion of the various institutional paradigms that pattern Coetzee's near-future projection of apartheid South Africa – as a necessary condition, sustained by a sophisticated stylistic architecture, for the resistance to colonial mastery that the novel performs on multiple levels. In this respect the figure of the protagonist has by and large been subsumed into the discourse of postcolonialism as a principle of deconstructive critique, a semantic vanishing point, escaping from all the camps, perpetually running from the medical officer's attempts to determine his truth.[11] It is a perspective that seems frequently to be confirmed by K himself, for example, when he tells the guard at the Jakkalsdrif labour camp that he simply does not 'want to be in a camp, that's all' (85), or when he muses in the final section of the book that 'perhaps the truth is that it is enough to be ... out of all the camps at the same time. Perhaps that is enough of an achievement, *for the time being*' (182, emphasis added).

But what happens if we apply some pressure on that italicized qualifying clause? Might it perhaps suggest something about a different time, one in which it is no longer enough simply to be 'out of all the camps at the same time?' It is a moment that invites us to reframe K's relationship with his socio-historical context in less metafictional terms, pointing to his situatedness in a milieu or lifeworld that is not simply the conceptual negative or the limitless 'outside' of the time of war, but that extends materially before, during and after it. Such a material view of K's sense of historical locatedness, or of his figuration within a material domain that extends beyond (and during) the time of the war, has cropped up occasionally in the criticism around the book. Dominic Head suggests, for example, that K's identification with the earth throughout the novel creates a sense of 'lingering realism' within the book's 'larger metafictional frame'.[12] Derek Wright proposes that the medical officer's description of K as 'a genuine little man of the earth' is representative of a 'special *chthonic* mythology' Coetzee has erected around his protagonist, linking him to 'a prehistoric earth *moving in geological time*'.[13] Indeed, the issue is already present in Gordimer's early review when she asks whether there is 'an idea of survival that can be realized entirely outside political doctrine', or 'a space between the camps'. Unusually, she discovers, the book posits an answer:

> The place is the earth, not in the cosmic but the plain dirt sense. The idea is the idea of gardening. And with it floods into the book, yet again, much more than it seemed to be about: the presence of the threat not only of mutual destruction of whites and blacks in South Africa, but of killing, everywhere, by scorching, polluting, neglecting, charging with radioactivity, the dirt beneath our feet.[14]

Gordimer is dubious about the efficacy of such a *longue durée* environmentalist perspective in the face of much more pressing transgressions against social and individual being in the contemporary moment of apartheid South Africa, and perhaps rightly so. But from the midst of our more widely articulated sense of the continuities between colonial-era destruction of life spaces and ecological ruination in the present,[15] K's attachment to a material reality that exists beyond, but also within the spaces of the camps comes more sharply into focus. Could it be that, as for the eccentric vegetarians in 'Meat Country', the times have caught up with Coetzee's perennially fugitive protagonist? Can the current climate of history – a time, as Bruno Latour notes, in which the 'massive event' of our knowledge that the earth can no longer support modernization has caused a widespread feeling 'that the ground is in the process of giving way'[16] – reveal K's closeness to the dirt to be political in more ways than we have expected? In order to examine these questions, we should look to an aspect of the narrative where the development of K's social being coincides most pointedly with a material reality that subtends the war: namely, the many instances of food and eating.

TIME FOR FOOD

Eating is an area where K's character undergoes a noticeable transformation over the course of the narrative. From the early stages of his fixation with the 'gleaming flank of roast pork' in the pages of a magazine he finds in the Buhrmanns' abandoned flat in Sea Point (16), to the end of the book when his subsistence needs have seemingly dwindled to a vision of extracting water from the earth with a teaspoon (184), a transformation occurs, as Daniele Monticelli notes, that appears to entail a 'progressive renunciation of food'.[17] For Monticelli, the protagonist's eating habits, as the basis for the radical challenge the book levels at 'the dehumanising force of biopolitical control', are the surest indicator of the 'the political relevance of K's outsideness' (635). Laura Wright, comparing K to Franz Kafka's 'A Hunger Artist', likewise reads his abstinence as 'the physical manifestation of ethical struggle' against the ravages of a violent order.[18]

It may seem uncharitable, in view of a present in which hunger is a pressing reality for so many, to construct a radical metaphysical politics on the meagre diet of a member of the precariat. But there is value in these attempts to recast K's seemingly apolitical outsidership in more positive terms, or to redeem him from a purely negatively defined freedom. K's transformative relationship with food also provides a key to understanding how the materially bound era he inhabits challenges 'the intensification of imperialist social relations in the times and spaces of the postcolonial world'.[19] One of the novel's conspicuous transformational food moments occurs when K kills a goat on the farm outside Prince Albert. This rather gruesome event takes place shortly after he reaches the farm and realizes that the wild-running goats will have to be 'caught, killed, cut up and eaten if he hoped to live' (52). He manages to drown one in the overflow of the concrete dam near the house and, slaughtering it with his penknife, hangs the carcass from the pantry ceiling in the abandoned farmhouse. The entire episode fills him with disgust:

> The thought of cutting up and devouring this ugly thing with its wet, matted hair repelled him. The rest of the goats stood on a rise some distance away, their ears pricked towards him. He found it hard to believe that he had spent a day chasing after them like a madman with a knife. He had a vision of himself riding the ewe to death under the mud by the light of the moon, and shuddered. He would have liked to bury the ewe somewhere and forget the episode; or else, best of all, to slap the creature on its haunch and see it scramble to its feet and trot off.
>
> (55)

The lesson K learns from the episode – if, indeed, 'there was a lesson, if there were lessons embedded in events' – is 'not to kill such large animals' (57). He makes a catapult for hunting birds; later, when he returns to the farm after jumping the fence at the labour camp, he uses it to kill a lizard, which he also eats (117). Cajetan Iheka points out that K's contrition, limited to 'large animals', complicates any attempt to enlist him into an organicist 'environmental ethic'.[20] As an ecological practice, the rejection of goat meat appears to be premised less on a moral estimation of the value of animal life than on material concerns around issues of scarcity, waste and the cost of labour. And yet, in the passage cited above, K's reaction appears also to be prompted by moral considerations of the first order. At first, he is seemingly disgusted on purely aesthetic grounds – the dead ewe is an 'ugly thing' that repels him with its 'wet, matted hair' (55). But the moment he becomes aware of the other goats standing on a rise nearby, 'their ears pricked towards him', he is impelled to recall the scene of the hunt, shuddering at the 'vision' of how he rode his quarry to death beneath the moon. The mute parliament of goats bearing witness to his misdeed – and it is in this moment that the *deed* becomes, in fact a *misdeed* – prompts in him the arrival of shame: a shame that resides not so much in a pang of fellow feeling for the goats, but rather in the image of himself as a figure of excess, a 'madman with a knife' (55).

If we untangle the mechanisms of shame embedded in this vignette, we notice that while it is K's night-time excess, in lurid technicolour, that is the moral focus of the episode, the surrounding moral perspective – what we might think of as the field of agency from which the judgement arises – is co-constituted between K and the goats. To draw again on Latour, we to have do here with what seems like a 'new distribution of the agents of geohistory',[21] a perspective within which K and the goats share not only a territory and an epoch, but also a principle (we might call it a footing) according to which moral agency is distributed. K's sense of transgression and his subsequent decision no longer to kill and eat goats arise from a vision of himself as a figure of violence, one that emerges not solely from his own introspection, but also from the point of view of the flock. Insofar as the goats do not need to cross over into the field of sentience for this collective perspective to occur, and stay in the background as timid creatures, they remain (in this instance) material or environmental actors. It seems, then, as if the texture of the social fabric within which K locates himself involves ecological factors in ways that may not sit comfortably with a modern perspective. K's social being extends beyond the institutional paradigms of the war through which he moves.

Another way of saying this is to suggest, borrowing the words of Amitav Ghosh, that the book and its protagonist seem attuned to the timescales of the epic in which, in many cultures across the world, 'there is a completely matter-of-fact acceptance of the agency of non-human beings of many kinds'.[22] But even if we are willing to read K as the inhabitant of a *longue durée* or geohistorical milieu that permeates and surpasses the temporality of the war, it is by no means clear what the politics of such a situation would entail. Dipesh Chakrabarty articulates some of the difficulty that arises when we try to imagine the social implications of co-inhabiting two incommensurable systems of time, the planetary and the human. What does it mean to 'pursue justice', he asks, when 'what seems "slow" in human and world-historical terms may indeed be "instantaneous" on the scale of Earth history'?[23] To approach these questions, we might look at another significant moment in the transformation of K's eating habits, one that focuses the matter precisely as an issue of food. After escaping from the labour camp, K returns to the farm and discovers 'a last handful of pumpkin and melon seed' in the shed beside the house (101). He plants them in an acre beside the dam and, as he tends them patiently through a season of risks, a profound dietary change comes over him. His need for food grows 'slighter and slighter'; when he does eat, the food 'has no taste, or taste[s] like dust': 'When food comes out of this earth, he told himself, I will recover my appetite, for it will have savour' (101). When the food finally does come out of the earth, the savour is returned in force. For readers who have grown progressively alarmed at K's asceticism, the moment arrives like a sumptuous feast in a land of famine. K cuts the first pumpkin into strips and roasts them over a bed of coals:

Beneath the crisply charred skin the flesh was soft and juicy. He chewed with tears of joy in his eyes. The best, he thought, the very best pumpkin I have ever tasted. For the first time since he had arrived in the country he found pleasure in eating … His teeth bit through the crust into the soft hot pulp. Such pumpkin, he thought, such pumpkin I could eat every day of my life and never want anything else.

(114)

The sensual enjoyment K experiences here, the vivid memories of 'salt, butter, sugar, cinnamon' that the taste of the pumpkin evokes (114), contradicts any notion we may retain of the protagonist as a spectral or abstracted principal of critique. In its visceral intensity, the experience unsettles the medical officer's later comment that K subsists in captivity on 'the bread of freedom', a kind of metaphysical food (146). It is surely no accident that shortly after this transformational awakening to the material pleasures of eating – a pleasure that seems primed, in its vegetable fixation, to turn the tables on the colonial heritage of meat-eating as a freedom ritual, such as Coetzee describes it in 'Meat Country' – K experiences a profoundly physical sensation of himself as occupying an alternative timescale. It is a sensation for which his previous work as a municipal gardener has in some small measure already prepared him. Lying in his burrow, he learns to love idleness, not merely as 'stretches of freedom reclaimed by stealth … from involuntary labour', but as a 'yielding up of himself to time': 'a time flowing slowly like oil from horizon to horizon over the face of the world, washing over his body, circulating in his armpits and his groin, stirring his eyelids' (115).

The pleasure K has in eating the pumpkin and melon that he has coaxed from the land extends here into a sense of corporeal locatedness within a temporal framework that exists 'beyond the reach of the calendar' (116). The slow, fossilized time of the burrow, 'flowing slowly like oil from horizon to horizon' (115), gestures towards planetary limits, rather than to the 'world-historical terms' of the war.[24] And yet, mindful of the view that K's seemingly ahistorical inscription into a kind of geological time may render him politically irrelevant, we should note that the book signals a strong awareness that K's removal from the social register of more conventionally time-bound human experience is not sustainable. Indeed, it dramatizes more than once K's failure to survive outside 'the cauldron of history' (151), for example when he tries to live in the rarified time of the mountain cave, facing 'the single huge block of the day', and ends up realizing that 'he might die' (69). In the burrow, subsisting on pumpkin, he falls victim to the consequences of malnutrition. He is visited, as Anthony Vital observes, by the material fact of 'organic life being inescapably time-bound'.[25] There is a 'continual taste of blood in his mouth' and his bowels run (117). He suffers from hallucinatory episodes and headaches (119). He eventually collapses into a feverish state (120).

But K's passage into an alternative time-scape is not reversed. The one thing he keeps with him, through his internment at the Kenilworth rehabilitation camp and back to Sea Point, is a packet of 'dried pumpkin seeds' from the farm (135). Seeds are here a fitting metonym for a sense of temporal situatedness that is at once immediately material (in its association with food, nourishment and the body), and that reaches back into the mists of early agrarian society, predating the war and its politics by millennia. Indeed, the pumpkin, carrying the 'imprint of colonial history' in being 'part of the bounty' Europe extracted from its conquests in the Americas, is precisely also a material trace, amidst the ravages of modernity, of older, pre-colonial forms of cultivation.[26] K's careful trafficking of seed back to the city suggests a form of eating that predates the time of the modern state and the mechanisms of control it has inherited from colonial history. That such a form of eating is a politically urgent activity in our times is articulated by Donna Andrews and Desiree Lewis, who describe how an increasingly monolithic corporate food industry leverages concern over food security to solidify its control over global food systems. Plotting in particular the entrenchment of corporate control, via a series of mega-mergers, over seed in South Africa, they point to the dangers of concentrating the power to produce food in the hands of corporations 'that own the information, knowledge and everything necessary for the development and sale of food'; against this encroaching mechanism of control, they describe 'the act of caring for seed' that happens in peripheral spaces outside the formal economy as 'integral to defending and sustaining cultural and bio-diversity'.[27]

Could it be then that although K's perilous induction into a material sense of time, one scaled according to the earth and its slow processes, does not equip him for survival in the midst of a late-colonial civil war, it has given him a prescient sense of the political urgency of finding ways to eat – and survive – both within and beyond the totalizing system of the camps? When K is reluctant to join the guerrillas in the war against the state, telling himself that 'there must be men to stay behind and keep gardening alive' (109), it might be less of a pacifist or isolationist act than we have been inclined to acknowledge. Perhaps he is not only turning his back on the war; perhaps he is also unwittingly taking a tentative step in the direction of a struggle that is to come. Perhaps his vocation as a gardener will make him more of a guerrilla than he had ever imagined becoming.

ACKNOWLEDGEMENTS

This chapter was written as part of the Andrew W. Mellon-funded project on 'Rethinking South African Literature(s)' in the Centre for Multilingualism and Diversities Research at the University of the Western Cape. I am grateful to the Mellon Foundation for its financial support of the broader project of which this is a part. The opinions expressed here are my own and are not necessarily attributable to the Mellon Foundation.

NOTES

1. Coetzee, *Life & Times of Michael K*, 3. Further references are cited parenthetically in text.
2. Coetzee, 'Meat Country', 43.
3. Ibid.
4. Esquibel and Calvo, 'Decolonize Your Diet: A Manifesto', 1, 2.
5. The only time the book alludes directly to K's race is when he is referenced as 'CM' – or 'coloured male', in apartheid bureaucracy's racialized categories of person. The charge sheet on which this designation appears, however, manages to get both his name ('Michael Visagie') and his age ('40') wrong (70).
6. Z. N., 'Much Ado about Nobody', 103.
7. Attwell, *J. M. Coetzee*, 100.
8. Gordimer, 'The Idea of Gardening'.
9. Attridge, *J. M. Coetzee*, 53.
10. Lazarus, *The Postcolonial Unconscious*, 3, 16, 11 (quoting Bhabha).
11. An afterlife of this idea can be found in Nthikeng Mohlehle's, *Michael K* (2018). Mohlehle's detects in the 'languid gaze' of his borrowed character 'a hint of mind-bending ideas that resisted forcefulness, ideas that presented only shadows of other ideas, which dissolved into each other as soon as they took shape, leaving a trail of suspicious weightlessness' (17).
12. Head, *J. M. Coetzee*, 110.
13. Wright, 'Black Earth, White Myth', 437, 438 (emphasis added).
14. Gordimer, 'The Idea of Gardening'.
15. See, for example, DeLoughrey's *Allegories of the Anthropocene*, which argues that 'catastrophic ruptures to social and ecological systems have already been experienced through the violent processes of empire' (7).
16. Latour, *Down to Earth,* 16, 19.
17. Monticelli, 'From Dissensus to Inoperativity', 630.
18. Wright, 'Minor Literature', 112.
19. Lazarus, *The Postcolonial Unconscious*, 17.
20. Iheka, *Naturalizing Africa*, 154.
21. Latour, *Facing Gaia* 143.
22. Ghosh, *The Great Derangement,* chap. 14, para. 4.
23. Chakrabarty, 'Anthropocene Time', 30.
24. Ibid.
25. Vital, 'Towards an African Ecocriticism', 98.

26. Ibid., 94.
27. Andrews and Lewis, 'Decolonising Food Systems', 5, 7.

WORKS CITED

Andrews, Donna and Desiree Lewis. 'Decolonising Food Systems and Sowing Seeds of Resistance', *The African Centre for Biodiversity*, July 2017: 1–11. https://www.acbio.org.za/sites/default/files/2017/07/Decolonising-Food-Systems-and-Sowing-Seeds-of-Resistance.pdf.
Attridge, Derek. *J. M. Coetzee & the Ethics of Reading: Literature in the Event*. Scottsville: University of Kwazulu-Natal Press, 2005.
Attwell, David. *J. M. Coetzee: South African and the Politics of Writing*. Berkeley: University of California Press, 1993.
Calvo, Luz and Catriona Rueda Esquibel. 'Decolonize Your Diet: A Manifesto'. *Nineteen Sixty Nine* 2, no. 1 (2013): 1–5.
Chakrabarty, Dipesh. 'The Seventh History and Theory Lecture: Anthropocene Time'. *History and Theory* 57, no. 1 (2018): 5–32.
Coetzee, J. M. *Life & Times of Michael K*. 1983. London: Vintage, 1998.
Coetzee, J. M. 'Meat Country'. *Granta*, 5 December 1995: 41–52.
DeLoughrey, Elizabeth. *Allegories of the Anthropocene*. Durham: Duke University Press, 2019.
Ghosh, Amitav. *The Great Derangement: Climate Change and the Unthinkable*. Gurgaon: Penguin Books, 2016.
Gordimer, Nadine. 'The Idea of Gardening'. *New York Review of Books*, 2 February 1984. https://www.nybooks.com/articles/1984/02/02/the-idea-of-gardening/.
Head, Dominic. *J. M. Coetzee*. Cambridge: Cambridge University Press, 1997.
Iheka, Cajetan. *Naturalizing Africa: Ecological Violence, Agency, and Postcolonial Resistance in African Literature*. Cambridge: Cambridge University Press, 2018.
Latour, Bruno. *Facing Gaia: Eight Lectures on the New Climatic Regime*. Translated by Catherine Porter. Cambridge: Polity Press, 2017.
Latour, Bruno. *Down to Earth: Politics in the New Climatic Regime*. Translated by Catherine Porter. Cambridge: Polity Press, 2018.
Lazarus, Neil. *The Postcolonial Unconscious*. Cambridge: Cambridge University Press, 2011.
Mohlehle, Nthikeng. *Michael K: A Novel*. Johannesburg: Pan Macmillan, 2018.
Monticelli, Daniele. 'From Dissensus to Inoperativity: The Strange Case of J. M. Coetzee's Michael K'. *English Studies* 97, no. 6 (2016): 618–37.
Vital, Anthony. 'Towards an African Ecocriticism: Postcolonialism, Ecology and *Life & Times of Michael K*'. *Research in African Literatures* 39, no. 1 (2008): 87–106.
Wright, Derek. 'Black Earth, White Myth'. *MFS: Modern Fiction Studies* 38, no. 2 (1992): 435–44.
Wright, Laura. 'Minor Literature and the "Skeleton of Sense": Anorexia, Franz Kafka's "A Hunger Artist," and J.M. Coetzee's *Life & Times of Michael K*'. *Journal of Commonwealth and Postcolonial Studies* 8, no. 1–2 (2001): 109–23.
Z. N. 'Much Ado About Nobody'. *The African Communist*, no. 97 (1984): 101–3.

PART THREE

Late and post-apartheid Coetzee

CHAPTER TEN

Foe

PATRICK FLANERY

If *Foe* (1986), Coetzee's fifth novel, is not always read as operating in the same allegorical mode as *Waiting for the Barbarians* (1980) or *Life & Times of Michael K* (1983), it is perhaps because its relationship to Daniel Defoe's *Robinson Crusoe* (1719) acts as a distraction, drawing readers' attention from its allegorical energies towards canonical and metafictional ones. This is not to suggest interpretation is a zero-sum game: readings of *Foe* that foreground (as Derek Attridge does brilliantly) the games of canonicity it stages tell us much about how the text functions stylistically, formally and in relation to canon formation – whether defined broadly or as entirely particular to individual readers. But returning to the book at this stage in Coetzee's career, after the manifestly metafictional *Slow Man* (2005) and as the subtly metafictional *The Pole* (2022) arrives as distilled exemplar of late style, it is difficult not to see *Foe* as seriously engaged in early experiments with properties of fictional composition, arrangement and performance.[1] For *Foe*, no less than *Slow Man* (perhaps more than *The Pole*), is a novel in which characters are both creations and playthings of a fictional author figure behind whom stands 'the real' Coetzee, plucking the primary and secondary strings of illusion.

In *Slow Man*, that figure is Elizabeth Costello, in *The Pole* an implied but remote author figure (who may or may not be J. M. Coetzee). In *Foe*, that figure is, at one degree, Daniel Foe, and at another, Coetzee himself. Readers with passing knowledge of the story of Robinson Crusoe's shipwreck, long stay on a tropical island and unequal power relationship with a Carib man he names Friday, will encounter in Coetzee's novel spectral equivalents of these narrative elements. We find ourselves in a territory of fiction at once familiar and unfamiliar. The immediate and most remarkable difference is that Coetzee's Robinsonade is almost entirely narrated not by Crusoe but by Susan Barton, who arrives from Defoe's final novel, *Roxana: The Fortunate Mistress* (1724). Flung upon the shores of the barren island home of 'Cruso' and Friday, whose tongue has been cut out – by slave traders, perhaps, as Cruso claims, 'to prevent him … telling his story'[2] – Barton has herself been literally cast away after journeying to Bahia in pursuit of her kidnapped daughter. Abandoning her search, boarding a ship for Lisbon and finding herself amongst mutineers, she is set adrift, with the captain's corpse, in a rowboat.

Other differences quickly proliferate: Cruso and Friday maintain terraces but grow nothing; Cruso (unlike Crusoe) has made no tools, salvaged no supplies from his wreck, kept no journal, done nothing to record time's passage. He shows little of the original Crusoe's work ethic, nor active will to escape an island populated by menacing 'apes' rather than useful goats. On the homeward voyage to Britain, Cruso dies, and on arrival in London, Susan seeks out Daniel Foe (the real author's birthname before adopting the pseudonym) to write her story as she and Friday live what feels like an impossibly itinerant existence, marking time on the fictitious Clock Lane until taking up residence in Foe's house when he absconds from creditors. This core relationship in some ways anticipates that of Mrs. Curren and Vercueil in *Age of Iron*; another forward echo is locatable in Susan's rhetorical question 'To whom am I writing?' (64), which anticipates Mrs. Curren's own question, 'To whom this writing then?'.[3] Susan Barton and Foe tussle over Susan's story, which Foe appropriates and embellishes.

From the beginning, Susan's narration is set in quotation marks, as if to suggest that she is overtly marked as a textual creature from the start, a *pre-made* but refashioned character as function of narrative form. The first two sections are addressed to Foe, and their foregrounded textuality provides a key to understanding Coetzee's Defoe project more broadly. The address to Foe in Section I, which appears as a memoir of Susan's time on the island, is first by implication: she uses second-person address ('the Cruso I told you of' [9]); by the end of the section this address is explicit: 'Do you think of me, Mr Foe ... as a bold adventuress?' (45). Section II appears as letters from Susan to Foe. The framing quotation marks are not present in Section III, which is narrated by Susan but not addressed to Foe. In the final Section, Susan's voice is replaced by an unnamed narrator. The extravagance of the game at play in *Foe* is confirmed in the Nobel Lecture, 'He and His Man', which suggests a complex relationship of origin and influence between Coetzee's Crusoe (as it is spelled in this later text) and Defoe.[4] In *Foe*, I want to suggest (as others have before) a less-mediated voice arrives in the novel's concluding section to help us see the stakes of the game, confirming its status as among Coetzee's most sophisticated metafictional works.

The novel's enigmatic final section offers us two endings. A voice (and a subjectivity we gradually realize is no longer Susan's) narrates its arrival at what we take to be the rooms where we last saw Susan and Foe. Here the narrator encounters a dead woman on the stairs and a couple lying in a bedroom, eyes shut, with receding lips and 'skin, dry as paper, ... stretched tight over their bones' (153). These bodies are not, however, decaying, 'but ... quietly composed', effectively embodied ghosts, while Friday himself lies, 'feet ... hard as wood', 'skin ... warm', with a 'faint' 'pulse in his throat' (153). The narrator lies next to Friday, trying to press open his mouth as if to make him speak. Friday 'stirs and sighs and turns', making a sound 'faint and dry, like leaves falling over leaves' before another sound comes from Friday's mouth like a 'faraway roar ... the roar of waves in a seashell; ... the cry of a bird ... sounds of the island'. Although the narrator detects a pulse, we are told the sounds coming from Friday arrive 'without a breath' (154).

After a section break, the exploration of the rooms is restaged: the narrator enters the building on Stoke Newington Church Street with its blue plaque from English Heritage commemorating Defoe.[5] He again passes the female body on the stairs, '[t]he couple in the bed', and Friday, this time with '[a]bout his neck ... a scar like a necklace' (155). A box contains Susan's manuscript, with the novel's first lines now clearly addressed to their recipient: 'Dear Mr Foe, At last I could row no further'. With that, the narrator 'slip[s] overboard ... drawn south toward the realm of the whales and eternal ice' in the waters off the shore of Cruso's island. Instead of swimming ashore, the narrator pushes down through a seaweed forest, 'petals floating around me' (these, we know, were cast by Friday during his time on the island), to a shipwreck on a filthy seabed 'like the mud of Flanders' (156). With the commemorative blue plaque, this detail suggests the final section is set not in the eighteenth century, but in the twentieth, from which we see 'the water ... still and dead' filling the ship's cabin, 'the same water as ... three hundred years ago' (156–7). Here the narrator finds the bloated corpses of Barton, the captain and, 'half buried in sand, his knees drawn up, his hands between his thighs ... Friday'. The narrator 'tug[s]' Friday's hair and inspects 'the chain about his throat' (157) – implicitly the chain that produced the 'scar like a necklace, left by a rope or chain' (155) that the narrator noticed on the physical iteration of Friday in Stoke Newington and 'had not observed ... before' (155), implicitly in the first exploration of the rooms in Part IV. The narrator tries to ask Friday 'what is this ship?', but the sound does not coalesce because this is a place 'where bodies are their own signs. It is the home of Friday' (157). Friday 'turns till he lies' facing the narrator and appears, like the corpses in London, with 'skin ... tight across bones, his lips ... drawn back' (157). Again, what emerges from his prised-back lips is a *breathless* stream that flows 'without interruption', 'northward and southward to the ends of the earth'. This is not the stream of life; it is '[s]oft and cold, dark and unending' (157). The voice of this final four-and-a-half-page section is a startling departure from Susan Barton's narration. I read this plunge to the depths as Coetzee-the-author projecting his imagination beyond the limits of realism to show us the stakes of representation and literary form with which he has been grappling throughout the novel.[6]

Foe is one of Coetzee's most cogent political allegories for Apartheid. Cruso's island offers a topographical scale model for Cape Town, with a diminutive Table Mountain in the form of 'a great rocky hill with a flat top, rising sharply from the sea on all sides except one' (7),[7] populated by grey, catlike apes 'with black faces and black paws' (21) that recall Vervet monkeys. Against these, Cruso arms Susan with a knife, warning her against venturing out alone.[8] Cruso's refusal to see any reason to change his life with his Black servant might be read as oblique commentary on a category of Apartheid-era white South Africans' building of structures that produce no life, living in a state of stasis and seeing no reason to change.[9] Susan pointedly concludes about Cruso: 'Growing old on his island kingdom with no one to say him nay had so narrowed his horizon – when the horizon all around us was so vast and so majestic! – that he had come to be persuaded he knew all there was to know about the world' (13). His 'heart was set on remaining to his dying day king of his tiny realm', such that he was paralyzed by 'indifference to salvation, and habit, and the stubbornness of old age' (13–14).

We might intuit a comparison with the white South African landowner in the years of the country's most acute emergency, surrounded by sublime landscapes and by Black employees whose voices he refuses to hear, believing he is lord of his little fiefdom. In March 1986, Coetzee profiled a range of Afrikaners in a fascinating article in the *New York Times*, its pull quote declaring that '[m]any Afrikaners, more moderate than their stereotype, still don't understand they live on the lip of a volcano'.[10] One year later, Coetzee would accept the Jerusalem Prize with a speech casting this 'failure of love' expressly in the language of servitude: 'a society of masters and serfs' could only transform through 'destruction of the unnatural structures of power' that had resulted in 'a deformed and stunted inner life'.[11] It is precisely these dynamics we see examined in *Foe*.

The final paragraphs of the address, however, also offer a way of interpreting *Foe*'s ending. Coetzee turns to Cervantes, 'the first of all novelists', wishing he too could 'quit a world of pathological attachments and abstract forces, of anger and violence, and take up residence in a world where a living play of feelings and ideas is possible'. Instead, Coetzee finds himself in 'a world of violent phantasms': the 'South African writer', he argues, could not at that moment make a similar departure as enacted in *Don Quixote* because 'the world his body lives in [...] impose[s] itself on him and ultimately on his imagination'.[12] The body, under this logic, has the ultimate claim, and in the case of *Foe* the claim pertains both to its author and to his characters. In an interview with David Attwell in *Doubling the Point*, Coetzee addresses *Foe*'s concluding section.[13]

'[H]ow', he asks, 'does a novel that is as much an interrogation of authority as *Foe* is find an end for itself?'[14] He also raises the entwined issues of 'power' and 'representation' in relation to Susan and Friday, wondering whether 'the endlessly skeptical processes of textualization' so disempower representation 'that those represented in/by the text – the feminine subject, the colonial subject – are to have no power either?'[15]

Susan at least has her book, which 'is not Foe's, it is hers, even in the form of the trace of her hunt for a Foe to tell it for her', Coetzee continues. But what of Friday, 'the true test' in Coetzee's formulation – '[i]s his history of mute subjection to remain drowned?', he asks, and continues: 'I return to the theme of power. The last pages of *Foe* have a certain power. They close the text by force ...: they confront head-on the endlessness of its skepticism.'[16] What follows is as fascinating a statement about his oeuvre as Coetzee has offered:

> Friday is mute, but Friday does not disappear, because Friday is body. If I look back over my own fiction, I see a simple (simple-minded?) standard erected. That standard is the body. Whatever else, the body is not 'that which is not,' and the proof that it *is* is the pain that it feels. The body with its pain becomes a counter to the endless trials of doubt. [....]
>
> Not grace, then, but at least the body. Let me put it baldly: in South Africa it is not possible to deny the authority of suffering and therefore of the body. It is not possible, not for logical reasons, not for ethical reasons [...], but for political reasons, for reasons of power. And let me again be unambiguous: it is not that one *grants* the authority of the suffering body: the suffering body *takes* this authority: that is its power. To use other words: its power is undeniable.[17]

The key here is one of verb *and* tense: is Friday's 'history ... *to remain drowned*?' *Already* drowned, and breathless at the end of the book – but *when*, we wonder, did this drowning occur? Do we imagine a trajectory, beyond his acquaintance with Susan, that saw him returned to slavery and subsequently drowned? Plausible, perhaps, but I want to offer an alternative that builds from how I read Friday's body in the novel's final section. 'Friday is body', Coetzee writes, but a body exists as both living and dead; Coetzee's emphasis is on the *suffering* body, tortured and maimed, its mouth in a speechless death grimace. What happens if we think of Friday as a body whose suffering is unignorable, but who remains beyond comprehension?

Why is Friday able to walk the cold lanes of England barefoot without any apparent discomfort (106), or to '[crush] under his soles whole clusters of the thorns that had pierced [Susan's] skin' (7), leaving her almost instantly unable to walk? Why are such details significant for Friday's characterization-as-body, notable as one of many specific differences between Coetzee's Friday and Defoe's Friday, who is 'frighted' by the Pyrenees' cold and snow?[18] In *Foe*, is Friday's physical, bodily resilience a valorizing (if essentializing) marker of great stamina, or of the hardening that occurred after years trapped on Cruso's rocky island? Hardly. To read Friday as a living body is, I contend, to ignore the novel's multiple references to spectrality,[19] and more specifically to Defoe's 1706 story 'A true relation of the apparition of one Mrs. Veal: the next day after her death: to one Mrs. Bargrave at Canterbury. The 8th of September, 1705'. In Defoe's supernatural fantasy, which Susan reports she has read to Friday (58–9), Mrs. Veal is a spectral apparition who appears, *in physical substance*, which is to say bodily, to her friend Mrs. Bargrave. In *Foe*, Susan refers twice to Mrs. Veal and Mrs. Bar*field* (134); there is no such thing as accident in the work of Coetzee. In place of an endpoint, a resting place with a sense of finality as Bar*grave* might be heard to suggest,

Coetzee offers us in Bar*field* a space of play or fecundity, even of battle, for which it might be possible to say elements of the law (the *bar*) are germane.

If *Foe* operates in a sporting field or pumpkin patch of the law, where certain rules pertain that govern specific forms of play and development (as well as the game we encounter as readers), they are up to us to discern. In Defoe's story of Mrs. Veal, her friend Mrs. Bargrave is accused of 'Hatch[ing] an Invention' when she tells people of Mrs. Veal's visit; doubters 'think the Relation of this Appearance to be a Reflection', a kind of spiritual contemplation or remembrance, but Mrs. Bargrave insists she saw, heard and touched her friend's 'Scowred Silk' gown.[20] The unnamed narrator believes Mrs. Bargrave's account; she is a witness rather than a fabulator. Unlike Defoe, she is no author of a supernatural *fiction*, but someone who believes her experience to be fact – and Defoe's fiction presents it as such. In *Foe*, this allusion suggests how we might understand Susan's accounts, she who is subjected to what appear to be supernatural workings of a fictional universe, who avers that 'ghosts can converse with us, and embrace and kiss us too' (134). Like Mrs. Bargrave/Barfield, Susan is (in her own mind) a truth teller and not, like Foe, an embellisher who would ventriloquize for Friday, add cannibals to the narrative stew, eliminate the woman entirely.

Like Defoe's Mrs. Veal, Coetzee's Friday is, in this reading, always already dead at the bottom of the sea where we find him at the close of the book. This Friday – who appears to inhabit Cruso's island and travel with Susan to England – is an embodied *apparition* of the dead and tongueless man in a wreck beneath the Caribbean waves. From his first appearance on the novel's first page, Friday is framed as belonging to the order of the supernatural, even the sacred, 'with a dazzling halo about him' (5). Later, Susan promises Foe that she and Friday 'should be as quiet as ghosts' (59) if they were to visit him. Later still, Susan recounts that 'townsfolk pay [Friday and her] no more heed than if [they] were ghosts' (87). Section III opens a field of discourse in which Susan seeks to engage Foe in discussion about her and Friday's ontological (or, one might say, hauntological) status as 'substantial' bodies. Susan is certain that Friday is *not* 'a substantial body', that he is instead 'what [she] make[s] of him …. He is the child of his silence, a child unborn, a child waiting to be born that cannot be born' (121–2).[21]

Alongside these spectral dynamics, the energies of migrancy and of an investment in dissident Protestantism are everywhere at play. Defoe's Mrs. Veal is fixated on French protestant Charles Drelincourt. We know from Defoe's text that Cruso's family name is originally Kreutznaer. In *Foe*, Susan recounts telling Cruso that her father was from the French minority in Flanders and 'fled to England', the surname Berton becoming Barton (10). Each of the four main characters in *Foe* is marked by migration, whether forced or voluntary; these marks are mapped onto the (spectral) body and/or the name by which these ghosts are known to one another.

Such a reading as I propose ignores another level of illusion: it would not be an exaggeration to say that what I read as the embodied *apparitions* of Friday, Susan and the younger woman who appears with the same name but who purports to be her daughter, as well as Cruso and Foe himself, are nothing more than fictional constructs *even within the world of the novel*.[22] One might conclude that Friday, like the younger Susan Barton, is 'father-born', the creation of a male author, although not in fact the creation of Foe but instead the author who stands behind them all, whose presence perhaps only Foe, as fabulator himself, begins fully to intuit. Susan believes she is a substantial body, initially certain she does not 'owe proof' of her status as 'a substantial being with a substantial history in the world' (131). She fails at first to recognize she is no more than a textual creation – not only as quiet as a ghost but an actual (textual) ghost arrived from an earlier text (Defoe's *Roxana*) to haunt the pages of Coetzee's novel (125–31).[23] She dismisses the younger Susan as 'a ghost, a substantial ghost, if such beings exist, who haunts me for reasons I cannot understand, and brings other ghosts in tow' (132). She criticizes Foe's '[lack] of skill in summoning ghosts' even as she starts to doubt her own existence:

> all my life grows to be story and there is nothing of my own left of me. I thought I was myself and this girl a creature from another order speaking words [Foe] made up for her. But now I am full of doubt. Nothing is left to me but doubt. I am doubt itself. Who is speaking me? Am I a phantom too? To what order do I belong?
>
> (133)

Foe refuses to be drawn, declaring that 'as to who among us is a ghost and who not I have nothing to say' (135). He disavows having called up Susan's daughter and maidservant Amy, but nonetheless acts in a way that shows the novel's hand, speculating that 'our worst fear' is that 'we have all of us been called into the world from a different order (which we have now forgotten) by a conjurer unknown to us, as you say I have conjured up your daughter and her companion (I have not)'; '[d]o we' – he continues – 'become puppets in a story whose end is invisible to us, and towards which we are marched like condemned felons?' (135).[24] The meditations on Susan's status continue, via what reads as a barely submerged reference by Foe to Dante's *Inferno*.[25] This purports to be a quotation in which a 'weeping' soul says to the poet: 'Do not suppose, mortal ... that because I am not substantial these tears you behold are not the tears of a true grief' (138). Susan, despairing, concludes the younger Susan and Amy are just 'ghosts haunting a ghost' (138–9). Susan has, at last, begun to realize her own artifice, the artifice of her fellows, even perhaps the artifice of all she has known of the world – that she is a ghost haunted by ghosts in a ghostly world.

The apparently *real* world of *Foe* is thus the playground of illusion, where the forms of fiction are marshalled to move in such a way that they seduce the reader into thinking they are reading a book variously invested in thinking (in a mode of realism) about literary canons, colonialism and racism, and the gendered power dynamics of creative authority. The book *does* engage with all of these, but in ways that entangle them with and even subordinate them to a concern with exploring the *limits* and *artifice* of realism, and the possibilities of a fiction that treats realism as a veil, a scrim of projections behind which the *real* action – of art's creation, the free-play of fiction in the field of its particular laws – occurs. Such manoeuvres are also in evidence in 'He and His Man', in which *he*, Crusoe, might or might not be writing 'his man', Defoe, into existence, or, alternatively, be mistaking the presence of Defoe in his, Crusoe's, own fictional consciousness as a figure of creation when *he*, Crusoe, is instead unconsciously 'conscious' of the existence of his *own* creator.

It is worth noting a few seemingly minor points: in Defoe's *Crusoe*, Friday does, in a textual sense, vanish. One minute he is baiting a bear and fighting off wolves, the next he is gone and forgotten as if his physical substance were not a thing of real substance. When Crusoe first sees a footprint in the sand, he looks at it 'like one Thunder-struck, or as if [he] had seen an Apparition' (130), and shortly thereafter considers that 'if ... this was only the Print of [his] own Foot, [he] had play'd the Part of those Fools, who try to make stories of Spectres, and Apparitions; and then are frighted at them more than any body'.[26] Crusoe later describes himself as 'a *Spectre-like* Figure'.[27] Again, in the first-person preface to Defoe's 1720 sequel, *Serious Reflections During the Life and Surprising Adventures of Robinson Crusoe*, the narrating Crusoe tells the reader: 'When I *was in my Island Kingdom, I had abundance of strange Notions of my seeing Apparitions*'.[28] And in *Roxana*, we find Susan Barton's progenitor 'dream[ing] continually of the most frightful and terrible things imaginable: Nothing but Apparitions of Devils and Monsters ... form'd meerly in the Imagination'.[29] In other words, the spectral apparition as genre of supernatural phenomenon already belongs in the world of Crusoe, and certainly in the world of Defoe, for whom fantasy was ripe with the potential for political allegory from the beginning of his novelistic career – as in *The Consolidator, or Memoirs of Sundry Transactions from the World in the Moon* (1705), legible in contemporary terms as a science-fiction satire.

The mobilization of apparitional, spectral energies in *Foe* serves a specific political purpose. Coetzee demonstrates the double-bind of representation across racial lines in a place and time of racialized inequality (which, we might say, is the always and everywhere spacetime of the human species to date). First, Coetzee escapes the bind of representing Friday's non-fluent English speech by rendering him mute.[30] He goes one step further in showing us the racism inherent in Susan's inability to know Friday, to think she cannot know him because she cannot hear his speech, can only observe what she takes to be his physical person (however insubstantial she judges him), which for her is nonetheless insufficient to tell her anything of his psychology.[31] The end point of that racist logic – either the speech of the Other must be represented in broken, un-syntactical, ungrammatical, comedic form (as in Defoe), or the absence of speech renders the Other fundamentally unknowable (as in Susan's view of Friday) – leads us to a position in which the Other can only be a racialized apparition whose real person is submerged and unreachable. That is the situation towards which the novel points us and the conundrum (for the white writer of conscience in the years of high Apartheid) it signals.

I see a trace of this species of argument in Gayatri Spivak's 1990 essay on *Foe*, in which she stages a comparable stand-off between the Eurocentric liberal humanist (Sartre stands in this subject position in her argument) who views the marginalized Other in racialized terms that insist on the ability to understand *across* differentials of power and race, and the 'view ... that only the marginal can speak for the margin'; this of course also risks, 'in its institutional consequences', leading to a 'legitimization of such an arrogance of conscience'.[32] Spivak sees Susan Barton as Coetzee's 'attempt[ing] to represent the bourgeois individualist woman in early capitalism as the *agent* of *other*-directed ethics' who is consequently 'involved in the construction of the marginal ... as object of knowledge'.[33]

The ideological importance of *Foe* was not lost on all reviewers at the time of first publication, nor was its potential as cogent political allegory for the civil-war stasis of Apartheid. Paul Grondahl, writing in the Albany, New York, *Times Union*, acclaimed *Foe* as 'a mesmerizing parable about apartheid' despite misreading Daniel Foe as a direct analogue for Coetzee – and rather too idealistically imagining the novel 'giv[es] voice to Friday' and, by extension, South Africa's oppressed majority.[34] Black novelist and lawyer Cyrus Colter, writing in the *Chicago Sun-Times*, saw *Foe* as 'an aberration ... an almost willful divergence from [Coetzee's] earlier stance into the vague, dry, austere (if often exquisite) allegorical format', which rather raises the question of how Colter might have (mis)read Coetzee's earlier books.[35] On the other end, English-born Australian novelist Elizabeth Jolley, writing in the *Sydney Morning Herald*, insisted the novel was 'not an allegory' since '[i]n an allegory each part of the text conveys one or more specific extra meanings' and '*Foe* must be read through the imagination and the emotions or left alone'.[36] Few reviewers came close to ascertaining what the final section of the novel might be attempting to do, but English novelist Jane Gardam, who had earlier published a novel titled *Crusoe's Daughter*, is an exception.[37] In her review for *The Sunday Times*, she concludes that, in Part IV of the novel, it is Coetzee himself who searches for Friday's body, 'seeking it in the waters off the island in the wreckage of a slave ship', and he who 'finds Friday with the chain still about his neck and from his dead mouth a stream is flowing that will reach the corners of the earth'.[38] One might cavil that it is less 'Coetzee himself' who goes diving than J. M. Coetzee – the author – who stands as always implied authorial consciousness and, unusually in Part IV, seems more immediately present than in any of his other books save, perhaps, *Diary of a Bad Year*, and the volumes that make up *Scenes from Provincial Life* (with the inevitable demurs about the fictionality of the Coetzeean self we encounter in those other books).

Why here and elsewhere the preoccupation with *Robinson Crusoe* and Defoe? Attwell suggests '[t]he appeal of Defoe and the Crusoe tradition seems always to have been linked in Coetzee's mind to questions of authorship – to the autobiographical investments that are hidden in realist stories, and to the possibility of an author's inventing a double life.'[39] He goes on to consider that the novel's conclusion 'dramatically illustrates the limits of representation', implicitly of Black subjectivity and Black oppression, 'that have been imposed on Coetzee by history', having 'discover[ed] that Friday's story is not his to tell'.[40] I don't disagree with Attwell's conclusion. In 1999, Coetzee provided an introduction for the Oxford World's Classics edition of *Robinson Crusoe* in which he again, as in the Jerusalem Prize speech, draws a connecting line between Defoe's projects and those of Cervantes. Both novelists present the fictional as factual, and although this is manifestly not what Coetzee himself is doing in *Foe*, it is possible to see the workings of a similar impulse in *Scenes from Provincial Life*. Crusoe, Coetzee says, 'pretended once to belong to history', but 'finds himself in the sphere of myth'.[41] Tellingly, he reads the preface to the second sequel to *Robinson Crusoe*, noting that '[t]he castaway returned in late life to the country of his birth seems ... to merge with the sixty-year-old Londoner, Daniel Defoe, from whose head he was born'.[42] Here Coetzee makes a claim as important for our understanding of Defoe, as for our understanding of *Foe*:

> Properly speaking, Defoe is a realist only in that he is an empiricist, and empiricism is one of the tenets of the realist novel. Defoe is in fact something simpler: an impersonator, a ventriloquist, even a forger .... The kind of 'novel' he is writing ... is a more or less literal imitation of the kind of recital his hero or heroine would have given had he or she really existed. It is fake autobiography heavily influenced by the genres of the deathbed confession and the spiritual autobiography.[43]

In the year before *Foe*'s publication, Coetzee delivered an inaugural lecture as Professor of General Literature at the University of Cape Town. This short text, 'Truth in Autobiography', was later revised and expanded for inclusion in *Doubling the Point* (1992),[44] but the original version's condensed consideration of Rousseau's *Confessions* illuminates Coetzee's thinking about literature and criticism as complexly related aspects of *discourse*. The lecture closes by framing a key question, 'one about *privilege*': 'What privilege do I claim to tell the truth of Rousseau that Rousseau cannot tell? What is the privilege of criticism by which it claims to tell the truth of literature?'[45] Privilege is interlocked with questions of authority, and in the case of *Foe* we might ask an analogous question: by what authority does Coetzee claim to tell Defoe's truth that Defoe cannot? If we consider *Foe* as engaged in a project of metapoesis as much as of metafiction, it bears reading alongside what Coetzee has written in a scholarly mode about Defoe's stylistics. In the 1980 essay 'The Agentless Sentence as Rhetorical Device', he teases out questions of authority in relation to *Robinson Crusoe*, asserting in an analysis of a particular passage that 'we cannot argue that because Crusoe's father uses short passives he is thinking of a universe without an author … The intentionality we attribute to Crusoe's father is one we *read into* him and *read out of* his language: it is an act of interpretation.'[46] '[T]he short passive', he argues, 'leaves an uneasy feeling: it opens up an area of vagueness that can simply be skated over' but that is also able to be 'exploited for their own ends by writers who take seriously the question of whether language is a good map of reality'.[47]

Foe is marked by the marshalling of passive constructions from the first paragraph of Susan's narration, which reaches a slowly dawning awareness that she may well be inhabiting a universe *with* an author. This gradual enlightenment and the refusal of an authoritative conclusion about Susan and the other characters' ontological status leave both Susan and the reader in a state of unease; the figure of authority is always receding out of view, until, for Susan, it is too late and she is dead in the rooms Defoe once inhabited.[48] What is ultimately at issue here, I think, is what Coetzee, in 'Truth in Autobiography', terms 'the life of the discourse itself'.[49] 'All forms of discourse may have secrets,' he continues, 'of no great profundity, which they nevertheless cannot afford to unveil'.[50] When asked in an interview by American novelist Joanna Scott a decade after *Foe*'s publication 'Who is speaking at the end of the novel? … Is it the author? A narrator?', Coetzee's response hints at one of those critical secrets on which hinges the life of the discourse – in this case, of the novel itself. Whose is the voice in Part IV of *Foe*? 'Goodness knows,' Coetzee is reported to have said, 'I don't know'.[51]

NOTES

1. See Cornwell, 'He and His Man'.
2. Coetzee, *Foe*, 23. Subsequent references parenthetically in the text.
3. Coetzee, *Age of Iron*, 5.
4. Coetzee, 'He and His Man', 5.
5. The text of the actual blue plaque says not, as in the novel, '*Daniel Defoe, Author*', but 'Daniel Defoe (1661–1731) Lived [*sic*] in a house on this site'; it was placed on the existing building in 1932. The narrating voice says, 'light does not penetrate these walls'; the four windows on the side of the building bearing the plaque, facing what is now 'Defoe Road', are indeed all bricked up. See English Heritage, online.
6. Patrick Hayes argues that *Foe*'s final section 'abandon[s] the discursive realm of the human subject entirely'; he locates a significant intertext in Adrienne Rich's poem 'Diving to the Wreck', from the 1972 collection of the same title ('Influence and Intertextuality', 162).
7. A point also made by Samuelson, 'Scenes and Settings', 32, and Zimbler, 'Under Local Eyes'.
8. '[T]he apes … would not be as wary of a woman as they were of him and Friday' (15, 21). If one were to read these creatures operating in Cruso's racist imaginary as surrogate analogues for what under Apartheid was termed the *swart gevaar* ('black peril'), the racism on which such allegory depends is explicitly Cruso's own and implicitly critiqued by the novel.
9. I ask the reader to hear resonances with Agamben's illumination of stasis as, in the words of Andrew van der Vlies, who reads Agamben alongside post-independence South African fiction in *Present Imperfect*, 'a

condition of civil war' (165–7). Matters of race are not straightforward: Defoe's Friday is Amerindian, and though Coetzee's Friday is, Susan tells us, 'black: a Negro [sic]', she qualifies this by describing his skin as 'not black but a dark grey' (6). His diminutive stature ('slight' and 'shorter than' Susan) might suggest the autochthonous Khoikhoi peoples of the Western Cape.

10. See Coetzee, 'Tales of Afrikaners'.
11. Coetzee, 'Jerusalem Prize Acceptance Speech', 97, 96, 97, 98. Coetzee is clear, however, that no easy, liberal 'fraternity' was a solution: '[t]he [...] essentially sentimental yearning that expresses itself in the reform movement [...] is a yearning to have fraternity without paying for it' (ibid., 97). Paton is here in view, as in the fact that Susan's voyage to Bahia in search of her kidnapped daughter evokes the trope of the provincial subject who travels to Johannesburg and disappears into what was often framed (as in Paton's *Cry, the Beloved Country* [1948]) as an urban jungle (115–16). We have evidence that Coetzee was engaging with Paton's novel during the mid-1980s; see 'Jerusalem Prize', 97.
12. Coetzee, 'Jerusalem Prize', 98–9.
13. Attwell invites Coetzee to 'comment on the importance of the body' in his fiction (*Doubling the Point*, 247), the question following his own interpretation of Friday in *Foe* (Friday 'mark[s] the limit of self-knowledge in Susan's case' and 'overwhelm[s] the narrator at the novel's close'; Friday's 'power is largely that of silence' [247]).
14. Coetzee, *Doubling the Point*, 247–8.
15. Ibid., 248.
16. Ibid.
17. Ibid.
18. Defoe, *Robinson Crusoe*, 244.
19. María López reads *Foe* as 'ghost story' but does not go as far as I am suggesting one might.
20. Defoe, 'Mrs. Veal'.
21. Chris Prentice reads these references to ghosts as evidence of 'Susan's sense of suspension in a state of unreality' ('*Foe*', 102).
22. In Defoe's *Roxana*, Susan's daughter is called 'Susanna'.
23. If Susan's relationship with Friday anticipates Mrs. Curren's relationship with Vercueil, then Susan's relationship with Foe in very significant ways anticipates Paul Rayment's relationship with Elizabeth Costello in *Slow Man*. See Attwell's nod in this direction in his article 'Coetzee's Estrangements'.
24. The explanation for the characters' existence that Foe proposes anticipates the world of the Jesus novels, in which Simón and David arrive in Novilla having forgotten the life and world from which they originated. See Bewes in this volume.
25. See Durrant, 'Bearing Witness to Apartheid'.
26. Defoe, *Robinson Crusoe*, 134.
27. Ibid., 214; emphasis original.
28. Defoe, *Serious Reflections*, 267.
29. Defoe, *Roxana*, 264.
30. Chris Prentice argues that 'Friday's silence enables the novel to focus on the problems of power and authority represented initially by Cruso, [...] but more centrally by Susan and Foe' ('*Foe*', 101).
31. She also, of course, sees his spear and on that account, and his race, imagines him a cannibal (6).
32. Spivak, 'Theory in the Margin', 2.
33. Ibid., 9–10.
34. Grondahl, '"Foe": Coetzee Continues to Grow as Writer', C6.

35. Colter, '"Foe" Fails to Befriend the Reader', 39.
36. Jolley, 'When a Woman Came to Crusoe's Island', 43.
37. Gardam's was not the only recent literary Robinsonade (of sorts) published in the period leading up to *Foe*'s appearance in 1986. Michel Tournier's *Vendredi ou les Limbes du Pacifique* (1967) won the Grand Prix du roman de l'Académie française. For a discussion of Tournier and Coetzee's Robinsades, see Carchidi, 'At Sea on a Desert Island'.
38. Gardam, 'Books: The Only Story'.
39. Attwell, *J. M. Coetzee and the Life of Writing*, 150.
40. Ibid., 160.
41. Coetzee, 'Daniel Defoe, *Robinson Crusoe*', 17.
42. Ibid., 18.
43. Ibid., 19.
44. The phrase 'doubling the point' also occurs in *Robinson Crusoe*. Although the idea of doubling and doubling back is elaborated in the revised version of 'Truth in Autobiography' that appears in *Doubling the Point*, the nautical imagery of 'a ship's course … doubled or bent upon itself' by 'sail[ing] round to the other side (of a cape or point)' (OED) suggests the ways in which the discourse of Defoe has sometimes surprising points of purchase in Coetzee's work.
45. Coetzee, 'Truth in Autobiography', 5.
46. Coetzee, 'The Agentless Sentence', 173.
47. Ibid., 174.
48. On the characters' status 'as the discursive texts they have been all along', see Macaskill and Colleran, 'Reading History, Writing Heresy'.
49. Coetzee, 'Truth in Autobiography', 6.
50. Ibid.
51. Scott and Coetzee, 'Voice and Trajectory', 99.

WORKS CITED

Attwell, David. 'Coetzee's Estrangements'. *NOVEL: A Forum on Fiction* 41, no. 2/3 (2008): 229–43.
Attwell, David. *J. M. Coetzee and the Life of Writing: Face to Face with Time*. Oxford: Oxford University Press, 2015.
Carchidi, Victoria. 'At Sea on a Desert Island: Defoe, Tournier and Coetzee'. In *Literature and Quest*, edited by Christine Arkinstall, 75–88. Amsterdam: Rodopi, 1993.
Coetzee, J. M. *Age of Iron*. London: Secker and Warburg, 1990.
Coetzee, J. M. 'The Agentless Sentence as Rhetorical Device'. In *Doubling the Point: Essays and Interviews*, edited by David Attwell, 170–80. Cambridge: Harvard University Press, 1992.
Coetzee, J. M. 'Daniel Defoe, Robinson Crusoe'. In *Stranger Shores: Literary Essays 1986–1999*, 17–22. New York: Viking, 2001.
Coetzee, J. M. *Doubling the Point: Essays and Interviews*. Edited by David Attwell. Cambridge: Harvard University Press, 1992.
Coetzee, J. M. *Foe*. London: Secker and Warburg, 1986.
Coetzee, J. M. 'Jerusalem Prize Acceptance Speech (1987)'. In *Doubling the Point: Essays and Interviews*, edited by David Attwell, 96–9. Cambridge: Harvard University Press, 1992.
Coetzee, J. M. 'He and His Man'. In *Lecture and Speech of Acceptance upon the Award of the Nobel Prize in Literature, Delivered in Stockholm in December 2003*. New York: Penguin Books, 2003.
Coetzee, J. M. 'Tales of Afrikaners'. *New York Times* March 9 1986: 19.

Coetzee, J. M. 'Truth in Autobiography'. Inaugural Lecture, 3 October 1984. New Series no. 94. Cape Town: University of Cape Town, 1984.

Colter, Cyrus. '"Foe" Fails to Befriend the Reader'. *Chicago Sun-Times*, 25 February 1987: 39. NewsBank: Access World News, infoweb-newsbank-com.eu1.proxy.openathens.net/apps/news/document-view?p=AWNB&docref=news/0EB36D54A791D13C.

Cornwell, Gareth. '"He and His Man": Allegory and Catachresis in J. M. Coetzee's Nobel Lecture'. *English in Africa* 34, no. 1 (2007): 97–114.

Defoe, Daniel. *The Consolidator, or Memoirs of Sundry Transactions from the World in the Moon: Translated from the Lunar Language*. London: B. Bragg, 1705.

Defoe, Daniel. *Roxana, The Fortunate Mistress, or, A History of the Life and Vast Variety of Fortunes of Mademoiselle de Beleau, afterwards called the Countess de Wintelsheim in Germany Being the Person known by the Name of the Lady Roxana in the time of Charles II*. 1724. London: Oxford University Press, 1964.

Defoe, Daniel. 'Frontispiece and Preface to Serious Reflections during the Life and Surprising Adventures of Robinson Crusoe (1720)'. In *Robinson Crusoe*. 1719. Oxford: Oxford University Press, 2008.

Defoe, Daniel. *Robinson Crusoe*. 1719. Oxford: Oxford University Press, 2008.

Defoe, Daniel. *A True Relation of the Apparition of One Mrs. Veal: The Next Day after Her Death: To One Mrs. Bargrave at Canterbury. The 8th of September, 1705*. London: Printed for B Bragg, 1706. Early English Books Online Text Creation Partnership, 2011. https://quod.lib.umich.edu/e/ecco/004844744.0001.000.

'double, v.' *OED Online*, Oxford University Press, June 2022, www.oed.com/view/Entry/57006.

Durrant, Samuel. 'Bearing Witness to Apartheid: J. M. Coetzee's Inconsolable Works of Mourning'. *Contemporary Literature* 40, no. 3 (1999): 430–63. JSTOR, https://doi.org/10.2307/1208885.

English Heritage, 'Blue Plaques, Defoe, Daniel (1661–731)'. https://www.english-heritage.org.uk/visit/blue-plaques/daniel-defoe/.

Gardam, Jane. 'Books: The Only Story – Review of "Foe" by J M Coetzee'. *Sunday Times* (London), 7 September 1986. NewsBank: Access World News, infoweb-newsbank-com.eu1.proxy.openathens.net/apps/news/document-view?p=AWNB&docref=news/0F92581851C70B3F.

Grondahl, Paul. '"Foe": Coetzee Continues to Grow as Writer'. *Times Union* (Albany, NY), March 29 1987: C6.

Hayes, Patrick. 'Influence and Intertextuality'. In *The Cambridge Companion to J. M. Coetzee*, edited by Jarad Zimbler, 152–67. Cambridge: Cambridge University Press, 2020.

Jolley, Elizabeth. 'When a Woman Came to Crusoe's Island'. *Sydney Morning Herald*, 13 December 1986. late ed., Saturday Review: 43. NewsBank: Access World News, infoweb-newsbank-com.eu1.proxy.openathens.net/apps/news/document-view?p=AWNB&docref=news/11BCF85518ECA938.

López, María. '*Foe*: A Ghost Story'. *Journal of Commonwealth Literature* 45, no. 2 (2010): 295–310.

Macaskill, Brian and Jeanne Colleran. 'Reading History, Writing Heresy: The Resistance of Representation and the Representation of Resistance in J. M. Coetzee's *Foe*'. *Contemporary Literature* 33, no. 3 (1992): 432–57.

Prentice, Chris. '*Foe* (1986)'. In *A Companion to the Works of J. M. Coetzee*, edited by Tim Mehigan, 91–112. Rochester: Camden House, 2011.

Samuelson, Meg. 'Scenes and Settings'. In *The Cambridge Companion to J. M. Coetzee*, edited by Jarad Zimbler, 29–44. Cambridge: Cambridge University Press, 2020.

Scott, Joanna and J. M. Coetzee. 'Voice and Trajectory: An Interview with J. M. Coetzee'. *Salmagundi* 114/115 (1997): 82–102. *JSTOR*, http://www.jstor.org/stable/40548963.

Spivak, Gayatri Chakravorty. 'Theory in the Margin: Coetzee's *Foe* Reading Defoe's "Crusoe/Roxana"'. *English in Africa* 17, no. 2 (1990): 1–23.

Tournier, Michel. *Vendredi ou les Limbes du Pacifique*. Paris: Gallimard, 1967.

Van der Vlies, Andrew. *Present Imperfect: Contemporary South African Writing*. Oxford: Oxford University Press, 2017.

Zimbler, Jarad. 'Under Local Eyes: The South African Publishing Context of J. M. Coetzee's *Foe*'. *English Studies in Africa* 47, no. 1 (2004): 47–59.

CHAPTER ELEVEN

Age of Iron

KATHERINE HALLEMEIER

When *Age of Iron* was published in 1990, it appeared remarkable in J. M. Coetzee's oeuvre for being set in contemporary South Africa. The action of Coetzee's sixth novel occurs in August and September 1986, and the dates at the novel's end, 1986–9, denote its historical genesis.[1] The novel's detailed descriptions of apartheid marked Coetzee's first foray into a realist mode that was distinct from, say, the speculative qualities of *Life & Times of Michael K* (1983) or the metafiction of *Foe* (1986). Nadine Gordimer's review of the former suggested that Coetzee's earlier works favoured allegory over realism 'out of a kind of opposing desire to hold himself clear of events and their daily, grubby, tragic consequences'.[2] Viewed in this light, *Age of Iron* was satisfactorily embroiled in events. Derek Attridge argues that part three of the book, for example, exposes the reader to 'the horror of the violence rending the townships and settlements in the traumatic year 1986 with a directness that brings Coetzee closer to historical reportage than anywhere else in his fiction'.[3] Yet the first-person epistolary novel does not necessarily present itself as an authoritative account of late apartheid. Like Coetzee's other fiction of the period, *Age of Iron* can be understood as part of a broader literary trend in the 1980s, one in which white South African writing questioned the authority granted to it by a predominately white international readership.[4] Mrs. Curren's final letter is riven with an awareness that her ways of 'knowing and ordering the world', in Justin Neuman's formulation, 'appear as failures or distant echoes'.[5] As other critics have noted, *Age of Iron* tests Mrs. Curren's belief in individual expression and liberal values in a historical moment that demands collective, revolutionary action.[6] 'Mrs. Curren's struggle to speak conscientiously, in the absence of any authority to do so,' Timothy Bewes remarks, 'is the story of the novel'.[7]

THE AMERICAN GOTHIC IN *AGE OF IRON*

While critics have read Mrs. Curren primarily as a retired classics professor whose writing draws on a humanist tradition,[8] this essay is also interested in her as a watcher of television. The televisual, I argue, focalizes Mrs. Curren's preoccupation with seeing as knowing and suggests how Coetzee's novel interrogates this association. In scenes where the reader watches Mrs. Curren watching others, the novel unsettles its protagonist's recourse to a logic of unveiling that is alternatively metaphorized in terms of lies and truth, ignorance and knowledge, and sin and redemption. The prevalence of this logic of revelation leads me to an unexpected conclusion: that Coetzee's first realist novel is a gothic novel. More precisely, it is a meditation on how the self-centering metaphors of the gothic relentlessly delimit white perception, producing a reality that is stultified and stultifying. Reading *Age of Iron* alongside Toni Morrison's theorization of the early American gothic romance, I tease out the fiction's self-awareness of how whiteness produces fantasies of blackness and externalizes violence. By reading allusions to Nathaniel Hawthorne and Emily Dickinson alongside the novel's descriptions of a decaying house and labyrinthine streets, I argue that an undead, transnational whiteness emerges as the novel's dull, inanimate horror.

Mrs. Curren, whose narrative begins the day after she receives a cancer diagnosis, regularly watches television in her Cape Town home. Television, Sean Jacobs notes, came 'relatively late to South Africa' as leaders of the National Party derided its 'foreign ideas' that 'normalized integration propaganda'.[9] In the years following the launch of a national television service in 1976, 'South African television was effectively an arm of the state.'[10] As Mrs. Curren dryly puts it, 'the land that is presented to me is a land of smiling neighbors.'[11] Consuming the news during the final years of a white nationalist imperial state proves to be a miserable experience:

> The parade of politicians every evening: I have only to see the heavy, blank faces so familiar since childhood to feel gloom and nausea [...] They with their fathers and mothers, their aunts and uncles, their brothers and sisters: a locust horde, a plague of black locusts infesting the country, munching without cease, devouring lives. Why, in a spirit of horror and loathing, do I watch them? Why do I let them into the house?
>
> (28)

Mrs. Curren's answer to the question, in 1986, centres on death: 'We watch as birds watch snakes, fascinated by what is about to devour us' (29). Watching television is an encounter with the murderous state in which Mrs. Curren lives and, at the end of the novel, in which she paradoxically narrates her own death. 'The reign of the locust family is the truth of South Africa,' and that family is a 'thanatophany', a manifestation of death (29). (The racist imaginary that equates death with specifically 'black' locusts is addressed later in this essay.) Thus, Mrs. Curren watches television while 'standing', for 'who would choose to face a firing squad sitting down?' (10). As she takes a stand and watches the news with an eye to the deathly truth of apartheid, Mrs. Curren lays claim to knowledge that exceeds state messaging. When she claims that 'we watch as birds watch snakes,' the implied 'we' includes those subjected by the South African state who apprehend the reality of its violence. That reality, as Njabulo S. Ndebele argued in his 1984 address on 'The Rediscovery of the Ordinary' (published in 1986), is spectacular: 'the most outstanding feature of South African oppression is its brazen, exhibitionist openness'.[12] At the same time, Mrs. Curren's knowledge of the 'truth' of apartheid, of the real death that the state deals, is self-consciously limited by what she does not see. When the Black woman employed as a domestic worker in Mrs. Curren's home, whom Mrs. Curren calls Florence, reports that she cannot send her son, Bheki, home because 'the police come in and shoot' (53), Mrs. Curren acknowledges that 'whatever Florence knows about it, whatever you know ten thousand miles away, I do not know' (53). The 'you' here is Mrs. Curren's daughter, the letter's addressee, who has emigrated to the United States. It is also implicitly the international reader, who by the mid-1980s had access to anti-apartheid films and television programming that had become crucial to liberation movements' strategies to isolate the regime. The 'we' that knows the truth of apartheid thus cleaves in at least three ways. It is not only people subjected by the South African state who watch its operations with horror and loathing, but also an international audience that has access to details of historical events that the South African state censors. More starkly, what it means to live and die within the borders of the state that devours is absolutely racialized: Mrs. Curren's metaphorical firing squad – a televised spectacle of white nationalism – is not the police that threaten Bheki. Mrs. Curren knows that those in power issue 'decrees like hammer blows: death, death, death' (29). She knows the state kills, but she does not know exactly whom it kills, where it kills and how it kills. What exactly she knows, as she watches television, is thrown into question: 'I say to myself that I am watching not the lie but the space behind the lie where the truth ought to be. But what is true?' (30).

As the novel progresses, it questions the epistemological distinction that Mrs. Curren initially makes between herself and her daughter by emphasizing how seeing is not knowing precisely because it is profoundly racialized. Mrs. Curren's attribution of greater knowledge to her daughter implies that truth corresponds with access to media that state censors prohibit. This conception of truth, however, is challenged when Mrs. Curren bears witness to the state-sanctioned killing of five Black children. After Florence receives an emergency phone call about Bheki, Mrs. Curren agrees to drive her 'I think, to Site C' (88). In a ruined 'hall or school' (100), Mrs. Curren sees the body of Bheki, who has been shot to death, as have four Black children whose bodies lie beside his and whose names Mrs. Curren does not know. She recounts these events, imbued with some historical detail, but also with copious allusions to Virgil's *Aeneid*, to her daughter/reader 'so that you will learn how things are' (103). Having 'seen black people in their death' (124), the white narrator positions herself as a potential source of truth, and, what is more, of a truth that exceeds whatever journalistic reporting has crossed international news wires. Yet this positioning is almost immediately qualified as Mrs. Curren asserts: 'I am the one writing: I, I. So I ask you: attend to the writing not to me. If lies and pleas and excuses weave among the words, listen for them. Do not pass them over, do not forgive them easily. Read all, even this adjuration, with a cold eye' (104). Read, in other words, for the truth behind the lie, behind the self-justifying subjective 'I' that lays claim to authority by virtue of having seen. Mrs. Curren's account is like the television screen. Following Marshall McLuhan's description of TV, each is exemplary of a 'cool medium' that 'provides a meager amount of information' and requires 'high participation or completion by the audience.'[13]

Scholars have taken up Mrs. Curren's challenge. Rachel Ann Walsh develops and qualifies earlier Lévinasian readings of the work to read with a cold eye the discourses of shame, childhood, maternity and classical humanism on which so much of Mrs. Curren's narrative depends. It is through such supposedly universal discourses, Walsh demonstrates, that Mrs. Curren repeatedly pathologizes Black people, and especially Black child activists.[14] While the racialization of these discourses is implicit to Walsh's analysis, I am interested in how the novel explicitly links them to Mrs. Curren's whiteness. Her injunction to the reader to track her words for lies is prefaced with the repetition of 'I'. The repetition harkens to an earlier passage in which she explicitly associates the repetition of 'I' with the '"I!" "I!" "I!"' (80) of 'I, a white,' and of 'whites' (79). Mrs. Curren invites us to read for the truth behind the lies of her (white) self. Coetzee's novel in turn would expose not some deeper truth of life under apartheid, but how the whiteness of the white writer – and the white reader – delimits the perception of life 'in these times, in this place' (130). What might seem to be historical realism transmutes into something different: the narrative of a white writer who apprehends how whiteness determines their reality, whether as critical spectator or self-interested witness.

Mrs. Curren's haunted sense that whiteness occludes her apprehension of both the truth behind the lie propagated by state media and the lie behind the 'truth' of her own confessions produces what I describe as the novel's gothic energies. The mode of the gothic, as Coetzee noted in a 1976 essay, aims 'to name, possess, and exorcise its obsession' as it 'yearns toward Eden, a time before inherited guilt, before parents'.[15] This definition resonates with Toni Morrison's definitive analysis of the genre in *Playing in the Dark*, a collection of essays based on lectures delivered the same year Coetzee's novel was published. The 'image of blinding whiteness' that Morrison finds repeated through early US gothic romance indexes the fantasy that 'one could be released from a useless, binding, repulsive past into a kind of history-lessness, a blank page waiting to be inscribed',[16] wherein one's self-definition as free was antithetical to, rather than dependent or parasitical on, 'a life of regularized violence' immanent to plantation slavery and genocidal colonialism.[17] For this fantastic romance to take hold, Morrison observes, the obsession to be exorcised is 'a dark and abiding presence'.[18] Morrison famously concludes: 'Even, and especially, when American texts are not "about" Africanist presences or characters or narrative or idiom, the shadow hovers in implication, in sign, in line of demarcation.'[19] As Coetzee's novel plays with these gothic tropes, it inverts them so that the white desire for history-lessness, the yearning towards Eden and the obsession with guilt emerge as the fearful yet compelling forces subjected to repeated, failed exorcisms. Such are the desires and obsessions that shadow Mrs. Curren as she watches the white glare of televised propaganda and as she reflects on her own account of bearing witness to Bheki's death.

Age of Iron's allusion to an exemplar of the genre clarifies its redeployment of the gothic mode. Shortly after imagining her suicide, Mrs. Curren offers a reading of Hester Prynne: 'She wears the A for so many years that people forget what it stands for' (114).[20] Mrs. Curren concludes her reading of Hawthorne with a question that applies to both her imagined self-immolation and her narrative: 'These public shows, these manifestations – this is the point of the story – how can one ever be sure what they stand for?' (114). *The Scarlet Letter*, according to Coetzee, was a text Hawthorne expressly conceived of as 'an act of expiation, meant to acknowledge inherited guilt and to put a distance between himself and his Puritan forebears'.[21] Mrs. Curren similarly attempts to find in the renunciation of innocence an act of expiation: 'what I cannot get over any more is that *getting over*' (126). The proclamation, she imagines, may be crucial to her own salvation: 'For the sake of my own resurrection I cannot get over it this time' (126). A yearning for innocence is implicit to the white narrative that acknowledges its complicity with violence. Thus in Mrs. Curren's rendering of the story of Hester Prynne, questions of sin and redemption culminate in a kind of stupor, as 'people forget'; the performance of moral virtue or failing is one more act of white self-definition that externalizes the violence of the colonial state. As Coetzee examined in his essay on confession, professions of guilt and innocence can be interrogated endlessly for truth.[22] *Age of Iron* suggests how interrogations of specifically white innocence and guilt, far from approaching truth, replicate the puritanical thinking that structures gothic fantasies.

The 'gloomy castles and labyrinthine underground passages' in Coetzee's novel do not, consequently, contain secrets to be uncovered, but obvious truths that are only dimly understood.[23] Mrs. Curren lives in a version of a gloomy castle, a building whose 'gutters sag' and whose 'roof tiles are heavy with moss' (15). She knows a truth: that the 'very bricks' have been 'made by the hands of convicts' (15). Evidence of the regularized violence of the apartheid state and its exploitation of criminalized, racialized people surrounds her on all sides. Yet, she retains an eerie image of the house as standing outside history, 'a site without a human past' (15). The pattern of knowing and not knowing repeats after visiting the (to her) labyrinthine streets of the settlements. Imagining Bheki's burial, Mrs. Curren has 'a gathering feeling of walking upon black faces. They are dead but their spirit has not left them' (125). Yet, she feels herself to be walking in a 'dead sleep': 'a child was taken and a doll left in its place to be nursed and reared, and that doll is what I call I' (109). She feels uncanny to herself, as she both perceives a cancer she cannot see and knows a killing whiteness without knowing. Gordimer suggested that Coetzee's commitment to allegory was symptomatic of a 'state of shock', meaning an inability to otherwise 'deal with the horror he saw written on the sun'.[24] *Age of Iron* shows that a state of shock is structural to whiteness as it is maintained within terroristic nations. During decades that saw the beginnings of a critical whiteness studies that continues to rehearse narratives of white innocence and white guilt, Coetzee's novel renders such narratives (which it rehearses) as a form of stupidity; they register not fine moral sensibility, but dull insensibility.[25]

Stupidity is a state which Mrs. Curren prefers to ascribe to the politicians she watches on television. 'They have raised stupidity to a virtue,' she writes, charting the etymological connections from stupefy to stupor to stupid to stunned to '*astonished*, to be turned to stone' (29). Yet their stupidity is also her own. Mrs. Curren is zombie-like, as she describes the '*dread*' that comes with a sleep that is not truly sleep: 'I am awake in my room in my bed, all is well. A fly settles on my cheek. It cleans itself. It begins to explore. It walks across my eye, my open eye. I want to blink, I want to wave it away, but I cannot. Through an eye that is and is not mine, I stare at it' (27). The passage alludes to Dickinson's 'I heard a Fly buzz – when I died –,' in which the fly is the reminder of the earthly world that is 'interposed' 'between the light – and me –' so that the speaker's 'I' 'could not see to see'.[26] The gothic trope of yearning towards a transcendent 'light' is defined against a shadow that, following Morrison, demarcates an Africanist presence. In Coetzee's rewriting, the fly itself – the sign of the earthly world – is that which cannot be fully seen. It is 'upon me, it is here' (27), yet the white I/eye precludes its perception, because the white I/eye privileges spectacles of innocence and guilt.[27] The cornea is like a television screen, manifesting stupefied and stupefying fantasies circumscribed by a gothic obsession with the expiation of sin.[28] Mrs. Curren's unblinking stare marks both a longing and a failure to see better, which is to say her stare remains trapped in the 'logic of visualization' that Katherine McKittrick identifies as central to the materialization of white patriarchal space.[29] This is also the logic of the gothic, which perpetually unveils that which it has kept hidden.

In his 1987 Jerusalem Prize Acceptance Speech, Coetzee asked: 'how do we get from our world of violent phantasms to a true living world?'[30] To Mrs. Curren, the obvious truth is that apartheid must end and that Mrs. Curren must '*do* something' to bring about its end (145). Here are some of the things Mrs. Curren does: she staunches the head wound of a Black child, John, after police push him off his bike; she tries to lodge a complaint against those police; she protests so vehemently when police arrive at the house looking for John that she is carried off bodily; after the police murder John, she tries to climb into the ambulance carrying his body; she tells the police that she lent John the pistol the police say he carried; she tries to warn John's community of the investigation. State agents are not only untroubled by her actions, but repeatedly try to ensure her well-being and supposed safety. A 'young woman in uniform' offers her tea, bundles her in a quilt and gives her a 'hug' (156). The presence of homicidal state agents who kill Black children produces a spectacle of white familial innocence. 'Vampirically' and in innumerable ways, Ruha Benjamin writes, 'white vitality feeds on black demise.'[31] Ending apartheid requires actions that effectively refuse and dismantle whiteness itself.

Coetzee's question in the 1987 speech followed from a reflection on the inescapability of whiteness in South Africa: 'You can imagine resigning, you can perform a symbolic resignation, but, short of shaking the dust of the country off your feet, there is no way of actually *doing* it.'[32] Mrs. Curren's daughter, notably, 'shook the dust of this country' from her feet in 1976 (139), the year of the Soweto youth uprisings, when images of Black school children who were murdered by the South African police were circulated nationally and internationally.[33] As Walsh notes, the daughter's departure is a 'rejection of mother and mother country'.[34] It is a refusal to remain part of a devouring family, and it converges with a wider international campaign of divestment and boycotts in the mid-1980s.[35] To adapt Christina Sharpe, the daughter refuses 'reconciliation to ongoing brutality' and attempts to rend the white 'kinship relations [that] structure the nation'.[36]

And yet, Mrs. Curren wonders, 'would I truly escape South Africa by running to you?' (127). White people, after all, are also stupid in the United States; as Coetzee concisely puts it, 'the gothic mode discovers itself in America', and the images that Mrs. Curren has of her daughter and grandchildren manifest the drive to expiate guilt and establish innocence.[37] Mrs. Curren imagines her daughter 'in a land where she will live and die in peace' (73). She contemplates a snapshot of her two grandchildren in a canoe, fully equipped with life jackets. The scene is one of eminent safety, of ostensible Edenic existence: they are 'two boys, seed planted in the American snow, who will never drown, whose life expectancy is seventy-five and rising' (195). The snow imagery self-consciously replicates the American gothic trope, as described by Morrison: 'Whiteness, alone, is mute, meaningless, unfathomable, pointless, frozen, veiled, curtained, dreaded, senseless, implacable.'[38] A narrative drive towards white settler redemption is thus rendered bathetic, a repeated, antiseptic, undead self-definition that continuously externalizes the violence it purports to confront. Mrs. Curren imagines how her world of the living dead will extend to her grandchildren, whom she imagines 'will die at seventy-five or eighty-five as stupid as when they were born' (195). If not dolls, or zombies, then 'white as grubs' (92), like white children in South Africa living lives of swimming lessons and walled gardens, 'spinning themselves tighter and tighter into their sleepy cocoons' (7). Such dullness to the reality of quotidian, catastrophic anti-Black violence, the novel suggests, is structural to white existence in an apartheid state. It is not transcended through individual knowledge or good works, emigration or denunciation. Its self-diagnosis only marks its continuance, and *Age of Iron*, in its international scope, questions whether national revolution is enough to abolish the global order whiteness sustains.

In early 1986, the year Coetzee began writing notes towards *Age of Iron*, he attended the forty-eighth PEN International Congress. Morrison gave the opening paper at a panel titled 'Alienation and the State', in which she considered the possibility that state machinations have created a world in which there is 'more past than future'.[39] As to the present, Morrison described her 'bone deep' knowledge that, had she lived the life the state planned for her, she would have 'never written a word'.[40] Her writing, she professed, 'has been bought and paid for' by 'Black children', both those children who 'got their brains shot out in the streets all over this country and had the good fortune to be televised' and by 'the mangled lives' of those children 'that went before them and were not televised': 'I am a read as opposed to unread writer because of those children. And I am clear on that point.'[41] As Morrison anticipates disagreement with her talk, her clarity is not something that she expects her predominately white audience to share. Nonetheless, Morrison exhorts listeners to imagine a living world beyond the state:

> It seems to me that it is a want of our imagination, not the state's, if we cannot both conceive of Eden, occupy it, and still have and do powerful work in it. It may be the nature of the state to rule and to contain its patriots, but it is not the nature of the writer to be ruled, and our imagination must have no limits.[42]

As Coetzee's novel tests how one vision of Eden rules and contains an international imperium of white compatriots, another Eden appears (if it appears at all) only in flashes. Like and unlike her daughter, Mrs. Curren attempts to rend the fabric of white international kinship: 'They are not my grandchildren,' she writes to their mother. 'The two boys whose lives have brushed mine are in any event already dead' (195). Mrs. Curren ends the novel living and dying with her 'shadow husband' Vercueil (189), a 'Coloured' man whom she first sees sleeping within 'a house of carton boxes and plastic sheeting' (3). The Dutch stem *kuil*, Susan VanZanten Gallagher notes, means 'hole in the ground'.[43] The word 'subaltern', Ruha Benjamin reminds us, literally means 'under the earth'. To be sure, Benjamin continues, 'racialized populations are buried people': 'But there is a lot happening underground. Not only coffins, but seeds, roots, and rhizomes. And maybe even tunnels and other lines of flight to new worlds, where alternative forms of kinship have room to grow and to nourish other life forms and ways of living.'[44] Vercueil responds to the spectacle of white nationalism on television by turning up the volume. 'It's just pictures,' he says, as he dances to the national anthem, mouthing words but 'not, certainly, the words I knew' (180).

NOTES

1. For a reading of these dates as marking the novel's fictional genesis, see Van der Vlies, '[From] Whom This Writing', 101.
2. Gordimer, 'The Idea of Gardening', 3.
3. Attridge, 'To Speak of This', 355.
4. Barnett, 'Constructions of Apartheid', 209.
5. Neuman, *Fiction Beyond Secularism*, 76.
6. See Hayes and Smuts.
7. Bewes, *The Event*, 141.
8. See Attridge and Walsh.
9. Jacobs, *Media*, 17–18.
10. Ibid., 18.
11. Coetzee, *Age of Iron*, 54. Further references cited parenthetically in text.
12. Ndebele, 'The Rediscovery', 143.
13. McLuhan, *Understanding Media*, 23.
14. Walsh, 'Not Grace', 177–8.
15. Coetzee, *Doubling*, 111.
16. Morrison, *Playing*, 35.
17. Ibid., 45.
18. Ibid., 33.
19. Ibid., 46–7.
20. A notebook entry for early manuscripts that would become *Age of Iron* dated 16 July 1986 suggests that Coetzee had Hawthorne in mind early on: 'She goes about the streets wearing a letter A'. Coetzee, *J.M. Coetzee Papers*.
21. Coetzee, *Late Essays*, 15.
22. Coetzee, *Doubling*, 293.

23. Ibid., 111.
24. Gordimer, 'The Idea of Gardening', 3.
25. See Milazzo and Moore regarding the limitations of concepts including white innocence and white guilt in the South African context.
26. Dickinson, '[I heard]', lines 12–16.
27. White stupidity in Coetzee's novel is not to be confused with 'white ignorance', which has been theorized as an epistemological phenomenon that can be overcome via a process of 'enlightenment'. See Mills, 'White Ignorance', 31.
28. In Ahmed's formulation, whiteness 'does' reification. See 'A Phenomenology of Whiteness', 150–3.
29. McKittrick, *Demonic*, 40.
30. Coetzee, *Doubling*, 98.
31. Benjamin, 'Black AfterLives Matter', n.p.
32. Ibid., 96.
33. The first entry in a notebook for early manuscripts that would become *Age of Iron* is 16 June 1986, the tenth anniversary of the Soweto Youth Uprising. Coetzee, *J.M. Coetzee Papers*.
34. Walsh, '"Not Grace,"' 179.
35. Attwell notes that an early draft of the novel recounts a son's response to his mother voting for the National Party in 1984. See *J.M. Coetzee and the Life of Writing*, 145–50.
36. Sharpe, 'Lose Your Kin', n.p.
37. Coetzee, *Doubling*, 111.
38. Morrison, *Playing*, 59.
39. Morrison, 'Alienation'. Morrison and Coetzee both read at an antiapartheid event held during the conference. Both taught at the University of Chicago in 1998, and Morrison invited Coetzee to Princeton to give the series of talks that would become *The Lives of Animals* (1999).
40. Ibid.
41. Ibid.
42. Ibid.
43. Gallagher, *A Story of South Africa*, 203.
44. Benjamin, 'Black AfterLives Matter', n.p.

WORKS CITED

Ahmed, Sara. 'A Phenomenology of Whiteness'. *Feminist Theory* 8, no. 2 (2007): 149–68.
Attridge, Derek. '"To Speak of This You Would Need the Tongue of a God": Coetzee's *Age of Iron*, Township Violence, and the Classics'. *Forum for World Literature Studies* 2, no. 3 (2010): 355–62.
Attwell, David. *J. M. Coetzee and the Life of Writing*. New York: Viking, 2015.
Barnett, Clive. 'Constructions of Apartheid in the International Reception of the Novels of J.M. Coetzee'. *Journal of Southern African Studies* 25, no. 2 (1999): 287–301.
Benjamin, Ruha. 'Black AfterLives Matter'. *Boston Review*, 16 July 2018: n.p. http://bostonreview.net/race/ruha-benjamin-black-afterlives-matter.
Bewes, Timothy. *The Event of Postcolonial Shame*. Princeton: Princeton University Press, 2011.
Coetzee, J. M. *Age of Iron*. New York: Penguin, 1990.
Coetzee, J. M. *Doubling the Point: Essays and Interviews*. Edited by David Attwell. Cambridge: Harvard University Press, 1992.

Coetzee, J. M. *J. M. Coetzee Papers*. Notebooks for *Age of Iron*. Harry Ransom Center. The University of Texas at Austin. Archives.
Coetzee, J. M. *Late Essays*. New York: Viking, 2018.
Dickinson, Emily. '[I Heard a Fly Buzz – When I Died –]'. In *Norton Anthology of American Literature*, edited by Nina Baym, 103. New York: W.W. Norton & Company, 2012.
Gallagher, Susan VanZanten. *A Story of South Africa*. Cambridge: Harvard University Press, 1991.
Gordimer, Nadine. 'The Idea of Gardening'. Review of *Life & Times of Michael K*, by J. M. Coetzee. *New York Review of Books*, 2 February 1984: 3–6.
Hayes, Patrick. *J.M. Coetzee and the Novel*. Oxford: Oxford University Press, 2010.
Jacobs, Sean. *Media in Postapartheid South Africa*. Bloomington: Indiana University Press, 2019.
McKittrick, Katherine. *Demonic Grounds*. Minneapolis: University of Minnesota Press, 2006.
McLuhan, Marshall. *Understanding Media*. 1964. Cambridge: MIT Press, 1994.
Milazzo, Marzia. 'On White Ignorance, White Shame, and Other Pitfalls in Critical Philosophy of Race'. *Journal of Applied Philosophy* 34, no. 4 (2017): 557–72.
Mills, Charles W. 'White Ignorance'. In *Race and Epistemologies of Ignorance*, edited by Shannon Sullivan and Nancy Tuana, 11–38. Albany: SUNY University Press, 2007.
Moore, Robyn. 'Resolving the Tensions between White People's Active Investment in Racial Inequality and White Ignorance: A Response to Marzia Milazzo'. *Journal of Applied Philosophy* 36, no. 2 (2019): 257–67.
Morrison, Toni. 'Alienation and the State I'. 48th PEN International Congress, 14 January 1986. https://soundcloud.com/penamerican/panel-on-alienation-pen-congress-1141986.
Morrison, Toni. *Playing in the Dark*. 1992. New York: Vintage, 1993.
Ndebele, Njabulo S. 'The Rediscovery of the Ordinary: Some New Writings in South Africa'. *Journal of Southern African Studies* 12, no. 2 (1986): 143–57.
Neuman, Justin. *Fiction beyond Secularism*. Evanston: Northwestern University Press, 2014.
Sharpe, Christina. 'Lose Your Kin'. *The New Inquiry*, 16 November 2016: n.p. https://thenewinquiry.com/lose-your-kin/.
Smuts, Eckard. 'J. M. Coetzee's *Age of Iron* and the Poetics of Resistance'. *Journal of Commonwealth Literature* 52, no. 1 (2017): 70–83.
Van der Vlies, Andrew. '"[From] Whom This Writing Then?' Politics, Aesthetics, and the Personal in Coetzee's *Age of Iron*'. In *Approaches to Teaching Coetzee's* Disgrace *and Other Works*, edited by Laura Wright, Jane Poyner and Elleke Boehmer, 96–104. New York: MLA, 2014.
Walsh, Rachel Ann. '"Not Grace, Then, but at Least the Body": Accounting for the Self in Coetzee's *Age of Iron*'. *Twentieth-Century Literature* 52, no. 2 (2010): 168–95.

CHAPTER TWELVE

The Master of Petersburg

DEREK ATTRIDGE

THE NOVEL

It is October 1869; an unnamed man gets out of an open carriage before a tall tenement building in St Petersburg. So begins Coetzee's seventh novel, a work whose subject and setting could not have been expected – and a work that makes expectation, and the unexpected, one of its themes.[1] The man is referred to as 'he', the narration is in the present tense, and, after a page of externalized description, we begin to see the scene from his perspective.[2] This shift to a personal view is signified by a single adjective: the young girl who shows the man up to the apartment he is looking for is described as having 'striking' dark eyes.[3] In the apartment, he explains to the girl's mother, Anna Sergeyevna, that he is the father of her recently deceased lodger, Pavel, and that he wishes to keep the room for a time. In making the arrangements, Anna mentions that her daughter Matryosha is at home in the afternoons, which prompts another conspicuous stylistic gesture, a single word paragraph: 'Matryona' (5). It is obviously the man's thought – at its most innocuous, he is mentally registering the girl's name (Matryosha being the familiar version of Matryona), but, by its salience on the page and its interruption of the narrative flow, something more consequential is suggested. At this moment, external narration and free indirect discourse (the reflection of a character's thoughts in the narration, as in the adjective 'striking') give way to interior monologue, a technique pioneered by James Joyce in *Ulysses* to create the illusion of fragmented thought processes.[4] The remainder of the novel will mix these narrative techniques to sustain a sense of intense intimacy with the character's thoughts and feelings, leaving moral judgement to the reader.

In these opening pages, we are invited to share the man's intense grieving for his dead son, which is prolonged in the chapters that follow. He visits Pavel's grave, spends afternoons in the apartment trying to reach him, puts on his white suit. We learn that the protagonist is a writer, though he is unable to write. Then, in a chapter titled 'Maximov', he is interrogated by the judicial investigator examining Pavel's death, and his name is revealed: Fyodor Mikhailovich Dostoevsky (33–4).

Coetzee expects his readers to have at least a modicum of knowledge about Dostoevsky and his fiction; those who know, or find out, more will enjoy an increased awareness of the subtleties of this novel – but we shall postpone that deeper investigation for the moment. The character is clearly related to the historical figure, but this is a fiction that need not – and does not – hew to the factual record. I shall refer to him as 'Fyodor' to keep the distinction between character and historical individual clear.

The plot is not complex; readers may be frustrated by the lack of external action and the relentless focus on Fyodor's attempts to communicate with, or somehow bring back to life, the dead youth, especially as it remains unclear what exactly he is attempting to achieve. The most significant events comprise Fyodor's relationships with Anna and Matryona, his involvement with the police investigation into Pavel's death (caused by a fall from a shot tower),[5] and his encounters with the revolutionary movement headed by Sergei Nechaev, with whom – it gradually becomes evident to Fyodor – Pavel was closely associated. Although the question of Pavel's death – was it suicide? was he murdered by the authorities? or by the Nechaevists? – is central to the narrative, and part of Fyodor's purpose is to find out the truth, readers who approach the novel as a whodunnit will be disappointed; its extraordinary richness lies not in the unravelling of the plot but in the themes explored and questions raised. There are many of these, and they are tightly interlinked, but for the purposes of this discussion I shall separate the most important of them before asking how they interrelate. I shall also refer to the style, where much of the novel's power lies, along the way, and end with some comments about the various contexts within which it is possible to read it.

THEMATIC THREADS

Mourning and guilt

Fyodor has come to St Petersburg from Dresden, where he has left his young wife, on hearing that his stepson Pavel Isaev – the son of his late first wife – has died. Since he has creditors in Petersburg, he has come incognito, using his stepson's surname (he consistently thinks of Pavel as his 'son'). He is in mourning, but it's not simple grief – he's buffeted by different emotions and desires during the hours he spends in Pavel's room – and his suffering is increased by his intense self-consciousness: every motion of his mind is complicated and qualified by other thoughts, every feeling is analysed without inhibition. He wants to believe that his son wasn't aware of his death when it was moments away; but he knows he wants this 'in order to etherize himself against the knowledge that Pavel, falling, knew everything' (21). He feels his love for his son as if it were a rope twisting and wringing his heart, and yet he 'reaches out and gives the rope another twist' (23). He senses that 'his son is inside him, a dead baby in an iron box in the frozen earth' whom he's unable to resurrect 'or – what comes to the same thing – lacks the will to do so' (52). He stays on in the apartment, but his reason for doing so is 'as obscure to others as to himself' (66). His mourning is complicated by feelings of guilt towards his stepson, with whom he had anything but an easy relationship – guilt that is increased when he read's Pavel's diary and realizes just how much the boy had disliked him. '[I]s there no word of forgiveness', he asks, 'however oblique, however disguised?' (219).

The language Coetzee employs to convey his character's mental and emotional states is very different from the precise, lapidary style we associate with his fiction. To take just one example: after Fyodor has read a manuscript of Pavel's, his thoughts are represented with a flair and colour that is almost Joycean:

> Young men in white playing the French game, croquet, croixquette, game of the little cross, and you on the greensward among them, alive! Poor boy! On the streets of Petersburg, in the turn of a head here, the gesture of a hand there, I see you, and each time my heart lifts as a wave does. Nowhere and everywhere, torn and scattered like Orpheus. Young in days, chryseos, golden, blessed. The task left to me: to gather the hoard, put together the scattered parts. Poet, lyre-player, enchanter, lord of resurrection, that is what I am called to be.
>
> (152–3)

The passage mixes self-indulgence with self-castigation, a lively sense of the boy's continuing presence with the painful awareness of his absence, poetic fancy with down-to-earth reality. The myth of Orpheus is put to double use: Pavel is like the dead musician, torn to pieces by the Maenads, while he himself has taken on the burden of resurrecting his son as Orpheus, thanks to his artistic skill, nearly succeeded in resurrecting Eurydice. The one way he might succeed is in achieving this is in his writing, but the words will not come. When they do come, at the end of the novel, it is not Pavel the golden youth who is brought to life.

Falling

This is also a novel about falling; in fact, *Falling* was one of its earlier titles.[6] Pavel's deadly fall has brought his stepfather to Petersburg, where he experiences falls of more than one kind; the anticipation of falling is repeatedly experienced; and the novel ends with a culminating fall.

Fyodor suffers from epilepsy, the 'falling sickness', which further intensifies his mental and emotional states, as well as operating metaphorically. (He knows he is making 'his own sordid and contemptible infirmity into the emblematic sickness of the age' (235).) A peculiarly powerful and positive vision of Pavel is followed immediately by the thought, '*Now there is sure to be a fit!*' (28). Waiting at the police station to retrieve Pavel's papers, he again 'has a premonition of an attack' – but, characteristically, at once recognizes that it would merely be device to extricate himself (31). A fit does arrive later, described in three pages of compelling prose; it first announces itself in a burst of joy as dawn breaks, then '[i]t is as if, at the moment when the sun comes forth in its glory, another sun appears too, a shadow sun, an anti-sun sliding across its face' (68). When he has recovered, he feels grateful that Pavel didn't suffer from the falling sickness – then experiences the bitter irony of what he has just thought (70).

A slighter fit overtakes Fyodor during a conversation with Nechaev and Katri (one of his associates) (97), and he has further premonitions while trying to hide the same clothes (164) and when he emerges into the street one snowy morning. On the latter occasion he reflects that 'a fit has been announcing itself for days without arriving', adding, 'Unless the entire state in which he lives can be called a fit' (174). He also expects to have a fit after failing to throw Nechaev's gun and poison – entrusted to Matryona – into the unfrozen river; but it doesn't arrive (215). When, watching Anna dress after they have made love, he feels he is 'within inches of falling into a love from which no reserve of prudence will save him', he calls it 'the falling sickness again, or a version of it' (226).

The motif of falling reaches a climax in the final chapter. The son he carries within him, he feels, is now 'whispering to him to fall', and he sees before him a choice: he can either 'cry out in the midst of this shameful fall, … call upon God or his wife to save him' or he can 'give himself to it' in the hope that he will become, instead of 'a body plunging into darkness', 'a body which contains its own falling and its own darkness' (234).

Gambling

Choosing to fall rather than being subject to a fall introduces the idea of risk. Fyodor is a compulsive gambler, a condition that has taken a heavy toll on his wife (84–5, 159). (It also lies behind the debts that keep him lying low in Petersburg.) Visiting Pavel's grave, he resists the finality of the boy's death: 'In a while, the wheel will roll, the numbers will start moving, and all will be well again' (8). Like his epilepsy, this compulsion takes on greater significance than a personal weakness.

The idea of gambling is central to an extraordinary chapter titled 'Ivanov'.[7] Fyodor, hearing a dog howling in the night, goes out to help it by unwrapping a tangled chain, but is aware that he could have gone further: 'Pavel will not be saved till he has freed the dog and brought it into his bed, brought the least thing, the beggarmen and the beggarwomen too, and much else he does not yet know of; and even then there will be no certainty' (82). Deciding not to help the dog further is a gamble: 'He is waiting for a sign, and he is betting (there is no grander word he dare use) that the dog is not the sign, is not a sign at all, is just a dog among many dogs howling in the night' (83). The only way to be sure not to miss the sign when it comes is to treat everything as a possible sign; '[t]hat is what Pascal would say: bet on everyone, every beggar, every mangy dog; only thus will you be sure that the One, the true son, the thief in the night, will not slip through the net' (84). But that is '[b]etting on all the numbers', so not gambling at all, and '[w]ithout the risk, without subjecting oneself to the voice speaking from elsewhere in the fall of the dice, what is left that is divine?' (84). After this debate with himself, he takes the smelly, shivering beggar he has discovered in the entryway – actually the police spy Ivanov – to his bed. (Later he learns that Ivanov has been murdered by the Nechaevists.)

Pavel, he tells Matryona, said to God, 'I will wager my life that you will save me' – but 'God did not intervene' (75). And in the final chapter, he thinks of himself as gambling to make God speak (237) and gambling, too, on the possibility that having missed Pavel's 'first word' he will hear his 'second word' (239) – a second word that he believes both will and will not come.

Possession

Epilepsy may feel like a kind of possession; Fyodor wonders if *seizure* is the wrong word to refer to his fits, 'whether the word has not all along been *possession*' (213). But possession is experienced in many other ways as well.[8] Fyodor, lying on Pavel's bed, in a rage at those who are alive, especially Matryona, tries 'to expel the demon that is taking him over' – though he knows 'that what he calls a demon may be nothing but his own soul flailing its wings' (16). He describes Nechaev as possessed by a 'dull, resentful, and murderous spirit'; Maximov prefers to call it possession by a demon (44). Later, Fyodor tells Anna that Nechaev has 'what the Greeks called a demon. It speaks to him. It is the source of his energy', and that '[t]he same demon must have been in Pavel, otherwise why would Pavel have responded to his call?' (113). Katri, too, thinks Fyodor, is 'a child in the grip of a devil' (92)

Both reading and sex are associated with possession. Maximov asserts that Fyodor's description of reading makes it sound like 'demon-possession' (47), as if 'the spirit of Nechaev might leap from the page and take complete possession of you' (48). During his lovemaking with Anna Sergeyevna, an image of his dying son appears to him, 'bursts upon him, possesses him, speeds on' (56); and on another occasion he finds it hard not to think of her during orgasm as possessed by the devil (231). And in the novel's climax, writing, too, seems to be a kind of possession.

Paedophilia

The relationship between generations is another major theme in the novel.[9] For the most part, it is the conflict between them that is stressed; but a different aspect emerges when it is a matter of an older man and a young girl.[10] From the start, Fyodor feels a strong but enigmatic bond with Matryona, in which looking plays a major part. We have noted signs of this from the first page, and there is a moment during a visit to the cemetery when '[s]omething flashes from his eyes towards her' and 'she turns away in confusion' (9). Again, back in the apartment, she 'raises her eyes for an instant, encounters his gaze exploring her, and turns away in confusion' (13); and, for a third time, after she has brought him some tea, 'He raises his eyes to her. Nothing is veiled. He stares at her with what can only be nakedness' (24) – and again she responds with embarrassment. The fourth meeting of eyes is more explicitly sexual, though not simply that: Fyodor is howling with grief when Matryona comes into the room in her nightdress, and '[h]e cannot fail to notice the budding breasts'. Their gazes lock, and 'something passes between them from which he flinches as though pierced by a red-hot wire' (28).

Fyodor has felt sexual desire of a more straightforward kind for Anna Sergeyevna from early in his stay, and one evening they make love in Pavel's room. What excites Fyodor in the act is not only the ardour of his partner but 'that they should be doing such fiery, dangerous work with the child asleep in the next room' (56). And the next evening he is sure that the 'avid glances he steals at the mother's throat, lips, arms' don't pass Matryona by (57). Later that night he goes into the room in which Anna and the girl are sleeping; bending over the daughter he realizes she is awake and 'watching his every motion with unremitting vigilance' (58).

Chapter 7 is titled 'Matryona'. In rehearsing to the girl an episode in Pavel's life that shows him to be thoughtful and generous, then heightening her pain by mocking the idea of a beneficent God, Fyodor is grooming her, though it's unclear (perhaps to him as well as to the reader) what for. 'Now she is ready' is his thought as he pats the bed next to him, then embraces her (75). The 'violation' is not physical but mental: he has a vision of Pavel inseminating Matryona, then, via a memory of an explicit Indian statue, of the girl experiencing a climax. He thinks that 'she might as well be sprawled out naked', and his mind moves to the erotic attraction some men feel to child prostitutes because of the 'flavour of innocence' about them (76–7). When the vision – which he also calls a 'fit' – is over, he embraces her once more, feeling 'the soft young bones fold, one over another, as a bird's wing folds' (78). The episode is deeply unsettling: Coetzee's writing risks alienating the reader, offering little to redeem his protagonist.

Another unsettling insight into Fyodor's desires is provided when, in a state of erotic arousal as he visualizes sex with Anna Sergevnya, it occurs to him that Matryona could wander into his room, and soon he is asking, 'Loving the mother, is one destined to long for the daughter too?' (128). He reassures himself that no one else knows of this paedophilic tendency – except the Pavel who is within him, and whom he hopes will be tolerant of his weakness.

When Fyodor promises to get rid of the incriminating parcel entrusted to Matryona, he sees – or imagines he sees – another look that disturbs him, this time 'a glance that is at once shameless and derisive', accompanied by a 'taunting, provocative smile' (213). A powerful passage follows, in which Fyodor likens this experience to a seizure during which he has remained conscious, and wonders whether all his fits in the past have been 'a mere presentiment of what is now happening, the quaking and dancing of the body in a long-drawn-out prelude to a quaking of the soul' (213). He calls it 'the death of innocence', and feels like a traveller overtaken by a mighty storm, to which his response is *'Let it all break!'*. But what is heading towards him remains uncertain.

After an encounter with Katri, whom he calls a 'child' when he first sees her (90), Fyodor is again beset by an image of paedophilia involving Pavel. He sees his son on his knees with the Finn, 'her bulky legs apart, her arms held wide to display her breasts and a belly round, hairless, barely mature' (107). And when Nechaev takes him into a cellar in which three children are sitting, his thoughts again move to child sex and his landlady's daughter: 'The sister younger than Matryona, but also, it strikes him, younger, more acquiescent. Has she already begun to say yes to men?' (182). Nechaev accuses him of 'doing it' to little girls, and, addressing the girl herself, associates him with men who 'drop tears when they hurt you, to lubricate their consciences and give themselves thrills' (193).

Near the end of the novel, after passionate sex, Anna Sergeyevna accuses Fyodor of using her as a route to her child, and in spite of his denial, her accusation rings true. She adds, 'I would never have gone so far if I weren't afraid you would use Matryosha in the same way' (232). Again, Fyodor hotly denies her imputation. They make love again, and in the morning, when they are still in bed together, Fyodor looks up to see 'the grave child at the door' (232). This penultimate chapter ends with his reflection: 'She sees all, she knows all' (233).

Writing, ethics and betrayal

The topic that braids together all these thematic threads, and highlights their ethical significance, is *writing*. From early in his stay in Petersburg, Fyodor tries to write, and writing remains an implicit ingredient in all his experiences. What it turns out he is trying to do, though he is not aware of it for a long time, is to write Pavel back into life. But something is blocking him; he sits at Pavel's desk but dares not write, since he believes that what would emerge from his pen would be 'vileness, obscenity, page after page of it, untameable' (18). When Matryona is ill and stays at home, 'he is less than ever able to give his attention to writing' (135). Above all, it is his attraction to Matryona that influences his writing self. After the third occurrence of a look that confuses her, he is provoked into ominous reflections:

> He is aware, even as it unfolds, that this is a passage he will not forget and may even one day rework into his writing. A certain shame passes over him, but it is superficial and transitory. First in his writing and now in his life, shame seems to have lost its power, its place taken by a blank and amoral passivity that shrinks from no extreme.
>
> (24)

The novel's conclusion, which we shall turn to in a moment, takes these reflections further.

Sex with Anna Sergeyevna provokes Fyodor into imagining becoming the author of an anonymous 'book of the night', 'of the kind one cannot publish in Russia'. His thoughts slide from the mother to the daughter, as he envisages a chapter in which 'the noble memoirist reads aloud to the young daughter of his mistress a story of the seduction of a young girl in which he himself emerges more and more clearly as having been the seducer', the effect of which is that the girl 'gives herself up to him in despair, in the most shameful of ways, in a way of which no child could conceive were the history of her own seduction and surrender and the manner of its doing not deeply impressed on her beforehand' (134). The potential closeness of fiction and illicit desires could not be more clearly stated and will be taken up again.

Pavel's writing also features importantly: Maximov taunts Fyodor with the text of the boy's unfinished novel, giving rise to the discussion of reading alluded to earlier, and we learn that Pavel used to read his stories to Anna and Matryona (136–7). Fyodor's own writing is inseparable from his desire to rescue Pavel: 'He will give a home to any word, no matter how strange, no matter how stray, if there is a chance it is an anagram for Pavel' (141). (We are reminded of the ethical obligation to take in every mangy dog.) Yet the word does not come: 'Stiff shoulders humped over the writing-table, and the ache of a heart slow to move' (153).

Eventually, in the multi-layered, disconcerting final chapter (whose title, 'Stavrogin', is unexplained), 'He unpacks the writing-case, sets out his materials' (235); it is in writing that he can become, as he hoped, 'a body which contains its own falling and its own darkness' (234). He has a different agenda now:

> No longer a matter of listening for the lost child calling from the dark stream, no longer a matter of being faithful to Pavel when all have given him up. Not a matter of fidelity at all. On the contrary, a matter of betrayal – betrayal of love first of all, and then of Pavel and the mother and child and everyone else. *Perversion*: everything and everyone to be turned to another use, to be gripped to him and fall with him.
>
> (235)

He senses a figure before him, a character for a new fiction. The figure has elements of himself and of Nechaev, but it is not them; if it is Pavel, it's 'Pavel as he might have been one day, grown wholly beyond boyhood to become the kind of cold-faced, handsome man whom no love can touch, even the adoration of a girl-child *who will do anything for him*' (240). Then he finds himself writing a description of a child who is clearly Matryona lying naked next to this man. He holds himself back from composing further, knowing this will be the worst of his falls, the most dangerous possession, 'a descent into representations that have no place in the world' (241).

Instead, he gets out Pavel's diary, and starts writing on the first blank page a story in which the protagonist is both himself and Pavel, a young man wearing a white suit who brings a girl back to his room to make love every week over a summer. The young man's pleasure is increased when he discovers the landlady's daughter observing them; he thinks of it as *'creating a taste* in the girl' (244). After an interruption by Matryona, Fyodor writes a version of the story he told her earlier of Pavel's generosity in befriending the weak-minded Maria Lebyatkin, although now the story is told by the young man about himself to the girl and has a different ending: an admission that his motivation was merely amusement.

Fyodor goes out, leaving the two pages of the diary open for Matryona to find. He sees himself as challenging God by corrupting a child. 'Time is suspended, everything is suspended before the fall' (249). In order to write, 'he has betrayed everyone, nor does he see that his betrayals could go deeper' (250), given up his soul. Writing is falling, gambling, being possessed, allowing one's illicit desires to feed one's creativity.

CONTEXTS

Intertextuality

I have outlined some of the main thematic strands of *Master* as they might be experienced by a reader with only a minimal knowledge of the life and work of Fyodor Dostoevsky. Knowing more adds a great deal to an appreciation of the novel.

Many features of Fyodor's character are taken straight from biographies of the novelist.[11] Dostoevsky suffered from epileptic fits, was a compulsive gambler, and had to leave Petersburg because of debts. He acquired a stepson, Pavel Isaev, on his first marriage, and remained the boy's main source of support when, after his first wife's death, he married a much younger woman, Anna Snitkina. His relationship with Pavel was indeed a troubled one. But there are significant departures from the historical record, too: most obviously, Dostoevsky was not in Petersburg in 1869, and Pavel outlived his stepfather by nineteen years. The novel is not an exercise in biography.

Most important for an enhanced enjoyment of Coetzee's novel is familiarity with the novel Dostoevsky was beginning in 1869: variously translated as *The Possessed*, *The Devils*, and *Demons*, it is an onslaught on the radical forces the author saw as endangering traditional Russian values.[12] Dostoevsky was horrified by the murder of a student activist by followers of the agitator Sergei Nechaev and incorporated a version of these events (using different names) in his novel. Coetzee restores Nechaev's name and gives a central place to the death of a young activist, possibly murdered by the Nechaevists (though he transfers the name of the original student, Ivanov, to the police spy). Dostoevsky's principal representation of evil is not the character based on Nechaev, however, but an amoral, intelligent, handsome young nobleman called Stavrogin, one of whose actions is to indulge in a mock courtship of a simple-minded woman, Marya Timofyevna Lebyadkin. A crucial chapter was to be a long (and unsuccessful) confession made by Stavrogin to a monk, during which he tells of his sexual preying on an eleven-year-old girl and his subsequent failure to prevent her suicide. The girl is called Matryosha.

Dostoevsky was forced to exclude the chapter from *The Possessed* (it is printed in modern editions as an appendix), but it is crucial to Coetzee's novel.[13] Coetzee appears to have asked himself, 'What series of events could lead a great writer to imagine a character like Stavrogin and produce a text as steeped in evil as his confession?' The current of paedophilia that runs through *Master* is part of the answer: Fyodor is working with some of his own blackest desires in conceiving his novel, the beginnings of which we see in the two sections written in Pavel's diary. In titling the chapter 'Stavrogin', Coetzee highlights how the threads of Fyodor's time in Petersburg are woven together in a feat of the darkest imagination.

Biography

Many readers find the wracking bouts of emotional stress that assail Fyodor over the course of the novel hard to justify: why is he so overwhelmed by the mental presence of his dead stepson, with whom he had such a difficult relationship? When the novel first appeared, the facts of Coetzee's private life were not widely known, and critics – including myself – were reluctant to adduce them in discussing his fiction.[14] Since then, Coetzee has made available to researchers a vast trove of materials, including manuscripts, notebooks and letters, and an extensive biography has been published.[15] It is thus public knowledge that Coetzee's son Nicolas died in 1989 at the age of twenty-two, after a fall from an eleventh-storey balcony, and that there is no absolute certainty about what happened, though it was probably an accident. Coetzee's anguish was made worse by the history of troubled relations between them.[16]

Knowing these facts, it is hard not to read *Master* – whatever one's views on the role of biography in literary interpretation – as the wrestling of a father with the sense of abiding loss after the death of a child. (Pavel was originally to be Fyodor's own son, and to be called Nikolai Stavrogin.[17]) And the betrayal implicit in the act of creating a work of fiction out of that struggle is a further cause of discomfort, made even worse by imagining the fictional writer's creation to be one of world literature's most chillingly evil characters.[18] One should not, I believe, allow this dimension of the novel to dominate one's reading, but there can be no doubt that it adds poignancy to the potent representations of the novelist's grief and pain.

History

The Master of Petersburg was published in 1994, one of the most significant years in the history of South Africa, Coetzee's home country. In that year, the first wholly democratic elections took place, resulting in the election of the African National Congress as the governing party and Nelson Mandela as the President. The novel was written, therefore, in the difficult years of the transition to democracy, which saw competing visions of the new South Africa in conflict, often violently so. Reading the novel in that context, one is made especially aware of the balance of ideological forces it presents. The Nechaevists are portrayed as ruthless and misguided, but we see them only from Fyodor's jaundiced position, and Nechaev's analysis of the systemic injustices of Russian society comes across with powerful conviction – even though Fyodor resists it. On the other side, the Russian authorities as embodied in Maximov and his spy Ivanov are far from models of good government. When Fyodor says, 'I am required to live – what shall I call it? – a Russian life: a life inside Russia, or with Russia inside me, and whatever Russia means. It is not a fate I can evade' (221), we are hearing Coetzee's discomfort as a writer in a national conflict to which he knows there are no easy solutions. Coetzee's next novel, which he was just beginning when *Master* was published, was *Disgrace* (1999), written, like Dostoevsky's *The Possessed*, out of that discomfort.

NOTES

1. See Attridge, 'Expecting the Unexpected: *The Master of Petersburg*', chapter 5 of *J. M. Coetzee and the Ethics of Reading*.
2. Third-person, present tense narration from a single perspective was to become Coetzee's favoured technique in later novels.
3. Coetzee, *The Master of Petersburg*, 2. Further references parenthetically in the text.
4. In *Ulysses* a similar one-word interruption on the opening page tells us we are privy to a character's thoughts: the sight of gold fillings in Malachi Mulligan's teeth elicits the name 'Chrysostomos', golden-mouthed, in Simon Dedalus's consciousness. Joyce, *Ulysses*, 3.
5. A tower used for the manufacture of shotgun ammunition, made by dropping molten lead from a height. There has never been a shot tower in St Petersburg. See Attwell, *J. M. Coetzee and the Life of Writing*, 187.
6. Attwell, *J. M. Coetzee*, 203.
7. I discuss the ethical implications of this chapter in *J. M. Coetzee*, 122–4. See also Fernie, *The Demonic: Literature and Experience*, chapter 27.
8. Jarad Zimbler discusses the use of the term *Master* and its relation to the terms *soul* and *spirit* in *J. M. Coetzee and the Politics of Style*, 181–6.
9. On fathers and sons, parents and children in *Master* see Lopez, *Acts of Visitation*, 265–74.

10. For a discussion of the role of desire in the novel and in novel-writing, see Bolin, 'The Sinister Mirror'. Coetzee's protagonist (spokesman?) in *Diary of a Bad Year* expresses some heterodox views on paedophilia (53–7).
11. Coetzee is particularly indebted to Joseph Frank's extensive biography of Dostoevsky, the fourth volume of which he reviewed. See Attwell, *J. M. Coetzee*, 188–9.
12. For more detail on the novel's allusions to *The Possessed*, see Scanlan, 'Incriminating Documents'. There are allusions to other novels by Dostoevsky; see Hayes, *J. M. Coetzee and the Novel*, 186–93, and Lawlan, 'The Master of Petersburg'.
13. Michelle Kelly provides some valuable comments on Coetzee's view on censorship in her essay on *Master* in Mehigan's *Companion*, 132–47.
14. My short postscript on the biographical background to *Master* was written under these self-imposed constraints (Attridge, *J. M. Coetzee and the Ethics of Reading*, 135–7).
15. Kannemeyer, *J. M. Coetzee*. See also Attwell, *J. M. Coetzee*.
16. See Kannemeyer, *J. M. Coetzee*, 452–7; Attwell, *J. M. Coetzee*, 191–2, 194–7. In *The Death of Jesus*, Coetzee returned to the theme of a father's grief at the loss of a son-figure with whom he had a difficult relationship.
17. Attwell, *J. M. Coetzee*, 191.
18. Rosemary Jolly notes another betrayal, Coetzee's betrayal of Dostoevsky, in associating him with paedophilia: see Jolly, 'Writing Desire Responsibly', 105.

WORKS CITED

Attridge, Derek. *J. M. Coetzee and the Ethics of Reading: Literature in the Event*. Chicago: University of Chicago Press, 2004.
Attwell, David. *J. M. Coetzee and the Life of Writing: Face to Face with Time*. Johannesburg: Jacana, 2015.
Bolin, John. 'The Sinister Mirror: Desire and Intensity in J. M. Coetzee's *The Master of Petersburg*'. *Review of English Studies* 65 (2013): 515–35.
Coetzee, J. M. *Diary of a Bad Year*. London: Harvill Secker, 2007.
Coetzee, J. M. *The Death of Jesus*. Melbourne: Text Publishing, 2019.
Coetzee, J. M. *The Master of Petersburg*. London: Secker and Warburg, 1994.
Fernie, Ewan. *The Demonic: Literature and Experience*. London: Routledge, 2103.
Hayes, Patrick. *J. M. Coetzee and the Novel: Writing and Politics after Beckett*. Oxford: Oxford University Press, 2010.
Jolly, Rosemary. 'Writing Desire Responsibly'. In *J. M. Coetzee in Context and Theory*, edited by Elleke Boehmer, Robert Eaglestone and Katy Iddiols, 93–111. London: Continuum, 2000.
Joyce, James. *Ulysses*. 1922. New York: Vintage Books, 1966.
Kannemeyer, J. C. *J. M. Coetzee: A Life in Writing*. Translated by Michiel Heyns. Johannesburg: Jonathan Ball, 2012.
Kelly, Michelle. '*The Master of Petersburg*'. In *A Companion to the Works of J. M. Coetzee*, edited by Tim Mehigan, 132–47. Rochester: Camden House, 2011.
Lawlan, Rachel. 'The Master of Petersburg: Confession and Double Thoughts on Coetzee and Dostoevsky'. *Ariel* 29 (1998): 131–57.
Lopez, María J. *Acts of Visitation: The Narrative of J. M. Coetzee*. Amsterdam: Rodopi, 2011.
Scanlan, Margaret. 'Incriminating Documents: Nechaev and Dostoevsky in J. M. Coetzee's *The Master of Petersburg*'. *Philological Quarterly* 76 (1997): 463–77.
Zimbler, Jarad. *J. M. Coetzee and the Politics of Style*. Cambridge: Cambridge University Press, 2014.

CHAPTER THIRTEEN

Disgrace

CHRIS HOLMES

LIVING WITH DISGRACE

In my second year of university teaching, a colleague from the Politics Department wandered into my office, leaning half-in, half-out, to say that he had heard from some of our shared students that I was teaching J. M. Coetzee's *Disgrace* (1999) in my class on postcolonial literature. He had some questions about that choice, he said. He really meant he had some *statements*. As those who read and write about Coetzee's extraordinary and contentious masterwork already know, *Disgrace* is a novel that leaves difficult conversations and intractable debates in its wake. Why, my colleague demanded, would anyone who cared about South Africa teach such a violently racist novel? What could possibly redeem a novel that planted a flag for afro-pessimism a mere five years after the transition to democracy in the country?[1]

My *esprit de l'escalier* had me wishing that I had argued for the value of Coetzee, the writer, to South Africa's literary tradition, and his role, however modest, in critiquing the Afrikaner minority government. But what became clear to me in the days after our piqued interaction was that my colleague was making a fundamental interpretative error, collapsing the author and the book's lead character into a single, objectionable persona, even as I could understand his discomfort with the novel's representation of the rape of a white woman by a gang of Black men. He seemed principally angry at Coetzee for having fashioned so convincing a racist, in a country recently unburdened of minority governance. I am writing this essay as a response not to my colleague, but to *Disgrace*'s history of inviting this kind of controversy and misreading. By treating fairly the criticisms of the novel's relationship to the violence it describes and to its racist principal character, David Lurie, I will show how *Disgrace* functions as a literary response to the very critiques it has engendered, while arguing that the novel's principal interest is in dismantling the logic upon which these critiques rely.

Disgrace presents as a philosophical novel tucked inside a campus drama, and finished off with an inverted *plaasroman*, with the urbane professor Lurie returned to the farm but finding there no idyll. A gloss of the novel's plot helps explain how animus for the main character can appear to cancel out all the formal features that work in dissonance to the main character's thoughts and feelings. The focus of the novel's free and indirect discourse, Lurie spends the novel careening towards self-destruction as a result of his egotism, lasciviousness, intellectual blindness and racism. Lurie begins his self-sabotage by sleeping with a coloured student, Melanie Isaacs. He is subsequently dismissed from the university where he teaches after refusing to take responsibility for his misuse of power in the coercive relationship with Melanie. He then enters an exile from Cape Town in the rural Eastern Cape where his daughter Lucy lives on a small plot of land that she tends with the help of a Black employee, Petrus. Soon after moving in with his daughter, there is an attack by a group of Black men, who rape Lucy and disfigure Lurie. Lurie's desire for revenge against the attackers, one of whom is a relative of Petrus, comes to a stalemate with Lucy, who seeks a détente with Petrus, to whom she ultimately deeds her land, retaining only a small plot of her farm for her own tending.

If one reads this merely as a mimetic dramatization of lived experience in post-Apartheid South Africa, as my colleague surely did, it is easy to see how each scene might be diagnosed as a metastatic afro-pessimism, or as a tirade against the growing pains of a newly democratic nation.[2] And yet the novel is much more than this husk of plot. *Disgrace*'s explicit literariness, allusiveness and ostentatious theorization of its own forms and structures expressly reject Lurie's way of reading and, most crucially for this argument, clear the intellectual landscape of Lurie's intellectual tyranny, making room for new contexts for imagining literature's relationship to the nation.

The problem for *Disgrace* as a novel born of the new South Africa is, as Anthony Uhlmann puts it, 'how to make something that addresses the ethical implications of otherness and conflicts, while constrained to think from within a particular disposition and situation'.[3] The disposition he refers to is Lurie's limited capacity to think outside of a mentality that has been shaped by racism and patriarchy of every manner. And the intimacy with which the narrative voice describes Lurie's inner life can leave us wedded to this disposition as readers. Thus, we get to the crux of the novel's pedagogical enigma: why read something that asks you to think alongside a mind that is closed off from the birth of possibility in the context of a newly postcolonial nation?[4] To invest the novel with meaning, are we condemned to simply sympathize with or denounce Lurie? Do we cast the novel off as irredeemable, perhaps even reprehensible, or might we be misjudging the root of pathos in the novel or the value of literature more broadly? In examining the critical treatments of the novel's representation of post-Apartheid South Africa, I will be offering a way of reading Lurie's seeming domination of the novel's imaginative landscape. The voice and mood of *Disgrace* draw us dangerously close to this protagonist's point of view, but the narrative preserves sufficient space to both identify the cognitive model that Lurie uses in his engagement with the world, and subsequently extinguish that model from the spaces in which he has existed.[5]

'A SENSE OF A VIOLATION'

The initial critical responses to *Disgrace* were largely positive, but some early reviews and commentaries found it impossible to separate the novel from the bluntness with which it narrates rape, abuse and racism with an arch ironic tone that appears designed to inflame and provoke. Indeed, the distinguishing narrative quality of *Disgrace*, its sardonic free indirect discourse, forged for some readers an uncomfortable linkage between Coetzee and Lurie. Gayatri Spivak and others have pointed to the novel's 'relentless focalization' on the unpleasant, highly pedantic, misogynist Lurie.[6]

The controversies seemingly courted by the novel are also inseparable from its milieu, composed just five years after the first democratic elections in 1994.[7] It is within this context that the rape of Lucy Lurie, and her subsequent decision to cede her land to Petrus have been understood by some critics as either the implicit racism of Coetzee the writer, or as signals of the novel's political unconscious – a deep cynicism or dissatisfaction with the seismic shifts in South African life. Nobel Prize winner Nadine Gordimer claimed in a review that 'there is not one black person who is a real human being' in the novel.[8] Aggrey Klaaste, writing in the Sowetan, felt *Disgrace*'s 'substance ... that of a typically disgruntled Afrikaner,' and found Coetzee 'totally cynical'.[9] For Athol Fugard, one of South Africa's greatest playwrights, the novel's violation comes in its denouement, Lucy's seeming acceptance of her rape as restitution for 'everything [the white minority] did in the past'.[10] Elleke Boehmer questions whether *Disgrace* can 'speak of atonement if it entails that women as ever assume the generic pose of suffering in silence'[11] while other critics understand this event as inseparable from an internal critique of Lurie's own sexual violence. Lucy Valerie Graham makes it clear that the novel enacts a doubling of the rapists in Lurie's treatment of his student Melanie. 'There will certainly be readers who protest against what they regard as the representation of black men as rapists in *Disgrace*,' Graham writes, 'but it is important to acknowledge that the novel dissolves clear boundaries of identity between Lurie and the men who rape Lucy.'[12] Carine Mardorossian furthers this line of thinking, arguing that *Disgrace* encourages readers to 'rethink ... the deeply racialized way in which rape is naturalized precisely as a black on white crime'.[13]

A submission from the African National Congress (ANC) to a 2000 South African Human Rights Commission hearing on racism in the media cited passages from *Disgrace*, concluding that 'J. M. Coetzee represents as brutally as he can, the white people's perception of the post-apartheid black man.' The report emphasized that 'five years after our liberation, white South African society continues to believe in a particular stereotype of the African.' In a special issue on the novel in the journal *Interventions*, Peter D. McDonald and David Attwell take different approaches to the quandary of race in *Disgrace*, and to the ANC's controversial response to the novel. For McDonald, the ANC's critique comes out of treating the novel purely at face value.[14] He goes on to argue that 'it is the instability of the literary' rather than the putative reportage about South African life that tests the reader of *Disgrace*; *Disgrace* 'is written in such a way as to risk putting contemporary expectations, especially with regard to reading texts called "literary", provocatively to the test'.[15] Attwell rejects what he sees as a misreading by those who position the ANC's response to the novel as definitively critical of Coetzee. 'The more interesting tension in the ANC document,' he argues, 'is between the attempt to *avoid* the philistinism of accusing Coetzee of racism, and wanting to use him nevertheless as celebrity witness to its prevalence – a project to which literature and literariness, are actually irrelevant'.[16] These 'impoverished' readings miss the fact (Attwell contends) that '*Disgrace* contains and sublimates race, by drawing it into larger patters of historical and ethical interpretation.'[17]

Some critics see *Disgrace* as explicitly challenging the reader's expectations for how a novel *about* South Africa should look, prompting them to reframe their expectations for how a novel speaks to its present moment in ethico-political terms.[18] Uhlmann claims the novel forces us to 'think about things that are not easy to think about, which are not easy to understand'.[19] Derek Attridge proposes that the novel's ethical impulse lies not in the false flags of 'the production of art and the affirmation of human responsibility to animals', but in the event of grace, 'a certain openness to experience and to the future'.[20]

Even the most persuasive examples of criticism that hold up *Disgrace* as an exemplary literary work do not whitewash the violence that moves the plot inexorably forward. As Tony D'Souza wrote in a retrospective for the National Book Critics Circle: '*Disgrace* is a pitiless and errorless book about the condition of the human experience ... while not altogether without hope, the book and its title is a condemnation of the basic state of modern humanity.'[21] While D'Souza's understanding of *Disgrace* as offering a critique of 'modern humanity' – a somewhat elementary reading echoed in the awarding of the Booker and Nobel prizes – rings true to what we understand to be the milieu of Coetzee's work, how precisely, and to whom, the disgrace of the title is meted out is the subject of much of the scrutiny of the novel.[22]

The irony of these controversies is that they have done little to unseat *Disgrace*'s place in the canon of world literature, where it often stands in for South African literature in a metonymic fashion.[23] Van der Vlies suggests that 'criticism of the novel in official circles in South Africa [had been] largely forgotten' by the time Coetzee was made a member of 'a prestigious state order in 2005'.[24] Amongst scholars, *Disgrace* is seen as carrying with it a library of criticism that rivals almost any contemporary novel in English. It is not uncommon to encounter in reviews and in prefatory material to monographs and collections Coetzee being wielded as a figure of the extremes. Coetzee is the 'most,' the 'least,' the postmodern conscience, the traitor, the historian, and the recluse – often all at once and in the same review. Some of the most important Anglophone critics of the twentieth and twenty-first centuries have turned to *Disgrace* as a laboratory for experimentation with the major literary theories of our time.[25] Indeed, this may partially explain the novel's pre-eminence with scholars – it appears readymade to respond to postcolonial, affect, trauma, critical race and narrative theories. This receptiveness to theory is matched by what can only be described as a machine of perpetual self-theorization, whereby the novel appears to be working through how it reads itself.

Disgrace dramatizes Lurie's thinking life by way of acting out a literary methodology for how to read the novel itself – as a narrative machine for clearing intellectual space within the novel's South African imaginary. The result is a contradiction between, on the one hand, the intellectual cocoon of Lurie's mind, inside which he remains 'a figure from the margins of history', and, on the other, the capaciousness with which the novel itself prompts new self-theorizations that are inexorably tied to the present and thus require a profoundly different perspective (167). Like much of Coetzee's work, the friction between Lurie's cognition, which appears hermetically sealed off from the present, and the novel's self-actualization, which works to puncture his imagination, sets in motion a parallel drama. In the case of *Disgrace*, that drama becomes essential to understanding the novel's relationship to its contemporaneous historical moment.

DISGRACE'S THINKING MINDS

Coetzee has made a career out of testing fiction's ability to dramatize the thinking mind.[26] The drama of his novels is inseparable from the antagonism between competing forms of thinking. This is most explicit in *Diary of a Bad Year*, where the space of the page is divided into two and sometimes three streams of thought, writing and dialogue, each one demonstrating a discrete mode of cognitive evaluation. While *Diary of a Bad Year* presents itself as a clash of ideas, it is, most explicitly, a conflict between ways of thinking – authoritative, dialogical, conspiratorial – a difference in process versus product. Although it is most transparent in *Diary*, Coetzee's warring ways of thinking are everywhere in his fiction.

I argue that *Disgrace*'s driving motivation is not to engage Lurie's spectacular failures of self-awareness, but to drive him from the narrative landscape, to push him further and further afield, so that his ways of interpreting have no purchase in South Africa, leaving space for the thinkers that the novel cannot yet imagine, but which it clearly anticipates. This restriction occurs geographically, with Lurie's marginalization as he is ostracized from the metropole *and* alienated from the life of the countryside, restricted to ever narrower physical spaces, ultimately bedding down with the dogs. It occurs too via his intellectual marginalization, effectively turning off the neural lights, one room at a time, in the machinery of Lurie's thinking mind.

This process of marginalization might best be literalized as a reader tearing out each chapter as she reads, propelling the narrative by removing its foundational ways of seeing and understanding the world. In this way, Lurie's intellectual life is closed, chapter by chapter, as the novel illuminates that which animates his mind and exposes the hegemonic structures that have dominated South African life. Just as Lurie's colleagues consider him 'a hangover from the past, the sooner cleared away the better,' so too does the novel enact the machinery of extinguishing, clearing away the hangovers from the age of cultural imperialism, while attending the arrival of new thinking minds, new protagonists through with which to read the nation (40). The result is a narrative that marks the change in who can matter in a body politic by extinguishing the very means for meaning-making that appear to propel the novel forward, and which have engendered so many caustic evaluations of the novel's politics. What remains is a story that invests not in Lurie's fall and redemption, but rather in his narrative extinguishment, a linguistic devaluation and physical decentering in order to make space for an emerging representation of the new citizenry that cannot be imagined from inside Lurie's imagination.

Lurie's pedagogical imagination offers us the blueprints for how to understand his own extinguishment on a micro-linguistic level.[27] This structure is most visible in his fetish for the perfective tense, via which he attempts to organize his exterior to match his interior world. He defines the tense for his students using the logic of completion, but his examples are macabre and portend his own disgrace: 'drink and drink up, burned and burnt. The perfective, signifying an action carried through to its conclusion. How far away it all seems! I live, I have lived, I lived' (71).[28] David's key example, to which he returns time and again, is the difference between burned and burnt up. The distinction is not only one of closure but also a fundamental change to the constitution of the thing being described. David is burned by the attackers who raped his daughter, doused with gasoline and set on fire. Looking at himself in the mirror, he sees a man if not fully extinguished, then at the very least burnt up.

The OED's remarkably fecund etymology for extinguish is worth attention here. The history of the word's forcefulness features literary examples, including 1590's 'to suppress': 'A booke conteyninge so disordered matter, that yt should be extinguished.' My theory of *Disgrace* as a self-extinguishing novel relies on an understanding that literature engages politics not only through expansion of ideas, but also by exchanging one mode of meaning-making for another. However, extinguishing is fundamentally different from censorship, an act of surveillance that Coetzee addresses in *Giving Offense* (1996). Self-extinguishing as a means of writing acts outside the gross impulses of the censor, locating the agency with the author and his novel rather than an external 'apparatus of regulation and control'.[29] Coetzee, as extinguisher, records the disordered matter of Lurie's attachment to ways of reading the nation that are unquestionably colonial, while extinguishing the pre-eminence of that vision. We see Lurie grasping for the language with which to restructure his prominence and meaning to each new place and space he is forced to inhabit, but like the rendering of the clinic dogs, a sublimation has occurred that moves Lurie and his way of reading into a different elemental state, his matter *matters* differently. As I move through three scenes – Soraya's assigned room for sex-work in Cape Town, the rape of Melanie Isaacs and subsequent academic trial at the university and the attack at Lucy's farm – I show how the novel has been structured in order to 'quench', 'obscure by superior brilliance', 'blot out', 'die out', all as a means of self-extinguishing that which it has so carefully dramatized in order to give space for intellectual meaning-making to which the novel does not have access.

EXTINGUISH: TO QUENCH (HOPES, PASSIONS, STRIFE, LIFE, MENTAL FACULTIES); TO SILENCE

Disgrace begins with ignominy. It is not merely that the narrative voice recounts Lurie's weekly engagement with a sex worker who takes on the persona of an 'exotic' type, stage-named Soraya, but also that Lurie believes that 'for a man of his age, fifty-two, divorced, he has, to his mind, solved the problem of sex rather well' (1). It is a grim assessment of desire, one which foreshadows Lurie's rationalization of his rape of Melanie Isaacs. It alerts the reader to Lurie's disordered thinking regarding his ownership of this space, the symbolically loaded 'Windsor Mansions', and of Soraya, whose pleasures are linked to her temperament, 'not effusive … rather quiet, quiet and docile'.[30] The apartment in Green Point, a suburb of Cape Town, 'has become an oasis of *luxe et volupté* ('abundance and sensuous delight'), a description drawn directly from the Baudelaire poem 'An Invitation to Journey' (*L'invitation au Voyage*).[31]

Baudelaire's poem plays like an orientalist dreamscape where vessels arrive filled with the luxuries of elsewhere having travelled from 'the ends of the earth' to 'Clothe the fields/With hyacinth and gold/(*luxe, calme, et volupté*)'. Lurie's comparison of the space of assignation and Baudelairean riches, '*luxe et volupté*', transforms the playacting of Soraya into a metonym for the room itself – full of riches and delights that are his alone.[32] Baudelaire, like Lurie, reads this space as structured for his delight – 'nothing but order', because of his imperial vantage: these are spaces prepared for his imagining. However, when Lurie's desire for Soraya can no longer accommodate the existence of her other clients, he calls her at home, at which points she cancels their commercial relationship: 'I demand you will never phone me here again' (9). He attempts a final act of dominance over her by correcting her grammar: 'Demand. She means *command*,' but there is only silence on the other end of the call. The novel furthers the extinguishing of Lurie from this space of his desirous imaginings with the omission of the word '*calme*' from Lurie's quotation of the Baudelaire. In this pregnant omission we find the novel's development of an intellectual disquiet, an unease with Lurie's position as the centre of the novel's thinking mind.

EXTINGUISH: TO RENDER VOID (A BILL, CLAIM, RIGHT, ETC.)

Much of the drama of the Cape Town section of the novel comes from Lurie's increasingly frenetic attempts to sustain an intellectual dominance in the spaces he inhabits. Lacking his Thursday retreats with Soraya ('the week is as featureless as a desert'), soon he turns his wandering eye to a student in his class, Melanie Isaacs (10). 'Clever enough, but unengaged,' Melanie presents an undistinguished landscape for Lurie's desire. He goes about renaming her 'Melaní: the dark one,' after judging Melanie 'not a good name for her' (16). She is suddenly exotic, with 'almost Chinese cheekbones', and as with the vessels on Baudelaire's canals, she is affixed with gold: 'the gold baubles on her belt match the gold balls of her earrings' (10).[33] In a perverse repackaging of Romantic conceptions of the aesthetic, Lurie tells Melanie that 'a woman's beauty does not belong to her alone', that it is her duty to share it (and with *him*) (16). He proceeds to rape Melanie soon after this first encounter, an act he cruelly differentiates as 'not rape, not quite that, but undesired nevertheless, undesired to the core ... like a rabbit when the jaws of the fox close on its neck' (23). His rationalization is nothing more than a confession with the veneer of metaphor to fold it within his literary universe.

The substitution of contractual sex for rape puts the lie to the transactionality of sex with Soraya, showing how both interactions rely on the imaginative eclipsing of the actual person. The subsequent deliberations – loosely understood as a trial for assault – have been compared to Coetzee's misgivings about the Truth and Reconciliation Commission.[34] Lurie refuses the committee's decision that he read a statement of guilt and show remorse. Even when the committee attempts to save him from himself, with an offer of counselling, Lurie makes it clear that he will not submit to any change to his ways of seeing the world: 'I am not receptive to being counselled' (49). His refusal to ape sincerity in reading a confession to the tribunal comes with the consequence of the loss of his position, and while the novel never gives us Melanie's direct testimony, the very thing we desire in building a picture of the novel's ethics, Lurie's claim to Melanie and to his place within the university have been rendered void.[35]

EXTINGUISH: TO PUT A TOTAL END TO ... BLOT OUT OF EXISTENCE

There is a perverse joke that sits jarringly in the middle of the farm attack. Lurie is locked inside a lavatory as he listens to the attackers loot the property. Having earlier in the novel admitted to knowing 'not a word' of Zulu or Xhosa, he finds that the attack clarifies his limitations:

He speaks Italian, he speaks French, but Italian and French will not save him here in darkest Africa. He is helpless, an Aunt Sally ... Mission work: what has it left behind, that huge enterprise of upliftment? Nothing that he can see.

(93)

The sardonic tone is unmissable here, and whether Lurie thinks in precisely these racist terms is less important than feeling the free indirect discourse flexing its devastating critique of Lurie's insufficiency in reacting to this event at Lucy's farm. And the distance of that voice from Lurie himself allows the novel to place the Romance languages alongside the colonial project in the most unflattering light. The attackers, now rapists, take the truck, the guns and do away with the guard dogs, but Lurie persists, the necessary catalyst of the novel's pathos. He will spend the horrible minutes of the attack still working on uses for the perfective tense: staring at his scorched visage, he finds 'everything is burned. Burned burnt' (94).

When David later visits his old Cape Town home, he will find that the perfective has come to extinguish not only him, but the 'arts and sciences' as well. The spaces of his home have been cleared of evidence of his existence, prepared for a 'raiding party' to move in:

He wanders through the house *taking a census of his losses*. His bedroom has been ransacked, the cupboards yawn bare. His sound equipment is gone, his tapes and records, his computer equipment ... The kitchen has been thoroughly stripped ... No ordinary burglary. A raiding party moving in ... Booty; war reparations; another incident in the great campaign of redistribution. Who is at this moment wearing his shoes? Have Beethoven and Janacek ... been tossed out on the rubbish heap?

(172)

We might take David seriously about the consignment of Beethoven to the rubbish heap, if he himself hadn't spent the better part of his exile reducing Byron to an opera featuring a rubber-band banjo, accompanied by a dog. The question is not how do we value these ur-texts of the European intellect, but how are they devalued by being *perfected* in David's imagination?

EXTINGUISH: *PASSIVE*: TO DIE OUT. 1599 INSCENDE … COMBURE, *TILL OF IT SELFE IT EXTINGUISHE*

David Attwell tracks *Disgrace*'s supposed pessimism with Coetzee's 'life and career becoming unmoored from South Africa'.[36] His increasing global mobility as a writer of world-prominence (prizes, residencies, lectures) and subsequent separation from South Africa created the 'ecology in which *Disgrace* was created'.[37] From these peripatetic years around the time of *Disgrace*'s publication, the seed of a life in Adelaide, Australia, is planted. Following his logic would explain why *Disgrace* transforms from a novel about his anxieties over the Truth and Reconciliation Commission in its early drafts, into its published form, the novel of self-extinguishment. As such, *Disgrace* becomes an announcement of his intention to 'bring to an end, cut off,' to extinguish the notion ever present in the early criticism that he speaks for South Africa.[38] The novels that follow bear this theory out quite directly, *mutatis mutandis*, relocating to Australia, an unnamed Spanish-speaking country, or moving into global waters. However, the writer, unlike the character he created, has always seen art as evolving in its capacity for making meaning. It is not a disappearing act he is after, but elemental change. Coetzee's greatest literary feat was to prepare *Disgrace* for sublimation – not unlike Lurie's dogs – a fundamental change of the contexts within which it is read. Like vapour from ice, the extinguished novel becomes more diffuse, more present, even as it abandons a certain authority to speak on behalf of the nation. *Disgrace*'s lasting legacy is its willingness to clear a path for the writers and thinkers yet to come.

NOTES

1. Afro-pessimism here refers to representations of the Global South as perpetually in a state of violent chaos and social decline. Its meaning is distinct from Frank Wilderson's use of the term to refer to slavery as the permanent condition for Black people in the United States in his *Afropessimism*.
2. As Andrew van der Vlies aptly puts it: 'Reading *Disgrace* as primarily or only about post-Apartheid South Africa arguably diminishes the novel's power and underestimates the demands it makes on the reader'. Van der Vlies, *J. M. Coetzee's* Disgrace, 17.
3. Ulhmann, *J. M. Coetzee*, 167.
4. Tony Morphet describes the discussions around teaching the novel as a fracture between literary appreciation and the political violation of norms that are seen as fundamental to a multiracial, democratic society:

    'The results of the departmental reading were startling … All readily agreed that the prose was distinguished, but the sense of a violation of the canons of a liberal and humanist study of literature was deep and intense … The book would be a danger to students. Nevertheless, we went ahead and taught it'. Morphet, 'Reading *Disgrace* in South Africa', 15.

5. While not a perfect scan, *Disgrace*'s opening line, 'For a man of his age, 52, divorced, he has, to his mind, solved the problem of sex rather well', echoes Austen's opening of *Pride and Prejudice*, 'It is a truth universally acknowledged, that a single man in possession of a good fortune, must be in want of a wife', well enough to tempt a comparison.

6. Spivak, 'Ethics and Politics in Tagore, Coetzee', 24.
7. David Atwell's locates the germ of *Disgrace* in Coetzee's 'misgivings about whether ordinary people were capable of living up to the spirit of moral triumph that was taking hold of the nation'. Atwell, *J. M. Coetzee and the Life of Writing*, 197.
8. In Donadio, 'Out of South Africa'.
9. Klaaste, *Sowetan*, 9.
10. Marais, 'J. M. Coetzee's *Disgrace*', 32.
11. Boehmer, 'Not Saying Sorry', 350.
12. Graham, 'Reading the Unspeakable', 443.
13. Mardorossian, 74. Panashe Chigumadzi reframes the question of *Disgrace*'s staging of a Black on white assault, to ask, 'What does the book have to say about the body of a black woman in South Africa? Or, if we try it another way: What questions does my body, the body of a black woman in South Africa, ask of David's story?' Chigumadzi, 'Rights of Conquest'.
14. McDonald, 'Disgrace Effects', 326.
15. Ibid., 330.
16. Attwell, 'Race in *Disgrace*', 334. Attwell claims that the 'least complex – and, arguably, least interesting – area of the novel's performance', is its 'socially mimetic function'. Attwell, 'Race in *Disgrace*', 332.
17. Attwell, 'Race in *Disgrace*', 340.
18. See Attridge, *Ethics of Reading*, 162–82; Marais, 'J. M. Coetzee's *Disgrace*'.
19. Uhlmann, *J.M. Coetzee*, 169.
20. Attridge, *Ethics*, 179, 182. It is possible to find commonality both with Timothy Bewes's position that 'Apartheid is ... a condition of possibility' for Coetzee's novels (Bewes, *The Event*, 159), while following Attridge's theory that the novels are 'not a lesson to be learned or a system to be deployed' (Attridge, *Ethics of Reading*, 190).
21. D'Souza, 'In Retrospect'.
22. Bewes puts disgrace in the larger context of shame, arguing convincingly that this is the great dilemma of the postcolonial writer, and the event of form in the contemporary novel. Bewes, *The Event*, 32.
23. Atwell details how *Disgrace* has overtaken Alan Paton's *Cry the Beloved Country* in that position. Atwell, *Life of Writing*, 191.
24. Van der Vlies, *Reader's Guide*, 78.
25. For excellent examples of theoretically driven responses, see Dancer, 'Between Belief'; Dickinson, 'Feeling, Affect, Exposure; and Babcock, 'Regrounding the Secular'.
26. Considering the difficulties of writing *Life & Times of Michael K*, Coetzee struggled not with 'how to write this story ... the problem is to *introduce consciousness into it*'. Attwell, *Life of Writing*, 114.
27. Marais' essay deals with Lurie's imagination outside of the binary choice of recuperation or dismissal.
28. Sanders argues persuasively that the grammar of *Disgrace* actively rejects the perfective tense. Saunders, '*Disgrace*', 371–2.
29. Coetzee, *Giving Offense*, xi.
30. Ibid.
31. In the poem, the speaker imagines the subject of his adoration as identical to the geography of the place to which he longs to travel:To love and die/In the land *that is like you!* ... There nothing but order and beauty dwell, Abundance, calm, and sensuous delight *(luxe, calme, y volupté)*. Baudelaire, 'An Invitation to Journey.'
32. Even Soraya's name has become 'a popular nom de commerce' (8).

33. Scholars have asserted that descriptions of Melanie point to her being coloured. But her 'exoticism' exists as a function of Lurie's intellectual disposition.
34. Atwell, *Life of Writing*, 197. See also Boehmer, 'Not Saying Sorry' for a discussion of reparations.
35. In a startling example of art outwitting criticism, the writer Michelle Cahill attempts to draw Melanie's voice out of the lacuna of *Disgrace*'s narrative in 'Letter to John Coetzee'. Cahill paints this revealed Melanie 'as eloquent and empowered, rather than as a silenced victim'. Graham, 'Intercepting Disgrace', 5.
36. Atwell, *Life of Writing*, 190.
37. Ibid., 190.
38. OED, 'Extinguish'.

WORKS CITED

Attridge, Derek. *Ethics of Reading*. Chicago: University of Chicago University Press, 2004.
Attwell, David. *J.M. Coetzee and the Life of Writing: Face to Face with Time*. New York: Viking, 2015.
Attwell, David. 'Race in *Disgrace*'. *Interventions: The International Journal of Postcolonial Studies* 4, no. 3 (2002): 331–41.
Babcock, David. 'Regrounding the Secular: Forms of World Sharing in J. M. Coetzee's *Disgrace*'. *MFS Modern Fiction Studies* 67, no. 3 (2020): 421–42.
Barnard, Rita. 'Prologue: Why Not to Teach Coetzee'. In *Approaches to Teaching Coetzee's* Disgrace *and Other Works*, edited by Laura Wright, Jane Poyner and Elleke Boehmer, 31–42. New York: MLA, 2014.
Baudelaire, Charles. 'Invitation to Journey'. Oxford Lieder. https://www.oxfordlieder.co.uk/song/2632.
Bewes, Timothy. *The Event of Postcolonial Shame*. Princeton: Princeton University Press, 2011.
Boehmer, Elleke. 'Not Saying Sorry, Not Speaking Pain: Gender Implications in *Disgrace*'. *Interventions: The International Journal of Postcolonial Studies* 4, no. 3 (2002): 342–51.
Chigumadzi, Panashe. 'Rights of Conquest, Rights of Desire: Panashe Chigumadzi Considers the Black Female Body through a Return to J. M. Coetzee's *Disgrace*'. *Johannesburg Review of Books*, 4 September 2017. https://johannesburgreviewofbooks.com/2017/09/04/rights-of-conquest-rights-of-desire-panashe-chigumadzi-considers-the-black-female-body-through-a-return-to-jm-coetzees-disgrace/.
Coetzee, J. M. *Disgrace*. New York: Penguin, 1999.
Coetzee, J. M. *Giving Offense: Essays on Censorship*. Chicago: University of Chicago Press, 1996.
Dancer, Thom. 'Between Belief and Knowledge: J. M. Coetzee and the Present of Reading', *Minnesota Review* 77 (2011): 131–42.
Dickinson, Phillip. 'Feeling, Affect, Exposure: Ethical (In)Capacity, the Sympathetic Imagination, and J. M. Coetzee's *Disgrace*'. *Mosaic: An Interdisciplinary Critical Journal* 46, no. 4 (2013): 1–19.
Donadio, Rachel. 'Out of South Africa'. *New York Times*, 16 December 2007.
D'Souza, Tony. 'In Retrospect: "Disgrace," Coetzee's Masterpiece'. *National Book Critics Circle*, 31 March 2008. https://www.bookcritics.org/2008/03/31/in-retrospect-disgrace-coetzees-masterpiece/.
Graham, Lucy Valerie. 'Intercepting *Disgrace*: *Lacuna* and Letter to John Coetzee'. *Safundi* 21, no. 2 (2020): 166–75.
Graham, Lucy Valerie. 'Reading the Unspeakable: Rape in J. M. Coetzee's *Disgrace*'. *Journal of Southern African Studies* 29, no. 2 (2003): 433–44.
Head, Dominic. *The Cambridge Introduction to J. M. Coetzee*. Cambridge: Cambridge University Press, 2009.
Klaaste, Aggrey. 'Odious Terre'Blanche Is a Cartoonist's Dream'. *Sowetan*, 3 April 2000: 9.
Marais, Mike. 'J.M. Coetzee's *Disgrace* and the Task of the Imagination'. *Journal of Modern Literature* 29, no. 2 (2006): 75–93.
Mardorossian, Carine. 'Rape and the Violence of Representation in J. M. Coetzee's *Disgrace*'. *Research in African Literatures* 42, no. 4 (2011): 72–83.
McDonald, Peter. 'Disgrace Effects'. *Interventions* 4, no. 3 (2002): 321–30.

Morphet, Tony. 'Reading Coetzee in South Africa'. *World Literature Today* 78, no. 1 (2004): 14–24.
Nixon, Rob. 'Review of Katie Kitamura's Gone to the Forest'. *New York Times Book Review*, November 2012. https://www.nytimes.com/2012/11/11/books/review/gone-to-the-forest-by-katie-kitamura.html.
Sanders, Mark. 'Disgrace'. *Interventions* 4, no. 3 (2002): 363–73.
Spivak, Gayatri Chakravorty. 'Ethics and Politics in Tagore, Coetzee, and Certain Scenes of Teaching'. *Diacritics* 32, no. 3/4 (2002): 17–31.
Ulhmann, Anthony. *J.M. Coetzee: Truth, Meaning, Fiction*. London: Bloomsbury, 2020.
Van der Vlies, Andrew. *J.M. Coetzee's* Disgrace: *A Reader's Guide*. London: Continuum, 2010.
Wicomb, Zoë. 'Culture beyond Color'. *Transition*, no. 60 (1993): 27–32.
Winicomb, Zoë. 'Translations in the Yard of Africa'. *Journal of Literary Studies* 18, no. 3/4 (2000): 209–23.
Wilderson, Frank III. *Afropessimism*. New York: Liveright, 2020.

CHAPTER FOURTEEN

J. M. Coetzee's apartheid-era criticism

XIAORAN HU

In a lecture named 'What Is a Classic?', given in Graz, Austria, in 1991, and published as the opening essay in the collection *Stranger Shores: Essays 1986–1999* (2001), J. M. Coetzee offers a 'personal' reading of T. S. Eliot's lecture of the same title given in London in 1944. Eliot's tribute to Virgil's *Aeneid* as the originary classic of Western European civilization, Coetzee argues, is open to scrutiny when read alongside Eliot's own life as well as 'the life of Europe' in his time.[1] For Coetzee, Eliot's flippant remarks about the then-raging war (being referred to only once as 'accidents of the present time') and his evasiveness about his American origins suggest a complicated, even if most likely unconscious, motivation behind his extolling of the Classical tradition. And, Coetzee argues, if one regards Eliot's entire poetic enterprise as a project of self-making, the oeuvre might be read as his attempt to redefine himself in a lineage of European literary tradition that can be traced back to Virgil.[2] But Coetzee proposes that there is another explanation, a starker one, for Eliot's enterprise of self-fashioning: to sidestep the reality of the provincialism of Eliot's own origins, 'the reality of his not-so-grand position', as Coetzee puts it, 'as a man whose narrowly academic, Eurocentric education had prepared him for little else but life as a mandarin in one of the New England ivory towers'.[3]

Far from downplaying Eliot, however, Coetzee finds in him a kindred spirit, 'using Eliot the provincial as a pattern and figure of [him]self'.[4] Coetzee proceeds to describe an incident he remembers from his teenage years in South Africa, when, as a fifteen-year-old, he experienced a moment of revelation on hearing the music of Bach for the first time. With a self-deprecatingly humorous remark, Coetzee draws a parallel between his encounter with Bach and Eliot's with Virgil. Such 'displaced' recognitions of Western European culture by writers of provincial descent in the present age are not a breach of the inherent value of a classic, if there is such value, but rather suggest the historical conditioning of classics of *all* kinds. Instead of some timeless qualities that guard a classic against the trials of history, it is in fact the multiple historical experiences and interpretations of a work, especially work of an interrogative or antagonistic nature, that truly constitute 'part of the history of the classic, inevitable and even to be welcomed'.[5]

In this way, Coetzee's Bach and Eliot's Virgil share similar attributes. They are examples of the ways in which the past may serve as shaping forces that are 'tangibly felt' in the lives of those who are living in their own historical presents.[6] The fact that a colonial writer's claim on a European classic might be a contestable issue only makes the classic more powerful. The function of criticism, as Coetzee concludes at the end of the lecture, is to participate in the interrogation of the classic in order to 'ensure its survival'. And criticism can be seen, in Coetzee's words, as 'one of the instruments of the cunning of history'.[7]

'What Is a Classic?' encapsulates one of Coetzee's enduring concerns in his critical works: namely, to explore the fraught relationship between literary aesthetics and historical experiences. His reading of Eliot is an example of the ways in which new critical energies arise out of the interplay between literary writing itself and a historical understanding of the socio-political forces that have shaped the writer as a person. Written near the end of the apartheid era, the lecture also has strong 'personal' relevance to the historical situation of Coetzee's own life. Residing in South Africa and working as an academic at the University of Cape Town between 1972 and 2002 – which is to say, throughout the period of the worst excesses of late-apartheid rule – Coetzee's readings of authors and works of diverse origins are in one way or another intricately bound up with his critical engagements, elusive and indirect as they are, with the political situation in South Africa. In this chapter, I will discuss these issues in Coetzee's apartheid-era criticism and illustrate some of his ideas about the interconnectedness between literary forms on the page and historical experiences of the writer, especially in relation to the dialectics between his own 'South Africanness' and his transnational or global scope.

In recent years, an increasing amount of scholarly attention has been paid to Coetzee's critical writing, seeing it as having independent value in his intellectual and literary importance rather than simply being subordinate to his fiction. His writing often engages with the complex relationship between criticism and fiction, too. In a chapter that discusses Coetzee' criticism, Carrol Clarkson points out that the 'critique of assumptions about the relation between fiction and critical writing' has been one of Coetzee's crucial concerns since the onset of his writing career.[8] Coetzee was in fact trained as a literary critic before he established his reputation as a novelist. Before the publication of his first novel, *Dusklands* (1974), he wrote a doctoral dissertation on Samuel Beckett, applying the method of statistical analysis to Beckett's style. Some of his earliest academic works, written in the United States, are published in revised form in the collection of essays and interviews *Doubling the Point* (1992). While these early writings clearly show Coetzee engaging with specific fields of scholarly and intellectual endeavour, including structural linguistics, computer programming and mathematics, crucial to his later development as a writer, they also indicate the beginnings of the constellation of a particular set of problems arising out of the encounter between his very Western intellectual background and the social realities and hyper-politicized intelligentsia of apartheid South Africa. The anxieties and critical debates surrounding such an encounter after Coetzee's return to South Africa in 1972 and before his emigration to Australia are in fact significant undercurrents in his intellectual development during this period.

Coetzee's supposed evasiveness about his political commitments, especially concerning the struggle against the apartheid regime, has been a topic of much debate among his critics. In an oft-cited review of his *Life & Times of Michael K* (1983), Nadine Gordimer expressed anxiety about the book's protagonist for not being an active participant in the making of history. 'A revulsion against all political and revolutionary solutions', Gordimer writes, 'rises with the insistence of the song of cicadas to the climax of the novel'.[9] Coetzee's own defence of his literary practice is based on the notion of the novel as a singular, autonomous discourse, independent from the dictates of history. In the speech 'The Novel Today' (1988), he argues that the novel 'operates in terms of its own procedures and issues in its own conclusions, not one that operates in terms of the procedures of history and eventuates in conclusions that are checkable by history'.[10] Often citing this statement, Coetzee's defenders have in various ways dismissed the criticism of his highly self-reflexive metafictions as a passive or politically 'irresponsible' gesture. David Attwell, for example, famously describes Coetzee's novels as works of 'situational metafiction', in which 'modern Western intellectual currents flow into the turbulent waters of colonialism and apartheid'.[11] While Coetzee's novels do, from time to time, show his deliberate withdrawal from direct commentary on South African politics, his critical works from the apartheid era are much more straightforwardly engaged in this respect. In an interview in *Doubling the Point*, Coetzee points out that the differences between writing fiction and criticism lie exactly in the fact that 'stories are defined by their irresponsibility', while criticism is implicitly bound up with 'a responsibility towards a goal'.[12] Some of his literary and cultural commentaries take the form of scholarly engagement, while some are essays, book reviews or lectures first published in a range of sources. The voice that emerges from this criticism actively and 'responsibly' explores the ways in which the inheritance of the European literary tradition, along with the influence of structural linguistics and post-structural theory, can or cannot be used to express the experience of South Africa's 'special' colonial and postcolonial situation.

Published in the late 1980s, towards the end of the apartheid era, when censorship control had started to loosen up, *White Writing* (1988) was Coetzee's first book-length critical study. It remains one of the most original academic engagements with white literary culture in colonial and early apartheid-era South Africa. Taking up the subject of landscape, the study examines the literary genres and forms (in English and Afrikaans) that inscribed the land from the early colonial period in the nineteenth century up to the point of the Nationalist Party's rise to power in 1948. Coetzee offers sensitive close readings of the writers he examines, tightly weaving his discussion of the formal and stylistic features of each work into a discussion of their historical situatedness. He gives a much-quoted definition of 'white writing' as 'generated by the concerns of people no longer European, not yet African'.[13] The emergence of a white South African literary culture, in Coetzee's analysis, results from the growing tension between writers' colonial experience and a literary language inherited from their European forebears. In the works of the first colonial travellers in the eighteenth and early nineteenth centuries, such as the travelogues of William Burchell and the verses of Thomas Pringle, the aesthetic taste nurtured on European picturesque art is problematized in its encounter with the South African landscape. As Coetzee suggests, the crucial question that these earliest colonial writers initiated in the history of colonial literature in South Africa is whether the heritage of their own European literary culture is adequate to describe the African landscape. Following the early, cautious attempts by Pringle to answer this question, Coetzee sees South African poetry in English until the mid-twentieth century as a project of strenuous effort. Works by Guy Butler and Sydney Clouts seek both a dialogue with, and a way to describe, an empty, alienating and unresponsive landscape.

This poetic vision of South Africa as an empty and silent land has its echoes in novels, too. In this regard, Coetzee pays his special tribute to the late-Victorian novelist Olive Schreiner and her classic anti-pastoral novel *The Story of an African Farm* (1883), which depicts an African farm that 'seems to lie outside history, outside society'.[14] 'Rather than taking Schreiner's farm as a realistic representation of an African stock farm', Coetzee suggests, it should be read 'as a figure in the service of her critique of colonial culture', especially 'in her assertion of the alienness of European culture in Africa'.[15] Coetzee reads Schreiner's critical stance alongside more conservative novelistic visions. Pauline Smith's farm, for example, shows a nostalgic longing for an idealized and stable order of peasant culture, while C. M. van den Heever's *plaasroman* ('farm novel' in Afrikaans) strives to depict an ideal (white) Afrikaner consciousness to illuminate a natural connection between farmers and land. On the one hand, Coetzee sees both Smith's and Van den Heever's literary creations as responses to the historical process of the increasing capitalist modes of production in rural farms that start to surface in the 1920s and 1930s. On the other, he traces their novelistic discourse to European sources both in England and in Germany. Sarah Gertrude Millin offers a much more problematic case for adopting conservative European discourses to depict South Africa. Adapting respectable European scientific and historical thought that involved a discourse of blood and degeneration, Millin's novels end up depicting race in a manner that is outdated and offensive to modern readers. Rather than reading this as Millin's own racial prejudice, however, Coetzee sees her writing as 'a response to formal problems that faced her as a colonial writer working in the medium of the novel'.[16]

The problems of appropriating European discourse to describe the local situation in South Africa start to take a different turn in the country's peculiar 'postcolonial' state after 1948. For writers including Coetzee, the surge in Afrikaner nationalism, as well as counter-ideologies of liberalism and radicalism, became the key discursive arenas where one had to find a literary voice. In a similar vein to Coetzee's analyses of white colonial writers' struggles over the tensions between their own experiences and the only available forms of thought and culture at their disposal in their time, his reviews of contemporary Southern African writers – many of them included in his collection of essays *Stranger Shores* (2001) – are also particularly concerned with exposing the tension between the inherent ambiguities of these writers' own experiences, and their proclaimed political and ideological commitments. Many of these essays were first published as reviews in the *New York Review of Books,* or as introductions. In similar fashion to his 'biographical' approach to reading T. S. Eliot (setting Eliot's literary aspirations against his 'life'), Coetzee's readings of his fellow Southern African writers often turn to their autobiographies and memoirs to point out the gaps surrounding the overt political motives of their writing. In reading Doris Lessing's autobiography, for example, he focuses on her attitude towards her commitment to the Communist Party in her youth. While Lessing clearly regrets this experience after witnessing the atrocities of the Stalin government, her exploration of a Communist past in her autobiography 'cannot get to the bottom of why she did what she did'.[17] Coetzee reads this obscurity as Lessing's gesture of confession; she does not intend to take a politically correct position, but rather to see the truth of the self as unfathomable and therefore unforgivable.[18] In his reading of anti-apartheid Afrikaans-language poet Breyten Breytenbach's memoirs, Coetzee observes that Breytenbach's constant, somewhat ambivalent exploration of his links with his own Afrikaner origins underpins his maverick attitude towards all political sides in both apartheid and post-apartheid South Africa.[19] The failure of their committed liberalism in the gradually left-leaning political climate in South Africa after the 1970s also manifests in the writings of Alan Paton and Helen Suzman. Coetzee points out that Paton's collection of essays, *Save the Beloved Country,* is 'boring and monotonous': 'neither his friends nor his foes are brought to life by his words'.[20] The veteran liberal parliamentarian Suzman's memoir, he writes, has 'a tired and incurious quality' and 'the air of a recital given so many times before that it has become affectless'.[21]

In the same collection, Coetzee's comments on Gordimer, who is perhaps the most prominent representative of the liberalist strain in South African literary culture, focus on the historical crossroads between failing liberalism and rising Leftist radicalism in South Africa during the 1970s. Instead of reading Gordimer's novels alone, Coetzee takes a comparative approach, focusing on her recourse to the Russian writer Ivan Turgenev in order to explain the conflicts between Gordimer's allegiance to a European literary-political tradition, and the growing demands from radical Black writers to repudiate such Eurocentric tradition altogether. Drawing on the similarities between 1850s Russia under the repressive rule of Tsar Nicholas I and South Africa under the apartheid regime, Coetzee points out the similarly ambivalent feelings that Turgenev and Gordimer share as liberals towards radicals. Like Turgenev, Gordimer can be read as 'sympathizing with [the radicals'] ardor and dedication while resisting their indifference toward what they saw as the museum of the past, yet all the while doubting her own right to reserve her position, or even to have any position at all'.[22]

Rather than offering a critique of Gordimer's alleged political commitment, Coetzee's reading argues that her ambiguous political orientation is in fact the driving force behind her creative and theoretical exploration of the form of the English novel against the backdrop of the changing political climate in apartheid South Africa. The idea that ambiguous and uncertain political positions might be a source of creative and critical power is explored more comprehensively in another of Coetzee's essay collections, *Giving Offense* (1996), which examines the subject of censorship. In the preface, Coetzee describes his overall approach to the censor as 'an uncertain critique [...] dominated by the spirit of Erasmus'.[23] Learning from Erasmus's refusal to take sides with either the Lutheran radicals or the Papacy, Coetzee defines such a stance of uncertainty as '*non*position' – 'a position not simply impartial between the rivals but also, by self-definition, off the stage of rivalry altogether'.[24]

The essays collected in *Giving Offense* were first published in academic journals between 1988 and 1993. Coetzee's analyses meticulously follow this principle of *non*position, revealing the relationship between the censor and literary productions under censorship as not one of rivalry but internalization. Writers working under the repressive eye of 'the censor' (of either a political or ethical nature) respond to the existence of 'the censor' in more complex ways than straightforward confrontation. Appropriating the metaphorical language of psychoanalysis, Coetzee describes the censor as a 'parodic version of the figure-of-the-father' who intrudes into 'the intimacy of the writing transaction' by force, thereby destroying the entire balance of the inner drama of the writer's self.[25] In the case of the famous trial of D. H. Lawrence's *Lady Chatterley's Lover*, for example, the author's main defence is his attempt to break social taboos that the progress of Western civilization over the years has gradually set upon the language of sex and the human body. Beyond the author's own defence, what Coetzee exposes in his reading is that Lawrence's work is in fact exactly the result of incorporating the idea, or 'the taint', of taboo itself, rather than drawing a *cordon sanitaire* around it.[26] In revealing the complex interactive dynamic between the writer and the censor of the authoritarian state, Coetzee turns to some controversial moments in some dissident writers' lives, such as the Soviet poet Osip Mandelstam's unpublished ode to Stalin, and Breyten Breytenbach's open apology to the then South African prime minister John Vorster. In both cases, the 'power' of the state over the writer shows itself not so much as an 'external' force as an 'internal' encroachment on the writer's selfhood, which eventually is manifested in their writing.[27] For more polemical writers like Solzhenitsyn and André Brink, the distinction between the discursive mode of the state's attack on them and that of their denunciation of the state is more and more blurry, as both have been in a long struggle with the censor throughout their writing careers. By attributing madness to the state, Solzhenitsyn is in fact mimicking the language of the repressive regime in its judgment of him. The antagonism between Solzhenitsyn and the Soviet state thus becomes an illustration of 'the dynamic of spiraling mimetic violence precipitated by a collapsing of distinctions'.[28] Similarly, Brink diagnoses South African society under apartheid as sick and mad, where the author himself and his language are eventually infected by the 'disease' of violence.[29]

The scope of the selection of texts in *Giving Offense* extends from literary writing to broader socio-political discussions, such as the American feminist Katherine McKinnon's opposition to pornography and the work of the apartheid theorist Geoffrey Cronje. The literary writers under discussion also cover a wide range of backgrounds, among which Eastern European writers, especially those working under the repressive Soviet regime, take a special place. While drawing on similarities between the historical conditions of censorship under authoritarian regimes like apartheid South Africa and Stalin's Soviet Union, Coetzee does not lose sight of the distinctiveness of the South African situation. In an interview about the collection, Coetzee states that it was not his intention to provide any general thesis among his eclectic choices of writers from diverse historical and cultural backgrounds;[30] yet the methodology adopted in *Giving Offense* is in a way representative of a prevailing comparative approach in his critical practice. In the same way as he approaches Gordimer, South African writers are often read alongside European, American or Russian writers. This comparative literary vision finds expressions in his novels too, starting from the parallel structure of the Vietnam War and Dutch colonialism in South Africa in his very first novel *Dusklands* (1974). As the rich intertextual sources in Coetzee's novels cover a vast range of nations and historical periods, decoding these sources in relation to his literary output has been one of the most significant aspects in scholarly studies of his work. In this light, his critical essays may provide a pathway for readers and critics to trace some of the important literary influences on his thinking and his novelistic practice.

Seeing himself as a writer benefiting from the long lineage of the history of English literature, Coetzee has shown his substantial critical attention to the legacies of canonical works in the English language, among which eighteenth-century prose, especially the founding figures of the genre of the English novel, Daniel Defoe and Samuel Richardson, takes a special place.[31] While his novel *Foe* is in some way a parody of Defoe's *Robinson Crusoe* and *Roxana*, Coetzee praises Defoe for both his originality in creating the 'realistic form' in the manner of 'fake autobiography',[32] and for Defoe himself as 'a business man trading in words and ideas' with a 'clear sense of what each word or idea weighs, how much it is worth'.[33] In reading Richardson's *Clarissa*, Coetzee knits together the image of the virgin protagonist Clarissa with the age-old Catholic-mystical tradition of the virgin-martyr. Beyond the Puritan-Protestant background of Richardson's own time, Coetzee's reading arrives at the conclusion that the rake Lovelace, whose rape of Clarissa leads to her eventual death, is in fact 'the dark side of the coin of which Dante the pilgrim-lover is the bright, ideal side' (33). This figure of the rake who idolizes a love object to the point of sexual violence finds its secular version in post-apartheid South Africa in Coetzee's own novel *Disgrace* (1999). Its protagonist David Lurie's problematic relationships with women in the novel are interwoven with his teaching and research of Romantic poets including Wordsworth and Byron. In both cases, great traditions of European culture such as Dante and Romantic poets become implicated in acts of violence committed by characters in the novels.

In exposing the patriarchal, colonialist and Eurocentric assumptions underlying literary discourses of a European origin, the nature of Coetzee's literary criticism is not totally distinct from that of his novels. While his novels do exhibit strong critical energies through which the politics of classical literary forms and elements are constantly put into question, his criticism often uses highly creative perspectives from which European canonical works can be read afresh. We can see such fresh approaches to literary classics in the essays collected in *Stranger Shores* (2001). In addition to earlier novelists and poets already mentioned, Coetzee carefully examines Dutch writers (Marcellus Emants, Harry Mulisch, Cees Nooteboom) as well as German figures (Rilke and Kafka) with a particular focus on issues of translation. However, the essays in this collection not only bring together discussions of various European and Southern African writers, but also include reviews of Russian writers (Dostoevsky, Skvorecky and Brodsky) as well as of some of his contemporaries, including fellow 'postcolonial' authors Salman Rushdie, Amos Oz and Naguib Mahfouz. Published mostly in the 1990s, before Coetzee's emigration to Australia in 2000 (which in many ways marked the start of a new phase in his writing), the selection of texts in this collection maps his global and comparative scope in thinking through the complex relationship between politics and literature during the apartheid era. It also directs readers to issues that will develop further after his departure from South Africa, both in his personal and intellectual life.

NOTES

1. Coetzee, *Stranger Shores*, 1.
2. Here Coetzee is alluding to Eliot's famous essay 'Tradition and Individual Talent'. See Eliot, *Selected Prose*, 37–44.
3. Coetzee, *Stranger Shores*, 7.
4. Ibid., 9. In his CNA Award acceptance speech in 1980, Coetzee defines white South African writers' efforts to build 'a new national literature' as in fact 'building on to an established provincial literature'. See Coetzee, 'SA Authors Must Learn Modesty', 16. For a discussion of Coetzee's extolment of the provincial, see Peter D. McDonald's chapter 'J. M. Coetzee: The Provincial Storyteller', in McDonald, *The Literature Police*, 303–20.
5. Coetzee, *Stranger Shores*, 16.
6. Ibid., 13.
7. Ibid., 16.
8. Carrol Clarkson, 'Coetzee's Criticism', 222. For recent works on Coetzee's criticism, see Kossew, 'Criticism and Scholarship'. For more general discussions of his role as a critic, see also, Mehigan and Moser, eds, *The Intellectual Landscape in the Works of J. M. Coetzee*, and Hayes & Wilm, eds, *Beyond the Ancient Quarrel*.
9. Gordimer, *Telling Times*, 402.
10. Coetzee, 'The Novel Today', 3. The piece was first delivered as a speech at a book festival sponsored by the anti-apartheid newspaper *Weekly Mail* in 1987. It was one of the very few occasions where Coetzee responded directly to the pressure being put upon him to display a public position. See Van der Vlies, 'Publics and Personas.'
11. Attwell, *J. M. Coetzee*, 11.
12. Coetzee, *Doubling the Point*, 246.
13. Coetzee, *White Writing*, 11.
14. Ibid., 4.
15. Ibid., 66.
16. Ibid., 138.
17. Coetzee, *Stranger Shores*, 247.
18. This idea of confession, in a secular context, as an endless chain of self-exploration without the possibility of closure echoes one of Coetzee's earlier articles 'Confession and Double Thoughts: Tolstoy, Rousseau, Dostoevsky', which is included in *Doubling the Point*.

19. Coetzee, 'The Memoirs of Breyten Breytenbach', in *Stranger Shores*, 249–60.
20. Coetzee, 'South African Liberals: Alan Paton, Helen Suzman', in *Stranger Shores*, 266.
21. Coetzee, 271.
22. Coetzee, 'Gordimer and Turgenev', *Stranger Shores*, 229.
23. Coetzee, *Giving Offense*, ix.
24. Coetzee, 84. Coetzee developed this argument in an earlier essay on Erasmus: Coetzee, 'Erasmus' *Praise of Folly*: Rivalry and Madness'.
25. Coetzee, *Giving Offense*, 38.
26. Coetzee, 48.
27. See the chapters 'Osip Mandelstam and the Stalin Ode' and 'Breyten Breytenbach and the Reader in the Mirror' in *Giving Offense*.
28. Coetzee, *Giving Offense*, 136.
29. Coetzee, 211.
30. See 'An Interview with J. M. Coetzee', 107–10.
31. Coetzee's strong interest in eighteenth-century prose can be dated back to the early 1980s, when he wrote several articles on the stylistic features of writers including Defoe, Gibbon and Newton, collected in *Doubling the Point*.
32. Coetzee, *Stranger Shores*, 19.
33. Coetzee, 22. Coetzee's Nobel Lecture, 'He and His Man' (2003), in which he gives a fictionalized account of Defoe's 'writing business', confirms the significance of this indebtedness.

WORKS CITED

Attwell, David. *J. M. Coetzee: South Africa and the Politics of Writing*. Berkeley: University of California Press, 1993.
Clarkson, Caroll. 'Coetzee's Criticism'. In *A Companion to the Works of J. M. Coetzee*, edited by Tim Mehigan, 222–34. New York: Camden House, 2011.
Coetzee, J. M. *Doubling the Point: Essays and Interviews*, edited by David Attwell. Cambridge, MA: Harvard University Press, 1992.
Coetzee, J. M. 'Erasmus' *Praise of Folly*: Rivalry and Madness'. *Neophilologus*, no. 76 (1992): 1–18.
Coetzee, J. M. *Giving Offense: Essays on Censorship*. London: The University of Chicago Press, 1996.
Coetzee, J. M. 'An Interview with J. M. Coetzee'. *World Literature Today*, vol. 70, no. 1 (1996): 107–10.
Coetzee, J. M. 'The Novel Today', *Upstream*, vol. 6, no. 1 (1988): 2–5.
Coetzee, J. M. 'SA Authors Must Learn Modesty', *Die Vaderland*, 1 May 1981: 16.
Coetzee, J. M. *Stranger Shores: Literary Essays*. London: Penguin, 2001.
Coetzee, J. M. *White Writing: On the Culture of Letters in South Africa*. New Haven: Yale University Press, 1988.
Eliot, T. S. *Selected Prose*. Edited by Frank Kermode. New York: Harcourt Brace Jovanovich, 1975.
Gordimer, Nadine. *Telling Times: Writing and Living, 1954–2008*. New York: Norton, 2010.
Hayes, Patrick, and Jan Wilm, eds. Beyond the Ancient Quarrel: Literature, Philosophy, and J. M. Coetzee. Oxford: Oxford University Press, 2018.
Kossew, Sue. 'Criticism and Scholarship'. In *The Cambridge Companion to J. M. Coetzee*, edited by Jared Zimbler, 138–51. Cambridge: Cambridge University Press, 2020.
McDonald, Peter D. *The Literature Police: Apartheid Censorship and Its Cultural Consequences*. Oxford: Oxford University Press, 2009.
Mehigan, Tim, and Christian Moser, eds. *The Intellectual Landscape in the Works of J. M. Coetzee*. Rochester, NY: Camden House, 2018.
Van der Vlies, Andrew. 'Publics and Personas'. In *The Cambridge Companion to J. M. Coetzee*, edited by Jared Zimbler, 234–48. Cambridge: Cambridge University Press, 2020.

PART FOUR

Late-style Coetzee

CHAPTER FIFTEEN

The Costello project

ANDREW VAN DER VLIES

In a 2018 interview, J. M. Coetzee relays with delight the story of a friend who, while lecturing on Australian literature, is asked to say something about the Australian writer Elizabeth Costello. 'I mention the story,' Coetzee explains, 'because it shows how a purely fictional being can start to take up residence in the real world'.[1] Indeed the status of fictional characters – as well as that of literary realism *tout court* – is at the heart of the book, published in 2003, that bears this fictional author's name. Presented as a series of 'eight lessons' (along with a curious postscript that grapples with the larger metaphysical problem of language's referentiality), *Elizabeth Costello* features a series of set-piece performances by this curmudgeonly writer that tests the borders of the anglophone novel of ideas, not to mention the patience of readers attuned to less philosophically lively, formally challenging, and bracingly intellectual fare. When Costello turned up as a character in *Slow Man* (2005), Coetzee's subsequent novel, some reviewers despaired. For Ron Charles, writing in the *Washington Post*, her intervention into the life of character Paul Rayment in that novel – declaring herself the author of the prose we have been reading – constituted 'postmodern tedium' that risked 'overwhelming everything else'.[2] What the *everything else* (circumscribed, elided or disavowed) in relation to a work of literary realism might – or ought to – be is precisely the question Coetzee's late-career work, arguably everything that follows the first outings of Elizabeth Costello, has been most interested in exploring.

What I am calling Coetzee's Costello Project includes all those fictions featuring this writer figure, one too easily regarded merely as a surrogate or only marginally mediated mouthpiece for Coetzee himself rather than a character whose outspoken forays into the realm of public-intellectual debate are more usefully regarded as Coetzee's working through, at arm's length, of a series of philosophical and aesthetic challenges that have long occupied his attention.[3] There are points of continuity with earlier work, including a preoccupation with non-human animal relations, complex investigations of the complicity of a protagonist with governing elites and powerful institutions, and the problem of writing itself, cast most particularly in relation to traditions of the novel. *Elizabeth Costello* continues Coetzee's long engagement with Defoe, whose method of 'supply[ing] the particulars, allow[ing] the significations to emerge of themselves' is invoked as a model for realism early in the first chapter – where Costello's 'blue costume' and 'greasy hair' serve as 'details, signs of a modest realism'.[4] In the same chapter, we meet a character whose surname, Moebius (11), alerts us to the illusionism at play: text is all (one) surface, not in any sense a report on the real.[5]

Coetzee's late-style problem is how to perform the barest modicum of realism without entirely breaking fiction's compact with the reader. *Elizabeth Costello*'s implied omniscient narrative voice, for example, labels a walk-on persona 'in the wider business a minor character' (5) about whom it is not important to know more, and informs us that '[t]here is a scene in the restaurant, mostly dialogue, which we will skip' (7).[6] Coetzee had noted in interview in the early 1990s that he preferred the term '[i]llusionism [...] for what is usually called realism', and that '[a]nti-illusionism' – a rejection of realism – was likely 'only a marking of time, a phase of recuperation, in the history of the novel'; the 'question', he suggested, was: 'what next?'.[7] The Costello Project's anti-illusionism, then, might be thought one of several 'phase[s] of recuperation' in a late-style exploration of the limits of the novel as form – succeeded in *Diary of a Bad Year* (2007) by the innovative division of narratives on the same page, the literalization of the death of the author in *Summertime* (2009) and the attenuated allegorical mode of the *Jesus* novels (2013–19).

Costello first appeared at a public event in London in 1996. Invited by PEN International to deliver an address titled 'What Is Realism?', Coetzee instead read a story about an ageing Australian writer delivering – as a prize acceptance speech – a lecture on the same topic.[8] This narrative, published in the journal *Salmagundi* the following year, forms the first chapter (or lesson) of *Elizabeth Costello*, titled 'On Realism'. Subsequent chapters had similar origins, including as the Tanner Lectures at Princeton University in 1997–8 (lessons 3 and 4, also published as *The Lives of Animals* in 1999)[9] and addresses at the University of California Berkeley (1999), Carl Friedrich von Siemens Stiftung in Munich (2001) and the Nexus Institute at Tilburg University in the Netherlands (2002), amongst other venues.[10] Across each of these instalments, Costello's biography gradually emerges: born in 1928 in 'Irish-Catholic Melbourne' (179), resident in London and Paris between 1951 and 1963, and celebrated chiefly for her fourth novel, *The House on Eccles Street* (1969), a reimagining of James Joyce's *Ulysses* from Molly Bloom's perspective – rather as Coetzee's *Foe* (1986) reimagines *Robinson Crusoe*. Costello's *chef d'oeuvre* is perhaps not coincidentally dated the same year as John Fowles's *The French Lieutenant's Woman*, whose famously frame-breaking authorial intervention occurs, like Costello's interruption of *Slow Man*, in chapter 13.[11]

That Costello is Australian seems significant, too. Coetzee had been planning a move from South Africa during the period of earliest composition and *Elizabeth Costello* is the first novel published after his formal emigration. It is as if the character Costello allowed Coetzee to test the subject position of 'Australian author' while the performative mode of the lessons' first outings simultaneously guaranteed a careful disavowal of any alignment with such a speaking position. Laura Wright suggests that Costello might best be read as a form of 'slanted' or 'off-kilter' drag,[12] a 'performative joke' that offers 'an answer in the form of a parody to all of Coetzee's earlier literary engagement with the ethics and challenges of voicing the other'.[13] Tellingly, too, almost all Costello's performances as public-intellectual figure are staged *outside* Australia, variously in the United States (on fictional college campuses in Pennsylvania and Massachusetts), on a cruise ship in the Southern Ocean, in South Africa (in Johannesburg and rural KwaZulu-Natal) and in Amsterdam.[14] These outings allowed Coetzee, Wright continues, to engage 'explicitly with the ways that all of "his women" – but particularly his woman Elizabeth Costello – refuse compliance with his interpretations and frustrate his all-too-conscious attempts to embody and narrate their experiences.'[15] Wright is here alluding to the title of Coetzee's Nobel Prize Acceptance Speech, 'He and His Man', delivered the same year as *Elizabeth Costello*'s publication, which performed a similarly complex – if differently coordinated – play between 'real' author and fictional character: the lecture was a story in the voice of Crusoe about 'his man' Defoe, where another writer might have offered the reverse.[16]

Two preambles to public readings from sections of *Elizabeth Costello* suggest the origins of the narratives and explain the payoffs Coetzee found in a form that blends metafiction, metalepsis and ventriloquism.[17] Introducing a reading from 'The Novel in Africa' (lesson 2) at the Centro Historica Mexico in Mexico City on 18 March 1998, Coetzee deadpanned: 'Once one has made a name for oneself writing stories, one begins to be invited to all corners of the globe to give lectures'.[18] While initially accepting this 'as a fact of life' (being a novelist was merely preparatory examination for 'the really important business of giving lectures'), he came to feel this was not his metier:

> They were bad lectures. The lecture form held no interest to me. The lectures I gave were a waste of time, of my time and of my audience's time. Then one day (as in a story) I said to myself, To hell with lecturing. I will tell stories. And it has been better ever since.[19]

Five years later, on 3 April 2003, prefacing a reading of what would shortly appear as *Elizabeth Costello*'s enigmatic eighth lesson, 'At the Gate', a self-conscious pastiche of (or homage to) Kafka, at the University of Oklahoma, Coetzee explained that its genesis was to be found in an event in Rome some years previously at which he had been asked at short (two hours') notice to participate in a gathering at which writers were to speak about their beliefs. If impromptu public speaking was second nature to Italians, 'brought up in a culture where the rhetorical tradition goes back unbroken to classical Rome', Coetzee suggested, for those like him with a 'chilly northern-European, Protestant inheritance, suspicious of rhetoric, suspicious of fluency in any guise, doubtful that it is possible to tell the truth without endless self-scrutiny, self-interrogation, revision after revision', the request was too much; he declined. However, he continues (again, with a dry humour that is not shared with the very serious Costello),

> being a conscientious Protestant, and therefore full of guilt about unfulfilled obligations, I continued to mull over the question: not the question of what I believe in but the question of how to act, what to say, when you are hauled before the bar, which you certainly will be, and told to present your case. From these concerns, years after the *coloquio* in Rome, 'At the Gate' emerged.[20]

Recalled again and again to a panel and asked to explain her beliefs in a scene that bears comparison with analogous scenes of interrogation in *Waiting for the Barbarians* (1980), *Life & Times of Michael K* (1983) and *Disgrace* (1999), Costello struggles to enunciate a response. 'Her books teach nothing, preach nothing; they merely spell out, as clearly as they can, how people lived in a certain time and place' (207), the text's disarming free-indirect prose informs the reader. At issue here are two key concerns that connect all the lessons in *Elizabeth Costello*, as well as *Slow Man* and subsequent Costello narratives ('A House in Spain', 'As a Woman Grows Older', 'Lies'): the problem of embodiment, and the tension between the discourses in which fiction and history (politics and opinion) operate. Both are questions that have long preoccupied Coetzee himself.

Alongside *Elizabeth Costello*'s implied omniscient narrator's observation that '[r]ealism has never been comfortable with ideas', that '[t]he notion of *embodying* turns out to be pivotal' (9), consider Coetzee's own observation in interview in the early 1990s that '[t]he body with its pain becomes a counter to the endless trials of doubt'.[21] Yet the represented body is distinct from the thing itself,[22] from real suffering in the world and real *bodies* suffering. '[E]*mbodying* turns out to be pivotal' in two senses, then: it is central to the illusionism that sustains realism (the reader suspends disbelief and imagines characters occupying the same ontological level as themselves); and it is pivotal in any distinction between realism ('never [...] comfortable with ideas') and other forms of prose that claim direct referentiality to the world. The latter is the target of *Elizabeth Costello*'s postscript, in which the problem of *any* direct experience of the world's mediation by language is posed.[23] Coetzee's protagonists have wrestled with these 'pivotal' divisions since the start of his career: it is arguably what drives Eugene Dawn mad in *Dusklands*' 'The Vietnam Project' (1974), a text in which photographs serve to represent the real more effectively and horrifyingly; what threatens to do so to Mrs Curren in *Age of Iron* (1990), her position of ironist (in a Rortyan sense) challenged by real suffering in the townships;[24] and what David Lurie must learn to accommodate in contradistinction to his aesthetic commitment to the Romantic sublime in *Disgrace*.

Costello's body itself provides what Michael Valdez Moses terms a 'thematic node' for each episode in *Elizabeth Costello*; their lessons 'thus dilate' (Moses argues) 'around a series of scenes representing the body in agony or in ecstasy, and more specifically the body at the moment that it literally opens up to the material world [...]'.[25] In a later instalment, 'As a Woman Grows Older' (2004), Costello's daughter Helen suggests that her mother's life is of value 'not because what you write contains lessons but because it is a lesson'.[26] It is so because of her compromised, difficult and halting attempts to speak a truth about real suffering beyond the vatic or merely cleverly postmodern (pace *The House on Eccles Street*) in moments that render Costello both vulnerable and ridiculous (her positions are political and emotional not philosophical or 'rational' in a sense valorized by the academy) in set-pieces in which, during performances in carefully described times and places, she rails against the industrial-scale farming of animals for slaughter (lessons 1, 3 and 4) and the dangers of representing evil (lesson 6), or defends a version of the Humanities that descends from Classical Hellenism (lesson 5). In Julian Murphet's astute reading, 'the *embodiment* at stake' in works like *Elizabeth Costello* 'is perilous and so "unstrung" as to be [...] effectively dualistic: ideas like ghosts in the novelistic machine, epiphenomenal and severed from causal efficacy on things as they are' while all around the characters in whose mouths we encounter these ideas 'the body of fiction is falling apart [...]'.[27] For Murphet, the key to understanding the difference between these novels of ideas and Coetzee's earlier quasi-allegorical mode is that the late works become 'allegories of [...] their own failure to amount to allegories'.[28] For Martin Puchner, they are less novels of ideas than of thinking; we see the processes, characters not only sharing opinions but having them tested in the space of the fiction, even losing faith in their own positions.[29] As Liz Anker notes, 'much of the philosophical argumentation that Costello undertakes ... can be seen as "bad philosophy" – riddled with hyperbole, false analogies, and incoherence [...]'.[30] The point then is less the content of Costello's opinions than the tensions she – not to mention her auditors, her son, his wife – intuits between these and her writing.

Whether it is possible for a writer to speak in a discourse whose terms are dictated by others – the state, organized religion, political movements – was a dilemma with which Coetzee himself grappled in the 1980s under pressure to align his fictions clearly with anti-apartheid politics.[31] There seemed little room for nuance or ambiguity in the actions or thoughts of his characters.[32] In response, he explored the attraction of the '*non*position', a refusal to take sides modelled on Desiderius Erasmus's careful navigation of the divide between Luther and the Catholic Church.[33] Attwell argues that Coetzee's engagement with Erasmus offers 'a meditation on what it is like to be a public intellectual in a time of violence, when reason is subordinate to contagion',[34] a dilemma that *Elizabeth Costello* recasts somewhat differently. Even as Costello herself rails against human exceptionalism cast as rationalism ('reason looks to me suspiciously like the being of human thought' [67]), her sister Blanche, who has taken religious orders and is now known as Sister Bridget, accuses her of committing to the 'wrong Greeks'; Elizabeth should have gone for 'Orpheus instead of Apollo', '[t]he ecstatic instead of the rational' (145).[35] Blanche also dismisses Erasmus, despite her Catholicism endorsing Luther's critique of Erasmus for having been 'seduced into branches of study that do not, by the standards of the ultimate, matter' (123). In lesson 4, set on the campus of Appleton College in Massachusetts where Costello's son John, an astrophysicist, teaches, John's wife, Norma, an under-employed philosopher who loses patience with Costello's 'rambling' lecture (75) and dismisses her arguments about animals as 'the kind of easy, shallow relativism that impresses freshmen' (91), charges: 'There is no position outside of reason where you can stand and lecture about reason and pass judgment on reason' (93). For Norma, Costello is finally no different from 'all the other crazy preachers and their crazy schemes for dividing mankind up into the saved and the damned' (113) – that is to say is not unlike Sister Bridget. The lesson here perhaps, as Coetzee himself came to realize in the 1980s, was that there was no ground on which to challenge discourses claiming to be finally authorized or self-evidently true that was not always ground already claimed.[36]

Blanche/Bridget and Norma are but two of the several antagonists or foils for Elizabeth; each of *Elizabeth Costello*'s lessons replicates a structure that has her *recognized* as writer, offer opinions in her own person (rather than as *writer*) and face a series of challenges in public debate or conversation with these foils. Elsewhere these antagonists include Emmanuel Egudu, a Nigerian novelist engaged – like Costello – to lecture on a cruise liner (embodiment is cast as a different kind of problem here, the African novel, Egudu claims, being uniquely *oral*), sundry academics, the (real) writers Robert Duncan and Paul West, and a panel of interrogators 'straight out of Kafka' (209), whose ontological status in relation to the novel's own 'real' is especially challenging. The parable-like eighth lesson sets the stage for the novel's afterword, in which Costello has perhaps morphed into Elizabeth, Lady Chandos, wife of the existentially despairing author of a complaint about the inefficacy of language to Renaissance humanist Francis Bacon ('All is allegory, says my Philip', she complains [229]) in Hugo von Hofmannsthal's 1902 'Letter of Lord Chandos to Lord Bacon'.[37]

Coetzee is here signalling his own long conversation with European Modernist progenitors, including Kafka and Beckett.[38] The latter returns as key intertext in *Slow Man* (as does Wallace Stevens),[39] but it is with Kafka that we see the most sustained engagement in *Elizabeth Costello*, not only in the setting of lesson 8, 'At the Gate', but also in the text about which Costello chooses to lecture at Appleton College, Kafka's 'A Report to an Academy' (*Ein Bericht für eine Akademie*, 1917). In this story an ape, Red Peter, addresses assembled scientists on his transformation to speaking subject nearly indistinguishable from themselves. In response to her son's query (why *this* topic), Costello returns us to the question of embodying: 'It is the embeddedness that is important [...]' (32); 'That ape is followed through to the end, to the bitter, unsayable end, whether or not there are traces left on the page' (33–4).[40] Reason as human exceptionalism is a target here, of course, but Kafka's story also provides Costello with a blueprint for the manipulation of character: Red Peter complains about being subject to experiment, being expected to mate with a female ape, being treated like an exhibit. Is there perhaps drily deadpan humour at play, then, in Costello's apparent invention of a character to whom 'she' makes similar things 'happen' in *Slow Man*, a character, Paul

Rayment, whose initials – PR – are exactly the inverse of Red Peter's? Indeed, Rayment complains at one point that Costello 'treat[s] everyone like a puppet' and she 'should open a puppet theatre, or a zoo':

> There must be plenty of old zoos for sale, now that they have fallen out of fashion. Buy one, and put us in cages with our names on them. *Paul Rayment: canis infelix.* [...] And so forth. Rows and rows of cages holding the people who have, as you put it, *come to you* in the course of your career as a liar and fabulator.[41]

Paul Rayment's name, of course, is heavily overdetermined: *Paul* suggests the apostle, and Costello's character has his own Damascene moment (he is knocked from a bicycle rather than a horse, though his accident also involves something Bright; 20); *Rayment* suggests both counsellor (which the novel renders ironic) and clothing – as if his post-amputation life is the afterlife (he does wonder about this; 233) and all that is left is his shell.

On one level, and setting aside Costello's frame-breaking intervention, *Slow Man*, Coetzee's first novel set in Australia (more specifically in Adelaide, where Coetzee had settled), might be read as a treatment of a migrant's loss. The amputation of Paul's leg is thus (also) metaphorical, but Rayment is a migrant, too, born in France and taken to Australia as a child, returning to France as an adult, before moving back to Australia (192). Paul is cared for most consistently by another migrant, Marijana Jokić (from Croatia). A retired photographer, he collects early photographic images of Australian colonial life, particularly those by another French migrant, Antoine Fauchery (1823–61). Marijana approves: 'Is good you save history. So people don't think this Australia is country without history, just bush and then mob of immigrants. Like me. Like us' (48). Her sixteen-year-old son, Drago, appropriates one of these prized prints and inserts one of his own ancestors digitally into the image. Costello observes (or narrates): 'What harm is there, thinks Drago, in inserting a Jokić into the national memory, even if somewhat prematurely [...]?' (221).

This is one of many instances of prosthetic supplementation or substitution in the novel,[42] from Paul's artificial leg to the mechanical ducks about which Marijana's husband Miroslav is an expert, and the blind woman Marianna who substitutes for Marijana in a tryst Costello arranges for Paul. When this attempt to coax him away from his infatuation with Marijana fails, Costello suggests Paul draw on models from the history of the novel to attempt to be a protagonist of his own narrative – these include *Don Quixote*, whose complex narrative conceits offer an analogue of sorts for *Slow Man* itself.[43] The whole course of the novel's treatment of Paul is rehearsed in Costello's rhetorical questioning of Drago:

> Mr Rayment has an accident as a result of which he loses a leg. He engages a nurse to look after him, and in no time has fallen in love with her. He has intimations that a miraculous, love-born reflorescence of his youth might be around the corner; he even dreams of engendering a son (yes, it is true, a little half-brother to you). But can he trust these intimations? Are they not perhaps a dotard's fantasies? So the question to ponder, given the situation as I have described it, is: what does Mr Rayment, or someone like Mr Rayment, do next?
>
> (138)[44]

Paul repeatedly fails to live up to the expectation of a major character as enunciated by this writer-character, but whether this is an existential or a metafictional dilemma is for the reader to ponder.

Paul, Attwell reminds us, 'is written into being by Costello, but he also resists'.[45] At the end of the book, Costello suggests she and Paul take a trip around Australia together: 'we could tour the whole land, the two of us, the whole of this wide brown land, north and south, east and west. You could teach me doggedness and I could teach you to live on nothing, or nearly nothing' (263). The suggestion of a tour is doubtless an allusion to Defoe's *A Tour Thro' the Whole Island of Great Britain* (1724–37), and possibly an intertextual allusion to 'He and His Man' (as Miroslav's facility with mechanical ducks echoes the duck decoys in Coetzee's Nobel lecture).[46] We leave them in stasis, however, and at odds.

Exhorting him to take charge of his life, Costello (imperfectly) invokes Wallace Stevens, though not by name (simply as 'the American poet fellow'): 'There weaves always a fictive covering from something to something' (158). Kenneth Pellow notes that the allusion is to 'Notes Toward a Supreme Fiction', in which Stevens suggests that '[t]he individual who wishes to be what some existentialists call "authenticated" ought, in Stevens's vision, to construct selves and counterselves [...] in order to isolate the most satisfactory version of self'.[47] There is a sense, then, in which *Slow Man*'s contribution to the Costello Project takes further the complex staging of a mirrored authorial self by splitting the imperfect stand-in into a more complex (and realistic) doubled double, male *and* female, writer *and* displaced metaphorical amputee, Australian and not. Costello's role in the novel is as 'a predator and a parasite', Attwell contends, suggesting that '[t]he authorial self and the self [that is] written into being are subject, it seems, to similar vulnerabilities of need'; 'the novel wants to undo the mystery around these roles and present them in terms that are ordinary and unflattering'.[48] At one point, Rayment finds Costello's *The House on Eccles Street* in a local public library and wonders 'What's wrong with her? Can she not make up characters of her own?' (119). As Pellow observes, '[t]he reference is to Costello's having pilfered characters and settings from James Joyce (also a notorious pilferer), but clearly the joke is as much on Coetzee, for borrowing from himself, as it is on Rayment'.[49]

The joke, one of many in what is by some measures Coetzee's funniest book (one hears *joke* in Jokić),[50] is also on any critic who tries too hard to pin down precisely what or who these characters might be beyond the page. At one point in *Slow Man*, Costello calls Rayment, Marijana, Miroslav, and Drago 'four people in four corners, moping, like tramps in Beckett' (141). Writing in 1970 about point of view in Beckett's *Murphy*, Coetzee described fictions as 'closed systems' or 'prisons' and suggested (in an extended metaphor about writing) that while a prisoner could 'spend his time writing on the walls [...] or making magic jokes about their unreality', they are still in prison.[51] What sometimes 'poses as a problem for the reader of choosing rationally among authorities', he concludes about *Murphy*, might in fact 'be a false problem, a problem designed to yield no solution, or only arbitrary solutions'. 'Fiction', Coetzee adds, 'is the only subject of fiction'.[52]

NOTES

1. Coetzee and Constantini, 'Las literaturas del sur', online.
2. Charles, 'Limping to love', online. Costello rings Paul Rayment's doorbell, seats herself on his sofa and 'recites' words that are very nearly – but not quite – the same as the opening of the novel (rendered in italics on their second iteration). See Coetzee, *Slow Man*, 81, 1. See also Currie, 'Postmodern Narrative Theory', 167.

3. In Attwell's words, Costello is 'an uncanny puppet through whom Coetzee is able to mirror back to society its expectations of the writer as public figure, and subject them to his own inscrutable, and occasionally unscrupulous, effects' (*Face to Face*, 104).
4. Coetzee, *Elizabeth Costello*, 4. Further references parenthetical.
5. See Wright, 'He and His Woman', 34.
6. Currie usefully discusses the 'two internal authors, one who is a character and the other who is a narrator [...]. The authorial narrator, the one who is more than just a focalizer of Costello's mind, is prominent only in the first chapter of the novel, and might be regarded as the primary voice' ('Postmodern Narrative Theory', 159). See also Effe's chapter in this volume.
7. Coetzee, *Doubling the Point*, 27. He has, arguably, remained committed to this 'anti-illusionism', which has turned out to be more than a marking of time.
8. Wicomb, '*Slow Man* and the Real', 16.
9. In a US edition that included responses, and in a UK edition that did not.
10. See Moses, 'King of the Amphibians', 26. On the complex textual history of the lessons, see: Flanery, '(Re-)Marking Coetzee & Costello'; Shillingsburg, 'Textual Criticism, the Humanities, and J. M. Coetzee'.
11. Currie makes a similar point in 'Postmodern Narrative Theory' (163–4).
12. Wright, 'He and His Woman', 30.
13. Ibid., 34.
14. See Steyn, 'Timely, Untimely, Timeless', 461. These settings exclude the more obviously allegorical setting of lesson 8, a teasingly ill-defined border town evoking Kafka-era Austro-Hungary, or indeed those lessons (6, 7) that include extended reminiscences.
15. Wright, 'He and His Woman', 20. See also Wright's chapter in this volume.
16. See further Poyner and Flanery chapters in this volume.
17. I am using Gerard Genette's definition of metalepsis here to refer to 'an intrusion by the diegetic narrator or narratee into the diegetic universe [...]', as quoted by Currie (165).
18. Coetzee, 'Centro Historica Mexico, 1998', 2.
19. Ibid., 2–3. On the development of Costello as character, see also Attwell, *Face to Face*, 213.
20. Coetzee, 'At the Gate', 2.
21. Coetzee, *Doubling the Point*, 248. The statement continues: 'Not grace, then, but at least the body' (ibid.). See also Moses, 'King of the Amphibians', 32.
22. This is a phrase that recurs in a number of Coetzee texts.
23. See Meffan, '*Elizabeth Costello*', 172.
24. Rorty, *Contingency, Irony, and Solidarity*, 187.
25. Moses, 'King of the Amphibians', 31. On embodiment, see also Vermeulen, 'Being True to Fact', and Mascia-Lees and Sharpe, 'Introduction', for an approach that considers the Costello Project's commitment to 'a "grounded metaphysics"' (85) sharing something with anthropological methodologies.
26. Coetzee, 'As a Woman Grows Older', 6. This 'pronouncement', novelist and critic Zoë Wicomb writes, 'I take to assert the heuristic value of reading' ('*Slow Man* and the Real', 7).
27. Murphet, 'Coetzee and Late Style', 95.
28. Ibid., 90.
29. Puchner, 'J. M. Coetzee's Novels of Thinking', 2–5. Attridge calls the represented opinions 'arguings' rather than arguments, 'events staged within the event of the work' (*J. M. Coetzee*, 197–8). In lesson 2, Costello 'is not sure, as she listens to her own voice, whether she believes any longer in what she is saying' (39).

30. Anker, 'Elizabeth Costello, Embodiment, and the Limits of Rights', 174.
31. See Van der Vlies, 'Publics and Personas', 236–9.
32. Nadine Gordimer was famously puzzled by the passivity of Michael K in a 1984 review of *Life & Times* ('The Idea of Gardening'). On this and other engagements with Gordimer that speak to the tension described here, see Van der Vlies, 'Writing, politics, position'. Attwell notes that Coetzee visited the Gordimer archives at the University of Indiana in Bloomington in preparation for writing the Tanner Lectures, suggesting another partial model for Costello (*Face to Face*, 217).
33. Coetzee, *Giving Offense*, 84.
34. Attwell, *Face to Face*, 101.
35. Blanche contends that Elizabeth's position 'enthrone[s] [...] the monster of reason' (123), something against which the latter herself inveighs in her defence of animals (69). Costello elsewhere takes issue with Jonathan Swift, her 'Age of Reason' models instead Rousseau and early Blake (as Coetzee's is Defoe), her Romantic models including Keats for his endorsement of negative capability, a forerunner for the brands of 'sympathetic imagination' (80) she appreciates in Rilke and Ted Hughes (95–103).
36. See Van der Vlies, 'Writing, politics, position', 65–8.
37. See Meffan, '*Elizabeth Costello*', 173.
38. See also chapters by Samolsky and Sheehan, respectively, in this volume.
39. And Conrad, specifically his story 'The Secret Sharer'. See Pellow, 'Intertextuality and Other Analogies', 544–6.
40. Costello regards herself as sharing with Red Peter similar forced performance before audiences whose expectations she can never satisfy (70–1).
41. Coetzee, *Slow Man*, 117. References hereafter parenthetical.
42. On prosthesis, in particular its theological usage and the resonances of substitution and transubstantiation in relation to the novel, see Wicomb, '*Slow Man* and the Real', 11–17, and Mehigan, '*Slow Man*', 201.
43. And to which Coetzee returns in *The Childhood of Jesus*; see Bewes's chapter in this volume.
44. 'Does he blindly follow the promptings of his desire as his desire strives to bring itself to fruition' Costello asks, 'or, having weighed up the pros and cons, does he conclude that throwing himself heart and soul into a love affair with a married woman would be imprudent, and creep back into his shell?' (138). See also Brittan's chapter in this volume on charity and care in *Slow Man*.
45. Attwell, 'Coetzee's Estrangements', 235.
46. *Doggedness* and living on *nothing* echo *Disgrace*, too. See Holmes in this volume.
47. Pellow, 'Intertextuality and Other Analogies', 546.
48. Attwell, 'Coetzee's Estrangements', 235.
49. Pellow, 'Intertextuality and Other Analogies', 544 n10.
50. On humour, see also Marsh's chapter in this volume.
51. Coetzee, *Doubling the Point*, 38. See also Coetzee, 'Eight Ways of Looking at Samuel Beckett', for reflections on monism and dualism, and illuminating asides about Melville and Kafka that are not irrelevant to the issues canvassed in this chapter.
52. Coetzee, *Doubling the Point*, 31.

WORKS CITED

Anker, Elizabeth. '*Elizabeth Costello*, Embodiment, and the Limits of Rights'. *New Literary History* 42, no. 1 (2011): 169–92.

Attridge, Derek. *J. M. Coetzee and the Ethics of Reading*. Chicago: University of Chicago Press, 2004.

Attwell, David. 'Coetzee's Estrangements'. *Novel* 41, no. 2/3 (2008): 229–43.
Attwell, David. *J. M. Coetzee and the Life of Writing: Face to Face with Time*. Oxford: Oxford University Press, 2015.
Charles, Ron. 'Limping to Love'. *The Washington Post*, 25 September 2005. http://www.washingtonpost.com/wp-dyn/content/article/2005/09/22/AR2005092201021.html.
Coetzee, J. M. 'As a Woman Grows Older'. *New York Review of Books* 51, no. 1 (2004): 11–14.
Coetzee, J. M. 'At the Gate, 2003', unpublished TS, Coetzee Papers, box 61.4. ('Coetzee, Long Works: *Elizabeth Costello*, public readings'), Harry Ransom Center, University of Texas, Austin.
Coetzee, J. M. 'Centro Historica Mexico, 1998', unpublished TS, Coetzee Papers, box 61.1 ('Coetzee, Long Works: *Elizabeth Costello*, public readings; "Novel in Africa", 1980–2000 [?]'), Harry Ransom Center, University of Texas, Austin.
Coetzee, J. M. *The Childhood of Jesus*. London: Harvill Secker, 2013.
Coetzee, J. M. *Doubling the Point: Essays and Interviews*. Edited by David Attwell. Cambridge, MA: Harvard University Press, 1992.
Coetzee, J. M. 'Eight Ways of Looking at Samuel Beckett'. *Samuel Beckett Today* 19 (2008): 19–31.
Coetzee, J. M. *Elizabeth Costello: Eight Lessons*. London: Secker & Warburg, 2003.
Coetzee, J. M. *Giving Offense: Essays on Censorship*. Chicago: University of Chicago Press, 1996.
Coetzee, J. M. 'He and His Man'. http://nobelprize.org/nobel_prizes/literature/laureates/2003/coetzee-lecture.html. Also in *Lecture and Speech of Acceptance Upon the Award of the Nobel Prize in Literature, Delivered in Stockholm in December 2003*. New York: Penguin, 2004.
Coetzee, J. M. 'A House in Spain'. *Architectural Digest* 57, no. 10 (October 2000): 68–76. Reproduced in *Three Stories*, 1–22. Melbourne: Text, 2014.
Coetzee, J. M. *The Humanities in Africa. Die Geisteswissenschaften in Afrika*. Munich: Carl Friedrich von Siemens Stiftung, 2001.
Coetzee, J. M. 'Lies'. *The New York Review of Books*, 21 December 2017. https://www.nybooks.com/articles/2017/12/21/lies/.
Coetzee, J. M. *The Lives of Animals*. London: Profile, 1999.
Coetzee, J. M. *The Lives of Animals*, introduction by Amy Gutmann, reflections by Marjorie Garber, Peter Singer, Wendy Doniger and Barbara Smuts. Princeton NJ: Princeton University Press, 1999.
Coetzee, J. M. *Slow Man*. London: Secker & Warburg, 2005.
Coetzee, J. M. and Soledad Constantini. 'J. M. Coetzee: Las literaturas del sur' (Madrid), 28 May 2018, https://www.youtube.com/watch?v=DW1QRdJ9rDg.
Currie, Mark. 'Postmodern Narrative Theory Reading Postmodern Narrative: Coetzee's *Elizabeth Costello* and *Slow Man*'. In *Postmodern Narrative Theory*, 2nd ed., 152–77. Basingstoke: Palgrave Macmillan, 2011.
Flanery, Patrick Denman. '(Re-)Marking Coetzee & Costello: *The* [Textual] *Lives of Animals*'. *English Studies in Africa* 47, no. 1 (2004): 61–81.
Flanery, Patrick Denman. 'Limber: The Flexibilities of post-Nobel Coetzee'. *Scrutiny 2*, 13, no. 1 (2008): 47–59.
Gordimer, Nadine. 'The Idea of Gardening'. *The New York Review of Books* 31, no. 1 (2 February 1984): 3–6.
Mascia-Lees, Frances E. and Patricia Sharpe. 'Introduction to "Cruelty, Suffering, Imagination: The Lessons of J. M. Coetzee"', *American Anthropologist* 108, no. 1 (2006): 84–7.
Meffan, James. '*Elizabeth Costello* (2003)'. In *A Companion to the Works of J.M. Coetzee*, edited by Tim Mehigan, 172–91. Rochester NY: Camden House, 2011.
Mehigan, Tim. '*Slow Man* (2005)'. In *A Companion to the Works of J.M. Coetzee*, edited by Tim Mehigan, 192–207. Rochester NY: Camden House, 2011.
Moses, Michael Valdez. '"King of the Amphibians": *Elizabeth Costello* and Coetzee's Metamorphic Fictions'. *Journal of Literary Studies* 25, no. 4 (2009): 25–38.
Murphet, Julian. 'Coetzee and Late Style: Exile within the Form'. *Twentieth-Century Literature* 57, no. 1 (2011): 86–103.

Pellow, C. Kenneth. 'Intertextuality and Other Analogies in J. M. Coetzee's *Slow Man*'. *Contemporary Literature* 50, no. 3 (2009): 528–52.
Puchner, Martin. 'J. M. Coetzee's Novels of Thinking'. *Raritan* 30, no. 4 (Spring 2011): 1–12.
Rorty, Richard. *Contingency, Irony, and Solidarity*. Cambridge: Cambridge University Press, 1989.
Shillingsburg, Peter. 'Textual Criticism, the Humanities, and J. M. Coetzee'. *English Studies in Africa* 49, no. 2 (2006): 13–27.
Steyn, Jan. 'Timely, Untimely, Timeless: Temporal Limits in J. M. Coetzee's *Elizabeth Costello*'. *Critique* 62, no. 4 (2021): 459–70.
Van der Vlies, Andrew. 'Writing, Politics, Position: Coetzee and Gordimer in the Archive'. In *J. M. Coetzee and the Archive: Fiction, Theory, and Autobiography*, edited by Marc Farrant, Kai Easton, and Hermann Wittenberg, 59–75. London: Bloomsbury Academic, 2021.
Van der Vlies, Andrew. 'Publics and Personas'. In *The Cambridge Companion to J. M. Coetzee*, edited by Jarad Zimbler, 234–48. Cambridge: Cambridge University Press, 2020.
Van der Vlies, Andrew. *Present Imperfect: Contemporary South African Writing*. Oxford: Oxford University Press, 2017.
Van der Vlies, Andrew. 'The Novelist has Entered the Room: J. M. Coetzee's Anti-Illusionism'. *Times Literary Supplement*, 2 September 2005: 9–10.
Vermeulen, Pieter. 'Being True to Fact: Coetzee's Prose of the World'. In *J. M. Coetzee and Ethics: Philosophical Perspectives on Literature*, edited by Anton Leist and Peter Singer, 269–89. New York: Columbia University Press, 2010.
Wicomb, Zoë. '*Slow Man* and the Real: A Lesson in Reading and Writing'. *Journal of Literary Studies* 25, no. 4 (2009): 7–24.
Wright, Laura. 'He and His Woman: Passing Performances and Coetzee's Dialogic Drag'. In *Reading Coetzee's Women*, edited by Sue Kossew and Melinda Harvey, 19–37. London: Palgrave Macmillan, 2019.

CHAPTER SIXTEEN

Diary of a Bad Year

KATARZYNA NOWAK-MCNEICE

Continuing many of the thematic concerns of Coetzee's earlier prose and pointing towards later interests, *Diary of a Bad Year* represents an intermediary bridging moment in the writer's career: in its experimentation with metafiction, it is a successor to *Foe*; in its investigation of writerly and readerly authority, *The Master of Petersburg*; it undertakes a metageneric play with the conventions of diary (reminiscent of *In the Heart of the Country*) and essay (echoing *Elizabeth Costello*). It also suggests preoccupations that will be explored in the books to follow: reflections on mathematics and the classics might be seen as precursors of these ideas in the Jesus novels. *Diary*'s play with generic conventions corresponds to its rejection of a monolithic novelistic authority and enables an examination of the meaning and effects of various narrative modes, which suggests a re-evaluation of the nature of human subjectivity.

Diary is divided into two chapters 'Strong Opinions' and 'Second Diary', which are followed by 'Notes', though its most striking feature is the division of the text on the page into two or three parts divided by a horizontal line. The discrete sections on each page correspond to three voices or authorial positions: the uppermost belongs to an elderly, celebrated author, JC, and is comprised of fragments of essays on a subject of contemporary topics ostensibly commissioned by a German publisher. These are his 'Strong Opinions' and are the most 'writerly' and formal in tone. In Part Two, the 'Second Diary', this top-most strand becomes more personal. The middle section on each page is more private and presents the first-person account of a relationship between JC and Anya, a young woman who lives with her boyfriend Alan in the same apartment building in Sydney. JC employs Anya as his typist; she is well aware of the ageing writer's infatuation, and will eventually play the role of a spiritual companion in the final sections, guiding the writer to his death.[1] The third strand is initially narrated by JC, to be taken over by Anya's subversive narration undermining the supposed harmony between and within the previous two strands.[2] In the 'Second Diary', these 'strong opinions' are presented in a more colloquial form, but because there is no 'First Diary', the chapter title suggests a revision of forceful and public opinions. The bottom-most part is Anya's first-person account: the reader witnesses her involvement with JC – whom she calls Juan or Señor C. – presented from her perspective, as well as her relationship and eventual break-up with Alan, apparently provoked by Alan's plot to rob JC of his money.

This three-part horizontal division of the text means that the reader is faced with a decision about whether to read the pages top to bottom; or follow the individual strands across pages before turning back to pick up another strand, or to go back and forth amongst them. Whatever reading strategy is chosen, it is the reader who exercises autonomy; they are forced to take an active part in the shaping of the narrative.[3]

Critics have noted the formal complexity of the novel, and while some commentators might have dismissed this as a simple postmodern trick (James Woods accusing Coetzee of making 'all the right postmodern noises'[4]), others have recognized an importance that reaches beyond it being simply a ploy. 'For every attempt made by the voice at the top of the page to homogenize, diagnose, and denounce modernity in general as instrumental, valueless, and Machiavellian', Patrick Hayes argues, 'there is a countervoice at the bottom holding it back.'[5] This creates a complex multivocal structure that rests on a balance created by the dynamic exchange of the evolving positions that the three layers of voices represent, none of them actually gaining a dominant position. This structure effectively displays resistance to master narratives, whose necessity has been forcefully argued by Coetzee on numerous occasions. Carrol Clarkson, for instance, claims that '[t]he "position" of the writer, then, is radically multiple – refracted through countervoices that transgress a supposed presence in time and space.'[6] Refraction and multiplication of the writerly positions, I want to argue, correspond to the multiplicity of reader's positions offered through the demand to assume a reading strategy – moving between horizontal and vertical division of the text – which will necessarily differ from one reading to the next.[7]

The move beyond the generic limits of a novelistic genre is suggested in the very title: *Diary of a Bad Year* brings to mind a private endeavour of keeping notes intended for a limited audience (possibly an audience of one), and it is misleading since a significant part of the novel strives to represent an essayistic form.[8] Arthur Rose reaches back to the origins of the essay as a genre to point out that its creator, Montaigne, aimed to take himself as 'the matter of [his] book'.[9] Comparing JC's essayistic self with Montaigne's, Rose points out that the integrity of JC's 'self-as-essay-matter' is compromised: 'The essay depends on the integrity of the "I writing" to validate its thinking-process. Exposing the rhetorical contingency of its moment of writing throws this integrity into disarray.'[10] The temporal dimension of the essay composition, Rose argues, is laid bare before the reader of *Diary*, not only as we read the essays and follow its strong opinions, but also when we partake in the editorial process behind the essays' formation, and as we learn of the opinions of their first critics, Anya and her partner Alan. Because not even JC remains convinced of his strong opinions, and because Anya's views influence his decision to abandon them in favour of softer opinions, the reader is witnessing a process of essay composition which normally remains hidden. In Rose's words, '*Diary of a Bad Year* inscribes a performance of production that leaves the text always open to revision'.[11] Such openness of the text not only exposes the artifice of an essayistic form, but also serves as a reminder that as readers we should never be seduced by the supposed finality of a text.

Diary of a Bad Year explores the limits of fiction as well as of criticism – arguably the larger goal of Coetzee's fiction and critical-writing project. My claim is that while exploring the limits of the authority of novelistic discourse and questioning the unity of the human 'I', *Diary* is invested in subverting the hegemony of anthropocentric discourse. It does so through both formal means as well as through the characters assuming a variety of ideological positions, explored and critiqued from within the text.

SUBVERSION OF AUTHORITY

Diary of a Bad Year tests the meaning of a 'public intellectual', and is concerned with the form of the novel, while also exploring the source of authority in fictional and nonfictional discourse, a recurring theme in Coetzee's oeuvre. Indeed, the subversion of authority and mistrust towards it is inscribed within the text, not only in the metatextual dramatizations of various critical positions, but also explicitly voiced by the narrator. At a pivotal moment in the book, JC abandons his primary strong opinions for another form altogether, that of a diary. After a disagreement with Anya, JC declares, 'I should thoroughly revise my opinions',[12] and in the hope of winning Anya back explains in a note to her: 'I am beginning to put together a second, gentler set of opinions' (145). The character of a writer, be it of strong opinions or a diary, dramatizes the effort to subvert or abandon altogether the hegemonic position of the narrator, and illustrates in writing such dialogic dispersion.[13]

The undermining of the hegemonic narratorial position also takes the form of irony. A case in point is JC's comments on boredom in which he refers to Nietzsche. For Nietzsche, boredom is the emotion demarcating a rather clear border between the human and its other: it is only the human, the supposedly higher, active and creative animal, who may experience boredom. JC corrects this view: 'While it may be so that only the higher animals are capable of boredom, man proves himself highest of all by domesticating boredom, giving it a home' (220). JC's irony lies in the fact that boredom might indeed be a category distinguishing 'higher animals', hence also humans, but it is humans who are the most boring – not bored – of all the creatures, willingly imprisoning themselves in their routine beliefs and accepted notions.

With respect to distinguishing features separating humans from nonhumans, JC's views contrast with those of Anya. Anya makes a connection between the human and the nonhuman in a humorous comparison between man (JC) and bird (a magpie she observes), implying an intimate link between the two. This suggests her acceptance of the continuity among animal species, human and nonhuman, which enables her to characterize them as 'Him and the magpie. Mr. Melancholy and Mr. Magpie, the amoro-dolorous duo' (225). In this description, the two merge in their figurativeness. Metonymically, they stand for what Anya distinguishes as their dominant qualities.

In contrast to the woman's cross-species comparison, JC's reaction reveals the more rigid categories in which he perceives himself and the bird: he describes the magpie as a 'he' and says, 'that is how I think of him, male to the core' (208), imagining a confrontation:

> He (…) walks in slow circles around where I sit. He is not inspecting me. He is not curious about me. He is warning me, warning me off. He is also looking for my vulnerable point, in case he needs to attack, in case it comes down to that.
>
> (207)

Attwell calls this 'a brilliant rendering of the interior life of a magpie',[14] even though we have no insight into the bird's way of looking at the world at all; Attwell's assumption re-draws the strict boundaries between the human and nonhuman that JC's description prose disavows. JC imagines the bird in much the same categories as Alan, Anya's partner, perceives him. JC hypothesizes about the bird's cognitive processes, thinking that '[h]e thinks I will die in that cage of mine, die of old age.' Following his own logic, JC presents the results: 'Then he can batter the window down, strut in, and peck out my eyes' (208). Interestingly, when JC imagines the bird's motivation and the consequences of his (i.e., the bird's) actions, he might as well be describing Alan, who is indeed plotting to rob him of his money. The bird is described as a 'schemer', which is a term Alan uses to differentiate himself and JC from Anya. Alan's perception of the world is rather mechanistic and crudely Darwinian, so JC's portrayal of the bird, coming close to Alan's, points to the limits of his perception of the species' interconnectedness. Even though he remains open to the animal's world in the sense that he takes the animal position into account, his vision contrasts with Anya's less intellectually rigorous, yet more accepting and inclusive attitude. The removal of a barrier between species enables a more nuanced perception of humanity, one that cannot be reduced to gender, intellect or social standing. The analogy between Alan and the bird suggests in turn an impossibility of establishing a clear-cut distinction between humanity and animality.

Such a human–nonhuman continuity comes to dominate JC's perception after he abandons his strong opinions in favour of softer ones, influenced by Anya's perspective on honour and individual responsibility. *Diary of a Bad Year,* in Rose's words, is 'concerned with the workings of "shame", and its relationship to "citizenship" and "responsibility",'[15] interrogating the connections between the political state, and private shame, simultaneously providing a reflection on the state of nature, thus re-introducing this element to the discussion about the state of humanity, which, importantly, cannot be separated from the state of nature. Anya becomes a catalyst of change for JC's opinions, from a Hobbesian understanding of the role of the political state and the state of nature ('By nature we belong to separate nations; by nature nations are in competition with other nations', JC forcefully claims (79)), to a 'softer', more private one, more inclusive both in terms of gender and species. Coetzee's novels bring to focus the characters who are wholly other, human and nonhuman animals alike, and endow them with a voice – as it does with Anya – or give them a meaning that disrupts simple binaries, while highlighting the ambivalence of the human–nonhuman divide and subverting the hegemony of the anthropocentric discourse.

Authority targeted and subverted in the 'Strong Opinions' takes various forms: from Australian policymaking, through Intelligent Design, neoliberalism, universities and the classics, to a novelist's responsibility to their audience; it also means imagining subject positions that are infrequent in fiction, as they undermine the unity of the human 'I', implied in any discourse.[16] One such strategy is introducing characters who make unorthodox alliances, renouncing not only their intellectual and scholarly but also their human superiority. 'Authority cannot be taught, cannot be learned', says JC; 'The paradox is a true one' (151). It is in this unwillingness to resolve the paradox that one might be tempted to hear the voice of the author, whose scepticism towards assumptions of authoritarian positions (such as the form of a public lecture) is well documented: 'I did not have a high opinion of opinions, including the opinion that […] I should not have a high opinion of opinions.'[17] Jane Poyner offers a perspective on this particular convergence, arguing that it is 'the slippage between the two, between author and author-protagonist, that energizes questions about the relationship between public intellectuals and the truths they promote'.[18] Undermining his own authority as a public intellectual, lecturer, reader and writer, JC accepts the possibility of other subjects, such as Anya, to assume agential positions that do not align with his, and in fact cast doubt on their validity. In this way, *Diary of a Bad Year* subverts the authority of the text.

TRANSGRESSING POSTCOLONIAL IDENTITY

Written after Coetzee's move to Australia, *Diary*'s engagement with the questions of postcolonial identity – and its ultimate dismissal of the very validity of the questions for the benefit of a wider question of truth and authority in writing – must be situated within the context of the author's later novels, in which the postcolonial society in question is no longer African but becomes global.[19] Poyner asserts that 'Coetzee moves beyond a specifically postcolonialist paradigm',[20] and while she admits that Coetzee's more recent works (including *Diary*) are not explicitly preoccupied with the questions of postcolonial identity, they are, nevertheless, 'important contributions to debates on intellectualism and the author's authority pertinent to the postcolonial field'.[21] Poyner points to the way 'Coetzee pares the problem of the author's authority via the radical defamiliarization of genre',[22] suggesting that one of the ways such defamiliarization works is through elaborate textual 'setups' which are meant to mislead the reader down the erroneous path of assuming correspondences between JC and the author; indeed, Van der Vlies categorizes *Diary of a Bad Year* as one of Coetzee's *autre*biographies, pointing to continuities between the character and the writer, and the disrupting differences between them.[23] Thus, for example, *Diary* contains sections ostensibly discussing specifically Australian issues (such as 22. 'On asylum in Australia', or 23. 'On political life in Australia'), inviting the reader to assume that it is the writer's voice that one hears in these comments, but it immediately frustrates this assumption by being set in Sydney, not Adelaide (the writer's place of residence). These setups, being more than mere ploys, perform a rigorous examination of the conditions of truth. Derek Attridge calls them '*arguings*' as opposed to arguments, and so, in contrast to presenting a fixed product of an intellectual process, they suggest a progression and are 'events staged within the event of the work' which 'invite the reader's participation'.[24] Using such narrative ploys, *Diary* places markers of postcolonial identity – nationality, religion, ethnicity, etc., – in dialogue with one another, asking the reader to investigate their usefulness as categories of identification (most eminently in the opening section of 'Strong Opinions', 'On the Origins of the State'), ultimately exposing their limits.

The questions of language and its authority also point to the limitations of postcolonial identification; this idea is dramatized in the figure of Anya and exemplified by her explicit disregard for the much stricter, if not ossified, identity categories used by JC. Characteristically, the reader learns of her nationality, education and linguistic quirks from JC's perspective: 'She likes to present herself as a Filipina …. In fact she has never lived in the Philippines …. She speaks French with an accent the French probably find charming but has not heard of Voltaire' (70–1). In 'Strong Opinions', Anya's education in international schools is deemed somewhat irregular, her nationality uncertain. And while JC comes to find his own language use problematic in 'Second Diary', he assesses Anya's linguistic abilities as lacking, though Anya treats languages like she does other identity markers and positions: she crosses between them lightly and with ease, never noticing the ragged borders that might seem insurmountable to others. Anya's language use is unorthodox, and it is contrasted with JC's musings on the matter of a mother tongue.[25] In 'Second Diary', the less forceful JC wonders whether we 'have a mother tongue? Do I have a mother tongue?', to which he gives a hesitant answer: 'Perhaps – is this possible? – I have no mother tongue' (195). His unwillingness to claim any as his mother tongue translates into an inability to transgress the boundaries imposed by the category of mother tongue.[26] When JC asks himself if his writing experience might have been different if he had worked in a language other than English, 'a truer, less questionable mother tongue' (196), he dramatizes the postcolonial position of an author painfully aware of the problematic status of the English language and its authority. Thus *Diary* undertakes the questions of the colonial authority of the English language, so thoroughly examined by Coetzee in other fictional works and essays. The sensation of entrapment in a (hegemonic) language also suggests a search for an answer in generic terms, for instance, of a demarcation between fiction and autobiography. As Mike Piero notes, in Coetzee's autobiographical writing 'the would-be artist is crafting a personality demonstrative of his otherness, […] also even in relation to the English which is his first language'.[27] A similar dramatization occurs in *Diary*, which ultimately forces the reader to examine their assumptions about the (post-)colonial authority of language and the identity categories it establishes.

Just as *Diary of a Bad Year* frustrates readers' possible assumptions about an identification between JC and the author, in a similar manner it frustrates our expectations of the novel's adherence to generic rules. *Diary* is certainly not the first novel in Coetzee's oeuvre that experiments with metageneric ploys and rejects any hopes for generic purity or narratorial authority; but it goes farther than its predecessors in its inclusion of nonhuman subjectivity and openness to readers' autonomy.

MULTIVOCAL METATEXTUALITY

The third thematic field, multivocal metatextuality, recognizes the centrality of an interrogation of the definition and value of high culture in *Diary of a Bad Year*, and an exploration of the limits of post-colonial authority in fiction and non-fiction writing. Multivocal and hybrid, the text is open to a number of subject positions, including nonhuman; it is the element of nonhuman animality that subverts distinctions between the narrators, JC and Anya, and between characters.

There are complex structural dependencies between the parts representing Anya's and JC's voices, which may be seen as oppositional, with Anya's boyfriend Alan not given a narrative stance yet clearly antagonistic to both Anya's and JC's positions. These various positions, dynamically changing throughout the course of the novel, account for different critical evaluations of the text. Stuart J. Murray calls the novel a 'polyphonic text' and notes that there is 'no "inner voice" to invite a readerly identification'; in fact, he suggests, it offers 'no ready identification'.[28] Polyphonic and hybrid as it is, *Diary* also suggests a different subject positioning, one that is not limited to a human subjectivity, and does so through its metatextual and metageneric interventions. Such a subject position is only representable in relation to other voices in the text, one whose presence undercuts the succession of the rather unambiguous binarisms that critics note. Even though animals necessarily speak through the human characters, their autonomy is acknowledged in a presence that cannot be reduced to a singular perspective but is represented and must be noticed from a variety of angles.

The difference in the positions occupied by the two narrators, Anya and JC, has been variously assessed: some critics situate it along the dividing lines between 'modern political culture' and an antiquated yet ethically commendable code of honour, the former postulated by Anya, the latter by JC (Hayes); or between public discourse and fictional writing (Attwell); they might also be seen as oppositional stances towards meta-cultural discourse. Proposing a wider claim that Coetzee's writing must be seen as an effort directed at transcending the understanding of culture as superior to politics, Hayes convincingly argues that the character of JC initially exemplifies the position of Kulturkritik, which signifies a perception of the cultural position as preferable to the terms of political debate in discussing issues that are inherently political. Inspired and encouraged by Anya, JC is persuaded to abandon this stance and to search for 'newer, up-to-date ones to replace his old opinions' (143). Hayes hence sees *Diary of a Bad Year* as an attempt to find a way out of the peculiar hegemony of the metacultural discourse, but he assesses the second part of the narrative, 'Second Diary', as unsuccessful in this regard, calling it 'uninspiring' and finding the position occupied by JC in it 'populistic'.[29]

While the gentler tone of the 'Second Diary' might indeed be seen as lacking in inspiration, I think it is rather a sense of defeat in the face of a discursive position that is not – and cannot be – accounted for in the binary pairing of culture versus politics. Anya's embodied experience is not contained in JC's textual practice, which is most clearly visible in the fragment in which Anya talks about being a victim of rape, refusing to describe the experience in detail.[30] This refusal gestures towards a rejection of a discursive position that might be appropriated by the narrator who occupies two thirds of the page. JC's retreat from the strong opinions of the first part might then be seen not as 'populist',[31] but as an admittance of an impossibility of clearly delineating two discursive positions as oppositional and thus reducing them to a set of binaries. Instead, the novel rehearses a variety of positionings, some of them nonhuman, in order to dramatize the multivocal chorus that constitutes it, including not just Anya and JC, but also the evolving stances both narrators assume.

CONCLUSIONS

The three headings under which I have discussed the novel are merely suggestions about *Diary*'s place in the development of Coetzee's thought in fiction and nonfiction alike. *Diary of a Bad Year* is an exercise in the exploration of novelistic authority, and it problematizes its foundations using metageneric tactics, irony and metatextual polyphony. It questions the seemingly unquestionable – such as the concept of the mother tongue. It proposes a revaluation of the centrality of human subjectivity, including a nonhuman subjectivity in its repertoire of subject positions, simultaneously opening the text to readers' autonomy. The novel suggests a fundamental interconnectedness between human and nonhuman animals, and while it continues Coetzee's earlier examinations of postcolonial identity and the sources of authority in postcolonial fiction, it becomes a voice in the wider debate about the human position in the Anthropocene.

NOTES

1. As Attwell points out, there is a hint of intertextual play when it comes to the character of Anya: 'the secretary in question is the near-namesake of the woman Dostoevsky engaged for a similar purpose and eventually married, the stenographer Anna Snitkina' ('Mastering Authority', 211).
2. A similar movement away from male-dominated perspective can be seen in what Danta points out is a change from Coetzee's reference to 'the Orpheus story' to later naming it 'the story of Eurydyce' in *Diary of a Bad Year*. (Danta, 'Eurydice's Curse', 20). As Kossew and Harvey argue, this reveals 'a change in perspective from the artist/creator to that of the Muse' (*Reading Coetzee's Women*, 9).
3. In this sense, *Diary* is also reminiscent of *Slow Man*, which, as Geertsema notes, is 'a novel that questions what being a novel might mean' ('Diary', 254).
4. Woods, 'Squall Lines'.
5. Hayes, *J. M. Coetzee and the Novel* 243.
6. Clarkson, *J. M. Coetzee: Countervoices*, 104.
7. Katy Iddiols points to the text's structure, which 'prevents us from drawing any definite conclusions about the novel'; Coetzee's deployment of a 'complex palimpsest-esque [sic] structure makes it very difficult to know whether to approach the text as memoir, fiction, theory, or a combination of the three' ('Disrupting Inauthentic Readings', 193.).

8. Benita Parry similarly argues that 'Coetzee's preferred modes, the diary, the journal and the letter – where the disingenuous transparency of the earliest forms of novel writing is problematized – make an apparently uncontested arena available to a speaking subject' (*Critical Perspectives*, 40).
9. Quoted in Rose, *Literary Cynics*, 164.
10. Rose, *Literary Cynics*, 164.
11. Ibid., 165.
12. Coetzee, *Diary of a Bad Year*, 142. Hereafter referenced parenthetically in the text.
13. Johan Geertsema argues that *Diary of a Bad Year* presents an impossible position, one that, however, is necessary from the ethical point of view: 'in *Diary of a Bad Year*, Coetzee strives to attain a position – one he realizes is impossible – that is not political but grounded in the aesthetic, and thereby has the potential to offer an ethically responsible response to the present in which he finds himself' ('*Diary*', 257).
14. Attwell, 'Mastering Authority', 218.
15. Rose, *Literary Cynics*, 178.
16. Clarkson claims that '[i]f the implication of an "I" is inevitable in any act of writing, Coetzee engages all strategies to question the presumed unitary authority of that "I"' (*Countervoices*, 42).
17. Quoted in Van der Vlies, *Present Imperfect*, 67.
18. Poyner, *J. M. Coetzee*, 169.
19. Dominic Head makes a similar point when he situates Coetzee's 'concern with his own ethnicity' at the heart of *Diary* (*Cambridge Introduction to J. M. Coetzee*, 19).
20. Poyner, *J. M. Coetzee*, 168.
21. Ibid.
22. Ibid., 13.
23. Van der Vlies, *Present Imperfect*, 73.
24. Attridge *J. M. Coetzee and the Ethics of Reading*, 197–8.
25. Paul Patton recognizes a recurring theme in *Diary* which is '[c]oncealment behind opinions"' ('Coetzee's Opinions', 59), to which a certain parallel might be found in *Elizabeth Costello*. Julian Murphet points to the formal opposition of novel versus Opinion, arguing that '[o]pinions, immaculate and unbroken, enjoy a spatial hegemony here; but fictional journals, written in parallel and linked by a law of desire, run skirmishes in the underbrush and find ways of modifying the oracular tone of the opinions, if not their content as such' ('*Diary*', 64).
26. The preoccupation with the language one might describe as one's first, or mother tongue, and the reasons to consider it as such appear also as the subject of *In the Heart of a Country* and is later taken up in the Jesus novels. It was also the central theme in Coetzee's address delivered at the University of Silesia in Katowice when granted the Doctor Honoris Causa in 2018 (J. M. Coetzee, *Doctor Honoris Causa*).
27. Piero, 'Coetzee, Blanchot, and the Work of Writing', 87.
28. Murray, 'Allegories of the Bioethical', 324.
29. Hayes, *J. M. Coetzee and the Novel*, 232.
30. In Lucy Valerie Graham's words, 'Coetzee chooses *not* to script women's experiences of rape' (*State of Peril*, 157).
31. Hayes points to a certain 'tendency in cultural criticism towards a "populist drift"' represented in the second part of *Diary* (*J. M. Coetzee and the Novel*, 232).

WORKS CITED

Attridge, Derek. *J. M. Coetzee and the Ethics of Reading: Literature in the Event*. Chicago: University of Chicago Press, 2004.
Attwell, David. 'Mastering Authority: J. M. Coetzee's Diary of a Bad Year', *Social Dynamics* 36, no. 1 (March 2010): 214–21.
Clarkson, Carrol. *J. M. Coetzee: Countervoices*. Houndmills: Palgrave Macmillan, 2009.
Coetzee, J. M. *Diary of a Bad Year*. London: Harvill Secker, 2007.
Coetzee, J. M. *Doctor Honoris Causa Universitatis Silesiensis*. Katowice: University of Silesia Press, 2018.
Danta, Chris. 'Eurydice's Curse: J. M. Coetzee and the Prospect of Death'. *Australian Literary Studies* 33, no. 1 (2018). https://www.australianliterarystudies.com.au/articles/eurydices-curse-j-m-coetzee-and-the-prospect-of-death.
Geertsema, Johan. 'Diary of a Bad Year'. In *A Companion to the Works of J. M. Coetzee*, edited by Tim Mehigan, 252–68. Rochester, NY: Camden House, 2013.
Graham, Lucy Valerie. *State of Peril: Race and Rape in South African Literature*. Oxford: Oxford University Press, 2012.
Hayes, Patrick. *J. M. Coetzee and the Novel: Writing and Politics after Beckett*. Oxford: Oxford University Press, 2010.
Head, Dominic. *The Cambridge Introduction to J. M. Coetzee*. Cambridge: Cambridge University Press, 2009.
Iddiols, Katy. 'Disrupting Inauthentic Readings'. In *J. M. Coetzee in Context and Theory*, edited by Elleke Boehmer, Katy Iddiols, and Robert Eaglestones, 185–97. London: Continuum, 2009.
Kossew, Sue and Melinda Harvey, eds. *Reading Coetzee's Women*. Cham: Palgrave Macmillan, 2019.
Mehigan, Tim, ed. *A Companion to the Works of J. M. Coetzee*. Rochester, NY: Camden House, 2013.
Murphet, Julian. 'Diary of a Bad Year: Parrhesia, Opinion, and the Novelistic Form'. In *Strong Opinions: J.M. Coetzee and the Authority of Contemporary Fiction*, edited by Chris Danta, Julian Murphet and Sue Kossew, 63–80. London: Continuum, 2011.
Murray, Stuart J. 2014 'Allegories of the Bioethical: Reading J. M. Coetzee's *Diary of a Bad Year*'. *Journal of Medical Humanities* 35, no. 3: 321–34.
Parry, Benita. 'Speech and Silence in the Fictions of J.M. Coetzee'. In *Critical Perspectives on J. M. Coetzee*, edited by Graham Huggan and Stephen Watson, 37–65. Houndmills: Macmillan, 1996.
Patton, Paul. 'Coetzee's Opinions'. In *Strong Opinions: J. M. Coetzee and the Authority of Contemporary Fiction*, edited by Chris Danta, Julian Murphet and Sue Kossew, 53–61. London: Continuum, 2011.
Piero, Mike. 'Coetzee, Blanchot, and the Work of Writing: the Impersonality of Childhood'. *Media Tropes Journal* 4, no. 2 (2014): 79–97.
Poyner, Jane. *J. M. Coetzee and the Paradox of Postcolonial Authorship*. Farnham: Ashgate, 2009.
Rose, Arthur. *Literary Cynics: Borges, Beckett, Coetzee*. London: Bloomsbury, 2017.
Van der Vlies, Andrew. *Present Imperfect: Contemporary South African Writing*. Oxford: Oxford University Press, 2017.
Woods, James. 'Squall Lines', review of *Diary of a Bad Year, The New Yorker*, 24 December 2007. https://www.newyorker.com/magazine/2007/12/24/squall-lines.

CHAPTER SEVENTEEN

The *Jesus* novels

TIMOTHY BEWES

A NEW KIND OF NOVEL?

The first sentences of J. M. Coetzee's 2003 novel *Elizabeth Costello* construct a problematic that has defined all of Coetzee's writing ever since:

> There is first of all the problem of the opening, namely, how to get us from where we are, which is, as yet, nowhere, to the far bank. It is a simple bridging problem, a problem of knocking together a bridge. People solve such problems every day. They solve them, and having solved them push on.[1]

The 'simple bridging problem' is not, of course, merely an issue of literary craft. Coetzee is not describing the personal challenges of the creative writer faced with the blank page, but the philosophical question of fictionality itself: its relation to reality, its capacity to address ethical issues and quandaries, its political significance and its ties to authorship. Once this series of relations has been made visible as a 'problem' – even one that must be put 'out of our mind' in order to write (*EC* 1) – there seems no going back to a world in which such relations were simply a matter of technical proficiency or critical interpretation and debate.

Coetzee's bridge image frames not only his own project, then, but the very possibility of writing in our period. Indeed, *Elizabeth Costello* evokes the question as a predicament that conditions every literary text, but that none is able to address directly. For a work of fiction can, by definition, do nothing other than 'assume ... that the bridge is built and crossed' (*EC* 1). Conventional novels have no business even alluding to the bridge, let alone narrating its traversal; reconstructing it is solely the work of readers or critics. The story begins only once 'we have left behind the territory in which we were' (*EC* 1). The interconnected stories (or 'lessons') of *Elizabeth Costello* are enabled by the bridge, but also limited and contained by it, for the mystery of the journey into fiction, established and preserved by Coetzee's framing image, ensures that a return journey is impossible. Once we have encountered the work that is *Elizabeth Costello*, how do we dare carry the lessons we find there (or indeed in any fictional work) back to the 'territory in which we were', the world of critical discourse?

Elizabeth Costello's completeness as a character, the coherence and consistency of her opinions, her philosophical commitment to animal rights, even her belief that 'the bottom has dropped out' of the presuppositions of realist fiction – presuppositions, she tells her audience at Altona College, dating from a time 'when we could say who we were' (*EC* 19) – all are expressed as a condition of the world in which she moves and talks. But that world is not ours – the world of the reader or critic. Elizabeth, her son John, her sister Blanche, even the various scholars and academics she meets, all live 'in the far territory, where we want to be' (*EC* 1). Thus, the 'problem' established by the opening of *Elizabeth Costello*, as critics such as Stephen Mulhall and Cora Diamond have noted, is that the representativeness of everything we encounter in the work (the characters, their opinions, the moral quandaries they entertain, even Elizabeth's speculations on the limits of realism in literature) is inherently dubious, confined to the fictional context in which it appears.[2] No point of view or proposition in *Elizabeth Costello* retains any normative value in our world, the world in which we sit holding the book in our hands.

Compare this framing passage with an image from early in *The Schooldays of Jesus* (2016), the second of Coetzee's so-called 'Jesus' trilogy, published thirteen years after *Elizabeth Costello*. Simón, the protagonist of the trilogy, is addressing his surrogate son, David, who has asked Simón about their origins:

> When you travel across the ocean on a boat, all your memories are washed away and you start a completely new life. That is how it is. There is no before. There is no history. The boat docks at the harbour and we climb down the gangplank and we are plunged into the here and how. Time begins. The clock starts running.[3]

A dominant theme of press reviews of the Jesus novels has been their 'bewildering' quality.[4] But much of the bewilderment disappears once we realize that these three works, published between 2013 and 2019, are Coetzee's attempt to resolve the 'bridging problem' of *Elizabeth Costello*. He does this not by narrating or explaining the passage from one bank to the other, nor by assuming the transition to be already completed, but with a work in which the journey is in process. The characters have left the near bank, but their arrival at the far one is incomplete.

This is to say that the schemas that explain works of literature, and by which we as readers and critics conventionally make our way back and forth between the two banks – schemas of realist representation, allegory, figurative abstraction, exemplarity and (its complement) exceptionality – have been suspended in the Jesus novels. Such schemas assume a relation of transmissibility between the world and the fiction, a relation that each theorizes in a different way. In interrupting these relations of transmissibility, it is as if the novel has, as Jennifer Rutherford writes of *The Childhood of Jesus*, 'slipped its form'.[5]

The question from David that prompts Simón's response – 'Am I a *huérfano*? [orphan]' (*S* 16) – is the existential question of a fictional character whose ontology, as with every fictional character, is nonbiological. But David's question also emerges from the space of ontological interrogation that the three novels open, and neither vacate nor resolve. Simón's response is the answer that a literary theorist familiar with, say, the work of Mikhail Bakhtin might offer; but it is not the sort of answer one expects from a fellow character in a novel. Descending the gangplank inaugurates the 'chronotope' of the novel – the spatio-temporal formation that defines the novel's setting and narrative. The work's characters are born at that moment; the narrator comes into being; the setting is established. Time itself, as Bakhtin puts it, 'thickens, takes on flesh, becomes artistically visible', and space 'becomes charged and responsive to the movements of time, plot and history'.[6] Although the Jesus novels contain very few historical indicators, their spatio-temporal organization is relatively conventional. Time and space enjoy a continuity such that, taken together, the three novels span a period of around five years. The narrative is set in two cities, Novilla and Estrella, located 475 kilometers apart (*D* 19); these locations are 'chronotopically' related to each other in realist time and space. However, Simón's reference to the 'gangplank' immediately makes this spatio-temporal framing a conceptual problem of the work, rather than a formal premise of it. Far from being put 'out of our mind', the 'simple bridging problem' of the Jesus novels is a continual preoccupation that structures and informs every conversation, action and event.

All this is to say that Coetzee's Jesus novels concern the novel form more directly and more intimately than any of his previous works, despite the fact that the problematic of the novel might be said to be this author's lifelong project.[7] The Jesus series takes place in a liminal space that precedes the formed fictional world of the novel as such. In offering us an image of that between-space in the societies of Novilla and Estrella, these texts also narrate, for perhaps the first time in the history of the novel (with an important exception – more on this later), the tentative early steps in the formation of a fictional world. Its characters are still in development. Its setting is created by the movement of the characters, rather than being merely inhabited by them. And the numerous ideational themes that seem to be suggested in the many conversations that take place over the course of the three books – the conflict between 'reason' and 'passion', the possibility of forgiveness, the relative claims to knowledge of art and science, the competing advantages and disadvantages of technical progress, the reality of history, the status of measurement, the limitations of arithmetic for grasping the 'essence' of numbers – do not cohere as answers but remain unresolved, caught between positions that never transcend the persons who embody them. As such, they neither propel the narrative nor explain it.

These works, as Derek Attridge puts it, 'mak[e] little use of the available novelistic resources to absorb and beguile the reader'.[8] Attridge is referring to the narrative qualities that theorists and practitioners of the novel have used to bring order and meaning to what is, in itself, disorderly and without meaning: life. Fictional characters have a consistency and a knowability that real people lack. Novelistic plots introduce causality and mystery into what is otherwise nothing but a sequence of events. Elements of physiological necessity – food, sleep, sex – are admitted only on condition that they are overlain with pleasure, sociability or narrative purpose.[9] Attridge's claim that such resources (consistency of character, narrative directionality and purpose, moments of pleasure and gratification) are relatively absent from the Jesus novels, along with their absorbing and beguiling effects, is demonstrably true, especially of *Childhood*. Novilla is a world bereft of novelistic definition. Simón's first attempts to establish sexual relations are met with 'goodwill' and 'benevolence', but no passion. 'It all remains a bit abstract', he says to Elena, an early object of his romantic attentions (56). The only food on offer in Novilla, initially, is utilitarian bean paste (26, 29). Simón's acquaintances seem incapable of 'irony'; they see no 'doubleness in the world', no 'difference between the way things seem and the way things are' (64). Attridge's observation holds true, for the most part, throughout the series. However, we begin to see 'beguiling' elements as early as the sixth chapter of *Childhood*, with the appearance of the unpredictable señor Daga, who one day causes a commotion at the docks where Simón works. Daga later befriends David, and Simón considers him a dangerous and malign influence. Given the blandness of the Novilla diet, it is perhaps a significant element in the novelistic progression of these works that when Simón attends a cooking class in Estrella he is (as Attridge observes) given a tray of spices to take home (*S* 183).[10] By *The Death of Jesus*, such novelistic resources are beginning to exert significant control over all the characters, as the search for David's 'meaning' emerges into relief as that novel's thematic centre of gravity.

David himself exists in these works as a point of resistance to the many ways in which the conventional novel navigates a passage (or constructs a bridge) between the two banks. He is in fact nothing less than the principle of a new kind of novel – one that would preclude such navigation and would thus successfully evade critical interpretation. I have referred already to the schemas of transmissibility by which novels enable and collude with the regime of literary interpretation. Each of the Jesus novels focuses on one of these schemas: *abstraction, exemplarity* and *the exception*. David's resistance to these schemas, which are the only ways the novel form could accommodate him (as with any character), is also, as I will outline below, the explanation for why he has to die in the third novel.

THE STORY

A sketch of the major events of the three novels would look something like this.

In *The Childhood of Jesus* (2013), David is five years old, Simón forty-five (C 2, 201);[11] they were assigned their ages and names in Belstar, a transition camp 'out in the desert' where they spent six weeks before arriving in Novilla (*Childhood* 5). Belstar is also where they learned Spanish, the only language spoken in this new world. David was separated from his mother during the journey and Simón has undertaken to reunite them. It seems that everyone they meet in Novilla has made the same journey; like Simón and David, they have been 'washed clean' of their memories (C 80). Only the slightest mental traces of a life before Novilla are present. Such traces become ever fainter as the trilogy progresses and by the third novel they have all but disappeared. Even Simón, whose memories of the world before Novilla seem to be stronger than anyone else's,[12] makes few if any references to that previous life in *The Death of Jesus*.

Soon after their arrival in Novilla, they meet Inés, whom Simón quickly identifies as David's 'true' mother. Inés leaves the comfortable life she shares with her two brothers and joins Simón and David as David's mother. When David reaches the age of six, he begins attending school. In the meantime, he has taught himself to read using a children's copy of *Don Quixote* from a community library that Simón has given him. However, in school David refuses to read. He also refuses (or is unable) to do conventional arithmetic and is declared by his teacher to have a 'deficit linked to symbolic activities' (205). Under the threat of having David sent to a remedial institution, the makeshift family leaves Novilla for a 'new life' in Estrellita, to the north.

Schooldays takes place in the 'sleepy provincial city' of (the now renamed) Estrella. David's first teacher in Estrella, a señor Robles, also identifies a 'cognitive deficit' in David after he is unable (or refuses) to identify the quality that two pens, or three pills, have in common – the fact of there being two of them, or three (S 30). The conversation recalls an episode in *Childhood* in which David is unable to perform a basic arithmetic exercise for his teacher, adding together three fish to five, except by visualizing each one in turn: 'This time ... this time ... it is eight' (C 224–5). David enrolls in an Academy of Dance run by a charismatic couple, Juan Sebastián and Ana Magdalena Arroyo. In an address to welcome the new parents, señora Arroyo outlines the school's mission, evoking 'shadow recollections' from the previous life, 'our former existence' – images that persist in the consciousness of children but that the child 'lacks words to express'. The Academy, she says, 'is dedicated to guiding the souls of our students toward that realm, to bringing them in accord with the great underlying movement of the universe, or, as we prefer to say, the dance of the universe' (S 68). The Arroyos welcome David's unconventional relation to numbers and language. Indeed, David feels 'recognized' by them and elects to become a boarder at the school, emerging over the course of the novel as its most gifted pupil. *Schooldays* ends with David performing the 'dance of Seven', which impresses even the sceptical Simón as 'extraordinary'. 'If ever in the future you are tempted to doubt him, remember this!' he says to himself (*S* 245–6).

The second book also includes a dramatic, ostensibly 'passionate' plot involving – finally – a character who does seem to have a novelistic quality of definition, a museum attendant and devotee of the Arroyos named Dmitri.[13] Dmitri kills Ana Magdalena, with whom he is in love, apparently during sex, though the motivation for the crime is never explained and remains mysterious even to Dmitri (*S* 250). Simón himself cannot 'imagine' the murder, and thus the novel, whose centre of consciousness is Simón, 'fails' or 'quails' (*S* 250) before its most novelistic event.

In *The Death of Jesus* (2019), also set in Estrella, David is ten and happily ensconced in the Academy community. That situation is upset by the appearance of Dr Julio Fabricante, the director of an orphanage, Las Manos, in the first chapter. 'To be an orphan, at the deepest level, is to be alone in the world,' Fabricante tells Simón and David (*D* 5). David self-identifies as an orphan and leaves Ines and Simón (and by extension, the world of the Academy) for Las Manos. He plays football in the orphanage team until a fall reveals that he has a 'neuropathic' illness. David weakens, is hospitalized and dies two-thirds of the way into the book, having spent his final weeks telling puzzled visiting schoolmates enigmatic stories featuring Don Quixote. The trilogy ends with the various characters unable to agree on the meaning of David's life. Simón, having long accepted that David is 'an exceptional child' (*D* 7), tells him before he dies: 'You lived through the Don's adventures. Don Quixote was you. You were Don Quixote' (*D* 104). He promises David that he will tell his story but will not try to 'understand' him. A pageant is staged at the Academy featuring episodes supposedly from David's life. David's disciples, the group of children who once gathered around his bedside, are now swollen in number to a hundred and march under a placard, 'Los Desinvitados' (*D* 152), taking his 'message' to the city's shopkeepers to proclaim, in David's name, 'the just price' (*D* 175). Meanwhile Dmitri, who has reappeared as an orderly in the hospital where David is treated, styles himself as David's 'most faithful follower' (*D* 178) and insists that 'he alone' is the bearer of David's message. In a letter to Simón, Dmitri tells him that David saved him by *not* forgiving him for killing Ana Magdalena (*D* 181). In a second letter he admits that there was no message, that what David uttered in his final moments with Dmitri was instead a question: 'Who am I and why am I here?' (*D* 190).

Such an event-oriented sketch fails to capture certain formal features that are indispensable to any attempt to grapple with the substance of these works. Most notable among these is their unremittingly dialogical quality. In his book-length study of the trilogy, Robert Pippin notes that Coetzee's narration in all three novels 'relies a great deal on' free indirect discourse. Thus Simón's mind and temperament constitutes the 'landscape' of these fictions just as much as Novilla and Estrella; even the third-person narration is 'often' focalized through Simón.[14] This important observation might be presented in even stronger terms, for in fact not a single instance of reported speech, observed action, or subjective reflection – which is to say, not a single moment of any of the three books – is not presented through Simón's consciousness. Simón is present in every scene because every moment in all three works is a biopsy of Simón's perception. Thus, even when the narration is not in free indirect discourse there is an all-encompassing frame of 'focalization' (to use Gérard Genette's term) that defines everything that takes place within it.[15] The Jesus novels are not simply narrated *from* Simón's point of view. Strictly speaking, I want to suggest, there is not a single moment of third-person narration in the Jesus novels.

We see this in the inflection given to the pronouns 'he', 'him' and 'his' throughout the trilogy. Technically, third-person pronouns are features of third-person narration. And third-person narration, observes the French linguist Émile Benveniste, 'is the only mode of utterance possible for instances of discourse not meant to refer to themselves but to predicate the process of someone or something outside the instance itself, and this someone or something can always be provided with an objective reference'.[16] Benveniste goes so far as to call the third-person pronoun a 'nonperson', meaning an object. Third-person pronouns are distinct from first- and second-person pronouns in 'never being reflective of the instance of discourse', which is to say that they are purely referential.[17] These definitions are well-established in the linguistic-theoretical literature on pronoun use. But Coetzee's mature fiction – from *The Master of Petersburg* onwards – invents a new use of the third-person pronoun, tied to the universality of free indirect discourse, in which 'he', 'him' and 'his' do not refer outside the instance of discourse, but operate precisely within its fold.[18]

It is with the same effect and rationale that the Jesus fictions are narrated exclusively in the present tense. In the opening paragraphs of *Elizabeth Costello*, shortly after a passage of conventional background information, Coetzee's narrator advises us, parenthetically, that there will only be 'present tense henceforth' (*EC* 2). That 'henceforth' will apply not just to the remaining pages of *Elizabeth Costello*, but to almost all of Coetzee's subsequent fiction.[19] The Jesus novels never violate this principle. Since *Elizabeth Costello*, then, Coetzee's novels have presented not narratives but fictions of consciousness. It would be a mistake to conceive of these fictions of consciousness as 'novels of ideas', for to do so would be to impose a separation between the narrative and the idea, where the former serves as the vehicle or transmitter of the latter. The effect of the universalization of free indirect discourse and the uninterrupted present tense is to abolish any such separation: ideas are present in Coetzee only as thoughts, which is to say, mental images. There is little character development and no revelation in the Jesus novels. The mystery of David remains intact; Simón is no wiser as the works conclude than when they began.

'PHILOSOPHICAL' ISSUES

Robert Pippin titles his essay on the Jesus novels – the first substantial treatment of the cycle as a whole – 'Metaphysical Exile'. The title paraphrases the German Romantic poet Novalis, who, in a fragment famously quoted by Martin Heidegger, said: 'Philosophy is really homesickness, an urge to be at home everywhere.'[20] For Pippin, this line provides the main justification for reading the Jesus novels in terms of the 'philosophy' that the books are 'filled with' (6). In this light, the philosophical tenor of the trilogy can be summarized as 'a treatment of the state of the human being as one of exile' (5).

At the level of 'content', Pippin is right: the novels are 'filled with' philosophy.[21] Simón's fellow stevedores in *Childhood* take philosophy classes on topics (for example, the question of the 'unity' that lies behind the apparent 'diversity' of things such as tables and chairs) that seem to restage certain of Plato's dialogues (*C* 119–20). Simón's conversations in Novilla often turn on the contrast between his commitment to a rationality grounded in an unspecified philosophical tradition (the 'Western' – we all recognize it) and the empiricism of his interlocutors, most of whom believe that 'nothing is invisible' (*C* 29) and 'nothing is missing' from their world (*C* 63).

One of the most significant discussions takes place early in *Childhood* between Simón and the foreman, Álvaro, at the docks. The question Simón introduces to Álvaro involves the 'higher' purpose of the labour the men undertake – unloading bags of grain by hand to be transported to warehouses that, we later learn, are infested by rats – a purpose higher than mere 'consumption', the survival of the organism: 'What is it all for, in the end? ... How does it fit into the larger picture?' (C 108). In posing the question, Simón is also invoking ideas from the old world that his comrades seem to have forgotten, such as 'history' (which is to say, change, progress), or 'justice' (the good society towards which we are all striving). In ten years, or even five, he tells Álvaro, grain is unlikely still to be unloaded by hand. Another of the stevedores, Eugenio, insists that unlike, say, 'climate', history 'is merely a pattern we see in what has passed. It has no power to reach into the present' (C 116).

Simón's questions and responses to Álvaro do have a 'philosophical' dimension, however, and the feelings of anxiety from which they emanate are recognizably contemporary. In our own period, for example, it is becoming clear just how devastating the logic of economic efficiency in the global shipping industry has been, in ecological as well as sociological terms. One of the effects of the shipping container – the innovation that follows, historically, upon that of the crane – has been, writes John Lanchester, to 'abolish geography and location as an economic factor: moving stuff from A to B is so cheap that, for most goods, there is no advantage in siting manufacturing anywhere near your customers. Instead, you make whatever it is where it's cheapest, and ship it to them instead.'[22] How reassuring it would be to take Coetzee's *Childhood* as a rejection of this economistic logic, to agree with Álvaro and the stevedores that there is no place for Simón's 'clever reasoning' on the wharf, to conclude that Simón's idea of 'history' is just an abstraction – a 'made-up story' involving further abstractions such as labour, commodities and means of production (C 114, 116) – whose first casualties, as Álvaro points out, would be the labourers themselves, not to mention the animals they put to use.

Another of the 'philosophical' issues broached in the trilogy is the problem of 'justice'; the primary context is Dmitri's trial for the murder of Ana Magdalena in *Schooldays*. Of course, the problem of justice is itself a 'bridging problem'. How to determine a punishment that would be commensurate with the crime when there is, by definition, no real repair possible – when crime and punishment exist in radically different realms? At his trial Dmitri refuses to offer any mitigating circumstances. His guilt is 'undeniable', he says, and he beseeches the judges to sentence him with 'the full weight of the law' (S 146). The judges respond to Dmitri's entreaty with what we might consider enlightened liberalism: '[W]hat does it ever mean to speak of *my guilt* or *your guilt* or *our guilt* in respect of some action or other? What if we were not ourselves, or not fully ourselves, when the action in question was performed?' (S 147). Their role, they tell Dmitri, is as much to 'save you the accused from yourself' as to 'shield [society] from rapists and murderers' (S 147). In other words, the judges take seriously both the difficulty of rendering justice and the obligation of doing so. Dmitri, however, rejects the logic of equivalence that underpins the project of justice, even in this most reasonable form. 'You cannot render justice! You cannot measure my guilt! It is not measurable!' (S 150). Only David seems to understand Dmitri's position and hopes Dmitri will be sent to the salt mines, the harshest possible punishment. 'I don't forgive you,' David tells him (S 157), a response that elicits Dmitri's admiration: 'He is really special, Simón, this boy of yours' (S 167).

It would be a mistake to suppose that Coetzee is addressing the question of what a fair criminal justice system might look like through the story of Dmitri's trial in *Schooldays* – or that a resolution of the two views of 'history' in contention in the episode at the docks might be elicited from an attentive reading of *Childhood*. Pippin, indeed, presents his reading as a rejection of such approaches. Simón's 'rational interrogation' of various aspects of his new life, says Pippin, 'is not met with anything like intimations of a possible answer ... The opacity is complete, absolute. Such is the state of metaphysical exile'.[23]

Pippin's detailed analysis contributes a great deal to our understanding of these books. However, with the theme of 'metaphysical exile' his account re-establishes the representational relations that all of Coetzee's 'late' works put into question, the Jesus novels more than any other. Pippin claims that such exile is a 'general condition of late modern life'.[24] Thus, Dmitri's lack of comprehension of his motives for killing Ana Magdalena is evidence of the 'land of exile' in which Dmitri – and by implication every modern subject – dwells.[25] But to say this is simply to replace one set of images (Novilla, Estrella, Simón, David, Inés, Dmitri, Daga, Álvaro, Eugenio, etc.) with a different image ('exile'), and one discursive practice ('fiction') with another ('philosophy'). Pippin attempts to give his argument more concretion by invoking certain actually experienced feelings: 'Not feeling at home in the world could arise when one, for example, contemplates the intertwining between physical passion, reproduction, and romantic love and is astonished by the strangeness of this conjunction, when one wonders whether desiring beauty matters all that much, or tries to understand what is meant for a life that we will die.'[26] 'Contemplates', 'wonders', 'tries to understand': in such moments, presumably, one is thinking or feeling 'philosophically' in a way that reflects, even captures, the exile of 'late modern' existence.

Pippin characterizes the mode in which this condition is evoked in the Jesus books as 'exemplarity' – an operation of 'compression' rather than 'abstraction' in which meaning and detail are compressed 'in an exemplar, a token of a type that embodies the type at its core, its essence'.[27] By such means, Coetzee's prose achieves the power of a 'philosophically relevant generality', he says. Pippin illustrates this logic with the 'love that Simón feels for David, and his anguish at not knowing how to express it', a love that is 'all the more powerfully expressed by the intensity of its compressed, infrequent expression in a few words or a single gesture ...'.[28] Pippin finds a further model for this in the music of J. S. Bach, the emotional substance of which is achieved with 'a compression of elements so well-formed that its implicit wealth can seem to some listeners like poverty'.[29]

Thus the 'philosophical' reading of Coetzee's Jesus books is another form of felicitous travel between the two banks. By its means, Coetzee's Jesus books are made to work like any other novel. It is as if the bridge from one bank to the other that is assumed to be 'built and crossed' in *Elizabeth Costello* had not, in the Jesus books, been dismantled; as if the enterprise of criticism, the discourse of philosophy and the writing and thinking subject who undertakes them were not just as implicated in this wreckage as the novel itself; and as if the extraordinary capacity for emotional honesty and expression in Bach were not regularly invoked throughout Coetzee's work precisely as something forever lost from our world.[30]

'BAD' INFINITY AND THE BIOGRAPHICAL FORM

A decade before Heidegger gave his lectures on metaphysics, Georg Lukács used the same line from Novalis as an organizing element in his early work *The Theory of the Novel*. For Lukács, the 'rift' between inside and outside, 'soul' and 'world', that makes philosophy necessary is also the constitutive gap that defines the 'productive possibilities' of the novel.[31] The gap is bridged by what Lukács calls 'form'. Lukács uses the same topographical figuration for this relation that we have seen elsewhere (in Bakhtin, in Coetzee himself) when he describes the formation of the novel as a journey along a road 'from dull captivity within a merely present reality – a reality that is heterogeneous in itself and meaningless to the individual – towards clear self-recognition' – after which moment 'the ideal thus formed irradiates the individual's life as its immanent meaning'.[32] The formless heterogeneity precedes the emergence of form but is also a suppressed element within it. Lukács refers to it as the novel's '"bad" infinity', for without form there is no principle of limitation in the novel. This heterogeneity is the great, untheorized category of Lukács's theory – and untheorized because it is untheorizable. As E. M. Forster points out, 'in daily life we never understand each other,' whereas 'people in a novel can be understood completely by the reader, if the novelist wishes'.[33] Lukács makes the same point when he describes the novel's use of biography:

> The novel overcomes its 'bad' infinity by recourse to the biographical form. On the one hand, the scope of the world is limited by the scope of the hero's possible experiences and its mass is organised by the orientation of his development towards finding the meaning of life in self-recognition; on the other hand, the discretely heterogeneous mass of isolated persons, non-sensuous structures and meaningless events receives a unified articulation by the relating of each separate element to the central character and the problem symbolised by the story of his life.[34]

From all that has been said above, it should be obvious that the Jesus novels do not achieve anything like a full realization of the 'biographical form' despite the fact that the cycle has all the structural components of a novel. No meanings are accorded to David's life until after his death. Those that emerge are based on apocryphal stories and rumours and are not confirmed by the text. During his life, David repeatedly expresses a desire to be 'recognized', but the substance or status of the recognition he obtains from the Arroyos and Dmitri remains unclear (*S* 231; *D* 161, 183). This is to say that, in the Jesus novels, the '"bad" infinity' remains active and unresolved; the 'heterogeneity' is a presence that threatens to emerge as the main event of these texts; and the 'ideal' of immanent meaning 'irradiating' a life is a perpetually receding prospect.

It is a paradox, of course, that these negative features converge in one individual: David. It is David who fails to attain biographical definition; it is through David that we experience these novels' refusal to deliver themselves over to a meaning that could be extracted from them; it is precisely David's insulation from the logic of abstraction-exemplarity-exceptionality that concretizes and personifies (exemplifies) the trilogy's refusal of that logic, or – we could also say – establishes his own exceptionality to it.

NUMBERS AND HOLES

Towards the end of *Childhood*, in a conversation between Simón and Eugenio, the peculiarity of David's relation to numbers is given a positive formulation. David, says Simón, sees numbers not as elements of arithmetic but as singularities. When David sees an apple, Simón explains, he sees 'not *one* apple, but just *an* apple'. When he sees two apples, he sees not two of the same, but 'an apple and an apple' (C 248). David, this is to say, has no ability to apprehend universal categories of knowledge. When señor Robles, beginning his mathematics lesson with the concept of the set, invites David to consider what two pens and two white pills placed next to each other on a table have in common, David responds: 'Two. Two for the pens and two for the pills. But they aren't the same two' (S 27). 'What if David is right?' Simón asks Eugenio. 'What if between one and two there is no bridge at all, only empty space? And what if we, who so confidently take the step, are in fact falling through space, only we don't know it because we insist on keeping our blindfold on?' (C 250).

It is impossible not to relate the absence of a bridge between the numbers to the absence of a bridge between the 'banks' in *Elizabeth Costello*. David himself makes the connection when he expresses a fear of 'holes' opening up 'between the pages' of *Don Quixote* (C 166). For most of *Childhood*, Simón dismisses this notion of holes as 'nonsense'. Simón's way of reading – a reading that, as he tells David, 'submit[s] to what is written on the page' (C 165) – is predicated upon a relation between the two banks that an attentive reader is in a position to reconcile, by 'hearing what the book has to say and pondering it – perhaps even having a conversation in your mind with the author' (D 9–10). True reading, he says, proceeds not on the basis of one book, but many, and a 'multitude' of heroes. A reader thereby has a chance of 'learning about the world – the world as it really is, not as you wish it to be' (D 9–10). Simón's method approaches the work with the assumption of a 'message' to be gleaned from it, a message that is not self-evident but that must be reconstructed in an attitude of attentiveness and humility (D 10). By contrast, David's way of reading proceeds on the understanding that Don Quixote is a real person (C 224), that his versions of events are as plausible as those of Sancho and that Cervantes's novel is 'a veritable history' (D 9). David's method has no need of schemas of representation and interpretation, but nor, apparently, does it accommodate or require the transcendent position of a critical, judicious, reading subject.

The conflict between these two methods of reading, David's and Simón's, is never resolved in the body of the Jesus trilogy. In the conversation with Simón, Eugenio identifies David's terror of the space between the numbers as a 'bad infinity', as opposed to the 'good infinity' of numerical order itself. Numbers 'fill all the spaces in the universe', Eugenio tells Simón, 'packed one against another tight as bricks. So we are safe. There is nowhere to fall' (C 250). And yet, in dying without leaving a message, David himself slips through the cracks of this suite of novels. David, this is to say, opens up a hole between the pages of the text in a way that Simón, not to speak of Eugenio, not to speak of all readers and critics of these novels, is powerless to forestall. What 'philosophical' readings of the Jesus novels have failed to consider is that, at least since *Elizabeth Costello*, Coetzee's writing has adopted a reverse relationship to form itself. Coetzee's post-*Costello* works, and perhaps his entire oeuvre, might be conceived of not as a positive struggle with the exigencies of form – a struggle for transmission in the face of formal obstacles and limitations – but a negative struggle, a project to evacuate every conception of a relation between the universality of ideas and the particularity of forms, to *prove* that a novel that takes place entirely in the space between the two banks is possible. A successful interpretation of a novel by Coetzee would thus register a failure – either a failure of the work or a failure of reading. The Jesus novels appear, then, as the culmination of a lifelong struggle to produce a novel that does not enclose a thesis of any kind within it, a work that does not close upon a meaning.[35]

WHY DAVID HAS TO DIE

Earlier in this essay I alluded to a prior work that, like the Jesus books, is not set in a fully developed fictional world but is diegetically constituted out of the very incompleteness of such a world. The referent of that claim is, of course, *Don Quixote* by Miguel de Cervantes (1605 and 1615).[36] Like David, the famous Dulcinea of Tobosa – Don Quixote's lady – is a person without biological origins. When David reads aloud a page from *Don Quixote*, chosen by Simón 'at random', the passage turns out directly to implicate David himself, for it concerns the ontology of Dulcinea, a figment of Don Quixote's imagination. Following a challenge to the authenticity of his adventures from a lugubrious clergyman, Don Quixote is asked whether Dulcinea is real or imaginary. He replies: 'I neither engendered nor gave birth to her, but I venerate her as one should venerate a lady who has virtues that make her famous through all the world' (C 217).[37]

The importance of *Don Quixote* to the Jesus books is impossible to overstate. From the moment of his first encounter with the *Illustrated Children's Don Quixote*, David refuses to accept Simón's patient explanations of the principles of fiction. 'He's not a windmill, he's a giant!', he insists, of the well-known encounter in the eighth chapter of *Don Quixote* (C 153). His question on hearing the story of Don Quixote's descent into the Cave of Montesinos concerns not merely whose account is correct, Sancho's or Don Quixote's, according to the logic of the work, but whether Don Quixote 'really' went under the ground for three days (C 165). Asked by señor León to write out the sentence 'I must tell the truth,' David writes instead *Yo soy la verdad*, 'I am the truth' (C 225). Almost every commentator on the passage has pointed out the echo of Jesus's declaration in the Gospel According to John. ('I am the way, the truth, and the life: no man cometh unto the Father, but by me.')[38] But the primary reference is to the novel's own fictional frame, as modelled by *Don Quixote*. David is rejecting the principle of reading that would consign him, a character in a novel, to mere fictionality – to the status of an abstraction, an example or an exception, the three primary modes of literary significance. All three modes assume a relation between a term and a type or set that the term respectively transcends, epitomizes or negatively confirms. David's freedom from these logics is captured most directly by Dmitri's final letter to Simón in *The Death of Jesus*: '[David] says you agreed he was exceptional, but have you any idea how exceptional he truly was? I don't think you do. He had a quick brain and was nimble on his feet; that was what exceptional meant to you. Whereas I ... knew from the moment my eyes alighted on him that he did not belong to our world' (D 189–90).

Among all the characters in these works, only Dmitri comprehends the degree to which David exceeds novelistic, 'biographical' conceptions of exceptionality like that which Simón so readily attaches to David. Over the course of the three novels, David is repeatedly denied any exceptional status with respect to various mundane rules and sets: {children forbidden entry to La Residencia} (C 72); {children lawfully obliged to attend school} (C 213); {children of normal intelligence} (C 225); {non-orphans forbidden to play for the Las Manos football team} (D 20); {people memorialized after their death because of good deeds they have performed during their lives} (D 103). Despite these refusals, none of these sets is able to accommodate him. '[A]gainst the rules', David bursts into Inés's apartment in La Residencia, for example (C 73–4). When he dies, however, it is not by any action or initiative but through 'bad luck'; he thus becomes an exception to the set {'ninety-nine cases out of a hundred' who do not succumb to germs in the air}. He is, as Simón puts it, 'the hundredth case, the bad-luck case' (*D* 110). Such bad luck, says Simón, 'is not worth talking about'. It is precisely this random quality of David's death that, along with the absence of a 'message', makes him an exception even to the ways novels produce and manage the exceptional beings that appear within them. David has to die because the principle of his existence cannot be sustained within a work that, through its own inner logic, is drifting ever closer to the 'far bank' of transmissible meaning and biographical form.

But we might put this another way. In her 2006 essay 'The Rise of Fictionality', Catherine Gallagher writes of a perverse and contradictory pleasure that arises from the reader's encounter with the limited unity and knowability of a fictional character 'forever tethered to the abstraction of type'. Faced with that typological being, the novel reader enjoys a contrasting sensation of living a life 'without textuality, meaningfulness, or any other excuse for existing'.[39] David dies, is killed, in order that this 'bad' infinity, what Gallagher calls the 'elation of a unitary unboundedness', may be saved – although not, as in Gallagher, for life, but for the novel.

NOTES

1. Coetzee, *Elizabeth Costello*, 1. Further references cited parenthetically in text, using the abbreviation *EC*.
2. Mulhall, *The Wounded Animal*, 172–83; Diamond, 'The Difficulty of Reality and the Difficulty of Philosophy', 43–89.
3. Coetzee, *The Schooldays of Jesus*, 17. Further references to the works of the trilogy, *The Childhood of Jesus*, *Schooldays*, and *The Death of Jesus*, indicated in parentheses using abbreviations *C*, *S* and *D*, respectively.
4. Theo Tait, reviewing *Schooldays* in the *London Review of Books*, wrote of being 'bewilder[ed]' by the shifting of 'co-ordinates' between what he took to be the 'utopianism' of *Childhood* and the relative 'normal[ity]' of *Schooldays*. Of the latter, he confessed, 'I don't pretend to understand this novel' (30c, 30d). See also Markovits; Preston.
5. Rutherford, 'Thinking through Shit in *The Childhood of Jesus*', 59.
6. Bakhtin, *The Dialogic Imagination*, 84.
7. Coetzee expressed this problematic as early as 1987 in the opening remarks to 'The Novel Today', a talk delivered at the Baxter Theatre in Cape Town (referenced elsewhere in this collection). (Coetzee, 'The Novel Today', 2.) Coetzee has apparently resisted efforts to republish this short essay – not, I suspect, because he has reneged on its concerns but the opposite: because it reveals all too nakedly the central preoccupations of his ongoing work.
8. Attridge, 'Reason and Its Others in Coetzee's Jesus Novels', 404.
9. E. M. Forster refers to these 'resources' as 'aspects of the novel', and writes with special clarity about people, plots and physiology. See *Aspects of the Novel*, esp. 56–7, 61–2, 86–7.
10. Attridge, 'Reason and its Others in Coetzee's Jesus Novels', 406.
11. There is some inconsistency in the reporting of Simón's age. In *The Death of Jesus*, Simón remembers his ascribed age on arriving at Novilla as forty-two, not forty-five (*D* 193).
12. 'I am beginning to think there is something in my speech that marks me as a man stuck in the old ways, a man who has not forgotten,' Simón tells Elena (*C* 143).
13. Several commentators (Attridge, 'Reason and its Others in Coetzee's Jesus Novels', 417 n15; Pippin, *Metaphysical Exile*, 64–5) have suggested that Dmitri is named for one of Dostoevsky's *Karamazov* brothers, a connection further substantiated by the presence of a character named 'Alyosha' – the name of another Karamazov brother – at the Academy of Dance.

14. Pippin, *Metaphysical Exile*, 31, 116.
15. Genette, *Narrative Discourse*, 189–94.
16. Benveniste, 'The Nature of Pronouns', 221.
17. Ibid., 222.
18. For a sense of the distinctive effect of this syntactical procedure, consider the radical change in focalization of a sentence as simple as 'He puts down the book' (C 154) if it were rendered as 'Simón puts down the book.' Consider too the fact that there is not a single instance of the latter formation in the entire trilogy. When 'Simón' is used as the subject of the sentence, it is always accompanied by a focalizing 'He', as in: 'He, Simón, joins the fore crew' (C 155). Again, the alternative rendering – 'Simón joins the fore crew' – is inconceivable within the syntactical pattern of the Jesus novels.
19. The few exceptions include the first-person narrative sections from JC's perspective in *Diary of a Bad Year* (the running text situated on the page between JC's essays and Anya's narrative) and certain passages in *Summertime*.
20. Heidegger, *The Fundamental Concepts of Metaphysics*, 5.
21. This is despite the fact that no actual philosophers are mentioned in any of the books (although in *Childhood*, David misnames Mickey Mouse's dog 'Plato'). The influence of Plato's dialogues on episodes in *The Childhood of Jesus* has been discussed by Ng and Sheehan, 'Coetzee's Republic'; Pippin, *Metaphysical Exile*, 43–8; Rabaté, 'Pathos of the Future'; and Uhlmann, *J. M. Coetzee: Truth, Meaning, Fiction*, 171–3.
22. Lanchester, 'Gargantuanisation', 3.
23. Pippin, *Metaphysical Exile*, 67.
24. Ibid., 124.
25. Ibid., 80.
26. Ibid., 12.
27. Ibid., 91.
28. Ibid.
29. Ibid., 92.
30. See, in particular, Coetzee, 'What Is a Classic?', 9–19; *Youth*, 93–4; *Diary of a Bad Year*, 221–2.
31. Lukács, *The Theory of the Novel*, 29, 88.
32. Ibid., 80.
33. Forster, *Aspects of the Novel*, 56–7.
34. Lukács, *The Theory of the Novel*, 81.
35. In an insightful discussion of the two ways of reading in *The Childhood of Jesus*, Peter Boxall paraphrases the meaning of David's engagement with Cervantes as follows:

> What David finds in Cervantes is not a series of oppositions – reality and fantasy, self and world, Don Quixote and Sancho – organised by the binding power of a human intelligence, but a new way of ordering thinking that turns around an anti-human continuity between such oppositions … This is a kind of thinking that does not separate human from nonhuman, nature from culture … but which turns around … a new, nonhuman adhesion between things in the universe.
> (Boxall, *The Prosthetic Imagination*, 344)

Boxall's account implies that the dispute between David's and Simón's ways of reading *is* resolved by the trilogy; that – as Boxall puts it – a 'seismic … shift from one epistemology to another' takes place when Simón recognizes that David's is 'a mind belonging to a different order, one which is attuned to the new world in which they find themselves' (ibid.). Such a 'shift' might then be extracted from the Jesus novels themselves as their 'message'. Simón's insistence upon there being a message is therefore borne out only on condition that its content is foreclosed from the work itself. Contrary to the account offered in the present essay, Boxall's reading would suggest that the Jesus novels are not the 'culmination' of Coetzee's project but a penultimate work, still dependent on the 'biographical form' and on schemas of 'transmissibility'.

36. Naturally, several other writers and works might also be mentioned. Among modern figures, Samuel Beckett and Gerald Murnane are especially important to Coetzee. See Coetzee's essays 'Eight Ways of Looking at Samuel Beckett' (202–17) and 'Reading Gerald Murnane' (259–71) in his *Late Essays: 2006–2017*. See also Uhlmann's fascinating discussion of Murnane's evident influence on Coetzee in *J. M. Coetzee: Truth, Meaning, Fiction*, 181–90.
37. See Miguel de Cervantes, *Don Quixote*, Part II, chapter 32.
38. John 14:6 KJV.
39. Gallagher, 'The Rise of Fictionality', 361.

WORKS CITED

Attridge, Derek. 'Reason and Its Others in Coetzee's Jesus Novels'. *Novel: A Forum on Fiction* 54, no. 3 (2021): 404–24.
Bakhtin, M. M. *The Dialogic Imagination: Four Essays*. Translated by Caryl Emerson and Michael Holquist. Austin: University of Texas Press, 1981.
Benveniste, Émile. 'The Nature of Pronouns'. In *Problems in General Linguistics*, translated by Mary Elizabeth Meek, 217–22. Coral Gables: University of Miami Press, 1971.
Boxall, Peter. *The Prosthetic Imagination: A History of the Novel as Artificial Life*. Cambridge: Cambridge University Press, 2020.
Coetzee, J. M. *The Childhood of Jesus*. London: Harvill Secker, 2013.
Coetzee, J. M. *The Death of Jesus*. London: Harvill Secker, 2019.
Coetzee, J. M. *Diary of a Bad Year*. London: Harvill Secker, 2007.
Coetzee, J. M. *Elizabeth Costello*. New York: Viking, 2003.
Coetzee, J. M. *Late Essays: 2006–2017*. New York: Viking, 2018.
Coetzee, J. M. 'The Novel Today'. *Upstream* 6, no. 1 (1988): 2–5.
Coetzee, J. M. *The Schooldays of Jesus*. London: Harvill Secker, 2016.
Coetzee, J. M. 'What Is a Classic? A Lecture'. In *Stranger Shores: Essays 1986–1999*, 1–19. London: Secker and Warburg, 2001.
Coetzee, J. M. *Youth*. London: Secker and Warburg, 2002.
Diamond, Cora. 'The Difficulty of Reality and the Difficulty of Philosophy'. In Stanley Cavell et al., *Philosophy and Animal Life*, 1–43. New York: Columbia University Press, 2008.
Forster, E. M. *Aspects of the Novel*. London: Penguin, 2005.
Gallagher, Catherine. 'The Rise of Fictionality'. In *The Novel Volume 1: History, Geography, and Culture*, edited by Franco Moretti, 336–61. Princeton, NJ: Princeton University Press, 2006.
Genette, Gérard. *Narrative Discourse: An Essay in Method*. Translated by Jane E. Lewin. Ithaca: Cornell University Press, 1980.
Heidegger, Martin. *The Fundamental Concepts of Metaphysics: World, Finitude, Solitude*. Translated by William McNeill and Nicholas Walker. Bloomington and Indianapolis: Indiana University Press, 1995.
Lanchester, John. 'Gargantuanisation', review of Laleh Khalili, *Sinews of War and Trade: Shipping and Capitalism in the Arabian Peninusula. London Review of Books*, 22 April 2021: 3–6.
Lukács, Georg. *The Theory of the Novel: A Historico-philosophical Essay on the Forms of Great Epic Literature*. Translated by Anna Bostock. Cambridge, MA: MIT Press, 1971.
Mulhall, Stephen. *The Wounded Animal: J. M. Coetzee and the Difficulty of Reality in Literature and Philosophy*. Princeton: Princeton University Press, 2009.

Markovits, Benjamin. '*The Childhood of Jesus* by J. M. Coetzee – Review'. *Guardian*, 2 March 2013. https://www.theguardian.com/books/2013/mar/02/childhood-of-jesus-jm-coetzee-review.
Ng, Lynda and Paul Sheehan. 'Coetzee's Republic: Plato, Borges and Migrant Memory in *The Childhood of Jesus*'. In *J. M. Coetzee's* The Childhood of Jesus: *The Ethics of Ideas and Things*, edited by Jennifer Rutherford and Anthony Uhlmann, 83–103. London: Bloomsbury, 2017.
Pippin, Robert. *Metaphysical Exile: On J. M. Coetzee's Jesus Fictions*. New York: Oxford University Press, 2021.
Preston, Alex. '*The Death of Jesus* by J. M. Coetzee Review – a Barren End to a Bizarre Trilogy'. *Guardian*, 31 December 2019. https://www.theguardian.com/books/2019/dec/31/the-death-of-jesus-jm-coetzee-review.
Rabaté, Jean-Michel. 'Pathos of the Future: Writing and Hospitality in *The Childhood of Jesus*'. In *J. M. Coetzee's* The Childhood of Jesus: *The Ethics of Ideas and Things*, edited by Jennifer Rutherford and Anthony Uhlmann, 33–56. London: Bloomsbury, 2017.
Rutherford, Jennifer. 'Thinking through Shit in The Childhood of Jesus'. In *J. M. Coetzee's* The Childhood of Jesus: *The Ethics of Ideas and Things*, edited by Jennifer Rutherford and Anthony Uhlmann, 59–81. London: Bloomsbury, 2017.
Tait, Theo. 'The Atom School'. *London Review of Books*, 3 November 2016: 30–1.
Uhlmann, Anthony. *J. M. Coetzee: Truth, Meaning, Fiction*. London: Bloomsbury, 2020.

CHAPTER EIGHTEEN

Later criticism and correspondence

NICK MULGREW

'There remains the matter of getting past Coetzee.'

– *Dusklands*, 14–15

Once, in my second-favourite Indian restaurant in Cape Town, I overheard a diner holding forth at length to his waiter about J. M. Coetzee. Coetzee, apparently, used to frequent its sister restaurant, near to the University of Cape Town. The wait-staff were not privy to this information, nor did they appear to care very much about it – yet the diner continued his monologue. 'Jay Em – John Maxwell – Coetzee, the greatest novelist of his generation – *in the world!* – used to come to your restaurant in Rondebosch. I saw him there many a time.' He had claimed to have known Coetzee's favourite dish. I wish I could remember what he said it was.

Episodes on this theme – South Africans seeking personal closeness to Coetzee – veer towards the comical. Wamuwi Mbao writes excruciatingly well on the clingy, sycophantic reception Coetzee receives at his rare public appearances in South Africa. There's one where past attendees of his classes, once-friends of his late journalist brother, and apparently even his childhood babysitter litter a crowd that drops 'bon mots and choice observations drawn from the novels with savage knowingness.'[1] Hedley Twidle, in an award-winning essay, relates his somewhat amusing failure to complete a career-defining article on Coetzee for a major London review: 'I found myself obsessed by minor details on the outskirts of his work', he writes, such as Coetzee's attempts 'to emulate the Mediterranean diet of Ford Madox Ford' by frying fish fingers in olive oil. For a writer so spare, so economical, 'these finer points of domestic economy seemed laden with meaning.'[2]

Apart from being a cautionary tale against a certain kind of literary biography, Twidle's essay also hints at an attitude specifically held about Coetzee, namely – as per Mbao – that Coetzee 'does not deal in explanations'. He is inscrutable. The studied, deliberate economy of his writing is echoed in a similar economy of the self. These perceptions of Coetzee – of a rigorously self-crafted, hard-to-pin-down intellectual – have perhaps become orthodoxy, which is strange because, over the first two decades of the twenty-first century, Coetzee has given over more of himself to the scrutiny of readers than they might have expected. During this time, in addition to the second and third of his trilogy of auto-fictional novels, *Youth* (2002) and *Summertime* (2009), and the fictional essays that make up the bulk of *Diary of A Bad Year* (2007), Coetzee has published two books of literary criticism and two of personal correspondence; four works that are, in sum, not only revealing of their subjects, but also of their writer – of John. It is on these works that I shall focus.

* * *

Inner Workings (2007) and *Late Essays* (2017) collect twenty-one and twenty-three critical essays respectively. None of the forty-four pieces is original to either collection: most were reviews, appearing first, sometimes in an earlier version, in the *New York Review of Books*; the remainder, save for two, appeared as introductions to translated or scholarly works. The essays range from four to twenty-three pages in length, and most concern a single work or writer, or a translation of their oeuvre. Five essays in total focus on Samuel Beckett; there are two each on Philip Roth, Robert Walser and Patrick White.

While it is difficult to categorize all the writers Coetzee writes about, if only because many of them were born into countries and eras defined by warfare, colonialism, exodus or other catalysts of societal re-definition, one sees in these later essays a broadening of Coetzee's gaze away from the predominantly southern African concerns of the earlier non-fiction.[3] One fact is immediately apparent, though: with the exceptions of Irène Némirovsky and Nadine Gordimer, these writers are all men. As fellow South African-Australian author Ceridwen Dovey writes, many of Coetzee's novels, from *In the Heart of the Country* to *Elizabeth Costello*, focus on the internal and intellectual lives of their woman protagonists who are in Dovey's opinion 'among the most intelligent [characters] I've encountered on the page'.[4] Hence, this lack of women writers may come as a disappointment. Readers attuned to anti- or post-colonial discourse will note that, with the exceptions of V.S. Naipaul and Hendrik Witbooi, the writers are of predominantly European heritage. That said, a large proportion of these writers are of Jewish descent, and as such reflect Coetzee's continuing interest in artists and art made by those on the receiving end of atrocity, as well as his interest in writers producing 'minor literatures', that is to say, writing within a major language but certainly not identifying with it in any simple nationalist sense.

Readers might be tempted to view these essays as a personal canon of sorts – a mapping of influences, in the way that the essays themselves map out the influences of their subjects and the genealogies of their texts. But despite Coetzee's assertion, very early on in his career, that he reads 'mostly the stuff that, crudely speaking, [he] can cannibalise',[5] there is no indication by Coetzee that this tendency still holds decades later, or that it applies in any way to the texts he writes about.

Either way, these are two disconnected collections, by which I mean that, as books, they have no internal logic, thematic spine or overarching sequence. They are composed of discrete critical essays, many of them reviews, collected for convenience's sake and grouped loosely by geographical region or subject. Having been written, presumably, on commission and for inclusion in other publications, they have jarring moments and sometimes end abruptly. Certain aspects have also changed from their initial appearances, such as their titles, and – in the case of essays from the *New York Review of Books* – the names or lists of books that mark out the essay's subjects at the outset. For example, an essay on five books by Paul Celan titled 'In the Midst of Losses' in the *New York Review of Books* is titled 'Paul Celan and his translators' in *Inner Workings*.[6] All of the essays have similarly austere titles: generally either a writer's name and the text or period at hand ('Robert Musil, *The Confusions of Young Törless*', 'Late Patrick White'), a writer's name and a short identification ('Hugo Claus, poet', 'Irène Némirovsky, Jewish Writer'), or even simply a writer's name ('Walt Whitman'). By condensing all of the essays' paratextual information into their titles, Coetzee strips down the textual form and presentation of the essay into its most essential components.

This is a typically Coetzean rhetorical strategy, one that is not accessible to most other writers. It is not borne simply of Coetzee's economy or sense of aesthetics, nor of a desire to make the essays vague, and their inquiries and aims therefore liable to being second-guessed. The play here is simple: as reviews and introductions to other texts, these are texts to guide or enrich reading; to provide perspective, context and understanding. To do this, Coetzee has to create a strong, in-built sense of textual authority; in other words, a sense of assured argument from the outset, built not just by what he writes, but *how* he writes, and how he presents that writing. Other writers, even an earlier Coetzee, might have to build up sufficient authority – usually by means of rhetorical strategies or peritextual manipulation (such as making a show of their knowledge of their subject matter, or having an impressive author biography running alongside their text) – in order to make the reader believe, accept or otherwise think valid, their argument. But Coetzee does not have to do this, by sole virtue of his being – and being seen to write like – J. M. Coetzee.

As such, Coetzee adopts an elevated, magisterial tone in these essays. Most notably this applies to his discussions of translation, given that it is the central subject of many of the longer pieces in each collection. Within the essays there are explications of certain texts' translation histories, in particular the works of Robert Walser and Johann Wolfgang von Goethe, while some (Paul Celan and Friedrich Hölderlin) are entirely given over to analysing the task of translation, and evaluating the efforts of those who have taken on that challenge.

Given the mimetic stakes – in addition to his interest in linguistics and own bilinguality – it is not surprising that Coetzee is an involved, productive and at times severe critic of translated texts. Indeed, while he admits perfect translation between cultures and periods of time can be 'an unattainable ideal',[7] there are standards to keep if literature is to bear witness. All of his points taken in sum, one might put together a guide for translative best practice. It is, for example, 'questionable professional practice' – even 'unacceptable' – to translate a work from an already existing translation (*IW*, 109; *LE*, 60). Likewise, do not imitate the translator of Italo Svevo who 'simply elides or synopsises passages' for economy's sake (*IW*, 8); nor the translator of Bruno Schulz, who 'universalizes' culturally specific idioms and allusions (*IW*, 69). Avoid using one language's conventions to transliterate another's (*IW*, 87), and certainly do not seek to 'improve' bad writing (*IW*, 92).

Even putting aside its meditations on the limits of translation, the essay on Celan is one of the most intriguing, detailing the hardships and suspicions, mostly borne out of anti-Semitism, that Celan worked under, as well as his treatment by a woman who was convinced that he was plagiarizing her dead husband (*IW*, 115). Coetzee's larger project here is to find a single answer for a number of questions; in other words, a locus for a number of inquiries. Discussing a poem about the murder of Rosa Luxembourg, as well as Celan's famously elusive Holocaust poem 'Death Fugue', Coetzee ponders whether it is a failure of poetics or mimesis if a reader requires prior information about a poem's subject in order to understand the work. If not, is there a limit to the demands a poem may put on its reader? 'Is it possible to respond to poetry', he asks, 'and 'even to translate it, without fully understanding it'? (*IW*, 117). Can literature 'offer a kind of knowledge different from that offered by history, and demand a different kind of receptivity' (*IW*, 117) and, if so, then does one approach the difficult task of translating various, sometimes intangible, layers of meaning, many of which are tied up in a writer's 'wrestling' with the very substrate of one particular language (*IW*, 131)? In comparison to these complex questions, Coetzee's precise language is necessary and welcome throughout.

Elsewhere Coetzee is particularly judicious when discussing form and genre. In *Inner Workings* he works to categorize and evaluate texts by his subjects' metrics, as well as (less successfully) by his own. He interrogates, to give only a few examples, the sufficiency of the term 'stories' to describe what are in fact collected fragments of larger works (*IW*, 86), whether travel writing can pass muster if it is not based on personal observation (*IW*, 101) and how historical fiction may be written about an imagined or alternate history (*IW*, 240–2, passim). It is not that Coetzee has set or is setting criteria on what genre and form are, but rather that he is attempting to understand the logic behind a text being called, considered or read as a particular genre or form, especially if such a text 'occupie[s] uneasy ground' between two genres or forms (*IW*, 216). This preoccupation with definition, however, does result in some strange assertions, such as that, 'despite its length', Nadine Gordimer's novel *The Pickup* should be considered a novella simply because of its 'narrower [thematic] range' compared with some of her earlier works (*IW*, 250). Coetzee offers no other justification or precedent for this opinion.[8]

When he does quote from other critics, they are seldom his contemporaries. The critics he tends to refer to are other prominent writers in the English-language canon, or critics contemporaneous with the subject. Writing on Nathaniel Hawthorne's *Scarlet Letter*, for example, he appeals to Henry James and Edgar Allan Poe (*LE*, 17–18). While most of the essays begin with lucid summations of texts or some kind of immersive, biographical note about their authors, Coetzee often gives no indication of sources: for example, in writing on *Madame Bovary*, he relates that Gustave Flaubert 'said or is claimed to have said' that '*Madame Bovary, c'est moi* [Madame Bovary is me]'; Coetzee does not indicate where he encountered the claim of the utterance (*LE*, 107).

These features, in sum, are claims to authority, latent suggestions that these are the kinds of facts that are so rote to Coetzee that they might as well be general knowledge. He, for instance, criticizes the critical edition of Walter Benjamin's *Selected Works*, the notes of which contain information that is 'sometimes out of date [...] or incorrect' (*IW*, 62), and that, he argues, make errors in their treatment of Greek, Latin and French. Likewise he has a habit of saying 'of course' about facts that many readers approaching his essays will in fact not know: in an overview of Benjamin's Arcades Project, he says that the story of the author's flight from Nazi-occupied France 'is by now so well known what it barely needs to be retold' (*IW*, 2, 40). Mercifully he retells it for anyone in the back rows.

* * *

In his introduction to *Inner Workings*, the scholar Derek Attridge argues that the essays show Coetzee 'speak[ing] in his own voice' (*IW*, ix). Yet Coetzee very seldom engages the first person, even if he does sometimes slip in under the guise of a 'reader' (*IW*, 264). Such aloofness might have to do with the essays' original places of publication: is his register a function of his own conception of himself, or the expectations of the editorial team of the *New York Review of Books*?[9]

The essays that were written as introductions or otherwise not as reviews are much more supple, and lighter in tone. There are two standouts in this regard. The first is the last of a series of four pieces in *Late Essays* on Samuel Beckett, a sequence that lays bare the construction of these collections as a retrospective assemblage of discrete writing jobs. Facts are repeated between them, paths retrodden. The last of them, however, titled 'Eight Ways of Looking at Samuel Beckett', is fresh and malleable, tracking Coetzee's encounters with Beckett via a number of philosophical inquiries and thought experiments. Here Coetzee grapples with certain Beckettian mysteries, in particular his 'existential homelessness' (*LE*, 203), casting light onto certain issues of embodiment touched upon in both writers' oeuvres. Coetzee is not afraid to inhabit (or ventriloquize) Beckett's voice, even entertaining an alternate history in which young Beckett's application for a lecturing position at UCT is accepted: 'Should we smile at the thought of Samuel Barclay Beckett, BA, MA, Professor of Romance Languages, University of Cape Town?' (*LE*, 217). It is about as close to playful as Coetzee gets, as close to an homage as he allows.

Also notable in the same volume is a short defence of Juan Ramón Jiminéz's *Platero and I*, as well as its eponymous subject, the narrator's beloved silvery donkey. A prose poem, *Platero and I*, 'is usually thought of a children's book' but in fact holds 'much that is beyond the range of interest of children', such as the 'mutual bond between man and beast', and the often hypocritical and superficial attachments human form to certain species of animals over others (*LE*, 130–1). But what Coetzee extols most here is the 'love' humans can (and must) have for animals, as well as the 'hard lessons' that such an emotional connection entails (*LE*, 132–3). This is a fitting coda to a long-running engagement with animal rights, such as in *The Lives of Animals* (which, stripped of the metafictional 'reflections' and academic responses to its two constituent stories by Peter Singer, Marjorie Garber, Wendy Doniger and Barbara Smuts, forms part of *Elizabeth Costello*). The topic of cruelty to animals also surfaces in Coetzee's appraisal of Arthur Miller's *The Misfits*, the only film to be discussed in either collection of essays. In particular, Coetzee considers the film's use of actual wild horses in scenes in which they are chased and wrangled: the horses' 'exhaustion and pain and terror' are not only evident but 'real', and as such, Coetzee argues, these scenes bring one 'close to the heart of film as a representational medium' (*IW*, 225).

In many respects, there is much in these essays about Coetzee that readers familiar with his work will already know. There is evidence of Coetzee's distaste for Soviet communism and political centrism (*IW*, 44–5 and 107), as well as his fascination with writers, like Irene Némirovsky and Antonio di Benedetto, who lived under the shadow of atrocity and brutality (*LE*, 113–18, passim and 150). Some readers, however, will find Coetzee awkward in his discussions of sex, sexual assault and rape. It is not that he avoids these topics, rather that his engagement is limited or uneven. While he deftly considers, for example, the narrative and ethical implications of the 'medico-legal orthodoxy' of early nineteenth-century Germany, in which it was argued that acts that resulted in conception could not be considered rape (*LE*, 92), there are instances where Coetzee's regular discursive rigour is lacking. Most troubling in this regard is a description of the action of Gabriel García Marquez's *Memories of My Melancholy Whores*. Here, Coetzee is too caught up with the 'brave' mission of the novel – its exploration of a 'continuity between sexual desire and the passion of veneration', and its attempts to 'show that paedophilia need not be a dead end for either lover or beloved' – to identify a scene where a man fondles a sleeping girl as sexual assault (*IW*, 264). Indeed, for a writer of such exactitude, he might be thought to be remiss in not describing sexual violence as sexual violence, whether it is the acts of Willie Chandran in V.S. Naipaul's *Half a Life* ('Soon he begins to visit African prostitutes, many of them, by Western standards, children' (*IW*, 283)), or 'a novel by Kawabata about ageing men who pay money to spend nights with drugged, sleeping girls' (*IW*, 268). These are euphemisms for acts of rape; acts that one might expect would demand Coetzee's interest in the ethical implications of depicting (or not depicting) atrocity. Perhaps Coetzee expects the immorality and horror of such acts to be implicit in their description, but it is still notable that he demurs from identifying sexual and gender-based violence as such, and chooses not to explore the ethics of the representation of these sexually violent acts. Coetzee writes, with regard to García Marquez, that 'to demand unequivocal answers [...] is to mistake the nature of the storyteller's art' (*IW*, 264). Perhaps, for a writer whose approaches to sexual desire and violence – from *Waiting for the Barbarians* to *Disgrace* – are manifest and complicated, the argument might also apply to his own work and speak for itself. Then again, when compared to the rigour with which he discusses representations of the Holocaust or questions of animal cruelty, readers may still be left wanting here.

* * *

When I think of Coetzee, I often think of a joke made at his expense. At the Adelaide Writers' Week in March 2010, Coetzee hosted a 'Meet the Author' session with the English writer Geoff Dyer. Introduced – perhaps a bit dryly – by Coetzee, Dyer took to the lectern. 'Thank you, John,' Dyer said. 'What an honour. If someone had told me twenty years ago that I'd be here in Australia and I'd be introduced by a Booker Prize-winning, South African, Nobel Prize-winning novelist, I don't know what I'd have said.' Cue applause. 'Well, what would I have said?' Dyer continued, after a moment's pause. 'I'd've probably said, well that's incredible – Nadine Gordimer is my favourite writer.'

Some might think this joke mean; others might regard Coetzee's response – there is not even a hint of recognition at Dyer's attempt at collegial humour – and conclude that he didn't care anyway. Of course, it is impossible to know what Coetzee thought in this specific situation, or in any of the other strange professional situations a writer encounters throughout their career: feuds, negative reviews, clingy readers, treacherous publishers, unethical journalists. That said, two collections of Coetzee's correspondence, one with the American writer Paul Auster and the British therapist Arabella Kurtz, can shine light on the experience of being J. M. Coetzee – or, rather, as he signs off his letters, John.

Here and Now, Letters: 2008–2011 (2013) tracks a budding friendship between Coetzee and Auster (and to a lesser extent their partners), bringing certain fragments of Coetzee's personal life – relatively unfiltered in comparison to his auto-fiction – into the body of his own oeuvre. From bouts of the flu to the 'purgatory' of jet lag, Coetzee offers insights into an extraordinary existence that to him (as well as to the other ultra-successful writer he is in conversation with) is quotidian.[10]

The volume is unexpectedly direct, attempting to mimic the verisimilitude of their correspondence as they (presumably) experienced it. There is no introduction to the volume, only the first letter, one from Coetzee telling Auster that he has been 'thinking about friendships' (*H&N*, 1), a septuagenarian's twist on the first-day-of-school tactic of asking the person closest to you if they want to be your friend. The letters are likewise of a considered tone and composition, as if the writers are themselves convinced of their import. Some are written over a number of days, with smaller notes sometimes dashed off to each other in the midst of composing a longer missive. Some letters never reach their destination, and are not replied to. The sequence is not always chronological: replies are sometimes staggered, owing to their mode of correspondence: Coetzee generally faxes his letters from Adelaide to Auster in New York (with a couple sent via e-mail, care of Auster's wife, the writer Siri Hustvedt), while Auster opts to post Coetzee typewritten pages.[11]

In addition to the tools of their trade, they write to each other about problems and occurrences they think the other will find interesting. The ways in which Coetzee and Auster write to each other – the latter even offers a numbered list of 'possible points to discuss'! (*H&N*, 15) – is as much evidence of a self-awareness on their parts that their correspondence will be pored over at some point, as it is of a sometimes awkward beginning to their conversation.[12] Auster is generally more forthcoming with sharing his experiences, while textual intimacies are mutually restrained.[13] Responding to one of Auster's many, often entertaining stories about bad reviews and unwanted public interactions, Coetzee confesses a paradox at the heart of his writing life: while he possesses a professional 'incapacity to get upset by what other people say about me', he is otherwise 'thin-skinned' in his 'everyday dealings' (*H&N*, 126). Where the professional and personal overlap is the trouble, as evidenced by one of the central happenings of *Here and Now*: a letter written to Coetzee by a reader in England, accusing him of anti-Semitism on the basis that one of the characters in *Slow Man* speaks in a derogatory manner about Jewish people. Despairingly he forwards the letter to Auster with a clipped note, seeking counsel: 'Paul, See below. What does one do? John' (*H&N*, 94).

Here they discourse on one of the aspects of literature (and art in general) that causes the most misunderstandings: the degree of separation between author and narrator, the creator and their creation. Auster offers comfort in labelling the sort of accusation Coetzee received 'absurd [and] idiotic', and yet 'a part of the world we live in' (*H&N*, 95). But Coetzee, having muddied many waters throughout his career, complicates matters further. Yes, he writes, 'one can write back explaining that characters in novels have a degree of independence from their authors', but there can be no expectation that this will be the final word. 'As a writer of a certain prominence,' he relates, 'I must expect to get all kinds of mail from readers', and this includes readers who do not have 'a sophisticated understanding of what fiction is or does' (*H&N*, 96). Therefore, he argues, the 'real question'

> is not whose hands are clean and whose are not. The real question arises out of the moment of being thrown onto the defensive, and out of the sinking feeling that comes next, the feeling that the goodwill between reader and writer has evaporated, the goodwill without which reading loses its joy and writing begins to feel like an unwanted, burdensome exercise. What does one do after that? Why go on, when one's words are being picked over for covert slights and heresies? It's like being back among the Puritans.
>
> (*H&N*, 96–7)

The ethical gaze is turned back on himself, and he then reflects it onto the world. This is an experience few writers will encounter, and perhaps a level of exasperation that few will ever feel. To have built up a career in as oppressive and censorial a regime as apartheid South Africa, to have given significant portions of this career – particularly in writing *Giving Offence* and in his work with centres of PEN International – to understanding and interacting with issues of censorship and injurious speech, and still, at the end of it all, to be unable to escape this problem. Given his professional and life experiences, it is perhaps not surprising that Coetzee is hyper-aware of, and constantly shifting, his approach to constructions of a narrative self.

The second volume of correspondence, *The Good Story: Exchanges on Truth, Fiction and Psychotherapy* (2015), is more revealing on this subject. Coetzee and Kurtz's conversation, occurring over roughly the same period as *Here and Now*, is more formal; this is in effect a book-length interview broken into chapters and introduced by an authors' note, which explains that the exchange is 'premised on the idea that something is to be gained by a therapist exploring their practice in the company of [...] a sympathetically disposed writer and literary critic'.[14] The other, unspoken point of the book, is to delineate different forms of storytelling, to compare and differentiate the functions, benefits and limits of fiction and therapy – in other words, the goal of the writer, and the goal of the therapist. They both deal with stories, of course, but to different ends. Coetzee worries about the 'serious real-world consequences' of life-stories (*TGS*, 4), while Kurtz works with life-stories other than her own – the one is concerned with the ethical and aesthetic dimensions, the other the practical and medical.

Kurtz is an able and candid interlocutor, her contributions to the book a balm to Coetzee's more chafing examination. Together the two explore notions of truth and selfhood in the work of Sophocles, Dostoyevsky, Cervantes, Marx, Eugene Marais, Melanie Klein and W. G. Sebald, as well as making forays into psychoanalytic theory and the psychology of groups, in particular societal 'silence' and revisionism among the white populations of South Africa, the United States and Australia (*TGS*, 96). Some of the exchange is interesting only for those interested in philosophical semantics, vis-a-vis psychotherapy and ontology. Likewise significant portions are given over to fancies born from Coetzee's dogged belief that he, a self-confessed 'amateur', 'may possibly have a contribution to make' to the field of group psychology (*TGS*, 131): he states at one point that there is almost 'nothing worth building on' in the work of Gustave Le Bon, and substitutes in for it stories from his childhood of being in a gang of small boys and from his life as a teacher at universities (*TGS*, 143–4, 164).

For Coetzee critics, the core question of the exchange, from which the many other topics radiate, is whether or not the narratives one tells or understands about oneself are necessarily fiction. Although he is driven by a childhood 'nostalgia for the one and only truth' (*TGS*, 68), Coetzee believes that thinking 'of a life-story as a compendium of memories which one is free to interpret' is 'characteristic of a writer's way of thinking', in contrast to how 'many people' see the story of their lives, 'as a history that is forever fixed' (*TGS*, 13). Regardless of how one conceives of their life's story, and regardless of whether one is a writer or not, the stories we tell about ourselves are all to 'serve our own interests, or what we imagine are our interests' (*TGS*, 60). For Coetzee, every seemingly autobiographical story is modified by the 'allure of self-invention' (*TGS*, 1), and is thus as much a fiction (in other words, a subjective fantasy) as any other narrative 'construction' (*TGS*, 3). In fact, he writes,

> I don't have much respect for reality. I think of myself as using rather than reflecting reality in my fiction. If the world of my fictions is a recognisable world, that is because (I say to myself) it is easier to use the world at hand than to make up a new one.
>
> (*TGS*, 69)

Here, out of a mixture of differences in outlook, as well as professional necessity, the two butt heads. Kurtz understands that the stories we tell about our lives may not be an accurate reflection of what really happened, and in fact 'may be more remarkable for their inaccuracies than anything else', but are nevertheless 'all we have to work with' in attempting to understand ourselves (*TGS*, 63). For a therapist, Kurtz explains, the point isn't whether or not someone's life-story is an objective factual account, but rather how their story reflects both 'subjective' and 'intersubjective' truth, both individual and interpersonally recognizable experience; how the story can then be reflected back at the patient, who, one should not forget, is someone who is in treatment for 'subjective distress' (*TGS*, 70).

This is an interesting discussion in part because it is obvious from the outset that the two might never see eye-to-eye. As much as they are attempting to see what understandings or contributions one can receive from the other, their professional aims are irreconcilable. Coetzee is concerned that writers modify and possibly compromise the 'truth' of stories by attempting to satisfy 'autonomous aesthetic criteria', instead using 'poetic tricks and devices' to persuade the reader that the compromised truth is still a truth (*TGS*, 8). Kurtz is concerned not whether a story is *a* truth, but whether it is to its teller *the* truth. This is a subtle difference, which Coetzee himself hints at but does not resolve when at one point he reminds himself to 'take to heart [Kurtz's] reminder' that a patient 'wants sympathy and understanding, not a disquisition on the difference between fictional truths and fictional fictions' (*TGS*, 142). For all of their grappling with the subject, Coetzee and Kurtz discourse about two different areas of truth, or more accurately, two different layers of truth. Coetzee is primarily concerned with what we might call factuality, whether or not a narrative *is* factual or non-factual; Kurtz with what we might call fictionality, whether a narrative *is intended* to be factual or non-factual.

This exchange is certainly not a therapy session in book form: Coetzee is not apparently in distress, and private details are few. It can nevertheless be read as Coetzee's managed and public attempt to understand his own view of the world, terminally self-aware of his own subjectivity, and given his interest in psychotherapy as a discourse. Although he is 'properly wary of using myself as an example' (*TGS*, 21), he does so anyway. *The Good Story* explains in part why Coetzee does not write about himself identifiably as himself – in the first person or otherwise – and why he is at pains to keep an authorial distance from his work. It isn't for obfuscation, or trickery, nor entirely to avoid occupational hazards like the ones he relates to Auster. Rather it is an unerring philosophical position, which he glosses from Gabriel Garcia Marquez: 'The I who tells the story will be no less a constructed figure than the actors in it' (*LE*, 263).

Near the outset of *The Good Story*, Kurtz submits that we might only 'know and understand ourselves fully through others, through the way we experience others and ourselves in relation to others, and the way others experience us': 'This,' she concludes, 'is what I read your book *Summertime* to be about' (*TGS*, 11). In addition to its critical clarity, this is notable for being one of only a few explicit mentions of a book written by Coetzee in another book (co-)written by Coetzee.[15] It is also a key to unlocking Coetzee's authorial stance. This is his (co-authored) book, so he had the power to erase Kurtz's reading of the novel, the third of his trilogy of auto-fictions. The author-subject, John Coetzee, is dead in *Summertime*; the book is a collection of voices and opinions about the dead man, compiled by a fictitious biographer. But this is not a traditional death-of-the-author situation, nor is it a straightforward comment on 'the malleability of memory', of which Coetzee admits his sense is 'simply too strong' (*TGS*, 21). Coetzee is inarguably writing about himself in his auto-fiction, as well as in many passages of his other books. To repurpose a passage from *Inner Workings* about Philip Roth's fiction about a child called Philip Roth (*IW*, 233): if the author John Coetzee had meant to write about a fictive person whose sole existence is between the pages of a novel, he would not have called that character John Coetzee. In some sense the John Coetzee whose life we read continues his life in the life of the John Coetzee who some years later not only exists in the novel, but writes it too.

Coetzee writes to Kurtz that he believes 'most exchanges between human beings to be exchanges between projected fictions' (*TGS*, 50) and that he himself is 'as divided, undecided and confused as can be' (*TGS*, 69). *Summertime* textually embodies these beliefs (as do the other auto-fictions), a writing about oneself from the perspective of 'the only ending one can seriously believe in': 'What an irony,' Coetzee writes, 'that to anchor oneself in a sea of fictions one should have to rely on death!' (*TGS*, 69).

So: John is dead, long live John? Not quite – or, perhaps, not all. For here is Coetzee's 'notion of [...] an ideal society':

> one in which, for each of us, our fiction (our fantasy) of ourself goes unchallenged; and where some grand Leibnizian presiding force sees to it that all the billions of personal fictions interlock seamlessly, so that none of us need stay awake at night wondering anxiously whether the world we inhabit is real.
>
> (*TGS*, 177)

In *Here and Now*, the reader learns that Coetzee does not, in fact, sleep very much. He gets only about four hours a night (*H&N*, 227).

* * *

What else may be gained from Coetzee's later criticism? For one, novelists, translators and critics can find all sorts of writerly tips and tricks. Some may be taken from Coetzee's professional experience. A successful novel, in his opinion, is one that, like psychoanalysis, 'exposes' the fantasies the characters hold about themselves, and 'that our seeming lives are not our real lives' (*TGS*, 191). Yet '[t]he novelist [still] has a duty to supply plausible psychological motives for the actions of his characters' (*LE*, 156). He finds 'too much self-aggrandisement in the idea – conjured up by artists themselves – of the artist as diagnostician of the age' (*TGS*, 60). The unspeakably atrocious may still, however, be written about 'by sideways motion', by narrative gestures through which 'the greater story somehow gets told' (*IW*, 143). Other insights come from his study of the practice of other writers. From Roth, Coetzee notes that a seasoned novelist 'knows that the stories we set about writing sometimes begin to write themselves, after which [our] declarations of authorial intent carry no weight' (*IW*, 229). From Walser, he understands how the very act of writing, of putting pen to paper or finger to keyboard, can bring about 'a frame of mind in which reverie, composition, and the flow of the writing tool became the same thing' (*IW*, 22–3).

The auto-fiction aside, there are other more personal insights into Coetzee's work. Most revealingly, he reveals that he has 'a pretty paltry visual imagination': he does not see anything in his mind's eye when he reads, but rather an 'aura or tonality' (*H&N*, 201). Likewise, the place in which he imagines his fiction taking place is 'pretty bare' – 'an empty cube, in fact' – in which items are only visualized if they are to figure in the narrative (*H&N*, 193). He also does not imagine the lives of his characters outside of the bounds of the narratives he composes.

In sum, these volumes are far more interesting than any promotional interview could ever be. Perhaps that is because, as Coetzee says to Auster,

> I have often felt oppressive boredom as I listen to myself mouthing off to interviewers. To my way of thinking, real talk only occurs when there is some kind of current running between the interlocutors. And such a current rarely runs during interviews.
>
> (*H&N*, 110)

A reader expecting overt candour from Coetzee, however, would be disappointed: these letters show that the perceptions of Coetzee as a calculated and possibly distant man are both true and not true. The level tone, the exacting intellectual inquiry? It's no show – that's just the way he is. He is as abstracting and critical of his own interests – sport, particularly cricket and previously chess (*H&N* 11, 30, 51, 162–3 passim) – as he is about the causes of the 2008 financial crisis, the factual basis of his English being called 'sud-africaine' by his French publishers, or the phenomenological basis of reading (*H&N*, 19, 72; *TGS*, 179). He worries that his thinking on certain subjects is 'airy-fairy', and he is 'embarrassed' to converse on topics over which he does not have mastery (*TGS*, 12).

The letters to Auster and Kurtz provide an answer to a mystery that Coetzee's readers have pondered over throughout his career. Namely, there is no great facade to Coetzee. He is as revealing and confessional a writer as any other, but only within the strict bounds of his literary output. There is little misdirection on his part with regard to his authorial intentions, only a complication, or perhaps an overlapping. Is *Here and Now* a sincere exchange of letters between friends? Yes, because Coetzee and Auster *are* friends, and that's what friends do. Is it also something of a meta-treatise on how correspondence between writers may be treated? Also yes, because they are writers, and that is what *writers* do. They discourse within *Here and Now* about the publication of the correspondence of Samuel Beckett, a writer close to both their hearts (*H&N*, 29, 32, 48). As such, it would be terminally naive to think they wouldn't have considered the aesthetics of their own correspondence. Likewise it would be naive to think Coetzee doesn't deeply consider his own constructions of himself within his work, fiction or non, critical or correspondence. It doesn't mean, though, that the constructions he creates aren't also him.

NOTES

1. Mbao, 'J.M. Coetzee Is Tired', online.
2. Twidle, 'Getting Past Coetzee', 10.
3. To list, there are six Germans (Walter Benjamin, Günter Grass, W. G. Sebald, Johann Wolfgang von Goethe, Friedrich Hölderlin, Heinrich von Kleist), two German-speaking Austrians (Robert Musil, Joseph Roth) and one German-speaking Swiss (Robert Walser); five US Americans (Walt Whitman, William Faulkner, Arthur Miller, Philip Roth, Nathaniel Hawthorn) and one US American-Canadian (Saul Bellow); three Englishmen (Graham Greene, Daniel Defoe, Ford Madox Ford) and one British-Trinidadian and Tobagoan (V. S. Naipaul); three Australians (Patrick White, Les Murray, Gerald Murnane); two Poles (Bruno Schulz, Zbigniew Herbert); and one writer each from Italy (Italo Svevo), Hungary (Sándor Márai), Romania (Paul Celan), Belgium (Hugo Claus), Spain (Juan Ramón Jiménez), France (Gustave Flaubert), France-via-Ukraine (Irène Némirovsky), Russia (Leo Tolstoy), Argentina (Antonio di Benedetto), Colombia (Gabriel García Marquez), modern-day Namibia (Hendrik Witbooi) and South Africa (Nadine Gordimer).
4. Dovey, *On J.M. Coetzee*, 9.
5. Watson, 'Speaking: J. M. Coetzee,' 24, in Dovey, *On Coetzee*, 43.
6. Coetzee, 'In the Midst of Losses', 4.
7. Coetzee, *Late Essays*, 61. Further references to essays from this collection will be cited parenthetically in text, using the abbreviation *LE*. References to essays from Coetzee's *Inner Workings* will be cited parenthetically using the abbreviation *IW*.

8. He is somewhat less inexact when discussing Philip Roth's *Nemesis*, of which he says, 'Despite its length (280 pages) it has the *feel* of a novella' (*LE*, 48; my emphasis).
9. And in this context, his relative lack of references would not be so problematic, with fact claims double-checked by the publication's editorial board.
10. Auster and Coetzee, *Here and Now*, 17, 186. Further references will be cited parenthetically in text, using the abbreviation *H&N*.
11. Auster moans at one point – in the year 2009 – about how 'Paris hotel rooms are not equipped with typewriters' (35).
12. Auster contrasts his openness with Coetzee with 'perhaps the closest male friend of [his] adulthood', whose mind is nevertheless almost inaccessible to Auster (4).
13. John usually wishes Paul a variation on 'All the best', while Paul graduates over the course of two years from offering a 'handshake', to giving 'Gramps' and his partner a pair of 'big hugs' (14, 182, 198).
14. Coetzee and Kurtz, *The Good Story*, v. Further references will be cited parenthetically in text, using the abbreviation *TGS*.
15. Others include references in *Here and Now* by Auster to the film adaptation of *Disgrace*, and a self-critical remark by Coetzee about *Giving Offence* as part of the conversation precipitated by the English reader's letter.

WORKS CITED

Auster, Paul and J. M. Coetzee, *Here and Now: Letters 2008–2011*. London: Faber and Faber & Harvill Secker, 2013.
Coetzee, J. M. 'In the Midst of Losses'. *New York Review of Books*, 5 July 2001: 4–8.
Coetzee, J. M. *Inner Workings: Essays 2000–2005*. London: Vintage, 2008.
Coetzee, J. M. *Late Essays: 2006–2017*. London: Harvill Secker, 2017.
Coetzee, J. M. and Arabella Kurtz. *The Good Story: Exchanges on Truth, Fiction and Psychotherapy*. London: Harvill Secker, 2015.
Dovey, Ceridwen. *On J.M. Coetzee*. Carlton: Black Inc., 2018.
Mbao, Wamuwi. 'J.M. Coetzee Is Tired: Wamuwi Mbao Reports from the Photographs from Boyhood Exhibition in Cape Town'. *Johannesburg Review of Books*, 5 February 2018.
Twidle, Hedley. 'Getting Past Coetzee'. *Financial Times*, 28 December 2012: 10–11.
Watson, Stephen. 'Speaking: J. M. Coetzee.' *Speak* 1, no. 3 (1978): 21–4.

PART FIVE

Style, Form, Ideas

CHAPTER NINETEEN

Coetzee's style

CARROL CLARKSON

I

In the opening scene of J. M. Coetzee's first novel, *Dusklands* (1974), Eugene Dawn's supervisor asks him to revise his essay. 'So what I would like you to do, first of all,' says the supervisor (whose name also happens to be Coetzee), 'is to set to work revising the *tone* of your argument'.[1] He goes on to give elaborate instructions:

> Keep this in mind: if you say that they don't know their jobs [...] that they don't understand what they are doing [...] then they have no choice but to throw you out the window. Whereas if you stress continually, not only explicitly but through the very genuflexions of your *style*, that you are merely a functionary with a narrow if significant specialism, a near-academic with none of the soldier's all-round understanding of the science of warfare; that, nevertheless, within the narrow boundaries of your specialism you have some suggestions to offer which may have some strategic fallout – then, you will find, your proposals will get a hearing.
>
> (3–4, emphasis in the original)

These are rather extravagant claims for the force of style itself, and if an element of wry humour in this passage deflects attention from the seriousness of the point, the question of style – as this chapter shows – touches a central nerve in Coetzee's writing practice. His own doctoral thesis, *The English Fiction of Samuel Beckett*, has the subtitle *An Essay in Stylistic Analysis*, and throughout his critical writings and fictions, Coetzee explores unexpected ethical dimensions of aesthetic choices that may, at first, seem insignificant.

'Coetzee's style' – perhaps most especially the pared-down quality of his prose – is often commented on in reviews, and it has also become a topic of sustained critical discussion.[2] Even the most cursory reading of Coetzee's writing confirms its precision, economy and syntactic lucidity, but the difficulty begins in the attempt to define 'Coetzee's style' in a comprehensive and critically meaningful way, and to develop a method of analysis up to the task. While his syntax has logical clarity, Coetzee's diction often carries historical freight. This, together with the intertextual allusiveness of words and phrases, means that his works read as palimpsests, and the intelligibility of the syntax is in counterpoint to a lexicon charged with emotive intensity – and with energies at times visceral, lyrical, transcendent, compassionate, erotic, cerebral, savage, spiritual. This makes one uneasy to speak *in general terms* about Coetzee's style as 'stark', 'lean' or 'austere'.

Throughout his writing life, Coetzee has experimented with literary forms and styles that generate voices, encounters and settings of extraordinary diversity, further compounding the difficulty of defining a signature style. I am thinking, for instance, of first-person sensibilities as distinct as those of Magda (*In the Heart of the Country*), the Magistrate (*Waiting for the Barbarians*), the Medical Officer (*Life & Times of Michael K*), Susan Barton (*Foe*), Mrs Curren (*Age of Iron*) and JC and Anya in *Diary of a Bad Year*. I am thinking of decidedly different styles of narrative setting that range from those embedded in particular historical and sociolinguistic landscapes (*Dusklands, Age of Iron, Boyhood* and *Disgrace*) to those in zones of politico-philosophical abstraction (*Waiting for the Barbarians*, the *Jesus* books). This list could go on, and each of these styles of storytelling invites a separate essay of its own.

Instead of attempting an overarching literary-critical analysis of Coetzee's style, then, the discussion that follows reads selected critical essays alongside his fiction to show how Coetzee provides the foundation for a philosophy of literary style. Through the conscious – and often metafictional – mobilization of the stylistic apparatus of a text, Coetzee raises ethical questions about the authority and answerability of the writer, troubles assumptions about the relation between fiction and autobiography, and he leads us to question received habits of thinking. Style itself, quite apart from its 'content' or 'theme', creates meaning, and generates ethical and political force.

As a way of finding a footing, I begin by consulting Coetzee's doctoral thesis, which presents style as 'linguistic choice within the economy of the work of art as a formal whole'.[3] Moving on from the doctoral thesis, the discussion shows why the problem of style for Coetzee is an ethical issue as much as it is an aesthetic one. We come to a keener understanding of Coetzee's insistence that 'all writing is autobiography', and gain an appreciation of why this insistence should matter.[4]

II

Coetzee's doctoral thesis, *The English Fiction of Samuel Beckett: An Essay in Stylistic Analysis*, considers different methods of stylistic analysis, contrasting literary stylistics with linguistically oriented stylistic approaches and statistical methods of description.[5] Coetzee reached the conclusion that stylostatistics and even linguistic stylistics prove incapable of producing the kind of analysis considered significant in literary criticism. Nevertheless, Coetzee's doctoral research would prove pivotal in his own development as a writer. In conversation with David Attwell in the early 1990s, Coetzee explains that his PhD and the essays he wrote on Beckett were not only 'academic exercises', but 'attempts to get closer to a secret, a secret of Beckett's that I wanted to make my own. And discard, as it is with influences' (*DP* 25). Coetzee's interest in style is articulated from the vantage point of a writer of fiction, and if his extensive critical writings in linguistics and stylistics strike the uninitiated as arcane, these essays and interviews also lead us to realize that Coetzee's professional engagement with the linguistic sciences is integral to his own creative practice.

At the time of writing his doctorate, Coetzee was seeking ways of mastering a craft that would occasion the kind of 'sensuous delight' he found in Samuel Beckett (*DP* 20), the 'magisterial freedom' he found in Rainer Maria Rilke ('Homage' 5), the 'pushing at the bounds of the possible' that he found in Robert Musil ('Homage' 5), the 'magic' that he found in Ezra Pound ('Homage' 6).[6] One of Coetzee's more technical linguistic essays ('Time, tense, and aspect in Kafka's "The Burrow"') is written with heightened 'analytic intensity'; but the experience of writing this essay, by Coetzee's own admission, was also 'a matter of grace, inspiration' (*DP* 199). When it comes to writing, what is the connection between the logical operations of linguistic structures (syntax, the aspect of a verb, pronouns) and their potential to create poetic affect? The aspect of a verb, for example, hardly seems a likely candidate for grace. But to what extent can linguistic and other 'purely formal elements' of a literary work be configured to generate meaning, to transmit the force of human experience?[7] These are the kinds of questions that provide the impetus for Coetzee's stylistic investigations.

The third chapter of the doctoral thesis offers extraordinary analytical readings of three of Beckett's texts, and these analyses help us to understand better what is at stake in Coetzee's own stylistic considerations. My brief outline here picks out just one thread of a complex discussion that includes quantitative linguistic analysis, transformational generative grammar, literary history and sociolinguistics (to name just a few of the fields that Coetzee incorporates in his doctoral study). At the risk of oversimplifying, then, Coetzee conducts his investigation along three different lines: diction (the choice of words), syntax and rhythm.

At the most basic level of diction, words are chosen for their meaning, yet even at a semantic level, aspects of the word are up for consideration:

> its degree of formality or colloquialism, its statistical rarity, its etymology, its emotive coloring, its allusiveness, its degree of abstraction. The breakdown depends on our sense of the social appropriateness of levels of language, the authority of scholarship, knowledge of literature, a conceptual scheme of reality.
>
> (EFSB 50)

Elsewhere in his critical writings, Coetzee insists on the physicality, the 'brute presence' of words, the idea that words are 'irreplaceable' in translation, that there is a *nom juste* (H 5). Stressing the materiality of the writing process, Coetzee foregrounds the verbal commitments an author is obliged to make in the act of producing a text. And even though the effect of the work is not entirely predictable, literary style is supervenient upon the tangible linguistic choices a writer makes within the context of the work as a whole.

At the level of syntax, although there is no magical correlation between patterns of thought and sentence structure, Coetzee draws attention to the pertinence of the readers' experience of literary convention and their expectations of 'the kinds of syntax and the kinds of meaning that usually occur together'. Much of the comedy in *Watt*, Coetzee argues, is the result of Beckett's pitching 'one social or functional register of language against another' (EFSB 89). It is one thing to produce isolated examples of certain linguistic choices at the level of diction and syntax, but what Coetzee is looking for is a 'generative principle' for Beckett's literary style. If there is one to be found, he suggests, it is at the nexus 'logic-syntax-rhythm' – where a 'rhythmical principle' may even take precedence over logic and syntax (EFSB 90–1). Coetzee defines rhythm in broad terms as 'any simple pattern of sound, syntax, or on occasion, meaning, set up by local repetition in the text', and draws diagrams of rhythmic structures in Beckett's writing (91). The relentless binary patterning, at all levels of the work (within a phrase, within a sentence, within a paragraph) is striking, but the point that stands out is the way Coetzee characterizes this binary pattern: he interprets it as a 'rhythm of doubt', a way of 'internalizing the philosophical debt to Descartes' (DP 47). That is to say, Coetzee registers the rhythms of a text (rather than the ideas expressed) as a manifestation of a particular – and highly sophisticated – subjectivity. Rhythm holds particular significance for Coetzee in his own writing, and it is on these grounds that he objects to the first German translation of *Waiting for the Barbarians*: 'it was a matter of rhythm – rhythm of speech but also rhythm of thought. The sensibility behind the German text, a sensibility embodied in particular in the speech of the narrator, felt alien to me'.[8] Again, it is worth noting here that it is the rhythm, a purely formal feature and not a set of beliefs or ideas, that for Coetzee embodies the sensibilities of the characters. In a self-reflexive moment in *Diary of a Bad Year*, JC reads *The Brothers Karamazov* and finds himself 'sobbing uncontrollably'. He tries to understand why he is so intensely moved and realizes that it has nothing to do with the substance of Ivan's argument. What grips him instead

> are the accents of anguish, the personal anguish of a soul unable to bear the horrors of this world. It is the voice of Ivan, as realized by Dostoevsky, not his reasoning, that sweeps me along.[9]

If the modulations of voice have the capacity to transmit such a powerful emotive charge quite apart from explicitly stated thoughts and arguments, then one way of approaching the question of style in Coetzee's works is to pay attention to the rhythms of his prose, as we see when we turn to *In the Heart of the Country*. Paying special attention to rhythm, my discussion asks what literary style can be made to *do* at a philosophical level of Coetzee's ethics of writing.[10]

III

Magda, the protagonist of *In the Heart of the Country*, addresses Anna, her servant: 'This is not going to be a dialogue, thank God,' exclaims Magda when Anna is unresponsive, 'I can stretch my wings and fly where I will.' In the 1978 South African (Ravan Press) edition of the novel, Magda's impassioned Blakean monologue switches between English and Afrikaans:

> Energy is eternal delight, I could have been another person, ek kon heeltemaal anders gewees het. I could have burned my way out of this prison, my tongue is forked with fire, verstaan jy, ek kan met 'n tong van vuur praat, but it has all been turned uselessly inward, nutteloos, what sounds to you like rage is only the crackling of the fire within, ek is nooit regtig kwaad met jou gewees nie, I have never learned the speech of men, ek wou slegs praat, ek het nooit geleer hoe 'n mens met 'n ander mens praat nie. It has always been that the word has come down to me and I have passed it on. I have never known words of true exchange, wisselbare woorde, Anna. Woorde wat ek aan jou kan gee kan jy nie teruggee nie. Hulle is woorde sonder waarde. Verstaan jy? No value.[11]

For a moment the passage sweeps the reader along in its exhilarating energies of self-expression, a voice seeking to transcend historical, political and social conformities. Yet Magda's supposedly free speech gives way to a tempestuous rhythm of inner polemic, lurching between English and Afrikaans, inner and shared worlds, a simultaneous cry for autonomy and reciprocity. See-sawing between English and Afrikaans in her address to her servant, Magda's voice plays out a double history of colonialism in South Africa; she embodies the conflicted and complicit histories each of these languages speaks, and recognizes the impossibility of encountering Anna in a language free of the master-slave dictates of apartheid South Africa. 'Sê vir my, Anna', Magda continues, 'hoe noem jy my? Hoe heet ek? […] Hoe noem jy my in jou gedagtes?'[12] Magda tries to coax Anna into calling her by name, but to no avail: 'Nee mies, kan nie.'[13] They are incarcerated in habits of being at once ideological and linguistic; templates of speech determine paradigms of thinking and ways of relating. One senses the abrasion of selves and the impossibility of reciprocity in the interlocutory fault lines of the colonial languages they speak. I am put in mind of the Bakhtin of *The Dialogic Imagination*: 'As a living, socio-ideological concrete thing, as heteroglot opinion, language, for the individual consciousness, lies on the borderline between oneself and the other. The word in language is half someone else's'.[14] In the sociolinguistic terrain of apartheid South Africa, the performative force of inherited languages and terms of address means that Magda is unable to take up autonomous linguistic agency to effect a change in the way she and Anna relate to each other.

Magda's challenges reflect Coetzee's own: a novel written in English and/or Afrikaans in South Africa is freighted with a colonial legacy; a literary writer – especially one concerned with modes of ethico-political resistance – will be caught between inherited and innovative modes of writing. Given that language operates in intersubjective fields, the writer has to use recognizable patterns of representation to be understood, but Coetzee appreciates that different modes of saying, new styles of writing, have to be invented if thinking and feeling are to find expression in ways that throw received social and ideological templates into question. This, in turn, demands interrogation of one's own creative practice.

A version of this dilemma has dogged literary-critical debates in South Africa, most especially during the apartheid years, where a literature preoccupied with its own artistic and linguistic processes is open to a charge of political irresponsibility. But language is not simply a neutral medium for representing a social reality, and if one takes the view that language itself is a politically and historically charged force *generating* social perceptions then 'drawing the procedures of representation into question' is a politically meaningful act (*DP* 202). It cuts to the quick of Coetzee's practice as he experiments with alternative modes of storytelling in tension with the exigencies of a particular historical, cultural and socio-linguistic landscape.[15] Coetzee insists that a questioning and challenging of inherited procedures of representation is part of a writer's ethical responsibility: it has to do with the writer's 'conscience'; even further, in Coetzee's preferred term, it is a 'transcendental imperative' (*DP* 340). For Richard Eldridge, philosophy and literature are 'forms of attention [...] modes of seeking orientation and clarification of commitment and emotion, and both begin within a specific, situated point of view'.[16] A writer's style is a way of rendering the world, of making it readable to others in a particular way. And, from a writer's perspective, since storytelling is a self-constituting commitment, it is critical to question where you are speaking *from* to explore the ways in which your style enables others to call you to account: these stylistic exposures of a writer's bearing are part of the ethical and political risk of literary representation.

IV

Coetzee's stylistic experiments with voice test different forms of narrative perspective, and hence different forms of authorial agency. These experiments include: unconventional combination of third-person, present-tense narration in the fictional autobiographies *Boyhood* and *Youth*, and inventive experiments with interviews, notes to self and reported speech presented as narrative in *Summertime*; the use of a hybrid version of *style indirect libre* that troubles the locus of narrative consciousness; the attribution to his fictional characters of names, initials, thoughts and facts we consider to be Coetzee's own; and the creation of protagonists whose motives and ideals are unclear, inconsistent and sometimes contradictory, even to themselves. The accumulative effect of these stylistic experiments in subjective displacement is that it is hard to locate an authoritative voice in a Coetzee text. This brings me to Coetzee's concept of 'countervoice', the nexus of aesthetic, political and ethical concerns.

'Writing is not free expression', says Coetzee in one of his interviews with David Attwell:

> There is a true sense in which writing is dialogic: a matter of awakening the countervoices in oneself and embarking upon speech with them. It is some measure of a writer's seriousness whether he does evoke/invoke those countervoices in himself, that is, step down from the position of what Lacan calls 'the subject supposed to know'.
>
> (*DP* 65)

These countervoices are *within* the self: the 'speech' is not an ordinary dialogue between two discrete and autonomous individuals. Instead, authorial consciousness becomes a site of relentless inner conference; psychological energies are refracted through the text in ways that make it difficult to locate a unitary narrative authority. On the one hand, Coetzee's works invite us to think of a Bakhtinian 'dialogic novel', 'in which' – in Coetzee's own definition of the term – 'there is no dominating, central authorial consciousness, and therefore no claim to truth or authority, only competing voices and discourses'.[17] On the other hand, matters are not quite this straightforward in the worlds of Coetzee's novels: it is not as if the characters articulate clear but contesting positions amongst which a reader can choose. Similarly, it is not as if any one of Coetzee's characters is a clear-cut correlate for Coetzee's own 'position', even if we could say with certainty what that might be. Coetzee's texts disturb assumptions about the distinction between autobiography and fiction, between writer and written selves, leading to difficulty in attributing accountabilities for and the commitments to the ideas, beliefs and values expressed. And what positions of affinity, or distance, or complicity will you, as reader, find yourself taking up in response to the literary address of the novel as a whole?

For Coetzee, a writer's willingness to question the presumed certitudes of narrative authority – 'awakening the countervoices in oneself and embarking upon speech with them' – is a measure of literary seriousness. This is at least one context in which we can speak about Coetzee's aesthetics and ethics of writing. Coetzee's remark in his 2003 Nobel Prize interview underwrites the ethical traction of these stylistic experiments:

> I would say that what you call 'the literary life' or any other way of life that provides means for interrogation of our existence – in the case of the writer fantasy, symbolization, storytelling – seems to me a good life – good in the sense of being ethically responsible.[18]

We are now in a position to appreciate that the characters in the novels operate as Coetzee's own countervoices rather than as entirely discrete subjectivities. It is through these character-countervoices and other formal experiments that Coetzee tests his *own* ideas, values and convictions.

One significant aspect of this ethics of storytelling is Coetzee's sustained attentiveness – in his critical work, and in the novels themselves – to the difficult *process* of writing. Coetzee's fictions are peopled with writers of reports, records, diaries, stories, letters, novels, poems, commentaries, confessions, essays, notes, librettos, autobiographical vignettes, marginalia, transcripts and statements of belief. Characters doubt their writing abilities; they wrestle with stylistic decisions and the consequences these choices might entail (as in the passage from *Dusklands* with which this chapter opened); they pitch their own idiolects against prevailing narratives and dominant discourses; they raise questions about the historical and political burdens of the words they use; they test alternative forms of expression (music, dance); register what cannot be said and think about animal sounds and signals that transcend the cultures and ideologies inherited through language. These writers are beset by self-doubt; they question their authority to write in the first place, and appreciate that different styles of rendering one's world generate different configurations of personal, political and ethical alignments.

It is important to stress Coetzee's attention to process and experiment here. A trial of different expressive attitudes demands an imaginative willingness to think differently: testing different styles is a way of discovering what sensibilities one can identify with, of finding a manner of thinking and relating to others. In other words, stylistic experiments put one's own subjective commitments to the test. In Coetzee's work, this opens up quite explicitly onto a question of what it is that imaginative literary writing (rather than abstract philosophical argument) is able to do. This is not to say that literature simply offers colourful allegories for *a priori* philosophical positions or stages recognizable philosophical arguments in a fictional setting. Literary writing – and the stylistic experiments that come with it – *breaks* new paths of thought, rather than following existing ones. The process of experimenting with different styles precipitates the writer into a field where certain meanings, resonances and orientations surface *as* language materializes, and not in some abstract zone prior to the commitments of form. 'It is naïve to think that writing is a simple two stage process: first you decide what you want to say, then you say it', Coetzee reminds us; instead, 'you write because you do not know what you want to say', and what that writing yields 'may be quite different from what you thought (or half-thought) you wanted to say in the first place. That is the sense in which one can say that writing writes us' (*DP* 18). This dual directionality of a writing act – that inaugurates both its agent and its object – is a core preoccupation that Coetzee articulates in a number of different contexts.

In his short essay, 'A Note on Writing', Coetzee considers the verb 'to write' as an instance of the middle voice; that is to say, neither passive nor active, but self-reflexive, as in a verb like 'to bathe' – which means to bathe oneself. To think of writing as an instance of the middle voice brings us closer to the claims for writing and autobiography that Coetzee reiterates in the first and last interviews in *Doubling the Point*: 'all writing is autobiography: everything that you write, including criticism and fiction, writes you as you write it' (*DP* 17); 'All autobiography is storytelling, all writing is autobiography' (*DP* 391). As writing inaugurates the readable proclivities of the writer, style itself makes a claim on the reader as a significant mode of understanding them. The refractive energies of Coetzee's countervoices question, as much as they disclose, the preoccupations of the writer. Magda, the Magistrate, Elizabeth Costello … these are all the inventions of one particular writer, raising countervoices of what it is that Coetzee does not know in advance.

V

Coetzee recognizes this reflexive quality of writing in Dostoevsky, and he takes a further philosophical step than Bakhtin does with his concept of the dialogic novel. For Coetzee,

'Dostoevskian dialogism grows out of Dostoevsky's own moral character, out of his ideals, and out of his being as a writer'; as such, his dialogism 'is only distantly imitable' (*SS* 145–6). In other words, writing styles the writer: a fictional world is configured as a here and now possible only from the particular stance of this individual writer, and in this exposure of the self, Dostoevsky's novels, for Coetzee, give voice to 'the most radical intellectual and even spiritual courage' (*SS* 145). The practice of writing sounds out – and exposes – the writer's own disposition: seemingly innocent or superficial stylistic choices give material form to the writer's manner of paying attention. And it is in modes of attention (rather than philosophies or theories) that Coetzee finds the greatest inspiration in other writers. With reference to the Polish poet, Zbigniew Herbert, Coetzee remarks:

> What one learns from Herbert is not a body of ideas but a certain style, hard, durable: a style that is also an approach to the world and to experience, political experience included. Ideas are certainly important – who would deny that? – but the fact is, the ideas that operate in novels and poems, once they are unpicked from their context and laid out on the laboratory table, usually turn out to be uncomplicated, even banal. Whereas a style, an attitude to the world, as it soaks in, becomes part of the personality, part of the self, ultimately indistinguishable from the self.
>
> (*H* 7)

What becomes increasingly clear is that the question of style in Coetzee has a greater depth of field than a problem of linguistic or aesthetic choice might at first seem to yield. Adopting one style over another is not simply a matter of saying the same thing in a different way – as the Mr Vincent of *Summertime* would have us believe when he recasts his interview with Margot as a continuous prose narrative.[19] Instead, as philosopher-critic Charles Altieri puts it, style 'is not primarily a matter of expressing emotional states. Its function is to ground such states, to anchor the self as value creator'.[20] If literary style is generated by a particular configuration of linguistic decisions, it also touches the very nerve of an authorial *ethos*, and it is in this sense that the commitments to form are nothing less than an act of transfiguration – of the object of representation, and of the writing self. In this context then, a responsiveness to the style of another writer is not merely a matter of aesthetics but a response to the other in the deepest ethical sense. For Coetzee, through a receptiveness to the style of another writer 'one makes oneself into the person whom in the most intractable, but also perhaps the most deeply ethical sense one wants to be'. This is part of a lifelong 'ethic of writing' that is in keeping with Coetzee's view that his work is a vocation as much as it is a craft (*H* 7). Whenever he speaks about the styles of other writers, we gain a deeper appreciation of Coetzee's awareness of what is *ethically* at stake in his own linguistic and aesthetic commitments. A writer like Pound evinces for Coetzee a consciousness of 'a technique both practical and spiritual' (*H* 6); what attracts Coetzee to Ford is 'as much the ethics of Tietjens as the aesthetics of *le mot juste*' (*DP* 20); he is interested in Joseph Brodsky's claim that 'making fine aesthetic discriminations teaches one to make fine ethical discriminations' (*SS* 158). In this sense, evil, and 'especially political evil, is always a bad stylist'.[21] Style, then, for Coetzee, follows the logic of the zeugma, operating simultaneously at levels of the political and the personal, the fictional and the autobiographical, the sensory and the spiritual, and this brings me to my closing remarks.

VI

Marion Milner writes about creative processes in her path-breaking study, *On Not Being Able to Paint* (first published in 1950). Although she focuses on drawing and painting rather than writing, her insights resonate with Coetzee's, and in a way that touches on several of the ideas raised in this chapter:

> Through the process of giving life to the portrayal of one's subject, of coming to see it as a whole through the discovery of patterns and rhythm and so coming imaginatively to appreciate its nature, one is actually creating something, creating the spiritual reality of one's power to love it – if it is lovable; or laugh at it or hate it – if it is laughable or hateful. Ultimately then it is perhaps ourselves that the artist in us is trying to create; and if ourselves, then also the world, because one's view of the one interpenetrates with one's view of the other.[22]

For Milner as much as for Coetzee, creative expression is a process of self-discovery: a world depicted in writing is one transfigured by the discriminating – and now perceptible – sensibilities of the writer. '[E]very new aesthetic reality makes man's ethical reality more precise', as Joseph Brodsky puts it.[23] And this is why the act of writing demands a certain spiritual courage: the writer's ethical reality becomes apparent, and more precise, even to the one who writes. In a letter dated 6 March 1974, Coetzee answers questions from Peter Randall of Ravan Press about the publication of *Dusklands*. 'I should like to be styled J. M. Coetzee on the title page', Coetzee writes.[24] '*Styled*'. That is to say, written *as*: the inaugural signatory commitment to a writing-life.

NOTES

1. Coetzee, *Dusklands*, 3. References hereafter cited parenthetically in the text.
2. See Zimbler's *J. M. Coetzee*. Attentive to salient South African literary-historical contexts, Zimbler coins the critically productive phrase 'poetics of reduction' to offer insightful analyses of stylistic features of Coetzee's first eight novels (from *Dusklands* to *Disgrace*). David James carefully chooses facets of Coetzee's style to develop sensitively nuanced and thought-provoking insights; see, for example, his poised reflections on 'the strange discrepancies between the damage of events and the graceful language of their expression'; a discrepancy that offers 'aesthetic amnesty to the very lyricism from which Coetzee has at times distanced his writing'. See James, 'Styles', 66. Robert Pippin's philosophically informed and critically innovative reading of the *Jesus* fictions takes issue with reviewers who label Coetzee's style as 'passionless', 'ascetic', 'parched' and 'etiolated'. Instead, Pippin finds the prose 'elegant, economical to the point of genius, and intense to the point of explosion' and argues that Coetzee achieves a 'philosophically relevant generality, not by abstraction but by compression, concretization, and so manifold allusiveness'. See Pippin, *Metaphysical Exile*, 90–2.
3. Coetzee, *English Fiction of Samuel Beckett*, Abstract. References hereafter parenthetically in the text (*EFSB*).
4. Coetzee, *Doubling the Point*, 17. References hereafter parenthetically in the text (*DP*).
5. See especially chapter 6 of *English Fiction*, 150–64. My book *J. M. Coetzee: Countervoices* explores the continuity between Coetzee's interest in the linguistic sciences and his aesthetic and ethical preoccupations as a writer; see its introduction for a discussion of Coetzee's account of different methods of stylistic analysis (4–5, 195 n4).

6. Coetzee, 'Homage', 5–6. References hereafter parenthetically in the text (H). First presented as a lecture at the University of California, Berkeley, on 12 November 1991, the lecture has moments of levity and offers a *caveat* in the opening remarks: 'The reader versed in the vicissitudes of autobiography will receive what I say with due caution' (5).

7. Anthony Uhlmann notes with critical acuity that 'Coetzee comes as close as anyone has to demonstrating how Beckett uses purely formal elements to create sense, a feeling of understanding, in the reader' (*J. M. Coetzee: Truth, Meaning, Fiction*, 39).

8. Coetzee, 'Roads to Translation', 149. In Coetzee's account of his own literary influences, he notes that 'the deepest lessons you learn from other writers are [...] matters of rhythm ('Homage', 6–7).

9. Coetzee, *Diary of a Bad Year*, 224–5.

10. In *Countervoices* (100–3), I discuss the contrapuntal rhythms across the three different bands of text in *Diary of a Bad Year*.

11. Coetzee, *In the Heart of the Country* (1978), 101, § 203. Future references use paragraph number only, and are made parenthetically, with reference either to the Ravan (1978) edition, or the text that was published by Secker & Warburg in the UK in 1977. The English dialogue in the UK edition of *In the Heart of the Country* closely resembles the Afrikaans in the Ravan edition. I purposely do not provide English translations of the Afrikaans phrases here, so that the reader experiences the performative rhythms of the code switching. Andrew van der Vlies provides meticulously detailed readings of the Ravan edition in relation to the British and US publications, and offers insightful discussion of 'the forces that mediated these different local and global instantiations'. See Van der Vlies, '*In* (or *From*) *The Heart of the Country*', 168. In a discussion that is at once personal and critically bracing, Rita Barnard considers Coetzee's complex relation to Afrikaans. Her essay opens onto questions of translation, identity and modes of (literary) self-expression. See Barnard, 'Coetzee in/and Afrikaans'.

12. *In the Heart of the Country* § 203. 'Tell me, Anna, what do you call me? What is my name? [...] What do you call me in your thoughts?' (Penguin).

13. 'No miss, I can't.' (§ 203 Penguin).

14. Bakhtin, *The Dialogic Imagination*, 293.

15. In 'Wisselbare Woorde', I take this idea further, especially when it comes to the problem of addressing the state (a problem that Eugene Dawn faces in the passage I quoted at the beginning of this chapter). Derek Attridge makes a path-breaking argument for the 'ethico-political' importance of Coetzee's 'formal singularity'. Attridge, *J. M. Coetzee and the Ethics of Reading*, 8.

16. Eldridge, 'Introduction', 6.

17. Coetzee, *Stranger Shores*, 144. Hereafter cited parenthetically (*SS*).

18. Coetzee, 'An Exclusive Interview', 3.

19. Margot is disconcerted, but Mr Vincent is insistent: 'that is what you told me word for word'. Margot still has misgivings, though: '*I don't know. Something sounds wrong, but I can't put my finger on it. All I can say is, your version doesn't sound like what I told you*' (*Summertime*, 91). In the end, she does not endorse Mr Vincent's rendition of their exchange. In the 'Author's Note' in *Doubling the Point*, Coetzee registers that he has made some revisions to essays originally published elsewhere. He has tried to 'respect the character of the originals' but adds: 'Style and content are not separable: it would be disingenuous for me to claim that my revisions have not touched the substance of the originals'. See Coetzee, *Doubling the Point*, vii.

20. Altieri, 'Style as the Man', 181. In 'Inner Worlds', I engage more fully with this essay, especially in relation to Coetzee's treatment of 'the self' in writing.

21. Brodsky, *On Grief and Reason*, 49, cited in *Stranger Shores* 158.

22. Milner, *On Not Being Able to Paint*, 158.

23. Brodsky, *On Grief and Reason*, 49.
24. Coetzee, letter to Peter Randall. Amazwi South African Museum of Literature, Makhanda, Eastern Cape. Thank you to J. M. Coetzee for permission to quote this letter.

WORKS CITED

Altieri, Charles. 'Style as the Man: What Wittgenstein Offers for Speculating on Expressive Activity'. *The Journal of Aesthetics and Art Criticism* 46 (1987): 177–92.

Attridge, Derek. *J. M. Coetzee and the Ethics of Reading: Literature in the Event*. Scottsville: University of KwaZulu-Natal Press, 2005.

Bakhtin, Mikhail. *The Dialogic Imagination: Four Essays*. Edited by Michael Holquist, translated by Caryl Emerson and Michael Holquist. Austin: University of Texas Press, 1981.

Barnard, Rita. 'Coetzee in/and Afrikaans'. *JLS/TLW* 25, no. 4 (2009): 84–105.

Brodsky, Joseph. *On Grief and Reason: Essays*. London: Penguin, 1995.

Clarkson, Carrol. 'Inner Worlds'. *Texas Studies in Literature and Language* 58, no. 4 (Winter 2016): 424–36.

Clarkson, Carrol. *J. M. Coetzee: Countervoices*. Houndmills: Palgrave Macmillan, 2009.

Clarkson, Carrol. 'Wisselbare Woorde'. In *Beyond the Ancient Quarrel: Literature, Philosophy, and J. M. Coetzee*, edited by Patrick Hayes and Jan Wilm, 199–214. Oxford: Oxford University Press, 2017.

Coetzee, J. M. *Doubling the Point: Essays and Interviews*, edited by David Attwell. Cambridge, MA and London: Harvard University Press, 1992.

Coetzee, J. M. *Dusklands*. 1974. London: Vintage, 1998.

Coetzee, J. M. *The English Fiction of Samuel Beckett: An Essay in Stylistic Analysis*. Doctoral Thesis, University of Texas, Austin, January 1969.

Coetzee, J. M. 'Homage'. *The Threepenny Review* 53 (1993): 5–7.

Coetzee, J. M. *In the Heart of the Country*. Johannesburg: Ravan Press, 1978.

Coetzee, J. M. *In the Heart of the Country*. 1977. London: Penguin, 1982.

Coetzee, J. M. Letter to Peter Randall, 6 March 1974. 98.8.1.36. Amazwi South African Museum of Literature, Makhanda, Eastern Cape.

Coetzee, J. M. 'Roads to Translation'. *Meanjin* (special issue) *Tongues: Translation: Only Connect* 64, no. 4 (2005): 141–51.

Coetzee, J. M. *Stranger Shores: Essays 1986–1999*. London: Harvill Secker, 2009.

Coetzee, J. M. *Summertime: Scenes from Provincial Life*. London: Harvill Secker, 2009.

Coetzee, J. M. and David Attwell. 'An Exclusive Interview with J. M. Coetzee'. *Dagens Nyheters*, 8 December 2003. https://www.dn.se/kultur-noje/an-exclusive-interview-with-j-m-coetzee/.

Eldridge, Richard. 'Introduction – Philosophy and Literature as Forms of Attention'. In *The Oxford Handbook of Philosophy and Literature*, edited by Richard Eldridge, 3–15. Oxford: Oxford University Press, 2009.

James, David. 'Styles: *Dusklands, Age of Iron, Disgrace, The Schooldays of Jesus*'. In *The Cambridge Companion to J. M. Coetzee*, edited by Jarad Zimbler, 64–83. Cambridge: Cambridge University Press, 2020.

Milner, Marion. *On Not Being Able to Paint*. London and New York: Routledge, 2010.

Pippin, Robert. *Metaphysical Exile: On J.cM. Coetzee's Jesus Fictions*. New York: Oxford University Press, 2021.

Uhlmann, Anthony. *Truth, Meaning, Fiction*. New York and London: Bloomsbury Academic, 2020.

Van der Vlies, Andrew. '*In* (or *From*) *the Heart of the Country*: Local and Global Lives of Coetzee's Anti-pastoral'. In *Print, Text, and Book Cultures in South Africa*, edited by Andrew van der Vlies, 167–97. Johannesburg: Wits University Press, 2012.

Zimbler, Jarad. *J. M. Coetzee and the Politics of Style*. Cambridge: Cambridge University Press, 2014.

CHAPTER TWENTY

Coetzee, religion and philosophy

ALICE BRITTAN

About midway through J. M. Coetzee's *The Schooldays of Jesus* (2016), the second novel in the Jesus trilogy, a middle-aged man named Simón enrols in an Elementary Spanish Composition class at a local institute of higher education. He is not a native Spanish speaker, but it is the language spoken in the unnamed country to which he arrived by boat a few years earlier, under mysterious circumstances, and he wants both to improve his writing skills and to find a new direction in his life. Simón's first assignment is to compose three paragraphs about himself, using a business letter as a model. He has no difficulty organizing his thoughts but finds it impossible to confine them to three paragraphs, so he hands in six, culminating in the following statement: 'I want to become a different person.'[1] 'Unusual content,' notes his instructor, a young woman named Martina, when she returns the assignment (*Schooldays*, 177). The next assignment is a three-paragraph letter of application for a dream job. Simón again hands in six and includes several strange disclosures that would not endear him to a potential employer. In the opening paragraphs of an application for a hypothetical job as a museum attendant, he freely admits that working in a museum has never been his dream, but that he is at 'a point of crisis' and needs to find a way to change his life (*Schooldays*, 178). Eventually, Martina runs out of patience with her dilatory and disobedient student. She confronts him, saying, 'This is more than I can deal with' (*Schooldays*, 182). Simón knows that his desire for existential guidance, for what was once called pastoral care, is 'a lot to expect of a teacher of prose composition, a lot more than she is paid to do' (*Schooldays*, 181). Then again, Simón's recent life has been so full of exorbitant demands that he has grown accustomed to them.

In the first novel of Coetzee's trilogy, *The Childhood of Jesus* (2013), Simón unhesitatingly assumed the role of godfather to Davíd, the young orphan he met on a boat, and he believes that the responsibility of a godparent is to lead a child to 'goodness'.[2] Davíd is a bright and creative child, but he is not easy to lead anywhere; throughout the trilogy he is described as exceptional and demands to be treated as an exception by everyone he meets. When it comes to Davíd, rules must be broken, even those of language and arithmetic. When asked to read and write, he makes up his own words; when asked to calculate how many fish Juan and Pablo have caught, he claims that he cannot answer the question because he cannot see the fish.[3] In addition to finding Davíd a mother – a stranger named Inés, plucked off a tennis court at random – Simón must protect his child from the teachers and state-sponsored rule enforcers who believe that five plus three always equals eight, and that 'the law is enough' (*Schooldays*, 256). At the end of *Childhood*, Inés, Simón and Davíd become fugitives, fleeing from their home in Novilla to the town of Estrella del Norte to escape the truancy officers who want to send Davíd to a boarding school-cum-juvenile detention centre. Given all that Simón has sacrificed for his unusual child, surely Martina can bend her assignment guidelines?

Simón explains to her that if Davíd no longer needs him then he has no one on whom to bestow the 'loving care' that pours out of him, 'sometimes as mere talk, sometimes as tears,' and that he feels adrift and alone (*Schooldays*, 180). Martina has no time for these esoteric problems. She works two jobs while also taking care of her husband and young child; managing spiritual crisis is well above her pay grade. She expels Simón from Elementary Spanish Composition, and although he nurtures the hope that she will change her mind, she does not.

I have taught *The Schooldays of Jesus* several times, both in Honours and graduate seminars.[4] Because these are not lecture courses, I have minimal control over the direction of the conversation, but if the opportunity arises, I always call my students' attention to Chapter 15, in which Simón strains Martina's patience. In general, my students' initial response to this episode is irritation. In Simón, they see a familiar figure: a middle-aged man who believes that he is entitled to make unreasonable demands on the time and energy of a young woman who works several jobs to make ends meet. They speak of women's emotional labour, of patriarchy, of the gig economy and the precariat. I nod: all true, all valid ways of understanding this scenario. What happens next depends on the kind of seminar I'm teaching. If *Schooldays* is the only work by J. M. Coetzee on the reading list, then I may not be able to shift the conversation, and Simón's need to give and receive goodness will be interpreted in a sinister light. The class might even decide that he is a double of Dmitri, the deranged museum attendant who strangled his mistress, the dancer Ana Magdalena. However, if this discussion is taking place in the seminar on Coetzee that I teach every few years, then Simón's crisis will probably get a second opinion. Because I structure the reading list chronologically, we read *Schooldays* towards the end of the term. By this point we have read eight or nine novels and encountered many people like Simón – men and women of several nationalities, ages and races. We are by now fluent in the language of loving care, which is central to Coetzee's evolving relationship with philosophy and religion, terms that are not easy to separate in his writing, or in general.

WHY NOT TRY TO BE LIKE A CHILD?

One of the enduring puzzles of the Jesus trilogy is that Jesus is never mentioned. God is scarcely mentioned either, and neither is religion nor theology. Philosophy is taught at the Institute, but like so much else in the new world that Coetzee imagines, it is dry and detached from real life.[5] Having been expelled from his Spanish class, Simón briefly attends a course in astrology, but leaves when the instructor announces: 'There is no beyond' (*Schooldays*, 183). Simón feels that 'whether or not there is a beyond, one would drown in despair were there not an idea of a beyond to cling to' (*Schooldays*, 183). But how can this *beyond* be expressed and experienced in a way that relieves Simón's despair? And why does despair exist in an imagined world where everyone's basic needs are met, which might even be understood as an afterlife and in that sense already a beyond? The *Jesus* books are filled with allusions to sources that demonstrate the longevity of these questions and the variety of forms in which they have been posed over the millennia, from Plato's *Republic* to the Gospels and *Don Quixote*, yet it is clear that Coetzee intends none of them as a skeleton key that opens all doors for all seekers. 'There is no such thing as a *llave universal*,' Simón is told at the beginning of *Childhood* when he and Davíd, fresh off the boat, find themselves locked out of the housing assigned to new arrivals; if there was one, 'our troubles would be over,' the housing administrator says (*Childhood*, 4).[6] This admonition is directed at Simón, but it applies to us as readers too.

If there is a universal key in the Jesus novels, it is not any of the novel's many intertexts, nor even the exceptional child, but the condition of childhood itself. 'Instead of waiting to be transfigured, why not try to be like a child again?' asks Simón's friend, Elena (*Childhood*, 143). Her advice comes shortly after a scene in which Davíd and Simón have a conversation about natural philosophy while attempting to unclog Inés's blocked toilet. The two discuss water and life cycles as Simón repeatedly plunges his arm into the toilet basin, which is overflowing with faeces, and probes into the S-bend with a length of wire. As Simón becomes increasingly smeared with excrement, Davíd asks difficult questions about mortality and the human condition, as young children often do, but also offers practical suggestions for how best to dislodge whatever is stuck in the pipe. 'What are dead bodies?' he asks. 'What are we like?' (*Childhood*, 133). Then he tells Simón, 'You can use the long fork in the kitchen,' and rushes off to get it (*Childhood*, 134). Fork in hand, Simón manages to retrieve a used sanitary pad from the depths of the plumbing and suddenly the water runs freely again. For me, as for Simón, the implications are clear. Water, blood, urine, faeces: these are the grounds of philosophy, not the arid or instrumental conversations that take place in the classrooms at the Institute. When you try to understand what a human being is like, you should do so in conversation with a kindergartener, while adapting a kitchen utensil into a tool that can solve an urgent problem with human waste disposal. In this conversation you will need to use the language of ideas, and you will need to speak of the heart and the soul, but you will also find yourself covered in someone else's shit, holding a fistful of blood, and then discover that there is no antibacterial soap with which to clean yourself.[7]

The more I reflect on the *Jesus* novels, the more I think about what might be the most famous lines from Coetzee's most famous novel, *Disgrace* (1999), which takes place in South Africa of the late 1990s, in the wake of the Truth and Reconciliation Commission hearings and the country's first fully democratic elections. David Lurie and his daughter Lucy, who was gang-raped by three Black men and decided not to terminate the resulting pregnancy, discuss the dangerous and humiliating sacrifices she is willing to make to continue to live alone on her small farm in the Eastern Cape. David, a professor and intellectual, is appalled by his daughter's refusal to prosecute her attackers or take practical steps to protect herself, and although Lucy will not explain her decisions, she is adamant in her commitment to them. 'Perhaps that is a good point to start from again,' she tells her horrified father, '[t]o start at ground level. With nothing. Not with nothing but. With nothing.'[8] 'Like a dog,' David replies. 'Yes,' she says, 'like a dog' (*Disgrace*, 205). In the 1970s, 1980s and 1990s, Coetzee stripped many of his characters down to nothing and then tried to imagine how they might start again. In novel after novel, he brings men and women to a point of crisis, and watches as they try to become different people. In general, they either fail or die, because the constraints they face are not just individual but systemic, and it is a central premise of Coetzee's apartheid-era novels that systems are more powerful than individuals, no matter how intelligent or brave.

Yet when I reverse the chronology of my Coetzee seminar and read *Disgrace* backward, as it were, I see a pattern that will eventually be radicalized in the *Jesus* novels. Lucy is not just starting at ground level like a dog, but like a child. I don't mean that her pregnancy will result in the birth of the messiah, the once and future king, or the chosen one whose coming is prophesied and salvific – although such nativity scenes are foundational within many folkloric and wisdom traditions, including Judeo-Christianity. I mean that in the trilogy Coetzee creates characters who are literally starting with nothing – no native language, no names, no memories, no documents, no family, no keys – and that whenever they try to cobble together some certainties, including a fixed address, they are upended by the charismatic little boy who lives by exceptions, not the laws that help people build systems. Here, as in *Disgrace*, Coetzee suggests that if we seek to transfigure either ourselves or our societies, to move towards rather than away from goodness, this might be how to begin. This is not a comforting thought, but anyone who turns to Coetzee for comfort has lost the plot before reading a single page.

The metaphysical conditions that Coetzee imagines in the *Jesus* novels are impossible, of course. But Coetzee is not alone in the attempt to tell the story of Jesus afresh, without even invoking Jesus or Judeo-Christianity other than in the titles of the books.[9] As the Irish Catholic priest-turned-poet John O'Donohue says, if the question of God has died in our time, it is because it 'has been framed in such repetitive, dead language'.[10] What would singular, vivacious language sound like? The *Jesus* novels are one way of trying to answer this question, which animates the writing of so many contemporary thinkers, from poets and novelists to theologians, philosophers and public intellectuals. This group includes people as different as Italian philosopher Giorgio Agamben, whose multivolume *Homo Sacer* project uncovers the theological origins of concepts like law, life, and sovereignty, and Norwegian writer Karl Ove Knausgård, whose multivolume *My Struggle* project builds on his earlier novel about the Old Testament, seeking the experience of the beyond in a world filled with despair but long deserted by prophets and angels.[11] Sometimes this diverse body of writing is referred to under the name of postsecularism, a term used loosely to describe precisely the impulse that O'Donohue identifies: the need to dissolve artificial oppositions between sacred and secular, faith and unbelief, antiquity and modernity, tradition and progress, and also to confront the messy reality embodied by the large number of people whom the poet Christian Wiman calls 'unbelieving believers'.[12] Wiman defines these as 'people whose consciousness is completely modern and yet who have this strong spiritual hunger in them'.[13] He could easily be talking about Simón. 'Something is missing,' he says towards the end of *Childhood*, 'I know it should not be so, but it is. The life I have is not enough for me. I wish someone, some saviour, would descend from the skies and wave a magic wand and say, *Behold, read this book and all your questions will be answered*' (*Childhood*, 239). The unbelieving believer knows that even the magic book is not a universal key, and many traditional believers know it too.

Postsecularism is a recent coinage, and has been invoked in Coetzee scholarship.[14] Yet I suspect that it is the kind of widely circulated academic terminology that Coetzee himself would distrust. It is impossible to spend any length of time reading his work without noticing the particularly cruel fates he visits upon scholars who believe that their coinages are equal to the pain and passion of life. Consider the 1990 work *Age of Iron*'s Mrs. Curren – a retired classics scholar dying of cancer during the State of Emergency of the mid-1980s, who presumes to lecture young Black revolutionaries on the dangers of the Spartan warrior code and ends up lying under a bridge in a pool of her own urine while feral children poke sharp sticks into her mouth.[15] Witness David Lurie, professor of Romanticism, whose skull is doused in kerosene and set on fire during the home invasion in which his daughter is raped: is there a more obvious way of forcing an intellectual to get out of his head?[16] He is succeeded by Elizabeth Costello, the Australian novelist who spends her last years on the international lecture circuit and then, after her death, finds herself in a purgatory where she comes before a committee that wants to know what she *believed* in life, not what she argued from behind a lectern.[17] If the Institute in the *Jesus* novels is not just a parody of Plato's *Republic* but also of the modern university, with its increasing reliance on sessional labour and utilitarian aims, the parody is already familiar to readers of Coetzee's earlier work. Above all, it echoes Lesson 5 of *Elizabeth*

Costello, 'The Humanities in Africa,' in which Costello's sister, a nun and former classics scholar, bluntly informs a group of graduating university students that the academic humanities are 'on their deathbed' because they enthrone intellect, reason and ignore the needs of the perplexed and hungry soul.[18] This is not a modern problem, she continues, but one that began during the European Renaissance, when the study of the human parted from the study of God. I am at 'a point of crisis,' writes Simón (*Schooldays*, 178). 'This is more than I can deal with,' responds Martina (182). And there you have it, says Sister Bridget, the death of the humanities.

The term postsecular may be recent, but the instinct it expresses is not. Particularly in times of crisis, personal or political or both, there are people who seek singular, vivacious language for the perennial needs of the soul. And not just language, but a lived commitment. As Wiman writes, 'there are some works that life electrifies with meaning, some sayings only action authenticates.'[19] By way of illustration, he names Dietrich Bonhoeffer, the dissident German theologian and Lutheran minister who returned to Germany from the United States at the beginning of the Second World War in full knowledge of what his resistance to the Nazi regime might cost.[20] He spent two years in jail before being executed in the chaotic final weeks of the war. To read the letters Bonhoeffer wrote in prison is an astonishing experience, not just because we know that his hopes of being released will never be fulfilled, but because of the courage with which he imagines a 'religionless Christianity'.[21] Bonhoeffer declares the Church obsolete, writes that Christianity may only have been a 'preliminary stage to a complete absence of religion', and imagines that in the future the word of God will have to be expressed 'in a new language, perhaps quite non-religious, but liberating and redeeming – as was Jesus' language' (153, 172). Unknowingly echoing Simone Weil, another war theologian who lived what she believed, Bonhoeffer notices that a '"Christian instinct" often draws me more to the religionless people than to the religious, by which I do not in the least mean with any evangelizing intention, but, I might almost say, "in brotherhood"' (154).[22] Also like Weil, who was writing from occupied France just a few years earlier, Bonhoeffer repeatedly returns to the simplest and most elemental teaching: take care of your neighbour.[23] Forget about 'antiquated' theological controversies or points of interpretation, he writes; they are 'now unreal' (*Letters*, 210). Understand that God wants us 'to manage our lives without him' (196).[24] In the absence of God, religion or Church, turn to 'the neighbour who is within reach in any given situation' (210).[25]

Dietrich Bonhoeffer was one of the most renowned theologians of the mid-century. Clive Staples Lewis (C. S. Lewis) was not, which is why in 1941 he was asked by the BBC to create a radio lecture series on Christian faith that would be accessible to all listeners. At the time, Lewis was a professor of Medieval and Renaissance Literature at Oxford, but he had fought in the trenches of the First World War and since 1940 had been giving regular talks to the pilots of the Royal Air Force, whose life expectancy was a matter of weeks. When Lewis accepted the BBC's offer, he did so in the conviction that most British people were 'post-Christian', with only the most conventional knowledge of Christianity, and little if any real faith.[26] This meant that his lack of theological training was an asset, as was his former atheism: he determined to speak to his listeners as a former soldier, an ordinary man, and to use words 'so that we can all understand what is being said'.[27] Lewis's talks between 1941 and 1944 were later published as *Mere Christianity*, so titled because he wanted to communicate the mere essence of the faith, with no concern for denominational or doctrinal differences, and to root everything he said in the homespun and the everyday. He spoke from life, explaining at the outset that there were certain topics he would not broach because he had no personal experience of them – birth control, for example. In tone and method, Lewis is very different from Bonhoeffer, but each seeks to revive Christianity by returning to its most basic practices, verified by action rather than by abstractions or jargon. In both cases, there is a search for fresh language, rather like Simón's when he tries to discuss what human beings are like while unplugging a toilet with the help of a fork and a five-year-old.

Less than a decade after his first BBC broadcasts, Lewis published the first volume of *The Chronicles of Narnia*, books in which he continues the work begun years earlier, except this time he addresses himself to the child reader. Many of those readers, including me, had no idea that Narnia had anything to do with the Bible, and I don't think this would have bothered Lewis, any more than Bonhoeffer was bothered by the possibility of a revitalized language of faith that might sound 'quite non-religious', and yet be redemptive for that very reason (*Letters*, 172). The letter in which Bonhoeffer wrote those words in the spring of 1944 was itself addressed to a child: to the son of his dear friend Eberhard Bethge, who was about to be baptized. In a series of letters, Bonhoeffer addresses the child directly, as a godparent giving spiritual advice to a new Christian. And how remarkable the advice: The Church into which you are about to be baptized is dead, and the faithful must now pray for a new language. There is something about the experience of addressing a child, as both Lewis and Bonhoeffer chose to do, that allows and even demands this demolition of conventionality. I can't help thinking of the years that Ludwig Wittgenstein spent teaching primary school in rural Austria, precisely because he wanted to expose the 'linguistic roots of our relationship with the world', and to do so 'through the figure of the speaking child'.[28] The most elite minds of the early-twentieth century couldn't keep up with him, but he chose to spend his youth not debating his fellow philosophers at Davos, but creating a dictionary for the young children he taught, so that they would know how to spell the basic words used in their daily lives.[29]

In the final scene of *Schooldays*, Simón finally takes the advice that Elena gave him in the first volume of the trilogy. Davíd has become a boarding student at a private Academy, where mathematics is learned not by practicing sums but 'dancing the numbers' down from the heavens to the accompaniment of live music (*Schooldays*, 207). When Davíd dances, he is visible to all as a 'pillar of grace', conjuring numbers into view as though they were gods, living entities, not units for counting fish or humans or time or money or anything else.[30] Simón is deeply sceptical of the Academy's experimental pedagogy, but he too would like to be a pillar of grace, in communication with the beyond, so he resolves to learn to dance. He is told that gold or silver slippers are required, but when he gets to the shoe store his size is unavailable, so he buys a child's pair and cuts the toes out. The effect is grotesque, clownish, the kind of outfit that embarrasses adults but amuses children, who have no fear of the ridiculous. Are the *Jesus* books Coetzee's attempt at a new language of faith, a religionless Christianity for a postsecular age with no universal keys? Perhaps. On the last page of *Schooldays*, we are told that as Simón dances in a child's shoes, 'Bliss washes over him' (260).

LOVING CARE

When Simón tells Martina that he is in crisis because he has no one on whom to bestow 'loving care', some readers will hear the echo of a cry sent out decades ago (*Schooldays*, 180). In Coetzee's apartheid-era novels, loving care is almost impossible. 'I have become an object of charity,' laments a dying Coloured man named Michael K in *Life & Times of Michael K* (1983), a novel in which K eludes apartheid's carceral systems by sacrificing every form of care, including food. 'I have escaped the camps,' he thinks in the novel's final pages; 'perhaps, if I lie low, I will escape the charity too'.[31] 'The spirit of charity has perished in this country,' says Mrs. Curren in *Age of Iron*, because 'those who accept charity despise it, while those who give give with a despairing heart'. 'Care,' she thinks: 'the true root of charity'.[32] Technically it's the opposite: charity is the true root of care, but let's not be pedantic or we might need to light our heads on fire. What's important is that both words derive from Greek *charis*, a word with many translations, and as important to Homer and Aristotle as to the authors of the Gospels and Epistles.[33] *Charis* is a root of Latin *caritas*, and also of the English words care, grace, charity and love. If this vocabulary proliferates in Coetzee's South African novels, usually in the context of failure, it comes even more sharply into focus in the novels he has written since emigrating to Australia in the early 2000s, including the *Jesus* trilogy. It would be reasonable to imagine that loving care is both easier and less important in a rich democracy with excellent public infrastructure, including healthcare and education, but it would also be wrong.

Like the war theologians Weil and Bonhoeffer, Coetzee has long been oriented to 'the neighbour who is within reach in any given situation'.[34] Here the word neighbour is not to be taken literally; it can refer to a vagrant or passer-by as readily as to people who share a property line. In every case, including Simón's, the kind of care that is being called for goes well beyond what can be required or legislated. When it comes to love, the law is never enough, and neither is a pay cheque nor a job description. A few years before the Jesus books, Coetzee published a novel called *Slow Man* (2005), whose protagonist, Paul Rayment, learns a great deal about care after he is hit by a car while riding his bicycle, sustaining injuries that require the partial amputation of one leg. Magill Road in Adelaide, Australia, is not quite the road to Damascus, and unlike his sainted namesake Paul does not hear the voice of Jesus calling him to a new faith.[35] Paul Rayment's transformation is slow, not sudden; human, not saintly. After his accident, he ceases to be a solitary, self-sufficient man who takes pride in his autonomy and instead becomes wholly dependent on what is described as 'frail care': a nursing subspecialty whose practitioners know how to clean an amputee's leg stump but are not paid to fill his heart or feed his soul (*Slow*, 18). Paul is an affluent man in an affluent welfare system, but he discovers that what he craves in his vulnerable state is not to become independent again, and not merely to have his damaged body protected from infection and pain, but to love and be loved.

Readers of any of Coetzee's other novels will recognize Paul's situation and feel a little queasy. Whatever form of love Coetzee writes about, whatever its etymology or English translation – *eros, caritas, agape*, charity, loving care, passion, blessing – we know that it is likely to make a character do something shocking, perhaps criminal.[36] We also know that in Coetzee's writing forms of love tend to blur into one another in a disturbing way; it is as though love moves at great speed, metamorphosing in transit, and our names do nothing more than identify temporary positions on a flight trajectory that we cannot predict or control. When Paul falls in love with his frail care nurse, a Croatian immigrant named Marijana, he reflects on this mystery: 'It all feels one to him, one movement: the swelling of the soul, the swelling of the heart, the swelling of desire' (186). As she stretches his stump and massages his torso, he thinks: 'He cannot imagine loving God more than he loves Marijana at this moment' (186). She straddles his body to knead the knotted muscles in his back and buttocks, intuiting where the pain is without needing to be told, and the scene is at once medical, maternal, erotic and divine. What kind of care is this, exactly? Here, as elsewhere in his writing, Coetzee is less interested in answering this question than in exploring how giving what cannot be asked, measured or paid for can help an individual, even an entire society, to begin again after trauma and loss. If there is an epiphany on Magill Road, it is this.

The letters that Paul writes to Marijana and her family after this epiphany are not exactly like his namesake's epistles, but they are not so different either. When he writes of his desire to become godfather to Marijana's three children, to 'take care of them, all of them, protect them and save them,' Paul evokes the language of love and gift that pervades the evangelist's own letters (*Slow*, 72). At the same time, there is something invasive about Paul's determination to become a godfather to near-strangers, especially when he imagines himself as 'co-husband' to Marijana and 'co-father' to her children (72). In the final pages of the novel, he seriously proposes moving into a shed in the family's backyard so he can 'watch over you' (251). Godfather or stalker? Benefactor or weirdo? Here, as in the Pauline epistles, love is strange and excessive. It moves a once-guarded man to wild generosity, just as it moves him to call his nurse on her day off because he has slipped in the shower and cannot get up even to use the toilet, eventually urinating on the floor. His need is great; so too is his new capacity to give. As Coetzee so often reminds us, that need is rooted in our hearts and souls, but also in our fragile bodies, which bleed and leak and suffer grievous injury even as we make desperate bids for transfiguration, because that is what human beings are like.

NOTES

1. Coetzee, *The Schooldays of Jesus*, 176. Subsequent references cited parenthetically.
2. Simón defines a godfather as someone who encourages a child to 'follow in the ways of goodness'; Coetzee, *The Childhood of Jesus*, 100. Subsequent references cited parenthetically.
3. On reading and writing, see Coetzee, *Childhood*, 165–6, 204–5. The story of Juan and Pablo takes places on 224–5.
4. I am indebted to all the students with whom I've read Coetzee in these seminars. In recent years, I'm particularly grateful to KP, David Lucia, Areej Alqowaifly and, above all, Brandi Estey-Burtt.
5. As several scholars have observed, philosophy at the Institute – and many philosophical dialogues that take place among the characters in the trilogy – closely invokes the content, tone and method of the dialogues of Plato's *Republic*. See Ng and Sheehan, 'Coetzee's Republic', 83–103; Uhlmann, 'Creative Intuition', 107–28.
6. This idea is reiterated on the last page of *The Death of Jesus*. After Davíd dies at the age of ten from an idiopathic infection, Simón finds his son's favourite book, *Don Quixote*. Inside the back cover, a children's librarian has written, '*What is the message of this book? What will you most of all remember of it?*' Two children have left comments, but by the handwriting Simón knowns that neither was Davíd. The final line of the novel is this: 'Now it will never be known what, in Davíd's eyes, the message of the book was, or what most of all he remembered from it.' Coetzee, *The Death of Jesus*, 196, 197. Italics in original.
7. This distrust of philosophical abstraction runs through much of Coetzee's writing. When in 1997 he was invited to give the Tanner Lectures in Human Values at Princeton University, he gave a series of talks about a fictitious Australian novelist, Elizabeth Costello, who attempts to make philosophical arguments for a university audience while also dealing with jet lag, fawning interviewers, her aging body, her alienated son and her angry daughter-in-law. The talks were later published as *The Lives of Animals*, which included essay-length responses by four prominent scholars: Wendy Doniger, Peter Singer, Barbara Smuts and Marjorie Garber. Each essay treats *The Lives of Animals* as though it were a work of philosophy, not a work of fiction. This decision has always struck me as ironic, given that Coetzee apparently found it impossible (or undesirable) to speak about human values without lodging those ideas within the vulnerable bodies and biased minds of a cast of literary characters. The irony deepens in the later novel *Elizabeth Costello*, in which 'The Lives of Animals' re-appears. No alert reader of this novel

can miss Coetzee's refusal to detach philosophical claims about human values, or ethics more broadly, from the embodied, fragile and wildly flawed humans who profess them.

8. Coetzee, *Disgrace*, 205. Subsequent references cited parenthetically.
9. Coetzee wanted to publish *Childhood* without a title on its front cover, thus hiding the word Jesus until the final page of the book, when the title would be revealed. His publisher refused the request. See Pecora, 'The Ambivalent Puritan', 128.
10. O'Donohue, 'The Inner Landscape of Beauty'.
11. See Agamben, *Homo Sacer* and Agamben, *The Kingdom and the Glory*; Knausgård, *A Time for Everything*.
12. Quoted in Thomas, 'A World of Strange Relations'. Wiman uses the term modern believer in the title of his critical memoir *My Bright Abyss*, 2013.
13. Quoted in Thomas.
14. For examples of recent scholarship exploring the meeting of sacred and secular, philosophy and religion in Coetzee's writing, see Faber, 'Post-Secular Poetics'; Pecora, 'The Ambivalent Puritan'; Estey-Burtt, 'Bidding the Animal Àdieu'; Wiegandt, 'The Creature-Feeling as Secular Grace'; Broggi, '"A Language I Have Not Unlearned"'; Farrant, 'Finitizing Life'; Forest, 'Challenging Secularity's Posthistorical "Destination"'; Googasian, 'Bothering to Believe'. The essays collected in Hayes and Wilm, eds., *Beyond the Ancient Quarrel* are also useful, although they are less concerned with Coetzee's attention to religion or the sacred.
15. Mrs. Curren invokes the Spartan warrior code in Coetzee, *Age of Iron*, 50, 80–1, 150; the episode in which children poke sticks into her mouth as she lies under a bridge in a pool her own urine takes place on 158–61.
16. Coetzee, *Disgrace*, 96.
17. Coetzee, *Elizabeth Costello*, 193–225.
18. Ibid., 123.
19. Wiman, *My Bright Abyss*, 47.
20. Ibid., 48–9.
21. Bonhoeffer, *Letters and Papers from Prison*, 153. Subsequent references cited parenthetically as *Letters* where necessary to disambiguate.
22. Weil, *Waiting for God*, 11–13, 36–7, 48.
23. Ibid., 50, 64.
24. In *The Weakness of God*, John D. Caputo pulls this thread of theological thought into the twenty-first century, drawing on Walter Benjamin's idea of God as a 'weak messianic force' rather than 'the overarching governor of the universe'. Caputo, 7, 9.
25. Bonhoeffer, *Letters and Papers*, 210. Also see 150.
26. Quoted in Norris, Foreword, xix.
27. Lewis, *Mere Christianity*, xv.
28. Eilenberger, *Time of the Magicians*, 255. Coetzee has a deep interest in the linguistic roots of our relationship to the world, as is clear in his close attention to language within his novels and essays. See Clarkson, *J. M. Coetzee*.
29. Eilenberger, *Time of the Magicians*, 255.
30. Coetzee, *Schooldays*, 246. Italics removed.
31. Coetzee, *Life & Times of Michael K*, 181,182.
32. Coetzee, *Age of Iron*, 22.

33. I write about the pre-Christian Greek origins of *charis* in Brittan, 'Death and J. M. Coetzee's *Disgrace*', 480–3.

34. Bonhoeffer, *Letters and Papers*, 210.

35. Paul explicitly refers to St Paul as his 'namesake, his name-saint'. Coetzee, *Slow Man*, 33. Subsequent references will appear parenthetically.

36. Examples are legion. Elizabeth Costello performs fellatio on an unresponsive dying man because she believes that she is offering him *caritas* (Coetzee, *Elizabeth Costello*, 151–5); David Lurie believes that his abusive affair with his student Melanie Isaacs was caused by *eros* (Coetzee, *Disgrace*, 52); Dmitri rapes and murders his mistress, Ana Magdalena, and blames the crime on love and passion (Coetzee, *Schooldays*, 168–73).

WORKS CITED

Agamben, Giorgio. *Homo Sacer: Sovereign Power and Bare Life*. Translated by Daniel Heller-Roazen. Stanford: Stanford University Press, 1998.

Agamben, Giorgio. *The Kingdom and the Glory: For a Theological Genealogy of Economy and Government*. Translated by Lorenzo Chiesa with Matteo Mandarini. Stanford: Stanford University Press, 2011.

Bonhoeffer, Dietrich. *Letters and Papers from Prison*. Translated by Reginald Fuller, edited by Eberhard Bethge. London: SCM Press, 1967.

Brittan, Alice. 'Death and J. M. Coetzee's *Disgrace*'. *Contemporary Literature* 51, no. 3 (2010): 477–502.

Broggi, Alicia. 'A Language I Have Not Unlearned': Cultivating an Historical Awareness of J. M. Coetzee's Engagement with Christianity'. *Literature & Theology* 32, no. 4 (2018): 252–74.

Caputo, John D. *The Weakness of God: A Theology of the Event*. Bloomington & Indianapolis: Indiana University Press, 2006.

Clarkson, Carrol. *J. M. Coetzee: Countervoices*. New York: Palgrave Macmillan, 2009.

Coetzee, J. M. *Age of Iron*. 1990. Toronto: Penguin, 1998.

Coetzee, J. M. *The Childhood of Jesus*. London: Harvill Secker, 2013.

Coetzee, J. M. *The Death of Jesus*. London: Harvill Secker, 2020.

Coetzee, J. M. *Disgrace*. New York: Penguin Books, 1999.

Coetzee, J. M. *Elizabeth Costello: Eight Lessons*. 2003. London: Vintage, 2004.

Coetzee, J. M. *Life & Times of Michael K*. 1983. Toronto: Vintage, 2004.

Coetzee, J. M. *The Lives of Animals*. Edited by Amy Gutmann. 1999. Princeton, NJ: Princeton University Press, 2016.

Coetzee, J. M. *The Schooldays of Jesus*. London: Harvill Secker, 2016.

Coetzee, J. M. *Slow Man*. Toronto: Viking, 2005.

Eilenberger, Wolfram. *Time of the Magicians: Wittgenstein, Benjamin, Cassirer, Heidegger, and the Decade That Reinvented Philosophy*. Translated by Shaun Whiteside. New York: Penguin Press, 2020.

Estey-Burtt, Brandi. 'Bidding the Animal Àdieu: Grace in J. M. Coetzee's *The Lives of Animals* and *Disgrace*'. *Literature & Theology* 31, no. 2 (2017): 231–45.

Faber, Alyda. 'The Post-Secular Poetics and Ethics of Exposure in J. M. Coetzee's *Disgrace*'. *Literature & Theology* 23, no. 3 (2009): 303–16.

Farrant, Marc. 'Finitizing Life: Between Reason and Religion in J. M. Coetzee's Jesus Novels'. *Journal of Modern Literature* 42, no. 4 (2019): 165–82.

Forest, Shannon. 'Challenging Secularity's Posthistorical 'Destination': J. M. Coetzee's Radical Openness in the Jesus Novels'. *Journal of Modern Literature* 42, no. 4 (2019): 146–64.

Googasian, Victoria. 'Bothering to Believe: Acts of Faith in J. M. Coetzee's Late Novels'. *Novel: A Forum on Fiction* 52, no. 2 (2019): 284–303.

Hayes, Patrick and Jan Wilm, eds. *Beyond the Ancient Quarrel: Literature, Philosophy, and J. M. Coetzee*. Oxford: Oxford University Press, 2017.

Knausgård, Karl Ove. *A Time for Everything*. Translated by James Anderson. New York: Archipelago Books, 2009.

Lewis, C. S. *Mere Christianity*. New York: HarperOne, 1980.

Ng, Lynda and Paul Sheehan. 'Coetzee's Republic: Plato, Borges, and Migrant Memory in *The Childhood of Jesus*'. In *The Childhood of Jesus: The Ethics of Ideas and Things*, edited by Anthony Uhlmann and Jennifer Rutherford, 83–103. New York: Bloomsbury Academic, 2017.

Norris, Kathleen. Foreword to *Mere Christianity*. Edited by C. S. Lewis, xvii–xx. New York: HarperOne, 1980.

O'Donohue, John. 'The Inner Landscape of Beauty'. Interview by Krista Tippett. *On Being with Krista Tippett*, 31 August 2017. Audio. https://onbeing.org/programs/john-odonohue-the-inner-landscape-of-beauty-aug2017/.

Pecora, Vincent. 'The Ambivalent Puritan: J. M. Coetzee'. In *Secularization without End: Beckett, Mann, Coetzee*, 85–152. Notre Dame: University of Notre Dame Press, 2015.

Thomas, Sally. 'A World of Strange Relations: Christian Wiman's *Survival Is a Style*'. *Public Discourse*, 20 August 2020. https://www.thepublicdiscourse.com/2020/08/61885/.

Uhlmann, Anthony. 'Creative Intuition: Coetzee, Plato, Bergson and Murnane'. In *The Childhood of Jesus: The Ethics of Ideas and Things*, edited by Anthony Uhlmann and Jennifer Rutherford, 107–28. New York: Bloomsbury Academic, 2017.

Wiegandt, Kai. 'The Creature-Feeling as Secular Grace: On the Religious in J.M. Coetzee's Fiction'. *Literature & Theology* 32, no. 1 (2018): 69–86.

Weil, Simone. *Waiting for God*. Translated by Emma Craufurd. New York: HarperPerennial, 2009.

Wiman, Christian. *My Bright Abyss: Meditation of a Modern Believer*. New York: Farrar, Straus and Giroux, 2013.

CHAPTER TWENTY-ONE

Coetzee, gender and sexuality

LAURA WRIGHT

PERFORMING GENDER AND 'THE PROBLEM OF SEX'

In nearly all of J. M. Coetzee's work, sex and sexuality are treated as problematic. When I teach his novels, my students often make me aware of the discomfort caused by the description of sexual encounters in his fiction. There are a number of rapes: in *Dusklands* (1974), Jacobus's of a 'Bushman' girl (who he describes as 'a rag you wipe yourself on and throw away'[1]); in *In the Heart of the Country* (1977), Hendrik's rape of Magda; and that rape of Lucy Lurie in *Disgrace* (1999)[2] that has attracted so much critical attention. Coetzee's fiction also includes scenes that are disturbing in their coercive ambiguity, instances that – as my students suggest – are 'rapey', 'rapish' or 'rapesque'. For example, in *Disgrace*, David Lurie's sexual encounter with his student Melanie is, in his own interpretation, 'not quite' rape 'but undesired nonetheless, undesired to the core'.[3] In *Waiting for the Barbarians* (1980), the Magistrate engages in a masturbatory bathing ritual centred on washing the body of a barbarian girl.[4] A woman fellates the unwilling eponymous protagonist in *Life & Times of Michael K* (1983).[5] Meanwhile in *Foe* (1986), Cruso ignores Susan Barton's rebuff and has sex with her, a transgression for which she excuses him, saying 'he has not known a woman for 15 years, why should he not have his desire?'[6] At the start of *Disgrace*, we learn that Lurie has 'solved the problem of sex' (1) through weekly visits to the sex-worker Soraya. The idea that sex constitutes a 'problem' is a theme writ large across Coetzee's opus. Sex is a problem for the very reason that it requires a reciprocity that is always impossible in the various contexts in which Coetzee situates his works – contexts that are acutely and self-consciously informed by their socio-cultural imbrication in patriarchal, colonial and white-supremacist politics. After foregrounding my discussion of the 'problem of sex' via an analysis of *Disgrace*, I then consider how this problem manifests in two of Coetzee's earlier works, *Life & Times of Michael K* and *Foe*, narratives that are infused with scenes of disturbing, violent and problematic sex. Both works, I suggest, explore ambivalent, gendered, performative spaces that challenge Western master narratives of heteronormative literary production and apartheid's specific legacy of white supremacy.

THE PROBLEM OF SEX

The novels of Coetzee's South African period explore various literal and imaginative spaces, from the eighteenth-century setting of *Foe*, in which Susan Barton fights for agency over her own story, to the allegorical outpost or floating signifier of empire in *Waiting for the Barbarians*, to South Africa before, during or after apartheid (from *Dusklands* to *Disgrace*). But in each of these, in the literal and implied histories and locations depicted, sex – particularly heterosexual sex – is more often than not a problem: the nature of consent is situated within particular postcolonial, gendered and racial politics that underscore the challenges Coetzee's characters face in connecting with one another as equals in mutually (often sexually) satisfying ways. Within such contexts, the line between consensual sex and rape is blurred by gendered and racial hierarchies that ensure unequal relationships of power. Coetzee's narratives often also challenge Western literary traditions' romanticization of rape. Nicola Moffat notes the ways that Western literary history figures 'rape as a seduction, popularized in English literature through metaphors of colonial expansion, hunting, and other masculine pursuits'; this 'is the extreme dichotomization of masculine and feminine sexuality, where being male has become synonymous with being a rapist inasmuch as being female has become synonymous with being a disenfranchised and passive victim', she argues.[7] In her reading of *Disgrace* as a self-reflexive narrative that 'presupposes and doubles back on ... "ambivalence", and ... also leaves a certain responsibility with the reader',[8] Lucy Valerie Graham has noted the ways that rape is characterized throughout canonical Western literature as 'unspeakable' or 'severed from articulation': 'literary references to hidden rape stories cannot but bring into relief the complex relationship between literary silences and the aftermath of actual violation,' Graham notes.[9] This lack of overt articulation, combined with *Disgrace*'s ambivalent depiction of problematic sex (as well as the discomfort and even revulsion that reading scenes of problematic sexual encounters engenders), serves to create a kind of Brechtian alienation effect, a theatrical 'representation that alienates ... allows us to recognize its subject but at the same time makes it unfamiliar'.[10]

In *Disgrace*, after his daughter Lucy – 'a latter day Magda, who ... knows well how to "husband" a farm' – is gang-raped,[11] David Lurie reflects on how to define 'rape': 'he remembers, as a child, poring over the word *rape* in newspaper reports, trying to puzzle out what exactly it meant' (159). Of Byron, his literary idol, he thinks that 'among the legions of countesses and kitchenmaids Byron pushed himself into there were no doubt those who called it rape' (160), even if they, unlike Lucy, did not have to fear for their lives after the encounter was over. The violent rape of Lucy at the hands of three strangers (who also set David on fire and lock him in a bathroom) forces him to reconsider his own actions in terms of what constitutes rape, and his recognition that rape can look like what he considered seduction, particularly in relation to his encounters with his student Melanie, is certainly implied in his thoughts about Byron. According to the Centre for Constitutional Rights, the rate of femicide in South Africa is five times the global average, with twenty-one women reported murdered in the first two weeks of June 2020.[12] It is understandable, then, that David is aware that his daughter must have feared that the rape 'would end with her throat being slit' (160) and up to this point in the novel, it is the overt violence that could lead to death, not the coercive supposed seduction in which he entraps Melanie, that David considers rape. It is not until after his daughter experiences this violence that David starts to shift ever so slightly in his perception of his own actions.

OUTSIDE OF ALL THE GENDERED CAMPS: *LIFE & TIMES OF MICHAEL K*

Coetzee's 1983 Booker Prize-winning novel *Life & Times of Michael K* begins with a description of Michael's hare lip, the first thing the midwife notices about him: 'the lip curled like a snail's foot, the left nostril gaped' (3). K, a man with a 'disfigurement' whose 'mind was not quick' (4), initially works as a gardener before, at the age thirty-one, embarking upon a quest to take his ailing mother from Cape Town to her childhood home in the countryside near Prince Albert. The narrative is set during a fictional South African civil war from which Michael, whose mother dies on the journey to the interior, unsuccessfully attempts to extricate himself: he is first conscripted into a labour gang, escapes to what he believes to be his mother's childhood farm and is later taken to a resettlement camp called Jakkalsdrif (Jackal ford). The narrative traces Michael's desire to 'be out of all the camps at the same time' (182) and the notion of 'camps' functions as a signifier of the labour and resettlement camps from which K escapes through various holes in fences as well as the 'rehabilitation camp' (131) where he is taken after he collapses. Further, Michael's assertion to the officer that he is 'not in the war' (138) and his refusal to remain imprisoned within its machinations constitute acts of resistance against state and culturally-sanctioned codifications of race, gender and sexual orientation.

Throughout the narrative, Michael is misnamed and mischaracterized. At Jakkalsdrif, the charge sheet lists him as 'Michael Visagie – CM – 40 – NFA – Unemployed' (70). His name and age are incorrect, which makes his racial classification (presumably 'coloured male') suspect as well. In addition to the medical officer misnaming him 'Michaels,' he is misrepresented to the admitting officer as 'an arsonist. He is also an escapee from a labour camp. He was running a flourishing garden on an abandoned farm and feeding the local guerrilla population when he was captured' (131). The medical officer desperately tries to glean Michael's story:

> I want to know your story. I want to know how it happened that you of all people have joined in a war, a war in which you have no place. You are no soldier, Michaels, you are a figure of fun, a clown, a wooden man ... You are like a stick insect, Michaels, whose sole defence against a universe of predators is its bizarre shape.
>
> (149)

The drive to know Michael's story, and his refusal (or inability) to tell it, prevails throughout the narrative, with various characters asking for him to explain himself and then creating false narratives about him when he does not offer what they expect.[13] Late in the novel, Michael describes the performance in which he is expected to engage, noting that 'if I had learned storytelling at Huis Norenius instead of potato-peeling and sums, if they had made me practice the story of my life every day, standing over me with a cane till I could perform without stumbling, I might have known how to please them' (181). The story that is true – or that perhaps comes closest to the truth – is that Michael wishes to remain outside of all defining systems, but to be outside is to be defined, erroneously, by others.

To my knowledge, no scholar has addressed the way that Michael K eschews and problematizes sex and gender norms, but it is clear that his refusals to participate in the war and to be codified in various camps are also indicative of a refusal of white, normative, male heterosexuality. Early in the novel, Michael moves his mother into a ransacked flat in Cape Town, where he discovers piles of magazines: 'he lay in bed, or lay in the bath, paging through pictures of beautiful women and luscious food. The food absorbed him more deeply' (16). It is food, not women, that Michael craves throughout the novel, even as he is thwarted in his attempts to grow his own crops or find the 'bread of freedom' (146) that the medical officer quips is all that he will willingly eat. Further, when the medical officer offers to fix Michael's cleft palate, Michael declines telling him that 'I was never a great one for the girls' (130). This lack of interest in women is further demonstrated near the end of the novel when a woman fellates Michael K against his wishes: 'he pushed her hand away and tried to struggle to his feet' (179), but he acquiesces only to feel 'the shame of the episode ... waiting like a shadow at the edge of his thoughts' (179). Further, *Life & Times of Michael K* opens with an epigram by Heraclitus, 'war is father of all and king of all,' and Michael views the orphanage where he lived as a child as his own father: 'my father was Huis Norenius. My father was the list of rules on the door of the dormitory' (104–5). He instead aligns himself with his mother, and with the maternal more generally, mourning the lack of maternal affection in the present moment of the novel: 'my mother is buried and not yet risen' (105). On the farm, after soldiers destroy his crops, Michael thinks 'I am like a woman whose children have left the house ... all that remains is to tidy up and listen to the silence' (111). Michael's lack of interest in heterosexual sex, his associations, as a cultivator of pumpkins, with the maternal, and his refusal to fight in the war constitute an affront to normative notions of a violent masculinity of the kind that underscores a narrative of rape as seduction and that was foundational to the white supremacist apartheid state that constituted South Africa at the time that Coetzee wrote the novel.

It is telling that Michael's final vision of companionship is not of life with a wife, but of travels with an old man. His vision manifests a minimalist homosocial space in which 'one can live' (184), even if such a connection is impossible in the present moment. At the end of the novel, Michael notes that his mistake 'was not to have plenty of seeds' (182) so that he could plant and grow a variety of crops instead of planting only pumpkins. He imagines going to the country with 'a little old man with a stoop and a bottle in his side pocket who muttered all the time into his beard, the kind of man the police ignored' travelling with him, of whom he notes, 'we could share a bed tonight; it has been done before' (183). Because the town's water supply has attacked and the pump destroyed, Michael imagines that the old man will wonder how they will get water. Michael thinks that he could lower a teaspoon 'down the shaft deep into the earth'. When he then brings up 'water in the bowl of the spoon' (184), he could give it to the man, feeding him, just as Michael's mother fed him 'with a teaspoon' (3) when he was a baby who, because of his harelip, could not suck from a bottle. This imagined vision occurs as Michael is near death, 'feeling that something inside him had let go or was letting go. What it was letting go of he did not yet know' (177).

Here, as elsewhere throughout the novel, the 'not yet' moment is invoked as designating the chronic state of many of Coetzee's characters' arrival, by the end of his novels, at a moment of *almost* becoming, of *almost* – but not yet – knowing something profound. This space of 'not yet' is indicative of the interregnum between the fall of apartheid and the rise of a new form of government. It is very much the imagined chronological time of *Life & Times of Michael K*, but it is also the space of waiting, for Michael K, a space of being 'a person who wants nothing' (179) except to exist beyond the rigid racial, sexual and social categorizations designated by apartheid. It is a space in which Michael cannot yet 'perform without stumbling' (181).

GENDERING *ROBINSON CRUSOE*, QUEERING COETZEE

As I note above in terms of the 'not yet' of *Life & Times of Michael K*, in Coetzee's works many of his protagonists often, almost, *but not quite* have epiphanies about why connection with various others is out of reach, and they even come to the brink of a transformational moment of epiphany, but the moment always proves elusive. The end of *Foe* finds a ghostly unknown narrator prying open the mouth of Friday, listening for his story, met with the sounds of the island. Jihan Zakarriya reads *Foe* as a performative text, 'an ecofeminist-inflected parody of cultural complicity' in which Susan Barton 'places herself in the dual role of exile/colonizer'.[14] Similarly, Jennifer Rickel notes that *Foe* 'stages' the project of writing back to Defoe 'via Susan since Friday does not speak. It imagines a scenario in which Friday, with Susan as his witness and sponsor, might parrot Cruso's supposedly universal narrative voice to establish himself as a fully developed person.'[15] It is from a metafictional performative position that both Susan and the mute Friday disrupt Defoe's *Robinson Crusoe* as a master Western novel and the idea of the single, monolithic author.

Much has been written about Coetzee's three female narrators:[16] *In the Heart of the Country*'s Magda, a white Afrikaner woman living with her widowed father in the Karoo at the start of the twentieth-century; *Foe*'s Susan Barton, a woman shipwrecked on Robison Crusoe's island who, after her rescue, entreats Daniel Defoe (Foe, in the novel) to write her story; and *Age of Iron*'s (1990) Mrs. Curren, a retired Classics professor living in Cape Town in 1986 during the violent uncertainty of the impending fall of apartheid. I argue that the liminal nature of these characters designates the transitory and shifting space of signification both for white women and for Coetzee's writing such subjects into history. That Coetzee engages via the narrative perspectives of white women seems indicative of his desire to distance himself from the racist patriarchy of South African history, opting instead for self-identification with the social and racial position white women occupy. Such a position is both complicit with and victimized by the institutions of apartheid and literary production.[17] It is from this performative narrative position that Coetzee perhaps comes closest to being able to move 'from the side of the oppressors to the side of the oppressed'.[18] Further, Elleke Boehmer notes that in his creation of Elizabeth Costello, the persona whose stories comprise numerous of his lectures, Coetzee queers himself, inhabiting the person of a woman novelist in an act I refer to elsewhere as 'dialogic drag'.[19] Boehmer notes that with Costello, Coetzee submits to the very 'femaleness, weakness, softness, eternal travail, that ... he has not only long associated with the body of woman but has also suspected of residing within himself, within his own ... "queer" body'.[20]

With regard to this queer body, Boehmer has explored the ways that the male body invokes desire in John, the protagonist in *Boyhood* (1998) and *Youth* (2003), the first two of Coetzee's three *autre*biographies. In *Boyhood*, she notes the 'tellingly excessive erotic description of ... the young male body'.[21] Boehmer argues that John's fixation on the legs of other young boys in the text 'represents, significantly, the narrator's first open acknowledgement of desire'.[22] While such eroticism is implicitly queer, the inclusion of explicitly queer characters in South African literature by white writers in the literature of the 'new South Africa' of the 1990s is, according to Brenna M. Munro, the product of the transition to a democracy that upended traditional apartheid heterosexual masculine hegemony to champion white LGBTQ+ identities as a means of white differentiation from the racist and patriarchal politics of the past. Several of the 1990s era works of Nadine Gordimer and Coetzee depict 'white, middle-class, middle-aged Anglo–South Africans whose struggle to adjust to the new era includes dealing with the revelation that their children are not heterosexual',[23] and in these depictions, Gordimer's *None to Accompany Me* (1994) and *The House Gun* (1998) and Coetzee's *Disgrace*, 'the queer kids often lead their families out of the ethnic enclave, into the larger rainbow nation'.[24]

Foe clearly predates Coetzee's more openly queer explorations, but both it and *Life & Times of Michael K* prefigure a queer male positionality predicated on an overt identification with women – in the form of Michael's mother Anna and *Foe*'s narrator, Susan Barton. In *Foe*, Susan's very existence constitutes a problem of sex: she is a female castaway who demands to be written into the story of *Robinson Crusoe*, and she is an affront to Foe, Coetzee's fictionalized version of Daniel Defoe, who is often considered the father of the English novel. As a 'woman alone',[25] Susan refuses to conform to either her culture's concepts of appropriate femininity or to Foe's attempts to turn her into his later protagonists Roxana or Moll Flanders instead of the female castaway she claims as her rightful position in her story – a story that she wants Foe to tell for her. Of the letters Susan writes to Foe before she meets him, she predicts the future: 'one day when we are departed you will tip them out and glance through them. "Better had there been only Cruso and Friday," you will murmur to yourself: "Better without the woman"' (71–2). In Defoe's 1719 novel, there is no woman castaway, and Crusoe repeats and rehearses the narrative of his shipwreck in chapters three, four and five, editing out and changing details in each telling. These revisions trace the narrative through three iterations: Crusoe's emotional and distressing memory of coming ashore, his narrated memory of transcribing the experience and, finally, the written, emotionless codified utterance of the event.

In the first, Crusoe even admits to his inability to describe his reaction: 'I walk'd about on the Shore, lifting up my Hands, and my whole Being, as I may say, wrapt up in the Contemplation of my Deliverance, making a Thousand Gestures and Motions *which I cannot describe*' (my emphasis).[26] In the second, Crusoe notes his keeping of a journal and describes his imagined memory of writing of the shipwreck in much more detail:

> I *must have said* thus. Sept. the 30th. After I got to Shore and had escap'd drowning, instead of being thankful to God for my Deliverance, having first vomited with the great Quantity of salt Water which was gotten into my Stomach, and recovering my self a little, I ran about the Shore, wringing my Hands and beating my Head and Face, exclaiming at my Misery, and crying out, I was undone, undone.
>
> (my emphasis)[27]

In the final telling, which comes directly from his journal, Crusoe adds the exact date and edits out the emotion conveyed in the previous telling: 'September 30, 1659. I poor miserable Robinson Crusoe, being shipwreck'd, during a dreadful Storm ... came on Shore on this dismal unfortunate Island, which I call'd the *Island of Despair*, all the rest of the Ship's Company being drown'd, and my self almost dead.'[28] The repetition of the experience serves as an illustration of the writing process: the first description seeks to convey what Crusoe feels in the moments after washing ashore; the second conveys what he feels he 'must have said' about that experience, after he starts to keep a journal; and the third constitutes the final product, the rational edited and revised telling, devoid of indescribable admissions and vomit, codified in an objective tone for an external audience.

Like Crusoe in Defoe's novel, Susan Barton repeats the story of her shipwreck and first moments ashore in *Foe,* but her repetitions function differently. The novel opens with her descriptive and simile-laden narration:

> at last I could row no further. My hands were blistered, my back burned, my body ached. With a sigh, making barely a splash I slipped overboard. With slow strokes, my long hair floating about me, like a flower of the sea, like an anemone, like a jellyfish of the kind you see in the waters of Brazil, I swam towards the island.
>
> (5)

The silent and tongueless Friday finds Susan and leads her to Cruso, to whom she repeats the story, saying 'then at last I could row no further. My hands were raw, my back was burned, my body ached. With a sigh, making barely a splash, I slipped overboard and began to swim towards the island' (11). After she meets Foe and he tries to shape her story into that of Roxana – even producing a missing daughter and confidante, Amy – Susan pushes back against being turned into his story, saying 'I am not a story, Mr. Foe. I may impress you as a story because I began my account of myself without preamble, *slipping overboard and striking for the shore*. But my life did not begin in the waves' (113, my emphasis). She continues by critiquing Foe's creation of her supposed daughter and of Amy: 'if these women are creatures of yours, visiting me at your instruction, speaking words prepared for them, then who am I and who indeed are you? I presented myself to you in words I knew to be my own – *I slipped overboard, I began to swim, my hair floated about me, and so forth*' (133, my emphasis). The final telling is read by an unnamed first-person narrator who finds her words written in a manuscript: 'with a sigh, making barely a splash, I slip overboard. Gripped by the current, the boat bobs away, drawn south towards the realm of the whales and eternal ice. Around me on the waters are the petals cast by Friday' (155). Susan's story moves from an initial focus on her physical body in the water shifting instead to focus on the boat, the sea and the inconvenient intrusion of Friday, whose story remains unspeakable and unknowable.

Zakarriya notes that Susan considers 'her body as a public domain to be owned and used by men',[29] but I disagree. Susan seeks to push back against the ways that patriarchy determines her bodily function and intellectual capacity. She has sex with Foe for pleasure, sitting astride him, which makes him uncomfortable, telling him: 'this is the manner of the muse when she visits her poets' (139). If she is having sex with Foe to bring about her own story, then she becomes an active participant in the creation of the narrative and not a passive victim who can be used and owned. Susan's frustration with her inability to assert her narrative in a way that can be heard is underscored by the fact that Friday's narrative is completely absent from the novel. Friday has no tongue – either because it was cut off by slavers, as Cruso suggests, or by Cruso, as Susan sometimes suspects. According to Robinson O. Murphy, in Coetzee's novel, Friday 'disavows all forms of intercourse with white heteropatriarchy in order to produce a political alternative that commands recognition of the inconvenient, unsanitized version of the Atlantic'. Further, Friday's castration – imagined, symbolic or literal – constitutes a 'refusal to be made intelligible and thereby appropriable to European interlocutors during the time of slavery'.[30] Susan asks Friday 'why did you not desire me?' (86) as she tries to discern his story. Just as various characters seek Michael K's story only to be met with silence, Friday never answers any of Susan's questions, resisting her attempts to interpret him and place him within the context of her experience. Instead, he plays the same tune over and over on his flute, driving Susan nearly to madness.

Friday finds Foe's robes and wigs, puts them on and dances around Foe's house. Susan notes that 'in the grip of the dancing he is not himself. He is beyond human reach ... Sometimes he seems to be singing' (92). Friday's mimicry of Foe, dressed in his clothes, dancing and singing, is a performative critique of the intellectual exercise of literary revision, a practice demonstrated by the narrative's retelling of Susan's initial description of her bodily presence in the water after the shipwreck, with her 'long hair floating' (5) to the final description of an unknown narrator diving down under the water, beneath the white petals, and swimming to the bottom of the sea to 'the home of Friday' (157). Friday refuses to revise, to modify, to perform a narrative that would conform to Defoe's willing slave version of his character; he plays the same tune over and over, whirling in Foe's robes, revealing to Susan his nakedness, though it is unclear what exactly Susan has seen: 'I saw and believed I had seen, though afterwards I remembered Thomas, who also saw, but could not be brought to believe till he had put his hand in the wound' (119–20). Friday's possible status as a 'slave unmanned' (119), according to Murphy, means refusing to make himself intelligible to Barton, which 'would mean complying with his own erasure; by refusing language altogether, Friday is unrepresentable to the would-be authors around him and so maintains a queer vantage from which to gesture toward an alternative story'.[31] In wanting Friday to alter his version – to enter narrative history – Susan behaves very much like Foe in his desire to define her in the context of his version of her, either Roxana or Moll Flanders.

Of the repetition of the tune that Friday plays, Susan complains 'But, alas, just as we cannot exchange forever the same utterances – "Good day, sir" – "Good day" – and believe we are conversing, or perform forever the same motion and call it lovemaking, so it is with music: we cannot forever play the same tune and be content. Or so at least it is with civilized people' (97). In an effort to get Friday to alter his tune, Susan plays a second flute in unison with him, adding and changing notes, turning Friday's original song 'into a new tune and a pretty one too, so fresh to my ear that I was sure Friday would follow me'. But he does not, and 'the two tunes played together formed no pleasing counterpoint, but on the contrary jangled and jarred' (97–98). Susan's comparison of discourse – 'utterances' – to sex – 'lovemaking' – situates writing, sex and music as creative performative acts in need of revision and adaptation: all three modes of expression require reciprocity between performer and audience, either the reader or listener, or, in the case of sex, the sexual partner. The utterance of Susan's coming ashore after the shipwreck, revised numerous times throughout the novel, is evidence of the revisionist nature of the history of Western literature and of history more generally: the story that is told is never the complete story; it is always a version of a kind of truth but never fully true.

Through their refusals to tell the stories demanded of them by their various audiences, Michael K and Friday offer a space of signification that must be read through alternately sexualized bodies marked by disability and trauma. Michael K's cleft palate and his starved body that, as the medical officer says, 'rejected the food that fed you' (163), and Friday's possible castration and mutilated tongue, situate both their speech and their sexuality unreadable within the context of their expected articulation. It is a place, as the unknown narrator of the final part of *Foe* notes, 'where bodies of their own signs. It is the home of Friday' (157) and a place where the medical officer (in *Life & Times*) states that Michael K is 'an allegory … of how scandalously, how outrageously a meaning can take up residence in a system without becoming a term in it' (166). Via the forced fellatio enacted upon Michael K and his rejection of bodily heterosexual companionship in favour of an esoteric homosocial fantasy, and via Friday's possible castration, the problem of sex is written on the bodies of these characters who eschew codification – of meaning, of utterance – in a heteronormative system that stages hierarchical racial and gender-based norms into which these characters refuse to be conscripted. And Coetzee's novels overdetermine the ways that other interlocutors, the medical officer in *Life & Times of Michael K* and Daniel Defoe in both *Foe* and literary history more broadly, misinterpret and revise their stories to fit their master narratives, demonstrating the problem of the monologic narrator via the lens of the problem of sex. Through this revelation, *Life & Times of Michael K* and *Foe* participate in a performance of racial and sexual resistance against Western literature's insistence that the 'white man's burden' constitutes the ur-text of imperialism.

NOTES

1. Coetzee, *Dusklands*, 61.
2. See Donadio, 'Out of South Africa', online.
3. Coetzee, *Disgrace*, 23. Further references are cited parenthetically in text. Many critics, me included, consider David's encounter with Melanie to be unquestionably an act of rape.
4. Coetzee, *Waiting for the Barbarians*, 28–30.
5. Coetzee, *Life & Times of Michael K*, 179. Hereafter cited parenthetically.
6. Coetzee, *Foe*, 30. Further references are cited parenthetically in text.
7. Nicola Moffat, 'Rape and the (Animal) Other', 415.
8. Graham, 'Reading the Unspeakable', 434.
9. Ibid., 439.
10. Brecht, *Brecht on Theater*, 192.
11. Ghosh-Shellhorn, 'Reading Coetzee Expectantly', 207.
12. Myeni, 'Our Bodies'.
13. This trope of the insistence upon the disclosure of stories and confessions is prevalent in much of Coetzee's work, including *Waiting for the Barbarians*, *Foe* and *Disgrace*.
14. Zakarriya, 'Sexual Identity', 221.
15. Rickel, 'Speaking of Human Rights', 166.
16. And about his women characters more broadly. See in particular Sue Kossew and Melinda Harvey's 2019 edited collection *Reading Coetzee's Women*.
17. Wright, 'Displacing the Voice', 13.
18. Quoted in Dean, 'Why Will He Not Join the Guerrillas', 684.
19. Wright, 'He and His Woman'.
20. Boehmer, 'Coetzee's Queer Body', 229–30.
21. Ibid., 224.
22. Ibid., 222.
23. Munro, 'Queer Family Romance', 398.
24. Ibid., 399.
25. Coetzee, *Foe*, 11. Hereafter cited parenthetically.
26. Defoe, *Robinson Crusoe*, 41.
27. Ibid., 60.
28. Ibid., 60–1. Emphasis in original.
29. Zakarriya, 'Sexual Identity', 222.
30. Murphy, 'Black Friday, Queer Atlantic', 182–3.
31. Ibid., 187.

WORKS CITED

Boehmer, Elleke. 'Coetzee's Queer Body'. *Journal of Literary Studies* 21, no. 3–4 (2005): 222–34.
Brecht, Bertolt. *Brecht on Theater*. Edited and translated by John Wilet. New York: Hill and Wang, 1964.
Coetzee, J. M. *Age of Iron*. New York: Penguin, 1990.
Coetzee, J. M. *Boyhood*. New York: Penguin, 1998.

Coetzee, J. M. *Disgrace*. New York: Penguin, 1999.
Coetzee, J. M. *Dusklands*. New York: Penguin, 1985.
Coetzee, J. M. *Foe*. New York: Penguin, 1987.
Coetzee, J. M. *In the Heart of the Country*. New York: Penguin, 1982.
Coetzee, J. M. *Life & Times of Michael K*. New York: Penguin, 1983.
Coetzee, J. M. *The Master of Petersburg*. New York: Penguin, 1994.
Coetzee, J. M. *Waiting for the Barbarians*. New York: Penguin, 1980.
Coetzee, J. M. *Youth*. New York: Penguin, 2003.
Dean, Andrew. 'Why Will He Not Join the Guerrillas?': J. M. Coetzee's *Life & Times of Michael K* and the Politics of the Postcolonial Novel'. *Modern Fiction Studies* 65, no. 4 (2019): 676–99.
Defoe, Daniel. *Robinson Crusoe*. Oxford: Oxford University Press, 2007.
Donadio, Rachel. 'Out of South Africa'. *New York Times*, 16 December 2007. https://www.nytimes.com/2007/12/16/books/review/Donadio-t.html.
Ghosh-Shellhorn, Martina. 'Reading Coetzee Expectantly: From Magda to Lucy'. In *Reading Coetzee's Women*, edited by Sue Kossew and Melinda Harvey, 205–19. Cham: Palgrave, 2019.
Gordimer, Nadine. *The House Gun*. New York: Picador, 2003.
Gordimer, Nadine. 'Living in the Interregnum'. In *The Essential Gesture: Writing, Politics and Place*, edited by Stephen Clingman, 261–84. New York: Penguin, 1989.
Gordimer, Nadine. *None to Accompany Me*. New York: Farrar, Straus, and Giroux, 1994.
Graham, Lucy Valerie. 'Reading the Unspeakable: Rape in J. M. Coetzee's *Disgrace*'. *Journal of Southern African Studies* 29, no. 2 (2003): 433–44.
Kossew, Sue. 'Women's Words:' A Reading of J. M. Coetzee's Women Narrators'. *SPAN* 37, no. 1 (1993): 12–23.
Moffat, Nicola. 'Rape and the (Animal) Other: Making Monsters in J. M. Coetzee's *Disgrace*'. *Signs: Journal of Women in Culture and Society* 43, no. 2 (2018): 401–23.
Munro, Brenna M. 'Queer Family Romance: Writing the "New" South Africa in the 1990s'. *GLQ: A Journal of Lesbian and Gay Studies* 15, no. 3 (2009): 397–439.
Murphy, Ryan O. 'Black Friday, Queer Atlantic'. *Research in African Literatures* 49, no. 2 (2018): 182–98.
Myeni, Thabi. 'Our Bodies Are Crime Scenes': South Africa's Murdered Women'. *Aljazeera*, 5 June 2021. https://www.aljazeera.com/features/2021/6/5/our-bodies-are-crime-scenes-south-africas-murdered-women.
Rickel, Jennifer. 'Speaking of Human Rights: Narrative Voice and the Paradox of the Unspeakable in J. M. Coetzee's *Foe* and *Disgrace*'. *Journal of Narrative Theory* 43, no. 2 (2013): 160–85.
Wright, Laura. 'Displacing the Voice: J. M. Coetzee's Women Narrators'. *African Studies* 67, no. 1 (2008): 11–31.
Wright, Laura. 'He and His Woman: Passing Performances and Coetzee's Dialogic Drag'. In *Reading Coetzee's Women*, edited by Sue Kossew and Melinda Harvey, 17–37. London: Palgrave Macmillan, 2019.
Zakarriya, Jihan. 'Sexual Identity and Disturbed Female Terrain in J. M. Coetzee's *Foe* and Jabra Ibrahim Jabra's *The Ship*: An Ecofeminist Reading'. *Journal of International Women's Studies* 18, no. 2 (2017): 219–32.

CHAPTER TWENTY-TWO

Coetzee and the nonhuman

DANIEL WILLIAMS

The nonhuman world has long constituted a fund of imaginative energy for J. M. Coetzee – a repertoire of image and analogy, an avenue for claiming literary-historical kin, a vehicle for philosophical rumination, a device for decentring plot's human concerns and a source of ethical gravity. Yet since Coetzee eschews fables where human relations are figured extensively in nonhuman terms, these topics have often seemed peripheral. Critics only began to contemplate the persistence of nonhuman themes in his work following *The Lives of Animals* (1999); most attention remains focused on *Disgrace* (1999). By contrast, we might identify four modes in which Coetzee has approached the nonhuman with remarkable range from the outset of his career. I term these the Schreiner, Adorno, Rilke and Dostoevsky modes, and discuss each in turn in what follows.

In the *Schreiner mode*, we confront the nonhuman's abiding indifference to human presence, a feature of Olive Schreiner's seminal 'South African' novel, *The Story of an African Farm* (1883), that Coetzee describes as necessitating 'a geological, not a botanical, gaze'.[1] Schreiner's stones – like the landscapes of Cape travel narratives and Coetzee's early imaginary – 'speak to those trained to read them, though what they mainly speak of is the insignificance of man'.[2] Creaturely life is here dwarfed by the inanimate, by long-run processes and desolate surroundings.

In the Heart of the Country (1977) typifies this mode in its arid setting – 'a theatre of stone and sun fenced in with miles of wire' – and its protagonist's 'stony monologue'.[3] By day the landscape 'belongs only to the sun' and to 'insects who eat sand and lay eggs in each other's corpses'; by night it welcomes 'a darkness that is complete, that lives in itself, ... that does not signify but merely is' (*IHC* 108, 9). In the veld among donkeys, chickens and flies, the nonhuman's oppressive unconcern – written to scales both massive and minute – frays Magda's sanity and frames the novel's shocking narrative.

Yet the indifference is Janus-faced. The nonhuman presents as an ontological conundrum – a zone of latent sense that might yield to 'metaphysical conquest' if not to colonial incursion (74). In a fantasy also entertained in *Dusklands* (1974), and episodically in later novels, humanity meditates the nonhuman's elusive being, often as a prelude to violence. Fancying herself 'a poetess of interiority', Magda 'ache[s] to abdicate the throne of consciousness and enter the mode of being practised by goats or stones' (35, 26). In anxious reflections joining introspection (of 'the molecular world inside') to exploration (of 'the prehistoric world outside'), she deems the existence of flowers and stones contingent on she who 'set[s] them vibrating with their own variety of material awareness that I am forever not they, and they not I' (35, 48). 'The farm, the desert, the whole world as far as the horizon', she desperately reasons, 'is in an ecstasy of communion with itself, exalted by the vain urge of my consciousness to inhabit it' (49).

Coetzee's early fiction shuttles between the poles of this roughly Hegelian dialectic between insistent opacity and inviting interiority. Yet if these works use the nonhuman as a conceptual fulcrum to reassert human powers, like Magda, their 'talent is all for immanence' (71). Their ludic metafiction might seem dated; what remains striking is their representation of the desolation to which the nonhuman consigns us. Magda's edifice of 'word-counters' is eclipsed by the thought of her body stripped to 'a clean white skeleton … with the spiders in my eyesockets spinning traps for the stragglers to the feast' – a macabre image making the portals of perception and identity (eye, I) a site for existential struggles postdating humanity (79). In a related image in the South African half of *Dusklands*, Jacobus Coetzee pictures himself as 'a spherical reflecting eye moving through the wilderness and ingesting it'.[4] But his deranged boasting about the remnants of his expedition – 'a mountain of skin, bones, inedible gristle, and excrement' – as well as his dominion over the uncountable wild – 'I am a hunter, a domesticator of the wilderness, a hero of enumeration' – is undermined by the text's proliferating objects (79, 80). In *Dusklands*, things pile up in parodic lists, catalogues of 'nonhuman witnesses' outlasting human eyes and events.[5]

The Schreiner mode's deep-time perspective appears wherever South Africa's landscape asserts itself, as in Coetzee's quasi-autobiographical fiction. One of its enduring tropes is the lithic: Eugene Dawn likens Vietnamese women to stones (*DL* 18); Jacobus and Magda obsess over their voice and being (*DL* 77–8, 95–6; *IHC* 26, 35, 114–15). The medical officer views Michael K as 'a stone, a pebble … enveloped in itself and its interior life'; Mrs Curren's moral etymologizing stresses the Afrikaners' 'message that turns people to stone'.[6] In *Disgrace*, Petrus's gravid name (from Greek *pétros*, 'rock') recalls the rape of Magda by Hendrik, his 'teeth grind[ing] like stones' (*IHC* 107).

The *Adorno mode* brings the nonhuman back into frontal view and human scale, registering the consequences of conflating human and nonhuman orders. 'The possibility of pogroms', Theodor Adorno observes,

> is decided in the moment when the gaze of a fatally wounded animal falls on a human being. The defiance with which he repels this gaze – 'after all, it's only an animal' – reappears irresistibly in cruelties done to human beings, the perpetrators having again and again to reassure themselves that it is 'only an animal', because they could never fully believe this even of animals.[7]

Waiting for the Barbarians (1980) offers the most sustained deployment of this analogical intuition.[8] The novel treats the gaze and voice as avenues of ethical appeal, viscerally recounting what happens when the 'substrate of life' uniting humans and animals is forgotten.[9] Its antagonists are divided by their approach to animal life: Colonel Joll enjoys killing en masse, producing (like his fictional forebear, Jacobus) a 'mountain of carcases', whereas the Magistrate's pleasure in hunting falters as his town succumbs to the 'empire of pain'.[10] A waterbuck's gaze immobilizes him, as does the stare of a horse that cannot proceed 'even under the severest flogging': 'I can swear that the beast knows what is to happen. At the sight of the knife its eyes roll' (62).

The desperate appeal of the animal gaze meets its obverse in the blank look of the barbarian girl – brutalized and nearly blinded by torture – whom the Magistrate adopts. She becomes an index of pain's 'unsharability'.[11] Unable to reconstruct an 'image of her as she was before', the Magistrate finds his overtures meet 'no answering life', as if 'caressing an urn or a ball, something which is all surface' (33, 49). Where the animal gaze is avoided by a reflex excuse ('it's *only* an animal …'), the girl's opacity risks soliciting the opposite of ethical attention – the 'intimate cruelties' through which Coetzee provocatively links lover and torturer (146). The animal voice, too, is a site of ethical concern. A parallel gradually becomes clear between birds, 'crammed alive into wooden cages, screaming with outrage', and barbarians under interrogation, causing 'the screaming which people afterwards claim to have heard from the granary' (57, 4–5).

When the Magistrate finds himself the object of Joll's tortures, the undiscussable facts of the Adorno mode's analogies become clear. Excised from the human sphere, reduced to homeostatic functions, the Magistrate is 'no more than a pile of blood, bone and meat that is unhappy' (85). His hand waving to ward off flies is 'as automatic as the flick of a cow's tail', and the townspeople recognize him only as 'the filthy creature who for a week licked food off the flagstones like a dog because he had lost the use of his hands', underlining the novel's reversible binaries (human/animal, civilized/barbarian) (116, 124). The voice of one whose official position involved adjudicating others' voices becomes, during a mock execution, merely 'the noise [that] comes out of a body that knows itself damaged perhaps beyond repair and roars its fright' (121) – the *logos* of human language reduced in pain to the *phonē* of nonhuman sound.[12]

The analogical mode recurs wherever Coetzee makes the treatment of animals – especially as institutionalized in zoos, farms and laboratories – a reference point for human degradations, as in the notorious juxtaposition of slaughterhouses and concentration camps in *Lives of Animals*. Indeed, in this text Elizabeth Costello may recall the Magistrate's plight when she surmises that living organisms are all 'full of being', opposing to philosophical rationality the 'heavily affective sensation … of being a body with limbs that have extension in space, of being alive to the world', an existential plenitude 'hard to sustain in confinement' (33). Through such analogies Coetzee registers – albeit tacitly or obliquely – the slippage that has beset comparisons between nonhumans and ethno-racial 'others' since antiquity. The disturbing undertones of the Adorno mode – does it endorse or criticize? – are audible across its range of figurative deployments. Jacobus confronts his servant Plaatje, whose 'eyes apologized like a dog's' (*DL* 103); Mrs Curren is wary of township children, 'rapacious as sharks' (*AI* 7). Michael K quails at a roadblock 'like a beast at the shambles' (*MK* 40). Melanie Isaacs submits during sex 'like a rabbit when the jaws of the fox close on its neck', while David Lurie's critics circle 'like hunters who have cornered a strange beast and do not know how to finish it off'.[13] If Coetzee's early fiction can seem reticent about the ethical bearing of these analogies, by *Lives of Animals* we find avenues of self-critique. The elderly Abraham Stern declines to attend dinner after Costello's first lecture, accusing her – and perhaps his author – of 'misunderstand[ing] the nature of likenesses' in comparing slain Jews to slaughtered cattle (*LA* 49–50).

In the *Rilke mode*, Coetzee is less concerned with the ethical ramifications of similitudes between human and nonhuman than with the metaphysical chasm separating them. He implicitly probes what being 'like a human' – what sets us apart, makes the chasm uncrossable – might entail. This ontological divide is often addressed in Rilke's poetry. The eighth Duino elegy, Coetzee writes, has the paradoxical goal 'to find words that will take us back to before words and allow us to glimpse the world as seen by creatures who do not have words, or, if that glimpse is barred to us, then to allow us the sad experience of standing at the rim of an unknowable mode of being'.[14] In his rendering of Rilke's key lines: 'What *is* out there, we know it from the animal's face alone; for even the young child we turn around and compel to look back, seeing form/formation [*Gestaltung*], not the open [*das Offne*], that in animal vision is so deep'.[15]

Coetzee stages his own version of 'the open' via beings whose radical otherness mediates between human and nonhuman. In *Foe* (1986), the site of such mediation is the manservant, Friday – specifically his tongue, mute because mutilated. The novel arcs around this awful lacuna, a synecdoche for what severs human from animal: speech, music, dreams, law, shame, knowledge of death. Yet *Foe* works according to the earlier rationale whereby human distinction appears less a mark of superiority than a makeshift: 'It is my commerce with the voices that has kept me from becoming a beast', says Magda in *In the Heart of the Country* (125). If in Coetzee's earlier fiction nonhuman opacity is figured as a threat, even a cause for violence, in *Foe*, Friday's muteness is a lure, drawing this text into reflections on the danger of ceding (human) distinction in the face of (nonhuman) unknowability. The 'true story' of Friday's tongue might emerge when 'by art we have found a means of giving voice' to him, a claim generalized in the thought that when humanity's veneer thins, when 'our vigilance relaxes', we might detect 'cracks and chinks through which another voice, other voices, speak in our lives'.[16]

In *Life & Times of Michael K* (1983), such voices are approached from the other side of the chasm, as it were, through the titular character whose defining characteristic is animalized (*hare-lip*), and who is likened to various creatures: rabbit, mole, mouse, squirrel, lizard, termite, 'an ant that does not know where its hole is', 'a snail without its shell' (83, 112). As Michael K flees urban unrest for the apparently deserted Karoo, the tropes of Schreiner's landscape acquire a spare intensity characteristic of the Rilke mode. This 'flat landscape of scrub and stone [where] there was nowhere one could hide' (45) forms the backdrop for inquiries into the mysteries of nonhuman life, and into questions of sentience, sustenance and suffering.[17] Perhaps Coetzee's deepest engagement with these topics, the novel explores two linked problems: humans rely on the nonhuman (sun, soil, water, plants, animals) for nourishment; and humans rely on other humans – on social structures – for survival. Michael makes a minimalist accommodation with both.

On one hand, he attempts a less and less invasive approach to nourishment. After a grisly episode hunting goats, Michael turns to gathering. He first 'nibbled at roots and bulbs', then 'broke open an ant-nest and ate grubs one by one', and finally 'ceased to make an adventure of eating and drinking' (68). When not on the farm, Michael forages yet more minimally – scavenging mealies and animal feed, considering whether 'to scoop up pocketfuls' of flour after sacks fall from a lorry (35). His 'life as a cultivator' begins, in symbolic fashion, with burying his mother's ashes, a ritual that shows how the human returns to, by mixing with, the nonhuman (59). Detailing the sublime exercise in subsistence carried out by this erstwhile Parks and Gardens employee – Michael grows pumpkins and melons, hiding them from roving armies – Coetzee aligns the conceits of paradisiacal garden and diabolical state of nature.

On the other hand, Michael's effort to exit social systems leads him to abjure food (and the obligations it compels) altogether. He cannot finally be 'a creature beyond the reach of the laws of nations' (151). Coetzee explores this theme via structures that recall the analogical mode: Michael drifts through prison camps, one named after an animal typically figured as vermin in South Africa (Jakkalsdrif, jackal's ford), another housed in a disused Cape Town racecourse. Though the camps strive to avoid the comparison to people 'shut up like animals in a cage' (88), they embody that paradoxical logic, theorized in Giorgio Agamben's *Homo Sacer*, of exceptional zones at once inside and outside sociolegal orders: their residents both belong to the human community and are held apart, like animals.[18] Without state certification, Coetzee's character JC later muses in *Diary of a*

Bad Year (2006), 'you do without an identity and condemn yourself to living outside the state like an animal (animals do not have identity papers)'.[19]

In defiance of these spaces with 'earth stamped so tight by the passage of ... footsteps' that 'nothing would ever grow there again', Michael K adopts a stark maxim for his earthly residence: 'A man must live so that he leaves no trace of his living' (104, 99). When gardening, he vows to use 'materials the insects would eat when one day he no longer needed them' (104). When embracing hunger, he approaches the lightest mode of nonhuman existence, aspiring to be not 'something heavy that left tracks behind it, but if anything ... a speck upon the surface of an earth too deeply asleep to notice the scratch of ant-feet, the rasp of butterfly teeth, the tumbling of dust' (97).

If the Rilke mode presumes that 'for an unmediated experience of the world we have to fall back on empathy with animals', or with putatively alien modes of being, its approach is existential rather than practical.[20] (Few could subsist as minimally as Michael K does.) This mode's ontological concerns – about (other) minds and souls, existence and endurance, recognition and relation – veer towards allegory and linger into Coetzee's late work. In 'The Old Woman and the Cats' (2013), the expediencies of approaching death are shrouded by Costello's mystical sense of 'accustoming myself to living in the company of beings whose mode of being is unlike mine, more unlike mine than my human intellect will ever be able to grasp'.[21] Bemused by such talk, her son John is unsure whether he detects, 'behind the black slit of the pupil' in a kitten's eye, 'a momentary flash, light glancing off the invisible soul hiding there', and prefers to believe in 'a vast distance fixed between the human and the rest'.[22]

In the *Dostoevsky mode*, by contrast, Coetzee addresses more concrete and commonplace ethical concerns, scrutinizing the possibilities and limits of attention, sentiment and sympathy – that faculty 'that allows us to share at times the being of another' (*LA* 34). Crucial here are scenes of instruction. An adult patiently explains the lives and deaths of animals; a child passionately rejects the 'lesson'. Or, drawn to a scene of cruelty or death, a child learns the unbearable – like Florence's daughter in *Age of Iron* (1990), witnessing her father in the slaughterhouse, 'her fingers gripping the mesh, [drinking] in the sight' (42); or *Boyhood*'s (1997) subject, watching Ros eviscerate a sheep of 'all the things that a sheep has inside it and that he has inside him too'.[23]

The paradigm for such scenes is Raskolnikov's fever-dream in Dostoevsky's *Crime and Punishment*, where the child throws its arms around a nag being flogged to death as his father urges, 'it's none of our business'.[24] In *The Master of Petersburg* (1994), Fyodor reasons unsuccessfully with Matryona: '"Animals don't find it hard to die", he says gently. "Perhaps we should take our lesson from them. Perhaps that is why they are with us here on earth – to show us that living and dying are not as hard as we think". ... He pauses, then tries again'.[25] A parent similarly deflects a child's question about neutering animals in *Boyhood*: 'There is no way of talking about what he has seen. "Why do they have to cut off the lambs' tails?" he asks his mother. "Because otherwise the blowflies would breed under their tails", his mother replies. They are both pretending; both of them know what the question is really about' (99).

Children are not privileged ethical agents in Coetzee; indeed, they can be models of cruelty. Yet childhood constitutes a proving ground where difficult questions about animal life are answered or dismissed – questions one would be naïve to raise as an adult. These fervent queries and foundering excuses introduce a tonal dialogism between child and adult – between emotional response and rational riposte, 'sentiment' and 'substance', to borrow JC's terms from *Diary of a*

Bad Year's 'On Dostoevsky' (225). Costello reprises this tension in *Lives of Animals* by occupying both positions, uncomprehendingly childish about how 'kindness, human-kindness' is complicit in the mass slaughter of animals, coldly adult in linking this 'crime of stupefying proportions' to the Holocaust (69).

A prominent locus of the Dostoevsky mode is *Age of Iron*, where a wide range of emotions are experienced by the terminally ill protagonist, Mrs Curren, to whom other beings appear as ethical claimants: the vagrant Vercueil and his dog, the domestic worker Florence, her activist son Bheki, his friend John. Referring to creatures evocative of death or the afterlife – flies, vultures, moths, butterflies, the extinct dodo and the crab that represents her 'pet' cancer – the novel examines several hierarchies of empathy (112). With its central voice 'beginning to feel the indifferent peace of an old animal … sensing its time is near', it wavers between radical privacy and empathic openness, pondering the risk of putting self-directed concern before other-directed responsibility, the pressures of biological life before the demands of relational life (158).

Several nonhuman metaphors organize the dialectic between these poles. On one hand, Mrs Curren considers the ontology of stones as a way of understanding her (and apartheid South Africa's) moral stupor. On the other, the paradoxical status of blood fortifies her ethical awareness. Sealed within beings, blood nevertheless links humans, animals and the inanimate, through the 'odour that blood has in common with stone, with oil, with iron' (*IHC* 71). As Mrs Curren reflects, 'blood is one: a pool of life dispersed among us in separate existences, but belonging by nature together: lent, not given: held in common, in trust, to be preserved' (*AI* 63–4). In a 'country prodigal of blood', nonhuman and human casualties alike scream for attention (*AI* 63).

The proximity of death (whether personal or political) in *Age of Iron* raises questions about the distinction between a singular, authentic death (for which Mrs Curren prepares: 'Must one die in full knowledge, fully oneself?') and plural, meaningless deaths (to which animals in slaughterhouses and people in burning townships are consigned) (141). Witnessing the bloody occupation of Florence's husband, Mrs Curren confronts a scene of numerical death that recalls the logic of *Dusklands*: 'the slaughtering, the plucking and cleaning, the freezing of thousands of carcasses, the packing of thousands of heads and feet, miles of intestines, mountains of feathers' (*AI* 42). She seems sympathetic to, if uncomfortable about, the 'universe of counting' that attends such labour. Yet the death of an individual chicken flummoxes her moral sensibility: 'At least it is not cattle he is slaughtering, I told myself; at least it is only chickens, with their crazy chicken-eyes and their delusions of grandeur' (44).

Such failures of empathy and ethical resolve in the face of number, abstraction and minimization ('it's *only* an animal …') link *Age of Iron* and South Africa's emergency years to the broader project of *Lives of Animals*. Indeed, Mrs Curren's emphatic word for the slaughterhouse – 'the *enterprise*' – recurs in her fictional cousin Elizabeth Costello's description of factory farming as 'an enterprise of degradation, cruelty, and killing which rivals anything that the Third Reich was capable of, indeed dwarfs it' (*AI* 44; *LA* 21). That same link between counting and moral oblivion appears in Costello's grim pun (discussing Treblinka) about 'numbers that numb the mind': 'We have only one death of our own; we can comprehend the deaths of others only one at a time. In the abstract we may be able to count to a million, but we cannot count to a million deaths' (*LA* 21). The failure of sympathetic imagination is likewise present in both. Costello remarks on the truly horrific realization about the camps: 'the killers refused to think themselves into the place of their victims, as did everyone else. They said, "It is *they* in those cattle-cars rattling past". They did not say, "How would it be if it were I in that cattle-car?" They did not say, "It is I who am in that cattle-car"' (*LA* 34).

If the Dostoevsky mode pushes these analogies into ethical territory, *Disgrace* questions the assumption that attention to nonhuman beings need not displace human claimants. Tracing the protagonist's development from emotional shallowness to ethical awakening, it explores themes of escape and expiation, and controversially sets the treatment of animals as the ground for other moral questions. Like *Age of Iron*, *Disgrace* is tinged with the fact of impending death, with 'the overriding truth uniting mankind: we are all going to die'.[26] Lurie puts it thus: '"I am going to end up in a hole in the ground …. And so are you. So are we all"' (189). At issue is the extent to which animals are included in that collective 'we all', not as 'stranger[s] in this breathing world' (in Lurie's quote from Byron), but as morally considerable entities (32).

Coetzee again avoids the stylistic temptation of using animals that elicit sympathy, preferring non-reciprocal animals exposed to desultory killing: farm animals and the watchdogs sheltered by Lurie's daughter on her Cape smallholding, dogs on 'short contracts' raised to be vicious (61). The figurative ground is thus prepared for the men who attack Lucy and her father. In Lurie's imagining, the men are like 'dogs in a pack' – the youngest a 'jackal boy', his relative the 'dog-man', Petrus – and they swap figurative space with animals: '*Go on, call your dogs! No dogs? Then let us show you dogs!*' (159, 202, 64, 160).

Like *Waiting for the Barbarians*, *Disgrace* makes us reckon with the representational elision of human brutality and human victims, even as animal death is savagely rendered. 'With practised ease', we read, one of the men

> brings a cartridge up into the breech, thrusts the muzzle into the dog's cage. … There is a heavy report; blood and brains splatter the cage. … One dog, shot through the chest, dies at once; another, with a gaping throat-wound, sits down heavily, flattens its ears, following with its gaze the movements of this being who does not even bother to administer a *coup de grâce*.
>
> (*D* 95)

While Lucy rejects the exceptional status of victim, Lurie struggles to surrender his singularity. But his expression of indifference – 'let it all go to the dogs' – literalizes the affective and ethical telos of *Disgrace*: by the novel's end his cynical demurrals and philosophical rationalizations cannot retain emotional coherence (107). After mocking the 'subculture' of animal-welfare types like Bev Shaw – their earnest pity anathema to his post-Romantic irony – Lurie, so to say, goes to the dogs (73). In wrenching scenes, he attends to animals at Bev's clinic with growing compassion. The man set alight in a mock sacrifice now drives to an incinerator and 'consigns the bodies in their black bags to the flames' (144).

By the novel's searing conclusion, Lurie accepts Lucy's claim that 'there is no higher life. This is the only life there is. Which we share with animals' (74). Where Mrs Curren confessed that 'with the best will in the world [she could] only half-attend' to human casualties, Lurie embraces the stance of 'fullest attention' to creaturely life (*AI* 39; *D* 142). Perhaps in an ironic nod to Lurie's beloved Romantics (foundational in the animal rights movement), Coetzee describes how Lurie has learned 'to concentrate all his attention on the animal they are killing, giving it what he no longer has difficulty in calling by its proper name: love' (*D* 219).[27] To dying animals, he offers the refrain Costello's son uses to comfort his weeping mother: 'There, there!' (*D* 81; *LA* 69). Lurie could almost be an object lesson from *Lives of Animals*, proof that in attending to fellow-creatures with the 'human-kindness' that constitutes our own struggles against necessity, we might, in Kafka's haunting words, find a way to 'make our living and our dying easier'.[28]

Yet amid this sentimental outpouring lurk darker references. 'What is being asked for', thinks Lurie, 'is, in fact, *Lösung* (German always to hand with an appropriately blank abstraction): sublimation, as alcohol is sublimed from water, leaving no residue, no aftertaste' (*D* 142). *Lösung* also translates Aristotle's *peripeteia* and in compound forms alludes to the Nazis' 'final solution' (*Endlösung*) and to salvation (*Erlösung*, a word used in Kafka's 'The Crossbreed' when the owner of a cat/lamb hybrid wonders, like Lurie, whether the 'knife of the butcher would be a release [*Erlösung*]').[29] Linking the undoing of animal life and the unravelling of plot, gesturing at a vision of death as both numerical insignificance and singular deliverance, Coetzee stretches the concerns of the Dostoevsky mode to the limit.

Indeed, each mode pushes tacit protocols to their limits, as a relevant novelistic statement often summarizes: 'there would be no resistance to my power and no limit to its projection' (*DL* 101); 'there seemed no limit to his endurance' (*MK* 35); 'There seems to be no limit to the shame a human being can feel' (*AI* 119). *Lives of Animals* presses a different logic to its extreme: 'there is no limit to the extent to which we can think ourselves into the being of another' (*LA* 80). Amplifying Coetzee's multimodal commitment to nonhuman themes, *Lives of Animals* is both the culmination of his sustained engagement and the inauguration of a late style. In *substance* these lectures clarify literary-philosophical bearings implicit earlier, surfacing allusions (notably to Rilke and Kafka) and addressing key topics in greater depth (animal cognition, vivisection, ethical eating).[30] In *form* they make us more aware of the rhetorical nesting of what in earlier work could plausibly be extracted as opinions. And they mark a watershed for critical attention to these topics in Coetzee, in literary studies and philosophy.[31]

Following *Lives of Animals*, the nonhuman in Coetzee's late work appears in projects dedicated to foundational inquiry. *Diary of a Bad Year* includes sections – 'On the origins of the state', 'On the slaughter of animals', 'On compassion' – where the status of the nonhuman is annexed to political questions. The *Jesus* novels address such issues in a more ethereal setting. The Dostoevsky mode endures, reasonably enough given the second novel's allusive use of names like Dmitri and Alyosha. In *The Childhood of Jesus* (2013), Simón bluffs about the fate of the euthanized carthorse ('He has a long journey to make, all the way to the great horse farm') after a hysterical Davíd tries to resuscitate the animal, his mouth on its 'vast nostril'.[32] *The Schooldays of Jesus* (2016) opens on a traumatic scene of cruelty, as boys pelt a duck with stones, breaking its wing, and Davíd dives into the dam to save it. Again, Simón's parental assurance – 'The duck isn't dead – see! – he just had a bump. He will soon get better' – proves hollow.[33] The duck's neck is wrung by a farmhand and its shallow grave is empty the following day.

Questions of animal ethics, especially as intuited by (and taught to) children, acquire a different cast in this world stripped down to necessities and first principles. In *Disgrace* and *Lives of Animals* Coetzee broods on the moment of death and the 'sacrificial animal'.[34] In the *Jesus* novels, there are intimations of other lives before or after, radicalizing Platonic and Wordsworthian intimations – that animals are '[b]orn with foreknowledge, so to speak', of death; that they 'have calculated the price and are prepared to pay it – the price of being on earth, the price of being alive'; that 'all creatures come into the world bringing with them the memory of justice' (*D* 83; *B* 102; *WB* 139). Unusually for Coetzee, animals in the *Jesus* novels are named – El Rey the carthorse, Bolívar the Alsatian, Blanco the pigeon, Jeremiah the lamb – so the cruelty of enslaving or eating them becomes less conscionable. Simón may concern himself with Davíd's education and quintessentially human topics, like arguing for meaningful work against 'bestial labour' unbefitting 'the pinnacle of creation' (*CJ* 113, 109). Yet Davíd often seems closer in spirit to animals. One cannot see him buying the claim that oxen 'wish us well', that they muse, '*If young Davíd needs to eat my flesh so that he can grow strong and healthy, then I willingly give it to him*' (*SJ* 76–7).

In this spirit, I close with a reflection that could stand as an epigraph to Coetzee's long-term engagement with the nonhuman. 'It is quite wrong', Socrates says in Plato's *Phaedo*,

> for human beings to make out that the swans sing their last song as an expression of grief at their approaching end. People who say this are misled by their own fear of death, and fail to reflect that no bird sings when it is hungry or cold or distressed in any other way – not even the nightingale or swallow or hoopoe, whose song is supposed to be a lament.[35]

A paradox: human *logos* fails when confronted by beings understood as lacking *logos* (language, reason, reflection): the human becomes nonhuman in a failure of empathy. Coetzee has come at this paradox in several modes, I've suggested. He employs the resources of *logos* and exceeds them via imagination, affect and sentiment. He scans the nonhuman voice and gaze for those echoes and reflections that make us consider the *kindness* of the animals we are.

NOTES

1. Coetzee, *White Writing*, 167.
2. Ibid.
3. Coetzee, *In the Heart of the Country*, 3, 12. Further references cited parenthetically, using the abbreviation *IHC* where necessary to disambiguate.
4. Coetzee, *Dusklands*, 79. Further references cited parenthetically using the abbreviation *DL* where necessary to disambiguate.
5. See Williams, 'Coetzee's Stones'.
6. Coetzee, *Life & Times of Michael K*, 135; *Age of Iron*, 29. Further references cited parenthetically using the abbreviations *MK* and *AI* respectively.
7. Adorno, *Minima Moralia*, 105.
8. See Williams, 'Vile Attentions'.
9. Coetzee et al., *The Lives of Animals*, 35. Further references cited parenthetically, using the abbreviation *LA* where necessary.
10. Coetzee, *Waiting for the Barbarians*, 1, 23. Further references cited parenthetically, using the abbreviation *WB* where necessary.
11. Scarry, *The Body in Pain*, 4.
12. See Arendt, *The Human Condition*, 129.
13. Coetzee, *Disgrace*, 25, 56. Further references cited parenthetically, using the abbreviation *D* where necessary to disambiguate.

14. Coetzee, *Stranger Shores*, 71.
15. Ibid.
16. Coetzee, *Foe*, 118, 30.
17. On hunger and the novel's 'anti-politics' see Moody, *The Art of Hunger*, 156–98.
18. See Agamben, *Homo Sacer*.
19. Coetzee, *Diary of a Bad Year*, 4. Further references cited parenthetically using the abbreviation *DBY*.
20. Coetzee, *Stranger Shores*, 71.
21. Coetzee, 'The Old Woman and the Cats', 10.
22. Ibid., 11, 21.
23. Coetzee, *Boyhood*, 98. Further references cited parenthetically, using the abbreviation *B* where necessary to disambiguate.
24. Dostoyevsky, *Crime and Punishment*, 59.
25. Coetzee, *The Master of Petersburg*, 188–9.
26. Coetzee, *Stranger Shores*, 176.
27. See Perkins, *Romanticism and Animal Rights*.
28. Kafka, *Letter to His Father*, 125.
29. Kafka, *Erzählungen*, 427.
30. Coetzee raises these topics when defending animal rights *in propria persona*: see 'Exposing the Beast'.
31. See Cavell et al., *Philosophy and Animal Life*; Cavalieri, *The Death of the Animal*; Mulhall, *The Wounded Animal*; and Leist and Singer, *J. M. Coetzee and Ethics*.
32. Coetzee, *The Childhood of Jesus*, 200, 199. Further references cited parenthetically, using the abbreviation *CJ* where necessary.
33. Coetzee, *The Schooldays of Jesus*, 7. Further references cited parenthetically, using the abbreviation *SJ* where necessary.
34. Danta, *Animal Fables after Darwin*, 159–85.
35. Plato, *Phaedo*, 85a.

WORKS CITED

Adorno, Theodor W. *Minima Moralia: Reflections from Damaged Life*. Translated by E. F. N. Jephcott. London: Verso, 1978.
Agamben, Giorgio. *Homo Sacer*. Translated by Daniel Heller-Roazen. Stanford: Stanford University Press, 1998.
Arendt, Hannah. *The Human Condition*. Chicago: University of Chicago Press, 1958.
Cavalieri, Paola. *The Death of the Animal: A Dialogue*. New York: Columbia University Press, 2009.
Cavell, Stanley, Cora Diamond, John McDowell, Ian Hacking, and Cary Wolfe. *Philosophy and Animal Life*. New York: Columbia University Press, 2008.
Coetzee, J. M. *Age of Iron*. 1990. New York: Penguin, 1998.
Coetzee, J. M. *Boyhood: Scenes from Provincial Life*. New York: Penguin, 1997.
Coetzee, J. M. *The Childhood of Jesus*. 2013. New York: Penguin, 2014.
Coetzee, J. M. *Diary of a Bad Year*. 2006. New York: Viking Penguin, 2008.
Coetzee, J. M. *Disgrace*. 1999. New York: Penguin, 2000.
Coetzee, J. M. *Dusklands*. 1974. New York: Penguin, 1996.
Coetzee, J. M. *Elizabeth Costello*. New York: Viking Penguin, 2003.

Coetzee, J. M. 'Exposing the Beast: Factory Farming Must Be Called to the Slaughterhouse'. *Sydney Morning Herald*, 22 February 2007. https://www.smh.com.au/national/factory-farming-must-be-called-to-slaughterhouse-20070222-gdpiwj.html.
Coetzee, J. M. *Foe*. 1986. New York: Penguin, 1988.
Coetzee, J. M. *In the Heart of the Country*. 1977. New York: Penguin, 1982.
Coetzee, J. M. *Life & Times of Michael K*. 1983. New York: Penguin, 1985.
Coetzee, J. M., et al. *The Lives of Animals*. Edited by Amy Gutmann. Princeton: Princeton University Press, 1999.
Coetzee, J. M. *The Master of Petersburg*. 1994. New York: Penguin, 1995.
Coetzee, J. M. 'The Old Woman and the Cats'. In *Cripplewood/Kreupelhout*, edited by Berlinde De Bruyckere and J. M. Coetzee, 7–28. Brussels: Mercatorfonds, 2013.
Coetzee, J. M. *The Schooldays of Jesus*. 2016. New York: Penguin, 2018.
Coetzee, J. M. *Stranger Shores: Essays 1986–1999*. New York: Viking Penguin, 2001.
Coetzee, J. M. *Waiting for the Barbarians*. 1980. New York: Penguin, 1982.
Coetzee, J. M. *White Writing: On the Culture of Letters in South Africa*. New Haven: Yale University Press, 1988.
Danta, Chris. *Animal Fables after Darwin: Literature, Speciesism, and Metaphor*. Cambridge: Cambridge University Press, 2018.
Dostoevsky, Fyodor. *Crime and Punishment*. Translated by Richard Pevear and Larissa Volokhonsky. New York: Vintage, 1993.
Kafka, Franz. *Erzählungen*. Edited by Michael Müller. Stuttgart: Reclam, 1995.
Kafka, Franz. *Letter to His Father/Brief an den Vater*. Translated by Ernst Kaiser and Eithne Wilkins. New York: Schocken, 1953.
Leist, Anton and Peter Singer, eds. *J. M. Coetzee and Ethics: Philosophical Perspectives on Literature*. New York: Columbia University Press, 2010.
Moody, Alys. *The Art of Hunger: Aesthetic Autonomy and the Afterlives of Modernism*. Oxford: Oxford University Press, 2018.
Mulhall, Stephen. *The Wounded Animal: J. M. Coetzee and the Difficulty of Reality in Literature and Philosophy*. Princeton: Princeton University Press, 2009.
Perkins, David. *Romanticism and Animal Rights*. Cambridge: Cambridge University Press, 2003.
Plato. *Phaedo*. In *The Collected Dialogues of Plato*, edited by Edith Hamilton and Huntingdon Cairns. Princeton: Princeton University Press, 1961, 40–98.
Scarry, Elaine. *The Body in Pain: The Making and Unmaking of the World*. New York: Oxford University Press, 1985.
Williams, Daniel. 'Coetzee's Stones: *Dusklands* and the Nonhuman Witness'. *Safundi* 19, no. 4 (2018): 438–60.
Williams, Daniel. '"Vile Attentions": On the Limits of Sympathetic Imagination'. In *The Link Between Animal Abuse and Human Violence*, edited by Andrew Linzey, 206–20. Brighton: Sussex Academic Press, 2009.

CHAPTER TWENTY-THREE

Coetzee, computers and binary thinking

REBECCA ROACH

J. M. Coetzee's first career was not as a writer but a programmer. He has acknowledged as much in his fictionalized autobiography *Youth* (2002), which traces the experiences of his namesake 'John', working in the nascent computer industry in Britain in the early 1960s. Finding the industry 'a tight little world defined by made-up rules', John eventually leaves Britain for the United States and a PhD in literature.[1] Aside from their appearance in *Youth*, the lack of computers, programmers and code in Coetzee's fiction would seem to indicate that they are largely irrelevant to the stuff of literature. Nevertheless, in this chapter I argue that computation plays a fundamental role in the development of Coetzee's literary project. In particular, computing comes to be associated with what he labels 'binary thinking' and becomes the foil by which literature is envisioned.[2] In what follows, I outline Coetzee's own involvement in the computer industry and discuss the uses to which he put this experience across his writing career via discussion of a number of his fictional and critical works.

YOUTH

Coetzee's second work of autobiographical fiction, *Youth*, is loosely based on his time employed in the British computer industry between 1962 and 1965. He worked first at American behemoth International Business Machines (IBM) as an applications programmer and later for the British 'Atlas 2/Titan' project, a joint endeavour between British electronics company Ferranti (later International Computers & Tabulators Ltd [ICT]) and Cambridge University to build a supercomputer (I have traced Coetzee's work during this period at length elsewhere[3]). *Youth* hews relatively closely to the historical record: John plans to utilize his University of Cape Town degrees in mathematics and literature while living in London, resigned to the reality that '[s]ince great artists are fated to go unrecognized for a while, he imagines he will serve out his probationary years as a clerk humbly adding up columns of figures in a back room'.[4]

Both Coetzee and John would use their knowledge of mathematics – appealing for its 'purity'[5] – in a less unassuming context than this suggests, however. Far from a humble clerk in a back room, the author and his protagonist would find themselves at the forefront of British computing in an era in which the industry was transforming the ways in which science, business, the arts and warfare were conducted. Yet as Coetzee depicts it, John's entry into the industry is largely a fluke; he rejects a job as scientific researcher because of its location, and applies to IBM because the newspapers are 'full of [their] advertisements'. John, indeed, 'has never laid eyes on a computer, except in cartoons, where computers appear as box-like objects spitting out scrolls of paper'.[6] Notably, both the reader's and John's initial impressions of this futuristic technology are mediated through older print media. When John's training begins, this view is compounded further: 'In his naïveté he had imagined that computer programming would be about ways of translating symbolic logic and set theory into digital codes. Instead the talk is about inventories and outflows ... He might as well be a clerk sorting cards into batches.'[7] As presented here, programming is not glamorous or engaged with sophisticated mathematics; in Coetzee's depiction, computing appears rather to be the modern-day equivalent of clerical drudgery.

In *Youth*, programming is a means to an end: paying the bills, while John develops his literary talents. The book acts as a *künstlerroman*-account of the young man's tussles with predecessors such as Henry James, Ezra Pound and T. S. Eliot, his attempts to write poetry and complete an MA dissertation on the work of Ford Madox Ford. Yet any easy split between computing and literature is difficult to uphold. *Youth* records John's attempts to write poetry using the powerful machines at his disposal. Making use of spare computing time to produce experiments in aleatory composition, John muses that 'if his heart is not in the right state to generate poetry of its own', he might 'at least string together pseudo-poems made up of phrases generated by a machine, and thus, by going through the motions of writing, learn to write again'.[8] The book mirrors young Coetzee's activities in detail here: he wrote a dissertation on Ford Madox Ford and 'generated' computer poetry on an IBM 1401 computer, amongst other models.[9] The results of the latter were first published in University of Cape Town literary magazine *The Lion and the Impala* in 1963.

Despite such detail, *Youth* is nevertheless circumspect concerning the degree to which Coetzee's programming and work with computers influenced his aesthetic practice. More than simply offering a means of composition, working within the logic of computer code and operations shaped his conception of literature's 'singularity'.[10] Coetzee's employment in the industry coincided with the business mainstream's adoption of computation as well as the increasing prominence of computers within popular culture. Public intellectuals, artists, writers and academics were also beginning to consider the social and cultural implications of computation, and Coetzee followed these developments closely. His reading in this period in London covered media theorists such as Howard Innis, Walter J. Ong and Marshall McLuhan, as well as volumes on game theory and automation, and literary uses of computing, something that *Youth* omits.[11] So too were Coetzee's own compositions at the forefront of practical experiments with the aesthetic and creative possibilities of computers internationally – his position gave him access to one of the most powerful computers in Britain (and the world) to do so – and his work with random number generation composition was of a theoretical sophistication little acknowledged in current histories of digital art and literature.[12] *Youth* recounts John's attempts, but it modestly underplays Coetzee's own reading and his intellectual and practical innovations.

Indeed, following his departure from Britain in 1965, the point at which *Youth* ends, Coetzee pursued a PhD at the University of Texas at Austin. There he would write a thesis on stylostatistics and the work of Samuel Beckett, drawing on a field that was benefiting from advances in computer power – exploiting computers' abilities to make quick counts to conduct stylistic analyses of literary works. He would continue to explore the theoretical implications of utilizing computers in the study of language and literature over the next decade and a half, publishing articles on 'Statistical Indices of "Difficulty"' (1969), 'Samuel Beckett's "Lessness": An Exercise in Decomposition' (1973) and 'Surreal Metaphors and Random Processes' (1979), as well as one further computer poem 'Hero and Bad Mother in Epic, a poem' (1978).

Despite this continued interest in computing, scholarship has not concerned itself with the details of Coetzee's involvement with the field. In part this is explained by his own tendency to present a simple binary between literature and computing – in *Youth* and elsewhere. Unlike at IBM, John talks of the work on the Atlas 2 project to 'reduce questions and answers to machine-readable code' as requiring 'mental ingenuity'.[13] Nevertheless, Coetzee also positions such work as bringing about the end of 'yearning', and John 'cannot help seeing a connection between the end of yearning and the end of poetry'.[14] The work on the Atlas 2 might be high level, but, like IBM's clerical programming, it remains in opposition to poetry. For John and a young Coetzee, programming was apparently a barren endeavour, beneficial largely for its ability to act as a foil to artistic activity.

COMPUTATION ± FREEDOM

Towards the end of *Youth*, John identifies the computer as a 'threat'; specifically, 'it will burn *either-or* paths into the brains of its users and lock them irreversibly into its binary logic'.[15] This characterization is one of more than sterility and is key to what makes Coetzee's relationship to computing so interesting. The binary logic that John discusses is explored by Coetzee in a number of essays across his career, including the recent 'On Literary Thinking'. Here he ponders young people's reliance on digital devices, noting:

> Binary logic is suited to electronic devices because the current in such devices flows through binary gates. A gate is open (YES) or it is closed (NO). The gate has no other state ... To the generation who handle digital devices with an ease that seems natural, the concept of freedom as having YES–NO choices without end is unproblematic.[16]

In Coetzee's move from discussing digital devices to binary logic, and to freedom, the latter step might seem a leap too far. To understand why Coetzee makes this leap and why he regards 'binary thinking' as so problematic, we need to understand the relationship Coetzee conceives between computation and the state in his work.

In the early years of the computer industry, just as today, there was a close relationship between technological advances and the security state. The first electronic computers had been developed under wartime collaboration between academia, industry and the military in Britain and America – whether Bletchley Park's Colossus or the US Army's ENIAC. While much of these earlier innovations remained classified at the time that Coetzee was working in programming, government and military funding for projects was widespread. Coetzee would himself work directly on such a project. As part of his role at ICT, he worked on the Atlas 2 computer based in Aldermaston, the UK's Atomic Weapons Research Establishment. Here he designed the either/or, YES-NO binary logic chain via which the supercomputer's supervisory programme would run.

In *Youth*, Coetzee underlines these ties between the computer industry and the military, which in the 1960s was largely focused around Cold War activities. While working at IBM, John aids a client called Mr Pomfret with calculations for the TSR-2 aircraft, a British Cold War military project. When working for International Computing, John also writes code at Aldermaston. Crucially, Coetzee also makes a link between the binary logic of computers and the binary logic utilized within a (cold) wartime setting in this work. As John notes to himself, 'by passing through these gates [at Aldermaston], by breathing the air here, he has aided the arms race, become an accomplice in the Cold War, and on the wrong side too'.[17] Binary logic dominates Cold War politics, reducing hitherto passive actions such as 'passing' and 'breathing' into choices. Far from offering freedom, it offers a restrictive 'life that consists in making a sequence of YES–NO decisions'.[18]

Nationality is also presented as a binary function in *Youth*. Despite their former colonial citizenry, as 'non-American foreigners', John and his Indian colleague Ganapathy are treated with suspicion at Aldermaston.[19] Nationality, cultural ties and colonial history are reduced to a simple us/them choice. In the case of John, such suspicion is not entirely without merit: offering his services, he 'writes to the Chinese Embassy in London. Since he suspects the Chinese have no use for computers, he says nothing about computer programming'.[20] Given the modern Chinese state's reliance on super-computation and AI, among other things to surveil their citizens, Coetzee might be suspected of exhibiting irony at the expense of his young protagonist here.

The binary thinking that computers embody and which facilitates Cold War politics occupied Coetzee's thinking after his time working in the industry. As a graduate student at the University of Texas at Austin, he would satirize the 'clear and systematic thinking' underlying American strategy in the Vietnam War: 'The Vietnamese who has seen a modern technology in action must be aware of the true direction of "the tide of history."'[21] The binarized biopolitics of the Cold War would enter into his personal life: he was arrested for participating in anti-war staff protests at the State University of New York at Buffalo, with the result that his visa (necessary to continue teaching in the United States) was not renewed.[22] Years later, back in South Africa, Coetzee would address this thinking in his first published novella, *Dusklands* (1974).

The first part of the work, 'The Vietnam Project', depicts an environment dominated by the computerized state: the department where protagonist Eugene Dawn works features RAND Whiz Kid strategy and a game theory-trained supervisor named 'Coetzee'. Such computer modelling, used to disastrous effect in the Vietnam War, had come to dominate military strategy, thanks to the expansion of computer power in the 1960s. Coetzee depicts the protagonist's descent into madness as closely associated with working in an environment dominated by binary thinking. The state's tendency to restructure experience in terms suitable for computer modelling is viewed with a suspicious eye in Coetzee's first published work. Decades before *Youth* was published, Coetzee's fiction grappled with the import of computation on the state and the individual.

APARTHEID COMPUTATION

It is to the South African context that we must turn to comprehend Coetzee's negative linkage of 'freedom' and computers more fully. Coetzee makes little mention of South African computing in *Youth*, apart from a (perhaps) satirical aside: 'There are no computers in South Africa that he knows of.'[23] However, in his fiction and nonfiction, Coetzee repeatedly makes associations between binary thinking and Apartheid, indirectly aligning computation against the freedom of the individual.

Apartheid functioned in large part through the computerization of the state. The passbook system, a hated symbol of the regime, was administered via computer databases and systems. Indeed, it was IBM and ICT, the two companies for which Coetzee had worked in the 1960s, that would provide the majority of these systems to the South African government.[24] Although he did not work in the South African industry, Coetzee's prior experience clearly influenced his attitudes towards state deployment of computation in his home country. Despite computers rarely appearing outright in Coetzee's writings, the nefarious effects that they can produce or support are everywhere apparent. The 'ideology of freedom' they promote, while curbing such freedom in practice, is most clearly articulated in his nonfiction. In his collection of essays on censorship, *Giving Offense* (1996), Coetzee discusses the logic behind apartheid bureaucrat and ideologue Geoffrey Cronjé's programme of 'Apartheid Thinking':

> There is something Cronjé is haunted by. Let me call it simply C. C is the sign of the undifferentiated but also of indifference ... In the algebra of mixing, C + W = C, C + B = C, C + C = C, even B + W = C. Unless there is apartness (Apartheid) asks Cronjé ... what can lie ahead but more and more mixing, more and more C?[25]

Coetzee characterizes apartheid according to the binary logic – or rather, the Boolean logic of and/or functions – on which digital computation is based. In *Youth* John speaks of having 'no respect for any version of thinking that can be embodied in a computer's circuitry'; here it is clear that the adoption of such thinking in a racialized setting can produce the doctrine of Apartheid.[26]

In another essay in the volume, 'The Work of the Censor: Censorship in South Africa', Coetzee notes that censorship utilizes the same mode of computational or binary thinking. Defining the censor's modus operandi as one of paranoia, he notes that this is 'an entry into an automatism, of which there can be no clearer illustration than the fact that, of all the pathologies, paranoia has been the most amenable to artificial stimulation'.[27] Here he draws on his knowledge of programming history to note that just such a programme has been written – PARRY in 1972. The binary thinking that manufactures such environments might not be coeval with digital computing, but Coetzee is keen to emphasize their associations.

Coetzee expanded on these associations in 2016, writing that '[i]n the language of ideology a life that consists in making a sequence of YES–NO decisions is called *being free to make choices*, and freedom is defined as *having unending choices before one*'.[28] While not mentioning the apartheid context that had so strongly exemplified his point, Coetzee indicates that the reduction of the world to a series of binary choices 'and the corresponding spread of a form of mental constraint that conceives of itself quite innocently as freedom' are concerning.[29] His answer, perhaps unsurprisingly, is that 'if God will not keep our children from the single vision of YES or NO then it is up to the poets to do so'.[30]

A VISION OF POETS

Across his nonfiction writing Coetzee utilizes computer languages and the logic they embody as a foil for the literary. Boolean logic becomes the example of what literature and 'literary thinking' are not. In a 1987 talk, 'The Novel Today', Coetzee explains:

> There is no addition in stories. They are not made up of one thing plus another thing, message plus vehicle ... On the keyboard on which they are written, the plus key does not work. There is always a difference; and the difference is not a part, the part left behind after the subtraction. The minus key does not work either: the difference is everything.[31]

Literature operates on a model distinct from simply arithmetic.[32] Literature becomes the remedy for binary thinking. Literature's remedial function is partly due to the imbrication of natural language in culture: as Coetzee has it, 'too protean to be tied down to single, pure meanings', natural language is not the 'perfect language' of mathematics.[33] Indeed, as he comments in a review on the subject of translation, 'human language is not a neutral code like a computer language. To be "English" is to be embedded in the English language and the English language's way of seeing the world'.[34] While one might contest Coetzee's description of computer code as 'neutral' (the overreliance on English and Roman script and the very existence of programming language wars indicates otherwise), his distinction does aim to oppose these two types of communication.

Coetzee utilizes computer logic, if not computers themselves, as a foil for literature in numerous of his fictions outside of *Youth*. However he also complicates any simple binary, as John's experimentation with programmed poetry demonstrated. I have written elsewhere about the presence of computational processes in *In the Heart of the Country* (1976/7), where key scenes in the novel are replayed with slight variation on a loop – like the running of a computer programme.[35] This novel was strongly influenced by Jean-Luc Godard's *Alphaville* (1965), a film about a dystopian society run by a computer – a machine that is ultimately destroyed when reprogrammed with avant-garde poetry. In *Alphaville*, the literary is deployed as a programme to defeat the machine; in Coetzee's novel, it is less the code itself than the mode of reading that is literary. The novel's recourse to 'recursive reading' suggests that programming in of itself is not literature's other; the other is rather, as I have been arguing, the binary logic that drives computation.[36]

Similarly, *Life & Times of Michael K* (1983) creates an opposition between the individual on the one hand and a biopolitical state governed by surveillance (resembling Apartheid South Africa) on the other. Yet the biometric data that would seem to fix Michael K is elusive: 'CM', the one apparent reference to his racial identity (as 'coloured male') that is so crucial to the regime, becomes a linguistic code that the reader must interpret.[37] The sympathetic Medical Officer in part two encourages Michael K to narrate his life with the entreaty that 'You've got a story to tell and we want to hear it', suggesting that narrative is an effective counter to database-driven surveillance.[38] Despite this, the novel is less positive: looking – reading – becomes uncomfortably close to surveillance. It is not storytelling per se that the novel holds above surveillance, but literature's resistance to binaries. The difference is between the YES-NO 'reading' of binary thinking and the interpretative ambiguity that 'literary thinking' facilitates.

We can even see this conception at play in Coetzee's most recent Jesus trilogy. *The Childhood of Jesus* (2013), *The Schooldays of Jesus* (2016) and *The Death of Jesus* (2019) follow the education of David, a young boy, and his relationship with his adopted father Simón. In a novel replete with mathematical discourse, one of the most significant binaries in the novel is between the creative arts – dance, music, storytelling – and the simple Boolean operations, or 'ant numbers' that drive computation.[39] In one notable exchange, when David insists that 'I don't want to read letters [...] I want to read the story', Simón responds, 'That is not possible.' He continues: 'A story is made up of words, and words are made up of letters.'[40] Recalling Coetzee's own 'message plus vehicle' figuration from 'The Novel Today', the exchange indicates both the additive operations at the heart of storytelling and also the limitations of binary thinking as a means of understanding literature. As Marc Farrant has noted, the *Jesus* trilogy stages 'the formal distinctiveness of the literary as a mode of linguistic practice resistant to propositional discourses'.[41] I would change this slightly to state that it stages the literary as a mode of linguistic practice resistant to computational discourses more particularly. Across Coetzee's oeuvre we find that literature – the vision of poets – promotes freedom from the troublesome binary thinking that computing fosters.

NOTES

1. Coetzee, *Youth*, 149.
2. Coetzee, 'On Literary Thinking', 1151.
3. See Roach, 'J. M. Coetzee's Aesthetic Automatism', and 'Hero and Bad Motherland: J. M. Coetzee's Computational Critique'.
4. Coetzee, *Youth*, 22.
5. Ibid.
6. Ibid., 44.
7. Ibid., 46.
8. Coetzee, *Youth*, 160.
9. Coetzee, 'Computer Poem', 2.
10. See Attridge, *The Singularity of Literature*.
11. Notes taken during this period record Coetzee's reading; they are held in his archive at the Harry Ransom Center at the University of Texas at Austin.
12. His experiments are absent from accounts such as Higgins and Kahn (eds), *Mainframe Experimentalism*; Funkhouser, *Prehistoric Digital Poetry*; and Wardrip-Fruin and Montfort (eds), *The New Media Reader*.
13. Coetzee, *Youth*, 143, 144.
14. Ibid., 144.
15. Ibid., 160.
16. Coetzee, 'On Literary Thinking', 1152.
17. Coetzee, *Youth*, 163.
18. Coetzee, 'On Literary Thinking', 1152.
19. Coetzee, *Youth*, 162.
20. Ibid., 153.
21. Coetzee, 'Misconception'.
22. Attwell, *J. M. Coetzee and the Life of Writing*, 59.
23. Coetzee, *Youth*, 44.
24. See Roach, 'Hero and Bad Motherland'.
25. Coetzee, *Giving Offense*, 176–7.
26. Coetzee, *Youth*, 149.
27. Coetzee, *Giving Offense*, 200–1.
28. Coetzee, 'On Literary Thinking', 1152.
29. Ibid.
30. Ibid.
31. Coetzee, 'The Novel Today', 3.
32. For more discussion of Coetzee's depiction of mathematics in his literature, see particularly Brits, *Literary Infinites* and Johnston, '"Presences of the Infinite": J. M. Coetzee and Mathematics'.
33. Coetzee, 'Isaac Newton and the Ideal of a Transparent Scientific Language', 194.
34. Coetzee, 'Going All the Way', n.p.
35. See Roach, 'Hero and Bad Motherland'.
36. For an expanded version of this argument see Roach, 'J. M. Coetzee's Aesthetic Automatism'.

37. Coetzee, *Life & Times of Michael K*, 70.
38. Ibid., 140.
39. Coetzee, *The Schooldays of Jesus*, 69.
40. Ibid., 191.
41. Farrant, 'Finitizing Life: Between Reason and Religion in J. M. Coetzee's Jesus Novels', 167.

WORKS CITED

Attridge, Derek. *The Singularity of Literature*. London: Routledge, 2004.
Attwell, David. *J. M. Coetzee and the Life of Writing: Face to Face with Time*. Oxford: Oxford University Press, 2015.
Brits, Baylee. *Literary Infinites: Number and Narrative in Modern Fiction*. London: Bloomsbury Academic, 2017.
Coetzee, J. M. *The Childhood of Jesus*. London: Vintage, 2014.
Coetzee, J. M. 'Computer Poem'. *The Lion and the Impala* 2, no. 1 (1963): 1–2.
Coetzee, J. M. *Giving Offense: Essays on Censorship*. Chicago: University of Chicago Press, 1996.
Coetzee, J. M. 'Going All the Way'. Review of *Reading Rilke: Reflections on the Problems of Translation* by William H. Gass. *New York Review of Books* 46, no. 19 (1999). https://www.nybooks.com/articles/1999/12/02/going-all-the-way/.
Coetzee, J. M. 'Hero and Bad Mother in Epic, a Poem'. *Staffrider* 1, no. 1 (1978): 36–7.
Coetzee, J. M. 'Isaac Newton and the Ideal of a Transparent Scientific Language'. In *Doubling the Point: Essays and Interviews*, edited by David Atwell, 181–94. Cambridge: Harvard University Press, 1992.
Coetzee, J. M. *Life & Times of Michael K*. London: Vintage, 2004.
Coetzee, J. M. 'Misconception'. Letter to the Editor, *Daily Texan*, 24 October 1967.
Coetzee, J. M. 'The Novel Today'. *Upstream* 6, no. 1 (1988): 2–5.
Coetzee, J. M. 'On Literary Thinking'. *Textual Practice* 30, no. 7 (2016): 1151–2.
Coetzee, J. M. 'Samuel Beckett's Lessness: An Exercise in Decomposition'. *Computers and the Humanities* 7, no. 4 (1973): 195–8.
Coetzee, J. M. *The Schooldays of Jesus*. London: Vintage, 2016.
Coetzee, J. M. 'Statistical Indices of "Difficulty"'. *Language and Style* 2, no. 3 (1969): 226–32.
Coetzee, J. M. 'Surreal Metaphors and Random Processes'. *Journal of Literary Semantics* 8, no. 1 (1979): 22–30.
Coetzee, J. M. *Youth*, Kindle edition 1.0. London: Vintage, 2002.
Farrant, Marc. 'Finitizing Life: Between Reason and Religion in J.M. Coetzee's Jesus Novels'. *Journal of Modern Literature* 42, no. 4 (2019): 165–82.
Funkhouser, Christopher. *Prehistoric Digital Poetry: An Archaeology of Forms, 1959–1995*. Tuscaloosa: University of Alabama Press, 2007.
Higgins, Hannah and Douglas Kahn, eds. *Mainframe Experimentalism: Early Computing and the Foundations of the Digital Arts*. Berkeley & London: University of California Press, 2012.
Johnston, Peter. 'Presences of the Infinite: J. M. Coetzee and Mathematics'. PhD Dissertation, Royal Holloway, University of London, 2013.
Roach, Rebecca. 'Hero and Bad Motherland: J. M. Coetzee's Computational Critique'. *Contemporary Literature* 59, no. 1 (2018): 31–48.
Roach, Rebecca. 'J. M. Coetzee's Aesthetic Automatism'. *MFS: Modern Fiction Studies* 65, no. 2 (2019): 309–38.
Wardrip-Fruin, Noah and Nick Montfort, eds. *The New Media Reader*. Cambridge: The MIT Press, 2003.

CHAPTER TWENTY-FOUR

Coetzee's humour

HUW MARSH

Early in Coetzee's *The Childhood of Jesus* (2013), Simón, bored with subsisting on bread and concerned about the health of his charge, David, asks his foreman, Álvaro, where he can buy meat to supplement his diet. Álvaro suggests that he could try catching rats. '"But who eats rats?", asks Simón, "Do you eat rats?"' "No", says Álvaro, "I wouldn't dream of it. But you asked where you could get meat, and that is all I can suggest."' This gives Simón pause: 'He stares long into Álvaro's eyes. He can see no sign that he is joking. Or if it is a joke, it is a very deep joke.'[1] In one sense it *is* a joke, but nothing in the novel suggests that it is a joke intended by Álvaro. Rather his extreme pragmatism brings to mind the deadpan grotesquery of Swift's *A Modest Proposal* (1729), in which an even less palatable scenario is offered as a logical solution to a problem. Nor is it a joke shared between characters in the storyworld, but instead, a moment of wry humour shared between narrator and reader in response to the absurd logic of the dialogue.[2] Álvaro's affect is flat and he offers advice seemingly without irony or judgement. Later, Simón asks Álvaro why the radio station in Novilla never broadcasts news: '"Oh,"' says Álvaro, '"is something going on?"' Again, Simón is 'ready to suspect irony', but 'there was none'; it is a question meant in good faith. Simón feels he is a 'misfit' in this new land, one in which irony does not exist and 'people have no secret yearnings he can detect, no hankerings after another kind of life' (64). When he attempts a joke about his colleagues' philosophy class (he asks if they have succeeded in working out what a chair is), they 'stare at him blankly', immune to his irony, and turn the joke back on him: '"Don't you know what a chair is?"' says one of them finally. '"Look down. You are sitting on one."' They 'burst out laughing', leaving Simón floundering and attempting belatedly to join in 'to show he is a good sport' (122). Shortly afterwards, another of the young men reports the Institute's life-drawing class is oversubscribed because '"people want to learn about the body"' and Simón once again 'searches for the irony' and finds none, just 'as there is no salt' (123) in the bland food they are served.

This sequence in *The Childhood of Jesus* describes a series of not-jokes and missed connections in which Simón's sense of humour is never in line with that of his interlocutors. It is itself a 'very deep joke' (37) about the nature of humour and humourlessness, and the role of humour as a mode of communication. Irony may not be intended by Álvaro and the other men, but we read it anyway; their earnestness is itself comic, as are Simón's stumbling attempts to joke with them. For Simón, irony is the 'salt' missing from his new life, but other citizens of Novilla appear not to want for it: like seasoning, its absence is only perceptible if one is habituated to its presence. Coetzee is not usually thought of as a humorous writer, but as we have seen in this example of writing that is both humorous and *about* humour, his reputation as the author of dour fictions emerges less from an absence of humour than from mismatched expectations and a misunderstanding about the diverse nature of the comic. In the discussion that follows, I do not seek to reclaim Coetzee as a 'comic novelist' – though I can see the humorous potential in doing so – but rather to describe some of the ways in which humour operates as an important but often misunderstood mode and subject for his writing.

Samuel Beckett has unsurprisingly been an important point of reference in scholarship on Coetzee and humour. These passages from *The Childhood of Jesus* might be read for their kinship with the deadpan dialogue found in Beckett's work; the forever out-of-sync interactions amongst Simón, Álvaro and the other stevedores bear comparison with what Laura Salisbury has described as Beckett's propensity for 'jokes which hold back from the instant of the comic payoff but are bound to the quivering temporality of the almost'.[3] In other words, there is clear comic intent in both Beckett and Coetzee, but this is a type of humour that often frustrates expectations. Its tone is easy to misread.[4] The youthful Coetzee recognized the humour in Beckett, and for him it was transformative. In *Youth* (2002) the narrator John describes his discovery of Beckett's novels, at a time when he was writing his MA thesis on Ford Madox Ford.[5] On first reading *Watt* (1953), he 'rolls about laughing' and the experience inspires reflection on his own writing: 'How could he have imagined he wanted to write in the manner of Ford, when Beckett was around all the time?' Beckett's prose avoids the 'element of the stuffed shirt' that he dislikes in Ford and offers the possibility of writing 'outside class, as he himself would prefer to be'.[6] Humour is fundamental to this encounter and the epiphany it instigates, and it has proven fundamental to Coetzee's subsequent writing.

In some critical accounts, Beckett inaugurated not a new direction in comic writing but rather the death of comedy. This is a formalist view focusing on dramatic comedy that does not fit most people's understanding of comedy's modern forms, but is symptomatic of the genre trouble that is frequently faced by humorous writing. We might instead recognize in Beckett a strand of humour that develops from nullity, irony and bleakness; this too is Coetzee's territory. In fact the sexual failure, the absence of the powerful phallus and the 'potent, energetic *gamos*' that Erich Segal laments in Beckett[7] are all topics for humour in Coetzee's fiction. Writing about an arid, mechanical and dismally humorous sex scene between Eugene Dawn and his wife Marilyn in *Dusklands* (1974), Attridge finds Beckettian resonances but concludes that 'where Beckett's heroes show winning hesitations, doubts, and recalibrations, Dawn's conviction never wavers. If we do laugh at his extraordinary representation of sex, it is fitfully and reluctantly'.[8] If Coetzee outdoes Beckett (never the most sunnily disposed of writers) in the bleakness stakes, and any amusement or laughter is muted and ironic, this might be, Attridge concludes, because such scenes are 'darkened by the external events that accompanied their composition'; his characters are 'subject to, or understood in the context of, exacting ethical and political responsibilities' in ways that are not always the case in Beckett.[9] In this example, even the self-effacing laughter at oneself that Simon Critchley identifies as a characteristically modern form of humour – more on which later – is conspicuously absent.[10] The aridity of the description places it closer to the mechanistic model of laughter proposed by Henri Bergson in his essay *Laughter* (1900).

For Bergson, we find it funny when a person reminds us of a machine, and the resultant mocking laughter has a corrective function, forcing individuals to step in line with social norms and behave in more vital, humanlike ways.[11] The description of sex in *Dusklands* can certainly be read in this way; its chilliness tallies with Bergson's assertion that 'laughter has no greater foe than emotion', that 'its appeal is to intelligence, pure and simple'.[12] Bergsonian humour is characterized by detachment and mockery, and when looked at alongside the classical definition, we arrive at two seemingly incompatible conceptions of humour: as celebration of the body and fecundity rather than the intellect (Segal and the classical tradition), or as an intellectual reaction to machinelike behaviour (Bergson). In some ways, however, these two conceptions of humour's role arrive at same place in their privileging of vital, non-mechanistic behaviour, whether through positive celebration or negative critique. Neither version appears adequately to account for the dry, ironic humour found in Coetzee's early writing, which is neither celebratory, nor exactly mocking.

Agnes Heller offers some useful insights through what she identifies as the constitutive humour and irony of existential comedy, arguing that in the comedies of Beckett, Ionesco and their descendants, the world 'manifests itself as absurd, chaotic, non-rational, and non-identical', but this is 'taken for granted' by the individual. Humour arises from the 'presentation of an absurd world in which one behaves "naturally"'.[13] Such comedies 'make fun of those of us who behave naturally in an absurd world' and the laughter they inspire is neither redemptive nor didactic; rather, it leaves 'an ambiguous, embarrassed aftertaste'.[14] This awkward, discomforting laughter is closer to the forms of humour we often find in Coetzee, in which the iniquities of the world are counterpoised in uneasy relation to the deadpan reactions of his characters. In *Waiting for the Barbarians* (1980) for example, the torturer Mandel asks the Magistrate when he will begin working for his keep. The Magistrate replies that he is a prisoner and that prisoners are maintained 'out of the public coffer'. '"But you are not a prisoner"', Mandel tells him, '"We have no record of you. So you must be a free man."'[15] According to Mandel's bureaucratic reasoning, the magistrate is free, but he is caught in a double bind because his freedom condemns him to life as an outcast. He provokes Mandel by asking him about the psychological effects of his work as a torturer, but is met only with violence and is left shouting, 'When are you going to put me on trial?' Mandel 'pays no heed'.[16] In the absence of a just or transparent system, the Magistrate falls back on the rule of law with which he is familiar, calling for his own trial on charges that have never been brought. This ironic reversal is not comfortable or consoling, but it resonates with Heller's comments on the ambiguous nature of existential comedy, in which revelations are restricted to the recognition of limitedness and not knowing, of 'feeling stupid, like a man who lost his way long ago but presses on along a road that may lead nowhere', as the Magistrate describes at the conclusion of the novel.[17] As with Mrs Curren in *Age of Iron* (1990), or even David Lurie in *Disgrace* (1999), there is bleak humour in the failure of Coetzee's protagonists to comprehend or adequately to account for the situations in which they find themselves.[18]

But this tone is not universal throughout Coetzee's work and diminishes in the later novels, where a gentler, more forgiving humour predominates. In the second of the *Jesus* trilogy, *The Schooldays of Jesus* (2016), Simón listens to Arroyo, the master of the Academy at which his ward, David, had previously been enrolled, composing a piece of music on a piano. Simón's mind turns to metaphysics and he asks himself, 'Where is the soul? When will the soul emerge from its hiding place and open its wings?' However, he is 'not on close terms with his soul' and is '[u]nable to see' it, nor has he

> questioned what people tell him about it: that it is a dry soul, deficient in passion. His own obscure intuition – that, far from lacking in passion, his soul aches with longing for it knows not what – he treats sceptically as just the kind of story that someone with a dry, rational, deficient soul will tell himself to maintain his self-respect.[19]

There is pathos in Simón's assessment of his own character and his reliance on the judgement of others over his own 'obscure intuition', but there is also humour in his determination to accept that he has a 'dry, rational, deficient soul'. This very dryness – and his trust of others' judgement – speaks to Schopenhauer's version of the incongruity theory of humour, which reasons that laughter 'results from nothing but the suddenly perceived incongruity between a concept and the real objects that had been thought through it in some relation'.[20] On this view, we recognize folly when an incongruity emerges from an individual's favouring of abstract knowledge or reason over their lived experience. One of Schopenhauer's examples is that of pedantry, which 'arises from a man's having little confidence in his own understanding, and therefore not liking to leave things to its discretion, to recognize what is right in the particular case'. In consequence, 'he puts his understanding entirely under the guardianship of his reason' and rigidly sticks to 'general concepts, rules, and maxims', an approach that 'can never accurately apply to reality's fine shades of difference and its innumerable modifications'.[21] The occasional tenderness and empathy in Coetzee's characterization prevent Simón from conforming to Schopenhauer's category of the 'foolish, absurd, and incompetent' pedant, but this and other flashes of interiority generate humorous but disquieting incongruities between external and internal perceptions.[22] His behaviour is a further example of what Heller describes as constitutive humour, but the laughter it inspires is of acceptance rather than harsh judgement: we are not invited to mock Simón for the dryness of his soul and are instead amused at his trust in the judgements of others at the expense of his own intuition and experience. This is a self-effacing and tragicomic form of humour.

Elsewhere in Coetzee's writing we see this same gentle comic mockery applied to the characterization of a version of Coetzee himself. In *Boyhood* (1997), the young John and his father are described as laughing at his mother, imagining the citizens of the local town, Worcester, mocking her as she trundles past on her bicycle: 'There is nothing funny about the jokes', he acknowledges, 'though he and his father always laugh together afterwards.'[23] Their derision wears his mother down and 'one day, without explanation, she stops riding the bicycle' and, when it disappears soon afterwards, '[n]o one says a word, but he knows she has been defeated, put in her place, and knows that he must bear part of the blame' (4). This is an early lesson in the power of scornful laughter, and the young John is repentant, promising himself that he will make recompense one day. Any humour in this scene is derived at John and his father's expense, and John acknowledges that his actions are motivated by selfishness: 'He does not want her to go. He does not want her to have a desire of her own. He wants her always to be in the house, waiting for him when he comes home' (4). Coetzee's excoriating appraisal of his character continues in *Youth* (2002), but here there is a good deal more noir humour in the young John's angst-ridden years of exile and self-pity. 'Happy people are not interesting', the narrator says early on: 'Better to accept the burden of unhappiness and try to turn it into something worthwhile, poetry or music or painting: that is what he believes' (14). The concluding qualification is loaded with the irony allowed by a future perspective, and the glimpses we are given of the artistic output inspired by this unhappiness are not promising. John later describes reading one of his compositions at a Poetry Society workshop, a poem that 'ends with the words "the furious waves of my incontinence"' – word-choice (he reflects wryly) thought 'unfortunate' for its associations with 'urinary incontinence or worse' (73). *Youth* is full of such moments, in which the dourness, seriousness and pretentiousness of the young John are offered as occasions for humour. Although, as Dooley notes, the character John's 'foolish beliefs are implicitly mocked by the narrator', it is a form of mockery quite unlike the boy's cruel ridicule of his mother in *Boyhood*.[24] Moreover, it is self-directed insofar as the *autre*-biographical texts involve a future Coetzee offering fictionalized versions of his younger selves.[25] The younger writer is not only a tormented, conventional *Künstlerroman* artist but also deeply ordinary and often foolish. To some degree at least, he turns the laughter on himself, avoiding the mockery that is so often a function of humour, for all its positive associations.[26]

Boyhood, then, describes mirthless humour and the callousness of childhood, while *Youth* gently mocks the pretentions of, well, youth, but it is *Summertime* (2009), the third volume of Coetzee's *Scenes from a Provincial Life* trilogy, that most consistently casts Coetzee – or a character who is a version of his younger self – as a comic figure, and moreover, that reflects more fully on the nature of humour. In one of the interviews that makes up the book, the interviewee, Julia Frankl, recounts to the biographer, Mr Vincent, her first meeting with the late writer John Coetzee, in which he helped her when she dropped some rolls of wrapping paper in the supermarket. As he returns these, '[f]or a second or two, through the length of the rolls, he could actually be said to have been prodding my breast', she remembers. It was an 'intimate, unexpected nudge' that may yet have faded and been 'lost among all the other personal moments' if not for the fact that a short time later she happened to drive past his home and see him shovelling sand.[27] She stops to speak with him and although she has not forgotten that he is guilty of the breast incident (her 'breast retained the memory'), she soon recasts it in her memory: '[T]en to one, I now told myself, it had been nothing but a clumsy accident, the act of a *Schlemiel*' (25). Later still she describes him as 'Mister Prod, Mister Nudge, the man shovelling sand from the back of the truck' (30). Leaving aside the multiple layers of fictionality complicating the relationship between Coetzee-as-author and Coetzee-as-character, as well as the fact that Julia has her own agenda in casting him as a fool, in this and other moments from *Summertime*, Coetzee is playing games with his public image, or what the biographer character describes as the '*image of him in the public realm as a cold and supercilious intellectual, an image he did nothing to dispel. Indeed one might even say he encouraged it*' (235). Julia describes John as a 'figure of comedy. Dour comedy. Which, in an obscure way, he knew, even accepted' (63), and the book is peppered with further moments that represent John as a mildly ridiculous figure, who, like Simón in the Jesus trilogy, has ideals and expectations that are at odds with others' perceptions. Another of his former lovers, Sophie Denoël, describes how he 'was the kind of man who is convinced that supreme felicity will be his if only he can acquire a French mistress who will recite Ronsard to him and play Couperin on the clavecin while simultaneously inducting him into the mysteries of love, French style' (241). She acknowledges that she is exaggerating, but also that she had been cast as the 'French mistress of his fantasy' and that their relationship was 'comical in its essence. Comico-sentimental. Based on a comic premise' (241).

In casting a version of himself as the *Schlemiel*, the put-upon and misguided fool, Coetzee practises a form of humour that moves away from the more detached irony of much of his earlier work and closer to the gentler pleasure described by Freud in his essay 'Humour' (1927). For Freud, such self-effacing humour 'never finds vent in hearty laughter' but its great value lies in its ability to keep the rampant ego in check without the usually damaging negative affect associated with the otherwise 'stern master', the super-ego. This form of amusement says, '"Look! here is the world, which seems so dangerous! It is nothing but a game for children – just worth making a jest about!"'[28] Coetzee's later work yields humour that is more likely to produce a smile of recognition than an ironic smirk, let alone a guffaw, and in this it is akin to the characteristically modern form mentioned earlier, which Critchley admires for its ability to produce a 'smile of knowing self-mockery and self-ridicule'.[29] For Critchley, such humour and the smiles it elicits are 'powerfully emblematic of the human, the quiet acknowledgement of one's limitedness'; it is 'the mark of the eccentricity of the human situation: between beasts and angels, between being and having, between the physical and metaphysical'.[30] As such, Coetzee's humour is not merely a touch of levity among the prevailing seriousness, but rather a fundamental part of his work's negotiation of questions of being. The self-effacing humour in *Scenes from a Provincial Life* is a further example of the 'very deep' jokes one finds throughout Coetzee's work, and it functions as a way of complicating the relationship between his public image and his (fictionalized) self-representations, and as a way of representing subjectivity with all its complexity, contradictions and failures. In this sense, it is part of a lineage of what Patrick Hayes terms Coetzee's 'fool-heroes',[31] a lineage within which I would include the Magistrate in *Waiting for the Barbarians*, Mrs Curren in *Age of Iron* and David Lurie in *Disgrace*, as well as Dostoevsky in *The Master of Petersburg* (1994) and Paul Rayment in *Slow Man* (2005), each of whom must reckon with their lack of mastery, their very human foolishness, even when they are without the self-awareness to identify it in themselves: '"This is not a comedy"', Rayment tells Elizabeth Costello in *Slow Man*, one of Coetzee's funniest novels.[32]

One further facet of Coetzee's humour requires us to consider the role of formal innovation and the layout of the page. In *Theory of the Gimmick* (2020), Sianne Ngai describes Coetzee's *Diary of a Bad Year* (2007) as an example of a novel that 'wants to represent the capitalist reification of thinking and embraces the gimmick as ideal form for the purpose'.[33] She elsewhere describes how 'we call things gimmicks when it becomes radically uncertain if they are working too hard or too little, if they are historically backward or just as problematically advanced, if they are wonders or tricks';[34] as such, they both index and invoke contemporary suspicions about the relationship between capital and labour. In the context of Coetzee's novel, Ngai discusses how 'suspicions of illegitimacy and meretriciousness surrounding value, time and labor [...] have concentrated around artworks "of ideas" in particular'.[35] Coetzee's book presents the essays of JC, another of Coetzee's near-but-not-quite analogues, at the top of the page, with his more intimate, first-person narration below, separated by a horizontal line. After the first five chapters, the first-person narration of JC's typist, Anya, joins these as the chorus at the bottom of the page, again separated by a horizontal line. JC's essays, presented as contributions to a volume entitled *Strong Opinions*, are therefore bracketed off from the ostensible plot of the novel, most notably the relationship between JC and Anya, and the later involvement of Anya's fiancé Alan, that develops through the text. Ngai argues that the 'emphasis with which the novel seems to want to detach its Opinions from the developing story of JC and Anya's complicated relationship' belies the fact that 'it is a relationship in which the Opinions figure prominently and which they in fact bring into being and mediate'.[36] In dividing them in this way, JC's opinions appear '*more reified than they actually are*' (in Ngai's terms), suggesting 'reification's centrality to the novel of ideas as a problem, even when it does not finally triumph'.[37] In other words, the book's form and the gimmick of the divisions between Opinions and first-person narration show the permeability of those divisions, enacting on the page the late-capitalist reification of thought. In addition to this effect, I would add that these divisions also represent the literal and figurative permeability of the hierarchical boundaries between high and low, mind and body, intellect and libido. One of the effects of the abrupt transitions between these sections is to create moments of comic bathos.

In the tenth of his Strong Opinions, JC reflects on 'National Shame' in relation to the so-called 'War on Terror' and the government-sanctioned torture of prisoners. Early on he invokes Demosthenes, and the seriousness and erudition of the piece are in keeping with what one might expect from Coetzee on this subject. But beneath this are JC's and Anya's reflections on less elevated matters, including their developing relationship. It is clear from the outset that JC has not hired Anya for her typing and secretarial skills and is perturbed but also aroused by her flirtations. When she asks whether he thinks she could do modelling, he reports that 'she puts her hands on her hips, tosses her hair, glances at me provocatively'.[38] Anya, for her part, suspects he is a dirty old man. 'There is a pair of panties of mine he pinched from the dryer, I am sure of it', she says, suspecting he uses them to conjure 'visions of my divine behind and makes himself come' (40). At the top of the page we have the public intellectual and the life of the mind, but as we move down the page and beyond those seemingly definitive dividing lines, we move metaphorically down the body and finally beneath the belt. As Ngai suggests of the gimmick, the effect can be read to undermine the reification of thinking, but it is also generative of bathetic humour, undermining the persistent idea of a Cartesian duality between the intellect and the body. This humour of bathos, literalized via the movement from high to low as one reads from top to bottom, recurs throughout the novel and, like the portraits of Coetzee as a figure of fun in *Scenes*, complicates his image as a writer as well as the conception of public versus private identities tout court. Whether or not we read JC as a version of Coetzee, as some of the details of the character seem to invite, the novel suggests that such moments of bathos are part of life and that the curated, public aspects of one's thought and character – one's Strong Opinions, presented for public consumption – cannot be bracketed off from the messier aspects of existence.

In the second, shorter section of *Diary* ('Second Diary'), the numbered sections at the top of the page become more personal in subject matter and tone, as well as more self-reflexive about the writing process. In the thirteenth, 'On the writing Life', JC discusses his image as a writer, beginning with the fact that when he was a literature professor he would find consolation by telling himself that he was 'not a teacher but a novelist'. 'But now', he says, 'the critics voice a new refrain': 'he is not a novelist after all, they say, but a pedant who dabbles in fiction' (191). He wonders whether this might be true and paints a derisory picture of his role as public intellectual, a worthy figure who is wheeled out for public occasions 'and then put back in the cupboard'. This, he says, is an 'appropriately comic and provincial fate for a man who half a century ago shook the dust of the provinces off his feet and sallied forth into the great world to practise *la vie bohème*' (191). Through several layers of fictionality, Coetzee again presents a wryly humorous version of himself and his role in the world; he is not, on this view, one of the great innovators of the novel or chroniclers of the contemporary moment but a pedant unable to rid himself of the dust of the provinces. In this and the other examples from his later works discussed above, Coetzee emerges as a humourist of serious intent who, in contrast to his reputation as sombre – even dry – writer, employs humour as a method to reveal the complex relationship between inner and outer lives, public and private reputations. There have always been humorous elements in Coetzee's writing, but these have mellowed and deepened over time, and the abiding suggestion is that despite our noblest intentions we are inherently comic and frequently foolish creatures.

NOTES

1. Coetzee, *Childhood of Jesus*, 37. Further references appear parenthetically in text.
2. Jerry Palmer describes comedy's strange internal reasoning as the 'logic of the absurd'. See Palmer, *Logic of the Absurd*, and Palmer, *Taking Humour Seriously*.
3. Salisbury, *Samuel Beckett*, 21.
4. As Roof notes, missing the tone of humorous writing has a literalizing effect, 'actually flattening a text to its complete opposite'. See Roof, *Tone*, 12.
5. Beckett's comic voice was the subject of some of Coetzee's earliest published work. See Coetzee, 'The Comedy of Point of View'.
6. Coetzee, *Youth*, 155.
7. Segal, *Death of Comedy*, 435.
8. Attridge, 'Sex, Comedy and Influence', 83.
9. Ibid., 86.
10. See Critchley, *On Humour*, 93–111.
11. Bergson, 'Laughter', 84, 90.
12. Ibid., 63–4.
13. Heller, *Immortal Comedy*, 103–4.
14. Ibid., 117.
15. Coetzee, *Waiting*, 136.
16. Ibid., 137.
17. Ibid., 169.
18. For a discussion of the interplay between the comic and the serious in *Age of Iron*, see Hayes, *J.M. Coetzee*, 130–64. Hayes's writing on the 'serio-comic' and 'jocoserious' in Coetzee is the most in-depth and thoughtful discussion of the topic to date.
19. Coetzee, *Schooldays of Jesus*, 194.
20. Schopenhauer, *World as Will*, I, 60.
21. Ibid.
22. Ibid.
23. Coetzee, *Boyhood*, 4. Further references cited parenthetically in text.
24. Dooley, *J.M. Coetzee*, 76.
25. For insightful discussions of *Scenes from a Provincial Life* as what Coetzee termed '*autre*biography', see Lenta, '*Autre*biography', and Van der Vlies, *Present Imperfect*, 54–65.
26. See, for example, Billig, *Laughter and Ridicule*.
27. Coetzee, *Summertime*, 22. Further references cited parenthetically in text.
28. Freud, 'Humour', 166.
29. Critchley, *On Humour*, 107.
30. Ibid., 109.
31. Hayes, *J.M. Coetzee*, 249.
32. Coetzee, *Slow Man*, 130.
33. Ngai, *Theory of the Gimmick*, 124.
34. Ibid., 49.

35. Ibid., 106.

36. Ibid., 125.

37. Ibid.

38. Coetzee, *Diary of a Bad Year*, 40. Hereafter referenced parenthetically.

WORKS CITED

Attridge, Derek. 'Sex, Comedy and Influence: Coetzee's Beckett'. In *J. M. Coetzee in Context and Theory*, edited by Elleke Boehmer, Robert Eaglestone and Katy Iddiols, 71–90. London: Bloomsbury, 2011.

Attwell, David. *J.M. Coetzee and the Life of Writing*. New York: Penguin, 2005.

Bergson, Henri. 'Laughter: An Essay on the Meaning of the Comic', translated by Cloudesley Brereton and Fred Rothwell. In *Comedy*, edited by Wylie Sypher, 61–190. New York: Doubleday, 1956 [1900].

Billig, Michael. *Laughter and Ridicule: Towards a Social Critique of Humour*. London: Sage, 2005.

Coetzee, J. M. *Age of Iron*. New York: Random House, 1990.

Coetzee, J. M. *Boyhood: Scenes from a Provincial Life*. Harmondsworth: Viking Penguin, 1997.

Coetzee, J. M. *The Childhood of Jesus*. London: Harvill Secker, 2013.

Coetzee, J. M. 'The Comedy of Point of View in Beckett's Murphy'. *Critique* 12, no. 2 (1970): 19–27.

Coetzee, J. M. *Diary of a Bad Year*. London: Vintage, 2008 [2007].

Coetzee, J. M. *Disgrace*. New York: Penguin, 2000 [1999].

Coetzee, J. M. *The Master of Petersburg*. New York: Viking, 1994.

Coetzee, J. M. *The Schooldays of Jesus*. London: Harvill Secker, 2016.

Coetzee, J. M. *Slow Man*. New York: Penguin, 2006 [2005].

Coetzee, J. M. *Summertime*. London: Viking Penguin, 2009.

Coetzee, J. M. *Waiting for the Barbarians*. London: Vintage, 2004 [1980].

Coetzee, J. M. *Youth*. London: Secker and Warburg, 2002.

Critchley, Simon. *On Humour*. London: Routledge, 2002.

Dooley, Gillian. *J. M. Coetzee and the Power of Narrative*. Amherst, NY: Cambria Press, 2010.

Freud, Sigmund. 'Humour' (1927), translated by Joan Riviere. In *The Future of an Illusion, Civilization and Its Discontents, and Other Works*, The Standard Edition of the Complete Psychological Works of Sigmund Freud, vol. 21, 160–6. London: Hogarth Press, 1961.

Hayes, Patrick. *J.M. Coetzee and the Novel: Writing and Politics after Beckett*. Oxford: Oxford University Press, 2011.

Heller, Agnes. *Immortal Comedy: The Comic Phenomenon in Art, Literature and Life*. Oxford: Lexington, 2005.

Lenta, Margaret. '*Autre*biography: J. M. Coetzee's *Boyhood* and *Youth*'. *English in Africa* 30, no. 1 (2003): 157–69.

Ngai, Sianne. *Theory of the Gimmick: Aesthetic Judgement and Capitalist Form*. Cambridge, MA: Belknap Press, 2020.

Palmer, Jerry. *The Logic of the Absurd: On Film and Television Comedy*. London: BFI, 1987.

Palmer, Jerry. *Taking Humour Seriously*. London: Routledge, 1994.

Roof, Judith. *Tone*. London: Bloomsbury, 2020.

Salisbury, Laura. *Samuel Beckett: Laughing Matters, Comic Timing*. Edinburgh: Edinburgh University Press, 2012.

Schopenhauer, Arthur. *The World as Will and Representation*. Translated by E. F. J. Payne. 2 volumes. New York: Dover, 2000 [1818–19].

Segal, Erich. *The Death of Comedy*. Cambridge, MA: Harvard University Press, 2001.

van der Vlies, Andrew. *Present Imperfect: Contemporary South African Writing*. Oxford: Oxford University Press, 2017.

CHAPTER TWENTY-FIVE

Education and the novels of J. M. Coetzee

APARNA MISHRA TARC

J. M. Coetzee's novels raise difficult questions about the impacts of Western colonial educational projects on children. In fictionally staged scenes, many ideals of Western education are exposed to be exploitative, violent, hypernormative, ethnocentric and harmful to their child subjects. Revealing educational theories, experiments and practices to mistreat impressionable children, across his novels Coetzee tests the limits of education. Numerous novels depict the historical and present pedagogical enactment of Western education that continues to take place in persistently colonial-style institutions. *Boyhood: Scenes from Provincial Life* (1997) recalls the author's bad schooldays through the third person fictional construction of young John. In *Life & Times of Michael K* (1983), the eponymous protagonist is placed as a child in Huis Norenius, an institution 'for various afflicted and unfortunate children'.[1] In *Age of Iron* (1990), Black children leave school en masse in the townships to fight for 'liberation before education',[2] much to pedagogue protagonist Mrs Curren's dismay. *Disgrace* (1999) follows the fall of Professor David Lurie and with him, misogynist attachments to humanist education in the wake of the dehumanizing colonial and Apartheid educational projects. Finally, the chapters of *Elizabeth Costello* (2003) are framed as lessons that deliberate the key role of education in instituting our deformed humankind.

Gestured to in previous novels, education takes centre stage in the recent *Jesus* trilogy, where education is explored in what Gayatri Spivak describes as 'scenes of teaching not only as event but task'.[3] These scenes, in Rita Barnard's words, 'alert us to the dangerous power of teaching: of bad teaching as well as powerful and good teaching'.[4] In this chapter I theorize scenes of teaching in the *Jesus* novels in terms of pedagogy. Pedagogy arises in highly relational and affecting scenes of teaching and *learning*, revealing both to be, as Barnard finds, 'a fraught and risky endeavor'.[5] Pedagogy, referring to the provision, fora, course and delivery of knowledge, is not to be confused with education. In *The Republic*, Pedro González explains, 'Plato distinguishes between education as pedagogy – the art of teaching – and the desire for learning.'[6] Pedagogy – from the Greek pedagogue ('pais' for 'boy'; 'agogos' for 'guide') – need not only take place in institutions. In the *Jesus* novels, Coetzee restages the pedagogical relation as a fraught interaction where the teacher's desire to impart forms of knowledge clashes with the student's desire to know and learn. Teacher and student are bound together in this largely unspoken, yet deeply felt, pedagogical knot of competing desires.

Simón is the primary parent and pedagogue in the *Jesus* stories and takes on the philosophical character of Greek philosophers Plato and Socrates. In the style of these men, Simón fields the child David's relentless curiosity and hard questions with what he acknowledges are 'dry little homilies'.[7] Frustrated by Simón's abstract philosophical teachings, David gravitates towards the passionate offerings of other teachers he meets along the way: the maternal Inés; the fictional Don Quixote; the charismatic but possibly dangerous Señor Daga; the passionate murderer Dimitri; the celestial Arroyos; and the physical 'Educator', Dr. Juan Fabricante. Seeking to provide pedagogical guidance for David, it is Simón who eventually learns from David; indeed, he attains a *child's* sense of how best he can grow, learn and live.

Coetzee's *Jesus* trilogy recasts educational ideas in literary depictions of pedagogy. In the singular relation of teacher and child, the author contemplates the philosophical and curricular aims of education across centuries of Western thought and culture. As Charlotta Elmgren suggests, the novels explore education largely through the adult provision of 'different educational options'[8] for a child. Through the narrative deliberation of strange, disturbing and familiar education options, the reader is offered musings on education as delivered through pedagogies of significant relation. With his mother's fostering pedagogy in mind, Coetzee pursues the ontological, epistemological, ethical and moral role of education in the life of a child across all three *Jesus* novels.

HOMEGROWN PEDAGOGY: *THE CHILDHOOD OF JESUS*

In my book *Pedagogy in the Novels of J. M. Coetzee* (2020), I find a precedent for pedagogy in infant-(m)other relations.[9] Without this primary relation, I argue, there is no education. The infant's visceral experience of radical dependency on and attachment to significant (m)others provides the child with the relational basis one needs to grow and learn throughout life. In his recent novels Coetzee relocates education in the maternal relation, one that emerges from his own educational history, as detailed in David Attwell's archival investigation of Coetzee's intellectual influences. In the chapter entitled 'Mother' of his 2015 literary biography, *J. M. Coetzee and the Life of Writing*, Attwell identifies Coetzee's mother as the author's first and enduring intellectual influence. A primary school teacher who introduced Coetzee to literature at an early age,[10] Vera Coetzee left a 'mark' on her son that is discernible in his authorship of female characters.[11] The mother's profession and ideas of education also find their way into parental characters (male and female) who teach in Coetzee's novels.

Vera Coetzee's educational ideas, influence and profession are traced in the passages contemplating education throughout Coetzee's novels. In *Summertime* (2009), the third instalment of the fictionalised memoir trilogy *Scenes from Provincial Life*, the late John Coetzee, a fictionalized version of the author, had been a university professor claiming to be 'reading here and there in educational theory and in the writings of the Dutch Calvinist school; he … had resisted them as he resists them now' (*Summertime* 252–3). John attributed his fierce resistance to Dutch Calvinism in the form of 'Kuypersim' to his mother's counter-pedagogy. According to her, 'the task of the teacher … is to identify and foster the natural talents of the child, the talents with which the child is born and which make the child unique' (*Summertime* 255).[12] At one point in 'John's' diary entries that bracket the stories of various narrators in *Summertime*, we read that John had noted to himself 'to be developed: his own homegrown theory of education' (*Summertime* 255).

Homegrown educational theory is plotted across the *Jesus* trilogy. The story of a five-year-old migrant child's education starts in *The Childhood of Jesus* (2013). David's educational journey then spans five more years across two sequels. Like an infant, David arrives in the world with no idea to whom he was born, with no name, history or home to speak of. Hostage to the adult community and positioned without memories, as a 'clean state', David is the epitome of the Platonic subject of pedagogy, apparently in need of someone to educate and lead him into the world. Similarly a refugee, Simón arrives with the orphaned David by boat to Belstar camp where together the two are transferred to the sanctuary city of Novilla. When asked by state authorities if he is David's guardian, Simón replies, 'I am responsible for him' (C 1), thus sealing the legal and modern *in locus parentis* pedagogical contract. Ironically, though taking on the calling to teach, Simón is just as much a 'clean slate' as David, with no memory of his prior life. The responsibility of teaching, to which Simón commits, is upended by David, his unruly student. Abandoned by his real family and history, David resists his de facto guardian's philosophical teachings. He wishes only for Simón to provide knowledge needed for answers to his 'true' questions: Who am I, Who are you to me? (C 33) and Why am I here? (C 17).

Attempting to respond to the child's existential desire to know who he is, Simón 'finds him' a mother, Inés (C 19), hoping she will put his unanswerable questions to rest. But simply having a mother is not enough for a child who desperately wants to know who he is. David's questions persist. As Simón also has no memory or knowledge of his or the child's family history, he falls back on Socratic-style philosophical teachings to fill in the gaps. These universalizing and moral teachings delivered by way of 'abstraction, explication, and digression' frustrate rather than appeal to the small child (C 124). The teacher soon realizes that none of his lessons are taking hold.[13] Determined to lift the child out of his 'ignorance' (C 33), Simón searches for another way to enlighten David.

To educate David, Simón goes to the library and brings home a children's version of *Don Quixote*.[14] David is initially enthralled with Simón's suggestion that they begin by 'reading the story aloud' by going through it 'word by word, looking at how words are put together' (C 152).[15] But the reading lessons go awry as the beginner-reader decides 'I can read' and 'I don't want to read your way' (C 165). Roundly dismissing the child's emergent, inventive readings, Simón instructs David to embark on 'real reading' by 'submitting to what is written in on the page' (C 165). Now literate, David rejects Simón's practice of close reading and embarks on a new and free period of enquiry that independent reading permits. 'He read the book so many times', Simon observes, 'that it sank into his memory. *Don Quixote* became part of him' (D 73). These solitary and meaningful re-readings will prove to sustain David across his life.

The book will accompany David wherever his education takes him including the compulsory state school(s) his parents are forced to enrol him in. In public school the 'clever child' who 'taught himself how to read and write' from *Don Quixote* infuriates his teacher, señor Leon (C 175). Slighted by this failure to recognize him, David withholds his academic abilities from señor Leon who he believes 'doesn't know how to teach' (C 212). Misunderstanding David, señor Leon attributes his refusal to learn from *him*, a punishing teacher, to 'a specific deficit linked to symbolic activities. To working with words and numbers'. Further, the teacher wrongly decides that David is unteachable: 'He cannot read. He cannot write. He cannot count' (C 204).

To cope with señor Leon's 'strict' (C 206) and mistaken reception of him, David resorts to saying 'crazy things' (C 206). His abnormal behaviour prompts the teacher to consult with an educational expert who recommends that David be placed in a 'first rate' (C 211) institution designed to remediate maladjusted children (C 208). Inés balks at the thought of sending her precocious and 'exceptionally intelligent' (C 229) son to the horrible Punta Arenas, 'a dumping ground for delinquents and orphans' (231).[16] 'My child,' she declares, 'is not going to that place, never, never, never' (C 231).

David's experience of misplaced ability and misunderstood behaviour is familiar to children unable to conform intellectually, ethno-culturally, and behaviourally (the three often and wrongly conflated) to the cultures and conventions of state educational institutions. Without considering the unique capacities of David, señor Leon's lessons render a curious and inventive child as deficient and wrong. Simón astutely suspects that David's troubles at school have a pedagogical rather than intellectual origin in a 'bad feeling between pupil and teacher' (C 226).

Defying the parents' explicit refusal to admit him to Punta Arenas, the school obtains a court order to override their decision. Without notice, the authorities come for David, effectively kidnapping him and taking him away in a car (C 253). Soon after, however, David 'escapes' the institution and is 'found' walking around 'in the street, in the dark, cold and naked' (C 241). David's torn clothing and eyewitness account of his brief time there confirm to Inés and Simón that the institute, which he claims is 'surrounded by barbed wire', is not the correct place for David, and they refuse to let anyone take him back (C 253).

'DANCING THE UNIVERSE:' *THE SCHOOLDAYS OF JESUS*

In *The Schooldays of Jesus* (2016), the family's search for an education for David continues. Fleeing Punta Arenas and the educational authorities in Novilla, the parents arrive in Estrella. There they ask three elderly and 'childless' sisters (S 22) to help them find a suitable educational environment for David. The sisters suggest that David receive mathematics tutelage from a water engineer señor Robles. The first and only lesson is a disaster when David refuses to accept the tutor's abstract conception of numbers. As with señor Leon, the tutor attributes the child's resistance to learn from him to a 'cognitive deficit.' 'This means', he tells Simón, 'that he is deficient in a certain basic mental capacity, in this case the capacity to classify objects on the basis of similarity' (S 30). Again, and mistakenly, another teacher suggests to his parents that what David needs to be successful at learning is not a teacher but a 'psychologist, preferably one who specializes in cognitive disorders' (S 31). Frustrated, Inés 'cancels the lessons' (S 31), prompting Simón to return to the elderly sisters for educational advice. This time the sisters suggest that the parents consider an alternative schooling system in Estrella operating through Academies: the Academy of Dance, the Academy of Music and the Atom School (S 23).

With the sisters' counsel, the parents choose for David the Academy of Dance whose mission involves 'guiding the souls of our students ... bringing them in accord with the great underlying movement of the universe' (S 68). At first resistant, David becomes enthralled with learning numbers through dance, in part because he is totally enamoured with his teachers, and particularly with Ana Magdalena Arroyo, the wife of the school's director. Not only does David thrive under the Arroyo's attentive, and experimental pedagogy but from them he learns to 'dance the universe' (S 68).

Privileging his own Socratic training, Simón is sceptical of the Arroyo's 'claptrap and mystical rubbish' (S 99) and of dance as a viable form of education. With Inés, he also wonders why the children are not learning basic reading and maths. To try to understand, he asks David to explain the principles of dance. David vehemently refuses: 'Never, because you don't believe in it' (S 103). Frustrated, Simón turns to señor Arroyo for answers to find none offered: 'If we wish to escape the cycle', the teacher tells him, 'perhaps we should be scouring the world not for the true answer but for the true question' (*S* 96). Sensing señor Arroyo's disapproval of his view of what education is to do and be in a life of a child, Simón gives David over to the Academy's training.

However, the principles of the Academy of Dance prove to be unsustainable without the pedagogy of their charismatic woman teacher. When David's Ana Magdalena is brutally murdered at the Academy, the ideals of education of the Academy die with her (*S* 255). While señor Arroyo is the 'great man, a true idealist' and mastermind of the Academy, Ana Magdalena pedagogically delivers 'the hard work' (*S* 54). David's reaction to his beloved teacher's death attests to the significance of her pedagogy, the care and inventiveness by which she fosters knowledge in his impressionable self. Yet the harm Inés witnesses her son experience at the Academy due to his teacher's loss confirms to her that dance teaches David nothing good (*S* 256). Inés withdraws David from another educational situation, finding it is 'high time he commences a normal education' (*S* 257).

LEARNING FROM DAVID: *THE DEATH OF JESUS*

The final novel of the *Jesus* trilogy replays the significance of pedagogy and the story ends tragically with David's abrupt death in *The Death of Jesus* (2019). Afflicted by a mysterious illness shortly after he enters a school for orphans run by 'Educator' Dr. Juan Fabricante (*D* 10), David embarks on his last experience of institutionalized education. To gain access to the football lessons offered at the school, David agrees to reclaim his formative orphan status and 'repudiate' (*D* 20) Simón and Inés. Devastated with David's decision, Simón worries that Dr Fabricante's football lessons will pedagogically turn his gentle child into a 'bully and savage' (*D* 31). Seeing that David is determined to enrol, Simón helplessly lets the child go.

Although he is revealed as a football virtuoso who finds new meaning for his life in sport, David is suddenly stricken with a mysterious illness. Learning is again interrupted, and this time terminally, by an incurable and fatal 'falling sickness' (*D* 56). Unable to play football, David is admitted for observation to hospital (*D* 51).

As death approaches, an education in school, dance or football all fail to give David reasons for his existence. Abandoning all, David seeks out and returns to the primary, maternal, home-grown pedagogy of his very first teacher, Simón. Together they retreat from the world back into the singular parental relation that makes education in the first place possible. Rereading *Don Quixote* together, the child once again asks the formative and ever-pressing existential question haunting him in each of his pedagogical encounters with others: 'Am I going to be recognized?' (*D* 103). Still unable to hear or bear the child's thoughts of mortal existence, Simón falls back upon philosophy and fiction.

> Recognized? Recognized as a hero? Of course. But you will first have to do deeds, the kind of deeds that people will remember you for, and those deeds will have to be good ones. Then someone will have to write a book about you describing your many deeds. That is how it usually happens. That is how Don Quixote was recognized.
>
> (*D* 103)

Somewhat comforted by Simón's response, David still finds his teacher missing the point: 'But who is going to write a book about my deeds? Will you?' (*D* 105). Buried in the question are the child's lifelong worries and experiences of misrecognition and of his unique self. Finally hearing that David's dying wish is to be recognized for who he is, Simón agrees to author the child's story. To this pedagogical pact made between teacher and student, David adds the condition that Simón writes the child's *real* story and not another mistaken version of it and him: 'When you try to understand me, it spoils everything. Do you promise?' (*D* 103–4). The last thing David clings to in the world is the book, *Don Quixote*, given to him by Simón, one David learns to read and reread outside of his formal education: 'My book, croaks the boy' (*D* 127), as his body succumbs to illness.

The final lesson is profoundly a pedagogical returning of the teacher to a child's first questions about (his) existence that Simón can only deliver if he promises to write what the child is really trying to say (*D* 107). After David's death, Simón is left to grapple with his grief, and with all he has learned and failed to learn from the uniqueness of the child David is.

As Coetzee's novels reveal, and in spite of all we are led to believe, our existing educational institutions have little to do with teaching or learning or even children. Without acknowledging the impact of pedagogy in our lives, the gift of intersubjective relation fostering teaching and learning with and from the Other, we have no means, no recourse to be held recognizable and responsible to each other. Without pedagogy of the (m)other, a child has no way to learn to know themselves, to grow into the world. The *Jesus* novels stress the need for exploring alternative models of education, in the face of deforming and punitive, even colonial, styles of teaching that still persist today. At the same time, the novels are a cautionary tale about all forms of education. In Coetzee's story of David and his teachers, we might acknowledge education as a flawed, rather than ideal, dialectical process whereby adult and child guide each other to read, dance, understand numbers, bear witness, and to question the world.

NOTES

1. Coetzee, *Life & Times of Michael K*, 4.
2. Coetzee, *Age of Iron*, 68.
3. Spivak, 'Scenes of Teaching', 17.
4. Barnard, 'Why Not to Teach Coetzee', 32.
5. Ibid.
6. González, 'Plato's Idea of the Teacher Coetzee', n.p.
7. *Schooldays*, 207. Further references to the works of the trilogy, *The Childhood of Jesus*, *Schooldays*, and *The Death of Jesus*, are in text and indicated in parentheses using abbreviations C, S and D, respectively.
8. Elmgren, *Poetics of the Child*, 149.
9. Mishra Tarc, *Pedagogy*, 1–20.
10. Attwell, 'Mother', 381. In his lecture 'Growing up with *The Children's Encyclopedia*', Coetzee credits his mother with initiating his literary education and lifelong love of English literature.
11. Attwell, 'Mother', 382.
12. An evangelical form of Calvinism developed by Abraham Kuyper (1837–1920), theologian and prime minister of the Netherlands (1901–5), was imported into South African public schools via Dutch missionaries. According to Baskell, Kuyper's racial purity slogan 'in isolation lies our strength' was used to establish the Christian National Education system, a key institution of apartheid. Baskell, 'Kuyper and Apartheid: A revisiting', 1280.
13. Curiously, Simón describes 'abstract' as having no relation to the real.

14. The library scene resembles the one Coetzee paints of his own mother who 'acquired' for her sons, 'a 10-volume set of [Arthur Mee's] *The Children's Encyclopedia*, second hand and disposed of by the public library'. See Coetzee, 'Growing up'.
15. Notably Simón's one-on-one 'method' of reading is common to parents teaching their children to read at home, one Vera Coetzee would be familiar with. The closeness of relation required for singular reading lessons cannot be replicated or achieved in institutions of mass schooling.
16. The reference to barbed wire harkens back and perhaps redresses Anna's depositing of Michael in a schooling institution akin to a prison or a concentration camp. Coetzee, *Michael K*, 104.

WORKS CITED

Attwell, David. *J. M. Coetzee and the Life of Writing: Face to Face with Time*. Melbourne: Text Publishing, 2015.
Attwell, David. 'Mother: *Age of Iron*'. *Texas Studies in Literature and Language* 58, no. 4 (2016): 378–91.
Barnard, Rita. 'Prologue: Why Not to Teach Coetzee'. In *Approaches to Teaching Coetzee's Disgrace and Other Works*, edited by Laura Wright, Jane Poyner and Elleke Boehmer, 31–42. New York: Modern Language Association, 2014.
Baskell, P. 'Kuyper and Apartheid: A Revisiting'. *HPT. Theological Studies* 62, no. 4 (2006): 1269–90.
Coetzee, J. M. *Age of Iron*. New York: Penguin, 1990.
Coetzee, J. M. *The Childhood of Jesus*. London: Harvill Secker, 2013.
Coetzee, J. M. *The Death of Jesus*. London: Harvill Secker, 2019.
Coetzee, J. M. *Elizabeth Costello. Eight Lessons*. New York: Vintage, 2004.
Coetzee, J. M. 'Growing up with the Children's Encyclopedia'. Unpublished lecture, 2018. https://www.youtube.com/watch?v=Qo30gEEbgfA.
Coetzee, J. M. *Life & Times of Michael K*. New York: Text Publishing, 1983.
Coetzee, J. M. *Lives of Animals. Tanner Lectures on Human Values*. Princeton, NJ: Princeton University Press, 1999.
Coetzee, J. M. 'The Novel Today'. *Upstream* 6, no. 1 (1988): 2–5.
Coetzee, J. M. 'On Men in Education'. *Mail and Guardian*, 10 December 2012. http://mg.co.za/article/2012-12-10-jm-coetzee-on-men-in-education.
Coetzee, J. M. *The Schooldays of Jesus*. London: Harvill Secker, 2016.
Coetzee, J. M. *Summertime*. New York: Penguin, 2010.
Elmgren, Charlotta. *JM Coetzee's Poetics of the Child: Arendt, Agamben, and the (ir)Responsibilities of Literary Creation*. London: Bloomsbury Publishing, 2020.
González, P. 'Plato's Idea of the Teacher'. *The University Bookman*, 2013. https://kirkcenter.org/essays/platos-idea-of-the-teacher/.
Mishra Tarc, Aparna. *Pedagogy in the Novels of J. M. Coetzee: The Affect of Literature*. New York: Routledge, 2020.
Plato. "*The Republic of Plato*". New York: Basic Books, 1991.
Spivak, Gayatri Chakravorty. 'Ethics and Politics in Tagore, Coetzee, and Certain Scenes of Teaching'. *diacritics* 32, no. 3/4 (2002): 17–31.

PART SIX

Contexts, Intertexts, Influence

CHAPTER TWENTY-SIX

Coetzee and the history of the novel

ANDREW DEAN

J. M. Coetzee is profoundly engaged with the history of the novel as a form, and his fiction bears the marks of an author self-consciously assessing what he is inheriting. This chapter will investigate key moments in Coetzee's theoretical engagement with the novel, understanding them as attempts to think through the limits and capacities of the form. Specifically, in the three sections that follow, I address the history of the novel in South Africa, the problem of endings and the materiality of writing. I show that at stake in each of these encounters are issues central to literary thought: politics, aesthetics and value.

Coetzee spent his twenties trying to break open the inner lives of novels. As a master's student at the University of Cape Town, he wrote a thesis on the work of Ford Madox Ford. In *Youth* (2002), he records the disillusionment he felt as he laboured over Ford's corpus. He even considered writing a report on 'what a let-down his subject had been, how disappointed he is in his hero'.[1] As a doctoral student at the University of Texas at Austin, he used statistical methods in his research on the works of Samuel Beckett. His conclusion at this time was that the statistical analysis of style could not access the intimate workings of the fictions themselves. 'Stylostatistics', Coetzee wrote, might end up measuring 'an aspect of our response rather than an aspect of the text'.[2]

Coetzee's early critical writing records the unusual ambitions he had as a scholar. It is as though he wanted to understand the deeper secrets of novels themselves; as though the works required a kind of attention and animation not supplied by critical methods. In these two very different academic projects, it was confronting the novels themselves that spurred his scholarship on. Perhaps Coetzee's interest, as he later observed to David Attwell, was more in 'the aesthetics of the *mot juste*' than in the ethical or moral terrain commonly associated with literary criticism as it was institutionalized in universities.[3]

Over the course of his career, Coetzee has written a great deal about the novel as a form. In published academic criticism, reviews and other non-fiction, he has drawn on everything from *Don Quixote* (1605–15) to Desiderius Erasmus, to modernist fiction and beyond.[4] As a result, undertaking scholarship on Coetzee can appear to require a forbidding range of reference. *The Master of Petersburg* (1994), for example, is deeply engaged with questions of perversion and eschatology in Fyodor Dostoevsky's *oeuvre*. *Life & Times of Michael K* (1983) draws on the work of Heinrich von Kleist.[5] *Age of Iron* (1990) is engaged with the tradition of epistolary novels like Samuel Richardson's *Clarissa* (1748).[6] *Foe* (1986) not only rewrites Daniel Defoe's *Robinson Crusoe* (1719) and *Roxana* (1724), but includes unannounced materials from Dostoevsky.[7] The

Jesus trilogy (2013–19), meanwhile, features an encounter with *Don Quixote* and characters who recall *The Brothers Karamazov* (1880), namely 'Aloysha' and an accused murderer named 'Dmitri'.[8]

Coetzee's fiction thinks through problems and opportunities presented by the history of the novel. I argue that this process in turn opens up the venturesome registers of thought and modes of encounter that distinguish Coetzee's most powerful fictions – and that these present new ways of conceptualizing the potential value of fiction in our lives. To focus this potentially vast topic, I survey three issues Coetzee has faced in his writing, exploring how he thinks through the history of the novel in order to address them. The first is political: how can a South African novelist undertake their task given the role that the novel has played in the colonial possession of South Africa? The second is aesthetic: how can a self-doubting novel come to an end? The third is material: how does a writer handle the legacies, in all its senses, of writing novels? The scale of Coetzee's career-wide engagements with the history of the novel means that I will only address a few examples from his *oeuvre*. Nevertheless, the outlines of the wider story of Coetzee's fiction will come into view: in the first section ('The Farm'), his thinking about the novel in South Africa; in the second section ('Endings'), his relationships with the early English novel and nineteenth-century Russian fiction; and in the third section ('Beginnings'), his handling of the legacies of modernism.

THE FARM

Coetzee's 1988 volume of literary criticism, *White Writing*, is animated by two primary interests: 'the great intellectual schemas, through which South Africa has been thought by Europe' and 'the land itself, South Africa as landscape and landed property'.[9] According to Coetzee, these 'intellectual schemas' are laid over the land, which in the process is turned into a colonial possession. The later phase of expropriation – Afrikaner nationalism from 1948 – is outside the scope of *White Writing*, even if the implications of Coetzee's argument are that fiction of this nature helped to lay the imaginative groundwork for what came later.

The literary genre of the *plaasroman* is of special interest to Coetzee. This distinctive mode of Afrikaans writing, in Coetzee's words, is a kind of colonial pastoral that 'concerned itself almost exclusively with the farm and *platteland* (rural) society'.[10] He argues that the form is ultimately nostalgic and conservative, 'hold[ing] up the time of the forefathers as an exemplary age when the garden of myth became actualized in history'.[11] It is stalked by the spectre of idleness, which would invalidate racial hierarchies and claims to rightful control of the land. The 'pastoral in South Africa therefore has a double tribute to pay', he writes. 'To satisfy the critics of rural retreat, it must portray labour; to satisfy critics of colonialism, it must portray white labour.'[12] Black labour is made invisible, along with the fact of expropriation that saw the 'pastoral home' of the black labourers 'only a generation or two ago' become the 'property of its [colonial] occupiers *by right*'.[13]

Outside of literary scholarship, Coetzee has spoken baldly about how South Africa has been written. In his acceptance speech for the Jerusalem Prize in 1987, he suggested that 'South African literature is a literature in bondage' and had become monstrous as a result. 'It is a less than fully human literature, unnaturally preoccupied with power and the torsions of power, unable to move from elementary relations of contestation, domination, and subjugation to the vast and complex human world that lies beyond them.'[14] This limited thematic and affective range makes South Africa's literature, in his words, written as if 'from a prison', as it is unable to lay claim to the deeper kinds of freedom involved in literary experiences. He concluded the speech by describing how

Cervantes and his character Don Quixote seek to shift 'from our world of violent phantasms to a true living world'.[15] While at the novel's end Quixote may give up his 'realm of faery' to the brute finitude of a life, Cervantes's 'subtle and enigmatic book' does not.[16] In this moment it is not that Coetzee imagines that the writer may be free to create art that will right the course of history, but rather, in a more deflated sense, that such a writer can at least write through consolation.

Coetzee's earliest fictions seek to clear a space from which to speak about South Africa. They are, in a way, metafictions about genres of colonial writing. The longer of the two stories in *Dusklands* (1974), 'The Narrative of Jacobus Coetzee', recreates the reception of a colonial travelogue. Coetzee's second novel, *In the Heart of the Country* (1977), is recognizably in the tradition of the *plaasroman*. In its 266 numbered sections, Magda narrates a series of events and fantasies or nightmares of her life on the farm. The combined effect of these events is to adduce what Zimbler calls a 'manichean reality', a structure that sits at the heart of the book's thinking.[17] Perhaps the most disturbing section of the novel deals with Hendrik's apparent rape of Magda. It takes place in different registers and locations across at least three numbered sections, each of which compounds into a newly gruelling literary experience.

In the Heart of the Country appears to draw from a limited supply of fictive possibilities. This is true even at the level of lexical choice. Certain words become notable in their repetition: '*desert, stony, stone, stone desert, flats, dry, dust, dusty, dull, dark, black, bush, pebble, green, grey, insect, tedium, monotony, loneliness, solitude, vacuum*'.[18] Through these seemingly standardized shifters, the narrative registers the extent to which Magda, rather than being a unique and self-sufficient character, is instead drawn from the history of literary expression in South Africa (and language in general). She has some understanding of this: 'I signify something', she writes, 'I do not know what'.[19] She asks soon afterward: 'Is it possible that I am a prisoner not of the lonely farmhouse and the stone desert but of my stony monologue?'[20] The technology of realist narration has stalled, becoming arbitrary, or at least is not fully realized. The second of the three consecutive accounts of Magda's father's interactions with Hendrik's wife begins: 'Or: As Klein-Anna makes her way homeward [...].'[21] There is a decided thinness to this way of speaking: the 'or' suggests that she is being made up out of interchangeable components.

The novel is structured according to what Coetzee later called in that Jerusalem Prize address, 'elementary relations of contestation, domination, and subjugation'. Magda reflects on the failure of communication itself:

> The language that should pass between myself and these people was subverted by my father and cannot be recovered. What passes between us now is parody. I was born into a language of hierarchy, of distance and perspective. It was my father-tongue.[22]

The possibility of undoing the voice of the father is fundamental to the novel (there might be 'a language lovers speak', Magda thinks).[23] Yet inhibiting the emergence of such a language is the asymmetry of colonial life, the profound harms that the colonial scene has done to human relations. Hegel's master-slave dialectic unexpectedly turns up here, falling out of the sky and into Magda's thoughts in the novel:

> *It is the slave's consciousness that constitutes the master's certainty of his own truth. But the slave's consciousness is a dependent consciousness. So the master is not sure of the truth of his autonomy. His truth lies in an inessential consciousness and its inessential acts.*[24]

The novel is concerned with showing how Magda's consciousness, caught in the grips of a Manichean struggle that extends to language itself, becomes a pathological interior world. Writing from a prison, the hope for a more humane future seems to rest on those strange airmen, who may be able to break Magda out of the prison of her own making. Magda, though, is left wondering why 'no one will speak to me in the true language of the heart'. She never gets her wish to be 'neither master nor slave, neither parent nor child' (*IHC* 145). Instead, she follows her destiny, which is to die 'in the petrified garden, behind locked gates, near my father's bones'.[25]

ENDINGS

In the final interview of *Doubling the Point* (1992), Coetzee reflected on his life to that point, dividing it into two parts. The first, in which he refers to himself as 'he', was his life as a young man – leaving South Africa and making his way as an academic. The second, in which he refers to himself as 'I', starts with his 'essay on confession' – this was 'the beginning of a more broadly philosophical engagement with a situation in the world'.[26] The essay that Coetzee is referring to is 'Confession and Double Thoughts: Tolstoy, Rousseau, Dostoevsky', which was submitted for publication in early 1983, around the same time that he sent the final typescript for *Life & Times of Michael K* to his publisher.

On the face of it, 'Confession and Double Thoughts' – which concerns specific literary strategies for handling confession – is an unusual text to mark such a decisive break in Coetzee's life. Yet it responded to profound issues in his understanding of the value of his own fiction. The central moment in the essay comes in his analysis of an episode of confession in Dostoevsky's *Devils* (1871–2). Coetzee wonders what may be required to achieve true self-forgiveness. Self-deception, he thinks, can mislead one into believing one has experienced grace. In Dostoevsky, 'the self cannot tell the truth of itself to itself and come to rest without the possibility of self-deception'. As we see in *Devils*, it is neither the 'sterile monologue of the self' nor 'the dialogue of the self with its own self-doubt' that makes 'true confession' possible. Rather, it is 'faith and grace'.[27]

Given the weight that Coetzee put on this essay in *Doubling the Point*, it is no surprise that it has been discussed extensively in the critical literature. The essay's focus might be a little unexpected, however, preoccupied as it is with the seemingly mechanical issue of endings. As Coetzee writes in the essay, he is interested in 'how the problem of *ending* is solved when the tendency of self-consciousness is to draw out confession endlessly'.[28] When Attwell asked Coetzee about confession and self-consciousness, he opted to 'translate' the question 'into practical terms': 'It becomes a question about closure'; 'How does a novel that is as much an interrogation of authority as *Foe* is find an end for itself?'[29] The kinds of endings that have been tried before, such as the postscript that concludes Dostoevsky's *Notes from Underground* (1864), Coetzee thinks to be dissatisfying. He wants 'an ending, not a gesture toward an ending'.[30]

The question of coming to an end clearly has political stakes, too. Coetzee said of the last few pages of *Foe* (1986) that they 'close the text by force, so to speak: they confront head-on the endlessness of [the novel's] skepticism'.[31] This skepticism has been partly the consequence of the quarrelling of two of the novel's main characters, Susan Barton and Foe, who each wish to put to use the mute character of Friday (drawn from *Robinson Crusoe*). The problem is repeatedly surveyed: who may tell the story of Friday, one that he cannot tell? How might that story be fairly told? In turn, how does the novel adjudicate between deepening incommensurabilities?

The ending of *Foe*, which drastically changes genre, has been interpreted in almost diametrically opposed terms. Where Gayatri Spivak imagined that the novel stages the 'full range' of the 'impossible position' of the white writer in South Africa,[32] more recent commentators, like Patrick Hayes, find that its ending engages a 'different form of literary knowing'.[33] Derived from Michael Holquist's account of Dostoevsky, Hayes argues that marginality is not able to be united as 'friends', but instead kept 'in a productive tension' – a less rapturous, and much more vexed, position.[34] The ending of the novel, I suggest, is more central to its political thinking than is generally true of most fictions, as the novel calls to a halt the loops of self-scrutiny that mark its first three chapters.

Life & Times of Michael K is similarly concerned with the problem of how to bring to an end a novel that traverses a range of different political thoughts. The problem that Coetzee faced throughout drafting the novel was how to account for K's position in relation to the political situation – both in the novel and in South Africa at the time. As I have shown elsewhere, Coetzee was scrutinizing how a reader would fit his novel into established political positions, especially as these positions pertained to apartheid.[35] The meaning he derived from the book as it then stood was a facile, liberal one (war is bad). According to this line of self-critique, he should have been brave enough to have K join the rebels to fight against the representatives of the repressive state.

The conclusion of *Michael K* as it was eventually written subtly manages shifts in tone and voice such that reading in schematic political terms becomes difficult. In place of such a reading emerges a deeply felt series of unusual and even comic passages, ones which sponsor no particular political position, but imagine a life beyond the political moment. The novel jokes with the reader about what we may expect:

(Is that the moral of it all, he thought, the moral of the whole story: that there is time enough for everything? Is that how morals come, unbidden, in the course of events, when you least expect them?)[36]

As a 'moral', this would not be a particularly good one – life on the farm, where there is time enough for everything. Yet the second sentence is crucial: had we not thought that meaning would come in the course of events? Is that not one of the pleasures of reading?

In a way that is difficult to account for, the novel ends up moving independently of K, who resists even the progress of a narrative that has only ever partially managed to contain him. 'And if the old man climbed out of the cart and stretched himself (things were gathering pace now) and looked at where the pump had been [...].'[37] The parenthetical insertion '(things were gathering pace now)' is truer of the novel than it is of K's situation. Where K will end up as the novel draws to its conclusion is in fact where he started: with a spoon in his mouth, enigmatically escaping our desire to insert him into some story about his meaning. 'In that way, he would say, one can live.'[38] K and the novel seem to part ways in work's final moments. In place of either political criticism or inapt endings, Coetzee develops an ending that cycles between restarting – learning how to live – and a comically hopeful, but already deflated, set of thoughts about an alternative life. He hoped that that life, unavailable though it may be, would be beyond the torsions of power.

BEGINNINGS

In a short reflection on his time as a doctoral student at the University of Texas at Austin in the 1960s, Coetzee recalled searching through the 'manuscript collection of the library'.[39] He was describing visits to what would later become the Harry Ransom Center, now one of the world's most important modern literary manuscript libraries. Its holdings were impressive even in its infancy, when he sought out 'the exercise books in which Samuel Beckett had written *Watt* on a farm in the south of France, hiding out from the Germans'. He reports that he 'spent weeks perusing [the notebooks], pondering the sketches and the numbers and doodles in the margins'.[40] Later, in the 1990s, Coetzee visited the Lilly Library at Indiana University to consult Nadine Gordimer's 'notebooks from the 1950s', which include 'reflections on reading Sartre, Camus, Merleau-Ponty and others on violence'.[41] What he found at the Lilly Library would eventually contribute to the lectures that comprised *The Lives of Animals* (1997) and *Elizabeth Costello* (2003).

The significance of what Jan Wilm has called 'archival dynamics' can be felt across Coetzee's work.[42] As Wilm points out, there are any number of examples of Coetzee engaging with 'archives of all sorts', including 'letters, diaries, manuscripts, [and] books'. In *Waiting for the Barbarians* (1980), there are even 'wooden slips on which are painted characters in a script [the Magistrate] has not seen the like of'.[43] The two stories of *Dusklands* are both explicitly drawn from research environments – the archive of South African travelogues in the case of 'The Narrative of Jacobus Coetzee', and the 'Harry S. Truman library', where Eugene Dawn writes in the 'The Vietnam Project'.[44] In *Foe*, the unnamed narrator who emerges in the final chapter opens a 'dispatch box with brass hinges and a clasp' and discovers fragile, yellowed paper on which is written the opening lines of the novel.[45]

There is agonism and disappointment in Coetzee's writing about scenes of writing – both others' and his own. He writes that he was 'disconcerted' by the 'flippancies' in Beckett's manuscripts.[46] In the fiction and *autre*biographies, the overwhelming presence of a writer at the level of the page often obstructs the creative process. In *Dusklands*, the obstructive author is Coetzee himself ('there remains the matter of getting past Coetzee').[47] The disenchantment that pervades *Youth* culminates with the author being unable to confront the page: 'He cannot begin writing until the moment is right, and no matter how scrupulously he prepares himself, wiping the table clean, positioning the lamp, ruling a margin down the side of the blank page, sitting with his eyes shut, emptying his mind in readiness – in spite of all this, the words will not come to him.'[48] In the event, he avoids writing altogether, unlike those authors who bravely 'pulled themselves together and wrote as best they could what had to be written'.[49]

Reading for the materiality of writing in Coetzee's work connects him with the history of the novel, with his sense of himself as a writer within a literary canon. There is ample room here to think in terms of what Harold Bloom described as an 'anxiety of influence', the Oedipal struggle that 'strong poets' undertake against earlier ones to create an 'imaginative space' for new writing.[50] Certainly, active contest is part of how Coetzee responded to the legacies of earlier writing. This is often dramatized in his novels and *autre*biographies, but nowhere more so than in *Foe*, where Susan Barton pleads with the Defoe character, 'Foe', to write the story in a more appealing way. The contest over writing is central to the book as a whole, as different ways of conceptualizing the value of literature and different claims on the capacity to tell stories are the source of seemingly unending quarrels. On one reading at least, overcoming Beckett was part of the process that Coetzee undertook to find a place from which he could begin.

Certainly, the materiality of writing in Coetzee's biographical life and in his fiction is a testament to the unusual significance of intertextuality for understanding his work. Hayes has described how Coetzee's fiction handles the complex notion of intertextuality, noting the different ways he draws on writers such as Beckett and Dostoevsky to think through moral and imaginative issues central to fiction – and in a way that moves beyond the philosophical registers that are ordinarily used to address such issues.[51] We might productively think of Coetzee's dramatizations of the author encountering the literary manuscript, and the displacements necessary to write, as particularly pressurized explorations of intertextuality.

In the closing pages of *The Master of Petersburg*, the Dostoevsky character confronts the travesties that motivate his writing. '*Perversion*', he thinks, unpacking his writing case, 'everything and everyone to be turned to another use, to be gripped to him and fall with him'.[52] He realizes that his writing may 'take children into dark places'.[53] When he does begin to write, what comes out channels the scarcely named paedophilic fantasies and desires that have hovered throughout the novel. Writing in his dead stepson's diary, he has a narrator make love to a 'girl', with the knowledge that the door is 'open a crack, and the child watching'. 'The pleasure is acute', Dostoevsky writes, 'it communicates itself to the girl'.[54] As Hayes suggests, moments such as these explore 'unruliness, and the elements of risk involved in taking literary writing seriously'.[55] Dostoevsky imagines his task to be to 'follow the dance of the pen'.[56] Coetzee in such moments faces the risk, pleasure and danger of writing at all – writing into a social world, writing into a living canon and writing when one cannot truly know oneself.

The history of the novel is alive in J. M. Coetzee's writing. The depth of his engagement with the form, I have suggested, is central to the distinctive scrupulousness of his work, the sense that he is working through literary concerns to their fullest possible extents. We have seen a few instances of this: the *plaasroman*, the problem of ending and what it means to follow in other writers' pen strokes. Yet it is the active nature of Coetzee's reception of the history of the novel that I wish to highlight in closing. For Coetzee, the novel is of far more than antiquarian interest. Rather, fiction and its histories are alive, enduring as imaginative monuments which we receive in our creative endeavours whether we like it or not. It is a mode of encounter that gives literature a new existence, from *Don Quixote* to Dostoevsky, Kafka to Kleist.

Perhaps it is no surprise that Coetzee supplies his own way of accounting for the presence of literary history in his own fictions. In 'What Is a Classic', he recalls one Sunday afternoon in the suburbs of Cape Town as a teenager, when he heard the music of J. S. Bach floating across the garden fence. 'As long as the music lasted, I was frozen, I dared not breathe. I was being spoken to by the music as music had never spoken to me before.' He asks of this experience: '[C]an I say that the spirit of Bach was speaking to me across the ages, across the seas, putting before me certain ideals?' Or was it that he was 'symbolically electing high European culture'?[57]

The answer is not so much one or the other, he argues through the rest of the essay, but hopefully something rather different, which relates to the classic. A classic is created by 'the process of testing' that takes place in a work's reception, as it is scrutinized in multifarious different ways to see what might survive, what it may still be able to say.[58] How might Bach sound for German nationalists? Or after the Second World War? In Coetzee's handling, powerful works generate their own interrogations over time – interrogations that ensure the continued vital existence of creative arts in our imaginative lives.

NOTES

1. Coetzee, *Youth*, 112.
2. Coetzee, 'The English Fiction of Samuel Beckett: An Essay in Stylistic Analysis', 159.
3. Coetzee, *Doubling the Point*, 20.
4. See Coetzee's essay, 'Erasmus: Madness and Rivalry', in *Giving Offense*, 83–103. For scholarship on Coetzee's relationship with Beckett, see Hayes, *J. M. Coetzee and the Novel*, esp. 33–71. For a general consideration of Coetzee, modernism and allegory, see Attridge, *J. M. Coetzee and the Ethics of Reading*, esp. 1–31.
5. For details of how Coetzee read Kleist, see Attwell, *J. M. Coetzee and the Life of Writing*, 129–47. See also Olivier, 'The Dertigers and the Plaasroman'.
6. For a discussion of *Age of Iron* and the epistolary novel, see Hayes, *J. M. Coetzee and the Novel*, 130–64.
7. For a discussion of the novel and Dostoevsky, see Hayes, 106–29. For a discussion of the eighteenth-century novel and canonicity, see Attridge, *J. M. Coetzee and the Ethics of Reading*, 65–90.
8. For a discussion of Coetzee's recent *Jesus* trilogy and its relationship with, for example, Cervantes and Plato, see Davies, 'Growing Up Against Allegory'.
9. J. M. Coetzee, *White Writing*, 10. For discussions of Coetzee's handling of the *plaasroman*, see Attwell, *J. M. Coetzee and the Life of Writing*, 64–78; Zimbler, *J. M. Coetzee and the Poetics of Style*, 56–86 (especially 56–64). For a more general discussion of the *plaasroman*, see Olivier, 'The Dertigers and the Plaasroman'.
10. Coetzee, *White Writing*, 63.
11. Ibid., 5.
12. Ibid., 4.
13. Ibid., 5.
14. Coetzee, *Doubling the Point*, 98.
15. Ibid.
16. Ibid., 98–9.
17. Zimbler, *J. M. Coetzee and the Politics of Style*, 86.
18. Ibid., 72–3.
19. Coetzee, *In the Heart of the Country*, 10.
20. Ibid., 22.
21. Ibid., 36.
22. Ibid., 106.
23. Ibid.
24. Ibid., 141.
25. Ibid.
26. Coetzee, *Doubling the Point*, 394.
27. Ibid., 291.
28. Ibid., 275.
29. Ibid., 247.
30. Ibid., 248.
31. Ibid.
32. Spivak, 'Theory in the Margin', 19.

33. Hayes, *J. M. Coetzee and the Novel*, 114.
34. Ibid., 128.
35. See Dean, '"Why Will He Not Join the Guerillas?": J. M. Coetzee's *Life & Times of Michael K* and the Politics of the Postcolonial Novel'.
36. Coetzee, *Life & Times of Michael K*, 183.
37. Ibid., 183.
38. Ibid., 184.
39. Coetzee, *Doubling the Point*, 51.
40. Ibid.
41. Attwell, *J. M. Coetzee & the Life of Writing*, 217.
42. Jan Wilm, 'The J. M. Coetzee Archive and the Archive in J. M. Coetzee', 225.
43. Ibid., 228.
44. Coetzee, *Dusklands*, 5.
45. Coetzee, *Foe*, 155.
46. Coetzee, *Doubling the Point*, 51.
47. Coetzee, *Dusklands*, 15.
48. Coetzee, *Youth*, 166.
49. Ibid., 167.
50. Bloom, *The Anxiety of Influence*, 5.
51. Hayes, 'Influence and Intertextuality', 152–67.
52. Coetzee, *The Master of Petersburg*, 235.
53. Ibid., 236.
54. Ibid., 244.
55. Hayes, 'Influence and Intertextuality', 166.
56. Coetzee, *The Master of Petersburg*, 236.
57. Coetzee, *Stranger Shores*, 9.
58. Ibid., 16.

WORKS CITED

Attridge, Derek. *J. M. Coetzee and the Ethics of Reading: Literature in the Event*. Chicago: Chicago University Press, 2004.

Attwell, David. *J. M. Coetzee & the Life of Writing: Face to Face with Time*. Oxford: Oxford University Press, 2015.

Bloom, Harold. *The Anxiety of Influence: A Theory of Poetry*. New York: Oxford University Press, 1973.

Coetzee, J. M. *Doubling the Point: Essays and Interviews*, edited by David Attwell. Cambridge, MA: Harvard University Press, 1992.

Coetzee, J. M. *Dusklands*. London: Vintage, 2004.

Coetzee, J. M. 'The English Fiction of Samuel Beckett: An Essay in Stylistic Analysis'. PhD dissertation, University of Texas at Austin, 1969.

Coetzee, J. M. *Foe*. London: Secker & Warburg, 1986.

Coetzee, J. M. *Giving Offense: Essays on Censorship*. Chicago: University of Chicago Press, 1996.

Coetzee, J. M. *In the Heart of the Country*. London: Vintage, 2004.

Coetzee, J. M. *Life & Times of Michael K*. London: Secker & Warburg, 1983.

Coetzee, J. M. *The Master of Petersburg*. London: Vintage, 2004.
Coetzee, J. M. Notebook, *Life & Times of Michael K*, 1979–82. Box 33, folder 5. The J. M. Coetzee Papers, Harry Ransom Center, University of Texas, Austin.
Coetzee, J. M. *Stranger Shores: Literary Essays, 1986–1999*. New York: Viking, 2001.
Coetzee, J. M. *White Writing: On the Culture of Letters in South Africa*. New Haven: Yale University Press, 1988.
Coetzee, J. M. *Youth*. London: Vintage, 2003.
Davies, Benjamin R. 'Growing Up against Allegory: The Late Works of J. M. Coetzee'. *Novel* 53, no. 3 (2020): 419–35.
Dean, Andrew. '"Why Will He Not Join the Guerrillas?": J. M. Coetzee's *Life & Times of Michael K* and the Politics of the Postcolonial Novel'. *MFS: Modern Fiction Studies* 65, no. 4 (2019): 676–99.
Hayes, Patrick. 'Influence and Intertextuality'. In *The Cambridge Companion to J. M. Coetzee*, edited by Jarad Zimbler, 152–67. Cambridge: Cambridge University Press, 2020.
Hayes, Patrick. *J. M. Coetzee and the Novel: Writing and Politics after Beckett*. Oxford: Oxford University Press, 2010.
Olivier, Gerrit. 'The Dertigers and the Plaasroman: Two Brief Perspectives on Afrikaans Literature'. In *The Cambridge History of South African Literature*, edited by David Attwell and Derek Attridge, 308–24 Cambridge: Cambridge University Press, 2012.
Spivak, Gayatri Chakravorty. 'Theory in the Margin: Coetzee's *Foe* Reading Defoe's "Crusoe/Roxana"'. *English in Africa* 17, no. 2 (1990): 1–23.
Wilm, Jan. 'The J. M. Coetzee Archive and the Archive in J. M. Coetzee'. In *Beyond the Ancient Quarrel: Literature, Philosophy, and J. M. Coetzee*, edited by Jan Wilm and Patrick Hayes, 215–31. Oxford: Oxford University Press, 2017.
Zimbler, Jarad. *J. M. Coetzee and the Politics of Style*. Cambridge: Cambridge University Press, 2014.

CHAPTER TWENTY-SEVEN

Coetzee's South Africans

JAN STEYN

J. M. Coetzee's work has situated itself within – and helped define – a South African literary tradition, yet Coetzee is more frequently associated with Samuel Beckett than with Olive Schreiner, with Dostoevsky than with Laurens van der Post. His works are more often noted for being Kafkaesque than for being Patonesque. He has avowed his foreign influences with a relative explicitness, laying claim (including directly in his fiction) to a literary heritage that includes Augustine, Rousseau, Defoe, Conrad, Joyce and Eliot, while his fellow South Africans have been afforded a quieter role and are often mentioned only in his critical writings. The South African writers discussed in this chapter are not simply a national subset of Coetzee's literary influences, however. As against the freedom represented by Coetzee's elective affinities with writers in the canons of world literature, Coetzee's South Africans often represent an obligation or constraint – they are those antecedents and peers to whom he *must* respond, and who are themselves responding to a shared history and landscape, albeit from varied perspectives and with diverse purposes.

FOREBEARS

South African influences are discernible in Coetzee's literary oeuvre from *Dusklands* (1974) to *Summertime* (2009), and even in the *Jesus* trilogy of the 2010s, but the author's engagement with the South African writers of earlier generations is most explicit in his teaching and nonfiction, particularly his academic monograph, *White Writing* (1988). Coetzee's introduction is careful not to overstate the book's reach, pointing out that it does not address more recent South African writing, and that even when accounting for these restrictions,

> they do not constitute a history of white writing, nor even the outline of such a history. Nor does the phrase *white writing* imply a body of writing different in nature from black writing. White writing is white only insofar as it is generated by the concerns of people no longer European, not yet African.[1]

These white writers – from the early explorers, missionaries and naturalists documenting the Cape Colony; to white landscape poets beginning with Thomas Pringle in the early nineteenth century and ending with Sydney Clouts in the mid-twentieth; to the differently problematic anglophone accounts of settler life in work by Schreiner, Pauline Smith, Alan Paton and Sarah Gertrude Millin; to the Afrikaans tradition of the farm novel (*plaasroman*) with C. M. van den Heever and Mikro as privileged exemplars – are remarkably diverse, notably representing two distinct languages and literary cultures. By discussing these together, Coetzee is arguing implicitly for a common problem of whiteness, a settler predicament shared by all writers, 'no longer European, not yet African', faced with South Africa's landscape and history.

Coetzee is unsparingly critical of, though rarely entirely unsympathetic to, these white writers and their aesthetic strategies. Millin's outright racism, Paton's denial of coeval status to his Zulu characters, Mikro's projection of racial and class hegemony into his Coloured subjects' thoughts and words, Schreiner's and Smith's effacement of Black farm labour, the tendency Van den Heever has to conflate farm and nature, all are objects of Coetzee's censure. But this is criticism of an especially interesting kind when considered alongside Coetzee's own writing, for, at least in those instances when his fiction deals with South African material or settings, Coetzee too is operating in this fraught field of 'white writing'. For example, an argument can be made that Coetzee's relatively stark, unmarked, deliberately delocalized style has at least something to do with avoiding the pitfalls he describes in his chapter on 'Simple Language, Simple People'. He sees Smith, Paton and Mikro make ethically and aesthetically unwise choices when giving voice to characters from a different race or culture.[2] And when Coetzee writes South African rural settings in the South African section of *Dusklands* or *In the Heart of the Country* (1977), *Life & Times of Michael K* (1983), *Boyhood* (1997), *Disgrace* (1999) and *Summertime* (2009), he is inevitably writing in reference to and often against the strategies of the *plaasroman* novelists and South African landscape poets.

Given his never-entirely-escapable position as white writer from South Africa, it follows that there are major figures in the national canon important to Coetzee's literary trajectory even when they appear as models to be studiously avoided rather than imitated. For a South African writer whom Coetzee does admire, however, one need look no further than Olive Schreiner, and specifically her most celebrated (though certainly not *only* noteworthy) work, *The Story of an African Farm* (1883).

Schreiner is a trailblazer for Coetzee in engaging the problem of how to depict South African people and landscape. Consider this oft-cited passage in Schreiner's preface to her novel's second edition:

> It has been suggested by a kind critic that he would better have liked the little book if it had been a history of wild adventure; of cattle driven into inaccessible kranzes by Bushmen; "of encounters with ravening lions, and hair-breadth escapes." This could not be. Such works are best written in Piccadilly or in the Strand: there the gifts of the creative imagination, untrammelled by contact with any fact, may spread their wings.[3]

Andrew van der Vlies points out that there is a commonality between Schreiner's refusal to adjust her fiction to metropolitan expectations and the program Coetzee lays out for South African writers in his 1981 acceptance speech for the CNA Prize (awarded to *Waiting for the Barbarians*): 'learn to dismiss the cries from metropolitan critics for, let us say, an "authentically South African" art which does not "ape European or American models" but "finds its own roots". Demands of this kind come out of a naive, idle, and typically metropolitan yearning for the exotic'.[4] Like Schreiner's, Coetzee's fiction refuses readymade exotic tropes – there are no 'cattle driven into inaccessible' ravines in Coetzee's novels either. But this is not to say that what Coetzee learns from Schreiner is a version of ethnographic realism. He is very clear in *White Writing* that Schreiner 'does not take on the task of comprehensively representing a South African sheepfarm', that her novel is rather best read as 'a figure in the service of her critique of colonial culture'.[5]

While Schreiner's relative disinterest in some of the fine-grained realities of the farm that is her setting is certainly a limitation, it is also a strength. Unlike the Afrikaans *plaasroman* tradition that follows Schreiner, she has no real attachment to the farm as a sacred locus for social identity. She avoids metropolitan exoticism and local sentimentalism alike. Coetzee, by comparison, is more drawn to the romance of the farm's claim upon his identity. In *Boyhood*, for instance, he writes of the Coetzee family farm, Voëlfontein:

> The secret and sacred word that binds him to the farm is belong. Out in the veld by himself he can breathe the word aloud: I belong on the farm. What he really believes but does not utter, what he keeps to himself for fear that the spell will end, is a different form of the word: I belong to the farm.[6]

This reversal of belonging – 'I belong to the farm' rather than 'the farm belongs to me' – is a familiar ethical move in both settler colonial discourses and in religious or ecocritical ones. In Coetzee's case, and especially in the concluding volume of the *Scenes from Provincial Life* trilogy, *Summertime*, the claims of belonging triggered by the locus classicus of (South African) white writing, the farm, go further. But it is worth noting that Schreiner's bracketing out of these attachments to the farm (as opposed to, say, Waldo's veneration of the land) allows for different claims and dynamics to surface.

There is something very appealing to Coetzee in the layers of temporality he finds in Schreiner's *The Story of an African Farm*: the first a chronography that spans 'prehistory to a posthistory after man' whereby 'lifespans of individuals and even of peoples constitute negligible intervals'; the second a 'scale of nonhuman time and distance on the farm too, by whose measure the plants and insects of the Karoo live'.[7] While Coetzee might find these temporal frames insufficient in capturing the social complexity (especially in as far as race and labour figure on Voëlfontein in his *autre*biographical writings and in the lives lived on the farms and smallholdings that appear in his fictions), they are nonetheless indispensable aspects. Take, for example, *In the Heart of the Country*, where Magda's fascination with her surrounds runs from the human and historical time through to vaster timescales experienced by fauna, flora and even rocks: 'Fascinating, this colonial history: I wonder whether a speculative history is possible, as a speculative philosophy, a speculative theology, and now, it would appear, a speculative entomology are possible, all sucked out of my thumb, to say nothing of the geography of the stone desert'.[8] Unlike his 'doubling' practice with characters such as David Lurie, Elizabeth Costello, *Diary of a Bad Year's* J.C. or the John Coetzee who appears in *Scenes from Provincial Life*, Coetzee maintains authorial distance from Magda, who, like *Duskland*'s Eugene Dawn or *Slow Man*'s Paul Rayment, can only sometimes be taken valuably as his representative. Nonetheless, in this instance, her fascination and his own track closely, and the (quasi-)spiritual appeal of the Karoo that is exemplified in Schreiner's work by Waldo is not entirely alien to Coetzee's work. Consider a passage such as the following from Schreiner's novel:

> To live on so, calmly, far from the paths of men; and to look at the lives of clouds and insects; to look deep into the heart of flowers, and see how lovingly the pistil and the stamens nestle there together; and to see in the thorn-pods how the little seeds suck their life through the delicate curled-up string, and how the little embryo sleeps inside![9]

While nothing could be more removed from Coetzee's prose – stylistically speaking – than Waldo's Romantic tributes to the nonhuman rhythms of life in the Karoo, in substance a passage like this finds several echoes in Coetzee's work. There is, for instance, Michael K., who after several hardships turns to a solitary existence farming the land – planting seeds and eating insects while the plants grow – and finds that 'time was poured out upon him in such an unending stream, there were whole mornings he could lie on his belly over an ant-nest picking out the larvae one by one with a grass-stalk and putting them in his mouth'.[10]

Unlike Schreiner's novel, however, labour and idleness are ever present categories in Coetzee's work. The first chapter of *White Writing*, 'Idleness in South Africa', is dedicated to outsider depictions of South African life, and particularly to those of the autochthonal natives by 'seamen, ship's doctors and [East India] Company officials' as well as poets, novelists, naturalists, missionaries, travel writers and (armchair) anthropologists.[11] These depictions, which are *'narrative'* (projecting Eurocentric cultural and historical values) rather than *'descriptive'* (a-historic and neutrally observational) by nature,[12] decry the idleness of the natives – predominantly 'bushmen' or 'Hottentots' but later, in an isomorphic configuration forwarded in anglophone prose, also the 'Boers' (as with Schreiner's Tant Sannie) – as they appear in a post-contact, post-settler world with its population boom and agricultural demands. Coetzee argues that, especially given apartheid discourses and legislation, figures of labour and idleness in South Africa remain powerful well into the twentieth century (two decades into the twenty-first century, we find no evidence of their decreasing relevance); he claims idleness 'as an authentically native response to a foreign way of life'.[13]

While Schreiner avoids the exoticism of Bushmen driving cattle into 'inaccessible kranzes', she does so by driving the Bushmen in her novel into an inaccessible past a time that has left a trace only through the survival of cave paintings.[14] For Coetzee, however, this (in)accessibility remains a question, and the disappearance of native languages and customs makes an ethical claim. While Michael K engages in a hybrid of settler and autochthonal practices, inhabiting his full South African heritage, the John Coetzee of *Summertime* responds even more strongly, setting out to learn the Khoi languages:

> From books. From grammars put together by missionaries in the old days. There are no speakers of Khoi languages left, not in South Africa. The languages are, for all practical purposes, dead. In South-West Africa there are still a handful of old people speaking Nama. That's the sum of it. The sum of what is left.[15]

Setting aside the self-flagellating humour in Coetzee's self-portrait as a self-important blowhard, it is worth noting that it is Voëlfontein that prompts this debt to the dead; Coetzee contributes a hauntological dimension to the farm in South African writing, a manner in which its being is caught up not just between town and country, or nature and cultivation, or even the class and racial struggles of the present, but in the demands and legacies of its past.

In addition to his debt to dead speakers, Coetzee's debt is also to dead writers – those missionary linguists who recorded the Khoi languages before they disappeared. Jonathan Crewe has noted that Coetzee, ever since *Dusklands*, has been engaged in mining 'the South African archive' as opposed to just 'South African literature for fictional materials',[16] and so these producers of the archives must also be counted among Coetzee's South African forebears. As with the missionaries, so with the travel writers, naturalists and ethnographers. Coetzee writes in *Youth*, 'Burchell may not be a master like Flaubert and James, but what Burchell writes really happened. Real oxen hauled him and his cases of botanical specimens from stopping-place to stopping-place in the Great Karoo; real stars glimmered above his head, and his men's, while they slept'.[17] These 'real' events, or rather the realism of their telling – the sheen of truth and reality mirrored in the telling details ('oxen ... cases of botanical specimens'), poetic mimesis of action ('from stopping-place to stopping-place') as well as the simple and contextually standard verbs ('hauled ... glimmered ... slept') describing Burchell's account in *Youth* – come from real 'contact with any fact' (as Schreiner's anti-colonial, anti-exoticizing preface has it) but also from the skill to relay this contact in a manner that feels true. For this latter skill, Coetzee can and does borrow from the archives of South African writing, but ultimately he must depend on the singular precision of his craft.

PEERS

South African writers of Coetzee's generation never lacked for a theme. For serious literary authors, apartheid was both an inexhaustible source of urgent material and inescapable interpretive lens for readers both inside and (for the lucky or enterprising) outside of the country. That such work had political heft was a given; the only question was how best to practice and promote one's art under the circumstances. Unsurprisingly, writers' solutions were manifold and, often, seen as competing, both ethically and aesthetically.

No other South African writer's path quite coincided with that taken by Coetzee, who was from the beginning focused on producing literature that would be received in an international context. Save for the rare incidences of Afrikaans in his work, this can be seen at the level of literary style and in the lexicon he chooses to describe South African material.[18] At the level of content, the comparative colonial frames of *Dusklands*, with Eugene Dawn's narrative of twentieth-century psychological warfare in Vietnam balanced against Jacobus Coetzee's eighteenth-century narrative of settler expeditions in South Africa, set the tone: Coetzee's novels resist the armchair-travel category of world literature that David Damrosch calls 'windows on the world'.[19] They are always in dialogue with philosophy, history, and the international literary canon, never simply produced for readers hoping to discover what another culture is like. This does not by itself set Coetzee apart from his peers – there are certainly other writers engaging the international literary canon and speaking to translational, or non-national themes – but it does mean that his trajectory as a writer is in a very real sense determined outside of a peer group: Coetzee is not easily assimilable into a literary movement. Consequently, his greatest interaction with his South African peers has been in his critical writing, his teaching and later (after his relative fame had been established) his support and endorsement of fellow South African writers.

Coetzee has always been interested in Afrikaans writers of his generation. He has translated works from Afrikaans, most notably Wilma Stockenström's novel, *The Expedition to the Baobab Tree* (1981, trans. 1983),[20] and has also written about Afrikaans literature, including in *White Writing* and in regular reviews and articles. These have always been diligent and attentive, if not always positive. A particularly critical example is his review of Jack Cope's *The Adversary Within: Dissident Writers in Afrikaans*.[21] Coetzee accuses Cope of failing to interpret the works in question qua literary texts, instead applying a political litmus test, only ever asking whether a work 'enters or stands aside from "the struggle against injustice, racism or other social evils"'.[22] Coetzee defends

André Brink, who is accused of writing insufficiently 'activist' prose, and he defends Bartho Smit on the grounds of *Christine* (1971) being a 'work of the highest artistic and moral quality'.[23] Other than serving as a catalogue of Afrikaans writers whom Coetzee has read and appreciated, the review is mainly noteworthy for the fact that despite expressing many reservations about Cope's analyses, Coetzee remains 'glad that an introduction to contemporary Afrikaans writing, in English, has been written', which speaks to his investment in this shadow-language of his formation. Other than Smith and Brink (who was Coetzee's colleague and, at times, co-teacher of writing seminars, at the University of Cape Town), Coetzee admired Karel Schoeman, whose *'n Ander Land* (1983, *Another Country*, trans. 1992) he once named as his book of the year.[24]

Coetzee highest admiration for an Afrikaans writer was perhaps reserved for his other colleague at the University of Cape Town, Breyten Breytenbach, whose poetry and creative nonfiction is stylistically far enough removed from Coetzee's own for it not to evoke a sense of rivalry, though thematically often very close. Coetzee wrote an important reflection on Breytenbach's memoirs, later included in *Stranger Shores*.[25] Here he notes Breytenbach's extraordinary trajectory as perpetual outsider and thorn-in-the-side of authority, first of the apartheid then of the African National Congress government. And he notes Breytenbach's right and poetic power to protest the corrupt and morally bankrupt political forces of the day: 'it remains the right of the poet to imagine a future beyond the dreams of the politicians, to have his prophetic say in the future. He even has the right to bite the hand that has fed him'.[26] What he finds most interesting in Breytenbach's work however is also what is most deeply explored in certain of his own novels: 'what it means to him to be rooted in a landscape, to be African-born'.[27] In that regard, Breytenbach's 1999 memoir *Dog Heart* and Coetzee's comments on this work are perhaps especially enlightening. There are remarkable thematic similarities between *Dog Heart* and Coetzee's own 1999 work, *Disgrace*, with both exploring the uncertainty of being 'rooted in a landscape' in South Africa in the immediate post-apartheid years, and linked by key events (farm attacks), and, of course, by dogs. So, when Coetzee asks why Breytenbach repeats stories of farm attacks when the 'circulation of horror stories is the very mechanism that drives white paranoia of being chased off the land and ultimately into the sea',[28] one has to imagine that he feels he too should have an answer, or perhaps even a justification, for this in *Disgrace*. In Breytenbach's case, the response is that there is a continuity between the present rural violence and historical rural violence perpetrated by the original settlers: 'farm murders, and crimes in general against whites – even the crime directed against the Breytenbachs when their home in Montagu is broken into and vandalised – are part of a larger historical plot which has everything to do with the arrogation of the land by whites in colonial times'.[29] While Coetzee expresses his doubts about Breytenbach's scholarship and historical method, especially when making a claim for the hybridity or 'bastardry' of the Afrikaner, such historical connections between new and old acts of violence have been figured and explored in much of Coetzee's work.

A single anglophone peer stands out above all others – Nadine Gordimer, South Africa's other literary Nobel Laureate, Coetzee's only real rival on the scene of South African letters, the writer that has most often been seen to represent an alternative path to Coetzee's own archivally informed, allegorical, self-reflexive, literarily-allusive, postmodern approach. In an interview with Stephen Watson, asked about the South African models for *Life & Times of Michael K*, Coetzee denies incorporating much of the writing by his South African peers ('[t]here aren't many South African writers I feel like cannibalizing'), but of Gordimer writes: 'I read Nadine Gordimer because I think she's extraordinarily accomplished'.[30] While Coetzee does not use, or cannibalize, Gordimer for his own work, he has written critically about her, and she about him.

In a review of *Life & Times of Michael K* in the *New York Review of Books*, Gordimer paints Coetzee (at least up until *Michael K*) as a writer of allegory and diagnoses this writing strategy as the result of the conflict between his 'inner compulsion to write' South Africa and his desire to 'to hold himself clear of events and their daily, grubby, tragic consequences in which, like everyone else living in South Africa, he is up to the neck':

> He seemed able to deal with the horror he saw written on the sun only – if brilliantly – if this were to be projected into another time and plane. His *Waiting for the Barbarians* was the North Pole to which the agitprop of agonized black writers (and some white ones hitching a lift to the bookmart on the armored car) was the South Pole; a world to be dealt with lies in between. It is the life and times of Michael K, and Coetzee has taken it up now.[31]

Even if *Life & Times of Michael K* brings Coetzee's writing to the politically engaged South Pole, there is nonetheless much that Gordimer finds wanting. Though Coetzee never responds directly to Gordimer, he does later in *Doubling the Point*, in an interview with David Atwell, intimate that Gordimer, albeit in a sophisticated fashion, wanted him to write a different kind of novel, one where Michael K would 'go off with the guerillas' and that ultimately his defence is that such a book, a 'book in the heroic tradition, is not a book [he] wanted-to-write, wanted enough to be able to bring off, however much [he] might have wanted to have written it – that is to say, wanted to be the person who had successfully brought off the writing of it'.[32]

While Gordimer is demonstrably frustrated by Coetzee's techniques of aesthetic distancing in a context that seems to demand politically engaged prose, the critique runs both ways. In two important essays, the first collected in *Stranger Shores*, the second in *Inner Workings*, Coetzee argues that Gordimer has written herself into an impasse, caring deeply about her irreconcilable affiliations to multiple readerships and multiple literary traditions, and, in particular, addressing herself to two distinct audiences that could not be simultaneously accommodated:

> inside South Africa, to a radical intelligentsia, mainly black; outside South Africa, to a liberal intelligentsia, mainly white; each (as she was acutely aware) listening with one ear to what she was saying to them, with the other ear to what she was saying to the other half.[33]

In the second essay, 'Nadine Gordimer', which confirms his regard for her oeuvre, Coetzee repeats and reframes the diagnosis:

> As stripper-away of convenient illusions and unmasker of colonial bad faith, Gordimer is an heir of the tradition of realism that Cervantes inaugurates. Within that tradition she was able to work quite satisfactorily until the late 1970s, when she was made to realise that [...] she was too European to matter to the people who mattered most to her. Her essays of the period show her struggling inconclusively in the toils of what it means to write *for* a people – to write for their sake and on their behalf, as well as to be read by them.[34]

If Schreiner was in some regards a model and proponent of not writing South Africa to cater to outside (metropolitan or imperial) fantasies and expectations, Gordimer, Coetzee's great peer, offered him a negative model for understanding why he did not wish to write South Africa to cater to inside (revolutionary or liberatory) fantasies and expectations. Her work served as a decades-long counterpoint to his own and clarified his project through contradistinction.

LEGACY

Coetzee casts a long shadow in contemporary South African letters, and it would be impossible to track the full extent of his influence on younger writers. He has had an obvious and demonstrable impact on new generations of writers with appetites for self-aware metafictional prose, or for stories with an allegorical feel but no easy one-to-one mapping to the real world, or for serious ethically engaging prose that avoids simplification and polemic. In some cases he has directly championed these writers' works, as with Ivan Vladislavić and Zoë Wicomb.[35] In other cases, he has had a direct influence on the themes and style taken up by those who follow him, as with Ceridwen Dovey.[36] Then there are those instances in which his influences come in the form of a negative model – a writer to react against, in whose footsteps *not* to follow – perhaps most strikingly in his direct heir to the creative writing program at the University of Cape Town, Imraan Coovadia, who accuses Coetzee of writing for theory-savvy cosmopolitan academics and thereby entirely bypassing important epoch-defining South African (or American, or Australian) concerns, including, for example, the AIDS epidemic.[37] Rather than conduct an exhaustive survey of South African writers whose writing has been impacted by J. M. Coetzee, I will use the final section of this chapter to look at just one particularly striking instance of Coetzee's literary influence: Marlene van Niekerk's playful tributes to *Elizabeth Costello*.

Van Niekerk is far from the most Coetzee-like of South African writers. Born in 1940, Coetzee writes novels, short stories, reviews and academic articles; born in 1954, Marlene van Niekerk writes all of those but also poetry, drama and personal essays. Where Coetzee's style is quiet, minimalist, controlled and consistent, Van Niekerk varies between the conventions of high lyricism, low drama, philosophical argument, sheer bathos and exaggerated polemic, depending on the occasion and character. Both are translators; but where Coetzee disappears into the text, hewing closely to the meaning and rhythms of the original, Van Niekerk likes to adapt and experiment in her translations. The South African edition of *In the Heart of the Country* aside, Coetzee writes in precise English and diligently avoids Afrikaans syntax or parallelism.[38] Van Niekerk writes an Afrikaans that recovers forgotten words, creates new ones, expands the language and is unafraid to creolize or mix in English or Dutch. And yet, when delivering her two inaugural lectures – first at the University of Utrecht in the Netherlands where she was named 'Africa Chair' of the Faculty of Arts and Humanities, then at her home institution, the University of Stellenbosch, when she was named full professor – Van Niekerk turns to Coetzee's *Elizabeth Costello* where she finds a kinship that goes beyond stylistic sensibility.

Coetzee's character, Elizabeth Costello, first appears as a bird. Before boarding her flight in 'The Fellow Traveller', the narrator notices an older woman wearing 'sturdy white shoes – travelling shoes – that incongruously made her look like Daisy Duck'.[39] For the listener, this may seem like an odd description. For the reader, there is a footnote citing Coetzee's *Elizabeth Costello* where the title character is first described as wearing white shoes that 'somehow make her look like Daisy

Duck'.[40] Van Niekerk's footnote goes on to explain the sustained allusion as 'a playful little homage to this South African author in whose compass all South African writers, literary theorists and critics should, to my mind, consciously move, and orientate themselves'.

Van Niekerk's audience, without recourse to the footnote, is unlikely to have understood that this old woman is meant to be Elizabeth Costello from this one clue alone, and so Van Niekerk keeps adding allusion after allusion, making the identity of this 'Fellow Traveller' an explicit riddle for the audience to solve, at one point even interrupting the story to directly ask the audience, 'Do I need to tell you who she was?'[41]

One of the benefits Coetzee reaps in ventriloquising and modulating parts of his own personality through Costello is that it emphasises the relevance of his works beyond South Africa; the Australian Costello (and her international travels) gives the South African Coetzee a global relevance. Like migratory birds, writers of Coetzee's ilk operate trans-locally; they have local meaning, but that is not their only sphere of influence. By reviving Costello for her inaugural speeches, translating her and giving her another afterlife, Van Niekerk manages to import some of this concern for the global, anxiety about the provincial and care about (taking) position – a vital and enabling legacy that Coetzee has bestowed on South African writers, with Van Niekerk perhaps only the most explicit in acknowledging her debt.

NOTES

1. Coetzee, *White Writing*, 11.
2. Steyn, 'Translations', 119–20.
3. Schreiner, *The Story of an African Farm*, 8.
4. Coetzee quoted in Van der Vlies, *Present Imperfect*, 61–2.
5. Coetzee, *White Writing*, 65–6.
6. Coetzee, *Boyhood*, 95.
7. Ibid., 64.
8. Coetzee, *In the Heart of the Country*, 21.
9. Schreiner, *Story of an African Farm*, 373.
10. Coetzee, *Life & Times of Michael K.*, 101.
11. Coetzee, *White Writing*, 15.
12. Ibid.
13. Ibid., 35.
14. Schreiner, *Story of an African Farm*, 37.
15. Coetzee, *Summertime*, 103.
16. Crewe, *In the Middle of Nowhere*, 42.
17. Coetzee, *Youth*, 137.
18. Zimbler, *J. M. Coetzee and the Politics of Style*.
19. Damrosch, *What Is World Literature?*, 15.
20. Stockenström, *The Expedition to the Baobab Tree*. For a discussion of this translation, see Steyn, 'Translations'.
21. Coetzee, Review of *The Adversary Within*.

22. Ibid., 85.
23. Ibid.
24. For a discussion of Coetzee's enthusiasm for Schoeman, see Kannemeyer, *J. M. Coetzee*, 360–1.
25. Coetzee, 'The Memoirs of Breyten Breytenbach'.
26. Ibid., 305.
27. Ibid., 306.
28. Breytenbach, *Dog Heart*, 312.
29. Ibid., 312–13.
30. Watson, 'Speaking J. M. Coetzee', quoted in Kannemeyer, *J. M. Coetzee*, 385.
31. Gordimer, 'The Idea of Gardening'.
32. Coetzee, *Doubling the Point*, 208.
33. Coetzee, *Stranger Shores*, 272.
34. Coetzee, *Inner Workings*, 256.
35. Always generous with serious writers, Coetzee has taken on the tedious labour of writing blurbs for books by these and other South African writers. For Wicomb's *David's Story*, he wrote, 'For years we have been waiting to see what the literature of post-apartheid South Africa will look like. Now Zoë Wicomb delivers the goods. Witty in tone, sophisticated in technique, eclectic in language, beholden to no one in its politics, *David's Story* is a tremendous achievement and a huge step in the remaking of the South African novel'.
36. Ceridwen Dovey, like Coetzee a South African transplant to Australia, writes on animals in a way strongly inspired by *Elizabeth Costello*. More generally, she attests to the feeling shared by many South Africans of her generation that Coetzee 'has always been there, an unseen but strongly felt presence' since her childhood. See Dovey, *On J. M. Coetzee*.
37. For the essay where Coovadia most clearly critiques his former teacher's work, among other things for its lack of grounding in a South African reality, see Coovadia, 'Coetzee In and Out of Cape Town'. For a summation of the scholarly argument this article prompted, see Popescu, 'The Argument over J. M. Coetzee'.
38. For an account of places where Afrikaans does play a role in Coetzee's fiction see Barnard, 'Coetzee in/and Afrikaans'.
39. Ibid., 119.
40. Coetzee, *Elizabeth Costello*, 4.
41. Ibid., 122.

WORKS CITED

Barnard, Rita. 'Coetzee in/and Afrikaans'. *Journal of Literary Studies* 25, no. 4 (2009): 84–105.
Breytenbach, Breyten. *Dog Heart*. Boston, MA: Harcourt, 1999.
Coetzee, J. M. *Boyhood: Scenes from Provincial Life*. New York: Viking, 1997.
Coetzee, J. M. *Doubling the Point: Essays and Interviews*. Edited by David Attwell. Cambridge, MA: Harvard University Press, 1992.
Coetzee, J. M. *Elizabeth Costello*. New York: Penguin Books, 2003.
Coetzee, J. M. *In the Heart of the Country*. New York: Penguin Books, 1976.
Coetzee, J. M. *Inner Workings: Essays 2000–2005*. London: Harvill Secker, 2007.
Coetzee, J. M. *Life & Times of Michael K*. New York: Penguin, 1984.
Coetzee, J. M. 'Review of *The Adversary within: Dissident Writers in Afrikaans* by Jack Cope'. *English in Africa* 10, no. 1 (1983): 85–9.

Coetzee, J. M. *Stranger Shores: Literary Essays*. London: Vintage, 2002.
Coetzee, J. M. *Summertime: Scenes from Provincial Life*. London: Harvill Secker, 2009.
Coetzee, J. M. *Youth: Scenes from Provincial Life*. New York: Penguin Books, 2003.
Coetzee, J. M. *White Writing*. New Haven, CT: Yale University Press, 1988.
Coovadia, Imraan. 'Coetzee In and Out of Cape Town'. *Kritika Kultura* 18 (2012): 103–15.
Crewe, Jonathan. *In the Middle of Nowhere: J. M. Coetzee in South Africa*. Lanman MD: University Press of America, 2016.
Damrosch, David. *What Is World Literature?* Princeton, NJ: Princeton University Press, 2003.
Dovey, Ceridwen. *On J. M. Coetzee*. Melbourne: Black Inc., 2018.
Gordimer, Nadine. 'The Idea of Gardening'. *New York Review of Books*, 2 February 1984. https://www.nybooks.com/articles/1984/02/02/the-idea-of-gardening/.
Kannemeyer, J. C. *J. M. Coetzee: A Life in Writing*. Translated by Michiel Heyns. Cape Town: Jonathan Ball, 2012.
Popescu, Monica. 'The Argument over J. M. Coetzee'. *Africa Is a Country*, 25 September 2013. http://africasacountry.com/2013/09/the-argument-over-j-m-coetzee/.
Schoeman, Karel. *Another Country*. Translated by David Schalkwyk. North Pomfret, VT: Trafalgar Square, 1992.
Schreiner, Olive. *The Story of an African Farm*. 1883. Boston, MA: Roberts Brothers, 1890.
Steyn, Jan. 'Translations'. In *The Cambridge Companion to J. M. Coetzee*, edited by Jarad Zimbler, 103–21. Cambridge: Cambridge University Press, 2020.
Stockenström, Wilma. *The Expedition to the Baobab Tree*. Translated by J. M. Coetzee. Brooklyn: Archipelago Books, 2014.
Van der Vlies, Andrew. *Present Imperfect: Contemporary South African Writing*. Oxford: Oxford University Press, 2017.
Van Niekerk, Marlene. *Die Sneeuslaper*. Cape Town: Human & Rousseau, 2009.
Van Niekerk, Marlene. 'The Fellow Traveler (A True Story)'. In *Van koloniale naar wereldliteratuur?* edited by Jerzy Koch and Ewa Dynarowicz, 117–39. Poznań: Nederlandse en Zuid-Afrikaanse Studies, Adam Mickiewicz Universiteit, 2009.
Van Niekerk, Marlene. Interview by Jan Steyn. *The White Review*, January 2016. http://www.thewhitereview.org/feature/interview-with-marlene-van-niekerk/.
Zimbler, Jarad. *J. M. Coetzee and the Politics of Style*. Cambridge: Cambridge University Press, 2014.

CHAPTER TWENTY-EIGHT

Coetzee's modernists

PAUL SHEEHAN

To write about literary modernism in the early 1970s, when J. M. Coetzee was developing his craft and finding his novelistic voice, was to be implicated in a project that had critical and pedagogical consequence. For it was in these years that the body of contestatory, confounding and formally daring work produced in the early decades of the twentieth century was being marshalled into a coherent, academy-friendly shape that could be taught and made historically legible. To that end, various critics, scholars and teachers were busy setting in motion the processes whereby *modernism* became reshaped as *modernist studies* – a shift that took place between, let us say, 1960 (Harry Levin's seminal, much-quoted essay, 'What Was Modernism?') and 1976 (Malcolm Bradbury and James McFarlane's critical anthology, *Modernism: 1890–1930*, which helped to demarcate the field for at least ten or fifteen years). Modernism thus becomes a 'bounded area of expertise, teaching, and professional practice' during these years, and forms the basis of a sub-discipline.[1]

On the other hand, to write *like* a modernist in the same period could only be seen as an act of hubris and impertinence, if not career suicide. The postwar generations understood that aesthetic modernism was anchored in some very specific, and very disruptive, historical changes – political, technological, sociological and philosophical changes, which had reoriented the West's understanding of itself. The Second World War, it is true, produced its own seismic upheavals, but the intellectual and ethical questions that it raised were not matters for which modernism could provide any useful answers. Indeed, even as modernist studies was emerging as a tangible thing, there were counter-forces in play that saw its objects of study as formalist, elitist, aloof and politically suspect. According to these adversarial voices, modernism belonged to the past, and that was where it ought to stay.

It is for these (and other) reasons that Coetzee's work was not initially seen as responsive to the modernist ethos in any deep-rooted way. Insofar as Coetzee was invoking some of the canonical names from the first half of the twentieth century, it was understood that he was doing so for his own eccentric or encomiastic reasons – *not* because he sought to revivify that particular tradition, or infuse it with elements that had been under-utilized the first time around. Although Coetzee's consuming interest in colonial violence, dispossession and subjection was apparent from *Dusklands* on, his earliest critics read this in terms of either French theory, German philosophy, and/or (especially after the appearance of *Foe*) Anglo-American postmodernism.[2] The modernist tradition did not figure significantly in Coetzee criticism until the 1990s.

The discord between modernism (now professionalized into modernist studies) and the emergent field of postcolonial theory was taken as a given.[3] In retrospect, it is possible to see Coetzee's great insight, the apprehension that shaped his career, as resting on the possibility that the two could be made to work. As he saw it, there were aspects of the modernist legacy worth reclaiming and rehabilitating, which could be used to expose and contest the assumed dynamics of power and the mandates of authority. The most urgent of these, for Coetzee, was the political dispensation in his native South Africa – a country riven by apartheid and also untouched by the upheavals of modernism. Looking back on his formative reading experiences, Coetzee declared that in 1960 there was 'no South African paternity' he could acknowledge.[4] It is possible, then, to see the kinds of manoeuvres that Coetzee was performing in 'The Narrative of Jacobus Coetzee' and *Foe*, and even as late as *Slow Man*, as having less to do with the metafictive apparatus of postmodernism, with its suspicion of realist orthodoxies and detachment from the social world, and more with modernist principles of reflexivity that seek closer proximity to the *real* – something that David Attwell calls 'bearing witness to the self in the act of writing'.[5] As a consequence, Coetzee's work has been variously described as 'ethical modernism', 'South African modernism' and 'modernist realism'.[6] But rather than attempt to restage or recapitulate the textual strategies of aesthetic modernism, Coetzee takes their lines of enquiry in new directions, re-tuning them to probe the disruptions of the post-1960s world.

In *Doubling the Point*, Coetzee describes himself, in his formative years, as a 'Western colonial whose imaginary identity had been sewn together ... from the tatters passed down to him by high modernist art'.[7] Coetzee's most elaborate ruminations on modernist writing were published in 1993, in a piece titled 'Homage' (given as a talk at the University of California, Berkeley, two years earlier). The emphasis, in this frank and probing memoir-cum-critical-enquiry, is on *style* – on rhythm and syntax, lexicon and idiom – to the detriment of any other aspect of literary-modernist practice. That modernism might be a crucible for ideas, or for polemical challenges, or cultural vivification does not figure in the piece.[8] Instead, what Coetzee recognizes in modernist stylistics is 'intensity and inwardness' (Rilke), 'exact registration of the sense-impression' (Pound) and 'finding a form for the movements of the mind' (Beckett).[9] In addition, Coetzee draws attention to the shape and tone of the sentence – a quality that he discerns, with uncommon critical acuity, in Musil, Joyce and Faulkner.[10]

In addition to this repertoire of stylistic resources, modernism provided Coetzee with a method. That method was Eliotian impersonality. As a nineteen-year-old university student, Coetzee's first, tentative moves towards authorship saw him publishing poems such as 'The Love Song', which merged Shakespearean diction with evocations of T. S. Eliot's 'Love Song of J. Alfred Prufrock'.[11] As theorized by the latter, impersonality set an important precedent for writing as a form of self-effacement, as a mode of engagement-through-detachment. In Coetzee, writes Attwell, this is part of his works' textual genesis: 'Typically, the novels begin personally and circumstantially, before being worked into fiction'.[12] Yet it is not 'effacement' that results so much as a relentless questioning of the notion of a 'knowable self' – a question also explored by Conrad and Ford, via their most famous narrators (Charlie Marlow and John Dowell, respectively).

If impersonality was, for Eliot, an antidote to the Romantic aggrandisement of the self, Coetzee saw its political uses. In the first place, it accords with a fundamental tenet of Continental theory, that writing 'writes you as you write it' (given explicit expression in *Foe*).[13] Impersonality is thus a way of displacing the authority and rhetorical facility that can accompany the act of writing. And second, it is the basis for a politics of style, a technique to countervail the 'judgementalism of the outsider', with its attestation of moral superiority, when confronting racial oppression, class inequality or colonial violence in its various guises.[14] Just as crucially, impersonality enabled

Coetzee to engage in historical exposition and conjecture – without, however, being indentured to the empirical or taking the high-modernist turn into myth.

Coetzee also demonstrated, in a move that now has critical weight behind it, that modernism was not reducible to a historical category but could also be renewed or reaffirmed in the changed literary field of the late twentieth century.[15] Thus, even as modernist studies consolidated itself as a sub-discipline, Coetzee treated its dicta as malleable and porous, with the potential to reach beyond the borders of the Northern Transatlantic.[16] In seeking to both document and reimagine South Africa, where English is a 'deeply entrenched foreign language', Coetzee brought to life a form of writing that would now be called 'transnational modernism'.[17] This insight enabled him to perform such feats as setting a novel in an unnamed and geographically indeterminate colonial town, whilst shining a severe and pitiless light on the imperial cruelties of his homeland (*Waiting for the Barbarians*); and situating another novel in a highly *determined* South African locale, yet rendering its social and administrative formations alien and inhospitable (*Life & Times of Michael K*). Elsewhere in Coetzee's oeuvre, there are instances of uncanniness, defamiliarization and dislocation that invoke the spirit of modernist *Verfremdung* whilst cleaving to the granular reality of the (post)colonial situation – most recently in *The Childhood of Jesus*, which demonstrates the plight of migrants or refugees in a strange, inscrutable land. A similar condition of estrangement is evident in *Age of Iron*, when its tormented narrator presents the Black townships as a kind of Dantesque underworld.

Coetzee's modernists not only cross national lines, but also media forms. For alongside his decisive encounters with literary modernism in the 1960s Coetzee underwent an 'immersion in film', devoting himself to the works of Ingmar Bergman, and to those of Jean-Luc Godard and other *nouvelle vague* luminaries.[18] *Youth* makes clear the parity between the two forms: John's discovery of Samuel Beckett's *Watt* in a London bookstore is preceded by a viewing of Pier Paolo Pasolini's *Gospel According to St Matthew*, the wild comedy of the former ('so funny that he rolls about laughing') offsetting the neo-realist desolation of the latter.[19] Like Beckett before him, Coetzee also nurtured creative ambitions, and even sought to adapt his own works along cinematic-modernist lines – an initiative that, to date, remains unrealized.[20]

In terms of literary modernism, the authors to whom Coetzee has been most consistently drawn possess distinct transnational identities: the Irishman, Samuel Beckett, who lived in Paris and wrote much of his postwar oeuvre in French; and the Czech-born Franz Kafka, a German-speaking Bohemian Jew who lived briefly in Berlin to fortify his writing. The modernist legacies of this duo have impressed themselves deeply upon Coetzee's work, as we will now see.

THE TRANSNATIONAL TURN: BECKETT AND KAFKA

If Samuel Beckett is generally regarded as Coetzee's preeminent literary forerunner, this is because of the sheer variety of ways in which the Irishman's writing manifests itself in his successor's work. In essays, reviews, interviews, introductions and autobiographical writings, Beckett is a steady, insistent presence, almost an accomplice. 'I have devoted years of my life to Beckett, as both academic and aficionado', writes Coetzee, '[i]t was time well spent'.[21] The sentiment is affirmed in *Doubling the Point*, where he attests to the 'sensuous delight' that Beckett has given him 'that hasn't dimmed over the years'.[22] It follows that the critical and other pieces written about Beckett began as ways of analysing and apprehending that delight.

Coetzee is equally forthright as to which part of the Beckett oeuvre he values the most: the novels (*not* the plays) written between 1945 and 1953, or from *Watt* to *The Unnamable*. The first of these features prominently in the PhD thesis that Coetzee produced in 1966–8, on 'The English Fiction of Samuel Beckett'. Unlike anything else in Beckett studies, before or (until recently) since, the thesis purports to be a 'stylostatistical' analysis of the *Watt* manuscripts and earlier works, using quantitative methods to establish finespun variations in Beckett's writing style.[23]

Almost as idiosyncratic as his thesis – though considerably more approachable – is the conference piece that Coetzee wrote, forty years later, titled 'Eight Ways of Looking at Samuel Beckett'. It begins with a kind of philosophical drama (Beckett is a dualist who does not believe in dualism); moves on to animal cruelty, via allusions to Melville (the white whale) and, more obliquely, to Kafka and his ape; and ends in bio-fiction, imagining what might have happened had Beckett migrated to South Africa in 1937, to take up a lectureship at the University of Cape Town. Beckett's transnational disposition is thus given a counter-historical spin, implicitly questioning how his reputation as thinker and canonized author might have fared had it been made in a colonial outpost, rather than a European metropole; and how he, Coetzee, might have come to writing, with this displaced Irishman as antecedent. There is also a further, speculative historical connection to be drawn between Beckett as a wartime *résistant*, later writing in the shadow of the Holocaust; and Coetzee's development of his critical-fictional voice, writing through and after apartheid (*his* particular 'holocaust').

For all this, though, Beckett's importance should not be taken for granted. In a 2011 interview, Coetzee warns against overestimating his involvement with Beckett ('There are writers who have meant more to me than he has').[24] From a strictly *modernist* point of view, however, Beckett has been exemplar, archetype and even lodestar. Although Coetzee has not devoted an entire novel to Beckettian themes or re-creations, as he has with Kafka, there are allusions and intimations scattered throughout the oeuvre. These inferences include the antagonistic father-son relationship in 'The Vietnam Project', recalling Moran and his son in *Molloy*; the Unnamable-like solipsism of Magda, whose monologue makes up *In the Heart of the Country*; the homeless man, Vercueil, in *Age of Iron*, a more laconic Western Cape descendant of Beckett's vagrants; as well as auto-fictive references to *Watt* (in *Youth*) and *Waiting for Godot* (in *Summertime*).[25]

But the key to Coetzee's ongoing kinship with Beckett, as he acknowledges in 'Homage', is the 'savage energy' of his predecessor's style, combined with syntactical control and lucidity.[26] That energy is all the more 'savage' for its paring-away capacity, reducing characters, situations and objects to their elemental particulars. Although Coetzee's relationship to realism is more intimate and immediate than Beckett's, his writing is marked by a similar commitment to 'spareness': 'Spare prose and a spare, thrifty world', as he puts it.[27] The style has proved to be remarkably versatile, adjusting and recalibrating itself to accommodate protagonists at either end of the class spectrum, from the well-educated (Elizabeth Curren, David Lurie, Elizabeth Costello, Paul Rayment) to the half- or barely educated (Michael K, Vercueil, Anya in *Diary of a Bad Year*, Simón in the *Jesus* trilogy). Pared-down prose, therefore, need not imply narrative reduction or constriction, or even stylistic inelegance. Extrapolating from Beckett, stylistic parsimony can be brought to bear on socio-political realities past and present, national and transnational.

'Eight Ways' concludes with a brief *rapprochement* between Beckett and Kafka. Both writers, says Coetzee, were lean, with piercing gazes; and in photographs of each, their inner being 'shines like a cold star'.[28] Beyond these physical resemblances, the juxtaposition acknowledges that it is not always easy to keep the two apart, insofar as they enrich Coetzee's work. The wider question that this raises, of 'literary paternity', becomes more complicated with the opening of the Coetzee archive at the Harry Ransom Centre, the University of Texas, in 2013. In the intervening years a great deal of light has been shed on Coetzee's method and forms of creativity, and also his modernist kinship.[29] As far as the latter goes, the work that has been the most profoundly affected is *Life & Times of Michael K*.

Since it was first published, thirty years earlier, *Michael K* had been read alongside Kafka and his 'Josef K.' protagonist. The early drafts, however, reveal another, pre-modernist intertext: Heinrich von Kleist's *Michael Kohlhass*, a story about the tribulations of a nineteenth-century horse dealer who seeks justice after being mistreated by a corrupt nobleman. The Kafkan surface of *Michael K* thus conceals a deeper, compositional tension. As the Kleist elements are reduced, through successive drafts, a nineteenth-century moral fable about injustice and outlawry is transformed into a modernist story about a marginal figure – an anonymous and insignificant outsider, who is not only struggling against material oppression but also trying to escape the pattern of meanings imposed on him, the pressure to 'have an identity'. The maddening entanglements of modern bureaucracy, so central to Kafka's depictions of individuals who feel lost, helpless and defeated, are instrumental in terms of how this pressure is applied. Ultimately, the Kleist plot about an outlaw or terrorist who sabotages government property devolves into a peripheral side-plot: the suspect(s) believed to be hiding out in the Jakkalsdrif labour camp, an incidental reminder of the book's pre-Kafkan origins.[30]

Kafka is also renowned for his animal tales, which brought to prominence a whole bestiary of humanized creatures (including dogs, apes, mice, beetles and moles or badgers), each of which assumes narrational duties. Coetzee reverses this: his K protagonist is an 'animalized' human being, likened alternately to a mouse, a squirrel and an ant (by others) and to an earthworm (by himself). In *Disgrace*, David Lurie's daughter, Lucy, rejects her father's proposal that she leave Cape Town for Holland, and decides to stay on at her smallholding and start from scratch – 'Like a dog,' says Lurie (also Kafka's penultimate line in *The Trial*).[31] In a narrative full of dogs, one stands out: the scruffy, disabled stray that Lurie 'adopts' and almost makes into a character, *à la* Kafka, when he considers putting him in his opera. Coetzee is more direct and polemical than Kafka, however, in *Elizabeth Costello*. Through his titular character a strident, yet controlled, case is made for human-animal 'sympathy', an ethical demand for imaginative recognition. The novel's concluding chapter, 'At the Gate', approximates Kafka's perplexing, dream-like texture, as Costello faces a panel of inquisitors to make a 'statement of belief'. A Kafka-conscious rewriting of (amongst other works) 'Before the Law' and filled with a 'purgatory of clichés', the episode none the less manages both to disorient and beguile.[32] Although stylistic concerns are not of paramount importance, for Coetzee's Kafka – tellingly, there is no mention of him in 'Homage' – in this instance he precisely captures the ineluctable menace and sinking darkness of Kafka's vision.

'MINOR' MODERNISTS: FROM FORD TO CONRAD

The two writers considered above do not exhaust Coetzee's invocations of, or engagements with, other modernist exemplars. A number of them appear in Coetzee's critical writings, without necessarily leaving any mark in his fiction; and a still smaller number has served provisional or intermediary purposes, in terms of Coetzee's writing career. Arguably the most important of the latter is Ford Madox Ford, whose fiction provided the basis for Coetzee's Master's thesis, 'The Works of Ford Madox Ford with Particular Reference to the Novels' (1963). If the expansive corpus of Ford's writing was ultimately disappointing for Coetzee, his encounters with it taught him the lesson of stylistic restraint.[33] Yet the understated economy of Fordian impressionism – the 'aesthetics of *le mot juste*', as Coetzee puts it – was no match for the more radical minimalism of Beckett's later example, nor for the monological intensity that made it so astringent.[34]

Vladimir Nabokov was another literary authority whom Coetzee, as a writer, outgrew ('I have no relation with Nabokov left,' he told Attwell in 1990).[35] Even as *Pale Fire* represented a high water mark in terms of reflexive narration and the 'fictionality of self', it led to where Coetzee did not want to go: the world of the textual imaginary, where irony and formal playfulness become ends in themselves.[36] A different kind of object-lesson was imparted by Patrick White, the Australian writer. In 'Homage', Coetzee commends White for producing something that he could not find in South African letters – namely, a modernist 'version of the land' that could guide and invigorate aspirant writers, one sufficiently vivid for them both to believe in and use as their own departure-points.[37] Much later, Coetzee declares all of White's novels, from the late 1940s on, to be 'fully achieved works', deserving of the reputation the author earned in the United States as 'an Antipodean William Faulkner'.[38] Conversely, the shadow cast by T. S. Eliot served another agenda. Overwhelmed by Eliot's role as 'arbiter of taste' in the 1950s and 1960s, Coetzee saw him – along with his lofty attitudes and overconfident dismissiveness – as an influence that needed to be shed, or at least tempered.[39] He works this out in a 1993 essay, 'What Is a Classic?' – a reply, of sorts, to Eliot's 1944 lecture of the same name. On the one hand, Coetzee punctures Eliot's ambition to be pioneer, prophet and sage all in one, particularly in his vision of a re-Christianized Europe. On the other, though, Coetzee is sympathetic to the modernist self-making that proceeded in tandem with Eliot's poetic development – a process that Coetzee's alter-ego, in *Youth*, will reckon with and try to emulate.[40]

Of the post-*Youth* texts, which emerge from Coetzee's new life as an Australia-based author, the work that continues the dialogue with modernism most purposively is *Elizabeth Costello*. Although it presents itself, via the subtitle ('Eight Lessons'), as something didactic and donnish – and, by implication, anti-modernist – the book features two rewritings of canonical works, with gender politics at the forefront of each. The first of these, folded into the narrative, is *The House on Eccles Street*, Costello's 1969 recasting of *Ulysses*, with Molly Bloom as the protagonist. Much is made, in *Elizabeth Costello*, of the impact and importance of this work, but precious little revealed of its stylistic or formal properties, or even how 'modernist' it is supposed to be.[41] Coetzee's dalliance with Joyce cannot but be tempered by his allegiance to Beckett, and to the virtues (if that is the word) of spareness, doubt and failure. Yet Joyce's attachment to, and incorporation of, naturalistic detail is arguably closer to the texture of Coetzee's novels than Beckett's relentless unpicking of realist convention. The vividness of *place* in Coetzee's writing, for example, even when it is geographically non-specific, makes his work a distant beneficiary of the Joycean aesthetic.

The second rewriting in *Elizabeth Costello* is more of a supplement or counter-text. The novel concludes with an extract from 'The Chandos Letter' (1902), which calls forth a late addition to Coetzee's pantheon of modernists: the Austrian poet and essayist, Hugo von Hofmannsthal. The Letter, writes Robert Pippin, 'is regarded as one of the most influential and telling documents of literary modernism' for diagnosing so acutely the crisis of language and meaning that Western culture was already confronting.[42] The passage quoted, a declaration of surrender to the natural world and the profusion of 'meanings' that it affords, is immediately followed by a 'Postscript', in which Coetzee imagines how Lord Chandos's wife might have reacted to the letter. Lady Elizabeth Chandos, who has the same initials as Coetzee's fictional author, writes as someone who has taken Costello's sympathetic imagination to the limit, at which point selfhood, embodiment and mental composure begin to lose their moorings. ('We are not meant to live thus,' she writes. 'We are not made for revelation.')[43] The crisis that Hofmannsthal announces, at the dawn of the last century, is thus converted in *Elizabeth Costello* into importunate questions about faith, belief, divination and the ethics of writing. These are not necessarily modernist questions *per se*, but they are annotated and examined in Coetzee's novel through a determinedly modernist analytic.

Finally, the modernist writer who is taken most for granted in Coetzee studies is actually a foundational influence. Joseph Conrad is often cited in relation to *Dusklands*, for its elucidation of the callous logic of imperial conquest; and to *Waiting for the Barbarians*, for its Kurtz-like, complicitous Magistrate. Less obvious Conradian traces can also be found in *The Master of Petersburg*, insofar as its subject, the politics of terror, is explored by Conrad at length in *The Secret Agent* and *Under Western Eyes*. Yet Coetzee has never written about or reviewed Conrad's work, nor made any formal acknowledgement of him as a precursor – even though the affiliation was noted from the outset. In a lengthy, 1974 review of *Dusklands*, Jonathan Crewe (against his editor's wishes) made a brief but pointed comparison of the 'Jacobus Coetzee' section with *Heart of Darkness*.[44] Crewe's remark is both apt and prescient, because Conrad – for all Coetzee's reticence in naming him as a forebear – is a transnational modernist, a Polish-born seafarer who settled in England, writing in what was effectively his third language. Like Beckett and Kafka, Conrad brings to modernism something that Coetzee, too, prizes: the potentiality of language and form to resist the matrices of power exuded by the nation.

Almost thirty years ago, Derek Attridge noted that Coetzee's novels 'appear to locate themselves within an established literary culture, rather than presenting themselves as an assault on that culture'.[45] This process of location involves, as we have seen, a resolute and ongoing dialogue with European modernism, making postcolonial or postmodernist readings of the work only partial or qualified, at best. It has also put Coetzee in a singular historical position, hinted at when he ascribes to Eliot's early poetry the 'feeling of being out of date, of having been born too late into an epoch'.[46] The same sense of belatedness haunts Coetzee's solicitations of literary-modernist practitioners and their legacies. In his fiction, though, he has used that belatedness in constructive ways, repositioning aesthetic modernism to make it both geographically diverse (South Africa, Russia, Australia) and responsive to the cultural and political climate of the last fifty years. In doing so, in putting the 'tatters ... [of] high modernist art' to productive use, Coetzee's own writing practice has furthered the development of a robust and demanding late-modernist poetics within the canons of world literature.[47]

NOTES

1. Latham and Rogers, *Modernism: The Evolution of an Idea*, 68–9.
2. For French theory, see Menàn du Plessis, 'Towards a True Materialism'; for German philosophy, see Steiner, 'Master and Man'; for Anglo-American postmodernism, see Wood, '*Dusklands* and the "Impregnable Stronghold of the Intellect"'.

3. The seminal text here is Achebe's 1975 critique of Conrad's impressionist methods in *Heart of Darkness*. See *An Image of Africa* and *The Trouble with Nigeria*. More recently, Gikandi has argued that modernism has actually *engendered* postcolonialism. See Gikandi, 'Modernism in the World'.
4. Coetzee, 'Homage', 7.
5. Attwell, 'Reading the Coetzee Papers', 376.
6. See, respectively, Attridge, 'Ethical Modernism: Servants as Others in J. M. Coetzee's Early Fiction'; Zimbler, *J. M. Coetzee and the Poetics of Style*; and Mulhall, *The Wounded Animal*, especially Chapter 10.
7. Coetzee, *Doubling the Point*, 24.
8. In the penultimate paragraph, Coetzee does provide a justification, of sorts, for the one-sidedness of his approach. When 'ideas' are critically dissected, he writes, they 'usually turn out to be uncomplicated, even banal'. Coetzee, 'Homage', 7.
9. Coetzee, 'Homage', 8.
10. Ibid., 5.
11. Kannemeyer, *J. M. Coetzee: A Life in Writing*, 100.
12. Attwell, *J. M. Coetzee and the Life of Writing*, 25.
13. Coetzee, *Doubling the Point*, 17.
14. Attwell, *J. M. Coetzee*, 42.
15. See Lazarus, 'Modernism and Modernity: T. W. Adorno and Contemporary White South African Literature'.
16. This line of thinking has recently gained critical support. See, for example, Friedman, *Planetary Modernisms: Provocations on Modernism across Time*, 2–5; Mao and Walkowitz, 'The New Modernist Studies'; and Jameson, *A Singular Modernity: Essays on the Ontology of the Present*, 150–2, 165–8.
17. Coetzee, 'Homage', 6.
18. Ibid., 5.
19. Coetzee, *Youth*, 155.
20. Although several novels have been filmed, *Waiting for the Barbarians* (2019) is the first to carry the credit 'Screenplay by J. M. Coetzee' – resulting in a film aesthetic that is closer to standard arthouse fare (slow, spare, suggestive) than to the formal ingenuity of cinematic modernism. On the latter, see Wittenberg, 'Editor's Introduction', in Wittenberg (ed), *J. M. Coetzee: Two Screenplays*.
21. Coetzee, 'Homage', 6.
22. Coetzee, *Doubling the Point*, 20.
23. Although it must have seemed unavailingly eccentric and rarefied in 1969, Coetzee's thesis appears to us now as an early example of digital humanities scholarship. In *Doubling the Point*, however, he dismisses the project as a 'wrong turning' and a 'false trail'. See Coetzee, *Doubling the Point*, 22.
24. Rainey, Attwell and Madden, 'An Interview with J. M. Coetzee', 847.
25. Coetzee, *Youth*, 155; *Summertime*, 112.
26. Coetzee, 'Homage', 6.
27. Coetzee, *Doubling the Point*, 20.
28. Coetzee, 'Eight Ways of Looking at Samuel Beckett', 31.
29. Attwell, 'Reading the J. M. Coetzee Papers', 374.
30. Coetzee, *Life & Times of Michael K*, 123–7.
31. Coetzee, *Disgrace*, 205.
32. Coetzee, *Elizabeth Costello*, 206. See also Van der Vlies's chapter in this volume.

33. James, 'By Thrifty Design: Ford's Bequest and Coetzee's Homage', 261.
34. Coetzee, *Doubling the Point*, 20.
35. Ibid., 28.
36. Ibid., 87. See also Coetzee, 'Nabokov's *Pale Fire* and the Primacy of Art'.
37. Coetzee, 'Homage', 7.
38. Coetzee, 'Patrick White, *The Solid Mandala*', 236, 235.
39. Coetzee, 'Homage', 5.
40. Coetzee, 'What Is a Classic? A Lecture', 7.
41. In her review of the novel, Margot Norris points out how unlike Molly Bloom Costello is ('an austere, humourless, exacting moralizer') but praises her creator for imagining a 'female intellectual … who violates every female stereotype'. See Norris, 'Not a Bit Like Molly Bloom', 1.
42. Pippin, 'Philosophical Fiction? On J. M. Coetzee's *Elizabeth Costello*', 3.
43. Coetzee, *Elizabeth Costello*, 228, 229.
44. Kannemeyer, *J. M. Coetzee*, 250.
45. Attridge, 'Oppressive Silence: J. M. Coetzee's *Foe* and the Politics of Canonisation', 169.
46. Coetzee, 'What Is a Classic?', 6.
47. Coetzee, *Doubling the Point*, 24.

WORKS CITED

Achebe, Chinua. *An Image of Africa* and *The Trouble with Nigeria*. London: Penguin, 1983.
Attridge, David. 'Ethical Modernism: Servants as Others in J. M. Coetzee's Early Fiction'. *Poetics Today* 25, no. 4 (2004): 653–71.
Attridge, Derek. 'Oppressive Silence: J. M. Coetzee's *Foe* and the Politics of Canonisation'. In *Critical Perspectives on J. M. Coetzee*, edited by Graham Huggan and Stephen Watson, 168–90. Basingstoke: Macmillan, 1996.
Attwell, David. *J. M. Coetzee and the Life of Writing: Face to Face with Time*. Oxford: Oxford University Press, 2015.
Attwell, David. 'Reading the Coetzee Papers'. *Texas Studies in Literature and Language* 58, no. 4 (2016): 374–7.
Coetzee, J. M. *Disgrace*. London: Secker & Warburg, 1999.
Coetzee, J. M. *Doubling the Point: Essays and Interviews*. Edited by David Attwell. Cambridge, MA: Harvard University Press, 1992.
Coetzee, J. M. 'Eight Ways of Looking at Samuel Beckett'. In 'Borderless Beckett / Beckett sans frontières', *Samuel Beckett Today/Aujourd'hui* 19 (2008): 19–31.
Coetzee, J. M. *Elizabeth Costello*. New York: Viking, 2003.
Coetzee, J. M. 'Homage'. *The Threepenny Review* 53 (1993): 5–7.
Coetzee, J. M. *Life & Times of Michael K*. London: Secker & Warburg, 1983.
Coetzee, J. M. 'Nabokov's *Pale Fire* and the Primacy of Art'. *UCT Studies in English* 6 (1974): 1–7.
Coetzee, J. M. 'Patrick White, The Solid Mandala'. In *Late Essays*, 234–42. London: Harvill Secker, 2017.
Coetzee, J. M. *Summertime: Scenes from Provincial Life*. Sydney: Knopf, 2009.
Coetzee, J. M. 'What Is a Classic? A Lecture'. In *Stranger Shores: Essays 1986–1999*, 1–16. New York: Viking, 2001.
Coetzee, J. M. *Youth*. London: Secker & Warburg, 2002.
du Plessis, Menàn. 'Towards a True Materialism'. *New Contrast* 13 (1981): 77–87.
Friedman, Susan Stanford. *Planetary Modernisms: Provocations on Modernity across Time*. New York: Columbia University Press, 2015.

Gikandi, Simon. 'Modernism in the World'. *Modernism/Modernity* 13, no. 3 (2006): 419–24.

James, David. 'By Thrifty Design: Ford's Bequest and Coetzee's Homage'. *International Ford Madox Ford Studies* 7 (2008): 243–65.

Jameson, Frederic. *A Singular Modernity: Essay on the Ontology of the Present*. London and New York: Verso, 2002.

Kannemeyer, J. C. *J. M. Coetzee: A Life in Writing*. Translated by Michiel Heyns. Melbourne and London: Scribe, 2012.

Latham, Sean and Gayle Rogers. *Modernism: Evolution of an Idea*. London and New York: Bloomsbury Academic, 2015.

Lazarus, Neil. 'Modernism and Modernity: T. W. Adorno and Contemporary White South African Literature'. *Cultural Critique* 5 (1986–7): 131–55.

Mao, Douglas and Rebecca L. Walkowitz. 'The New Modernist Studies'. *PMLA* 123, no. 3 (May 2008): 737–48.

Mulhall, Stephen. *The Wounded Animal: J. M. Coetzee and the Difficulty of Reality in Literature and Philosophy*. Princeton and Oxford: Princeton University Press, 2009.

Norris, Margot. 'Not a Bit Like Molly Bloom'. *James Joyce Broadsheet* 74 (2006): 1.

Rainey, Lawrence, David Attwell and Benjamin Madden. 'An Interview with J. M. Coetzee'. *Modernism/Modernity* 18, no. 4 (2011): 847–53.

Robert Pippin. 'Philosophical Fiction? On J. M. Coetzee's *Elizabeth Costello*'. *Republic of Letters* 5, no. 1 (2017): 1–14. https://arcade.stanford.edu/rofl/philosophical-fiction-jm-coetzees-elizabeth-costello.

Steiner, George. 'Master and Man'. *The New Yorker* 12 July (1982): 102–3.

Wittenberg, Hermann. 'Editor's Introduction'. In *J. M. Coetzee: Two Screenplays*, edited by Hermann Wittenberg, 7–27. Cape Town: UCT Press, 2014.

Wood, W. J. B. '*Dusklands* and "The Impregnable Stronghold of the Intellect"'. *Theoria* 54 (1980): 13–23.

Zimbler, Jarad. *J. M. Coetzee and the Politics of Style*. New York and Cambridge: Cambridge University Press, 2014.

CHAPTER TWENTY-NINE

Coetzee's *Mitteleuropa* and Austro-Hungary

RUSSELL SAMOLSKY

ANCESTRAL RELATIONS

Boyhood, J. M. Coetzee's fictionalized autobiography, ends with the boy, John, asking himself a weighty question: 'How will he keep them all in his head, all the books, all the people, all the stories?'[1] The 'books' John refers to is really one book, *Through a Dangerous Malady to Eternal Healing*, many copies of which he has found salted away in his great aunt's storeroom. Originally written in German by his maternal great-grandfather Balthazar du Biel, who was born in the historical region of Pomerania and came to South Africa to work as a missionary, this strange volume had been translated into Afrikaans by John's great aunt, who devoted her life and savings to getting it printed only to find that no bookseller would take it. John tries to read the book but finds it too boring: 'No sooner has Balthazar du Biel got underway with the story of his boyhood in Germany than he interrupts it with long reports of lights in the sky and voices speaking to him from the heavens.'[2]

No one, John knows, will ever read this book, yet Coetzee preserves or encrypts a memory of it at the end of *Boyhood*: why is it so important for him to do this? And why does this unread, almost unreadable, book impose the obligation of remembering upon him? One answer may well be that although Coetzee draws on the history of his extended paternal ancestry in writing his first novel, *Dusklands*, it is to this maternal genealogical line that he traces his literary talent. What in Balthazar was probably madness, however, Coetzee transmutes into canonical strangeness. While Coetzee shares an ancestral relation with central Europe and the German language, 'Coetzee's *Mitteleuropa*' does not signify a geographical locale with which he is intimately familiar. Unlike 'Coetzee's South Africa' or 'Coetzee's Australia', 'Coetzee's *Mitteleuropa*' is rather a country of the mind or intricate set of Middle European-inflected textual worlds.

This is not to say that central Europe itself did not exert an attraction. In *Youth*, the second volume of fictionalized biography, John remarks: 'There are two, perhaps three places in the world where life can be lived at its fullest intensity: London, Paris, perhaps Vienna … [but] Vienna is for Jews coming back to reclaim their birthright: logical positivism, twelve-tone music, psychoanalysis'.[3] Coetzee chose London, where he would pursue his quest to become a writer, but he had also already chosen Freud and Kafka, two Jews from the Austro-Hungarian Empire, as intimate companions. In London, John also carries the poetry of Rilke and Hölderlin, which, if *Youth* is to be believed, he makes a show of reading in the hopes of attracting that woman who will perceive his 'exceptional spirit'.[4] Coetzee speaks here too of his growing feel for German: 'He approves of the way in which every syllable in German is given its due weight. With the ghost of Afrikaans still in his ears, he is at home in the syntax … There are times, reading German, when he forgets he is in a foreign language.'[5] It was this linguistic intimacy that opened up a body of literature that was to have a profound influence on his subsequent writings.

COETZEE'S *MITTELEUROPA* AND AUSTRO-HUNGARY

The range of Coetzee's encounter with this literature is perhaps best exemplified by a striking number of deft, exactingly evaluative and biographically informed essays that focus on central Europe and the Austro-Hungarian Empire. Spanning the period from the eighteenth century to the present, these essays – on writers such as Johann Wolfgang von Goethe, Friedrich Hölderlin, Heinrich von Kleist, Robert Walser, Walter Benjamin, Gunther Grass and W. G. Sebald – give us a sense of Coetzee's studied engagement with the whole arc of Middle European literature. *Inner Workings* opens with a cluster of central European writers born in the late nineteenth century, working in different linguistic and literary-historical traditions, but with a shared concern with exploring, as Derek Attridge observes, 'the passing of the world into which they had been born' and 'the shock waves of the new world that was emerging'.[6] Adding to Attridge's observation, Andrew van der Vlies remarks that what is particularly notable about this group of central European writers is that five were born in Austro-Hungary: Robert Musil, Joseph Roth, Bruno Schulz, Sándor Márai and Italo Svevo. Indeed, as van der Vlies observes, 'one finds references to Austro-Hungary … throughout Coetzee's oeuvre'.[7] One especially pertinent reference that may help account for his interest in Austro-Hungary is a line from Freud's diary, which Coetzee cites in his essay on Joseph Roth: 'Austro-Hungary is no more. I do not want to live anywhere else … I shall live on with the torso and imagine that it is whole'.[8] Freud's wish fulfilment, his imaginary re-membering of the old empire in which Jews had lived as one among a number of ethnicities, could not hold, and the empire gave way before the violence unleashed by the rise of ethnic states.[9]

One hallmark of these essays is Coetzee's particular interest in the problems posed by translation. His first collection, *Stranger Shores* (2001), contains essays on translating Rainier Maria Rilke and Franz Kafka; *Inner Workings* (2007) features an essay on Paul Celan's translators; and his *Late Essays* (2017) contains a piece on translating Hölderlin. Each of these deal with the difficulties of translation and demonstrate Coetzee's meticulous eye for the correct German word. This chapter will reflect on the question of translation, but with regard to its etymological meaning of 'carried across'. More specifically, I shall examine some of the ways in which Coetzee has translated *Mitteleuropa* into the world of his novels.

TRACES OF *MITTELEUROPA*

One abiding influence that Coetzee encountered in his early twenties was the Austrian writer Robert Musil, with whom he shared an affinity, a similar 'intellectual formation', Coetzee in mathematics and Musil in engineering.[10] What Coetzee found in Musil was the example of a writer who was himself engaged in a number of difficult translations. According to Musil, Coetzee claims, we function in the 'real' world only by blinding ourselves to the 'the irrational that lies mysteriously under our feet'.[11] There is a way in which we live only by fictitiously bridging the unbridgeable.

We function rationally only by 'crossing a bridge whose piers are joined by something that does not "really" exist'.[12] However, this does not mean that we can only live by wholly banishing the irrational, but rather by assuming a 'reserve toward the real world'.[13] We can only speculate on how profoundly Musil impacted the young Coetzee, but he must surely have stuck a strong chord. What is apparent is that Coetzee's fiction maintains a definite reserve towards the real, and often works to surpass the logical pushing beyond the limits of the real, and gesturing by means of the analogical towards an opening to the ethical.

In Kafka, Coetzee encountered another writer whose nightmare logic or illogic surpassed the real. Kafka was in fact a prior and profound influence whom Coetzee had been reading in German since his adolescence. It would be, Coetzee has said, 'foolish for me to deny that Kafka has left his traces on me'.[14] Indeed, the nature and extent of these traces has emerged as a significant topic in the study of Coetzee's oeuvre. We might safely surmise that both Kafka and Musil guided Coetzee towards his suspicion of realism as the predominant literary mode. In his essay on Bruno Schultz, a writer who like Kafka was a Jew born in the Austro-Hungarian Empire, Coetzee approvingly cites Schultz on the nature of Kafkan narrative:

> Kafka's procedure, the creation of a *doppelgänger* or substitute reality, stands virtually without precedent ... Kafka sees the realistic surface of existence with unusual precision, he knows by heart, as it were, its code of gestures ... but these to him are but a loose epidermis without roots, which he lifts off like a delicate membrane and fits onto his transcendental world, grafts onto his reality.[15]

Schultz's analysis does not uncover the full mystery of Kafka's process but, Coetzee remarks, 'as far as it goes it is admirably put'.[16] His analysis also corresponds with Coetzee's account of his own:

> By profession I have been a trader in fictions. ... [and] I don't have much respect for reality. I think of myself as using rather than reflecting reality in my fiction. If the world of my fictions is a recognizable world, that is because ... it is easier to use the world at hand than to make up a new one.[17]

Let me now explore the subtle ways in which Coetzee, like Kafka, transmutes reality into the plenum of his fictional worlds by literalizing Kafka's fiction in the making of his own.

In *Waiting for the Barbarians*, we find Coetzee composing the landscape of a wholly new fictional world and Empire that is also imbued with traces from the Kafkan world. In contrast to Freud or Roth, however, and their lament for the loss of the security afforded by the late Austro-Hungarian Empire, Coetzee draws on Kafka in his composition of the security apparatus of his fictional Empire. Set at the brutal juncture of two scopic regimes: the old order of spectacular punishment and the new panoptic order of bureaucratic surveillance and torture, *Barbarians* begins with the arrival of Colonel Joll at a town on the border of the Empire. Joll represents the Third Bureau, 'the most important division of the Civil Guard nowadays. That is what we hear, anyhow, in gossip that reaches us long out of date from the capital'.[18] The message long out of date recalls the long out of date transmission of messages in Kafka's 'The Great Wall of China', and Joll, with his mixture of refinement and barbarity, is reminiscent of the officer in 'In the Penal Colony'. Joll has refined torture to a procedure in which degrees of pressure inevitably draw out the truth: 'First I get lies, you see – this is what happens – first lies, then pressure, then more lies, then more pressure, then the break, then more pressure, then the truth.'[19] Degrees of increasing pressure equals degrees of increasing pain and by these increments the truth has no choice but to emerge. Joll's procedure recalls Kafka's torture machine with its flesh inscribing needles that after hours of pressure produces an ironic 'enlightenment'. However, *Barbarians* ends with a counter-procedure or manoeuvre that turns Joll's mounting degrees of pressure against itself. In Kafka, the problem of getting to the truth is often figured in terms of a problem of the impossibility of closing the distance. In *Barbarians*, Coetzee literalizes this problem when the Barbarians deploy this tactic to defeat Joll's army of Empire. The Barbarians appear and disappear like a mirage that reflects Joll's fantasmatic projection of them as the enemy. But having being turned into the enemy, the Barbarians defeat Joll by cunning use of degrees of distance: 'They lured us on and on, we could never catch them. They picked off the stragglers'.[20]

ACTS OF TRANSLATION

Writing about translations of his novels, Coetzee claims 'sometimes [to] use words with the full freight of their history behind them, and that freight is not easily carried across to another language ... I do tend to be allusive, and not always to signal the presence of allusion.'[21] With his *Life & Times of Michael K*, however, Coetzee again invokes the strong presence of Kafka. Why does he do this? He does not seem to be inviting an agon with Kafka as literary precursor; in fact, with respect to the impact of Kafka, Coetzee has said, 'I ... acknowledge it with what I hope is a proper humility. As a writer I am not worthy to loose the latchet of Kafka's shoe.'[22] But Coetzee is also concerned with another translation of authority or centrality, claiming that

> it is as much possible to center the universe on the town of Prince Albert in the Cape Province as on Prague. *Equally* – and the moment in history has perhaps come at which this must be said – it is as much possible to center the universe on Prague as on Prince Albert. Being an out-of-work gardener in Africa in the late twentieth century is no *less* but also no *more,* central a fate than being a clerk in Hapsburg Central Europe.[23]

Even as he shifts the axis from Prague to Prince Albert, however, Coetzee does so by carrying Kafka, and the freight he bears, across, and this is no easy translation.

Surprisingly, the impetus for *Life & Times of Michael K* was provided not only by Kafka but by another 'K' from *Mitteleuropa,* Heinrich von Kleist, and his great novel, *Michael Kohlhaas.* Coetzee's notebooks and manuscript drafts show him trying to write some version of Kleist's bandit narrative into contemporary South Africa; although vestiges of it remain, the novel ultimately followed another path.[24] Coetzee was attracted to the pace of Kleist's prose, but a later essay reveals another tactic of Kleist's narrative echoed in his own. Coetzee cites Goethe's insight that 'Kleist had a tendency to locate important events offstage ... then to base his dramatic action on the repercussions of those events'.[25] Coetzee too deploys this device in which crucial events take place off the page, which gives his novels their beguiling sense of unexpectedness. 'Kleist's originality', Coetzee adds, 'lies in creating a vehicle in which invisibility and indeed inscrutability of the originating action becomes the engine of the narrative, as the characters onstage struggle to work out what has truly happened.'[26] In both Kleist and Coetzee, it is not only characters but readers who struggle to resolve competing accounts or to determine what truly happens. 'In truth', Coetzee asserts, 'there is no solid ground in Kleist's stories, no ultimate place where we as readers can take a stand and be sure of ourselves.'[27]

The problem of standing on solid ground both in its literal and hermeneutical sense is the focus of *Michael K*, and here too Coetzee digs into this by evoking Kafka's stories. Indeed, readers quickly register that the novel's protagonist is figured in a vexed personified relation to the anxious creature in 'The Burrow'. While Kafka's creature is personified by his reports of ramifying anxieties with regard to his life in the burrow, we witness the seeming transmogrification of Michael K from a human gardener into a burrowing creature. Early on K is presented as becoming an animal: With the 'black coat clinging to his body like a pelt, he stood and ate ... chewing as quickly as a rabbit, his eyes vacant'.[28] By the middle of the novel, K too hollows out a burrow, though nothing so ingeniously elaborate as Kafka's creature. We are told '[h]e also ate roots. ... as though he had once been an animal'.[29] Kafka's animal creature with his hyper-conscious interrogation of itself and Michael K with his submersion or burial of his more conscious self would seem to have exchanged places. But Coetzee is also literalizing or translating Kafka's story into the human realm of a South Africa beset by war for ethical ends. The worries that confront Kafka's creature underground, his fear of attack and his fear for his stores of food, have their above-ground correlates for Michael K.

Coetzee draws not only on Kafka but also Freud with regard to K's primal relation to ground or earth. '[T]races of my dealings with Freud,' Coetzee remarks, 'lie all over my writings'.[30] One such trace is Michael K's encounter with the Freudian death-drive high in the mountains; having sought refuge, K comes close to succumbing to the death-drive and a return to the inorganic. It is not the green and brown vegetal earth that he now longs for but the yellow and red of the dry mineral earth. If he were to die sitting at the mouth of his cave, he considers that he would soon be desiccated by the wind, and 'preserved whole, like someone in the desert drowned in sand'.[31] Lying in what would become a tomb, K comes face to face with a death-driven vision of his own fossilization: 'It came home to him that he might die ... that his story might end with his bones growing white in this faroff place'.[32]

K does not succumb on the mountainside but returns to define himself as an earthworm or mole, that is, as a gardener. Although he would be unaware of it, K's definition of himself as a mole invokes his difference from two famous Middle European moles: Hegel deploys the figure of the 'old mole' burrowing through earth towards light to describe the advancing of spirit through history to its teleology of self-consciousness; and Marx, inverting Hegel, names the old mole as the figure of materialist revolution. Unlike these moles, K is not greatly engaged with tending to the course of history. In fact, hidden in his burrow, K considers joining a group of guerillas that have come down from the mountains but decides not to, which he rationalizes by claiming that he must stay behind to keep gardening, or at least the prospect of gardening, alive. But, we are also told that, '[b]etween this reason and the truth he would never announce himself, however, lay a gap wider than the distance separating him from the firelight' of the guerillas.[33] The problem of truth, in this case self-knowledge or self-confession, is again figured in terms of distance, but here distance plays the role of evasion. At the end of the novel Michael K offers his answer: unlike Josef K trapped in his trial, he has passed through his own trials to pronounce his judgement that 'the truth' is 'perhaps ... that it is enough to be out of the camps, out of all the camps at the same time'.[34]

For Coetzee, K can only be thought of as a hero in terms of his resistance to accepted notions of the heroic: 'But insofar as this resistance claims a social meaning and value, I see no great distance between it and the resistance of the book *Michael K* itself, with its own evasions of authority, including its ... evasion of attempts by its author to put a stranglehold on it.'[35] In Michael K, Coetzee fashions an extraordinary character who goes as far as he can to evade the narrator who supports his being, the medical officer who would know his being, the author who calls him into being, and the book that would contain him. But in creating a character who flees authority, does Coetzee not also ensure that the inverse is also true? If K and *Michael K* resist Coetzee's stranglehold, must it not also be said that Coetzee resists the stranglehold of K and *Michael K* on him as author? 'How many people are there left who are neither locked up nor standing guard at the gate?' K asks.[36] Perhaps this question also applies to Michael K and Coetzee himself as allegory of the captive relation between character and author, or author and book.

AT THE GATES

It is at the gate that we again encounter Coetzee's literalization of Kafka, as well his further engagement with the literature of *Mitteleuropa*. John, the son of Australian author Elizabeth Costello, is waiting 'at the gate' when his mother's flight arrives.[37] Invited to give a lecture at an American college, she has chosen to speak on the lives of animals. Standing before her audience, Costello tells them that she feels like Red Peter, the educated ape from Kafka's story 'Report to an Academy'. In doing so, Costello both replicates and inverts the position of Red Peter who stands before the academy relating the story of his evolution from an ape to something not all that distant from a human. If Red Peter attains the ironic heights of addressing the learned members of the academy, Costello, it would seem, takes up the ironic position of the educated ape before her academic audience. But this is not what Costello intends. She invokes her placing herself in the position of Red Peter, literally that is, without irony. Costello speaks without irony because she wishes to address as sympathetically as possible the suffering lives and deaths of animals. Her target is the endless industrialized generation and slaughter of animals, which she provocatively compares to the industrialized slaughter of Jews in the Nazi death camps.

It is not only Kafka that Coetzee draws on in *The Lives of Animals* but also Hölderlin and Rilke. Coetzee speaks of Hölderlin's great subject as the withdrawal or retreat of the gods, and this is perhaps a source for another of his inversions.[38] Costello proclaims that men went to war with the majestic animals and defeated them. Bereft of their powers, animals withdrew into the only thing left them: the resistance of silence. But perhaps too their withdrawal is also a withdrawal from the gods themselves, whom Costello surmises, humans might have invented to sanctify the eating of meat. If Hölderlin is a speculative source, Rilke is a cited one.[39] Indeed, Costello offers an analysis of Rilke's 'The Panther' in which she charges Rilke with dissolving the bodily panther into the representation of something else – a vital force whose will is stupefied by the loping circuit imposed on it by the bars of the cage. The caged panther is further trapped in the cage of Rilke's poem. Against Rilke's poem, she calls on Ted Hughes' 'The Jaguar', which embodies the jaguar who then embodies the reader: 'When we read the jaguar poem ... we are for a brief while the jaguar. He ripples within us, he takes over our body, he is us'.[40]

If Costello presents us with the limits of Rilke's poem, Coetzee also sees 'The Panther' as preparing the way for our reading of the eighth of his *Duino Elegies*, in which Rilke laments human estrangement from the open world of animal perception. What Coetzee profoundly takes away from Rilke is the 'drama of a poet at the height of his powers striving to find words for intuitions at the limit of his grasp'.[41] While Rilke gestures back to a world before words, Coetzee also perceives Kafka as pressing up against the limits of language and perhaps 'report[s] back on what it is like to think outside language itself'.[42] Along with his uncanniness, perhaps, Coetzee's own pushing at limits is a legacy carried over from Middle Europe.

Coetzee often positions his protagonists as pressing up against intuitive or other limits. He has Costello, for example, think her way into her death, which leaves her simultaneously dead and alive, trapped in the contradiction of knowing what she cannot know. And if this were not enough, Coetzee later places her at the very gate of the afterlife itself. Indeed, in the episode titled 'At the Gate', Costello is required to write a petition on what she believes in order to pass through. As we might infer, 'At the Gate' echoes Kafka's parable, 'Before the Law', and in a strange reversal Kafka's allegory is brought to theatrical life. If Kafka grafts the skin of this world onto his transcendental reality, the skin of Kafka's transcendental reality is similarly draped over the space before the gate at which Costello finds herself. But this world before the afterworld also appears to Costello to be composed of a theatrical mashup of twentieth-century *Mitteleuropa*, stretching from an obscure town on the Austro-Italian border to the camps of the Third Reich.

Slow Man, Coetzee's second novel to feature Elizabeth Costello, is again concerned with *Mitteleuropa* and translation. Having emigrated to Australia in 2002, we might assume that Coetzee would choose to write a novel about South African immigrants. Instead, he takes up the theme of immigration, of being caught between two worlds, by bringing together Paul Rayment, an aging Australian whose leg has been amputated after an accident, and the Jokić family who are migrants from Croatia. Marijana, the mother of the family, begins to take care of Paul, and he responds by falling in love with her. What unfolds is a story that takes up the themes of the ethics of care and the erotic, as well as identity and the quest to enter Australian history. The theme of translation or traversing two linguistic worlds is manifest in Marijana's Croatian-inflected English, which Paul describes as a 'rapid, approximate Australian English with Slavic liquids and an uncertain command of *a* and *the,* coloured by slang she must pick up from her children, who must pick it up from their classmates'.[43]

But *Slow Man* is a novel about being caught between two worlds in a further sense. A third of the way through the story, Elizabeth Costello visits Rayment and recites (with a slight difference) the first lines of the novel we are reading. Both we readers and Rayment are suddenly thrown into perplexity: we readers are perplexed about the nature of the novel we are reading, and Rayment about the very nature of his existence. Suspecting that he is becoming a character in her book, Rayment complains, 'You treat me like a puppet ... You should open a puppet theatre, or a zoo ... put us [characters] in cages with our names on them'.[44] If Costello accused Rilke of trapping the panther in the cage of his poem, Rayment now accuses Costello of trapping him in the cage of her novel. Reading through Costello's notebook, Rayment is struck by the mind-bending thought that he did not survive his accident and has been 'translated to what ... he can only call *the other side*'.[45]

In *Slow Man*, Coetzee blends the immigrant novel with its theme of being borne across with the metafictional novel that unfolds the process of literary inspiration and the scene of literary composition. In this, he twice has recourse to *Mitteleuropa*: first, through the Jokić family and their Croatian history, and second through Kafka and his parable 'Before the Law'. When Rayment asks at the end of the novel why she perseveres with him, Costello answers, 'You were made for me, Paul, as I was made for you'.[46] Her answer alludes to the guard's famous proclamation in Kafka's parable, 'This gate was made only for you. I am now going to shut it'.[47] *Slow Man*, then, concludes with a question and a reversal: will Rayment pass through the door of authorship that allows this novel to be written or will he shut it? If Costello found herself an author before the gate, Rayment finds himself a character before the law of literary composition. Or, put differently, in Coetzee's hands, Kafka's story is transmuted into a parable on the nature of authorship itself.

One of the ways that I have traced the influence of Middle European writers on Coetzee is through his acts of translation or carrying across. Indeed, it is only a slight exaggeration to playfully claim that all of Middle Europe went into the making of Coetzee's novels.[48] This, as we have seen, has not been a straightforward or literal carrying across but rather one of creative inversion or revision or reimagining. In demonstrating this, this chapter also represents an instance of Coetzee's claim that 'all translation is criticism'.[49]

NOTES

1. Coetzee, *Boyhood*, 166.
2. Ibid., 41, 118. We have to be cautious in taking Coetzee's fictionalized biography as the truth of his factual biography, but J. C. Kannemeyer has corroborated these details (30–1).
3. Coetzee, *Youth*, 41.
4. Ibid., 72.
5. Ibid., 76.
6. Coetzee, *Inner Workings*, xi.
7. Coetzee, *Late Essays*, 68.
8. Coetzee, *Inner Workings*, 79. Graham and Macmillan cite this line in their review, which examines Coetzee's increased focus on writers from the Austro-Hungarian Empire.
9. Speculating on Coetzee's fascination with Austro-Hungary, Van der Vlies remarks, 'There is also something of the nostalgia for a home imagined lost after empire's demise, a capacious supra-national identity, that is powerfully suggestive for … the writer who chafes at being categorized as citizen of a single country rather than a more expansive republic of letters' (*Present Imperfect*, 69).
10. Coetzee, 'In Conversation'.
11. Ibid.
12. Coetzee, *Doubling the Point*, 234.
13. Ibid., 235.
14. Sévry, 'An Interview', 5.
15. Coetzee, *Inner Workings*, 75.
16. Ibid.
17. Coetzee and Kurtz, *The Good Story*, 69.
18. Coetzee, *Waiting for the Barbarians*, 2.
19. Ibid., 5.
20. Ibid., 147.
21. Coetzee, 'Roads to Translation', 143.
22. Coetzee, *Doubling the Point*, 199.
23. Ibid.
24. For a fine commentary on the genesis of *Michael K* that draws on Coetzee's archive, see Atwell's *J. M. Coetzee and the Life of Writing*.

25. Coetzee, *Late Essays*, 94.
26. Ibid.
27. Ibid., 90.
28. Coetzee, *Michael K*, 139.
29. Ibid., 102.
30. Coetzee, *Doubling the Point*, 245.
31. Coetzee, *Michael K*, 69.
32. Ibid. K's fasting also alludes to the astonishing feats of fasting in Kafka's 'The Hunger Artist'.
33. Ibid., 109–10.
34. Ibid., 182.
35. Coetzee, *Doubling the Point*, 206.
36. Coetzee, *Michael K*, 182.
37. Coetzee, *Elizabeth Costello*, 59.
38. Coetzee, *Late Essays*, 76.
39. Coetzee, *Elizabeth Costello*, 188.
40. Ibid., 98.
41. Coetzee, *Stranger Shores*, 72.
42. Coetzee, *Doubling the Point*, 198.
43. Coetzee, *Slow Man*, 27.
44. Ibid., 117.
45. Ibid., 122.
46. Ibid., 233. In his manuscript notes on *Slow Man*, Coetzee identifies this line as citing the end of Cervantes' *Don Quixote*; however, it also alludes to 'Before the Law' ('Slow Man', 13).
47. Kafka, 'Before the Law', 4.
48. In making this play, I am, of course, in no way equating Coetzee with Kurtz.
49. Coetzee, *Doubling the Point*, 90.

WORKS CITED

Atwell, David. *J. M. Coetzee and the Life of Writing*. New York: Penguin, 2015.
Coetzee, J. M. *Boyhood: Scenes from Provincial Life*. New York: Penguin, 1997.
Coetzee, J. M. *Doubling the Point: Essays and Interviews*. Edited by D. Atwell. Cambridge: Harvard University Press, 1992.
Coetzee, J. M. *Elizabeth Costello*. New York: Penguin, 2003.
Coetzee, J. M. 'In Conversation: J.M. Coetzee with Soledad Constantini'. 2018. https://www.youtube.com/watch?v=4VNk52t-YPM&t=3450.
Coetzee, J. M. *Inner Workings: Literary Essays 2000-2005*. New York: Viking, 2007.
Coetzee, J. M. 'J. M. Coetzee Papers'. Austin, TX: Harry Ransom Center.
Coetzee, J. M. *Late Essays: 2006–2017*. New York: Viking, 2017.
Coetzee, J. M. *Life & Times of Michael K*. New York: Penguin, 1983.
Coetzee, J. M. 'Roads to Translation'. *Meanjin* 64, no. 4 (2005): 141–51.
Coetzee, J. M. *Slow Man*. New York: Viking, 2005.
Coetzee, J. M. 'Slow Man' Manuscript Notes. Coetzee Papers, Harry Ransom Center, University of Texas, Austin, box 39, folder 2.

Coetzee, J. M. *Stranger Shores: Literary Essays, 1986–1999*. New York: Viking, 2001.
Coetzee, J. M. *Waiting for the Barbarians*. New York: Penguin, 1980.
Coetzee, J. M. *Youth*. New York: Penguin, 2002.
Coetzee, J. M. and Arabella Kurtz. *The Good Story*. New York: Penguin, 2015.
Graham, Lucy Valerie and Hugh Macmillan. *Acta Scientiarum* 31, no. 1 (2009): 109.
Kafka, Franz. 'Before the Law'. Trans. Willa and Edwin Muir, 3–4. In *Franz Kafka: The Complete Stories*, edited by Nahum M. Glatzer. New York: Schocken Books, 1983.
Kannemeyer, J. C. *J. M. Coetzee: A Life in Writing*. Translated by Michiel Heyns. London: Scribe, 2012.
Sévry, J. 'An Interview with J. M. Coetzee'. *Commonwealth* 9, no. 1 (1986): 1–7.
Van der Vlies, Andrew. *Present Imperfect: Contemporary South African Writing*. Oxford: Oxford University Press, 2017.

CHAPTER THIRTY

Coetzee, Israel, Palestine

LOUISE BETHLEHEM, DALIA ABU-SBITAN AND SHIR DANNON

BETWEEN JERUSALEM AND RAMALLAH: COETZEE AND THE TRAVAILS OF THE APARTHEID ANALOGY

On 9 April 1987, J. M. Coetzee took to the podium to accept the Jerusalem Prize for the Freedom of the Individual in Society, an award presented biennially since 1967 in association with the Jerusalem International Book Fair. His acceptance speech began interrogatively: 'How does it come about that someone who not only comes from but also lives in so notably unfree a country as my own is honoured with a prize for freedom?' he asked.[1] The question needed little response. The decision to bestow a literary prize championing freedom on a dissident white South African writer would have seemed self-evident at the time. That this rationale flattened the complexity of Coetzee's interrogation of the relation between writing and resistance in apartheid South Africa seemed not to matter.[2] For the duration of the prize-giving ceremony, held under the patronage of Israel's cultural, intellectual and political elite, Coetzee's focus on 'the *crudity* of life' in the land of his birth held racism at a safe remove for his Hebrew-speaking audience.[3] Apartheid designated an *elsewhere* whose *South African* coordinates Coetzee himself effectively put on display. Scant reference was made to the debates concurrently taking place in the background regarding the military ties between Israel and the apartheid regime,[4] or to associated readings of Coetzee's work, and South African texts more generally, as allegories for the perceived predicaments of the Israeli state.

In recent years, the 'apartheid analogy' that compares the Israeli occupation of Palestine with the white South African regime – a comparison sometimes also used to reference Israeli policies within the 1967 borders – has become increasingly prominent in the global public sphere as a component of non-violent Palestinian resistance.[5] The analogy has also generated considerable scholarship, much of it concerned with the discursive and epistemic reframing that it affords in relation to what is conventionally called the Israel-Palestine conflict.[6] This chapter offers a different perspective. It analyses how Coetzee's imbrication within what Soske and Jacobs term 'the politics of an analogy' in the Hebrew public sphere reflects Jewish-Israeli mobilizations of apartheid as a trope that recurs across the Israeli political spectrum.[7] Proceeding on the basis of Louise Bethlehem's argument that the transnational circulation of anti-apartheid expressive culture provides historiographic leverage over conjunctures beyond South Africa's borders, the discussion below investigates how Coetzee's reception on the part of Jewish Israelis sheds light on the political consciousness, fears and disavowals of *this* constituency.[8] Two moments, in particular, condense these dynamics: Coetzee's appearance in Jerusalem in 1987, noted above, and the public response to the Hebrew translation of *Disgrace* in the early 2000s. However, our focus on these conjunctures should not be taken to imply that we discount the participation of Palestinian citizens of Israel in Hebrew public discourse,[9] or that we view the histories of Israelis and Palestinians as anything other than relational.[10] In the concluding section of the paper, we thus turn to Coetzee's appearance in Ramallah almost three decades after he first appeared in Jerusalem. We use Coetzee's performance in the context of the 2016 Palestine Festival of Literature (PalFest) to move the analysis beyond the Jewish-Israeli public sphere and to reflect on Coetzee's reprise of the apartheid analogy in the context of transnational solidarity efforts with the Palestinian struggle.

COETZEE IN HEBREW TRANSLATION: THE EARLY YEARS

J. M. Coetzee first came to the attention of Hebrew-speaking Israeli readers with the translation of *Waiting for the Barbarians* (*Mehakim Labarbarim*) in 1984, *Life & Times of Michael K* (*Hayav Uzmanav Shel Michael Kof*) in 1985, as well as *In the Heart of the Country* (*Belev Ha'aretz*) and *Foe* (*Oyev*), both in 1989. The two earliest translations appeared in the showcase series *Sifriyah La'am* (People's Library) of the *Am Oved* (A Working People) publishing house, a body originally founded in the pre-state era as the literary organ of the Jewish labour federation associated with the dominant centre-left workers' party, *Mapai*, the predecessor of the current Israel Labour Party.[11] Deeply enmeshed in the socialist Zionist hegemony, *Am Oved* retained its cultural pre-eminence during the early 1980s despite the 1977 defeat of the socialist left that brought Menachem Begin's right-wing *Likud* party to power for the first time. Publishing South African authors was not a novelty for the publishing house. Immediately before the release of the Hebrew translation of *Waiting for the Barbarians*, *Am Oved* had published translations of Nadine Gordimer's *July's People* (*Mishpakhat Yuly*, 1983) and *Burger's Daughter* (*Bito Shel Burger*, 1984), both recognizably 'committed' works of anti-apartheid 'struggle' literature.

If the chief editor of *Sifriyah La'am*, Avraham Yavin, initially entertained high hopes for the public impact of the first Hebrew translation of a novel by Coetzee, he was apparently disappointed. In a short newspaper commentary that appeared at the end of 1985, he expresses regret that *Waiting for the Barbarians* failed to resonate more powerfully with its Israeli readership despite what he identified as its capacity to transcend the South African context. Had it been attacked for its content, he speculates wryly, for instance by right-wing *Likud* member of Knesset (parliament), Miriam Glazer-Ta'asa, it might have fared better.[12] In a piece published in the literary and cultural monthly *Iton77*, the reviewer Ehud Ben Ezer took up Yavin's response and amplified it satirically. He reframed the plot of *Waiting for the Barbarians* for hypothetical scrutiny by Glazer-Ta'asa, the former deputy Minister of Education, Culture and Sport to whom Yavin had alluded, as if the novel were set in an Israeli context. The ruse was topical. Glazer-Ta'asa's vigorous attacks on the radical feminist poet Yona Wallach, and the absurdist playwright Hanoch Levin, had stirred heated public debate concerning freedom of expression. Despite the sarcasm that Ben-Ezer directs at the Israeli political right (for 'the failure' of the 1982 Israel-Lebanon War among other things), the review ends on a note of consolation. 'As for myself', Ben-Ezer writes, 'reading this South African book as an allegory [...], I was comforted by a single fact: that the IDF [Israel Defence Force] nevertheless still remains an army of the people.' He contrasts this 'army of the people' with the military regime that is depicted in Coetzee's text.[13] A tangible sense of liberal Zionist exculpation goes hand in hand with a reaffirmation of the constitutive militarism of Israeli society.[14]

RESURGENT ALLEGORY

Ben-Ezer's self-consolidating assimilation of Coetzee's text within the ideological priorities of liberal Zionism proceeds with unsurprising ease. Israeli commentators of various ideological leanings had, after all, debated analogies between Israel and South Africa as far back as 1953, when *Am Oved* published Alan Paton's *Cry, the Beloved Country* (1948) in translation. A Hebrew adaptation of the novel, based on Kurt Weill and Maxwell Anderson's Broadway musical *Lost in the Stars* (1949), was staged the same year at Habima National Theatre. Paton's story had a momentous impact on the Israeli public; Eitan Bar-Yosef has shown how the stage production reflected contemporary debates concerning the racialized divide between Israeli Jews of *Ashkenazi* (European) descent versus their *Mizrahi* (North African or Middle Eastern) compatriots.[15] For their part, Nitzan Tal and Louise Bethlehem have argued that reviews of the novel served to highlight debates over Israeli socialism, state appropriation of Palestinian land and Jewish suffering during the Holocaust.[16] What emerges into view here is a process of vernacular allegorization that extends to Coetzee's early translations in Hebrew. The comparative impulse on display precedes formal literary critical invocations of allegory in Anglophone scholarship, such as Teresa Dovey's analysis of Coetzee's 'Lacanian allegories'[17] or David Attwell's concept of 'situational metafiction' that would prove so formative for Coetzee studies.[18] If anything, the tendency is closer to Nadine Gordimer's reflections in her notoriously mistrustful 1984 review of *Life & Times of Michael K* where she invokes allegory as 'a *discovered* dimension, the emergence of a meaning not aimed for by the writer but present once the book is written'.[19] The emergent dimension of allegory is necessarily contingent as well as deeply contextual. In the days immediately before Coetzee was awarded the Jerusalem Prize, Israeli journalists and political commentators had recourse to well-established uses of the apartheid analogy in Israeli public discourse that had recently been triggered anew by the revelations concerning Israel's military ties with South Africa noted above. Despite the vigorous recruitment of the analogy by the Israeli left, these broad-ranging comparisons with South Africa did not extend as far as referencing the 670 Palestinian prisoners then on hunger strike in Israeli jails.[20]

Where Coetzee's literary corpus was concerned, the tendency to assimilate the dissident South African other to the liberal Israeli self betrayed certain limits regarding what could not (yet) be said. A few days before the prize-giving ceremony, the expatriate Israeli poet and academic Yossi Gamzu, then Professor of Hebrew at the University of the Witwatersrand in Johannesburg, published an interview with Coetzee in what was at the time the most widely circulated Israeli newspaper, *Yedioth Acharonoth*. 'As a Jew, the descendant of a people who have survived the sword', Gamzu remarks to his addressee, 'it seems to me that you never cease examining what might be called "the psychology of the fugitive"'. Having laid claim none too subtly to histories of Jewish persecution, Gamzu bluntly reminds Coetzee that he is a non-Jew before going on to question him about his affinity for what Gamzu calls 'the fugitive experience'. Needless to say, Coetzee is dismissive of Gamzu's terminology but more is at stake here than Coezee's rebuttal suggests.[21] Gamzu's choice of words in the Hebrew interview that stands as the enduring record of this encounter is particularly revealing. Gamzu uses the biblical phrase 'sridey herev' (literally, 'survivors of the sword') taken from Jeremiah 31.2: 'Thus saith the LORD, The people which were left of the sword found grace in the wilderness [....].' Although the Holocaust allusion is clear, Gamzu does not invoke the usual Hebrew term for Holocaust survivors, grounding his claims instead in the Hebrew Bible as the foundational text of Israeli nationalism. At the same time, Gamzu's focus on Jewish flight and survival occludes some of the enduring consequences of the post-Holocaust establishment of the State of Israel for the Palestinians. Those who have 'survived the sword' are never designated 'refugees' in the Hebrew text. Gamzu's circumlocution strains to ward off any reference to the Palestinian *Nakba* and with it to the disavowed figure of the *Palestinian* refugee, whether in exile or internally displaced within the boundaries of the Jewish state.[22]

PESSIMISM AND PORTENT

After the flurry of responses to the initial translation of Coetzee's work in Hebrew, Coetzee would not again feature prominently in Israeli public discourse until the translation of *Disgrace* (*Ḥerpa*) appeared in the autumn of 2000. Much had changed in the intervening period. In South Africa, the optimism of regime change was tempered by the sombre revelations of South Africa's Truth and Reconciliation Commission. Coetzee's novel rapidly achieved notoriety in that country for what was variously construed as its endorsement of white self-abasement on the one hand, and its alleged racism on the other.[23] The pessimism of the novel was not lost on its commentators in the Hebrew press, either. Writing in *Yedioth Acharonoth*, Arianna Melamed sees an unbridled political violence as informing all interpersonal relations in the version of post-apartheid South Africa that Coetzee depicts. Lucy Lurie, she argues, 'is a victim because she is white and because she has nowhere else to go'. To strengthen the parallel with the Jewish Israeli subject, Melamed exhorts her readers to consider 'what will happen here if the occupation is not brought to an end' – a statement that combines liberal guilt with palpable existential dread.[24] Local allusions continue to saturate Tzur Erlich's review of the novel in *Makor Rishon,* an organ of the religious nationalist political camp. In a manner indicative of right-wing Israeli dissatisfaction with the 1993 Oslo Accords between Israel and the Palestinian authority, Erlich draws an explicit parallel between Coetzee's Black South African character, Petrus, and the Palestinian leader, Yasser Arafat – to the detriment of both. In this reading, Petrus bears direct responsibility for sending rapists to violate Lucy as a 'clear hint' of her new subordinate status – a sequence of actions that Erlich calls, in an abrupt segue to his own local context, 'the continuation of Oslo by other means'.[25] The suspension of the South African setting of the novel in the interests of inflammatory nationalist responses to Oslo and to the second *Intifada* is complete.

In 2002, the Hebrew journal of visual cultural and critical theory, *Plastika*, devoted a cluster of articles to readings of *Disgrace*, including an intervention by literary historian, cultural theorist and anti-occupation activist Hannan Hever, which set out the implications of the novel for the oppositional Israeli intellectual.[26] What is at stake in *Disgrace*, Hever argues, is Coetzee's scepticism regarding the capacity of political negotiation to effect the complete elimination of apartheid. With the Oslo Accords clearly in mind, Hever calls for the adoption of a 'Coetzee-like sobriety' in the face of the shared fallacy of Zionist, post-Zionist and non-Zionist imaginings of political settlement,[27] namely that achieving 'an all-encompassing, Messianic solution' to the Israeli-Palestinian conflict is possible.[28] Against the backdrop of the ongoing violence of the second *Intifada*, he observes that *Disgrace* strives to contain political violence within frameworks 'so different from those already known that they are rendered almost incomprehensible'.[29] In this spirit, Hever calls for oppositional Israeli intellectuals to imagine the Palestinian right of return – an anathema for secular liberal and religious nationalist Zionism alike – as 'a basic structural shift which cannot be cleansed, in advance, of the failures and contradictions that will attend it'.[30] Hever's reading of *Disgrace* uses the novel as pretext – or perhaps as a deeply secular proof-text – to convey a radical arc *within* Jewish-Israeli intellectual culture. His intervention is incompatible with exculpatory uses of the apartheid analogy typical of much of the Hebrew-language reception of Coetzee's South African *oeuvre*. Yet Hever shares this much with his political opponents: The South African text is mobilized in the interest of internal debate within the Jewish-Israeli national community, abrogating any consideration of *Palestinian* responses to ongoing effects of the *Nakba* and occupation that the apartheid analogy might have been expected to generate.

This tendency would later be repeated in unexpected quarters beyond the Israeli public sphere. Between April and July 2010, the Jewish-American writer Paul Auster conducted an exchange of letters with Coetzee that touched briefly on Israel and Palestine in the context of a longer correspondence, later anthologized. Auster first raises the Israeli-Palestinian conflict, linking his waning optimism regarding a two-state solution to the assassination of Yitzhak Rabin, the 9/11 attacks and 'the growth of militant Islam'.[31] Coetzee responds by noting the 'huge injustice' done to the Palestinians who 'have been made to bear the consequences of events in Europe for which they were in no way responsible [....]'[32] This articulation of support for the Palestinian cause notwithstanding, he goes on to observe that: 'There is such a thing as defeat, and the Palestinians have been defeated. [...] They must accept defeat, and accept it constructively.'[33] While neither Coetzee nor Auster repudiates Palestinian suffering, both writers disparage the Palestinian political leadership.[34] Despite Auster's Jewishness, and despite the lines of identification that Coetzee derives from his indebtedness to 'the Jewish element in Western culture', on the one hand, and his loyalty to Jewish friends, on the other,[35] each confesses to having 'tangled thoughts' or 'divided feelings' in relation to Israel and Palestine.[36] Their respective condemnations of Israeli policy or of Jewish Israeli conduct proceed by way of historical analogy. 'There is only one word that will describe what has been done of late in Lebanon and Gaza', writes Coetzee, 'and that word is *schrecklich* [dreadful]. *Schreklichkeit*: an ugly hard word – a Hitlerian word – for an ugly, hard, heartless way of treating people'.[37] He proceeds to enunciate a teleological philosophy of history that reinforces his moral condemnation of Israel: 'For any of us who might be inclined to entertain the essentially progressive notion that the history of humankind teaches lessons that we should heed if we want to become better people, the question that must give us pause is: What kind of lesson has history taught Israel?'[38] For his part, Auster, newly returned from the Second International Writers Festival at Mishkenot in Jerusalem, laments that: 'The Arabs [sic] are *citizens*, and yet their fellow citizens want nothing to do with them [...] I would not go so far as to call Israel an apartheid state, but it is very close to a Jim Crow society, which is depressing enough.'[39]

Coetzee does not comment on the analogy that Auster offers, nor on the one that he skirts. Instead, he recalls South African history to mind, invoking F. W. de Klerk's recruitment of the military establishment to back the South African leader's implementation of far-reaching political reforms as a possible precedent for the Israeli case. Whatever its contradictions, Coetzee's willingness to allow this segment of his private correspondence with Auster to enter the public sphere under his proper name makes his observations on Israel and Palestine consonant in one crucial respect with his public intellectual appearance at the 2016 session of PalFest, and with his earlier appearance in Jerusalem, for that matter. Both unfold without recourse to what Andrew van der Vlies calls 'the mask of a writer-character persona' that has sometimes accompanied Coetzee's public appearances elsewhere.[40] When judged in relation to Coetzee's participation in PalFest, however, the overall tenor of the Auster-Coetzee exchange appears out of step with the heightened global support for the Palestinian struggle that forms such a crucial backdrop to Coetzee's eventual appearance in Ramallah.

PERFORMING SOLIDARITY IN RAMALLAH

A decade and a half after the Oslo Accords animated Jewish-Israeli readings of *Disgrace*, the stakes of the apartheid analogy had shifted considerably. The World Conference against Racism in Durban, South Africa, in 2001, as well as the call for Boycott, Divestment and Sanctions (BDS) on the part of Palestinian civil society in 2005, lent impetus to various international solidarity movements with the Palestinian cause – often on the basis of direct comparison with the anti-apartheid struggle.[41] Increasingly prevalent appeals to the analogy among Palestinian activists and their supporters provided fertile ground for the mobilization of J. M. Coetzee himself – rather than his texts – on the part of the Palestinian literary 'counterpublic'.[42] This is not surprising. Without national sovereignty, Palestinian literary culture cannot lay claim to the publishing institutions of a nation-state. Additionally, since the translation of Coetzee's work into Arabic occurred across a range of cultural centres on the part of Egyptian, Iraqi and Syrian translators, there is no direct uptake between the Arabic translation of Coetzee and a distinctly Palestinian readership.[43] Instead, the symbolic importance that Coetzee holds for Palestinian constituencies would be channelled through the embodied repertoires of solidarity activism rather than through the resources of print culture.

As a Nobel Laureate and a writer of South African descent, Coetzee's presence was well suited to the ethos of the Palestine Festival of Literature, whose resistance to what its organizers have designated the 'cultural siege' of Palestine was transnationally conceived from the outset.[44] At the same time, Coetzee's address at the close of the 2016 session in Ramallah opens with a caveat. Although he begins by foregrounding his South African descent, Coetzee warns his listeners that he finds the application of the term 'apartheid' to 'the way things are here' to be unproductive since it threatens to provoke 'inflamed semantic wrangle' in the place of analysis. Jacques Derrida once rather notoriously argued that the Afrikaans signifier constituted an 'untranslatable idiom, a violent arrest of the mark'.[45] Coetzee seems, by contrast, to fear the term's volatile capacity for reattribution. This is not to say that he rejects the comparative basis of the apartheid analogy (although he fails to name it as such); instead, Coetzee applies a single analytic framework – 'a system of enforced segregation based on race or ethnicity put in place by an exclusive self-defined group in order to consolidate colonial conquest' – across what he pointedly terms 'two colonial conquests' to collapse the distance between apartheid South Africa, on the one hand, and 'Jerusalem and the West Bank', on the other.[46] 'Draw your own conclusions', Coetzee exhorts, aware that his words will carry weight in the global public arena.[47] But he speaks in the flesh to a particular audience – to the women and men we see sitting in the garden of the Khalil Sakakini Cultural Centre in Ramallah who are caught in the photographer's lens as Coetzee is pictured ascending to the podium.[48] Coetzee's use of inference privileges what Émile Benveniste terms *énonciation* (the act of saying an utterance) over *énoncé* (the utterance itself).[49] Stated in a different theoretical vocabulary, the performativity at stake here has site-specific force. Coetzee's *performance of analogy* resonates with the activist staging of PalFest as an itinerant literary festival that unfolds across the spaces of historical Palestine where it is frequently the object of Israeli regimes of surveillance and restricted mobility.[50] 'It was important for PalFest', observes its founder Ahdaf Soueif, 'that it should try to travel in the same manner as its Palestinian audience'.[51] This site-specific performativity is a prominent dimension of the visual cultural record that accompanies Coetzee's participation in the festival. The African-American writer and intellectual Saidiya Hartman is pictured exiting a turnstile at the Qalandia checkpoint used by Israel to control Palestinian access to Jerusalem.[52] In another image, J. M. Coetzee looks on in Hebron, his passport held slightly ajar as if in readiness for inspection, as a nearby Israeli soldier scrutinizes the passport of Pulitzer Prizewinner Benjamin Moser.[53]

The apartheid analogy localizes constituencies in Israel and Palestine, throwing their political conflict into sharp relief. Through charting J. M. Coetzee's imbrication in the discursive relays that eddy around Jerusalem or Ramallah, each of us deferring to the cadences of her most intimate language – South African English, Palestinian Arabic or Hebrew – we have sought to argue that Coetzee's standing in each arena cannot easily be disentangled from the dynamics of analogy. What circulates alongside 'Coetzee' in Israel and Palestine is the catachrestic capacity of the Afrikaans signifier 'apartheid'; its volatile capacity to inform struggles for equality that play out at a remove of time and space from South Africa. The partisan recruitments of J. M. Coetzee that this chapter has considered differ strongly from one another. The task of understanding how apartheid South Africa functions as a trope in the political imagination of Israelis and Palestinians is served precisely through their divergence.

NOTES

1. Coetzee, 'Jerusalem Prize Acceptance Speech', 96.
2. For a discussion of this, see Attwell, *J. M. Coetzee*, 15–17.
3. Coetzee, 'Jerusalem Prize Acceptance Speech', 99, emphasis in the original.
4. Following the disclosure of a report to the United States Congress concerning Israel's military collaboration with South Africa (*Ha'aretz 'Hadu'ah 'al Drom Africa'*), the jurors disagreed over whether their commendation at the prize-giving ceremony needed to reference these ties. Horvitz, '*Amos Elon mul Prof. Avineri: Vikuah Drom Afrikani*' [Amos Elon vs. Prof. Avineri: A South African Debate], 6.
5. For the longer history of its use, see Fischer, 'Palestinian Non-Violent Resistance and the Apartheid Analogy', 1124–39.
6. Feldman, *A Shadow over Palestine*, 7; Soske and Jacobs, 'Introduction', 5.
7. Soske and Jacobs, eds., *Apartheid Israel*.
8. Bethlehem, 'Restless Itineraries', 47–69.
9. The case of Palestinian writer Anton Shammas who translated Athol Fugard, John Kani and Winston Ntshona's 1973 play *The Island* into Hebrew and Arabic for performance at the Haifa Municipal Theatre in 1983, and whose 1986 novel *Arabesques* was written in Hebrew, underscores our caveat. See 'Israeli Jewish Theatre Here and Now!', Haifa Municipal Theatre, 1983.
10. Lockman, *Comrades and Enemies*, 8. We are grateful to Omri Grinberg for discussion of this point.
11. Neiger, *Motsi'im L'or Ke'metavkhey Tarbut* [Publishers as Cultural Brokers], 215.
12. Kim, '*Hasefer Hamochmatz shel Hashana*' [The Overlooked Book of the Year], 21.
13. Ben-Ezer, '*Mhakim Labarbarim*' [Waiting for the Barbarians], 7. Hebrew translations throughout by Louise Bethlehem.

14. Years later, Coetzee's exchanges with Paul Auster on Israel and Palestine would fundamentally underestimate the centrality of this ethos for Zionist ideology. Auster and Coetzee, *Here and Now*, 139–56. See discussion below.
15. Bar-Yosef, 'Zionism, Apartheid, Blackface'.
16. Tal and Bethlehem, 'South African Text; Zionist Palimpsest'.
17. Dovey, *The Novels of J. M. Coetzee*.
18. Attwell, *J. M. Coetzee*, 17.
19. Gordimer, 'The Idea of Gardening'.
20. See the exchange in *Yedioth Acharonoth* between Peace Now activist and intellectual Avishai Margalit, who drew strong equivalences between Israel and South Africa and journalist Amos Carmel who rebutted them. Margalit, *'B'emtsa Haderekh Lagehinom'* [Halfway to Hell]; Carmel, *'Hashura Hatahtona'* [The Bottom Line]. For the hunger strike, see *Ha'aretz*, 'Bagada Nimshakhot Hafganot Hizdahut Alimot' [Violent Solidarity Protests Continue in the West Bank], 5.
21. Gamzu, 'J. M. Coetzee: Eykhut Sifrutit'.
22. *Al-Nakba*, literally the 'disaster' or 'catastrophe', refers to the 1948 exodus of Palestinians who fled their homes or were expelled from them following the declaration of the state of Israel.
23. See Marais, 'Very Morbid Phenomena', 32–8; McDonald, 'Disgrace Effects', 321–30.
24. Melamed, *'Al Herpa Ve'al Kalon Ve'ma Shebeineihem'* [On Disgrace, Shame and What Lies between Them].
25. Erlich, *'Herpat Hayeynu At': 'Al Herpa me'et Coetzee'* [You Are Our Life's Disgrace: On *Disgrace* by Coetzee].
26. The intervention was reprinted in translation in 2002 in the South African literary journal *Scrutiny2: Issues in English Studies in Southern Africa* in the context of a symposium on *Disgrace*, together with two other contributions originally published in *Plastika* by visual cultural theorist Ariella Azoulay and by one of the authors of the present paper, Louise Bethlehem. See Hever, *'Facing Disgrace'*, translated by Louise Bethlehem, 42–6. Citations refer to the English translation of the text.
27. Hever, *'Facing Disgrace'*, 45.
28. Ibid., 42–3.
29. Ibid., 43.
30. Ibid., 46.
31. Auster and Coetzee, *Here and Now*, 139.
32. Ibid., 144.
33. Ibid.
34. Coetzee laments the absence of a 'great man, a man of vision and courage' going so far as to suggest that 'the leaders whom the Palestinian have produced thus far strike me as midgets' (Auster and Coetzee, *Here and Now*, 145). Auster concurs: 'If, instead of Arafat, there had been a Middle Eastern Gandhi to frame the political discourse, I am convinced the Palestinians would have had a country of their own twenty or thirty years ago' (Auster and Coetzee, *Here and Now*, 150).
35. Auster and Coetzee, *Here and Now*, 146–7.
36. Ibid., 144, 146, 149, 150.
37. Ibid., 145.
38. Ibid., 145–6. It is perhaps surprising that Coetzee's invocation of Nazism and of the Holocaust escaped comment on the part of the Israeli reviewers of the translated correspondence in contrast with the outrage elicited by his earlier comparison between slaughterhouses and concentration camps in *Elizabeth Costello: Eight Lessons*. In a review of *Elizabeth Costello*, Arianna Melamed complains that Coetzee has 'so allowed his heroine to be blinded by her high moral principles that she endorses the very thing

against which she has preached. The dehumanization of [Holocaust] victims albeit in the name of the believer's lofty ideas is also evil'. Melamed, '*Lo Kol Coetzee Zahav*' [Not Every Coetzee is Gold].

39. Auster and Coetzee, 153, emphasis in original.
40. Van der Vlies, 'Publics and Personas', 246.
41. See Clarno, *Neoliberal Apartheid*, 2–3; Allen 'What's in a Link?'
42. Warner, 'Publics and Counterpublics', 86.
43. *Waiting for the Barbarians* seems to have appeared in three different translations, first on the part of The Supreme Council of Culture in Egypt in 2000; and subsequently in the translation of Iraqi novelist and literary translator, Ibtisam Abdallah, for *Ālmrkz āltqāfy āl'rby* [The Arab Cultural Center], a publishing house with branches in Morocco and Lebanon, and by the Syrian critic and translator, Sakhr Al-Hajj Hussain, for the *Ward* publishing house in Damascus. Together with several later works by Coetzee, *Disgrace* was issued by the publishing arm of the Egyptian Ministry of Culture, the General Egyptian Book Organisation (GEBO), in the translation of Abed Elmaqsoud Abed Elkareem in 2009. That we have not been able to find any of these volumes in circulation in East Jerusalem is itself a reflection on the political complexities that we are charting.
44. PalFest, *2016 Festival Report*, 2; Soueif, 'Introduction', 4. All the same, Coetzee's participation in PalFest was not entirely uncontroversial. The exiled Syrian literary critic and translator Subhi Hadidi, who covered the event approvingly, nevertheless noted the sense of 'annoyance' felt in certain quarters regarding Coetzee's inclusion in the 2016 cohort since Hadidi felt that Coetzee did not 'deal directly with the topic of apartheid', or at least not 'in the ways available in the novels of Nadine Gordimer'. See Hadidi, '*Kwytzī ū'abārtīd isrā'īl*'. Translation from the Arabic by Dalia Abu-Sbitan.
45. Derrida, 'Racism's Last Word', 292.
46. Coetzee, 'Draw Your Own Conclusions', 35.
47. Ibid.
48. PalFest, *2016 Festival Report*, 19.
49. Benveniste, 'The Formal Apparatus of Enunciation', 141–5.
50. Peteet, *Space and Mobility in Palestine*.
51. PalFest, *2016 Festival Report*, 3.
52. Ibid., 9.
53. Ibid., 26.

WORKS CITED

Allen, Lori. 'What's in a Link: Transnational Solidarities across Palestine and Their Intersectional Possibilities'. *South Atlantic Quarterly* 117, no. 1 (2018): 111–33. https://doi.org/10.1215/00382876-4282064.

Attwell, David. *J.M. Coetzee: South Africa and the Politics of Writing*. Berkeley: University of California Press; Cape Town: David Philip, 1993.

Auster, Paul and J. M. Coetzee. *Here and Now – Letters 2008–2011*. London: Faber & Faber, 2013.

Bar-Yosef, Eitan. 'Zionism, Apartheid, Blackface: *Cry the Beloved Country* on the Israeli Stage'. *Representations* 123, no. 1 (2013): 117–53. https://doi.org/10.1525/rep.2013.123.1.117.

Ben-Ezer, Ehud. '*Mhakim Labarbarim*' [Waiting for the Barbarians]. *Iton 77*, no. 72–3 (1986): 7.

Benveniste, Émile. 'The Formal Apparatus of Enunciation'. In *The Discourse Studies Reader: Main Currents in Theory and Analysis*, edited by J. Angermuller, D. Maingueneau and R. Wodak, 141–5. Amsterdam/Philadelphia: John Benjamins Publishing Company, 2014.

Bethlehem, Louise. 'Restless Itineraries: Anti-Apartheid Expressive Culture and Transnational Historiography'. *Social Text* 36, no. 3 (2018): 47–69.

Carmel, Amos. *'Hashura Hatahtona: Israel Vedrom Africa – Bekhol Zot Yesh Hevdel'* [The Bottom Line: Israel and South Africa – Nevertheless a Difference]. *Yedioth Acharonoth, 24 Sha'ot [24 Hours]* (Tel Aviv), 9 April 1987: 19.

Clarno, Andy. *Neoliberal Apartheid: Palestine/Israel and South Africa after 1994.* Chicago: University of Chicago Press, 2017.

Coetzee, J. M. 'Draw Your Own Conclusions'. In *This Is Not a Border: Reportage & Reflection from the Palestine Festival of Literature*, edited by A. Soueif and O. R. Hamilton, 35. New York: Bloomsbury, 2017.

Coetzee, J. M. 'Jerusalem Prize Acceptance Speech'. In *Doubling the Point: Essays and Interviews*, edited by D. Attwell, 96–9. Cambridge, MA; London: Harvard University Press, 1992.

Derrida, Jacques. 'Racism's Last Word', translated by Peggy Kamuf. *Critical Inquiry* 12, no. 1 (1985): 290–9.

Dovey, Teresa. *The Novels of J. M. Coetzee: Lacanian Allegories.* Johannesburg: Ad. Donker, 1988.

Erlich, Tsur. *'Herpat Hayeynu At': 'Al Herpa Me'et Coetzee'* [You Are Our Life's Disgrace: On *Disgrace* by Coetzee]. 24 May 2010. http://tsurehrlich.blogspot.com/2010/05/blog-post_24.html.

Feldman, Keith. *A Shadow over Palestine: The Imperial Life of Race in America.* Minneapolis: University of Minnesota Press, 2015.

Fischer, Nina. 'Palestinian Non-Violent Resistance and the Apartheid Analogy'. *Interventions* 23, no. 8 (2021): 1124–39, https://doi.org/10.1080/1369801X.2020.1816853.

Gamzu, Yossi. 'J. M. Coetzee: Eykhut Sifrutit, Mevukha Ustirot Ideologiot' [J. M. Coetzee: Literary Quality, Bewilderment and Ideological Contradictions]. *Yedioth Acharonoth* (Tel Aviv), 3 April 1987: 3.

Gordimer, Nadine. 'The Idea of Gardening'. *The New York Review*, 2 February 1984. https://www.nybooks.com/articles/1984/02/02/the-idea-of-gardening/.

Ha'aretz. 'Bagada Nimshakhot Hafganot Hizdahut Alimot 'Im Ha'asirim Hashovtim' [Violent Solidarity Protests Continue in the West Bank with the Striking Prisoners]. 11 April 1987: 5.

Ha'aretz. 'Hadu'ah 'al Drom Africa: Israel Mesapeket Neshek, Madrikhim Yeda Tekhni' [Report on South Africa: Israel Provides Weapons, Technical Support and Knowledge], 1 April 1987: 1.

Hadid, Subhi. 'Kwytzī ū'abārtīd isrā'īl' [Coetzee and Israel's Apartheid]. *Al-qds al-ʿrbī, Al-qds al-ʿrbī*, 29 May 2016. https://www.alquds.co.uk/%EF%BB%BF%D9%83%D9%88%D9%8A%D8%AA%D8%B2%D9%8A-%D9%88%D8%A3%D8%A8%D8%A7%D8%B1%D8%AA%D9%8A%D8%AF-%D8%A5%D8%B3%D8%B1%D8%A7%D8%A6%D9%8A%D9%84/.

Hever, Hannan. 'Facing Disgrace: Coetzee and the Israeli Intellectual', translated by Louise Bethlehem. *Scrutiny2: Issues in English Studies in Southern Africa* 7, no. 1 (2002): 42–6.

Horvitz, Moshe. *'Amos Elon Mul Prof. Avineri: Vikuah Drom Afrikani'* [Amos Elon Vs. Prof. Avineri: A South African Debate]. *Koteret Rashit*, 8 April 1987: 6.

'Israeli Jewish Theatre Here and Now!' *1983 Season Program*, The Haifa Municipal Theatre, 1983.

Kim, Hanna. *'Hasefer Hamochmatz Shel Hashana'* [The Overlooked Book of the Year]. *Yedioth Acharonoth* (Tel Aviv), 27 December 1985: 21.

Lockman, Zachary. *Comrades and Enemies. Arab and Jewish Workers in Palestine, 1906–1948.* Berkeley: University of California Press, 1996.

Marais, Mike. 'Very Morbid Phenomena: "Liberal Funk," the "Lucy-Syndrome" and J. M. Coetzee's *Disgrace*'. *Scrutiny2: Issues in English Studies in Southern Africa* 6, no. 1 (2001): 32–8.

Margalit, Avishai. *'B'emtsa Haderekh Lagehinom'* [Halfway to Hell]. *Yedioth Acharonoth* (Tel Aviv), 7 April 1987: 19.

McDonald, Peter D. 'Disgrace Effects'. *Interventions* 4, no. 3 (2002): 321–30.

Melamed, Ariana. *'Al Herpa Ve'al Kalon Ve'ma Shebeineihem'* [On Disgrace, Shame and What Lies between Them]. *Yedioth Acharonoth* (Tel Aviv), 28 September 2000. https://www.ynet.co.il/articles/1,7340,L-143448,00.html.

Melamed, Ariana. *'Lo Kol Coetzee Zahav'* [Not Every Coetzee Is Gold]. *Yedioth Acharonoth* (Tel Aviv), 4 April 2006. https://www.ynet.co.il/articles/0,7340,L-3194976,00.html.

Mitgang, Herbert. 'Coetzee Wins Writing Prize'. *New York Times*, 16 December 1986. https://www.nytimes.com/1986/12/16/books/coetzee-wins-writing-prize.html.

Neiger, Moti. *Motsi'im L'or Ke'metavkhey Tarbut* [Publishers as Cultural Brokers]. Jerusalem: Min Yerushalaim, 2017.

PalFest [Palestine Festival of Literature]. *2016 Festival Report*, 29 March 2017. https://www.scribd.com/document/343439665/PalFest-2016-Report.

Peteet, Julie. *Space and Mobility in Palestine*. Bloomington, Indianapolis: Indiana University Press, 2017.

Soske, Jon and Sean Jacobs, eds. *Apartheid Israel: The Politics of an Analogy*. Chicago: Haymarket Books, 2015.

Soske, Jon and Sean Jacobs. 'Introduction: Apartheid/Hafrada: South Africa, Israel and the Politics of Historical Comparison'. In *Apartheid Israel: The Politics of an Analogy*, edited by J. Soske and S. Jacobs, 1–12. Chicago: Haymarket Books, 2015.

Soueif, Ahdaf and Omar Robert Hamilton, eds. 'Introduction'. In *This Is Not a Border: Reportage & Reflection from the Palestine Festival of Literature*, 1–5. New York: Bloomsbury, 2017.

Soueif, Ahdaf and Omar Robert Hamilton, eds. *This Is Not a Border: Reportage & Reflection from the Palestine Festival of Literature*. New York: Bloomsbury, 2017.

Tal, Nitzan and Louise Bethlehem. 'South African Text; Zionist Palimpsest: Israeli Critics Read Alan Paton's *Cry, the Beloved Country*'. *Journal of Modern Jewish Studies* 19, no. 4 (2020): 450–71. https://doi.org/10.1080/14725886.2019.1693116.

Van der Vlies, Andrew. 'Publics and Personas'. In *The Cambridge Companion to J. M. Coetzee*, edited by J. Zimbler, 234–48. Cambridge: Cambridge University Press, 2020.

Warner, Michael. 'Publics and Counterpublics'. *Public Culture* 14, no. 1 (2002): 49–90. https://www.muse.jhu.edu/article/26277.

CHAPTER THIRTY-ONE

Coetzee's Russians

JEANNE-MARIE JACKSON

Of J. M. Coetzee's many engagements with literary traditions beyond South Africa's, his debt to Russian writers is especially robust across his fiction, criticism and scholarship alike. His affinity for Russia's so-called 'Golden Age' of nineteenth-century literature and ideas is most famously developed in *The Master of Petersburg*, the 1994 novel in which Coetzee reimagines Dostoevsky's life leading up to the composition of his 1872 masterwork, *Demons* (Бесы, in Russian). The familiar but inexhaustible themes of Coetzee's book, written as apartheid ended – truth's displacement by politics, art's exploitation of intimacy, the perils of self-awareness chief among them – are in many ways definitive of the early and middle stages of his career.[1] Poised uncertainly between the great reforms of Tsar Alexander II and the world-changing revolution to come, Russia in the 1860s offers a grand existential canvas for Coetzee to work through persistent personal and historical anxieties. He is not alone in his sense of comparability between the twilights of the Russian empire and South African apartheid.[2] Numerous of Coetzee's literary compatriots, including Nadine Gordimer, Alex La Guma and Christopher Hope, reached back beyond the Soviet period to ground their representational concerns in a context of extreme inequality and rising state repression.[3]

But while his gratitude to 'Mother Russia' for providing 'the standards towards which any serious novelist must toil' is a well-known facet of his fiction,[4] it is Coetzee's lesser-studied critical *oeuvre* that offers perhaps the clearest guide to the significance of Russian writers to his thought. To this end, this chapter looks back to Coetzee's 1985 essay 'Confession and Double Thoughts: Tolstoy, Rousseau, Dostoevsky' (first published in the academic journal *Comparative Literature*), seeing it as a template for his writing about Russian writers over roughly the next decade. In its emphasis on the fraught mechanism of confession for arriving at a truthful understanding of the self, the essay elaborates a structural pattern that echoes through Coetzee's later treatments of Russia and its frustrated proximity to 'truth' more broadly.[5] Coetzee's Russians are marked again and again by burning commitments to an *ultimate*, non-contingent source of moral authority, and therefore also exemplify the deflations of discovering that all candidates for this role are subject to doubt. Drawing on an admirable awareness of Russian philology and literary history to trace fine distinctions amongst writers, Coetzee nonetheless adheres to a common critical mission: he outlines comparable 'redoubling' structures in Russian writers across different contexts, implicitly linking them through their failure to reach absolute truth and self-knowledge in a secular context. Coetzee turns to Russian writers to elaborate a vision of self-awareness as self-entrapment – and thereby also enforces a more controversial, continuous reading of Russian history, spanning its imperial and Soviet periods. Coetzee's Russians and Coetzee's Russia, we might say, evolve in a closed loop.

THE ARCHITECTURE OF THE 'DOUBLE THOUGHT'

'Confession and Double Thoughts: Tolstoy, Rousseau, Dostoevsky' takes its cue from Augustine's *Confessions* in establishing shame as both a motor of and barrier to self-knowledge. The essay begins with Saint Augustine's story of stealing pears as a child for the thrill of the transgression, through which 'the knowledge of its own desire as a shameful one both satisfies the desire for the experience of shame and fuels a sense of shame'.[6] In Coetzee's reading, the upshot of Augustine's self-castigation is that the pursuit of self-knowledge it foments – the revelation not only of wrongdoing, but of deep, existential *wrongness* – means little without the promise of God's absolution. More relevant to Coetzee's literary interests, absolution also offers a formal conclusion to the process of self-narration. 'Confession is one element in a sequence of transgression, confession, penitence and absolution', he continues. 'Absolution means the end of the episode, the closing of the chapter, liberation from the oppression of the memory.'[7] When he turns to the authors named in the essay's title, it is with the intention of charting 'whatever they take to be the secular equivalent of absolution'. Confession, in this new context, is defined by its 'underlying motive to tell an essential truth about oneself'.[8]

Coetzee thus sets up an intractable problem that is at once literary and moral: how can the narrativized pursuit of self-knowledge truly *get anywhere* in the absence of a divine authority? By introducing the notion of secular 'equivalence' to Christian divinity at the essay's outset, he juxtaposes the singularity of divine absolution with the fungibility of its secular substitutions. In effect, this means that an 'equivalent' of absolution is intrinsically *not* that there can be only one God, but many alternatives. As a result, the would-be equivalents to absolution do not have a clear end point, forcing confession to double back on itself in perpetuity as it strains towards truth. Coetzee attributes the fullest expression of this bind to Dostoevsky, and in particular to the same novel to which he will later return in *Master of Petersburg*. The chief confession within *Demons*, by a character named Stavrogin, 'raises the question … of whether secular confession, for which there is an auditor or audience, fictional or real, but no confessor empowered to absolve, can ever lead to that *end of the chapter* whose attainment is the goal of confession'.[9] Coetzee sets forth the lack of such an ending as his essay's introductory concern.

'Confession and Double Thoughts' thus performs impressive intellectual gymnastics to get to a nowhere that is more-or-less declared at its outset ('and so on endlessly', he writes in relation to the young Augustine on its first page).[10] The essay is structured not in chronological order of the main works it discusses – Rousseau's *Confessions* (1782), Dostoevsky's *Demons* (1872), Tolstoy's *The Kreutzer Sonata* (1889) – but in order of their degree of ineffectiveness at reaching some higher truth via confession and the self-knowledge each work displays. Coetzee begins, in fact, with the last published of these texts, establishing a point of departure from rather than working towards the possibility of confessional 'success'. In this sense, 'Confession and Double Thoughts' is structured like the secular confessions it treats, appearing to pursue an ultimate truth but instead slipping deeper into its elusiveness. In *The Kreutzer Sonata*, an unnamed narrator recounts the confession of a fellow train traveller named Pozdnyshev, who has jealously murdered his wife. Coetzee uses the text as an example of a narrative that works against the moral revelation it pronounces. I focus here not on Tolstoy's text, but on Coetzee's claims for its failures and achievements, both of which are captured by his statement that '[t]he moment when everything becomes reversed' for Pozdnyshev (*navyvorot*' 'turned inside out') 'is the moment of illumination that opens his eyes to the truth and makes true confession possible'.[11] Pozdnyshev locates his own turning point in a new awareness of the moral collapse of educated Russian society. Crucially, though, Coetzee reads this explanation as inadequate to explain the events leading up to his wife's murder.

As an experiment in confession's inadequacy to achieve self-knowledge *vis-à-vis* a reader instead of a priest-confessor, Coetzee instead offers an alternate reading of *The Kreutzer Sonata* that stresses Pozdnyshev's unconscious but nonetheless self-betrayed phallic obsession. 'My argument', Coetzee writes,

> is merely that Pozdnyshev and Pozdnyshev's interlocutor and Tolstoy and Tolstoy's public operate within an economy in which a second reading is possible, a reading that searches in the corners of Pozdnyshev's discourse for instances where the truth, the 'unconscious' truth, slips out in strange associations, false rationalizations, gaps, contradictions.[12]

In other words, Coetzee is not suggesting that his psychoanalytic reading is *more* true than the Christian, moralistic one that Tolstoy presents through Pozdnyshev, but that Tolstoy's failure to pre-empt Coetzee's reading renders the confession's truth value moot. Coetzee cites an idiosyncratic range of Russian literary criticism by English writers who share his interest in irony to echo a conviction familiar among mid-century British critics in particular that Tolstoy's late work lacks self-reflexivity.[13] 'At all levels of presentation, then, there is a lack of reflectiveness', Coetzee pronounces.[14] The salient point here is that Coetzee reads for literary values that radically depart from Tolstoy's own: he prioritizes awareness over conviction, and interpretive density over bold declaration.

It should not be difficult to imagine an entirely different way of reading *The Kreutzer Sonata*, one prioritizing openness to moral conversion or revelation in spite of textually inbuilt temptations to doubt. This would align with Tolstoy's own late theory of artistic value, which he elaborates in a treatise called *What Is Art?* through the idea of 'infectiousness' (the usual translation of the Russian word заразительность, or *zarazitel'nost'*, from the verb заразить or *zarazit'*).[15] Nor is it surprising that Coetzee's interpretive method should reflect the broadly poststructuralist norms of literary studies during the time of his academic training – loosely, a priority on uncovering texts' subversion of their apparent meaning.[16] Indeed, Coetzee references Paul de Man at numerous points throughout 'Confession and Double Thoughts', with particular regard for his influential reading of Rousseau's *Confessions*. He is, furthermore, fully aware of the difference between his own terms and Tolstoy's: 'Just as one effect of seeing the light has been to make it easy for Pozdnyshev to discard his earlier self', Coetzee writes, 'so it would seem that the effect of "knowing the truth" has made it easy for the Tolstoy of 1889 to turn his back on the earlier self who had regarded the attainment of truth as perilously beset with self-deception and complacency, and to see the problematics of truth-telling as trivial compared with the truth itself'.[17] Where the late Tolstoy locates the value of art in its communication of feeling and capacity to effect moral transformation, Coetzee is concerned with such effects' unreliable rhetorical architecture.

What are the implications of this paradigmatic difference for Coetzee's broader sense of Russian literature and history, and particularly its capacity for dramatic change? His focus on the slippery mechanics of secular confession as against its professed result suggests that ultimate truth must transcend or is even incongruent with narrativization. At the same time, Coetzee is drawn to the unyielding pursuit of truth that characterizes Russian literature for Coetzee and so many others.

Why return again and again to a quest whose appeal is its failure? And more importantly, what does Coetzee achieve as a critic by reading *Russians'* failures in such meticulous ways? The key as far as 'Confessions and Double Thoughts' is concerned is his scepticism of transformation, brought about in *The Kreutzer Sonata*'s Pozdnyshev by the alignment of the character's internal self with an external force. The force, that is, of truth itself, in the form of God and what Coetzee refers to as a 'truth-directedness' that seeks him out.[18] Coetzee bases his reading of truth's externality to the self in Tolstoy's use of impersonal Russian constructions, most notably in his description of Pozdnyshev's moral conversion. 'The self does not change (does not change itself)', Coetzee concludes, 'rather, a change takes place in the site of the self: "When and how the change took place in me [*soversilsya vo mne etot perevorot*] I could not say."'[19]

Coetzee is right that Tolstoy's language here does, in a literal English translation, seem odd: the verb for 'to take place' is written in the past-tense reflexive form with the noun for 'change' as its subject, and the person in whom it has occurred is identified as an indirect object by the dative case. This means, in theory, that Pozdnyshev in Tolstoy's grammatical formulation is the *recipient* of change and not the one who wills it to happen, which to Coetzee suggests that moral transformation serves as a 'contemptuous, disregarding' means of effectively 'short-circuiting self-doubt and self-scrutiny in the name of an autonomous truth'.[20] The upshot is that Coetzee establishes a mutually exclusive relationship between truth and doubt, and between dramatic change and self-awareness. It is debatable whether Coetzee's grammatical evidence is as strong as his essay suggests, however; impersonal constructions are common in Russian, and to determine how significant Tolstoy's use of them really is would require his works to be painstakingly cross-referenced with those by other Russian writers of his time.[21] Nevertheless, the apparent rigour of Coetzee's philology bolsters the arc of the essay as a whole, which winds through discussion of Rousseau to arrive at Dostoevsky's status as chief exemplar of truth's self-reflexive deferral. Unlike Coetzee's Tolstoy (or Rousseau), Coetzee's Dostoevsky is *aware* of the ways in which confessional narratives undermine the goals of their exposition. In Dostoevsky's late work, he asserts, 'confession itself, with all its attendant psychological, moral, epistemological and finally metaphysical problems, moves to the centre of the stage'.[22] All three Dostoevsky works featured in 'Confession and Double Thoughts' – *Notes from Underground, The Idiot* and *Demons* – predate *The Kreutzer Sonata*, and so it is again worth noting that the essay creates a strong sense of building from an achieved Tolstoyan truth at the cost of self-awareness, towards a Dostoevskian *desire* for truth kept burning by an eagle-eyed attention to the fraught nature of its pursuit. This, in turn, upsets any notion that Russian literature as a tradition can be imagined in terms of moral or metaphysical advancement.

As a result, Coetzee ends up re-inscribing the view that positive moral change is possible only through some sort of conversion or radical break, even as he argues against its credibility in Tolstoy's case. The conversion at the heart of *The Kreutzer Sonata* stands in, albeit ineffectively, for the absolution that must punctuate a confession for it to work. This, in turn, leaves meta-reflexivity – an awareness of the failings *of* awareness, or what Coetzee terms 'hyperconsciousness' – as the only mode of undeceived narrative exposition.[23] In other words, Coetzee's Dostoevsky shares a broad critical paradigm with Coetzee as a critic. In *Notes from Underground*, this means that the narrator's confession of having wronged a prostitute 'reveals nothing so much as the helplessness of confession before the desire of the self to construct its own truth'.[24] In *The Idiot*, Coetzee foregrounds the Christ-like main character Prince Myshkin's identification of what he calls a 'double thought' (in Russian, двойная мысль or *dvoinaia mysl'*), but which Coetzee writes is 'better imagined as a doubling back of thought, the characteristic movement of self-consciousness'.[25] Again, Coetzee's reading here is stronger than it might appear. Dostoevsky's Myshkin adopts this term to describe the experience of holding contradictory impulses within oneself, which might also be interpreted as a moral stalemate in which there remains hope that one's better inclinations will find traction. (The Russian word for 'ambivalent', двойственный or *dvoistvennyi*, unsurprisingly shares a root with the 'double' thought.) Coetzee, though, describes it as an infinite regression that 'undermines the integrity of the will to confess by detecting behind it a will to deceive, and behind the detection of this second motive a third motive (a wish to be admired for one's candour), and so on'.[26]

Given the problems of performed self-knowledge that, in Coetzee's eyes, Dostoevsky sets forth, it should come as no great shock that he sees the Russian writer as finding resolution only in 'faith and grace', which often accompanies the relinquishing of selfhood at death.[27] Nothing short of an inarticulable move beyond truth's effortful narrativization will do. 'Because of the nature of consciousness', Coetzee summarizes Dostoevsky's findings across his corpus, 'the self cannot tell the truth of itself to itself and come to rest without the possibility of self-deception'.[28] This leaves Coetzee in a tighter bind than the Russians he reveres: secular mechanisms of self-knowing are inadequate to their goal, yet he is stuck with them. Unlike Tolstoy or Dostoevsky, for whom a turn to truth as God seems differently possible, Coetzee's guiding principle is a doubt from which he can imagine no real relief.[29]

THE DOUBLE-THOUGHT AS A MODEL OF RUSSIAN HISTORY

As Coetzee's criticism evolves, many of the key turns from 'Confession and Double Thoughts' echo through his discussion of other Russian writers. The essay resonates most obviously in familiar meta-reflexive formulations: in a piece from 1990 called 'Censorship and Polemic: Solzhenitsyn', for example, Coetzee declares his wish to avoid the 'Charybdis [a Greek sea monster] of denouncing denunciation itself and the rhetoric of the denunciatory mode'.[30] Similarly, in 'Osip Mandelstam and the Stalin Ode', from 1991, he directs readers 'to the representation of the project of representation itself'.[31] More significant is the general pattern in which they partake of Russians' striving towards truth, giving it literary form, and then falling prey to self-deception, which in turn gives way to a sense of Russian history that emphasizes 'redoubling' rather than change. In Coetzee's Russian literary tradition, writers on both sides of the Russian Revolution and across genres and forms are subject to a comparable thwarting of their admirably grand aims, with their differences absorbed into this larger similarity.

In 'Censorship and Polemic: Solzhenitsyn', this similarity is presented as a lineage connecting Tolstoy and Solzhenitsyn, both of whom were censored by state authorities: Tolstoy mainly by the Russian Orthodox church, and Solzhenitsyn for clinging to it after it, in turn, was banned. This pairing links the nineteenth-century Russian aristocracy (Tolstoy) with a relatively poor post-revolutionary childhood (Solzhenitsyn), as well as Tolstoy's anti-Orthodox Christian anarchism and collectivism with Solzhenitsyn's conservative and deeply individualized Orthodox faith. After he argues against an Oedipal framework for understanding the relationship between the writer and the state – for abandoning, that is, the paternal 'myth of a higher-order state' – Coetzee argues that '[t]he challenge that a Tolstoy or a Solzhenitsyn chooses to issue to the state [...] is: Who truly speaks for the people and who is the pretender? – a question framed in terms of representation, not priority'.[32] Again, it is debatable whether this is a fair way to imagine Tolstoy's populism: the ambitions behind his relationship with 'the people' are pedagogical more than representative, as evidenced by his work with peasant schooling, and later, his preaching to his followers at his estate.[33] And yet in emphasizing the two writers' broad affinity in being censored rather than the dramatic social and political differences underlying which of their texts were censored and why, Coetzee advances a narrative of Russian history that turns on Soviet embellishment and not upending of imperial precedents. Beginning with the creation of a secret police force under Tsar Alexander I (1801 to 1825) and moving quickly through a history of political criticism in the nineteenth century, he concludes that 'in the Soviet era the bureaucracy of control built up under the Tsars was not only massively extended [...] but also given a new Marxist-Leninist theoretical underpinning'.[34]

This interpretation is not necessarily wrong, but it is controversial: it downplays complicating factors in order to connect the faulty mechanics of secular confession to the perfidy of Russia's claims to political advancement. In Coetzee's analysis of Soviet *samokritika*, the practice of performing one's guilt and desire for improvement before state authorities, the tension between 'truth' and self-awareness reappears as the thread connecting Russian writers across time. When he sets up the challenges confronting Solzhenitsyn's efforts to preserve a 'true' self from official co-optation, Coetzee briefly references some lesser-known writers' compelled confessions in the 1950s. 'Any later retraction', he notes of one, based on the claim that the confession was insincere because made under duress, 'is robbed of its force beforehand by the fact that the confession addresses unambiguously the question of its own sincerity'.[35] This sounds like his description of Dostoevsky's failed efforts to achieve self-knowledge in 'Confession and Double Thoughts', with the false truth of Soviet dogma now weighed against the more subtle, established falsity of belief in a 'real' self that exists apart from its discursive performance. Coetzee concludes that despite Solzhenitsyn's faith in his powers of resistance to state lies and manipulation, he is ultimately 'an actor in a dynamic over which he has no control'.[36] Solzhenitsyn here mirrors at least Coetzee's *version* of Tolstoy, whose moral confidence in *The Kreutzer Sonata* is bought with self-delusion. Solzhenitsyn's enabling delusion extends for Coetzee to his sense of himself *as* Russian rather than Soviet, as he insists on 'the opposites of a true (old) Russia [...] and a false (Soviet) Russia, against whose all-prevailing violence and lies he will do battle'.[37] In 'Censorship and Polemic', Coetzee thus again makes clear that truth claims narrativized as rupture – be it a personal conversion or political revolution – are intrinsically flawed.

Coetzee's other essays on Russia unfold along a similar logic of an ever-more-complex search for a truth that cannot be undone, and so cannot be written. In 'Osip Mandelstam and the Stalin Ode', he explores the problematic 'sincerity' of the infamous 1937 poem in which Mandelstam seems to glorify Stalin, and whose writing was intended to save Mandelstam from being persecuted for political disloyalty. Coetzee rejects longstanding attempts to see the ode as 'not coming from [Mandelstam's] true self' by virtue of madness, in favour of a reading that foregrounds 'a madness like Hamlet's, a madness that knows itself' and that can be traced by 'seeking for signs of reflection within the ode upon the ode's own madness'.[38] Later, in a 1996 review of Joseph Brodsky's essay collection, *Less Than One*, Coetzee applies his analytic pattern of truth-seeking that unfolds as truth's inevitable secular un-zipping to a critique of literary studies. 'None of the schools of criticism that rule the academy wants to deal with poetry in its own right',[39] he bemoans, in what Brodsky saw as poetry's 'truly metaphysical status'.[40] And yet Coetzee holds out little hope for the rectification of this oversight. Implicating himself in the question of whether 'academic critics' can 'take a lesson from Brodsky', he rejoins with: 'I fear not. To operate at his level, one has to live with and by the great poets of the past, and perhaps be visited by the Muse as well.'[41] Finally, in the memorable 1997 essay 'Gordimer and Turgenev', Coetzee returns to the Russian nineteenth century to depict claims of ultimate truth as a cover for conflicted historical allegiances. The quest for truth is offset by meta-awareness *of* this quest's contingency, creating an endless tunnel of doubt. In relation to Turgenev, this means wondering, 'what aspect does the politics of being above politics take on in *Fathers and Sons*?'[42] As concerns Gordimer, it means charting her stake in opposing truth claims to observe how she winds up 'doubting her own right to reserve her position, or even to have any position at all'.[43]

In sum, Coetzee appears to turn to Russia to imagine a recurrent and lofty truth-seeking authorial agency, only to see his subjects entangled in pushing truth farther away. Much as confession in the absence of God leads to either self-delusion or redoubled anxiety, the appearance of a historical break between imperial Russia and the Soviet Union, for Coetzee, is window dressing on the negative continuity from one to the other. Despite his rich engagement with changing philological and historical details, Coetzee's reading of Russian literature holds remarkably consistent across his critical *oeuvre*. At a moment of unusual plainness in 'Confession and Double Thoughts', Coetzee remarks that 'one of the minor functions of [his] readings is to bring the notion of *the* truth into question'.[44] It is this aim that he furthers throughout his critical writing on Russian literature, holding fast all the while to admiration of Russian writers who refuse to rest easy with such relativism. Coetzee's Russians, then, in a formula that keeps on giving, exemplify both the enduring appeal and elusiveness of final moral authority.

NOTES

1. For a discussion of this novel, see Attridge's chapter in this volume.
2. For a brief treatment of *Master of Petersburg*'s relationship to *Demons*, see Adelman, 'Stalking Stavrogin'.
3. For a thorough treatment of the connections between literary South Africa and, respectively, the nineteenth-century Russia and the Soviet Union, see Jackson, *South African Literature's Russian Soul*, and Popescu's *South African Literature beyond the Cold War*.
4. Coetzee, *Diary of a Bad Year*, 227.
5. Some of these ideas were rehearsed in Coetzee's inaugural professorial address, 'Truth in Autobiography', at the University of Cape Town in 1984.
6. Coetzee, 'Confession and Double Thoughts', 193.
7. Ibid., 194.
8. Ibid.
9. Ibid., 195.
10. Ibid., 193.
11. Ibid., 195.
12. Ibid., 199.
13. In addition to Davie as quoted in 'Confession and Double Thoughts', see Bayley, *Tolstoy and the Novel*.

14. Coetzee, 'Confession and Double Thoughts', 200.
15. In English, see Tolstoy, *What Is Art?*
16. Testifying to this interest in De Manian 'irony' or texts' inbuilt self-contradiction, Coetzee is demonstrably well-versed in structuralist and poststructuralist linguistics. See Attwell's introduction to *Doubling the Point*.
17. Coetzee, 'Confession and Double Thoughts', 201.
18. Ibid., 203.
19. Ibid.
20. Ibid., 204.
21. For an overview of the moral implications of Tolstoy's poetics, see Morson, *Hidden in Plain View*.
22. Coetzee, 'Confession and Double Thoughts', 215.
23. Ibid., 216.
24. Ibid., 220.
25. Ibid., 222.
26. Ibid., 222–3.
27. Ibid., 230. It is also worth noting here that Coetzee's characteristic formal and epistemological explanation for Dostoevsky's interest in deathbed confession omits an equally compelling historical one, that Russians from the Middle Ages through the eighteenth century confessed less often than their European counterparts, relying instead on localized and communally oriented penitential rituals. For a fascinating exploration of this topic, see Zhivov's 'Handling Sin in Eighteenth-Century Russia'.
28. Coetzee, 'Confession and Double Thoughts', 230.
29. For a brief account of the relationship between Christianity and choice in Tolstoy and Dostoevsky as against their postcolonial counterparts, see Jackson, 'The Russian Novel of Ideas in Southern Africa'.
30. Coetzee, *Giving Offense*, 117.
31. Ibid., 107.
32. Ibid., 118–19.
33. For a classic, accessible overview in English of Tolstoy's investment in peasant education, see Tolstoy, 'Tolstoy and the Russian Peasant'. For an illuminating and unconventional treatment of Tolstoy's influential teachings at his Yasnaya Polyana estate, see Bunin, *The Liberation of Tolstoy*.
34. Coetzee, *Giving Offense*, 124. Some of this anxiety that relates to the continuity and thereby expansion of censorship regimes is no doubt due to Coetzee's own position in apartheid-era South Africa. For a lively and thorough discussion of its own history of censorship, see McDonald, *The Literature Police*.
35. Coetzee, *Giving Offense*, 127.
36. Ibid., 140.
37. Ibid., 142.
38. Ibid., 106–7.
39. Coetzee, *Stranger Shores*, 133.
40. Ibid., 130.
41. Ibid., 134.
42. Ibid., 225.
43. Ibid., 229.
44. Coetzee, 'Confession and Double Thoughts', 213.

WORKS CITED

Adelman, Gary. 'Stalking Stavrogin: J.M. Coetzee's The Master of Petersburg and the Writing of The Possessed'. *Journal of Modern Literature* 23, no. 2 (1999–2000): 351–7.
Bayley, John. *Tolstoy and the Novel*. Chicago: University of Chicago Press, 1988.
Bunin, Ivan. *The Liberation of Tolstoy: A Tale of Two Writers*. Translated by Thomas Marullo. Evanston: Northwestern University Press, 2001.
Coetzee, J. M. 'Confession and Double Thoughts: Tolstoy, Rousseau, Dostoevsky'. *Comparative Literature* 37, no. 3 (1985): 193–232.
Coetzee, J. M. *Diary of a Bad Year*. New York: Penguin, 2007.
Coetzee, J. M. *Doubling the Point: Essays and Interviews*. Edited by D. Attwell. Cambridge, MA: Harvard University Press, 1992.
Coetzee, J. M. *Giving Offense: Essays on Censorship*. Chicago: University of Chicago Press, 1996.
Coetzee, J. M. *The Master of Petersburg*. New York: Viking, 1994.
Coetzee, J. M. *Stranger Shores: Literary Essays*. New York: Viking, 2001.
Coetzee, J. M. *Truth in Autobiography*. Cape Town: University of Cape Town Press, 1984, 1–6.
Jackson, Jeanne-Marie. 'The Russian Novel of Ideas in Southern Africa'. In *Transnational Russian Studies*, edited by A. Byford, C. Doak and S. Hutchings, 232–46. Liverpool: Liverpool University Press, 2020.
Jackson, Jeanne-Marie. *South African Literature's Russian Soul: Narrative Forms of Global Isolation*. London/New York: Bloomsbury, 2015.
McDonald, Peter D. *The Literature Police: Apartheid Censorship and Its Cultural Consequences*. Oxford: Oxford University Press, 2010.
Morson, Gary Saul. *Hidden in Plain View: Narrative and Creative Potentials in War and Peace*. Stanford: Stanford University Press, 1988.
Popescu, Monica. *South African Literature beyond the Cold War*. London: Palgrave, 2010.
Tolstoy, Alexandra. 'Tolstoy and the Russian Peasant'. *The Russian Review* 19, no. 2 (1960): 150–6.
Tolstoy, Leo. *What Is Art?* Translated by Richard Pevear and Larissa Volokhonsky. London: Penguin, 1995.
Zhivov, Viktor. 'Handling Sin in Eighteenth-Century Russia'. In *Representing Private Lives of the Enlightenment*, edited by A. Kahn, 123–48. Oxford: Voltaire Foundation, 2010.

CHAPTER THIRTY-TWO

Coetzee's Latin America

MAGALÍ ARMILLAS-TISEYRA

Speaking to the writer Mr Foe of events prior to her arrival on Cruso's island in *Foe* (1986), Susan Barton asserts that Bahia is 'a world in itself, and Brazil is an even greater world'; Bahia, she says, cannot be 'held down in words'.[1] Although often inconspicuous, Latin America is integral to the conceptual geography of Coetzee's work. 'The Vietnam Project' in *Dusklands* (1974), for instance, invokes US operations in Central America. In *Youth* (2002), 'John' learns Spanish to read César Vallejo, Nicolás Guillén and Pablo Neruda, and then uses Neruda to generate the lexicon for his computer poems; in *Summertime* (2009), John teaches Neruda in translation at the University of Cape Town. The eponymous protagonist of *Elizabeth Costello* (2003) discusses Jorge Luis Borges's 'La biblioteca de Babel' ('The Library of Babel', 1941). In *Diary of a Bad Year* (2007), the ageing writer J.C. invokes Gabriel García Márquez's reflections on writerly inspiration, while Anya calls J.C. 'Señor C' on the misunderstanding that he is Colombian (he has a diploma from Columbia University). There is also the suggestively unspecified setting of the novels in the *Jesus* trilogy, where characters speak Spanish in a place that is not Spain. As a critic, Coetzee has reviewed Borges and García Márquez; these writers, along with Reinaldo Arenas, Antonio di Benedetto, Carlos Fuentes, Mario Vargas Llosa and even indigenous foodways in Mesoamerica, form part of his extended archive of reference.[2]

Recent years have seen more direct interaction. While Penguin Random House publishes his fiction in Latin America, Coetzee has for the past decade worked closely with the independent Argentinian press El Hilo de Ariadna, which publishes his essays as well as the series 'Biblioteca Personal' (Personal Library) – translations of works selected and introduced by Coetzee, inspired by Borges's project of the same name.[3] They have also published two story collections, *Tres cuentos* (*Three Stories*, 2016) and *Siete cuentos morales* (Seven Moral Tales, 2018), and in May 2019, nearly a year before it was available in the UK or United States, co-published *La muerte de Jesús* (*The Death of Jesus*) with Literatura Random House.[4] These ventures are part of a larger effort to foster connections across the southern hemisphere or 'South', understood by Coetzee as a space of shared physical (biogeographical) and historical experience. From 2015 to 2018, Coetzee presided over the 'Literaturas del Sur' (Literatures of the South) seminars, conducted under the Cátedra Coetzee (Coetzee Chair) at the Universidad Nacional San Martín (UNSAM) in Greater Buenos Aires, and has since been involved in similar events in Australia. He has helped facilitate the translation and publication of Australian and southern African writers by UNSAM Edita in Argentina, and of Latin American writers in Australia with Giramondo's 'Southern Latitudes' series. James Halford consequently argues that Coetzee's 'Australian period' (following his emigration to Australia in 2002) should be seen as Coetzee's 'Southern period'.[5] But 'South' is expansively understood, as Derek Attridge makes clear when he includes Latin America – a diffuse regional designation comprising South America, the Caribbean, Central and parts of North America – in Coetzee's South.[6]

Like this fluid South, Coetzee's Latin America is less a distinct location than a nexus of overlapping ideas about the history of the southern Atlantic, the global hegemony of English, and the promise of South-South literary exchanges. This chapter will disentangle and describe this agglomeration. First, it outlines the historical basis for comparison between southern Africa and Latin America, focusing on the role of Brazil in Coetzee's work. These connections are the background for comparison of Coetzee with writers such as Borges, discussed in the second part. Finally, it looks at the reception of Coetzee in Latin America alongside Coetzee's activities in the region, which together constitute a larger 'Southern turn'.

TRANSATLANTIC CROSSINGS: LATIN AMERICA IN COETZEE'S FICTION

Latin America has not appeared overtly as a setting in Coetzee's fiction; this includes the stories in *Tres cuentos* and *Siete cuentos morales*.[7] To the extent that the novels of the *Jesus* trilogy invoke Latin America, they evince only a glancing relationship to the material realities of the region.[8] Rather than affirm a Latin American setting, the Spanish language and names create a sense of locational ambiguity familiar to much of Coetzee's work.[9] Following Rebecca Walkowitz, Spanish in the *Jesus* novels serves to decentre English – emphasized by recurring reference to Miguel de Cervantes's *Don Quixote* (1605–15), as progenitor of the modern novel – and in this sense contributes to the novels' metanarrative interest in translation and the unevenness of the global publishing market.[10] But Latin America is nevertheless crucial to Coetzee's work.

While Coetzee derives the island in *Foe* from Daniel Defoe's *Robinson Crusoe* (1719), its topography and ecology differ significantly, and Coetzee abandons Defoe's Caribbean location.[11] In drafting *Foe*, Coetzee considered several alternatives, including the Atlantic coast of southern Africa, before situating the island near Bahia (and the port city of Salvador) on Brazil's Atlantic coast.[12] These variations echo the history of *Robinson Crusoe*: Defoe himself moved the story of the castaway Alexander Selkirk that inspired the novel from the Juan Fernández archipelago in the southern Pacific (near Chile) to the Caribbean, adding Robinson's time trading in enslaved people and as a plantation owner in Brazil. Yet *Robinson Crusoe* and *Foe* present very different visions of Brazil. Defoe's, as the grounds for a plantation whose value compounds during Crusoe's absence, is largely blank. In *Foe*, Brazil is a space filled with people and events, significant as the part of the story Susan largely declines to tell. In recasting Friday as Black, moreover, Coetzee brings questions of race and the history of slavery in the Americas to the fore. No longer coded as indigenous and therefore associated with the natural landscape of the island, and – crucially – missing his tongue, Coetzee's Friday is, to cite Gayatri Spivak, 'wholly other'.[13] The illegibility of Friday's difference is most explicit in the scenes where Susan and Foe attempt to teach Friday to write, and Friday produces a series of signs neither comprehends.[14] In sum, Coetzee amplifies elements of Defoe's story to the point of distortion, making it the raw material for very different reflections on coloniality, racial difference and the ethics of writing.

Taking this condensed discussion of *Foe* as benchmark, references to Latin America in Coetzee's work serve to evoke the complex historical entanglements between the region and Africa from which emerge the ethical and philosophical questions Coetzee explores. Already linked by the transatlantic trade, Latin America and Africa had by the end of the eighteenth century become, per Mary Louise Pratt, 'parallel sites of European expansionist initiatives'.[15] These corresponding processes produced striking resemblances, particularly between sites of intensive settler-colonial projects. Coetzee's observations about the 'literature of the empty landscape' in *White Writing* (1988), for instance, resonate with the discourses of the so-called Conquest of the Desert, the displacement and massacre of indigenous people by which the state established control of the national territory in nineteenth-century Argentina.[16] Latin America and Africa are further linked by the geopolitics of the Cold War, which included direct contact in the form of Cuban assistance to Agostinho Neto's People's Movement for the Liberation of Angola (MPLA) (Operation Carlota, 1975–91), initiated to counter the South African invasion of Angola (Operation Savannah, 1975–6) as part of the Border War (1966–90). This period also saw collaboration between the apartheid government and dictatorial regimes in Argentina, Brazil, Chile, Uruguay and Paraguay. Post-apartheid, South Africa's Truth and Reconciliation Commission (1996–2003) drew on earlier commissions in Latin America, including those in Argentina (1983–4) and Chile (1990–1).[17] Such corresponding experiences of state violence and investment in transitional justice, per Ariel Dorfman – whose play *Death and the Maiden* (1990) was staged in Johannesburg in 1992 and is cited in the *Truth and Reconciliation Commission of South Africa Report* (1998–2003) – make South Africa a 'mirror' of a country such as Chile, and vice versa.[18]

These layered historical connections surface in *Summertime* in the form of Adriana Teixeira Nascimento, a Brazilian dance teacher whom 'John' pursued in the 1970s. Adriana remembers John's affections with embarrassment. 'He was not in love with me', she says, but 'with some idea of me, some fantasy of a Latin mistress that he made up in his own mind'.[19] Adriana and her family arrived in Cape Town from Luanda, having first fled the military dictatorship in Brazil. In Cape Town, Adriana's husband is attacked and dies, leaving her to contend with a hostile bureaucracy while also negotiating the racial hierarchies of apartheid, within which she is not (or does not feel) entirely legible. Yet Adriana remembers her many 'Coloured' students fondly. Noting that Latin America was then popular in South Africa, she says: 'They had romantic illusions about Latin America, Brazil above all. Lots of palm trees, lots of beaches. In Brazil, they thought, people like themselves would feel at home. I said nothing to disappoint them.'[20] While the details of Adriana's life serve to register more recent connections between southern Africa and Latin America, this passing observation invokes deeper ties.

The statement 'I said nothing to disappoint them' alludes to the pervading ideology of white supremacy in which both apartheid and Brazilian racial hierarchy are embedded.[21] The point is not that Adriana's students are naïve, but rather that the structures of oppression that condition their lives are continuous with those experienced on the other side of the Atlantic. For Adriana's students, Brazil figures an alternative via which to denominate the structures that govern their lives. This moment illuminates a history in common and suggests bases for transatlantic solidarity. It is contrasted to John's romantic illusions of Brazil, outlined later in the novel. He imagined Brazil as a paradise of racial intermixture, wishing a 'Brazilian future' for South Africa; as one colleague drily remarks, 'He had of course never been to Brazil.'[22]

In saying nothing to her students about race in Brazil, however, Adriana interrupts (practically, not thematically) possible connections. One reason for this silence is suggested at the end of Adriana's interview, where John's biographer intimates that Adriana was the inspiration for Susan

Barton.[23] While the claim is fictional, Adriana does resemble Susan in her limited ability to engage with questions of race. Adriana's silence is not exactly shared by *Summertime* itself. Within the novel, her silence makes space for the juxtaposition of her students' and John's versions of Brazil. In so doing, *Summertime* emphasizes Brazil's function as a space of desire, a site for the projection of alternatives that serve (indirectly, even clumsily) to name the present condition. This is similarly the case with Susan's partial descriptions of Bahia, which are expressions of her desire for autonomy.[24] With these examples from *Foe* and *Summertime* in mind, Brazil appears in Coetzee's work both as a stand-in for larger histories of racial exclusion and violence, and as the name for ideas about possible, better futures. Yet, as placeholder, Brazil itself – and, by extension, Latin America – remains largely absent.

COETZEE AND LATIN AMERICA: WORLD-LITERARY CIRCULATION AND COMPARISON

Critics have long compared Coetzee's work to that of Latin American writers with similarly broad international dissemination, including Roberto Bolaño, García Márquez and Borges.[25] These writers have been accorded a place in what Coetzee terms the 'repertoire of world literature', despite being from the so-called periphery, where a writer's world-literary status is never assured.[26] In *Diary of a Bad Year*, J.C. references García Márquez's *El olor de la guayaba* (*The Fragrance of Guava*, 1982), a volume of conversations in which García Márquez discusses his writing process, paying particular attention to the difficulties of writing in 'a continent unprepared for successful writers'.[27] García Márquez contends that while these material realities pressure the production and circulation of the work, they should not limit its imaginative scope.

Coetzee's approach to these challenges is consonant with that laid out by Borges in 'El escritor argentino y la tradición' ('The Argentine Writer and the Tradition', 1951), where Borges rejects the notion that Argentinian writers should restrict themselves to 'Argentinian' topics (the gaucho, the countryside), instead claiming 'the whole of Western culture' as a tradition to which he has a right. Borges's assertion, per Mariano Siskind, is fundamentally cosmopolitan, while also keenly aware of the marginal position from which it is articulated.[28] Coetzee's work is similarly characterized, to paraphrase David Attwell, by the global reach of his intellectual connections, as shaped by the fact of his South African birth.[29] Borges and Coetzee's shared interest in using fiction to explore philosophical arguments offers rich grounds for comparison.[30] Borges's play with authorial personae in 'Borges y yo' ('Borges and I', 1960), for instance, informs Coetzee's in the Nobel lecture, 'He and His Man'(2003), and with the figure of Elizabeth Costello.[31] In one interview, Coetzee delightedly relays the story of a friend who, lecturing on Australian literature, is asked to discuss Costello as an Australian writer. 'I mention the story', he explains, 'because it shows how a purely fictional being can start to take up residence in the real world'.[32] Such blurring of fiction and reality would similarly have delighted Borges, who explores this idea in 'Tlön, Uqbar, Orbis Tertius' (1940).[33] Finally, in taking *Don Quixote* as an intertext in the *Jesus* novels, Coetzee is also playing with Borges's ludic engagement with Cervantes in 'Pierre Menard, autor del Quijote' ('Pierre Menard, Author of the Quixote', 1939).[34]

Perhaps the most striking similarity between Coetzee and Borges is the facility with which their work can be read with little or no reference to the context from which it emerges. Writing in the

1980s about the international reception of Borges, Beatriz Sarlo observed that Borges's reputation had 'cleansed him of nationality', generating a version of Borges that could be explained by and within Western culture. But, Sarlo declares, 'there is no writer in Argentine literature more Argentine than Borges'. The Argentine-ness Borges embodies is one of animating contradiction: he is at once cosmopolitan and national (or, in the vocabulary of Coetzee scholarship, provincial). His work exists at the edge – in Spanish, *en las orillas* (on the shore) – between cultures, genres and languages.[35] There is of course a rich body of scholarship that looks at Coetzee's work in context, particularly his relationship to Afrikaner identity.[36] My contention, however, is that comparisons of Coetzee and Borges prove most fruitful when they turn from shared interests (their cosmopolitan or philosophical investments) and ask instead what reading one writer might reveal about the other.

Paratactic juxtaposition of Coetzee and Borges – a comparison that does not attempt to coordinate through subordination or narratives of influence – illuminates each writer's complex relationship to place and the history of their countries of origin. This is particularly true of work set in the rural expanses of South Africa or Argentina. In 'Historia del guerrero y la cautiva' ('The Story of the Warrior and the Captive Maiden', 1949) and 'The Narrative of Jacobus Coetzee' (*Dusklands*, 1974), for instance, each looks to the settler frontier, marking their relationship to it via a (partially fictionalized) ancestor.[37] From 'Biografía de Tadeo Isidoro Cruz (1829–74)' ('A Biography of Tadeo Isidoro Cruz', 1949) to 'El Evangelio según Marcos' ('The Gospel According to Mark', 1970), from *In the Heart of the Country* (1982) to *Disgrace* (1999), rural spaces figure as sites of violence or the disintegration of social order.[38] Both writers are also keenly attuned to these spaces as sites of desire, specifically of desire for belonging when one is part of a settler colonial project; or, as Coetzee puts it in *Boyhood* (1997), when one is an 'uneasy guest'.[39]

These tensions are at the centre of Borges's 'El Sur' ('The South', 1953). Here, the librarian Juan Dahlmann, immigrant German on his father's side and settler *criollo* on his mother's, suffers a blow to the head. As he perishes in a hospital, Dahlmann reimagines his death as a knife fight with a gaucho in a frontier town.[40] Such romantic attachments to place and past likewise inform the melancholy of Coetzee's 'Nietverloren' (2002; 2014), which situates these in the context of the transformation of South Africa's rural economies in the latter half of the twentieth century.[41] A South African writer and two friends from the United States visit a struggling farm in the Karoo, Nietverloren – from the Dutch, 'not lost' – now functioning as a tourist attraction. As the narrator bitterly explains, without mention of the family farm to which he no longer has a claim, the only real money to be made these days is in 'The tourist crop' ('Cosechar turistas').[42] Written across continents and several decades apart, 'The South' and 'Nietverloren' both turn on their protagonist's attachment to the rural as the figure for a form of belonging that, not least because it seeks to forget the violence on which it is founded, cannot be sustained in the present. In a review of Borges's *Collected Fictions*, Coetzee argues that in stories such as 'The South' Borges intends to situate himself within the tradition of Argentinian mythmaking.[43] Yet Borges is not so much participating in national mythmaking as reflecting on this process and its consequences, a set of concerns that has been similarly important to Coetzee. Both are in this sense writing from the 'shore', at once inside and outside of the worlds about and for which they write, whether this is the 'world' of world literature or their worlds of origin.

LATIN AMERICA AND COETZEE: RECEPTION AND THE SOUTHERN TURN

Just as Coetzee is an attentive reader of Latin American writers, Latin Americans have long read Coetzee. Per Francisco Goldman, Coetzee was one of García Márquez's favourite contemporaries; when Coetzee was awarded the Nobel, García Márquez joked that he received so many congratulations, he felt he had won the prize a second time.[44] Carlos Fuentes was also an admirer and invited Coetzee to take part in the conference 'Geografía de la novela' (Geography of the Novel) in Mexico in 1998. Here, Coetzee delivered a lecture that would become part of 'The Novel in Africa' in *Elizabeth Costello* and was introduced to writers such as Juan Villoro and Carlos Chimal.[45] Both have gone on to write about Coetzee's work for venues such as *Letras libres*, where Coetzee is a frequent point of reference. The number of conferences, symposia and publications on his work demonstrate sustained and attentive engagement with Coetzee throughout the region.

Coetzee is an increasingly active participant in these exchanges. In addition to his work with 'Literatures of the South', he has been the subject of and attended conferences in Mexico, Colombia and Chile, where he also awards an annual prize in his name, and regularly attends festivals throughout the region. His influence also registers beyond literary circles: the Argentinian film *El ciudadano ilustre* (*The Distinguished Citizen*, 2016), in which a Nobel-prize-winning writer – the fictional Daniel Mantovani – returns home to Argentina after forty years, takes inspiration from Coetzee. Per Oscar Martínez, the actor who played Mantovani, Coetzee was one of the models for the role.[46] While there are significant differences between Coetzee and Mantovani, Martínez's physical bearing and delivery of Mantovani's speech at the Nobel ceremony that opens the film speaks to a familiarity with Coetzee that underscores the reach of his reputation. Coetzee's appearances in the region receive extensive media coverage, and he uses this to promote the work of writers from the African continent as well as South-South literary exchanges.[47] The latter in particular moves the focus from Latin America proper to the question of Coetzee's South.

Invoked as both a physical location and metonymic association, Coetzee's South is an amorphous concept comprising a complicated assortment of ideas. Its difficulties are compounded by the fact that, while Coetzee has spoken widely on the topic, his thinking has not yet been systematically articulated in writing. The archive for engaging with Coetzee's South consists of recordings of public appearances, statements relayed by attendees and expansions on both by critics. Broadly speaking, Coetzee's South overlaps with such frameworks as Meg Samuelson and Charne Lavery's 'oceanic South', Samuelson's 'blue southern hemisphere', Isabel Hofmeyr's turn towards the Indian Ocean in South African literary and cultural studies, Joseph Slaughter and Kerry Bystrom's work on the (global) South Atlantic and the South of Raewyn Connell's Southern Theory. All of these frameworks understand the South in locational or latitudinal as well as relational terms. In the latter sense, South-ness is a dynamic condition produced by relations – to quote Connell, of 'authority, exclusion and inclusion, hegemony, partnership, sponsorship, appropriation' – with the North.[48] For Coetzee, however, the South also has material specificity: 'the South is a real part of the world', he explained in an interview with María Soledad Constantini (founder of El Hilo de Ariadna) in 2018, 'a part of the world with a climate and flora and fauna of its own; indeed, with more than just natural features in common, with strong commonalities of history and culture'.[49]

There is apparent solidity in Coetzee's insistence on the biogeographic specificity of the South, which extends metonymically to include history and culture. But it can tend towards the rhapsodic, as in Coetzee's opening address to the April 2016 'Literatures of the South' seminar at UNSAM:

> What is left [when social scientific terms such as 'periphery' and 'Third World' have faded] is the real South, the South of this real world, where most of those present in the room were born and most of us will die. It is a unique world – there is only one South – with its unique skies and its unique heavenly constellations. In this South the winds blow in a certain way and the leaves fall in a certain way and the sun beats down in a certain way that is instantly recognizable from one part of the South to another.[50]

These lines emphasize the unique but also unitary nature of the South, as recognizable to a certain kind of viewer. Yet, when the logic of analogy slips into claims of identity, it threatens to obscure very real political, economic and cultural differences between locations within the South – not least of which is their varyingly uneven relations with the North. My intent here is to demonstrate the difficulties critics face when speaking about Coetzee's South. The lines discussed above are, after all, part of a speech at an event bringing together people to explore their commonalities, and Coetzee prefaced his remarks by emphasizing that he spoke as a writer and not a theorist.[51]

Rather than attempt to fix a definition of Coetzee's South, it is more useful to understand Coetzee's Southern turn in the context of his relationship to the North and, by extension, the global dominance of the English language. As he explained in an interview at the Museo de Arte Latinoamericano de Buenos Aires (MALBA) in 2017:

> I am here principally to promote literary exchanges between countries of the South; and it is a particular pleasure to me that this story, 'The Glass Abattoir' ['El matadero de cristal'] and others [the collection *Siete cuentos*] will be coming out as work from a South African-Australian writer published by an Argentine publisher without any intervention from the world's North.[52]

The goal, as Coetzee elaborated in his 2018 interview with Constantini, was to bypass the 'cultural gatekeepers of the metropoles of the North', which mediate cultural exchanges from and within the South and, most importantly, determine 'which stories by the South about itself will be accepted into the repertoire of world literature and which will not'.[53]

If 'Literatures of the South' furthers this goal, it does not necessarily follow that Coetzee's decision to publish first or exclusively in Spanish functions in the same way. While English dominates the global publishing market, Spanish is hardly a minor language. It has its own imperial history, both in Latin America (and Asia and Africa) as well as within Spain itself; as Attridge puts it, 'Spanish is no more and no less a marker of Southern-ness than English'.[54] And yet, Coetzee's move to publishing first in Spanish does constitute an act of resistance to English-language hegemony. Coetzee himself has framed this decision as the result of a progressive disenchantment with the United States and Britain, where early experiments with releasing his novels first in Dutch gave way to publication in Spanish and 'letting the North wait its turn'.[55] It marks, as Samuelson argues, the emergence of a new internationalism for Coetzee, one 'no longer authorized by the Anglosphere'.[56] In this sense, Coetzee's move to Spanish is principally a move away from English. Spanish is therefore not a synecdoche for Latin America (where it is one of many languages spoken), nor does it stand for South-ness in and of itself. It is instead Coetzee's *choice* of Spanish, expressed as an insistence on particularity and illegibility, that reflects a specifically *Southern* perspective, one shaped by his long-standing engagement with Latin America.

CONCLUSION: LATIN AMERICA AS AXIS

What, then, is Coetzee's Latin America? It is, as I have elaborated, a nexus of overlapping histories and associations that, much like Coetzee's South, is amorphous, shifting and, like Susan Barton's Bahia, cannot be held down in words. In this abstract sense, Latin America informs Coetzee's fiction, where places such as Brazil have long functioned as metonyms for larger histories of racial exclusion and settler colonialism. The historical connections between Africa and Latin America, as well as their putatively peripheral positions in the world system, also inform the comparison of Coetzee's work to that of Latin American writers. But to say that Latin America is an agglomeration of ideas for Coetzee is not to discount its importance as a physical – or, per Coetzee, 'real' – place. Over the last two decades, Latin America has become the generative space from which Coetzee has attempted to renegotiate the terms of his engagement with the cultural circuits of the North, whether via his efforts to grow networks for South-South exchange or in his use of Spanish to decentre English. Latin America has been, in short, the axis of Coetzee's Southern turn.

NOTES

1. Coetzee, *Foe*, 122–3.
2. See Coetzee, 'J. L. Borges, *Collected Fictions*', in *Stranger Shores*, 139–50; 'Gabriel García Márquez, *Memoirs of my Melancholy Whores*', in *Inner Workings*, 257–71; 'Antonio di Benedetto, *Zama*', in *Late Essays*, 134–51; 'Emerging from Censorship', in *Giving Offense*, 34–47; 'Meat Country', 44–5.
3. Spanish translations of Coetzee's novels appear under the imprint Literatura Random House. In Brazil, Companhia das Letras has published many of Coetzee's novels; Penguin Random House acquired majority ownership in 2018.
4. While *Siete cuentos* is not available in English, the Australian house Text Publishing released the English version of *Three Stories* in 2014. They also published *The Death of Jesus* in English in October 2019.
5. Halford, 'Southern Conversations 2'; see also Samuelson, 'An International Author'.
6. Attridge, 'The South According to Coetzee'.
7. Most of the material in the Spanish-language collections is available in English. *Tres cuentos* contains Spanish translations of three previously published works: 'Una casa en España' ('A House in Spain', 2000), 'Nietverloren' (as 'The African Experience', 2002) and 'Él y su hombre' ('He and His Man', 2003). In *Siete cuentos*, 'Una mujer envejece' was published as 'As a Woman Grows Older' in the *New York Review of Books* (15 January 2004). Of the three more recent Elizabeth Costello stories, 'La anciana y los gatos' ('The Old Woman and the Cats') was published in the catalogue for a collaboration between Coetzee and the Belgian artist Berlinde De Bruyckere; 'Mentiras' ('Lies') appeared in the *NYRB* (21 December 2017); and Coetzee has read versions of 'El matadero de cristal' ('The Glass Abattoir') in public several times, including at the 2018 Melbourne Writers' Festival and at the Museo de Arte Latinoamericano de Buenos Aires (MALBA) in 2017. Another story from this collection, 'El perro' ('The Dog') appeared in the *New Yorker* (4 December 2017). At the time of writing, only 'Una historia' (A Story) and 'Vanidad' (Vanity) are not easily available in English.
8. See Ng and Sheehan, 'Coetzee's Republic'.

9. See Harvey, 'The Escape from Place in Coetzee's Late Novels'; Miklos, 'El Evangelio según Coetzee'; Attwell, *J. M. Coetzee and the Life of Writing*, 209–22.
10. Walkowitz, *Born Translated*, 3–23.
11. Coetzee, *Foe*, 122–3.
12. See Attwell, *J. M. Coetzee*, 128; Attwell and Easton, eds., *Scenes from the South*, 64.
13. Spivak, 'Theory in the Margin', 4; see also Attwell, *J. M. Coetzee*, 124–36; Attridge, *J. M. Coetzee and the Ethics of Reading*, 65–90.
14. Coetzee, *Foe*, 151–2.
15. Pratt, *Imperial Eyes*, 11–12.
16. Coetzee, *White Writing*, 9–11; Pratt 37–9.
17. See Bystrom 'South Africa, Chile, and the Cold War' and 'The Cold War and the (Global) South Atlantic'.
18. For more on *Death and the Maiden* and the TRC, see Bystrom, 'Literature, Remediation, Remedy'.
19. Coetzee, *Summertime*, 193–4.
20. Ibid., 182.
21. See Milazzo, 'On the Transportability, Malleability, and Longevity of Colorblindness'.
22. Coetzee, *Summertime*, 232–3.
23. Ibid., 200–1.
24. See, for instance, Susan's description of 'free women' in Bahia (114–15).
25. See Loy, 'The Precarious State of the Art'; Forest, 'Challenging Secularity's Posthistorical "Destination"'; Brits, *Literary Infinities*; Galván, 'Borges, Cervantes, and Coetzee, or The Fictionalization of the Author' and Rose, *Literary Cynics*.
26. Coetzee and Constantini, 'In conversation'.
27. García Márquez and Mendoza, *The Fragrance of Guava*, 25–6.
28. Siskind, 'El cosmopolitismo como problema político', 90–1; see also, Núñez Faraco, 'The Argentine Writer and the Tradition'.
29. Attwell, *J. M. Coetzee*, 215–16.
30. The philosophical dimensions of Coetzee's work are also a topic of interest to Latin American scholars; see Lazo Briones, *Las encrucijadas de J. M. Coetzee*; Herrera Rodríguez, '*Escenas de una vida de provincias de J. M. Coetzee*'; Maciel, 'A vida dos outros'; Lums, 'Coetzee, o de la complejidad' and Santoveña Rodríguez, 'La ética imposible de J. M. Coetzee'.
31. Borges, 'Borges and I', in *Collected Fictions*, 324. In addition to the eponymous novel and the Costello stories in *Siete cuentos*, see *The Lives of Animals* and *Slow Man*.
32. Coetzee and Constantini, 'J. M. Coetzee: Las literaturas del sur' (Madrid).
33. Borges, 'Tlön, Uqbar, Orbis Tertius', in *Collected Fictions*, 68–81.
34. Borges, 'Pierre Menard, Author of the Quixote', in *Collected Fictions*, 88–95.
35. Sarlo, *Jorge Luis Borges*, 1–6.
36. See Barnard, 'Coetzee in/and Afrikaans'; Attridge, 'J. M. Coetzee's *Boyhood*, Confession, and Truth'; Attwell, *J. M. Coetzee and the Life of Writing*, 11–24; Jolly, *Colonization, Violence, and Narration in White South African Writing* and Sanders, 'Undesirable Publications'.
37. Borges, 'The Story of the Warrior and the Captive Maiden', in *Collected Fictions*, 208–11; 'The Gospel According to Mark', in *Collected Fictions*, 397–401.
38. Borges, 'A Biography of Tadeo Isidoro Cruz (1829–1874)', in *Collected Fictions*, 212–14.

39. Coetzee, *Boyhood*, 79.
40. Borges, 'The South', in *Collected Fictions*, 174–9.
41. See Attwell, *J. M. Coetzee*, 40–54.
42. Coetzee, 'Nietverloren' (2002). In *Tres cuentos*, trans. Marcelo Cohen, 47–68; and *Three Stories*, 25–43.
43. Coetzee, 'J. L. Borges, Collected Fictions', 147.
44. Goldman, 'In the Shadow of the Patriarch'.
45. Fuentes, 'Desgracia y fortuna de J. M. Coetzee'.
46. Reinoso, 'La Argentina al desnudo en la mirada de un nobel ficticio'.
47. Gigena, 'Nueva ola africana'.
48. Connell, *Southern Theory*, viii–ix.
49. Coetzee and Constantini, 'In Conversation'.
50. Qtd. in Halford, 'Southern Conversations'.
51. Ibid., n.p.
52. Coetzee and Kazumi Stahl, 'Lectura John M. Coetzee en MALBA'.
53. Coetzee and Constantini, 'In Conversation'.
54. Attridge, 'The South According to Coetzee'.
55. Coetzee and Constantini, 'J. M. Coetzee: las literaturas del sur'. For more on the publication of Coetzee's work in Dutch, see Walkowitz, *Born Translated*, 3–4 and 51–5; Walkowitz, 'Comparison Literature' and Attridge, 'The South According to Coetzee'.
56. Samuelson, 'An "International Author"', 138.

WORKS CITED

Attridge, Derek. *J. M. Coetzee and the Ethics of Reading: Literature in the Event*. Chicago: Chicago University Press, 2004.

Attridge, Derek. 'J. M. Coetzee's *Boyhood*, Confession, and Truth'. *Critical Survey* 11, no. 2 (1999): 77–93.

Attridge, Derek. 'The South According to Coetzee'. *Public Books*, 25 September 2019. https://www.publicbooks.org/the-south-according-to-coetzee/.

Attwell, David. *J. M. Coetzee and the Life of Writing*. New York: Penguin, 2016.

Attwell, David and Kai Easton, eds. *Scenes from the South: From the Collections of the Harry Ransom Center and Amazwi South African Museum of Literature to Mark the Occasion of J. M. Coetzee's 80th Birthday*. Makhanda: Amazwi South African Museum of Literature, 2020.

Barnard, Rita. 'Coetzee in/and Afrikaans'. *Journal of Literary Studies* 25, no. 4 (2009): 84–105.

Borges, Jorge Luis. 'The Argentine Writer and the Tradition' (1951). Translated by Ester Allen. In *Selected Non-Fictions*, edited by E. Weinberger, 420–7. New York: Penguin, 2000.

Borges, Jorge Luis. *Collected Fictions*. Edited and translated by A. Hurley. New York: Penguin, 1998.

Brits, Baylee. *Literary Infinities: Number and Narrative in Modern Fiction*. New York: Bloomsbury, 2018.

Bystrom, Kerry. 'The Cold War and the (Global) South Atlantic'. In *The Global South and Literature*, edited by R. West-Pavlov, 69–82. New York: Cambridge University Press, 2018.

Bystrom, Kerry. 'Literature, Remediation, Remedy (The Case of Transitional Justice)'. *Comparative Literature* 66, no. 1 (2014): 25–34.

Bystrom, Kerry. 'South Africa, Chile, and the Cold War: Reading the South Atlantic in Mark Behr's *The Smell of Apples*'. In *The Global South Atlantic*, edited by J. R. Slaughter and K. Bystrom, 124–43. New York: Fordham University Press, 2018.

Bystrom, Kerry and J. R. Slaughter. 'The Sea of International Politics: Fluidity, Solvency, and Drift in the Global South Atlantic (Introduction)'. In *The Global South Atlantic*, 1–30.

Coetzee, J. M. *Boyhood*. New York: Viking, 1997.
Coetzee, J. M. *The Childhood of Jesus*. New York: Viking, 2013.
Coetzee, J. M. *The Death of Jesus* (2019). New York: Viking, 2020.
Coetzee, J. M. *Diary of a Bad Year*. New York: Viking, 2008.
Coetzee, J. M. *Disgrace*. New York: Viking, 2000.
Coetzee, J. M. *Dusklands*. 1974. New York: Penguin, 1985.
Coetzee, J. M. *Elizabeth Costello*. New York: Viking, 2003.
Coetzee, J. M. *Foe*. New York: Viking, 1986.
Coetzee, J. M. *Giving Offense: Essays on Censorship*. Chicago: Chicago University Press, 1996.
Coetzee, J. M. 'He and His Man'. J. M. Coetzee Nobel Lecture, 7 December 2003. https://www.nobelprize.org/prizes/literature/2003/coetzee/lecture/.
Coetzee, J. M. *In the Heart of the Country*. New York: Penguin Books, 1982.
Coetzee, J. M. *Inner Workings: Literary Essays, 2000–2005*. New York: Penguin, 2007.
Coetzee, J. M. *The Lives of Animals*. Princeton: Princeton University Press, 1999.
Coetzee, J. M. 'Meat Country'. *Granta* 52 (1995): 43–52.
Coetzee, J. M. *La muerte de Jesús*. Translated by Elena Marengo. Buenos Aires: El Hilo de Ariadna and Literatura Random House, 2019.
Coetzee, J. M. *Late Essays, 2006–2017*. New York: Penguin, 2017.
Coetzee, J. M. 'The Old Woman and the Cats'. In *Cripplewood/Kreupelhout*, edited by B. De Bruyckere, 7–27. Brussels: Mercatorfonds, 2013.
Coetzee, J. M. *The Schooldays of Jesus*. New York: Viking, 2016.
Coetzee, J. M. *Siete cuentos morales*. Translated by Elena Marengo. Buenos Aires: El Hilo de Ariadna and Literatura Random House, 2018.
Coetzee, J. M. *Stranger Shores: Literary Essays, 1986–1999*. New York: Penguin, 2001.
Coetzee, J. M. *Summertime*. New York: Viking, 2009.
Coetzee, J. M. *Three Stories*. Melbourne: Text Publishing, 2014.
Coetzee, J. M. *Tres cuentos*. Translated by Marcelo Cohen. Buenos Aires: El Hilo de Ariadna, 2016.
Coetzee, J. M. *Slow Man*. New York: Viking, 2005.
Coetzee, J. M. *White Writing: On the Culture of Letters in South Africa*. New Haven: Yale University Press, 1988.
Coetzee, J. M. *Youth*. New York: Viking, 2002.
Coetzee, J. M. and Anna Kazumi Stahl. 'Lectura John M. Coetzee en MALBA'. 11 September 2017. https://www.youtube.com/watch?v=U5Ms65oo2wI&feature=youtu.be.
Coetzee, J. M. and Soledad Constantini. 'In Conversation: J.M. Coetzee with Soledad Constantini' (Bilbao). 29 May 2018. https://www.youtube.com/watch?v=4VNk52t-YPM.
Coetzee, J. M. and Soledad Constantini, 'J.M. Coetzee: Las literaturas del sur' (Madrid). 28 May 2018. https://www.youtube.com/watch?v=DW1QRdJ9rDg.
Connell, Raewyn. *Southern Theory: The Global Dynamics of Knowledge in Social Science*. Cambridge: Polity Press, 2007.
Chimal, Carlos. 'Sudafricanos profundos: J. M. Coetzee en México'. *Letras libres*. 21 December 2003. https://www.letraslibres.com/mexico-espana/ciencia-y-tecnologia/sudafricanos-profundos-jm-coetzee-en-mexico.
Dorfman, Ariel. 'Whose Memory? Whose Justice? A Meditation on How and When and If to Reconcile' (2010 Mandela Lecture). In *Writing the Deep South: The Mandela Lecture and Other Mirrors for South Africa*, 3–19. Johannesburg: Picador Africa, 2011.
Duprat, Gastón and Mariano Cohn, dir. *El ciudadano ilustre*. 2016. Argentina: Aleph Media, Televisión Abierta, Magma Cine, and A Contracorriente Films.
Forest, Shannon. 'Challenging Secularity's Posthistorical "Destination": J. M. Coetzee's Radical Openness in the Jesus Novels'. *Journal of Modern Literature* 42, no. 4 (2019): 146–64.
Fuentes, Carlos. 'Desgracia y fortuna de J. M. Coetzee'. *La Jornada Semanal*, 4 June 2000. https://www.jornada.com.mx/2000/06/04/sem-fuentes.html.

Galván, Fernando. 'Borges, Cervantes, and Coetzee, or The Fictionalization of the Author'. *European Journal of English Studies* 20, no. 2 (2016): 179–91.

García Márquez, Gabriel and Plinio Apuleyo Mendoza. *The Fragrance of Guava* (1982). Translated by Ann Wright. London: Verso, 1983.

Gigena, Daniel. 'Nueva ola africana'. *La Nación*, 30 September 2016. https://www.lanacion.com.ar/cultura/nueva-ola-africana-la-literatura-secreta-que-llega-a-las-playas-del-idioma-espanol-nid1942661/.

Goldman, Francisco. 'In the Shadow of the Patriarch'. *New York Times*, 2 November 2003. https://www.nytimes.com/2003/11/02/magazine/in-the-shadow-of-the-patriarch.html.

Halford, James. 'Reading Three Great Southern Lands: From the Outback to the Pampa and the Karoo'. *The Conversation*. 11 July 2016. https://theconversation.com/reading-three-great-southern-lands-from-the-outback-to-the-pampa-and-the-karoo-60372.

Halford, James. 'Southern Conversations: J. M. Coetzee in Buenos Aires'. *Sydney Review of Books*. 28 February 2017. https://sydneyreviewofbooks.com/essay/southern-conversations-j-m-coetzee-in-buenos-aires/.

Halford, James. 'Southern Conversations 2: Writing the South in Sydney'. *Sydney Review of Books*. 25 February 2020. https://sydneyreviewofbooks.com/essay/southern-conversations-2/.

Harvey, Melinda. '"In Australia You Start Zero": The Escape from Place in J. M. Coetzee's Late Novels'. In *Strong Opinions: J. M. Coetzee and the Authority of Contemporary Fiction*, edited by C. Danta, S. Kossew and J. Murphet, 19–34. New York: Continuum, 2011.

Herrera Rodríguez, Camilo. 'Escenas de una vida de provincias de J. M. Coetzee: Una mirada a la novela autobiográfica desde la analítica existencial de Martin Heidegger'. *Perseitas* 5, no. 2 (2017): 421–39.

Hofmeyr, Isabel. 'The Black Atlantic Meets the Indian Ocean: Forging New Paradigms of Transnationalism for the Global South – Literary and Cultural Perspectives'. *Social Dynamics* 33, no. 2 (2007): 3–32.

Hofmeyr, Isabel and Michelle Williams, eds. *South Africa and India: Shaping the Global South*. Johannesburg: Wits University Press, 2011.

Jolly, Rosemary. *Colonization, Violence, and Narration in White South African Writing: André Brink, Breyten Breytenbach, and J. M. Coetzee*. Athens: Ohio University Press, 1996.

Lavery, Charne. 'Thinking from the Southern Ocean'. In *Sustaining Seas: Oceanic Space and the Politics of Care*, edited by E. Probyn, K. Johnson and Nancy Lee, 307–18. London: Rowman & Littlefield, 2020.

Lazo Briones, Pablo, ed. *Las encrucijadas de J. M. Coetzee: Miradas filosóficas de un creador literario*. Mexico City: Universidad Iberoamericana, 2016.

Loy, Benjamin. 'The Precarious State of the Art: Writing the Global South and Critical Cosmopolitanism in the Works of J.M. Coetzee and Roberto Bolaño'. In *Remapping World Literature: Writing, Brook Markets, and Epistemologies between Latin America and the Global South*, edited by G. Müller, J. J. Locane and B. Loy, 91–116. Berlin and Boston: De Gruyter, 2018.

Lums, Rafael. 'Coetzee, o de la complejidad'. *Letras libres*. 30 September 2010. https://www.letraslibres.com/mexico-espana/coetzee-o-la-complejidad.

Maciel, Maria Ester. 'A vida dos outros: J.M. Coetzee e a questão dos animais'. *Alteria: Revista de Estudos de Literatura* 21, no. 3 (2011): 91–101.

Miklos, David. 'El Evangelio según Coetzee'. *Letras libres*. 11 October 2013. https://www.letraslibres.com/mexico-espana/libros/el-evangelio-segun-coetzee.

Milazzo, Marzia. 'On the Transportability, Malleability, and Longevity of Colorblindness: Reproducing White Supremacy in Brazil and South Africa'. In *Seeing Race Again: Countering Colorblindness Across the Disciplines*, edited by K. W. Crenshaw, L. C. Harris, D. M. Ho Sang and G. Lipsitz, 105–27. Berkeley: University of California Press, 2019.

Ng, Lynda and Paul Sheehan. 'Coetzee's Republic: Plato, Borges, and Migrant Memory in *The Childhood of Jesus*'. In *J. M. Coetzee's The Childhood of Jesus: The Ethics of Ideas and Things*, edited by A. Uhlmann and J. Rutherford, 83–104. New York: Bloomsbury, 2017.

Núñez Faraco, Humberto. 'The Argentine Writer and the Tradition'. In *Jorge Luis Borges in Context*, edited by Robin Fiddian, 99–105. New York: Cambridge University Press, 2020.

Pratt, Mary Louise. *Imperial Eyes: Travel Writing and Transculturation* (1992). 2nd ed. New York: Routledge, 2008.
Reinoso, Susana. 'La Argentina al desnudo en la mirada de un nobel ficticio'. *Clarín*, 14 August 2016. https://www.clarin.com/cultura/argentinidad-desnudo-mirada-Nobel-ficticio_0_Hy3dz_0K.html.
Rose, Arthur. *Literary Cynics: Borges, Beckett, and Coetzee*. London: Bloomsbury, 2017.
Samuelson, Meg. '"An 'International' Author, but in a Different Sense": J. M. Coetzee and "Literatures of the South"'. *Thesis Eleven* 162, no. 1 (2021): 137–54.
Samuelson, Meg and Charne Lavery. 'The Oceanic South'. *ELN: English Language Notes* 57, no. 1 (2019): 37–50.
Sanders, Mark. 'Undesirable Publications: J. M. Coetzee on Censorship and Apartheid'. *Law and Literatures* 18, no. 1 (2006): 101–15.
Santoveña Rodríguez, Marianela. 'La ética imposible de J. M. Coetzee'. *Acta Poética* 30, no. 2 (2009): 217–31.
Sarlo, Beatriz. *Jorge Luis Borges: A Writer on the Edge*. London: Verso, 1993.
Siskind, Mariano. 'El cosmopolitismo como problema político: Borges y el desafió de la modernidad'. *Variaciones Borges* 24 (2007): 90–1.
Spivak, Gayatri Chakravorty. 'Theory in the Margin: Coetzee's *Foe* Reading Defoe's *Crusoe/Roxana*'. *English in Africa* 17, no. 2 (1990): 1–23.
Villoro, Juan. 'J. M. Coetzee: El trazo de la sombras'. *Letras libres*, 30 November 2003. https://www.letraslibres.com/mexico-espana/jm-coetzee-el-trazo-las-sombras.
Walkowitz, Rebecca. *Born Translated: The Contemporary Novel in the Age of World Literature*. New York: Columbia University Press, 2015.
Walkowitz, Rebecca. 'Comparison Literature'. *New Literary History* 40, no. 3 (2009): 567–82.

CHAPTER THIRTY-THREE

Coetzee's Australians

MICHELLE CAHILL

NOTES FOR AN ESSAY

'A short interview with Coetzee'

on Gadigal Country, Sydney   23 February 2020

My father has suffered a stroke and is being nursed in a coastal town in New South Wales when an email arrives from Lucinda Evangeline Wright inviting me to write a chapter on 'Coetzee's Australians'. She mentions that it might be an idea to interview him. How would that go, I wonder? Coetzee, the distinguished recluse, the novelist of ethical and philosophical enquiry, has a reputation for declining interviews. What questions should, or could, I possibly ask of the master? His command of narrative logic appears only to be surpassed by his command of its indeterminacy. His virtuosity, complexity of narrative structures, allegory, pastiche, metafiction – all of this would need to be addressed, in relation to the country in which we both now reside. It seems an enigma that as a woman of colour, a marginal author slash critic, I should be asked to write an appraisal of his Australian characters and contexts.

Most readers agree that Coetzee's later novels, written in Australia, are somewhat arcane and self-reflexive, remixed with reincarnations. These complexities and hauntings are bewildering for a critic to navigate, provoking seemingly unanswerable questions. Elizabeth Curren, a retired Classics lecturer dying of cancer, has witnessed the brutality of the South African security forces against Black youth in *Age of Iron* (1990). To what extent does she re-animate or inhabit her Australian successor, Elizabeth Costello? Can characters be revivified as heteronyms? Coetzee, like his forerunners, Pessoa, Borges and Rhys, would have us believe so.

Elizabeth Costello (2003) transforms a series of eight Platonic-styled prose lectures delivered by an ageing Melbourne-born author into narrative. Blending philosophy, poetics, ethics, autobiography and fiction, it asks powerful questions about realism, analogy, the Holocaust and animal rights. To complicate matters, Elizabeth Costello makes a guest appearance in *Slow Man* (2005): just when we are convinced that Coetzee has committed himself to realism, he code-switches to metafiction, extemporizing with diegetic frames to forge a transcendent intertextual parody set in his current hometown, Adelaide. What transpires hinges on the corollary of the phantom limb: a synecdoche for the writing life cut away from origin, mentored and tormented by the figure of Costello, playing with her creation in a one-way yet empathetic duet. I think of *Slow Man* fondly as a kind of Australian *Foe* (1986). The authorial voice in the novel, with its informal tone, colloquialisms and embattled protagonist, pays homage in Coetzee's idiosyncratic way to the lives of atypical 'Aussie' characters. Following a bicycle accident, Paul Rayment is literally on his last leg, being tended by a married Croatian nurse, Marijana, whom he begins to desire, and to whose children he acts out the part of godfather.

My father is lying by the Pacific Ocean. He is bedridden, unable to speak, although for most of his life, and when I was growing up, my father held strong opinions. Guilty for being absent, I reflect on paralysis and the many registers of silence. The strong opinions in Coetzee's *Diary of Bad Year* (2007) belong to an ageing Sydney-based author who hires a beautiful Filipina, Anya, to be his typist. Coetzee complicates the power relations between the polarities represented: Caucasian and Asian, intellectual and sensually desirable, youth and age, the tragic and the comic. The novel defies being read sequentially as the geometry of the page disrupts a chronological unfolding of the story, even though the diaries offer themselves as temporal accounts, or in formalist terms, as 'fabula'. And in the *Jesus* trilogy we encounter parodies of Coetzee's earlier novels and of other novelists – Cervantes and Dostoevsky cast their shadow spirits, there is a dog called Plato and throughout it all a quasi-improvisation of Socratic dialogue. Coetzee's ironic doubles reduce the considerable authority of Western philosophy's understanding of the subject. A ventriloquized, malleable and theoretically decentred voice is crucial to his praxis, revising the canon.

Coetzee walks a tightrope between first and third person, innovation and repetition, between genders and genres, between pedagogy and cliché, urban centres and province. He is the most careful incendiary, one capable of making a real author's real novel become the subject of critique for which he cannot be blamed. Perhaps because my mind cannot hold this undertaking as a plausible entity, I don't dwell on Lucinda's proposed request for very long – but can't seem to push it away either. For days and weeks it oscillates within me, hovering like an irrepressible doubt. Upon dismissing the idea, it faithfully returns, as if I am being asked to defend a plea – what do I believe? – so that, ultimately, I do not even know if I am for Coetzee or if I am against him. I write back, expressing some interest. My focus for the foreseeable future, however, is creative, writing new poems and an urgent revision of my novel, required under contract with my publisher.

'Violations of innocent children. The extermination of whole peoples.'

on Guringai Country, Dangar Island   7 March 2020

Today is my sister's birthday, and we are on Dangar Island. Everyone is relaxed, talking. My mind is wandering, soothed by the rippled surface of the river, yet turning to the past, to the violence of white language appropriating First Nation's language names, to the frontier wars erased by the textbooks, to colonial, historical shame. I had been for a walk up the hill to Flat Point before the others arrived. The plaques in the memorial park seem gravely wrong in failing to question Terra Nullius. The plaque reads that Governor Phillip led the first European exploration into Pittwater and Broken Bay in 1788, a month after the settlement of Sydney was founded. He took a longboat and a cutter, reaching Dangar Island on 7 March. Having succeeded in catching mullet, he upheld the conventions by which European occupation and exploitation are recorded, naming it Mullet Island.

As we stroll through lush greenery after lunch, I wonder how this island has changed; how the crimes of our history can be narrated, so it can be decolonized; and what that might mean for a critical practice. There are many islands and castaways in Coetzee's *oeuvre*. In the *Jesus* trilogy, the past has been erased and the characters have no memory; their names, numbers and ages are assigned.

Lucinda has sent a follow-up email and I have been wondering if I am, after all, sufficiently skilled, and sufficiently visible as 'an Australian writer' to write about Coetzee. What does it mean to be visible or invisible? At the most basic level the mainstream tokenizes some minority writers, trading them as commodities so they become hypervisible in the vortex of dominant culture, while others slip under the radar. In my work the slippages between writing subject and writing self have cultivated counter-voices in heteronymic tension, palimpsestic writing and Pessoa-like masks. Crossing genres and national boundaries, I am malleable, fragmented and contingent. There is activism inherent in the course of my work as a settler immigrant. Can I write about Coetzee without compromising my task?

Lesson 8 in *Elizabeth Costello*, 'At the Gate', allegorizes manifest and invisible thresholds, the gates to eternal life *and* the borders of a nation-state like Australia. Alternatively, it may be read as a portal for one author passing, and another author arriving, as they journey through narrative space: Coetzee standing in the auditorium at Princeton University to deliver The Tanner Lectures in 1997, slipping into a story of Elizabeth Costello facing a secular literary community after extensive world travels and professional lecture tours. The lecture chapters of *Elizabeth Costello* are a hall of mirrors, exploring the restricted capacity of realism to debate ideas and probing the power of language to reveal or conceal truth, to foster real things. Whose opinions are we to believe in *Elizabeth Costello*? Should they be Elizabeth Costello's, Emmanuel Egudu's or Sister Bridget's? Can the Australian continent be realized in prose because the frogs of the Dulgannon mudflats vividly described by Costello are real?

At a pivotal moment, a tribunal of European judges asks Costello to comment on the genocide of Tasmanian Aboriginals. Her responses at first are hesitant and equivocal. I read this as a performance of the colonizer's strategy since Costello is shrewd and non-committal: she is almost in 'contempt of court'.[1] Eventually, she confesses a position that seeks not to appropriate culture as a white settler, preferring silence until she is appointed by First Nation's peoples: 'When the old Tasmanians summon me, if they choose to summon me, I will be ready and I will write to the best of my ability', she says.[2] Significantly enacted in Coetzee's first Australian novel, this scene may be considered a defining statement on his positioning as a guest on Aboriginal lands.

In a letter to Paul Auster dated 27 May 2009, Coetzee writes of the monolingual dominance he experienced after migrating to Australia:

> I began to feel my own situation more acutely after moving to Australia, which despite the fact that within its territory there are scores of Aboriginal languages still clinging to life, and despite that fact that since 1945 it has encouraged massive immigration from southern Europe and Asia is far more 'English' than my native South Africa. In Australia public life is monolingual. More importantly relations to reality are mediated in a notably uninterrogated way through a single language, English.

The effect on me of living in an environment so saturated with English has been a peculiar one: it has created more and more of a skeptical distance between myself and what I would loosely call the Anglo *weltanschauung*, with its inbuilt templates of how one thinks, how one feels, and how one relates to other people, and so forth.[3]

> *'Well your little Filipina typist can't do it for you. Your little Filipina typist with her shopping bags and her empty head.'*

Westfield Shopping Complex, Sydney   2 July 2020

Sitting at a table in Expresso Warriors, I sip my latte, flicking through *Diary of a Bad Year*. I can imagine a chorus of WhatsApps and Tweets firing off with the hashtags #JMC, #JMCoetzee #Anya #DiaryofaBadYear #caucasity! 'Wait, it's powerful', I want to reply. 'Hooray for Anya', 'LOL', 'LMAO'. It's a pity that some readers may take Anya's character too literally as representing a subjugation or a reduction of Filipina women. This points to the risk-taking when white men write Black, Asian and minority ethnic (BAME) characters. According to Rachel Isom, however, the novel makes space for Anya's voice, allowing Coetzee 'to explore heteroglot exchanges' that undermine the apparent monologues of white.[4] Señor C's 'strong opinions' are slated to be published with 'six eminent writers (who) pronounce on what is wrong with today's world'.[5] We learn this ironically. Anya's asides compete for the main narrative. Her erotic agency weakens patriarchal power. I love that Coetzee allows Anya to mock Señor C. Tauntingly, in her tomato-red smock, she reverses assumptions, through the too often abusive exchange that passes between racially and educationally privileged white men and women of colour.

For all his privilege, it would be foolish of me to deny that Coetzee has not left substantive traces on me as a reader and a writer. I once wrote a sycophantic email to the master: 'You have no idea how much I admire your work', I raved, 'No one has written sustained poetic novels such as yours: not Dostoevsky, not Emily Brontë'. Don't mistake me. Although there is a hard clarity in his work that I can trust, I'm not obsessed with Coetzee's prose, nor do I revere the man, the writer. Even if he has cast himself obliquely, allegorically, as a master, I am not in awe. On the pretext of seeking permission to quote from *Disgrace* (1999) and *Foe*, I sent him my short story, 'Letter to John Coetzee', written in the voice of Melanie Isaacs. This short intervention, or interception, published in my collection *Letter to Pessoa* (2016), challenges the reductive depiction of Melanie in *Disgrace* and what that might mean for women of colour.

The response I received from John Coetzee was brief, stern even, but with a hint of humour in the ellipsis of a verb. He gave me permission to cite our emails for a paper that I delivered in Prato, at the 'Coetzee's Women' symposium, convened by an Australian contingent from Monash University and hosted in a grand palazzo. I gave a paper concerning the function of games in literary subversions. It was at Prato that I met Lucinda ... but I digress.

Anya is not merely a typist for Señor C; she becomes the key character, her shrewd intuitions and body language exposing his pretences. As Issom suggests, she interprets across boundaries created by whiteness, marriage and patriarchy. She debunks the narrative reduction of the seductive, clueless Asian, whereas by contrast Elizabeth Costello is a clever portrayal of the white middle-class feminist. Despite their alterity both characters are in service to the narrative project. When called to defend her lectures on politics and ethics, Costello speaks to a shared inheritance: 'I am a writer and what I write is what I hear. I am a secretary of the invisible, one of many secretaries over the ages'.[6]

'I borrowed a bicycle and rode down to the coast a couple of times.'

Yuin country, Bundanon Trust   11 September 2020

It is rather beautiful here; it will be difficult to leave. I am quite charmed, especially by the birds and the colour of the rocks in the evening. The landscape cradles one and there is so much history. Walking along the dams and to the river, there are many wombats and kangaroos, and they too seem imbued with traumas of the past. I have broken the ice, so to speak. Although politely declining to meet in Adelaide for an interview, J.M.C. has agreed to answer electronic questions presented to him through email.

Coetzee was in residency here at Bundanon in 1999 as part of the Sydney Writers' Festival. He rode a bicycle to the coast, he tells me. It is a stunning stretch of forest trails to the mouth of the Shoalhaven river. The road was burned badly in the December fires, but there is re-growth now. Yesterday, I saw some yellow-tailed cockatoos among the scarred trees.

I ask Coetzee what he thinks of art, inspiration and if was he aware of Sidney Nolan's 'Deaths in Custody' paintings or Boyd's work with Aboriginal subjects in the 'Brides' series, and, following on from this, how he sees himself in relation to Aboriginal Australia. His response, delivered at 3 am Adelaide time, touches on his sense of estrangement, Australian art and his relationship to Aboriginal Australia, which he described as being 'an indirect one, mediated through my interest in First Peoples in Africa and, to a lesser extent, in South America'. He also wrote:

> Strictly speaking, no Australian artist has inspired me because the phenomenon of inspiration is pretty much foreign to me. However, I do remember my first contact with Australian painting, which took place sometime in the early 1960s, when I was living in England. There was a big exhibition of Australian art at the Tate Museum, and I remember being immensely impressed with the work of Sidney Nolan and Arthur Boyd. I know Boyd's Brides paintings, but I don't think I have ever seen Nolan's Deaths in Custody. I also admire Fred Williams very much, and, in a different way, Jeffrey Smart.[7]

Whilst here, I've been reading Nolan's letters to Albert Tucker, with whom Nolan was a friend for about 40 years until they snubbed each other at an exhibition in London. I feel, through his letters, that I rather like Nolan. In 1950, from his studio in Wahroonga, the suburb where I live in Guringai country, he wrote the following, which I now share with Coetzee: 'One of the main surprises was the strong impact the Aborigines made on us. They give you the key to the whole situation … They show you that the country is a gentle, dreaming one, the barrenness and harshness is all in our European eyes and demands. In fact, one feels a barbarian at the gates.'[8]

'… the essay, should be about his Australian novels.'

Ngunnawal and Wiradjuri country, Yass   9 September 2020

Driving to Adelaide the fastest way possible, I take the Hume Highway from Sydney, my car packed with a suitcase, shoes, jars of spices, fruit, vegetarian food and four boxes of books, including

Woolf's *Mrs Dalloway, To the Lighthouse* and *The Waves*; Valleri Luiselli's *The Story of My Teeth*; Vahni Capildeo's *Measures of Expatriation*; Joshua Poteat's *The Regret Histories*; Alice Oswald's *Memorial* and Jean Rhys' Paris novels. J. M. Coetzee's 'Australian' novels are carefully placed in a wide, shallow box about four inches high, with handles; two neat piles with *The Death of Jesus* at the top of one pile and *Diary of A Bad Year* at the top of the other. The label on the box reads 'Fresh Australian Produce'.

Lucinda has given me an extension to write the essay, so it's a thing, not a mere speculation that partly fizzled out. I have committed myself now.

Coetzee prises open the complexities of power, history, authorship, torture, hospitality, global migration and displacement. And yet, there has also been controversy surrounding his treatment of post-apartheid South Africa, and particularly about interracial rape in the novel *Disgrace*. Some attribute this to his disillusionment with the new South Africa.[9] Surely I must proceed carefully, as a woman author and poet, as a writer of colour, as an immigrant Australian, one who is scarcely herself representative of Australians.

At Yass, the tree-lined river parks and cafés have closed early. Supplies sold in supermarkets across the state have been diminished by the pandemic; yet the Woolworths store keeps the largest range of supermarket condoms I have seen. A few hours on, and I turn left onto the Sturt Highway, passing Tarcutta's lush farmland. I am reminded of Josephine Rowe's edgy, poetic short fictions, *Tarcutta Wake,* and the truck stop café which Bruce Dawe and Les Murray wrote poems about; Murray having lived in Nabiac, a coastal town 700 kilometres north. Narrandera was my planned overnight stay, but darkness sets in fast and with it, fatigue. HiLux utes and cargo vans are parked in rows outside the motel. A cluster of new virus cases fills today's news bulletins. South Australia is in hard lockdown, the borders closed, even for an author who is adept at building fictional bridges and navigating sea journeys; an author who shifts his/her/their characters from Cape Town to London, from Melbourne to Pennsylvania, from Amsterdam to Adelaide, from Novilla to Estrella or from Calcutta to Gravesend.

A local footnote on 'Coetzee's Australians'

on Kaurna Country, Provost Street, Adelaide   6 October 2020

Few cities have preserved native trees as close to the CBD, yet the eucalypts and mallee of Adelaide's parklands are contrasted with tamed European gardens and rose beds. During my stay, I visit the national parks, beyond which lie remote communities and the outback.

I love the trees glittering in the breeze at sunset, the delicate bush scents of the parklands. A pleasant ride along the river past the zoo takes me to the art gallery. In Kerryn Goldsworthy's essay 'Acts of Writing', she cites Coetzee describing his first impressions of the city: 'It was March, it was hot, but there were shaded walks to be had along the Torrens River where black swans glided serenely. "What kind of place is this?" I asked myself. "Is this paradise on earth?"'[10]

In his *Late Essays: 2006–2017* (2017), Coetzee reviews the work of Australian writers Patrick White, Les Murray and Gerald Murnane. He discusses these in terms of the canon and its fidelity to nationalism, emphasizing White's British background as heir to the English-language modernists, and in the context of Australia's cultural cringe. He probes into Murray's outsider status and exposes his appropriation of Aboriginal consciousness in 'The Buladelah-Taree Holiday Song Cycle'.

Coetzee powerfully calls out 'Murray's assimilation of the white rural poor with the people whose lands they took over; his reluctance to, in the parlance of today, "say sorry" for the historic crimes of colonialism', pointing to veiled hubris in Murray's posture with officialdom.[11] By contrast, the Murnane essay places him as the most experimental and European-influenced of the 1950s white, male-dominated, puritanical settler culture.

Yet these are major white male writers in the Australian and world canon, and I am neither inclined nor qualified to add much to the copious critical attention that their work and Coetzee's essays have attracted. As a minority writer speaking through cumulative microaggressions and the repetitive traumas of white supremacy and settler colonialism, my task focuses on how the Nobel laureate has supported First Nations peoples, and asylum seekers, as well as Black, indigenous and people of colour (BIPOC) writers.

First Peoples and refugees are prioritized in the essay passages 'On Apology' and 'On Asylum in Australia' in *Diary of A Bad Year*. Restitution for colonial invasion in South Africa has been 'in one sense better than in Australia' because of the transfer of government and property to Black Africans, Coetzee's protagonist argues.[12] Through his alter-ego, Señor C, Australia's processing of refugees is exposed as 'a system of deterrences, and indeed, a spectacle of deterrence'.[13] By 2016, Coetzee was a signatory along with sixty other authors to an Open Letter petitioning the Australian government to amend its abuses of human rights in detaining refugees offshore. Thomas Kenneally described this as comparable to Émile Zola's 'J'accuse' letter of 1898 in defence of Alfred Dreyfus, who was incarcerated by the French government for treason on Devil's Island off French Guiana. In September 2019, Coetzee published a review of *No Friend But the Mountains: Writing from Manus Prison* by Behrouz Boochani, translated from the Farsi by Omid Tofighian. A Kurdish-Iranian journalist detained since 2014, Boochani had kept a cell phone hidden in his mattress, typing his autobiographical account by text messages that were sent to a collaborator outside the gulag. Coetzee's seminal essay on the book, appearing in *The New York Review* and fittingly titled 'Australia's Shame', offers an historical account of Australia's inhumane criminalizing of others. Coming from a Nobel Prize laureate and a member of Sydney PEN, the article generated international pressure to close the camps. It is likely to have assisted Boochani's gruelling escape from Manus Island through six time zones to attend the World Literary Festival in Christchurch, defying Australia's offshore prison regime.

Coetzee has been generous in writing blurbs for the Indian-Australian author Aashish Kaul, among several other minority writers, including for myself. He was photographed with Australian performance poet Omar Musa on Facebook. His literary engagements have helped marginal communities, creating rhizomic networks that resist the myopia of global neo-liberal literary agendas. The J.M. Coetzee Centre for Creative Practice has run programs involving Aboriginal educators, as well as public seminars. Additionally, Coetzee has presented at several Australian-curated academic conferences, in collaborations with Western Sydney University as well as seminars that he directed, in Comparative Literature, at Argentina's Universidad Nacional de San Martín, a state university in San Martin, Buenos Aires. Reading events resulted from these colloquiums, as did publications. *A Book of Friends* was edited by his partner, Dorothy Driver, to honour his eightieth birthday; it accompanied new editions by Text Publishing in Melbourne of several Coetzee novels, each with introductions by Australian authors, creating a local merchandising of his most esteemed works.

It strikes me that the establishment is melded to Coetzee's work, which ironically deals with marginality.

To write, to inhabit and renew the voices of my kin, those who have been repressed in written history and in the canon, having faced the barriers of how race, gender and class determine agency and authorship – this is my task. Who gets to tell what story, and thereby shape literary genre? As a woman of colour, I am not endorsed to write freely across aesthetic, political and ethical terrains, nor do I enjoy the same privilege, fuelled by cultural nostalgia for the dominance of European philosophy and literature, that have enabled Coetzee to flourish as an experimental and formal provocateur.

> *'To be an orphan, at the deepest level, is to be alone in the world.'*

Vivonne Bay, Kangaroo Island   15 November 2020

I lie in my bed and hear the wind and rain howl and the sea rolling as dawn breaks and the house trembles. When I draw the curtains, sunlight's golden ribbon illuminates the far shore, and the headland, Cape Gantheaume. There is something about this remote coastline that nurtures the writing life. When I walk along the beach, I may see someone in the distance standing by the steps, or else there may be no one for miles. I look for the white-bellied sea eagles riding thermals high above the cliffs, performing their *jeté battu* as they hover in search over the dunes.

Upstairs in the stone cottage, my laptop is open to a chapter in my novel where a child dies on an ocean steamer in 1924 after leaving Calcutta. It's a reimagining of Virginia Woolf's novel *Mrs Dalloway*, from the Indian perspective of Daisy Simmons, the Eurasian wife and mother. Her presence diminished, she is a half-caste in Woolf's imperial closet. Have I derived from Coetzee's *Foe* the concept of breaking narrative frames to expand Daisy's historical identity and agency? Here is an excerpt from my narrator Mina's diaries, describing the essay-novelistic genre that was pioneered by Woolf, and expanded by Coetzean palimpsests:

> She was perhaps one of the first to attempt the novel-essay. In *A Room of One's Own* she invents Shakespeare's sister as a character to argue a place in fiction for women. Like Virginia, I'm not blindfolded by the trick of narrative. Maybe it has to do with its emphasis on symmetry being predictable in some way; how it suppresses the malleable nature of experience we encounter in our lives. Colonialism is part of our history, a fact that cannot be altered. But is it right to assume that a story alone can liberate Daisy of race and gender? Without an argument, without a history, Daisy's story is exotic, or historical fiction. Or it might be a fable.

How to stretch narrative time and space? How to house the inner life of Daisy Simmons? How to make history and discourse accountable? Variously, the hegemonies of European history, philosophy and epistemes are subsumed and subverted in *The Childhood of Jesus* (2013), *The Schooldays of Jesus* (2016) and *The Death of Jesus* (2019), by hybrid associations and speculative asymmetries. Wildly autonomous and post-Platonic, these novels defy a recognizable interpretation, suggesting there is a *'llave maestre'* but 'no such thing as a *llave universal*'.[14] They can be read as the other life of composite fictional characters beyond the books where they first appear.

'Coetzee's star burns so brightly in the firmament now'

Vivonne Bay, Kangaroo Island   18 December 2020

The clouds have spilled, and the evening sky is draped in violet hues. Honeyeaters and emu wrens are nesting, pigmy possums rattle through the leaves. A sign of recovery: a koala grunting in the eucalypt trees. The books I brought with me are piled in small stacks like mani stones. I am trying to decipher the *Jesus* trilogy under the southern ocean's starlit skies.

Ngarrindjeri and Tangane people call this place Karta, island of the dead, separated from the mainland. It was rediscovered and colonized by the French and the British in 1803. American sealers abducted Tasmanian Aboriginal women to hunt and fish here; some of their descendants still live on the island. How many drowned? Considering the historical slaughter of animals, land clearing for farming and the devastating bush fires, this post-apocalyptic coast reminds me of suffering's presence in our lives. I also think of the Biloela Tamil family deported to Christmas Island in 2019 and the Australian government's subsequent Kafkaesque handling of their visa applications. Aboriginal ancestors, environmental activists, Buddhist meditators, refugee activists and readers of Coetzee might envision a world where living beings are freed from humiliations and sufferings.

Critical reception of the *Jesus* trilogy found the novels to be perplexing in their refusal to correlate specifically with either refugees or with Jesus, the Nazarene, though the novels are replete with Biblical allusions and vocabulary. I encounter them as textual space, labyrinthine and algorithmic in genre, philosophical in theme. Palimpsestic allegories of allegories, these novels shimmer with sparks from a constellation of Coetzee's creations: David the savant is enigmatic and purposely bewildering, as Friday had been. His strange arrival by boat with Simón and Inés on the island of Novilla is like a remix of *Foe's* castaways. Inés dresses him curiously as Susan dressed Friday upon arrival in England in a blousy shirt with 'a frilly front' that hangs over his thighs, in 'blue shoes with straps instead of laces, and brass buttons on the side'.[15] Robert Kusek extensively details inter-textual wormholes that connect the story to Dante, Goethe, Plato and Voltaire, the strained echoes of Dosteoevsky's *The Brothers Karamazov* and *The Idiot*.[16] Cervantes, too, is present, not only in the quixotic unpredictability of narrative turns, but in the single book that David reads, *Don Quixote*. Borrowed from the City of Novilla Library, it is marked with two comments describing the meaning of the book, neither of which is in David's hand. The names of Simón and of Bolivar the dog are redolent of Gabriel García Márquez's *The General in His Labyrinth*, a novel about the Venezuelan anti-Spanish liberator Simón Bolivar's last months of life. In an interview with María Alvira Samper, Gabriel García Márquez, who is to some extent considered the Cervantes of Colombia, says, 'I have written only one book, the same one that circles round and round and continues on'.[17]

Perhaps it is no accident that only the stars that are numbers shine in Novilla, while dark numberless stars are ubiquitous as ants, according to the dying David.[18] David believes there are holes between the pages of a book into which characters may disappear. These fictions are mercurial and ironic, spun with the dark matter of narrative possibility rather than semantic closure. In his review of *The Childhood of Jesus*, Patrick Flanery describes the characters as 'living in an entirely Coetzean universe, reincarnated after the death of their previous selves'.[19] This could very well be the case.

***

The sea is a stunning blue today. I am supposed to take the ferry back on Monday, and drive north; but although my father is dying and death may pass like a comet, I don't really wish to leave. I sit at my desk and write an email to John Coetzee. His novels and Virginia Woolf's novels are close by, each a perfect shell. On such a day as this, Crusoe, Friday and Susan Barton might have been washed ashore from a shipwreck off course from Madagascar. Perhaps, if I walk over the hill following the Harriet River, I will find the empty terraces sheltered from the wind, dug out of the levelled earth and walled with a thousand stones waiting to be tilled and sown. There is space here, for the imagination to breathe, to shapeshift, stretching as thin and as protean as clouds.

NOTES

1. Coetzee, *Elizabeth Costello*, 203.
2. Ibid., 204.
3. Auster and Coetzee, *Here and Now*, 73.
4. Isom, 'Do You Think I Can't Read between the Lines?', 7.
5. Ibid., 22.
6. Coetzee, *Elizabeth Costello*, 199.
7. Coetzee, Personal correspondence with Michelle Cahill, 14 September 2020.
8. Tucker and Nolan, *Bert & Ned*, 110.
9. Glenn, 'Gone for Good'.
10. Goldsworthy, 'Acts of writing', 33.
11. Coetzee, *Late Essays*, 252.
12. Coetzee, *Diary of a Bad Year*, 107.
13. Ibid., 112.
14. Coetzee, *The Childhood of Jesus*, 11.
15. Ibid., 107.
16. Kusek, 'Thirty Years After'.
17. Quoted in Palencia-Roth, 'Gabriel García Márquez', 56.
18. Coetzee, *The Death of Jesus*, 117.
19. Flanery, 'The Childhood of Jesus'.

WORKS CITED

Auster, Paul and J. M. Coetzee. *Here and Now: Letters 2008–2011*. London: Harvill Secker, 2013.
Boochani, Behrouz. *No Friend but the Mountains: Writing from Manus Prison*. Sydney: Picador Australia, 2018.
Cahill, Michelle. "Letter to John Coetzee." In *Letter to Pessoa & Other Short Fictions*. 55–62. Sydney: Giramondo, 2016.
Cahill, Michelle. *Daisy & Woolf*. Sydney: Hachette, 2022.
Coetzee, J. M. *The Childhood of Jesus*. Melbourne: Text Publishing, 2013.
Coetzee, J. M. *The Death of Jesus*. Melbourne: Text Publishing, 2019.
Coetzee, J. M. *Diary of a Bad Year*. New York: Penguin, 2007.
Coetzee, J. M. *Disgrace*. London: Secker and Warburg, 1999.
Coetzee, J. M. *Elizabeth Costello*. London: Vintage, 2003.

Coetzee, J. M. *Foe*. New York: Viking, 1986.
Coetzee, J. M. *The Schooldays of Jesus*. London: Harvill Secker, 2016.
Coetzee, J. M. *Slow Man*. 2005. Melbourne: Text Publishing, 2020.
Coetzee, J. M. Personal Correspondence with Michelle Cahill. 14 September 2020.
Flanery, Patrick. '*The Childhood of Jesus* by J. M. Coetzee'. *The Washington Post*, 2 September 2013.
Glenn, Ian. 'Gone for Good: Coetzee's *Disgrace*'. *English in Africa* 36, no. 2 (2009): 79–98.
Goldsworthy, Kerryn. 'Acts of Writing'. In *Adelaide: A Literary City*, edited by K. Goldsworthy, 19–38. Adelaide: University of Adelaide Press, 2013. https://www.jstor.org/stable/10.20851/j.ctt1sq5x41.
Isom, Rachel. '"Do you Think I Can't Read between the Lines?": Discourse of the Unsaid in J. M. Coetzee's *Diary of a Bad Year*'. *Journal of Commonwealth Literature* 53, no. 1 (2018): 7–20.
Kusek, Robert. 'Thirty Years After … *The Childhood of Jesus* by J. M. Coetzee'. *werkwinkel* 8, no. 2 (2013). https://repozytorium.amu.edu.pl/bitstream/10593/13755/1/1_Kusek.pdf.
Palencia-Roth, Michael. 'Gabriel García Márquez: Labyrinths of Love and History'. *World Literature Today* 65, no. 1 (1991): 54–8.
Rowe, Josephine. *Tarcutta Wake: Stories*. Brisbane: University of Queensland Press, 2012.
Tucker, Albert and Sidney Nolan. *Bert & Ned: The Correspondence of Albert Tucker and Sidney Nolan*. Melbourne: Miegunyah Press, 2006.

PART SEVEN

Intermediation, adaptation, translation

CHAPTER THIRTY-FOUR

Coetzee and photography

HERMANN WITTENBERG

In his youth, J. M. Coetzee had ambitions to become a professional photographer and this early interest in images persisted in later life, leaving multiple traces in the fictions. As he put it in an interview that accompanies *Photographs from Boyhood*, the catalogue for an exhibition of his early experiments with the camera, '[t]he marks of photography and of the cinema, are all over my work, from the beginning'.[1] Coetzee's fascination with the camera and his work in the darkroom where he manipulated optics, light and chemistry is not only visible in novels such as *Slow Man* (2005) where photography is a major motif, but an attentiveness to images pervades the oeuvre as a whole. Already with his debut work, *Dusklands* (1974), Coetzee declared his interest in 'images, particularly photographs, and their power over the human heart'.[2] In 'The Vietnam Project' the disintegration of the protagonist is made visible through his obsession with a number of photographic prints, but photography also pervades the 'Narrative', for example when Jacobus Coetzee uses a lens analogy when he imagines himself as 'a spherical reflecting eye moving through the wilderness and ingesting it', and figures himself as 'a transparent sac with a black core full of images'.[3] The next novel *In the Heart of the Country* (1977) is strongly imprinted by modernist cinema and the techniques of montage, as acknowledged by Coetzee who discerned the 'more fundamental influence' on his style as being 'film and/or photography'.[4] Photographic or cinematic images feature in most of Coetzee's following fictions, for example a daguerreotype in *The Master of Petersburg* (1994) which triggers strong feelings of loss, an old family picture in *Age of Iron* (1990) that allows complex meditations on the exclusions of colonial photography, or the dunce-cap press photograph in *Disgrace* (1999) which graphically illustrates David Lurie's public fall from grace. An interest in images continues in the late fictions such as *The Schooldays of Jesus* (2017), where Dmitri murders his lover, but then remorsefully turns himself in to the police after seeing her photograph on the front page of a newspaper.

Considerable scholarship has concerned itself with such photographic moments in the fictions,[5] as well as the influence of specific images on the genesis of particular novels.[6] But images are not only frequently referred to as content material in the story lines, but also shape the style of narration. Indeed, significant moments in Coetzee's writing derive their force from the suggested presence of a camera lens where a photographic and cinematic visuality shapes narration and point of view. Moreover, optical devices, lens metaphors, light effects and camera analogies play an important role in the fictional work, and while such narrative effects are not always readily noticeable to readers, they are crucial to a fuller understanding of Coetzee's authorship. This chapter traces examples of some of these lesser visible 'marks of photography' in two of the middle-period fictions, giving insight into Coetzee's fascination with optics and the mechanics of the analogue camera.

NARRATING THROUGH THE LENS

The influence of the camera and the medium of film can be seen in an exemplary moment in *Life & Times of Michael K* (1983). During the period of an extended creative impasse while attempting to write his fourth novel, Coetzee suddenly found it generative to narrate his story as if imagined through a cinematic lens.[7] In effect, he was using the model of the screenplay as a drafting tool in the creative process, a writing technique that would help him craft more vivid and rapidly unfolding prose.[8] The extent to which Coetzee was thinking himself into the story *visually* is evident in his notebooks and manuscripts, for example in the following note to himself: 'The scene on p. 46 is better shot from the <u>outside</u> of the shop, through the window (and the letting down the window)'.[9] This is the scene where Michael K has escaped from the Worcester work gang and tries to buy some provisions from a shop at the railway station. In the final published version the experimentation with a screenplay format had long been absorbed into narrative prose, but traces of the camera are still discernible:

> He peered through the glass and knocked; he held up the ten-rand note to show good faith; but the old woman, without so much as a look, disappeared behind the high counter ... Beyond the rack of paperback books, through the sweets in the display cases, he could still see the edge of the black dress. He shielded his eyes with his hands and waited. There was nothing to hear but the wind across the veld and the creaking of the sign overhead. After a while the old woman brought her head up over the counter and met his stare. She wore glasses with thick black rims; her silver hair was drawn back tight. On shelves behind her K could make out canned food, packets of mealie-meal and sugar, detergent powders. On the floor in front of the counter was a basket of lemons. He held the banknote flat against the glass above his head. The old woman did not budge.[10]

The scene is a narrated as a classical over-the-shoulder shot (OTS),[11] which allows us to 'see' and experience the event through Michael K's subjectivity. The simulated camera, like Michael K himself, is prevented from entering the shop's interior, but still allows indistinct and partial views of the inside, creating a strong sense of spatial depth. Lighting, which is vital in all film, is foregrounded as a constitutive element of the scene: in order to see anything in the dark interior, K 'shielded his eyes with his hands and waited', giving his eyes time to adjust from the outside glare to a lower luminosity inside. His eyes, like the adjusted exposure settings of a camera lens, can now begin to 'make out' some of the details of the dim interior. Coetzee's interest in light effects and optics is also reflected in the multiple refractive and partially transparent surfaces in this scene: the window of the shop door itself, the glass display cases with sweets through which he peers and the thick spectacles of the shopkeeper through which she stares back. The scene as a whole derives its force by being shot from the '<u>outside</u> of the shop', where the subjective camera position emphasizes the fact that Michael K's is being kept out. He is an observing outsider, not just literally in this scene, but more generally in the story as a whole.

As evident from the above example, the device of the camera enables and underpins narration through large sections of *Life & Times of Michael K*, but its influence reaches much further into the oeuvre. An exhaustive account of Coetzee's photographic and cinematic visuality is beyond the scope of this chapter;[12] instead, after a discussion of *Foe* (1986), I consider the implications of optics, as lens-mediated forms of seeing and narrating, for the work as a whole.

THE RIPPLE IN THE GLASS

Foe is set in the early eighteenth century, well before the invention of photography in the 1830s. There was, however, a broad interest in optics during the seventeenth and early eighteenth centuries, with considerable scientific and popular experimentation in ocular apparatuses, lenses and refractive visual devices. Isaac Newton's influential *Opticks: or, A Treatise of the Reflexions, Refractions, Inflexions and Colours of Light* (1704) appeared not long before Daniel Defoe's *Robinson Crusoe* (1719), the text to which Coetzee's *Foe* most directly responds. While cameras and photographs are obviously absent from Coetzee's re-imagination of Defoe's narrative, *Foe* is centrally concerned with matters of representation, truth and point of view – the position from which one sees, and the perspective from which one writes. Coetzee's fiction insistently foregrounds the authorizing power and legitimating operations of writing and story-telling and their power to establish versions of the truth that may silence and occlude alternative stories and points of view.

What is of interest here is that Coetzee makes such points of view literally visible through an optical device. The scene occurs when Susan Barton climbs up the steps to Foe's attic and sits down at the author's writing desk. As she looks out of the window, she quite literally adopts Foe's point of view. It is in this moment that she notices the imperfections in the hand-made glass pane that alter the field of vision before her eye, creating distortive optical effects: 'There is a ripple in the window-pane. Moving your head, you can make the ripple travel over the cows grazing in the pasture, over the ploughed land beyond, over the line of poplars, and up into the sky'.[13] Even though the glass pane may be fully transparent, it acts as a lens or filter through which the world is subtly altered and transformed, emphasizing that what we see through a rectangular frame (a window or a photograph) is not identical with actuality. Looking out from the study window, the point of view of the author, Foe (the second person 'you' addressed in this passage), twists and warps the outside world. It is a disruption of verisimilitude that is not confined to the visual field but also extends to his writing. As will become apparent, the ripple in the glass can be read as a figure more generally for the operations of fiction itself.

The window pane moment in *Foe* might, on one level, be discounted as an insignificant detail in the novel, yet it could also be read as doubling back on the effects of realism that Coetzee diagnosed as characteristic of Defoe's fictional craft. Defoe was adept in crafting stories that purported to be true accounts, forms of story-telling that Coetzee characterized as 'faking an authentic record'.[14] Defoe's canny disguise of his stories' fictiveness followed a technique described as follows in *Elizabeth Costello*:

> Supply the particulars, allow the significations to emerge of themselves. A procedure pioneered by Daniel Defoe. Robinson Crusoe, cast up on the beach, looks around for his shipmates. But there are none. 'I never saw them afterwards, or any sign of them,' says he, 'except three of their hats, one cap, and two shoes that were not fellows.' Two shoes, not fellows: by not being fellows, the shoes have ceased to be footwear and become proofs of death, torn by the foaming seas off the feet of drowning men and tossed ashore. No large words, no despair, just hats and caps and shoes.[15]

The ripple in Foe's window pane might initially be read as Coetzee emulating, or perhaps even 'faking', Defoe's realism; it is an example of the many concrete 'particulars' or small details inserted into the narrative so as to create the illusion of a historically true account. Coetzee admired Defoe as 'a fascinating and absorbing writer',[16] and in *Foe* we see that he paid his dues to Defoe in the form of a secret optical puzzle, which is only decodable through a palindromic process of visual inversion. This enigmatic moment occurs when a destitute Susan Barton is forced to dispose of Mr Foe's household possessions, which includes selling 'the one mirror not taken by the bailiffs, the little mirror with the gilt frame that stood on your cabinet'.[17] The mirror provides the clue to understanding an immediately preceding moment when Susan notices a 'trunk with the initials M. J. on the lid', prompting her to ask: 'who is M. J.?'.[18] The obvious answer to Susan's puzzled question lies in the absent mirror: its prior presence in the text allows us to see the inverted initials of Coetzee's own name inscribed on Defoe's trunk – a subtle optical insinuation of his own authorial presence in *Foe*. Signs in mirrors, like the photographic negatives that Coetzee was so familiar with in his darkroom work, need to be read and decoded in reverse, thereby creating a 'signature effect' in which we can recognize the true identity of the text's author.[19] Coetzee in effect was staking a claim in Defoe's house of fiction, marking it with his own veiled presence.

The optical devices in the novel, both the 'ripple in the window pane' and the 'little mirror', point to the way that *Foe* as a whole can be read as a refracted engagement with Defoe's authorship, even in the very act of distorting *Robinson Crusoe*. The fictional premise of Coetzee's text functions then as a 'ripple': in reading *Foe*, we still recognize some of the basic contours and narrative elements of Defoe's original novels, even as these have become warped and altered into something entirely different. The signature effect in the mirror similarly signals Coetzee's authorship, through which he has put his own mark on the story. It is a figure for the way Defoe's authorial power over the island narrative has been disrupted and literally inverted, reversing a patriarchal and colonial fantasy with Coetzee's feminist, postcolonial re-envisioning.

If we consider that the scene with the ripple in the glass was the original opening gambit of the novel, the small imperfection in the windowpane assumes larger significance as an optical figure for what Coetzee was attempting to achieve in *Foe*, reflecting the blurred relationship between truth and fiction, and posing the vexed question of realism. In the first manuscript version of *Foe*, the scene is even more elaborated and rich in details. Susan Barton is in this version a chamber maid in Foe's household, secretly reading the manuscript of *Robinson Crusoe* in the author's attic as it is being written, and writing her own counter-narrative in her basement room below:

> Sometimes, when the family is out, or when Mrs F is asleep, I come up and sit at the table and eat an apple and look out through the windows at the pasture with the five cows, and the ploughed land beyond, and the line of poplars. There is a ripple in the windowpane; moving my head, I can make the ripple travel over the brindled backs of the cows, and over the green grass, and up into the sky.[20]

The key sentence describing the 'ripple' survived almost unchanged over several versions into final publication, and the novel invokes the optical device again when Susan reflects on Foe's fictional craft, and the uneasy gap between the actual world in front of his eyes and his fictional inventiveness:

> To tell the truth in all its substance you must have quiet, and a comfortable chair away from all distraction, and a window to stare through; and then the knack of seeing waves when there are

fields before your eyes, and of feeling the tropic sun when it is cold; and at your fingertips the words with which to capture the vision before it fades. I have none of these, while you have all.[21]

What is significant here is that Susan recognizes that telling 'the truth in all its substance' is not a matter of simply recording the world in a direct, seemingly unmediated manner. Reality is not accessible in a transparent way, akin to looking through a clear window. Instead, truth in storytelling involves transformations, and the manipulation of actuality. As Coetzee had already put it in an early notebook entry, 'Fiction is about <u>what is possible</u>. That's what is wrong with realism.'[22] For this author, then, who throughout his oeuvre has been interested in questions of literary realism and has pursued forms of non-realist fiction in different ways, 'the truth in all its substance' is not reducible to a faithful, documentary reproduction of actuality, but in the 'knack of seeing waves' in the stillness of the scene before one's eyes, creating ripples the space-time fabric of the world.[23]

THE OPTICS OF REALISM

If we take the ripple in the glass as a key figure for Coetzee's authorial strategy, we also recognize that a fictional world emerges out of defamiliarized actual historical particulars in each of the novels. The 'Narrative of Jacobus Coetzee', part two of *Dusklands* (1974), is set in the eighteenth century northern Cape, but through fictionalizing processes the genre of the colonial travelogue is blurred and distorted. *In the Heart of the Country* (1977) is shot through with defamiliarizing strategies that shift the story of a Karoo farm into a highly attenuated stream of consciousness where our sense of what is real and what is imagined is continually thrown in doubt. Even a novel such as *Waiting for the Barbarians* (1980) is actually, as an earlier article has shown, a fictionalized version of a specific geographic location: the ancient and now ruined frontier settlement of Lou-lan on the Lop Nur lake in western China's Taklamakan desert.[24] Coetzee's fictional method in *Waiting for the Barbarians* is not unlike that of Defoe, who was 'faking an authentic record'.[25] It is a fictional method which Susan Barton, in an earlier manuscript version, sees as follows:

> I used to think that the story of Crusoe was entirely fantasised. I have discovered that whole passages are copied from the books he keeps on his table, histories of voyages to the New World, or narratives of shipwreck, or stories of captivity among the Moors. I begin to understand why he writes such a clean hand.[26]

The details that Coetzee culled from such geographic and historical accounts were then lightly 'blurred' so as to disguise their origin. Coetzee's stories are thus never 'entirely fantasised', as he has Susan Barton put it.

Life & Times of Michael K similarly offers some recognizable particulars of a Cape Town setting, only for the realist rug to be pulled from under our feet as the geography of the city morphs into a dystopic location. As Coetzee noted during the novel's composition, 'What I need is a liberation from verisimilitude!'[27] But instead of sharply cutting out any description of the novel's Cape setting, Coetzee's anti-realism is achieved through a blurring of temporal referentiality. In *The Master of Petersburg* (1994), Coetzee simulates a nineteenth-century Russia, only to alter key particulars in Dostoevsky's life, changing dates, inventing characters and encounters that did not historically occur. *Disgrace* (1999) would also subtly change the particulars of its university setting: while still recognizable as the University of Cape Town, the novel also transforms the institution in small but significant ways, a change signalled by the fictional name: the Cape Technical University. The subtle shift from the historical givens to their fictionalized versions is particularly apparent in the autobiographical memoirs, *Boyhood*, *Youth* and *Summertime*, where Coetzee takes increasing liberties with biographical truth. The geriatric author figure JC in *Diary of a Bad Year* is a prime example of such transformational shifts that disrupts the real: JC is a somewhat altered, distorted and aged version of Coetzee, only partially identical with the author.

Speaking to Joanna Scott about his approach to writing, Coetzee explained that his novels consistently blurred the line between history and fiction, or what 'people call confusing the real and the imaginary'.[28] Writing his novels involved taking a 'fictional leap' from the given world, but Coetzee also conceded that attempting to leap too far into a wholly invented new world, or 'trying to write out of a world that so unfamiliar' might mean that you could 'fall on your face'.[29] He compared himself to Dostoevsky, who wrote fictions that 'imagine or reimagine history, imagine or reimagine the scene around him'.[30] More recently, in conversation with Arabella Kurtz, Coetzee reflected on his approach to writing fiction: 'I think of myself as using rather than reflecting reality in my fiction. If the world of my fictions is a recognisable world, that is because (I say to myself) it is easier to use the world at hand than to make up a new one'.[31] For Coetzee, fiction is thus a transformational endeavour in which reality is 'used', not with the aim of 'reflecting' it accurately, but with a view to rework and reshape given worlds into new fictional possibilities.

WRITING BEYOND PHOTOGRAPHY

In conclusion, we can understand Coetzee's shift from photography to writing more than just as a biographical event that came to fruition on the now legendary date of 1 January 1970, when he began writing *Dusklands*. David Attwell aptly characterized Coetzee's literary beginnings in *Dusklands*, as a 'revolt against what he saw as realism's unadventurous epistemology',[32] a fictional strategy that would be pursued in different ways in each of the subsequent novels. Although Coetzee had initial ambitions to be a photographer, anti-realist prose fiction ultimately came to be his preferred creative medium as he reached the end of his twenties – and this shift is not disconnected from how the camera and the printed word involved different representational possibilities. Teju Cole, in a recent interview with Coetzee, speculated that abandoning the camera 'wasn't a matter of the eye (a matter of aesthetics)' but 'a matter of breaking through the pervasive and intolerable violence of the society (a matter of ethics) – a breakthrough that eluded you in photography, nice as the pictures were, but that you were eventually able to make in writing'.[33] Cole's suggestive question allows us to see how writing became the medium that allowed Coetzee to craft a distinctive anti-realist aesthetic, an aesthetic that he could not realize with the camera. Unlike prose fiction, photography lent itself much less readily to an adventurous and radical engagement with the real, an idea caricatured in *Slow Man* when Marijana naively conceives of photography as a form of uninventive copying: 'You point camera, click, you make copy. That is how camera works. Camera is like photocopier'.[34] As an artistic medium, photography of course has the potential of far exceeding a mere reproductive representation of the world, but as Coetzee himself conceded, he himself did not have 'the eye of an artist-photographer'.[35] Rather than document the world mimetically through the lens, prose fiction gave Coetzee an endlessly inventive creative medium that could transform the world he was experiencing. The figure of the ripple in the window is thus an apt way of thinking about

Coetzee's larger strategy of disrupting the illusion of realism, namely the idea that the world can be represented and written about as if it is being seen through a transparent window: looking through this fictional lens, the author's gaze bends, blurs and transforms historical particulars and even the biographical self, making the illusionistic quality of writing itself visible.

NOTES

1. Coetzee, 'Remembering Photography', 178.
2. Coetzee, *Dusklands*, jacket.
3. Coetzee, *Dusklands*, 84.
4. Coetzee, *Doubling the Point*, 59. See Wittenberg, 'Godard in the Karoo', for a more detailed discussion.
5. See variously: Castillo, 'Coetzee's *Dusklands*'; Amir, 'What Used to Lie Outside the Frame'; Powers, 'Emigration and Photography in J. M. Coetzee's *Slow Man*'; Kossew, 'J.M. Coetzee and the parental punctum'; Wicomb, '*Slow Man* and the Real'; Louvel, 'Photography as Critical Idiom and Intermedial Criticism'; Gilburt, 'Cinematic and Photographic Aesthetics in the Novels of J.M. Coetzee'.
6. See Lucy Valerie Graham's discussion of press photographs as an influence on *Disgrace*: 'Intercepting *Disgrace*: Lacuna and "Letter to John Coetzee"'. Also my work on the 'Khamieskroon killer' photograph in *Life & Times of Michael K*, forthcoming.
7. For a more extended discussion of cinematic modes of writing in the novel, see Wittenberg, 'Film and Photography in J. M. Coetzee's *Life & Times of Michael K*'.
8. Coetzee discusses the influence of cinema on his writing in some detail in *Doubling the Point*, specifically referencing the impact of film on the compositional process of *In the Heart of the Country*, 59–60.
9. HRC, 33.5, 22 July 1981. Original emphasis.
10. Coetzee, *Life & Times of Michael K*, 61.
11. For a discussion of the conventions of the over-the-shoulder shot and its pervasiveness in classical cinema, see Bordwell, *Poetics of Cinema*, 58.
12. For a fuller discussion of photographic aspects of Coetzee's fictions, see Wittenberg's forthcoming *Through the Lens. Photography and Film in the Fictions of J. M. Coetzee*.
13. Coetzee, *Foe*, 50.
14. Scott, 'Voice and Trajectory', 87.
15. Coetzee, *Elisabeth Costello*, 13.
16. Scott, 'Voice and Trajectory', 99.
17. Coetzee, *Foe*, 93.
18. Ibid.
19. For a more detailed discussion of signature effects in a work, see Jacques Derrida's essay 'Signature Event Context', in *Limited Inc*.
20. HRC, 10.1, 1 June 1983.
21. Coetzee, *Foe*, 51–2.
22. HRC, 33.3, 24 November 1974. Original emphasis.
23. For a comprehensive discussion of Coetzee's engagement with questions of realism, see Marc Farrant's chapter, '"The aura of truth": Coetzee's archive, realism and the problem of literary Authority'.
24. Wittenberg and Highman, 'Sven Hedin's "vanished country"', 103–27.
25. Scott, 'Voice and Trajectory', 87.
26. HRC, 10.1, 1 June 1983.

27. HRC, 33.5: 2 March 1981.
28. Scott, 'Voice and Trajectory', 99.
29. Ibid., 100.
30. Ibid.
31. Coetzee and Kurtz, *The Good Story*, xx.
32. Attwell, *Life of Writing*, 61.
33. Cole, 'Io, fotografo', 35.
34. Coetzee, *Slow Man*, 245.
35. Coetzee, 'Remembering Photography', 176.

WORKS CITED

Amir, Ayala. '"What Used to Lie Outside the Frame": Boundaries of Photography, Subjectivity and Fiction in Three Novels by J. M. Coetzee'. *Journal of Literary Studies* 29, no. 4 (2013): 58–79.
Attwell, David. *J. M. Coetzee and the Life of Writing. Face to Face with Time*. Johannesburg: Jacana, 2015.
Bordwell, David. *Poetics of Cinema*. New York: Routledge, 2008.
Castillo, Debra A. 'Coetzee's *Dusklands*: The Mythic Punctum'. *PMLA* 105, no. 5 (1990): 1108–22.
Coetzee, J. M. *Diary of a Bad Year*. London: Harvill Secker, 2007.
Coetzee, J. M. *Disgrace*. London: Secker and Warburg, 1999.
Coetzee, J. M. *Doubling the Point: Essays and Interviews*. Edited by David Attwell. Cambridge: Harvard University Press, 1992.
Coetzee, J. M. *Dusklands*. Johannesburg: Ravan Press, 1974.
Coetzee, J. M. *Elisabeth Costello*. London: Harvill Secker, 2003.
Coetzee, J. M. *Foe*. Johannesburg: Ravan Press, 1986.
Coetzee, J. M. *Life & Times of Michael K*. Johannesburg: Ravan Press, 1983.
Coetzee, J. M. 'Remembering Photography'. In *Photographs from Boyhood*, edited by H. Wittenberg, 171–8. Pretoria: Protea Books, 2020.
Coetzee, J. M. *Slow Man*. London: Secker & Warburg, 2005.
Coetzee, J. M. and Arabella Kurtz. *The Good Story. Exchanges on Truth, Fiction and Psychotherapy*. New York: Penguin, 2015.
Cole, Teju. 'Io, fotografo di un mondo bianco e nero. L'intervista a J. M. Coetzee', *La Repubblica* 9 February 2020: 34–5.
Derrida, Jacques. *Limited Inc*. Evanston: Northwestern University Press, 1988.
Farrant, Marc. '"The Aura of Truth": Coetzee's Archive, Realism and the Problem of Literary Authority'. In *Coetzee and the Archive Fiction, Theory and Autobiography*, edited by Marc Farrant, Kai Easton and Hermann Wittenberg, 163–78. London: Bloomsbury, 2021.
Gilburt, Iona. 'Cinematic and Photographic Aesthetics in the Novels of J. M. Coetzee'. PhD Thesis, University of the Western Cape (2017).
Graham, Lucy. 'Intercepting *Disgrace*: Lacuna and "Letter to John Coetzee"'. *Safundi* 21, no. 2 (2020): 166–75.
Harry Ransom Centre (HRC). J. M. Coetzee Papers. Austin: University of Texas.
Kossew, Sue. 'J.M. Coetzee and the Parental Punctum'. In *J.M. Coetzee's The Childhood of Jesus: The Ethics of Ideas and Things*, edited by J. Rutherford and A. Uhlmann, 149–64. New York: Bloomsbury Academic, 2017.
Louvel, Liliane. 'Photography as Critical Idiom and Intermedial Criticism'. *Poetics Today* 29, no. 1 (2008): 31–48.
Powers, Donald. 'Emigration and Photography in J. M. Coetzee's *Slow Man*'. *Journal of Postcolonial Writing* 49, no. 4 (2013): 458–69.

Scott, Joanna. 'Voice and Trajectory: An Interview with J. M. Coetzee'. *Salmagundi*, no. 114/115 (1997): 82–102.

Wicomb, Zoë. '*Slow Man* and the Real'. *Journal of Literary Studies* 25, no. 4 (2009): 7–24.

Wittenberg, Hermann. 'Film and Photography in J. M. Coetzee's *Life & Times of Michael K*'. *Texas Studies in Literature and Language* 58, no. 4 (2016): 473–92.

Wittenberg, Hermann. 'Godard in the Karoo: J. M. Coetzee's Screenplay Adaptation of *In the Heart of the Country*'. *English in Africa* 41, no. 2 (2014): 13–34.

Wittenberg, Hermann and Kate Highman. 'Sven Hedin's "Vanished Country": Setting and History in J. M. Coetzee's *Waiting for the Barbarians*'. *Scrutiny2* 20, no. 1 (2015): 103–27.

CHAPTER THIRTY-FIVE

Coetzee and the visual arts

SEAN O'TOOLE

PALPABLE, LEGIBLE, INTELLIGIBLE

'Writers are not like painters', states the unnamed protagonist of J. M. Coetzee's novel *Youth* (2002) during one of his gauche reflections on art and human intimacy; writers, he proposes, are 'more dogged, more subtle'.[1] The word 'writer' is a capacious noun encompassing many possible and interconnected modes of expression, but for the lovelorn young mathematician in Coetzee's second autobiographical fiction, it merely denotes novelist and poet. When *Youth*'s setting shifts from post-Sharpeville South Africa to early 1960s London, the narrator's out-dated tastes are enlarged by his encounters with the new art – American poetry, electronic music and abstract expressionism – championed on the BBC's Third Programme radio service (Y 49). The narrator comes to appreciate poet Joseph Brodsky, composer Anton Webern and painter Robert Motherwell, but not critic Harold Rosenberg, who argued that 'new painting calls for a new kind of criticism'.[2] There is also no mention in *Youth* of critic David Sylvester, whose 1959–60 interviews on the Third Programme were important in cultivating broader English interest in new American painting. Critics, we infer, are not like writers: their method is less dogged, less subtle, less important.

Coetzee, as distinct from the unpublished poet and gloomy littérateur of *Youth*, is a distinguished literary critic. His literary reviews, essays and correspondences have been collected in nearly a dozen volumes and collectively evidence his method of paying close and interested attention to the subject at hand. Couched in Coetzee's remote and astringent prose style, his literary criticism especially exhibits none of 'the uglier side of Grub Street', as Coetzee put it in 2010 letter to Paul Auster, the hack reviewer's resort to 'animosities', to 'fawning and backbiting' and to 'saying clever things at other people's expense'.[3] This is true of his small output of film and art criticism too. Over the course of his career, Coetzee has shown consistent interest in images and visuality, both in his fiction and nonfiction writing. David Lurie, the protagonist of *Disgrace*, recalls the 'women in gauze veils' appearing in *The Rape of the Sabine Women* (1639–40), a painting by Flemish Baroque artist Peter Paul Rubens, as informing his youthful understanding of rape.[4] The narrator of *Youth* describes a transfixed encounter with abstract-expressionist painter Robert Motherwell's *Elegy for the Spanish Republic 24* in the Tate Gallery, its central element a 'menacing and mysterious' black shape (Y 92). Coetzee has also produced expository writing on artists William Kentridge, Roger Palmer and J. H. Pierneef.

While uneven in focus, consistency, ambition, form and yield, Coetzee's art writings – including his corpus of novels and diverse output of formal art and literary criticism, letters and essays – would easily fill a modest volume. This makes the silence around his art writing all the more noticeable. In 2015, scholars Robert Kusek and Wojciech Szymański expressed surprise at this lacuna in an essay exploring Coetzee's then recent collaboration with Belgian sculptor Berlinde De Bruyckere. With the exception of a handful of essays investigating the cinematic inspirations behind Coetzee's works, they noted, 'neither literary critics nor experts in visual studies have, so far, shown substantial interest in the links between Coetzee's *oeuvre* and the issues of – largely speaking – visuality'.[5] This oversight persists, and in certain respects perpetuates the bias of *Youth*'s diffident narrator, who is 'unsure of what the study of literature ought to be' (Y 26–27), and so settles on endorsing shop-worn ideas of creative castes. He privileges writers over painters, and painters over the obtuse commentators motivated by them; in this schema, words trump images and art exceeds its interpretation.

Coetzee's lifelong engagement with art and images – first as an adolescent photographer, later as an impressionable colonial in London, still later as a novelist and academic of sustained creative and intellectual ambition – challenges these assumptions. They also undercut the fictional authority of *Señor* C., the elderly South African writer of *Diary of a Bad Year*, who declares: 'The truth is, I have never taken much pleasure in the visible world.'[6] Images are everywhere in, and have repeatedly fertilized, Coetzee's thinking. The marks of both photography and cinema, he told Hermann Wittenberg in 2017, 'are all over my work, from the beginning'.[7] Images abound, as does the corollary labour of making sense of them. 'Through images, even blank images, stream torrents of meaning (that is the nature of images)', Coetzee remarked at a 2006 symposium on Samuel Beckett.[8] The job of seizing that meaning – of rendering it an adequate language and form; of making the image palpable, legible and intelligible in a charismatic personal style – is the subject of this brief essay.

The difficulty and fullness of the labour I have just described was impressed on Coetzee when he was a student enthralled by American poet Ezra Pound. Among the constellation of early influences enumerated by Coetzee's ambiguous proxy in *Youth*, Pound and Polish writer Zbigniew Herbert stand out. Indeed, Coetzee has repeatedly invoked them in his writings. In his correspondence with De Bruyckere (discussed later), Coetzee sends a poem by Herbert entitled 'Apollo and Marsyas' by way of reflecting on the idea of a tortured body.[9] Herbert and Pound are discussed at length in an autobiographical essay appearing in *The Threepenny Review*. Published in 1993, its contents foreshadow the biographical revelations appearing in *Youth*, such that the disclosures of the novel can plainly be received as facts.

Of Pound, Coetzee states in his 1993 essay:

> What Pound can teach – Pound more than any other poet I know, because Pound was conscious of what he was doing as a technique both practical and spiritual – is that the reading eye and inner ear, the eye and ear of the mind, must be slowed down so as to be prepared for the image.[10]

Coetzee's interest in the image – the palpable image capable of ekphrastic description; but also the synaesthetic image, one audible to 'the reading eye and inner ear, the eye and ear of the mind' – informs all of his writing; but for the purposes of this essay, I will concentrate on select works that broadly operate as formal art criticism. Beyond the yield of particular texts, I am interested in Coetzee's search for an adequate form to express his interest in art and image making, as well as his laconic style as a writer. Much in the way Coetzee was motivated to communicate what Pound can teach, so too, I believe, can Coetzee's criticism, not simply through exposition but something more nebulous, though in Coetzee's case also defining: style.

***

In 1976, Coetzee published a Roland Barthes-like semiotic analysis of Captain America, the alter ego of Steve Rogers, an award-winning but frail artist transformed into a super soldier. Written in a showy, epigrammatic style, Coetzee's essay 'Captain America in American Mythology' is replete with rhetorical flourishes of a self-confident intellect. 'Captain America is a great flag-wrapped phallus striding out, like all heroes of adventure since Achilles, in quest of a foe worthy of all that bulging, displaced potency', writes Coetzee.[11] The costumed superhero, he adds, is an embodiment of 'the Calvinist categorical imperative of absolute urgency and absolute stringency'; he is also thoroughly of the 'gothic mode', an American innocent always negotiating 'the maze of the old European psyche'.[12] The essay's insights have not curdled with age, particularly given the hegemony of the Marvel Comics universe in contemporary Hollywood cinema, but this is not what makes Coetzee's early essay interesting. Rather, it is the structuralist method and demystifying mode of analysis that Coetzee adopts that make the essay worthy of consideration.

Mystification and its opposite, elucidation, were central to debates around the meaning of postwar art criticism. Important critics like Susan Sontag and Harold Rosenberg frequently deliberated on this. 'The aim of all commentary on art now should be to make works of art – and, by analogy, our own experience – more, rather than less, real to us', declared Sontag in her landmark 1964 essay 'Against Interpretation'.[13] Rosenberg advanced much the same position in 1959:

> Mystification attends each fresh move in art, each new coalescence in politics ... In these circumstances, criticism cannot divide itself into literary criticism, art criticism, social criticism, but must begin in establishing the terms of the conflict between the actual work or event and its illusory context.[14]

Coetzee's criticism, particularly his essays gathered in *White Writing* (1988), enacts this ambition of criticism as a supple diagnostic tool attuned to the zeitgeist.

The seven essays in *White Writing* variously engage with two of Coetzee's broad concerns: the European intellectual schemas applied to South Africa by early visitors and settlers; and land, both as social fact and mythical projection. While principally an act of literary archaeology, the collection includes two essays about visual representations of the land. 'The Picturesque and the South African Landscape' is a methodical examination of the use of the post-Claudian romantic sublime by white artists to resolve problems of landscape representation in South Africa. Its principal subject is the historical and ideological contexts of the picturesque and sublime, and the stunted output of local painters working in this mode. Its procedural form masks an ambition, at once laboured but ruthless, to demystify failure of vision as much as of language. 'Reading the South African Landscape' deals chiefly with South African landscape poetry in English; this poetry, argues Coetzee, has had to cultivate a geological not botanical gaze in response to the arid topography it encounters. The essay includes a substantial discussion of landscape painting and its origins in travel and the imperial eye – 'the eye that by seeing names and dominates'.[15]

White Writing appeared at a time of intense historical anxiety and cultural revisionism. William Kentridge's essay 'Landscape in a State of Siege', also published in 1988, similarly dwells on the predicament of the romantic landscape tradition, in particular work by J. H. Pierneef (1886–1957) and J. E. A. Volschenk (1853–1936), South African painters born of Dutch immigrants whose unpeopled landscape studies achieved the status of Afrikaner folk art. 'These paintings, of landscape in a state of grace, are documents of disremembering', asserts Kentridge.[16] But Kentridge's overall focus is the urban landscape, a shift in temporality and location that Coetzee is mindful of and picks up on in his 1999 essay on Kentridge and an earlier essay from 1995 on Roger Palmer. Despite his antique interests – the essays in *White Writing* barely touch on the neo-colonial period in South Africa's history, as he concedes in the introduction – Coetzee is a persuasive critic of art and photography invested in representing the landscape.

The land figures prominently in Coetzee's analysis of Kentridge's early stop-animation films, films more often remarked upon for their opposing protagonists (artist Felix Teitelbaum and industrialist Soho Eckstein) and social context of the end of white-minority rule. Of *Felix in Exile*, Kentridge's fifth film in his *Drawings for Projection* series (1989–ongoing), Coetzee writes that it is 'about the recovery of the past of the South African landscape', and 'very much in line with the master project of unburying the national past'.[17] The reversion to landscape as a theme in Coetzee's art writing from the 1980s and 90s points to his limitations as a formalist art critic drawn to a familiar set of themes; conversely, his acute focus and specialization straddles disciplinary fiefdoms, and encompasses literature, art and cultural theory. It is perhaps for this reason that *White Writing* has been so extensively quoted. Art historian Nic Coetzee's controversial 1992 revisionist reading of Pierneef's Johannesburg Station Panels (1929–32) is replete with references to his (unrelated) namesake.[18] Coetzee's 1988 essay on the picturesque was republished in *Fifty-One Years: David Goldblatt* (2002), a book that accompanied photographer David Goldblatt's international travelling exhibition of the same name (2002–4). *White Writing* remains an important reference point for art historians and scholars of visuality interested in making sense of South Africa's fraught tradition of landscape painting.[19]

Coetzee's interest in addressing art and visuality in the blunt expository mode of his essays on Captain America and South African landscape painting in *White Writing* started to wane by the 1990s.[20] 'I no longer see opening up the mystifications in which ordinary life is wrapped as a necessary aim, or indeed obligation, of criticism', Coetzee remarked in an interview with David Attwell published in 1992, adding: 'a demystifying criticism privileges mystifications. It becomes like Quixote scouring the plains for giants to tilt at, and ignoring everything but windmills'.[21] Coetzee's diminishing interest in using the academic and literary essay to explore his earlier 'relentless suspiciousness of appearances'[22] coincided with what Terry Eagleton in 2003 identified as the domestication of cultural theory in the last two decades of the twentieth century: 'Socialism lost out to sadomasochism. Among students of culture, the body is an immensely fashionable topic, but it is usually the erotic body, not the famished one.'[23]

Art criticism was not immune from this cultural drift. Signification, a central of prop of postwar structuralist analysis, remains a valuable apparatus of critical analysis; but in a materialist economy founded on commerce, authorship also signifies. Coetzee signifies. One senses this in his procedural essay appearing in a 1999 monograph devoted to Kentridge by prestigious art publisher Phaidon. Coetzee largely operates as a describer of Kentridge's early films and their underlying concerns. One is reminded here of Senor C., the aging South African writer exiled in Australia, who expresses little 'conviction' in recreating the visible world in words. Coetzee's contribution at this strategic moment of international emergence for Kentridge following his 'discovery' in the mid-1990s is measured and insightful, but also fatally polite. Ultimately, though, it is Coetzee's name that signifies, not his literary style, which Coetzee in 1969 defined as the 'the linguistic choice within the economy of the work of art as a formal style'.[24] It is uncharitable to speak of Coetzee's essay on Kentridge as a failure, but it lacks a certain doggedness and subtlety, and lapses into journalism and lugubrious promotion – a hallmark of a great deal of art criticism, let it be said.[25]

***

'What more is required than a kind of stupid, insensitive doggedness, as lover, as writer, together with a readiness to fail and fail again?' conjectures the narrator at the close of *Youth*. 'What is wrong with him is that he is not prepared to fail' (Y 167). Coetzee, by distinction, is willing to negotiate failure, again and again. In 2012, Berlinde De Bruyckere, an artist best known for her sculpture practice featuring distortions of organic forms rendered in wax, animal skins, hair, textiles, metal and wood, approached Coetzee to cooperate on her presentation in the Belgian pavilion at the 55th Venice Biennale. Coetzee was invited to serve as the curator of her exhibition, as well as to contribute towards two related art books, *We Are All Flesh* and *Cripplewood/Kreupelhout* (both 2013).

We Are All Flesh features textual excerpts from various novels by Coetzee presented alongside colour photos of De Bruyckere's animalistic and wounded sculptures. 'The excerpts do not describe the images, while the images do not illustrate the excerpts', note Kusek and Szymański in a thorough analysis of the project. The tension between word and image, writer and artist, is central to the book's creative torque. Among its chief virtues as a project is the way it reiterates the granular beauty and forensic precision of Coetzee's writing. 'He feels like a crab pulled out of its shell, pink and wounded and obscene', reads a culled fragment from *Boyhood* appearing on a page next to an illustration of a 2011 sculpture titled *Unintentionally Keloid*.[26]

De Bruyckere's cooperation with Coetzee aimed to draw the crab from his shell. In certain respects, Coetzee obliged: he was a diligent collaborator. Besides giving permission for his fictional writing to be cleaved from its original context and impressionistically repurposed in *We Are All Flesh*, he also agreed to provide 'a parallel text' in the form of an original short story to *Cripplewood/Kreupelhout*. Entitled 'The Old Woman and the Cats', it features the writer's alter ego Elizabeth Costello, a logician and vegetarian with a 'passion for exactitude'.[27] The book also compiles a select number of letters exchanged between the writer and artist between September 2012 and March 2013, as well as a short piece of writing by Coetzee which, like the lone sculpture of fallen tree installed in the Belgian pavilion, is entitled *Kreupelhout*. 'The cripplewood tree that cannot straighten itself, that grows bent, at a crouch; from whose limbs we cut crutches for those who can only creep; a tree of knotted limbs, gnarled, snarled', reads an excerpt of Coetzee's lexicographic description.[28]

In other respects, the collaboration was stunted like the tree that cannot straighten itself. De Bruyckere makes clear in her correspondence that she requires something more 'delicate' than curatorial assistance during the working process and hopes Coetzee might serve 'as a source of inspiration'.[29] Coetzee came to function as an idealized rather than actualized inspiration. The image of the fallen tree that dominated her installation drew on an encounter in Burgundy several years earlier. The cripplewood suggested by Coetzee in his correspondence is abandoned in favour of an elm tree by the artist. Nonetheless, De Bruyckere's collaboration with Coetzee attracted considerable interest, in part due to the strangeness of Coetzee functioning as a curator. One art critic likened it to 'a joke from some art world Onion – as unbelievable as Thomas Pynchon appearing on "Oprah" or Joan Didion doing a Reddit AMA'.[30] A substantial queue formed outside the Belgian pavilion during the preview. Coetzee, however, was not in attendance – he was in Norway, participating in a literature festival. The crab, briefly pink and exposed in an obscene environment, had returned to his shell.

The time period between Coetzee's contributions to the books by Kentridge and De Bruyckere, 1999 and 2013, witnessed a remarkable shift in the form and style of his criticism. Where the former essay is expository, an elucidation of means and outcomes in a dispassionate style, his contributions to *Cripplewood/Kreupelhout* are more formally diverse, idiosyncratic and dialogical. Where his earlier criticism is couched in a rational form that operates adjacent to fiction, his late style, a style inaugurated with the publication of *Boyhood* in 1997, is marked by a transference of criticism into the habitat of Coetzee's fictions and correspondence. Mystification becomes an aspect of Coetzee's late style as a writer occasionally drawn to engage with artists and remark on visuality. In the manner of W. G. Sebald, Coetzee tramples the boundaries between fiction and nonfiction, merging storytelling, fictive biography, essay and philosophical rumination in order to attain 'lift-off' into 'the realm of the imaginative'.[31]

Clarity of statement, a defining virtue of Coetzee's writing, however, remains. Coetzee's scrubbed and laconic sentences have frequently been a subject of commentary. John Updike, a mellifluous critic emblematic of a patrician style in post-war American literary criticism, described Coetzee as 'austere', 'penetrating' and 'astringent'. James Wood, another insightful *New Yorker* critic, has described Coetzee's prose as 'chaste, exact, ashen'. Similarly, Okwui Enwezor, a curator and historian whose background as a poet lent his early art criticism from the 1990s brio and panache, has also commented on Coetzee's 'dry, standoffish writing', describing it as 'bloodless' and 'cauterized'.[32] Style might seem an unremarkable foundation on which to base an appraisal of Coetzee's authority as a critic. However, Coetzee has himself stated: 'Style and content are not separable.'[33] Although taken out of context, his statement nonetheless echoes an assertion by philosopher Martha Nussbaum:

> Style itself makes its claims, expresses its own sense of what matters. Literary form is not separable from content, but is itself a part of content – an integral part, then, of the search for and the statement of truth.[34]

Truth here is multifarious: it is syntactical, logical and ethical. Ethics matter deeply to Coetzee, and his writing is an expression of this attitude. Can style enunciate an ethical outlook?[35] In his admiring appraisal of Zbigniew Herbert in his *Threepenny Review* essay, Coetzee (implicitly) addresses the attitudinal implications of his much remarked-upon laconic style:

> What one learns from Herbert is not a body of ideas, but a certain style, hard, durable: a style that is also an approach to the world and to experience, political experience included. Ideas are certainly important – who would deny that? – but the fact is, the ideas that operate in novels and poems, once they are unpicked from their context and laid out on the laboratory table, usually turn out to be uncomplicated, even banal. Whereas a style, an attitude to the world, as it soaks in, becomes part of the personality, part of the self, ultimately indistinguishable from the self.[36]

This attitude, this saturated sense of style, is what I recognize in Coetzee's small but fascinating body of writing about art: a hardness and durability that proposes a way of looking at images, of being in the world with them; also, of finding an adequate language and form to make images palpable, legible and intelligible, on the page, but also in the eye and ear of the mind.

NOTES

1. Coetzee, *Youth*, 11. Further references cited parenthetically in text, using the abbreviation Y.
2. Rosenberg, *The Tradition of the New*, 35.
3. Auster and Coetzee, *Here and Now*, 19 February 2010.
4. Coetzee, *Disgrace*, 160.
5. Kusek and Szymanski, 'An Unlikely Pair: Berlinde De Bruyckere and J. M. Coetzee', 15.
6. Coetzee, *Diary of a Bad Year*, 192.
7. Coetzee, *Photographs from Boyhood*, 178.
8. Coetzee, 'Eight Ways of Looking at Samuel Beckett', 22.
9. De Bruyckere and Coetzee, *Cripplewood/Kreupelhout*, 46, 45 and 48.
10. Coetzee, 'Homage', 6.
11. Coetzee, *Doubling the Point*, 107. 'Captain America in American Mythology' was first published in *University of Cape Town Studies in English*, No. 6, 1976.
12. Coetzee, *Doubling the Point*, 111.
13. Sontag, *Against Interpretation*, 14.
14. Rosenberg, *The Tradition of the New*, 11.
15. Coetzee, *White Writing*, 174.
16. Christov-Bakargiev, *William Kentridge*, 46. 'Landscape in a State of Siege' was first published in *Stet 5* (no. 3), November 1988.
17. Coetzee, *Kentridge*, 84.
18. Coetzee, *Pierneef, Land, and Landscape*, 50, 51 and 111.
19. See for example Foster, *Washed with Sun: Landscape and the Making of White South Africa*, who substantially draws on Coetzee, notably on 245 and 253–4.
20. Coetzee, *Diary of a Bad Year*, 192.
21. Coetzee, *Doubling the Point*, 106.
22. Ibid.
23. Eagleton, *After Theory*, 2.
24. Quoted in Clarkson, *J. M. Coetzee: Countervoices*, 4.
25. See especially Coetzee, *William Kentridge*, 93.
26. De Bruyckere and Coetzee, *We Are All Flesh*, 46.
27. De Bruyckere and Coetzee, *Cripplewood/Kreupelhout*, 8.
28. Ibid., 42.
29. Ibid., 29.
30. Farago, 'J. M. Coetzee, Curator?'.

31. Coetzee, *Inner Workings*, 145, 148. Given Coetzee's pronounced early interest in photography, his circumspect appraisal of the German author's 'endearingly amateurish' (145), and mischievous use of, photography in his fictions is striking, even conspicuous.
32. See Updike, 'The Story of Himself'; Wood, 'Squall Lines'; Enwezor, 'The Enigma of the Rainbow Nation', 40–1.
33. Coetzee, *Doubling the Point*, vii.
34. Nussbaum, *Love's Knowledge: Essays on Philosophy and Literature*, 3.
35. Carrol Clarkson has persuasively analysed the relationship between Coetzee's literary style and ethics, notably in 'Not I': 'A careful consideration of an aspect of literary style (rather than the more obvious discussion of a novelistic "theme") has the potential to become a way of thinking through questions more readily associated with moral philosophy.'
36. Coetzee, 'Homage', 7.

WORKS CITED

Auster, Paul and J. M. Coetzee. *Here and Now: Letters 2008–2011*. New York: Viking, 2013.
Cameron, Dan, Carolyn Christov-Bakargiev and J. M. Coetzee. *William Kentridge*. London: Phaidon Press, 1999.
Christov-Bakargiev, Carolyn. *William Kentridge*. Brussels: Société des Expositions du Palais des Beaux-Arts de Bruxelles, 1998.
Clarkson, Carrol. *J. M. Coetzee: Countervoices*. Houndsmills: Palgrave Macmillan, 2009.
Clarkson, Carrol. 'Not I'. *Arcade*, 2015. https://arcade.stanford.edu/content/not-i.
Coetzee, J. M. *Diary of a Bad Year*. London: Harvill Secker, 2007.
Coetzee, J. M. *Disgrace*. London: Martin Secker & Warburg, 1999 (Vintage, 2000).
Coetzee, J. M. *Doubling the Point: Essays and Interviews*. Edited by D. Attwell. Cambridge, MA: Harvard University Press, 1992.
Coetzee, J. M. 'Eight Ways of Looking at Samuel Beckett'. *Samuel Beckett Today/Aujourd'hui* 19 (2008): 19–31.
Coetzee, J. M. 'Homage'. *The Threepenny Review* 53 (1993): 5–7.
Coetzee, J. M. *Inner Workings: Essays 2000–2005*. London: Harvill Secker, 2007.
Coetzee, J. M. *Photographs from Boyhood*, edited by H. Wittenberg. Pretoria: Protea Book House, 2020.
Coetzee, J. M. *White Writing: On the Culture of Letters in South Africa*. New Haven: Yale University Press, 1988.
Coetzee, J. M. *Youth*. London: Secker and Warburg, 2002.
Coetzee, N. J. *Pierneef, Land, and Landscape: The Johannesburg Station Panels in Context*. Johannesburg: CBM Publishing, 1992.
De Bruyckere, Berlinde and J. M. Coetzee. *Cripplewood/Kreupelhout*. New Haven and London: Mercatorfonds, 2013.
De Bruyckere, Berlinde and J. M. Coetzee. *We Are All Flesh*, Ghent: MER Paper Kunsthalle, 2013.
Eagleton, Terry. *After Theory*. London: Allen Lane, 2003 (Penguin, 2004).
Enwezor, Okwui. 'The Enigma of the Rainbow Nation'. In *Personal Affects: Power and Poetics in Contemporary South African Art*, edited by S. Perryer, 24–43. New York: Museum of African Art, 2004.
Farago, Jason. 'J.M. Coetzee, Curator?'. *New Republic*, 7 February 2013. https://newrepublic.com/article/112302/jm-coetzee-curate-venice-biennale.
Foster, Jeremy A. *Washed with Sun: Landscape and the Making of White South Africa*. Pittsburgh: University of Pittsburgh Press, 2008.
Kusek, Robert and Wojciech Szymanski. 'An Unlikely Pair: Berlinde De Bruyckere and J.M. Coetzee'. *Werkwinkel: Journal of Low Countries and South African Studies* 10, no. 1 (2015): 13–32.
Nussbaum, Martha C. *Love's Knowledge: Essays on Philosophy and Literature*. New York: Oxford University Press, 1990.

Rosenberg, Harold. *The Tradition of the New*. New York: Horizon Press, 1959.
Sontag, Susan. *Against Interpretation*. New York: Farrar, Straus & Giroux, 1966 (Vintage, 2001).
Updike, John. 'The Story of Himself'. *The New Yorker*, 7 July 2002. https://www.newyorker.com/magazine/2002/07/15/the-story-of-himself.
Wood, James. 'Squall Lines'. *The New Yorker*, 16 December 2007. https://www.newyorker.com/magazine/2007/12/24/squall-lines.

CHAPTER THIRTY-SIX

J. M. Coetzee and the work of music

GRAHAM K. RIACH

What is a work? In the philosophy of music, this question is one of the thorniest. Take Johann Sebastian Bach's *Goldberg Variations*. We hear them through performances, perhaps now most often recorded performances, each derived from the score; but we would more readily say that the performances are *of* the variations, rather than saying they *are* the variations. Likewise, the score: it gives directions for the performance of the work, but few would say that the book in front of them *is* the *Goldberg Variations*, as destroying that copy would not destroy the work. Amid conflicting interpretations, the prevailing philosophical model for the nature of works is Platonist, according to which musical works are abstract objects. This is to say that they have no physical or temporal extension, unlike the score – a physical object made up of signs which depict or point to the work – or the performance, a token, translation or realization of the work in time.[1] To think through the relationship between works and their instances, this chapter examines some of J. M. Coetzee's descriptions of listening to music. In the examples I offer, mainly from *The Schooldays of Jesus* (2016) and the essay 'What Is a Classic?' (1993), there is a trope in which listening to music is described in terms of seeing or imagining a spatial structure. This figure allows the consideration both of the nature of musical works – and of the work of music – in Coetzee's writing. These descriptions have at least three consequences: they draw our attention to a commonly experienced but rarely described dimension of aesthetic experience, help us think about the work-performance relationship in both music and literature, and suggest how aesthetic experience might mediate between an artwork and its societal outsides.

The dominant analytical approach in musicology privileges the written score as giving best access to the work, and so situates ultimate meaning outside the immediate phenomenological experience of performed music. As Nicholas Cook puts in, 'in a nutshell, musicology was set up around the idea of music as writing rather than music as performance'.[2] However, in recent years, there has been a swing towards performance: Carolyn Abbate, one of the strongest advocates for performance, insists that we must approach music in all its unruly singularity. Borrowing terminology from philosopher Vladimir Jankélévich, she claims that when we focus on the 'gnostic', 'the abstraction of the work', we risk forgetting the 'drastic' experience of 'real music'.[3] By privileging the 'low hermeneutics and soft hermeneutics' of the gnostic, our attention is diverted from the visceral dimensions of performance towards '"something else," something behind or beyond or next to this mental object [the material acoustic phenomenon]'.[4] The drastic involves 'a category of knowledge that flows from drastic actions or experiences and not from verbally mediated reasoning', whereas the gnostic 'implies not just knowledge per se but making the opaque transparent, knowledge based on semiosis and disclosed secrets, reserved for the elite and hidden from others'.[5]

The terms of this debate will look familiar to critics following discussions in literary studies about critical and post-critical approaches.[6] On the one hand, we have an approach to reading and analysis shaped by a largely German tradition of critical theory that emphasizes history, ideology and critique, and the paradigmatic axis of scores/texts; on the other, a mostly French tradition that privileges Bergsonian temporality, performance, empiricism and the syntagmatic axis of unfolding experience.[7] This distinction was cast memorably by Derek Attridge as being between 'allegorical' and 'nonallegorical' forms of reading: the former involves taking 'the literal meaning of the text to be a pathway to some other, more important, meaning' usually found in 'historical, biographical, psychological, moral or political' domains; the latter resists moving 'too quickly beyond the novel to find its significance elsewhere', preferring the phenomenological description of the reading experience as it unfolds in time.[8]

Gnostic and drastic perspectives, however, are not so easy to disentangle. Stephen Rings considers how written criticism about music can create or modify drastic experience. For Rings, the verbal description of musical works can perform a deictic function by 'directing, contextualizing and focusing our aural attention', and so creating experiences of musical presence that would otherwise not have come about.[9] In his words, musical description can 'lead to the "dawning of an aspect" in Ludwig Wittgenstein's sense', that is to say, a verbal description can cause an abrupt shift in how we experience a piece of music, by drawing our attention to it in new ways.[10] When this aspect dawns, aesthetic experience can be created or enhanced, giving previously inaccessible experiences of pleasure, awe, presence or other kinds of intensification. Rings focuses on the critical analysis of music, ranging from the purple descriptive mode favoured by Jankélévich – 'a gossamer poetics of oblique approach and retreat'[11] – to less colourful academic prose. His argument can be extended, both in that fictional descriptions can perform this deictic function, and also in that the effect of deixis is not limited to specific moments of single pieces. If our attention is pointed towards, say, a textural or structural effect in one piece, we learn a way of hearing that can be exported to other pieces. In Coetzee's writing, the description of musical experience fulfils a deictic function, but does so unusually; first in that it is less concerned with describing features of particular pieces, and more with what happens to us when we hear music. Our aesthetic experience is therefore not simply enhanced for a particular piece but rather enhanced for pieces in general. Moreover, by describing aesthetic experience, while framing it in variously ironized narratives, Coetzee creates an unstable state in which drastic proximity and gnostic distance become fused.

My first examples are drawn from Coetzee's *The Schooldays of Jesus* (2016), the second part of the Jesus trilogy, between *The Childhood of Jesus* (2013) and *The Death of Jesus* (2020). *The Childhood* recounts the experience of a man called Simón and a boy called Davíd, who have arrived by boat in a city called Novilla. Simón is not Davíd's biological father, but he takes on the role of his guardian; later a woman called Inés takes on the mother's role. By the end of the book, the trio leaves Novilla to avoid problems with the authorities caused by David's unwillingness to participate in the school system. Music is present to some extent: Davíd tries music lessons; Simón has a tepid affair with Davíd's music teacher Elena; Davíd sings a passage from Schubert's 'Erlkönig' on the bus; we learn that Simón finds the music in Novilla 'lacks weight' and Simón hears, from behind a closed door in The Institute for Further Studies, 'a woman singing mournfully to the accompaniment of a harp'.[12] In *Schooldays*, the action moves to the city of Estrella and the role of music becomes more prominent. In a continued attempt to evade the authorities, Simón and Inés enrol Davíd in an Academy of Dance run by Ana Magdalena and her husband Juan Sebastián Arroyo (a literal Spanish translation of Johann Sebastian Bach; Anna Magdalena was the name of Bach's second wife). The couple teaches according to a philosophy in which certain dances are thought to accord with particular numbers, and as 'music enters us and moves us in dance, so the numbers cease to be mere ideas, mere phantoms and become real'.[13] According to the school's philosophy, a child 'still bears deep impresses of a former life', and by dancing they can gain access to that life and to what lies beyond the visible world, 'namely the realm of the numbers themselves' (68). Numbers, like musical works, are often held to be types of abstract object, and here that abstract sphere can be accessed through embodying the numbers in 'music-dance'.[14]

Stolidly rational, Simón is sceptical of the school's philosophy – 'claptrap [...] a load of mystical rubbish' (99) – and at a performance at the Academy of Dance finds the dancing rather boring. The music, however, has a different effect on him. He closes his eyes and concentrates:

> The upper notes of the organ are tinny, the lower notes without resonance. But the music itself takes possession of him. Calm descends; he can feel something within him – his soul? – take up the rhythm of the music and move into it. He falls into a mild trance.
> (70)

Simón begins to experience a heightened state of presence, which draws him into a state of trance. The music, in the sense of the sounds in the room,[15] is nothing special – the notes are 'tinny' at the top end and 'without resonance' at the bottom – but these sounds are distinct from the 'music itself', which is at once a ravishing force which 'takes possession' of him, and a haven into which some part of him can move. The drastic dimension of the performed music here gives Simón access to an altered state, and as his immersion in the music deepens, he opens his eyes and finds himself on the brink of an epiphany, of seeing a logic behind the performance that 'he cannot quite grasp, though he feels on the edge of doing so' (70). Whether or not this logic is really there, what is important to note for now is that he feels it to be there, and this is an important part of how we experience artworks.

The passage above leaves Simón on the cusp of discovery, but at the end of the novel he takes one further step. Simón goes to the Academy of Dance for a lesson, and while Arroyo plays the piano, Simón dances:

> Arroyo inverts the tune, varies it, elaborates: while the pulse remains steady, the little aria begins to reveal a new structure, point by point, like a crystal growing in the air. Bliss washes over him; he wishes he could sit down and listen properly. [...] It is cool in the studio; he is conscious of the high space above his head [...] there is only the music. Arms extended, eyes closed, he shuffles in a slow circle. Over the horizon the first star begins to rise.
> (260)

The experience described here is not that of a nearly graspable logic, but rather of perceiving a tertiary object that appears over time, a 'structure', which emerges 'point by point, like a crystal growing in the air'. This structure is not part of the performance, although it is accessed or perhaps realized through the performance. Further, it is unclear whether Simón sees it at all, or if it is the narrating voice which offers this image to the reader only. Spatial metaphors are often used to describe non-spatial artforms – we say a melody goes up and down, or that a plot closes – and while these are not literally true, spatial metaphors are so integral to our way of understanding the world that they constitute an important part of aesthetic experience. What is this structure? Perhaps it is a synaesthesic visualization of the kind provided by some computer media players, in which certain pitches, timbres and harmonies produce visual manifestations. Another possibility, as Arroyo is improvising on the aria by taking liberties with the melody, voicings and so on, is that the crystallization is rather an abstract of the underlying harmonic structure: the effect would be similar to the visual representation of literary plots, as found in Freytag's Pyramid or Northrop Frye's U-shaped and inverted U-shaped plots.[16] The philosophy of the academy, in which 'music-dance' grants access to 'the realm of the numbers themselves', suggests a third possibility, namely that the music has given a glimpse – or rather a visual analogue – of some abstract structure (the work?) that accompanies the auditory experience of music.

In describing the experience of 'seeing' a temporal artform, Coetzee points our attention towards this dimension of encountering artworks. This amplifies its effect, but here also ironizes it. In Coetzee's writing, as Michelle Kelly reminds us, ideas can be taken completely seriously while also being disallowed by their narrative framing through a 'particular narrating consciousness or worldview'.[17] In part, Coetzee's description is a deictic gesture that singles out a component of aesthetic experience and so focalizes it in our attention. As Rings suggests, this singling out can create or alter drastic experience, rather than just describing it. Coetzee imbues these rather abstract thoughts with a visceral, drastic dimension: the reader experiences the structure along with Simón as it forms, with the rhythm of the passage controlled by semi-colons, colons and commas to create a gradual unfolding of experience. Further, as we finish the novel and are invited to partake of its epiphanic ending ('Bliss washes over him [...] Over the horizon the first star begins to rise'), Coetzee draws on art's capacity to grant us revelatory experience, while also asking us to question it. In my case, at least, a sense of presence was intensified: the work seemed to have inevitably led up to this moment and so seized into a momentarily graspable structure, and along with the star's rise, an aspect dawned. Coetzee's description opens a space in which we can examine our experience of epiphany and our spatial conception of the novel as it comes to a close by making them explicit objects of thought. However, by experiencing them along with the ludicrous, shuffling Simón, we are also encouraged to view our drastic experience from the outside in and think about how art causes drastic experience in us, even as we experience it. We are required, in other words, to sustain a doubled state of gnostic distance and drastic immediacy, of the thought-object of the work and the unfolding singularity of performance.

Another of Coetzee's descriptions of listening to music, from his essay 'What Is a Classic?', adds a further dimension to our understanding:

> In Bach nothing is obscure, no single step so miraculous as to surpass imitation. Yet when the chain of sounds is realized in time, the building process ceases at a certain moment to be the mere linking of units; the units cohere as a higher-order object that I can only describe by analogy as the incarnation of ideas of exposition, complication, and resolution that are more general than music.[18]

The description is similar: a piece of music, when experienced in time, seems to either reveal or create a thought-object. We might think here of similar moments in Coetzee's writing, such as when Mrs Curran in *Age of Iron* plays a recording and '[b]ar by bar the Goldberg Variations erected themselves in the air', or, in *Disgrace*, when 'the shade of a melody, having hovered for days on the edge of hearing, unfolds and blessedly reveals itself' as David Lurie composes his opera.[19] In 'What Is a Classic?', as in *Schooldays*, Coetzee's description operates by resemblance, here through analogy, nearing metaphor. This descriptive mode – perhaps characteristically for an essay – is neither solely that of drastic experience, nor precisely that of gnostic hermeneutics, but rather a combination of the gnostic and drastic with deictic implications. A state of thinking-feeling is elicited through a rhetorical structure that begins with the procataleptic 'nothing [...] no', to the turn at '[y]et', and then the build from 'ceases to be' through to 'cohere' before expanding out into 'more general than'. In this passage, it is neither the work nor the harmonic structure of the piece that is revealed in crystalline form; it is rather the 'incarnation of ideas of exposition, complication and resolution that are more general than music'. This 'incarnation' – the religious overtones, as for 'blessedly' in *Disgrace*, are surely no accident – appears to be of something already known that art brings temporarily into our grasp. How else would we recognize these ideas if we did not bring some foreknowledge of them? Music here provides a resonating space for conscious thought and a sounding chamber for some unthought formal or narrative gestalt impulse. Whether it is in fact the case that this higher-order object exists and becomes perceptible to us, or whether some aspect of that experience only leads to believe that we have perceived such a thing, it remains the case that the experience does happen. As a result, our own knowledge – thought or unthought – feels realized in art and our affective and cognitive vistas widen. The sensation is closer to recognition than discovery, as if some previously known but never explicitly thought knowledge had been made accessible, or perhaps better that such knowledge realizes itself through an encounter with an artwork.

It is, moreover, exactly the tension between drastically embodied experience and the way that experience takes on gnostic meaning that Coetzee explores in 'What Is a Classic?'. On the one hand, we have the sublime 'stunned overwhelmedness' on hearing Bach's music – 'a disinterested and in a sense impersonal aesthetic experience'; on the other, we have an awareness that such responses are bound up with 'the masked expression of a material instinct', one current in a 'tide of communal feeling that found in Bach a vehicle for its own expression'.[20] If experiencing a work can conjure up abstract objects through which we recognize without ever having seen, then Bach (as a cultural phenomenon) here becomes a conduit through which a culture articulates itself to itself, both in the romantic reconstruction of Bach and in Coetzee's critical retrospection on his provincial affiliation to the classic. For Coetzee, the status of a classic is assured by its endurance in the face of sustained critical enquiry across generations, as each finds in the work resources for the present, affordances that only become actualized through critical engagement. A classic is, in Coetzee's reading of Eliot, to be understood in 'allegorical terms'; that is, the work will 'bear the weight of having read into it a meaning for Eliot's own age'.[21] Coetzee finds in Bach's music both a profound and moving drastic experience and a gnostic vehicle through which to explore the figure of the classic for onetime residents of former colonies.

To draw together my earlier thinking on abstract objects in aesthetic experience and the idea that works might 'bear the weight' of allegorical readings, I offer a final, speculative, suggestion. The experience of a 'higher-order object' – one that happens as much in reading works of literature as it does when listening to music – provides one spur for 'allegorical' readings. From his descriptions of listening to Bach, or the Bach-adjacent Arroyo, Coetzee is clearly aware that artworks can lead us to believe we have perceived some hidden structure. This, accompanied by the feeling of recognition or fulfilment that often accompanies it, contributes to why critics often attach that experience to domains of knowledge outside the text. Attridge notes the importance of allegorical consciousness to drastic experience in noting that 'one may be doing justice to the singularity and inventiveness of a literary work by responding to its invitation to allegorize', as 'in so doing we are working through the operations of its meaning'.[22] Further, as Coetzee points out in his *Late Essays*, some texts even require allegorical reading to realize them fully. For him, *The Scarlet Letter* is:

> not an allegory – that is to say, it is not a story whose elements map closely onto the elements of another story taking place in some other, parallel realm. It does, however, rely on being read in an allegorical spirit: without the Judaeo-Christian tradition of allegorical reading behind it, it would be a bare little fable indeed.[23]

One route to allegorical consciousness is through a drastic experience in which an object seems to be revealed to us. What is required to understand the work of music in Coetzee – and it is a feature that his descriptions of music often point us towards – is a dialectical tacking between gnostic, allegorical readings and those that recognize the drastic, embodied experience of art. Or rather, these two halves are so inseparable that even to speak in terms of halves or dialectics risks a misstep. The experience of music is, in Michael Gallope's words, 'a stubborn amalgam of form and sensation' in which 'the interaction of the two halves is irresolvable by one side or the other', and the same might readily be said about allegorical and nonallegorical impulses in reading works of literature.[24] To fully apprehend the layered components of aesthetic experience requires imbricating drastic and gnostic knowledge, while never claiming one as an artefact of the other.

Distinguishing too sharply between gnostic and drastic reading risks obscuring how allegorical readings can intensify drastic experience and underplaying the role of drastic experience in allegorical consciousness. Gnostic reading is always one step ahead of the text, it disenchants, unveils and unmasks, but might miss some of the most immediate experiences of a text experienced in time. The resurgent drastic reading is sensitive to epiphany, presence and embodiment, but susceptible to accusations of obfuscation, false consciousness and naïveté. The gnostic, however, is enfolded in the drastic, offering us new ways of experiencing the text in time. Meanwhile, the drastic experience of perceiving a higher-order object as we listen or read is one component in what leads us to allegorize. In analysing the moments of musical experience presented above, I hope to have shown that Coetzee uses the deictic capacity of language to direct our attention to a particular facet of musical experience, and that attending to this invitation can refresh our aesthetic sensorium, illuminate discussions of the work-performance relationship and open out onto much larger questions about what we do when we read.

NOTES

1. See Dodd, *Works of Music*.
2. Cook, *Beyond the Score*, 1.
3. Abbate, 'Music – Drastic or Gnostic?', 505, 531.
4. Ibid., 516, 505.
5. Ibid., 510.

6. See Felski, 'Introduction'; Kramnick, 'Criticism and Truth'.
7. See Gallope, *Deep Refrains*, 19–20.
8. Attridge, *J.M. Coetzee & the Ethics of Reading*, 60, 43.
9. Rings, 'Talking and Listening with Jankélévitch', 219.
10. Ibid., 222.
11. Gallope et al., 'Vladimir Jankélévitch's Philosophy of Music', 222.
12. Coetzee, *The Childhood of Jesus*, 64, 120.
13. Coetzee, *The Schooldays of Jesus*, 68. Further references cited parenthetically in text.
14. Axel Englund suggests that Coetzee's fiction often portrays music as a 'means of closing the Cartesian gap to reconnect spirit and matter', noting that 'live music enacts the notion that the roots of the soul are located in the body'. Englund, 'Intimate Practices: Music, Sex, and the Body in J. M. Coetzee's *Summertime*', 100, 107; Coetzee, *The Schooldays of Jesus*, 243. For other engagements with music in Coetzee's works, see Lachman, 'Opera and the Limits of Representation in J. M. Coetzee's *Disgrace*'; Sheils, 'Opera, Byron, and a South African Psyche in J. M. Coetzee's *Disgrace*'; Attridge, 'Age of Bronze, State of Grace'; Sánchez, 'The Limits of Reason in J. M. Coetzee's *The Schooldays of Jesus*'; Dooley, '"The Origins of Speech Lie in Song"'; Kelly, 'Other Arts and Adaptations'; Holland, '"Plink-Plunk" Unforgetting The Present In Coetzee's *Disgrace*'; Bruyn, 'Polyphony beyond the Human'.
15. On the unstable boundary between music and sound, see Bruyn, 'Polyphony beyond the Human'.
16. Freytag, *Freytag's Technique of the Drama*; Frye, *The Great Code*; Improvization challenges discussions of the work, unless the work is taken to be ontologically thin, made up of a general structure rather than a precise set of pitches, rhythms, timbres and so on. For more on improvization, see Davies, *Musical Works and Performances*, 16.
17. Kelly, 'Other Arts and Adaptations', 190.
18. Coetzee, 'What Is a Classic?', 9.
19. Coetzee, *Age of Iron*, 30; Coetzee, *Disgrace*, 183.
20. Coetzee, 'What Is a Classic?', 11, 14–15.
21. Ibid., 5.
22. Attridge, 'Against Allegory: *Waiting for the Barbarians, Life & Times of Michael K*, and the Question of Literary Reading', 76.
23. Coetzee, *Late Essays*, 17.
24. Gallope, *Deep Refrains*, 19.

WORKS CITED

Abbate, Carolyn. 'Music – Drastic or Gnostic?' *Critical Inquiry* 30, no. 3 (2004): 505–36.
Attridge, Derek. 'Against Allegory: *Waiting for the Barbarians, Life & Times of Michael K*, and the Question of Literary Reading'. In *J. M. Coetzee and the Idea of the Public Intellectual*, edited by J. Poyner, 63–82. Athens: Ohio University Press, 2006.
Attridge, Derek. 'Age of Bronze, State of Grace: Music and Dogs in Coetzee's *Disgrace*'. NOVEL: A Forum on Fiction 34, no. 1 (2000): 98–121.
Attridge, Derek. *J.M. Coetzee & the Ethics of Reading: Literature in the Event*. Chicago: University of Chicago Press, 2004.
Bruyn, Ben De. 'Polyphony Beyond the Human: Animals, Music, and Community in Coetzee and Powers'. *Studies in the Novel* 48, no. 3 (2016): 364–83.
Coetzee, J. M. *Age of Iron*. London: Secker & Warburg, 1990.
Coetzee, J. M. *The Childhood of Jesus*. London: Harvill Secker, 2013.

Coetzee, J. M. *Disgrace*. London: Secker & Warburg, 1999.
Coetzee, J. M. *Late Essays: 2006–2017*. New York: Viking, 2006.
Coetzee, J. M. *The Schooldays of Jesus*. New York: Viking, 2017.
Coetzee, J. M. 'What Is a Classic?' *Current Writing* 5, no. 2 (1993): 7–24.
Cook, Nicholas. *Beyond the Score: Music as Performance*. Oxford; New York: Oxford University Press, 2013.
Davies, Stephen. *Musical Works and Performances*. Oxford: Oxford University Press, 2001.
Dodd, Julian. *Works of Music: An Essay in Ontology*. Oxford; New York: Clarendon, 2007.
Dooley, Gillian. '"The Origins of Speech Lie in Song": Music as Language in Coetzee's *Age of Iron*'. *Le Simplegadi* 18, no. 20 (2020): 26–34.
Englund, Axel. 'Intimate Practices: Music, Sex, and the Body in J. M. Coetzee's *Summertime*'. *Mosaic: An Interdisciplinary Critical Journal* 50, no. 2 (2017): 99–115.
Felski, Rita. 'Introduction'. *New Literary History* 45, no. 2 (2014): v–xi.
Freytag, Gustav. *Freytag's Technique of the Drama: An Exposition of Dramatic Composition and Art*. Translated by Elias J. MacEwan. Chicago: Scott, Foresman & Co., 1900.
Frye, Northrop. *The Great Code: The Bible and Literature*. New York: Harcourt Brace Jovanovich, 1982.
Gallope, Michael. *Deep Refrains: Music, Philosophy, and the Ineffable*. Chicago: University of Chicago Press, 2017.
Gallope, Michael, Brian Kane, Steven Rings, James Hepokoski, Judy Lochhead, Michael J. Puri and James R. Currie. 'Vladimir Jankélévitch's Philosophy of Music'. *Journal of the American Musicological Society* 65, no. 1 (2012): 215–56.
Holland, Michael. '"Plink-Plunk" Unforgetting the Present in Coetzee's *Disgrace*'. *Interventions* 4, no. 3 (1 January 2002): 395–404.
Kelly, Michelle. 'Other Arts and Adaptations'. In *The Cambridge Companion to J. M. Coetzee*, edited by J. Zimbler, 187–205. Cambridge: Cambridge University Press, 2020.
Kramnick, Jonathan. 'Criticism and Truth'. *Critical Inquiry* 47, no. 2 (22 December 2020): 218–40.
Lachman, Kathryn. 'Opera and the Limits of Representation in J.M. Coetzee's *Disgrace*'. In *Borrowed Forms: The Music and Ethics of Transnational Fiction*. 113–36. Liverpool: Liverpool University Press, 2014.
Rings, Steven. 'Talking and Listening with Jankélévitch'. *Journal of the American Musicological Society* 65, no. 1 (2012): 218–23.
Sánchez, Patricia Álvarez. 'The Limits of Reason in J.M. Coetzee's *The Schooldays of Jesus*'. *Miscelánea: A Journal of English and American Studies* 60 (2019): 107–26.
Sheils, Colleen M. 'Opera, Byron, and a South African Psyche in J. M. Coetzee's *Disgrace*'. *Current Writing: Text and Reception in Southern Africa* 15, no. 1 (2003): 38–50.

CHAPTER THIRTY-SEVEN

Adapting Coetzee for the stage and screen

ED CHARLTON

Adaptation is not quite translation. In Walter Benjamin's view, translation describes a form of kinship between languages. It is, he notes, 'ideational', an abstract commitment to the idea of 'true language'.[1] By comparison, the art of adaptation is more often about interpretation than ideas. Even as it retains something of the same repetition function, adaptation does not always uphold translation's (imperfect) obligation to fidelity. In the various acts of revision, parody, popularization and hybridization potentially at stake, adaptation permits and often even urges less than loyal influences to assert themselves. The pleasure that comes from this pursuit of 'repetition with difference', as Linda Hutcheon once put it, tends to be more inward looking, a play with hermeneutics rather than lofty ideas like true language.[2]

As a prolific adaptor and literary translator, J. M. Coetzee complicates this separation. Whether citing the influence that *Waiting for the Barbarians* (1980) draws from Cavafy or the canonical figures borrowed in *Foe* (1986), Coetzee's interest in adaptation and the 'poetics of reciprocity' is well established.[3] So too is his allied affection for metafiction and reflexivity. As critical engagement with Coetzee's comparatively modest work in literary translation has risen, however, his avant-garde credentials have begun to shift. Assessing the assumptions that drive his translations, Jan Steyn finds that Coetzee depends on 'the now-unpopular notion of "fidelity"' both to guide his practice and defend the translatability of his own fiction.[4] Rebecca Walkowitz presses further this second point when she describes his novels as 'born translated'.[5] By this, she means that, as a world writer, Coetzee anticipates translation of his writing as 'a condition of its production'.[6] Whatever else may be said of this provocation, like Steyn, Walkowitz discovers in Coetzee's writing relatively orthodox ideas about fidelity and the kinship between languages.

It is not my aim to adjudicate on this precise point. I am interested instead in the corollary role that adaptation may play in working through Coetzee's ideas about representation more generally. The point here is that just as critical readings of Coetzee's translations help adjudicate on his attitude to language, so a comparable attitude to adaptation may unfurl related ideas on writing, performance and the potential limits of artistic representation at large. To begin, this means augmenting Walkowitz's already unusual claim to suggest that Coetzee's novels are also born adapted – that is, written *as* and *for* adaptation. This first point is hardly controversial given his record in intertextual revision. In order to sustain the second, however, this chapter looks beyond Coetzee's play with intertextuality, thinking about his intermedial legacy on the stage and screen.

This is sometimes an arduous task. Not quite comparable with the 'ridiculous figure ... picking away at tunes on a child's banjo', as Katherine Lachman casts would-be librettist David Lurie in *Disgrace* (1999), many intermedial adaptations of Coetzee's fiction appear, nonetheless, to be 'lacking in fire' – to borrow directly from the novel.[7] The 2008 film version of *Disgrace* offers much evidence for this benumbing tendency. Based on a screenplay by Australian producer Anna Maria Monticelli, directed by husband Steve Jacobs and starring John Malkovich as Lurie, it is likely the most widely viewed adaptation of Coetzee's fiction, but it is also the most lamented. Even Ian-Malcolm Rijsdijk's comparatively charitable review raises complaints that are difficult to discount. Principle among them is the film's scenography. Location, or rather located-ness, has proven a topic of general controversy in Coetzee's fiction, which tends to favour an inexact geography.[8] Moving between Cape Town and the small village of Salem, outside Makhanda (Grahamstown), *Disgrace* is unusual, therefore, in its specific appeal to place. Monticelli and Jacobs's adaptation has been derided, however, as a typically Australian film, with critics querying the appeal the pair make to the 'poetic realist' aesthetic of Australian cinematic culture.[9]

This is an exegetic critique as much as a cinematographic one. In Coetzee's original text, Lurie's retreat into the austere hills of the Eastern Cape is designed to reflect the character's own 'atrophied interiority'.[10] Chosen by Jacobs for their scenic appeal, the Cederberg mountains north of Cape Town offer an environment of some comparable hostility, but the landscape is necessarily lacking in the exhausted atmospherics of the area around Salem, to say nothing of the region's specific history of racial conflict.[11] This environmental inconsistency is arguably indicative of the film's other failings, like its optimistic ending, which undoes the ambiguity of Coetzee's original, reducing it to little more than a story about 'a man and his dog', as Rijsdijk puts it.[12] Similarly, even accepting Lurie's ridicule as a plausible pretence, it is hard to look past the film's amateurish costuming, which leaves Malkovich's character looking more like a court jester after the attack on the farm than a figure of contradictory ethical interest.

When it comes to cinematic adaptations, *Disgrace* is by no means unique in attracting such heavy criticism. To date, there have been two other notable examples: a reworking of *In the Heart of the Country* (1977) by Marion Hänsel entitled *Dust* (1985), and Ciro Guerra's *Waiting for the Barbarians* (2019). In addition, Alex Harvey directed a television film of *The Lives of Animals* (1999) for the BBC in 2003.[13] None has attracted the critical benevolence enjoyed by Coetzee's novels. Guerra's adaptation, starring Mark Rylance as the Judge and Johnny Depp as Colonel Joll, is the most promising. Based on a script drafted by Coetzee in 1995, it resists the urge to undo the novel's transcendent setting, even if cinematographer Chris Menges' Moroccan landscapes tempt a generically orientalist reading of its allegory. There are other minor flaws, too, like Judge's relationship with the Girl, played by Gana Bayarsaikhan, which resists the novel's original play with impotence and authority; but generally, Guerra's film delivers a recognizable repudiation of imperial anxiety and misrule.

By contrast, Hänsel's adaptation has been broadly disparaged by its critics, Coetzee among them. Comparing the film with his novel, Coetzee regrets that *Dust* 'retains virtually none of the sequence divisions and indeed none of the quite swift pacing'.[14] Lindiwe Dovey and Teresa Dovey have also pointed to the film's incongruous setting in Spain, even if they accept the cultural boycott under apartheid that necessitated its relocation. Nonetheless, '[t]he landscape, architecture, and furnishings of the house ... are quite obviously not that of a farm in the Karoo', they insist, disappointed by the scenography's inability to register 'the feelings and meanings of the text'.[15] It is worth exercising some caution here. People and places are not as pliable as the human imagination, and cinematic adaptations often risk blunt accusations of inaccuracy when forced to locate their source text spatially and temporally in ways that the original may resist. Like the plot contractions that cinematic adaptation demands, these complaints are usually the product of various practical constraints rather than essential diegetic ones, and suggest a relatively narrow understanding of what fidelity constitutes.

When it comes to a work like *In the Heart of the Country*, however, the formal contradictions at work in the novel perhaps help mitigate *Dust*'s own less than radiant achievements. Building on Coetzee's stated affection for the avant-garde style of filmmakers like Ingmar Bergman and Jean-Luc Godard, Hermann Wittenberg claims that the novel's original tendency towards 'narrative discontinuity' is indebted above all to French cinema's *nouvelle vague*.[16] This explains why other critics have been tempted to read *In the Heart of the Country* like a filmscript, its numbered sections taken to be expository scenes on a cinematic storyboard. Nonetheless, such outward continuities do not always enable an easy transfer from the literary to the cinematic. This, Coetzee discovered in his own faltering efforts to adapt the novel into a screenplay in 1981.[17] Published in 2014, alongside his screenplay of *Waiting for the Barbarians*, this early attempt at cinematic adaptation is described as a product of 'creative reverse-engineering' by Wittenberg.[18] This is not to mistake its technical reproduction for any aesthetic achievement. Coetzee makes clear his own misgivings, complaining of its stubbornly 'static' tempo. In search of formal compensation, he suggests a suite of extra-diegetic features (whether a 'musical motif' or 'change in the pitch-level of the soundtrack') to help distinguish Magda's fantastical imagination from any realist rendering of her experience: 'This can in fact be done *more* easily on the screen than on the page', he insists.[19] Few have found encouragement in these assurances. Early efforts to adapt the novel for the screen consistently failed, with producers insisting on their own script and Coetzee demanding onerous revisions by return.[20]

What emerges above all from these faltering efforts, however, is a sense of the way in which Coetzee's approach to the novel is also bound up with his ideas about other arts, and, indeed, other artists' ideas about his own writing. If nothing else, the hazy boundaries that separate his understanding of the textual sphere from a visual medium like cinema make adaptations of his writing more challenging, not less. There seems to be little value, therefore, in pursuing further the type of evaluative criticism seen above. More profitable is a critique that sets Coetzee's own ideas about the art of adaptation at its centre. For in 'climbing in the wake of poets', to return us to *Disgrace*, his writing is defined just as much by 'the great archetypes of the mind, [the] pure ideas' about artistic representation visible from the summit as any of the technical gear deployed along the route.[21]

To describe Coetzee as novelist of ideas is nothing new. Martin Puchner readily places him in a genealogy that includes the likes of Dostoevsky, Zola and Musil, but he also insists upon Coetzee's awkwardness in their company.[22] Looking to novels like *Elizabeth Costello* (2003) and *Diary of a Bad Year* (2007), it is clear they are about ideas, about the separation of the human from the non-human, about violence, grace, and divinity. More significantly, though, they are about the representation of these ideas, about the ways in which ideas are 'generated from the matrix of individual interests out of which their speakers act in the world', to borrow from *Elizabeth Costello*.[23] Indeed, for Puchner, this is their 'primary drama'.[24] The phrase partly betrays Puchner's critical preference for the theatrical, but it is also suggestive of Coetzee's plausible debt to Platonic dramaturgy as much as to *The Possessed*. Take, for instance, the descent made by *Dusklands* (1974) into a series of propositional meditations, or the philosophical idealism that, according to Ileana Dimitriu, organizes his more recent work. In each, Coetzee defers to the anti-theatrical form as well as the metaphysical concerns of Plato's dialogues, all the time bolstering his ideas with a similarly displaced Socratic authority.[25]

It is not necessary to rehearse the ancient quarrel that plagues this 'dramatic Platonism' to accept the influence that such an anti-theatrical attitude holds over Coetzee's writing, philosophically as well as formally.[26] Most evident is the suspicion that Coetzee shares of the mimetic sphere, something indexed by Plato in the 'multiple frames of narration' that structure his tetralogies.[27] Coetzee repeats this diegetic manoeuvre to a greater or lesser extent across his fiction. *Diary of a Bad Year*, which according to Attwell gives up entirely on the 'business of verisimilitude', offers an intense comparison, but there are visible signs everywhere of this mutiny against 'the realism he feels bound to produce'.[28] Coetzee's complaint here is not necessarily with realism in the abstract, so much as its specific hold over the sphere of ideas and their representation. In much the same way that Plato's anti-theatricalism works to 'dislodge' his philosophy from its drama (as Puchner has it), then, Coetzee's metafiction allows him to 'evoke and critique' realism's incursions into thinking as such.[29]

Jan Wilm helps ratify this formal mutualism, insisting on the Platonic ambition that underpins much of Coetzee's writing. His novels are generally characterized by 'direct questioning between characters in monologue', Wilm observes. This is not merely a structural observation; such a Socratic form 'has the function of discursively opening up arenas of thinking and philosophizing', Wilm further explains.[30] In this way, Plato's dramaturgy also makes viable the adapted return of Coetzee's ideas on representation to the performative arena itself. Consider the outwardly monologic form of Elizabeth Costello's public lectures, which provide the basis for Harvey's version of *The Lives of Animals*. In their original telling, these soliloquies uphold a broadly Platonic impulse: Costello regularly shuts down the debate, either refusing to answer questions or responding with carefully rehearsed 'blocks of dialogue'.[31] Similarly, in *Elizabeth Costello*, the narrator often abets her Socratic authority, at times skipping over supposedly extraneous conversation in order to extract Costello's ideas from the drama of their reception. For all its other shortcomings, Harvey's adaptation gives formal representation to exactly this anti-theatrical impulse. Cutting between the long, formal recitation of Costello's ideas about animal ethics and short sequences from the novel's two dinner scenes (first at her son's home and later at Appleton College, each an allusion to the setting of Plato's *Symposium*), Harvey's adaptation helps similarly to shelter her from critique. Those clamouring to challenge Costello are denied extended focus, each forced instead to raise their complaints in small asides spliced awkwardly between her general speechmaking. Here, adaptation's 'doubled response', as Linda Hutcheon and Michael Hutcheon put it, seems to magnify the novel's own Platonic premise, evoking and critiquing the realist form that Coetzee feels bound to reproduce.[32]

Nonetheless, the specific achievements of Harvey's adaptation do not settle the wider tension between Coetzee's introspective, monologic tendencies and the dialogic demands that intermedial adaptations often make of his writing. To date, there have been at least six theatrical versions of Coetzee's novels, but none has attempted to adapt those more perorational works to which Puchner defers in accounting for Coetzee's ideas about representation.[33] Instead, this theatrical interest has resulted in two adaptations of *Foe*, the first directed by Mark Wheatley and staged at the West Yorkshire Playhouse in 1996 and the second by Peter Glazer at the University of California,

Berkeley in 2003. There has been an adaptation of *Waiting for the Barbarians* by Alexander Marine for the Baxter Theatre in Cape Town (2012), as well as versions of *Disgrace* – by a Dutch theatre company, Toneelgroep (2011); Kornél Mundruczó (2012); and (controversial) French-Senegalese director Jean-Pierre Baro (2016). Choreographer and dancer Jeanette Ginslov has also staged two separate interpretations of *In the Heart of the Country* at the 1998 National Festivals of Arts in South Africa and the Jozi Arts Festival in 2006.

In many of these works, Coetzee's ideas about the limits of representation are relegated in favour of more straightforward concerns over agency and selfhood. Wheatley and Glazer, for instance, each make extended use of dialogue drawn from Coetzee's novel to approach the question of voice that also drives his revision of *Robinson Crusoe*. In both productions, however, this question serves as a prompt to experiment with the separate resources available to the stage. In reviewing these adaptations, Kareesha Naidoo and Hermann Wittenberg draw attention to the use of non-naturalistic theatrical devices by the directors in their separate efforts to unsettle the singularity of their characters. For example, in his collaboration with Theatre de Complicité, Wheatley deploys a series of disembodied voices located somewhere off-stage. These ghostly voiceovers serve to fracture Cruso's integrity, even they also narrate his plight for the audience. Glazer maintains a similar sense of rupture by including three separate versions of *Foe*'s principal narrator, Susan Barton. In this way, Glazer comes closer to finding a theatrical equivalent to the narrative instability at the heart of Coetzee's novel, but this is largely secondary to the play with theatrical representation driving the production more generally.

Wittingly or otherwise, these productions do at least gesture at the representational limits that also govern them in their adaptive aims. Most obviously, for Wheatley and Glazer alike, the silent, stubborn alterity of a character like Friday regularly proves an awkward, if not impossible, idea to dramatize. In this context, however, the Handspring Puppet Company's adaptation of *Life & Times of Michael K* (1983), conceived and directed by Lara Foot in 2020, is arguably much more suggestive.[34] One of South Africa's most successful theatrical exports, Handspring are well-versed in the art of adaptation, having crafted puppets in the likeness of Büchner's Woyzeck and Marlowe's Faustus. In fixing Coetzee's Michael K as a roughly hewn, wooden figurine, they also discover a highly suggestive theatrical account of this outwardly mute, impassive character. For like the misidentifications endured originally by Michael K, who has his thoughts ventriloquized by the third-person narrator in the opening section, before being subjected to the medical officer's speculative analysis in the second, the puppet's unchanging wooden form means that he must rely on the ascriptions of the onlooking audience, who are asked to animate the character from the outside.[35] As elsewhere in Handspring's theatre-making, Foot makes use of cinematic backdrops and live narration to share Michael K's internal thoughts, but his unchanging wooden form ensures that he cannot entirely escape the audience's projections. Ultimately, this immutability actively extends the struggle over self-representation that is also pivotal to Coetzee's novel.

As an interpretive object, the puppet is not without precedence in Coetzee's writing and thinking. Pointing, for instance, to scenes from *The Schooldays of Jesus* (2016), Marc Farrant suggests that Coetzee's *Jesus* trilogy owes an important debt to Heinrich von Kleist's essay 'On the Marionette Theatre' (1810).[36] Here, Kleist establishes a dissimilarity between the general beauty of the puppet's movements and the divine grace of the dancer. While the essay begins by distinguishing the self-consciousness of the latter from the materiality of the former, it proceeds by challenging this separation between mind and matter, arguing in favour of their interdependence.

As Farrant informs us, Coetzee's interest in Kleist's ideas here is longstanding, with references to this essay on marionettes first appearing in Coetzee's preparatory notes for *Foe*.[37] Once noted, it is possible to see how this debate over the material limits of art and artistic representation, especially the representation of human consciousness, informs Coetzee's approach to figures like Friday and Michael K.

Equally significant, however, is the way in which this deliberation appears to encourage the adapted return of Coetzee's ideas about representation to the stage, especially in the form of theatrical objects like puppets. Foot's version of *Life & Times* provides obvious evidence for this return, but it also joins up with a lively tradition of operatic adaptation that has sought to discover in its own technical apparatus a possible approach to these ideas about the limits of artistic representation. Beginning with Philip Glass's *Waiting for the Barbarians* (2005), this corpus now includes two operas adapted by Belgian composer Nicholas Lens: *Slow Man*, performed in Poland in 2012, and *Elizabeth Costello*, which is yet to be staged publicly. Arguably, opera's blend of music and song as well as dramatic action – its multiple 'sign systems' – distinguishes its technical agility from other performative media.[38] This is not exactly why Hutcheon and Hutcheon claim opera as 'the Ur-adaptive art', nor is it to dismiss the rich talent of the cinema screen and theatre stage.[39] It is, instead, to point to the ways in which opera's layered form of representation, each element conscious of its own limits, lines up alongside Coetzee's ideas about artistic representation at large.

This metatheatrical appeal is in partial evidence in Glass's *Waiting for the Barbarians*. Like much of the composer's music, it is a highly repetitive, cyclical work. Held together by tremolos and pulsating phrases from the strings, the sense of looming violence running through Glass's adaptation swells and fades in ways that echo the seasonal drift of Coetzee's original tale. Unlike the novel, however, Christopher Hampton's two-act libretto challenges Coetzee's allegorical formula by drawing critiques of the Iraq War into its lyrics. As Hampton noted ahead of a performance in Austin, Texas, in 2007, 'so much of [the novel] seems applicable to what we're going through at the moment', in particular 'the way in which phony external threats [are] being played up to shore up a rather shaky administration at home'.[40] His revisions reflect something of the interpretive latitude available to live performance. Nonetheless, even as Hampton finds new contemporary resonance in Coetzee's novel, his revision arguably undoes exactly the paradox of its allegory, which depends on 'the very leanness of its literal saying', as Julian Murphet puts it, 'to make the highest and most ponderable of universal claims'.[41] In this sense, Hampton's situated appeal risks a symbolism that, strictly speaking, corrupts the ambition of his source.

This paradox provides fewer challenges for Lens in his adaptations of *Slow Man* and *Elizabeth Costello*, both allegories that 'fail to amount to allegories'.[42] More significantly, as novels that 'take flight from the very comforts of novelistic writing', they also seem to land somewhere amid the other arts.[43] Not only did Coetzee collaborate directly with Lens on these adaptations, writing a libretto for both operas, but the pair were already in correspondence long before *Slow Man*'s original publication in 2005.[44] There is no way to assess the specific impact of these exchanges, but the novel's play with performativity arguably anticipates its adaptation for the stage, with Paul Rayment as the puppet and Elizabeth Costello the puppet master. Michelle Kelly even casts Costello as the librettist, with Paul and Marijana taking up leading roles in her operatic experiment.[45] If nothing else, this metatheatrical appeal ensures that Coetzee's subsequent operatic achievements compare favourably with David Lurie's more ridiculous ambitions. More generally, however, there is a sense across this intermedial tradition of the difference (to rework Hutcheon) that a repetition of Coetzee's fiction writing makes to our understanding of its representational limits, rather than its possibilities.

NOTES

1. Benjamin, 'The Task of the Translator', 77.
2. Hutcheon, *A Theory of Parody*, 142.
3. See Attwell, 'Interview', in *Doubling the Point*, 58.
4. Steyn, 'Translation', 105.
5. Walkowitz, *Born Translated*, 3.
6. Ibid., 4.
7. Lachman, *Borrowed Forms*, 116; Coetzee, *Disgrace*, 195.
8. See Wittenberg and Highman, 'Sven Hedin's "Vanished Country"'.
9. Wade Major, qtd. in Rijsdijk, '(Dis)placed', 10.
10. Rijsdijk, '(Dis)placed', 22.
11. For more on Salem, see Cornwall, 'Disgraceland'.
12. Rijsdijk, '(Dis)placed', 25.
13. Harvey's film can be accessed through his personal website: alexanderharvey.org.
14. Coetzee, *Doubling the Point*, 60.
15. Dovey and Dovey, 'Coetzee on Film', 61.
16. Wittenberg, 'Godard in the Karoo', 21.
17. It is worth noting that Coetzee resists the urge to read his original novel as a screenplay. See Coetzee, *Doubling the Point*, 59.
18. Wittenberg, 'Godard in the Karoo', 20. For more on the screenplays, see Coetzee, *Two Screenplays*. For commentary on Coetzee's adaptation of *Waiting for the Barbarians*, see Wittenberg, 'Coetzee in California'.
19. Coetzee, qtd. in Wittenberg, 'Godard in the Karoo', 22. Emphasis original.
20. For more, see Wittenberg, 'Godard in the Karoo', 13–33.
21. Coetzee, *Disgrace*, 22–3.
22. Puchner, 'J. M. Coetzee's Novels of Thinking', 1.
23. Coetzee, *Elizabeth Costello*, 9.
24. Puchner, 'Novels of Thinking', 5.
25. For more on *Dusklands*, see Attwell, '"The Labyrinth of My History"'. For more on idealism, see Dimitriu, 'J. M. Coetzee's *The Schooldays of Jesus* (2016)'.
26. Puchner, *Drama of Ideas*, 33.
27. Ibid., 34.
28. Attwell, *J. M. Coetzee and the Life of Writing*, 235–6.
29. Puchner, *Drama of Ideas*, 33.
30. Wilm, *Slow Philosophy*, 152–3.

31. Coetzee, *Elizabeth Costello*, 9. For a review of Costello's debating habits, see Northover, 'Elizabeth Costello as a Socratic Figure'.
32. Hutcheon and Hutcheon, 'Adaptation and Opera', 307.
33. In 2016, Polish director Krzysztof Warlikowski wove the 'Eros' section from *Elizabeth Costello* into a wider revision of the Phaedra myth entitled *Phaedra(s)*.
34. The original staging of *The Life & Times of Michael K* at the Baxter Theatre, Cape Town, in 2020 was postponed after extensive rehearsals.
35. For more on ventriloquism in *Life & Times of Michael K*, see Alderman, 'Ventriloquism and Idleness'.
36. See Farrant, 'Finitizing Life'.
37. Ibid., n. 20.
38. Hutcheon and Hutcheon, 'Adaptation and Opera', 310.
39. Ibid., 305.
40. Quoted in Faires, 'An Opera for Wartime'.
41. Murphet, 'Coetzee and Late Style', 89.
42. Ibid., 90.
43. Ibid., 86.
44. Kelly, 'Other Arts and Adaptations', 199–200.
45. Ibid., 200.

WORKS CITED

Alderman, Richard. 'Ventriloquism and Idleness in J. M. Coetzee's *Life & Times of Michael K*'. *Textual Practice* 30, no. 4 (2016): 599–619.
Attwell, David. *J. M. Coetzee and the Life of Writing: Face to Face with Time*. Oxford: Oxford University Press, 2015.
Attwell, David. '"The Labyrinth of My History": J. M. Coetzee's *Dusklands*'. *Novel* 25, no. 1 (1991): 7–32.
Benjamin, Walter. 'The Task of the Translator'. In *Illuminations*, edited by H. Arendt, 70–82. London: Pimlico, 1999.
Coetzee, J. M. *Disgrace*. London: Sacker & Warburg, 1999.
Coetzee, J. M. *Doubling the Point: Essays and Interviews*. Edited by D. Attwell. Cambridge, MA: Harvard University Press, 1992.
Coetzee, J. M. *Elizabeth Costello: Eight Lessons*. London: Sacker & Warburg, 2003.
Coetzee, J. M. *Two Screenplays*. Edited by H. Wittenberg. Cape Town: UCT Press, 2014.
Cornwall, Gareth. 'Disgraceland: History and the Humanities in Frontier Country'. *English in Africa* 30, no. 2 (2003): 43–68.
Dovey, Lindiwe and Theresa Dovey. 'Coetzee on Film'. In *Coetzee's Austerities*, edited by G. Bradshaw and M. Neill, 57–78. Farham: Ashgate, 2010.
Dimitriu, Ileana. 'J. M. Coetzee's *The Schooldays of Jesus* (2016): A Novel of Ideas?'. *Current Writing: Text and Reception in Southern Africa* 30, no. 1 (2018): 55–68.
Faires, Robert. 'An Opera for Wartime'. *Austin Chronicle*, 19 January 2007.
Farrant, Marc. 'Finitizing Life: Between Reason and Religion in J. M. Coetzee's Jesus Novels'. *Journal of Modern Literature* 42, no. 4 (2019): 165–82.
Hutcheon, Linda. *A Theory of Parody: The Teachings of Twentieth-Century Art Forms*. Chicago, IL: University of Illinois Press, 2000.
Hutcheon, Linda and Michael Hutcheon. 'Adaptation and Opera'. In *The Oxford Handbook of Adaptation Studies*, edited by T. Leitch, 305–23. Oxford: Oxford University Press, 2017.

Kelly, Michelle. 'Other Arts and Adaptations'. In *The Cambridge Companion to J. M. Coetzee*, edited by J. Zimbler, 187–205. Cambridge: Cambridge University Press, 2020.
Lachman, Katherine. *Borrowed Forms: The Music and Ethics of Transnational Literature*. Liverpool: Liverpool University Press, 2014.
Murphet, Julian. 'Coetzee and Late Style: Exile within the Form'. *Twentieth Century Literature* 57, no. 1 (2011): 86–104.
Naidoo, Kareesha and Hermann Wittenberg. 'Between Text and Stage: The Theatrical Adaptations of J. M. Coetzee's *Foe*'. *South African Theatre Journal* 30, no. 1–3 (2017): 30–45.
Northover, Richard Alan. 'Elizabeth Costello as a Socratic Figure'. *English in Africa* 39, no. 1 (2012): 37–55.
Puchner, Martin. *The Drama of Ideas: Platonic Provocations in Theater and Philosophy*. New York: Oxford University Press, 2010.
Puchner, Martin. 'J. M. Coetzee's Novels of Thinking'. *Raritan* 30, no. 4 (2011): 1–12.
Rijsdijk, Ian-Malcom. '(Dis)placed: Place and Identity in the Film *Disgrace*'. *African Cinema Unit Yearbook* 1, no. 1 (2014): 9–28.
Steyn, Jan. 'Translations'. In *The Cambridge Companion to J. M. Coetzee*, edited by J. Zimbler, 103–21. Cambridge: Cambridge University Press, 2020.
Walkowitz, Rebecca L. *Born Translated: The Contemporary Novel in an Age of World Literature*. New York: Columbia University Press, 2015.
Wilm, Jan. *The Slow Philosophy of J. M. Coetzee*. London: Bloomsbury, 2016.
Wittenberg, Hermann. 'Coetzee in California: Adaptation, Authorship, and the Filming of *Waiting for the Barbarians*'. *Safundi* 16, no. 2 (2015): 115–35.
Wittenberg, Hermann. 'Godard in the Karoo: J. M. Coetzee's Screenplay Adaptation of *In the Heart of the Country*'. *English in Africa* 41, no. 2 (2014): 13–33.
Wittenberg, Hermann and Kate Highman. 'Sven Hedin's "Vanished Country": Setting and History in J. M. Coetzee's *Waiting for the Barbarians*'. *Scrutiny2* 20, no. 1 (2015): 103–27.

CHAPTER THIRTY-EIGHT

Coetzee and translation

JAN WILM

I

From his first full-length fiction, *Dusklands* (1974), to the late stage of his writing career, translation has been key to J. M. Coetzee. It has been central to his development as a writer, to his hermeneutic interests, his international reputation and canonization and to his narrative cosmos – even if his novels and *autre*-biographies infrequently address translation directly. There is no fully fledged translator character in his storyworlds (as in Javier Marías's *A Heart So White*, 1992), nor does his work narrate a character's actual translation of a text (as in Gerbrand Bakker's novel *The Detour*, 2010) – even if (like Marías and Bakker) Coetzee has worked as a literary translator himself.[1] His *oeuvre*, however, features various thematic and aesthetic engagements with translation. Frequently these emerge in an indirect way, as translation is staged more equivocally, through implicit address, the metaphorizing of the phenomenon of translation or the fusing of translation into the genesis of a work.

In *J. M. Coetzee and the Life of Writing* (2015), David Attwell makes the argument that Coetzee is an inherently biographical writer. Following this approach, it is tempting to argue that all of Coetzee's work is concerned with the act and art of writing, or, as Coetzee himself writes about Samuel Beckett's aesthetic, 'Fiction is the only subject of fiction.'[2] While some of Coetzee's characters are, in fact, writers (Daniel Foe, Fyodor Dostoevsky, Elizabeth Costello), and while most of his characters do write at some point (which does not necessarily make them writers), most are *not* professional writers. Yet, writing is at the core of Coetzee's work, the way it is at the core of the modernist (and late- or post-modern) tradition of a self-reflexive, self-referential aesthetic. It might, therefore, be unsurprising that Coetzee is everywhere concerned with writing. It is, however, still an underexplored area in Coetzee Studies that throughout his *oeuvre* the author is almost equally concerned with questions of translation: with the problems of interpretation related to translation as to writing, and with the politics and ethics of transposing a literary work from one language and culture into others.

II

Coetzee is a writer whose literature has grown from philological as well as academic interests. It engages with post-structuralist theories, with the theories of reading, deconstruction, feminism, ethics and animal ethics, with post-colonialism; it has been informed by his academic career and research.[3] Similarly, Coetzee's translational interests have been shaped in large part through translational activities, both personal and academic. As Jan Steyn notes, 'Coetzee has translated works from Dutch and Afrikaans [...], he has edited works in translation; he has critiqued the translations of others; he has taught books in translation and a translation workshop to university students; he has written about the theory of translation.'[4]

The translation workshop to which Steyn refers took place when Coetzee was employed at the University of Buffalo. In 'an introduction to the course' he intimated how writing and translation were intricately linked: 'I do not recommend the course for students who have done no original writing.'[5]

Shortly after, in 1970 Coetzee published a translation of the poem 'Ballade van de gasfitter' ('Ballad of the Gasfitter') by the Dutch poet Gerrit Achterberg (1905–62). Subsequently in 1977, he published the essay 'Achterberg's "Ballade van de gasfitter": The Mystery of I and You', in which he details key concerns about translation. This is an inventive essay hybrid, consisting of Coetzee's translation of the poem, whose fourteen sonnets are interspersed with commentary on the individual translations and on the phenomenon of translation as practice.[6] The final section of the essay offers an insightful glance into the translator's workshop, when Coetzee writes:

> A literary work is, among other things, a structure in which form has become meaning. When form is disrupted, meaning is also disrupted. Such disruption is inevitable, for there is never enough closeness of fit between languages for formal features of a work to be mapped across from one language to another without shifts of value. Thus the work continually presents its translator with moments of choice.[7]

Coetzee is not restating a platitude; he is highlighting the essentially ethical dimension of translation, since the translator has an obligation to a source text in a way that a writer does not. The translator has to be 'deeply sensitive to the effects of translation, and to the authority of the translator'.[8] Because no language is free from cultural, historical and ideological associations, the translator must interrogate both the source language and their own language, and decide on interpretations that have a direct effect in the target language.

Coetzee's reflections on the myriad choices required of translators reflect the influence of contemporaneous engagements with the ethics of reading, such as those formulated by J. Hillis Miller (amongst others), which Coetzee was reading during his time in the United States. In a 1999 essay on Rainer Maria Rilke, Coetzee concludes that 'translation turns out to be only a more intense and more demanding form of what we do when we read'.[9]

As Steyn suggests, to Coetzee, translating and reading are so inextricably linked that naturally 'the translation embodies the interpretation'.[10] What Steyn does not highlight is a key aspect of Coetzee's interests in translation: the ethical dimension of carrying across a literary text from one language to another. This aspect of translation makes the practice dissimilar to reading. Whereas reading is individual and private, translation is a form of public interpretation, even if not (or not only) under the translator's own name (as is the case of literary criticism), but under the name of the original work's author. Translation is not so much a form of writing literature as it is a form of *writing reading*.[11]

Acutely aware of such theoretical ideas, Coetzee has frequently reflected on translation in both his fiction and critical writing, and in the latter has implied a general scepticism of translation *tout court*, a position related to his general scepticism of authorial explication, which consists of another form of uttering ('writing') a reading into the public field.[12] In the Achterberg essay, Coetzee refers to translation as nearly paradoxical when noting 'the impossibility of "full" translation, that is a mapping of all the significations that may inhere in the original'.[13] Here, Coetzee is writing like the Walter Benjamin of 'The Task of the Translator' (1923), in which Benjamin ponders the idea that there might exist those 'linguistic creations' which men may 'prove unable to translate'.[14] Here, Benjamin and Coetzee converge, although they differ in one crucial aspect. Where Benjamin's thoughts arise from the belief that all works are theoretically translatable, Coetzee's seem to spring from the idea that literary texts are not ever really translatable, which foregrounds his relatively conservative translational views of fidelity rather than, for example, the foreignization Lawrence Venuti speaks of.[15] In the Achterberg essay, Coetzee suggests that a translation, like a reading, is always provisional, the relationship between original and translation one in which the translation is always *near*, yet never *here*. Coetzee is conscious of one of the meanings inherent in the etymology of 'translation', namely 'to remove', and therefore to him, '[s]omething must be "lost"' in translation.[16]

As a proponent of fidelity, in a 2002 essay on the work of Joseph Roth, Coetzee criticizes Roth's translator, Michael Hofmann, for taking liberties. He notes that 'Hofmann seems to have decided that he can better render Roth in English by recasting or condensing his German rather than translating him word for word'.[17] Coetzee's view of translation seems so rigorously bent on fidelity to the original that even an improvement constitutes a near-unethical act of destruction. The question whether Coetzee's literalist conception of translation is realistic or useful is a matter of a personal poetics, but is not every translation, if it is a type of reading, also always a lesson that is taught to the author, always part improvement and destruction into another language, another context?

Of the latter Coetzee seems especially aware. In 2005, in the essay 'Roads to Translation', published in the Australian journal *Meanjin*, he returns to the matter of translation in the most explicit way yet:

> The necessary imperfection of translation – brought about in the first place by the incapacity of any given target language to supply for each single word in the source language a corresponding single word that would cover, precisely and without overlap, the denotation of the original and its major connotations to boot – is so widely accepted that the translator becomes accustomed to aiming for the best possible translation rather than a hypothetical perfect one.[18]

Of course, Coetzee's scepticism is not born out of a dismissal of translation, but out of the opposite, a deep and lifelong engagement with translation in a theoretical and practical way. This highlights his ethical concerns for the philological task of the translator as well as the epistemological dimensions linked to both task and phenomenon.

He addresses the epistemological dimensions in the 2001 essay 'Paul Celan and His Translators', where Coetzee raises 'important' questions about the Romanian-born German language poet: 'Does poetry offer a kind of knowledge different from that offered by history, and demand a different kind of receptivity? Is it possible to respond to poetry like Celan's, even to translate it, without fully understanding it?' The linking of these questions is significant, as it implies that the epistemological dimension of literature is intricately tied to translation also. This is perhaps especially germane to the Jewish Celan, whose poetry constitutes a deconstruction of the language spoken by the architects of the Holocaust. Thereby, Celan's poetry is innately historical, even when it is not as overtly political as his most famous engagement with Shoah, 'Todesfuge' ('Death fugue', 1948). If such a poetry is translated into English, for example, does the deconstruction of language then become a deconstruction of English; and is one even able (is one allowed?) to deconstruct one language in another language? Celan's originality – his frequent use of compounds and neologisms and his 'knotted, compacted syntax' pose great problems to translators, as Coetzee notes. 'In this sense', he observes, any attempt to translate Celan's 'later poetry must always fail' even if 'two generations of translators have striven, with striking resourcefulness and devotion, to bring home in English what can be brought'.[19]

Coetzee's views may today be read against ideas of translation as alienizing and foreignizing. The translation carries across but does not carry home. Coetzee implies that the translator's task is not only to carry a text to a new place and a new language, but also to turn the foreign place, the foreign language, into a new home for the text. Such a view turns a translation into another *version* of the source text, no more superior or inferior to the 'original' than a draft. This deconstruction of the temporality and hierarchy of original/translation is implied by Jorge Luis Borges, who writes that 'there can only be drafts. The concept of the "definitive text" corresponds only to religion or exhaustion'.[20]

Coetzee's critique of translation belies his alignment with Borges, as he never delegitimizes translation, but attempts to reflect upon fossilized views of translation. By highlighting the transitory nature of translation and by viewing translation as a form of reading, Coetzee's implication is that translation, like reading, is always singular, unrepeatable, in transit. No reading is ever finished, every translation is present and open to the future. They imply the next reading, the next translation.

III

An occupation of futurity, translation has been part of Coetzee's formation as a writer in the past. He has worked as a translator, not only on the already mentioned poems, but also as the translator of a novel from Afrikaans, Wilma Stockenström's *Die Kremetartekspedisie* (1981), the translation of which was published as *The Expedition to the Baobab Tree* in 1983. Before, however, Coetzee translated a novel by the Dutch naturalist Marcellus Emants, which was published as *A Posthumous Confession*. Coetzee began the translation in 1968; that is, 'before he actually turned to writing fiction'.[21] The translation was only published in 1975; that is, after the publication of *Dusklands* and during the writing of *In the Heart of the Country* (1977). One can only speculate about how this translation influenced the form of these fictions, both of which include material presented in pseudo-translation. The second part of *Dusklands*, 'The Narrative of Jacobus Coetzee', includes a double distancing device through two forms of 'translation', one metaphorical and the other literal – the metaphorical translation, as the text was '[e]dited [...] by S. J. Coetzee'; the literal translation, as it was '[t]ranslated by J. M. Coetzee'.[22] These forms of estrangement are more than post-modernist gimmicks, since they allow for certain liberties, not only in matters of style – the story is informed both by nineteenth-century travel writing as well as modernist writers like Beckett – but liberties also in matters of plot, as the deliberate inconsistency concerning poor Klawer's doubling of his death could be seen as a translation error. In this sense the translation that is feigned as being part of this text's genesis has direct existential and equivocal dimensions for Klawer: what he gains in translation are a few pages' worth of life; what he loses in translation, however, *is* his life – twice.[23]

Translation is an even stronger element in *In the Heart of the Country*, concerning style and diegesis as well as the book's status in Coetzee's *oeuvre*; his second book was the first to be translated. After its publication in 1977, a French translation appeared in 1981 by Sophie Mayoux. To Mayoux he explained the meaning of the many Afrikaans words[24] which frequently pierce the English narration. While Coetzee could be sure that South African readers would have little problem in understanding both languages, his growing international relevance confronts him with possibilities of translating the parts in Afrikaans himself.

This happens even before the book's publication, in 1975. When his South African publisher, Peter Randall, informs him that 'manuscripts were being invited for consideration' for a prize, Coetzee is acutely aware of how the novel might fail to be considered favourably, since 'one of the judges'[25] was the Nigerian writer Chinua Achebe, who spoke no Afrikaans. Coetzee writes to Randall: 'If it is necessary, I am prepared to translate the Afrikaans, but that entails a lot of work, since literally every second page is affected.'[26] Possibly, this leads Coetzee to prepare a version with the dialogue translated into English, while Randall's concerns about 'a negative effect on sales'[27] may also have contributed to Coetzee's decision. Ultimately, the book was first published in London by Secker & Warburg and only a year later in South Africa by Ravan Press in a version 'in which all the dialogue [...] is given in Afrikaans'.[28]

The question is why in Coetzee's original version – published as the second version in South Africa – the book mixes English and Afrikaans in the first place. In a letter to the agent Celia Catchpole in London, Coetzee notes that the dialogue in Afrikaans is written

> in a *patois* which stands in roughly the same relation to literary Afrikaans as the speech of Faulkner's crackers and poor Negroes to literary American English. In preparing the English text I was unable to find a stylistic variety which was non-regional and yet had a rural, traditional flavour; I therefore translated it into a rather colourless colloquial English. For this reason, and for other reasons, I prefer this mixed or bilingual version to the English version, though it is obviously unsuitable for publication anywhere but in this country.[29]

The reference to Faulkner is crucial, as Coetzee implicitly places himself in a tradition of literary giants on a global literary scale. What is further insightful is that he voices a disinclination to translated dialogue if it is too close to spoken language. His general critique of translation is echoed in these statements, and as argued before, his critique of translation is borne not from a lack of knowledge, but because of his experience as a translator, here peculiarly of his own work.

This is, then, a book *about* translation, though in subtler ways than through topical representations of translation. Translation is a part of the English version, as its production includes the Afrikaans parts which have undergone a self-translation; but translation is also very much a part of the reception of the Afrikaans version in which the Afrikaans dialogue is not translated into English. As a South African (or any other reader who speaks Afrikaans or Dutch) goes about the reading of this largely English text, he or she is forced to translate those instances where the text veers into Afrikaans. Thereby, a reader is forced to produce *micro-translations* on their own, having to switch back and forth between languages. In doing so, this reader may even come to reflect on the acts of translation they produce, perhaps even on the phenomenon of translation more generally. In crucially different ways, translation is inscribed into both versions of the novel, in their reception and even in their publication history.[30]

After *In the Heart of the Country* was published, scholarship on Coetzee grew and with it the number of translations of his work. Coetzee has commented on the translatability of his style: 'Sentence by sentence, my prose is generally lucid, in the sense that the syntactic relations among words, and the logical force of constructions, are as clear as I can make them.'[31] This translatability allows the argument to view his works as 'born translated' in the way Rebecca Walkowitz does, as works evincing through their style a 'commitment [...] to keep being translated',[32] open to the future. Such a view might argue that works like *Waiting for the Barbarians* or Coetzee's *Jesus* trilogy, with its allegorically flavoured spaces 'eschew [...] the idiosyncrasy of the local for the interchangeability of the global'.[33]

Adopting Walkowitz's argument by focusing on another significance with which she imbues her term *born translated*, one sees that Coetzee's works are *born translated* in the sense that all of them feature some dimension of translation in some form. What Walkowitz leaves largely unconsidered is that a translation, which has no recourse to the local peculiarities of space (and to specifics of the time in which a story takes place), is necessarily writ in water. It is a text that is swimming between departure and destination, unable to grasp the specific homes of time and place – in much the same way that it is so difficult to pin down works like *Waiting for the Barbarians* or the *Jesus* novels; all eschew specific lexica and use translation intra-textually to destabilize the reader's ability to fix the diegeses once and for all in time and place.

The great danger of translating such novels is that the translation may unwittingly introduce fixed and undesired localities and temporalities. A translator may, consciously or unconsciously, work the heavy cargo of history and geography of their own time and place into a novel which painstakingly tries to float free from historical and geographical peculiarities. This is partly why Coetzee was disappointed by the first German translation of *Waiting for the Barbarians*, by Brigitte Weidmann, in 1984. Her version infuses the novel with terms that – judging from Coetzee's marginal notes to Weidermann's version – smacked too much of twentieth-century vernacular.[34] The novel was re-translated in 2001 by Reinhild Böhnke, who has been Coetzee's German translator since 1997, and the German in her translation of *Waiting for the Barbarians* sounds as non-local and omnitemporal as Coetzee's English in his novel.[35]

IV

Similar ambiguity-making strategies concerning time and place, which are at play in *Waiting for the Barbarians*, also abound in Coetzee's *Jesus* novels, and here the phenomenon of translation assumes even more importance. Here, Coetzee uses a metaphorical understanding of translation and literalizes it, namely the idea of bearing across, of being borne across in the first of the *Jesus* novels. Like *Waiting for the Barbarians*, the *Jesus* trilogy takes place in a near no-place, something which is much more possible in the medium of literature than, for example, in film, which has to be filmed somewhere and more directly carries traces of time and place.

In the *Jesus* novels, the reader is immediately estranged by the clash between the Spanish-language feeling of the place and the narrative language of English, something which harks back to a similar effect in Beckett's trilogy, which in the original is narrated in French, while Beckett country is peopled by Irish-sounding characters.

The *Jesus* novels are written in English and the characters speak English; but in the near-utopian space, Spanish is spoken and institutions have Spanish names. Walkowitz argues that there are books to which '[t]ranslation is not secondary or incidental', but that translation is instead 'a condition of their production'.[36] She cites *The Childhood of Jesus* as an example, since the book 'is born translated in at least two ways: it appeared first in Dutch, and it pretends to take place in Spanish'.[37] That it appeared first in Dutch has been true of the last five of Coetzee's works, as his affectionate relationship with his Dutch publisher Eva Cossee has allowed the book to be translated and published *before* it appeared in English. The last of the Jesus novels, *The Death of Jesus*, was first published in Spanish, and Coetzee's next novel, *The Pole* – a work which again puts translation at the centre of its narrative – was first published in Spanish translation in Argentina as *El Polaco*. More than gregarious gestures to his international publishers, this practice destabilizes traditional temporalities and hierarchies of translated works and of the idea of the original – both of an original work and an original language, since the original language in which a book was written is now no longer recognizable merely by being first.

Walkowitz's description that *The Childhood of Jesus* '*pretends* to take place in Spanish' is intriguing, and the novel's strategies that suggest so are part of a project of mystification to imply that what we are reading is, in fact, a translated text, that this world in which the novel takes place is, metaphorically speaking, a *translated world*. As with 'The Narrative of Jacobus Coetzee', Coetzee enables the interpretation that the text has undergone a translation and that something was lost during the process of reading. This gives justification to the flatness of description in the *Jesus* novels and to the often wooden dialogue between the characters. The dialogue often sounds more written than spoken which self-reflexively underlines the textual dimension of the character's world, but also subtly avoids the endowment of characters' dialogue with any kind of othering qualities and social markers such as race or class.[38]

The issue of translation in the *Jesus* novels is also underscored by their prominent featuring of Miguel de Cervantes' *Don Quixote* – itself a text that feigns to have been translated from the Arabic by Cide Hamete Benengeli. In *The Childood of Jesus*, however, translation becomes part of the diegesis through the way in which a metaphorical sense of translation is literalized in the text. Metaphorically speaking, the characters in the novel have been translated from one place to another. Literally speaking, translation is part of their existence.[39]

So, Coetzee stages translation as the existential phenomenon which Jacques Derrida reads into 'Benjamin's concept of translation as an after-life or survival',[40] and he picks up on notions delineated by Salman Rushdie and subsequently by Homi Bhabha, who views 'the transnational as the translational'.[41] While Coetzee stages translation as a phenomenon of survival and a situation of futurity, he also dramatizes this after-life as an impoverished life, a life that lacks excitement, that lacks, above all and necessarily, 'originality'. In *Childhood*, part of the staging of these people's translation is to show that if translation is like survival, then the truth of the obverse may have to be considered as well: that survival of the 'transnational'—even the survival of the migrant—is a survival after having been borne across, during which *something must be lost*.

In the title essay of his collection *Imaginary Homelands*, Rushdie puts a spin on the idea of something having to be lost in translation: 'It is normally supposed that something always gets lost in translation; I cling, obstinately, to the notion that something can also be gained.'[42] Coetzee's theories and poetics of translation as they emerge in his critical writing and in his fiction affirm Rushdie's statement wholeheartedly, even if in 'translated' fashion. While something is always necessarily lost in translation, the source text being at once embodied and destroyed in and through the translated work, the very existence of a translation is a positively productive and affirmative fact, a doubling of the source text, a deepening of the original's interpretation, a striving for a new home of significance and always and forever an invitation to the next reading, the next translation.

NOTES

1. I explicitly exclude the magistrate's translation of the poplar slips excavated from the desert, because it is entirely unclear if these 'texts' are literary in nature, and because the magistrate lacks basic knowledge about the semiotic system he is working with.
2. Coetzee, *Doubling the Point*, 38.
3. See Hayes and Wilm, 'Ancient Quarrels, Modern Contexts', 8; see also Wilm, 'The J. M. Coetzee Archive and the Archive in J. M. Coetzee'.
4. Steyn, 'Translations', 103.
5. Qtd. in Steyn, 'Translations', 104.
6. The Achterberg poem along with other poems from the Netherlands are collected in the book *Landscape with Rowers: Poetry from the Netherlands*, which was published in 2004 and became the first book to appear after Coetzee receiving the Nobel Prize in Literature in 2003, although he had worked on the poems long before that.
7. Coetzee, *Doubling the Point*, 88.
8. Clarkson, *Countervoices*, 57.
9. Coetzee, 'William Gass's Rilke', 70. See also Steyn, 'Translations', 109.
10. Steyn, 'Translations', 110.
11. For more on the ventriloquistic aspects of translation, see, for example, Briggs, *This Little Art*.
12. 'I don't believe in the principal of authorial explication [...]' (letter to Peter Randall, 22 February 1974; qdt. in Wilm, *The Slow Philosophy of J. M. Coetzee*, 25).
13. Coetzee, *Doubling the Point*, 90.
14. Benjamin, 'The Task of the Translator', 245.
15. See Steyn, 'Translations', 105; Venuti, *The Translator's Invisibility*.
16. Coetzee, *Doubling the Point*, 88.
17. Coetzee, 'Joseph Roth, the stories', 92.
18. Coetzee, 'Roads to Translation', 145.
19. Coetzee, 'Paul Celan and His Translators', 117.
20. Borges, 'The Homeric Versions', 57.
21. Toremans, 'The Transnational Rebirth', 45. See also Kannemeyer, *J. M. Coetzee*, 358–60.
22. Coetzee, *Dusklands*, 51.
23. See Wilm, *The Slow Philosophy of J. M. Coetzee*, 25–6; 164.
24. Kannemeyer, *J. M. Coetzee*, 308.
25. Ibid.
26. Coetzee qtd. in Kannemeyer, *J. M. Coetzee*, 308.
27. Attwell, *J. M. Coetzee and the Life of Writing*, 286.
28. Coetzee, qtd. in ibid., 288.
29. Ibid.

30. See the chapter on *In the Heart of the Country* in this volume.
31. Coetzee, 'Roads to Translation', 143. See also Steyn, 'Translations', 118–20.
32. Walkowitz, *Born Translated*, 31.
33. Ibid.
34. See Wilm, *The Slow Philosophy of J. M. Coetzee*, 212.
35. See also Coetzee, 'Roads to Translation', 149–51.
36. Walkowitz, *Born Translated*, xi.
37. Ibid.
38. See also Steyn, 'Translations', 119; and Coetzee, *White Writing*, 116.
39. Elsewhere Coetzee has used the term 'translated' in this metaphorical way too, when Paul Raiment reads the account of Elizabeth Costello writing about Paul's accident and subsequent life (Coetzee, *Slow Man*, 122).
40. Trivedi, 'Translating Culture vs. Cultural Translation', 283.
41. Bhabha, *Location of Culture*, 173.
42. Rushdie, 'Imaginary Homelands', 17.

WORKS CITED

Attwell, David. *J. M. Coetzee and the Life of Writing*. Oxford: Oxford University Press, 2015.
Benjamin, Walter. 'The Task of the Translator'. In *Selected Writings, Volume 1: 1913–1926*, edited by M. Bullock and M. W. Jennings, translated by Harry Zohn, 153–63. Cambridge, MA and London: Belknap Press of Harvard University Press, 1996.
Bhabha, Homi. *The Location of Culture*. London and New York: Routledge, 1994.
Borges, Jorge Luis. 'The Homeric Versions'. In *On Writing*, translated by Eliot Weinberger, 57–63. London: Penguin, 2010.
Briggs, Kate. *This Little Art*. London: Fitzcarraldo Editions, 2017.
Coetzee, J. M. *Doubling the Point: Essays and Interviews*. Edited by D. Attwell. Cambridge, MA: Harvard University Press, 1992.
Coetzee, J. M. *Dusklands*. 1974. London: Vintage, 1998.
Coetzee, J. M. 'Joseph Roth, The Stories'. In *Inner Workings: Literary Essays 2000–2005*, 79–93. London: Harvill Secker, 2007.
Coetzee, J. M. 'Paul Celan and His Translators'. In *Inner Workings: Literary Essays 2000–2005*, 114–31. London: Harvill Secker, 2007.
Coetzee, J. M. 'Roads to Translation'. *Meanjin* 64, no. 4 (2005): 141–51.
Coetzee, J. M. *Slow Man*. London: Secker & Warburg, 2005.
Coetzee, J. M. 'William Gass's Rilke'. In *Stranger Shores: Literary Essays 1986–1999*, 60–73. London: Harvill Secker, 2001.
Clarkson, Carrol. *Countervoices*. Basingstoke: Palgrave Macmillan, 2009.
Hayes, Patrick and Jan Wilm. 'Ancient Quarrels, Modern Contexts'. In *Beyond the Ancient Quarrel: Literature, Philosophy, and J. M. Coetzee*, edited by P. Hayes and J. Wilm, 1–14. Oxford: Oxford University Press, 2017.
Kannemeyer, J. C. *J. M. Coetzee: A Life in Writing*. Translated by Michiel Heyns. London: Scribe Press, 2012.
Rushdie, Salman. *Imaginary Homelands*. London: Penguin, 1992.
Steyn, Jan. 'Translations'. In *The Cambridge Companion to J. M. Coetzee*, edited by Jarad Zimbler, 103–21. Cambridge: Cambridge University Press, 2020.
Stockenström, Wilma. *The Expedition to the Baobab Tree*. Translated by J. M. Coetzee. Johannesburg: Jonathan Ball, 1983; Brooklyn: Archipelago Books, 2014.

Toremans, Tom. 'The Transnational Rebirth of a Dutch Classic: J. M. Coetzee's Translation of Marcellus Emants' *Een nagelaten bekentenis*'. *Journal of Dutch Literature* 5, no. 1 (December 2014): 44–54.

Trivedi, Harish. 'Translating Culture vs. Cultural Translation'. In *In Translation: Reflections, Refractions, Transformations*, edited by P. St-Pierre and P. C. Kar, 277–87. Philadelphia and Amsterdam: John Benjamins, 2007.

Venuti, Lawrence. *The Translator's Invisibility: A History of Translation*, 2nd ed. New York: Routledge, 2008.

Walkowitz, Rebecca L. *Born Translated: The Contemporary Novel in an Age of World Literature*. New York: Columbia University Press, 2015.

Wilm, Jan. 'The J. M. Coetzee Archive and the Archive in J. M. Coetzee'. In *Beyond the Ancient Quarrel: Literature, Philosophy, and J. M. Coetzee*, edited by P. Hayes and J. Wilm, 215–31. Oxford: Oxford University Press, 2017.

Wilm, Jan. *The Slow Philosophy of J. M. Coetzee*. London: Bloomsbury, 2016.

INDEX

Abbate, Carolyn 408
Aboriginal Consciousness 378–9
Achterberg, Gerrit 24, 426–7, 432 n. 6
Adelaide 8, 23, 24, 154, 174, 185, 212, 239, 373, 377–9
Adelaide Writers' Week 212
Adelaide, University of 23, 154, 174, 212
Adorno, Theodor 9, 255, 256, 257
African National Congress (ANC) 18, 145, 149, 310
Afrikaans (language) 16–21, 33, 36, 40 n. 51, 47, 72, 78 n. 26, 82, 86, 161, 162, 224–5, 230 n. 11, 296, 305–6, 309–10, 312, 314 n. 38, 327, 328, 342, 343, 426, 428, 429
Afrikaner(s) 16–18, 72, 147, 149, 162, 249, 363, 400; Afrikaner nationalism 17, 162, 296
Afro-pessimism 7, 147, 148, 154 n. 1
Agamben, Giorgio 236
allegory/allegorical 4, 8, 91–2, 98, 104, 121, 127, 131, 173, 192, 252, 259, 311, 332, 333, 338, 339, 412, 416, 420
Altieri, Charles 230
Anderson, Maxwell 339
Andrews, Donna, 109
animals 97, 98, 107, 149, 172, 173, 177 n. 35, 183, 184, 186, 187, 197, 211, 256, 257, 258–63, 314 n. 36, 332, 381. *See also* Coetzee, *Lives of Animals*
Anthropocene, the 7, 98
anti-Semitism 209, 213
apartheid 4, 8, 10, 16, 20, 25 n. 17, 33, 43, 44, 48, 69, 72, 91, 94–5, 104–6, 117, 121, 127, 128, 130, 132, 159–66, 163, 213, 224, 225, 235, 238, 245, 248, 249, 270–1, 285, 299, 308, 309, 310, 349, 416; anti-apartheid movement/ actions 44, 47, 48, 72, 94, 134 n. 39, 172, 381; post-apartheid South Africa 5, 7, 10, 22, 310, 314 n. 35, 340, 378. *See also* Israel
Arafat, Yasser 340, 344 n. 34
archive(s) (the) 5, 6, 17, 24, 29, 30, 32, 35, 38, 300, 308–9, 359, 364. *See also* Harry Ransom Center
Arenas, Reinaldo 359

Attridge, Derek 4, 7, 18, 21, 29, 31, 34, 36, 49, 50, 91–3, 98, 115, 127, 149, 185, 193, 210, 230 n. 15, 276, 323, 328, 360, 365, 408, 412
Attwell, David 4, 14, 16, 17, 21, 23, 30–2, 35–9, 41 n. 38, 68–9, 74, 82, 83–4, 95, 98, 104–5, 117–18, 122, 124 n. 13, 149, 154, 155 n. 16, 161, 172, 175, 176 n. 3, 187 n. 1, 179 n. 32, 183, 186, 187 n.1, 222, 226, 286, 295, 298, 318, 322, 339, 362, 392, 400, 418, 425
  J. M. Coetzee and the Life of Writing: Face to Face with Time 4, 16, 37, 38
Auden, W. H. 56
Augustine, Saint *Confessions* 350
Auster, Paul 212, 341–2, 375–6; Auster and J. M. Coetzee, *Here and Now*, 212–13, 216, 217, 344 n. 34
Australia 6, 8, 10, 11, 20, 23–5, 49, 154, 160, 165, 169, 170, 174, 175, 184–5, 212, 214, 236, 239, 240, 312, 323, 327, 333, 359–60, 373–86, 400, 416, 427
Austria, Austrians 160, 217, 238, 322, 328. *See also* Austro-Hungary (empire)
Austro-Hungary (empire) 10, 176 n. 14, 327–36
autobiography 5, 8, 15–16, 29–42, 122, 123, 162, 164, 185–6, 222, 226, 227, 230 n. 6, 267, 327, 373; *autre*biography 6, 16, 29–31, 35, 38–9

Bach, J. S. 18, 159, 198, 301, 409, 410–12; *Wohltemperierde Klavier* 18; *Goldberg Variations* 407, 411
Bakhtin, Mikhail 192, 199, 226, 227; *The Dialogic Imagination* 225
Barnard, Rita 16, 17, 18, 24, 230 n. 11, 285
Baro, Jean-Pierre 419
Barthes, Roland, 398
Baudelaire, Charles 152
Baxter Theatre (Cape Town) 21, 22, 202 n. 7, 419
Bayarsaikhan, Gana 416
Beckett, Samuel 5, 9, 15, 19, 33, 37, 61, 75, 81, 160, 173, 204 n. 36, 203, 210–11, 217, 221, 222–4, 268, 276, 277, 295, 300, 301, 303, 318, 319–20, 322, 323, 393, 425, 428, 430; *Murphy* 175; *Watt* 223

Beethoven, Ludwig van 153–4
Begin, Menachem 338
Benedetto, Antonio di 211, 359
Benjamin, Ruha 131, 133
Benjamin, Walter 210, 328, 415, 427, 431
Benveniste, Émile 196, 342, 345
Bergman, Ingmar 417
Bergson, Henri 9, 276–7, 408; *Laughter* 276
Bethlehem, Louise 339
Bewley, Marius 82
Bible, the 85, 238, 339–40
Biko, Steve 20, 46–7, 95
binary (thinking) 9, 33, 155, 184, 186–87, 223, 257,
    266–74
Black Consciousness 20, 43, 46, 94
Black Lives Matter 67
Blake, William 85, 224
body, the 73, 74, 76, 109, 117–18, 119, 124 n. 13,
    163, 171–2, 176 n. 21, 239, 240 n. 7, 249, 251,
    256, 257, 275, 277, 280, 281, 332, 398, 400
Boehmer, Elleke 16, 34, 149, 249
Boehmer, Elleke, Robert Eaglestone, and Katy Iddiols,
    J. M. Coetzee in Context and Theory 5
Bolivar, Simón 381
Bonhoeffer, Dietrich 237, 239
Boochani, Behrouz 11, 379
Borges, Jorge Luis, 359, 360, 362–3, 373, 428;
    Collected Fictions 363
Boxall, Peter 203–4 n. 35
Boyd, Arthur 377
Brecht, Berthold 71, 246
Bradbury, Malcolm, and James MacFarlane
    Modernism: 1890–1930 317
Breytenbach, Breyten 9, 162, 163, 310
Brink, André 20, 163–4, 310
British Broadcasting Corporation (BBC) 237, 238,
    387, 416
Brodsky, Joseph 165, 228, 229, 354–5, 397
Brontë, Emily 58
Browning, Robert 58, 59
Bruyckere, Berlinde de 398, 401–2
Buffalo, State University of New York 19, 33, 270,
    426
Burchell, William 17–18, 37, 161, 309
Burroughs, William *Cities of the Red Knight* 21
Byron, George Gordon 154, 164, 246, 261

Cajetan, Iheka 107
Calvin, John 85; Calvinism 86, 286, 290 n. 12, 399
cancer 20, 34, 128, 236, 260, 373
Cape Town 15–18, 117, 128, 147, 151, 152–3,
    247–9, 258, 301, 321, 359, 361, 391, 416

Cape Town, University of (UCT) 4, 5, 7, 15, 18,
    20–22, 5,6–64, 207, 211, 267, 268, 310, 312,
    320, 392
Capildeo, Vahni *Measures of Expatriation* 378
Carmel, Amos 340
Cartwright, Justin 24
Carpenter, Edward, 103
castaway(s) 15, 86, 122, 360, 375 381
Catchpole, Celia 429
Catullus (poet) 59
Cavafy, Constantine 20, 96, 415
Cavey, Charne 364
Celan, Paul, 208, 209, 328, 427–8
censorship 21–2, 31, 43, 44, 46, 81, 96, 146 n. 13,
    151, 161, 163, 164, 213, 271, 353, 354,
    356 n. 35. *See also* South African Publications
    Control Board (SAPCB)
Cernuda, Luis 85
Cervantes, Miguel de 117, 122, 200, 203, 214, 297,
    311, 362, 374, 381; *Don Quixote*, 201, 360, 431
Chakrabarty, Dipesh 108
Christian Institute, the 44
Christianity 237–8, 322, 350, 351, 353, 356 n. 29
cinema 387, 388, 398, 415–23
Clarkson, Carrol 34, 40–1 n. 51
Coetzee, Gisela 19, 81
Coetzee, Jack (Zacharias) 16
Coetzee, John Maxwell
  Background, Early Life and Education 16–22
  Awards
    Fulbright Scholarship 19; Booker Prize 6, 7, 15, 22,
    23–4, 44, 48, 103, 104, 150, 212, 246; CNA
    Prize 20, 93, 306; Geoffrey Faber Memorial
    Prize 20, 93; James Tait Black Prize 20, 93;
    Jerusalem Prize, 10, 117, 122, 124 n. 11, 131,
    296, 297, 337, 339; Nobel Prize 4, 5, 12, 15,
    17, 55, 150, 212, 310, 342, 362, 379; Order of
    Mapungubwe 23
  Discarded manuscript
    'The Burning of the Books' 21
  Films
    Disgrace 416; *The Lives of Animals* 416; *In the
    Heart of the Country* (as *Dust*), 416–17; *Waiting
    for the Barbarians* (screenplay by J. M. Coetzee)
    67, 324 n. 20
  Lectures
    Nobel Lecture, 'He and His Man' 14, 24, 116,
    170, 175, 362; Inaugural lecture, UCT,
    'Truth in Autobiography' 15, 30, 122;
    Princeton, 'Growing Up with *The Children's
    Encyclopaedia*' 18, 49, 290 n. 10; 'The Novel
    Today' 94; 'The Old Woman and the Cats' 259,

INDEX

366 n. 7, 401; Tanner Lectures, Princeton 170, 240 n. 7; Graz, 'What Is a Classic?' 159

Poetry 56–64 and *see* below

'The Love Song' 57; 'Trivial Verses' 59–60; 'Five Night Thoughts' 61–2; 'Computer Poem' 63–4

Publications

Novels and *Autrebiographies*

Age of Iron 3, 5, 7, 8, 9, 11, 19, 73, 116, 127–35, 138, 172, 222, 236, 239, 249, 259, 260, 261, 277, 280, 282 n. 18, 285, 295, 319, 320, 373, 387, 411

Diary of a Bad Year 3–4, 8, 10, 23, 24, 49, 122, 146 n. 10, 150, 170, 181–9, 203 n. 19, 207, 222, 224, 230 n. 10, 259–60, 262, 280, 281, 307, 320, 359, 362, 374, 376, 378, 379, 392, 398, 417, 418

Disgrace 3, 4, 5, 7, 8, 11, 12, 14, 15, 18, 22, 23, 87, 94, 145, 147–57, 164, 171, 172, 212, 218, 222, 229 n. 2, 235, 236, 245, 246, 249, 253 n. 13, 255, 256, 261, 262, 277, 280, 285, 306, 310, 321, 337, 340–1, 342, 344 n. 26, n. 43, 363, 376, 378, 387, 391, 393 n. 6, 397, 411, 413 n. 14, 416, 417, 419

Dusklands (including 'The Vietnam Project' and 'The Narrative of Jacobus Coetzee') 6, 16, 19, 20, 21, 24, 30, 34, 43, 44–5, 55, 67–79, 82, 160, 164, 172, 207, 221, 229, 229 n. 1, 245–6, 255, 256, 260, 270, 276–7, 297, 300, 305, 306, 308, 309, 317, 323, 327, 359, 363, 387, 391, 392, 418, 425, 428

Foe 3, 5, 7, 8, 10, 11, 14, 15, 30, 43, 48, 49, 115–26, 127, 164, 169, 170, 181, 217, 222, 245, 248–52, 258, 295, 298, 299, 300, 317, 318, 338, 359, 360–1, 362, 373–4, 376, 380, 381, 388, 389–90, 415, 418, 419, 420, 425

In the Heart of the Country/ From the Heart of the Country 7, 10, 11, 15, 18, 20, 21, 34, 43, 45, 46–7, 78 n. 24, 81–9, 93, 181, 188 n. 26, 208, 222, 224, 230 n. 11, 249, 255, 258, 272, 297, 306, 312, 320, 323, 338, 363, 387, 391, 416, 417, 419, 428, 429, 430

Life & Times of Michael K 3, 5, 6, 7, 8, 10, 11, 15, 18, 21, 48, 92, 103–11, 115, 127, 155 n. 26, 160, 171, 172, 177 n. 32, 222, 238, 245, 246–8, 249–50, 251, 252, 256, 257, 258, 259, 272, 285, 291 n. 16, 295, 298, 299, 306, 308, 310, 311, 319, 320, 321, 330, 331, 332, 334 n. 24, 338, 339, 388, 391, 412, 418, 419, 420, 422 n. 34, 427

Scenes from Provincial Life trilogy – *see also* below *Boyhood*, *Youth*, and *Summertime*) 15, 29, 33–67, 39 n. 3, 122, 279, 280, 286, 307

Boyhood 6, 9, 15, 16, 17–18, 29, 31, 33, 34, 35–6, 37–8, 39 n. 3, 40 n. 47, 222, 225, 249, 259, 278–9, 285, 306, 307, 327, 363, 392, 401

Youth 6, 9, 15, 18–19, 29, 31, 33, 34, 35–6, 37, 39 n. 3, 55, 57, 59, 61, 62–3, 207, 225, 249, 267–71, 272, 276, 278–9, 295, 300, 309, 319, 320, 322, 327–8, 359, 392, 397–8, 401

Summertime 4, 6, 19, 24, 29, 33, 34, 35, 36, 37, 38, 39 n. 3, 40 n. 51, 55, 57, 62, 69, 170, 203 n. 19, 207, 215, 216–17, 225, 228, 230 n. 19, 279, 286, 305, 306, 307, 308, 320, 359, 361, 362, 392

The *Jesus* novels trilogy, and *see* below *The Childhood of Jesus*, *The Schooldays of Jesus*, and *The Death of Jesus* 24, 38–9, 124 n. 24, 170, 181, 188 n. 26, 191–205, 222, 229 n. 2, 233, 234–6, 238, 239, 262–3, 272, 272, 277, 279, 285–6, 289, 290, 296, 305, 320, 359, 360, 362, 374, 375, 380, 381, 408, 419, 430, 431

The Childhood of Jesus 3, 5, 8–9, 15, 24, 38–9, 177 n. 43, 192, 193, 194, 196, 197, 198, 199–200, 202 n. 4, 203 n. 21, 203 n. 35, 233–4, 235, 236, 241 n. 9, 262, 272, 275, 276, 286–7, 319, 380, 381, 408, 431

The Schooldays of Jesus 8, 24, 192, 194–5, 197–8, 202 n.4, 233–4, 237, 238–9, 262, 272, 277, 288–9, 380, 387, 407, 408–9, 411, 419

The Death of Jesus 8, 10, 24, 193, 194, 195, 199, 201–2, 240 n. 6, 289–90, 359, 378, 408, 431

The Costello novels 169–80 and *see* below: *The Lives of Animals*, *Elizabeth Costello*, *Slow Man*

The Lives of Animals 5, 8, 11, 49, 170, 211, 240 n. 7, 255, 257, 260, 262, 300, 332, 416, 418

Elizabeth Costello: Eight Lessons 8, 16, 24, 31, 32, 43, 49, 98, 161–79, 181, 188 n. 25, 191–2, 206, 208, 211, 227, 236–7, 240 n. 7, 242 n. 36, 249, 300, 312–13, 314 n. 36, 320, 321, 322–3, 344 n. 38, 359, 364, 366, 373, 375, 417, 418, 420

Slow Man 8, 24, 115, 123, 143, 169, 170, 171, 173–5, 175 n. 2, 177 n. 44, 183, 187n. 3, 213, 239, 240, 280, 307, 318, 333–4, 335 n. 46, 373–4, 387, 392, 420

The Master of Petersburg 7, 10, 22, 30, 77, 137–46, 196, 259, 280, 295, 301, 323, 349, 350, 387, 391

The Pole (published first in Spanish as *El Polaco*, to be published in English in September 2023) 115, 431

Waiting for the Barbarians 3, 5, 7, 10, 11, 20, 21, 24, 48, 67, 73, 77, 91–101, 115, 171, 212, 222, 223–4, 245, 256–7, 261, 277, 280, 300,

306, 311, 319, 323, 324 n. 20, 329–30, 338, 345 n. 3, 391, 415, 416, 417, 419, 420, 430

Collections of essays, interviews etc.
Doubling the Point: Essays and Interviews, 1986–99 (ed. David Attwell) 16, 17, 30, 31, 35, 37, 64 n. 2, 69, 70, 117–18, 122, 124 n. 13, 125 n. 44, 160, 161, 165 n. 18, 166 n. 31, 227, 230 n. 19, 298, 311, 318, 319, 324 n. 23, 356 n. 16, 393 n. 8
Giving Offense: Essays on Censorship 22, 31, 151, 163, 164, 271, 356 n. 34
Inner Workings: Literary Essays, 2000–2005 31, 208, 210, 215, 211, 328
Late Essays: 2006–17 208, 328, 378, 412
Stranger Shores: Literary Essays, 1986–99 18, 31, 159, 162, 164, 311, 328
White Writing: On the Culture of Letters in South Africa 8, 17, 31, 64 n. 2, 161, 296, 305, 308, 309, 361, 399, 400
Coetzee, J. M., and Arabella Kurtz, *The Good Life: Exchanges on Truth, Fiction and Psychoanalysis* 213–17
Coetzee, J. M., and Paul Auster, *Here and Now*, see under Auster

Translations
Afrikaans/English dialogue in *In the Heart of the Country* 230 n. 11, 429–30
Into Arabic *Waiting for the Barbarians* 342, 345 n. 43
Into Dutch, 365, 368 n. 55, 426, 431
Marcellus Emants, *A Posthumous Confession* (translated by J. M. Coetzee) 428
Into Hebrew *Waiting for the Barbarians, In the Heart of the Country, Life & Times of Michael K, Foe* 338–9
Disgrace 340
Into German *Waiting for the Barbarians* 223–4
Into Spanish *Death of Jesus* 359–60, 366 n. 3
El Polaco 115, 431

Coetzee, Nicolas 19, 22, 81, 144–5
Coetzee, Philippa (née Jubber) 19, 20, 22, 33–4, 81
Coetzee, Vera (née Wehmeyer) 16
Colter, Cyrus 121
computers/computing 267–74. See also binary (thinking); IBM; ICT
confession/confessional 15, 30, 31, 34, 35, 76, 122, 130, 144, 153, 162, 165 n. 18, 217, 227, 253 n. 13, 298, 349, 350–4, 356 n. 27, 428
Connell, Raewyn 364
Conrad, Joseph 69, 305, 318, 323; *Heart of Darkness* 67, 323, 324 n. 3

Constantini, María Soledad 364, 365
Cook, Nicholas 408
Coovadia, Imraan, 312
Cope, Jack *The Adversary Within: Dissident Writers in Afrikaans* 309–10
correspondence 16, 21, 31, 44, 46–9, 185, 207–20, 341, 344 n. 30, 397, 398, 402, 420
COSAW (Congress of South African Writers) 21, 22
Cossee, Eva 38, 421
Crewe, Jonathan 36, 67, 68, 75; *In the Middle of Nowhere: J. M. Coetzee in South Africa* 38
Cronje, Geoffrey 164
cycling 23, 24

dance/dancing 83, 133, 194–5, 202, 227, 238, 351, 274, 288–90, 409–10, 419
Dante Alighieri 58, 164, 319, 381; *Inferno* 120
Dawe, Bruce 378
Dean, Andrew 16
Defoe, Daniel 7, 76–7, 115–26, 164, 166 n. 31, 169, 170, 177 n. 35, 249–51, 300, 305, 389–90, 391; *A Tour Thro' the Whole Island of Great Britain* 175; *Robinson Crusoe* 7, 15, 115–26, 249–52, 360, 389; *Roxana* 7, 115, 119–20
De Klerk, F. W. 341
Depp, Johnny 416
Derrida, Jacques 7, 43, 342
Dickinson, Emily 7, 83, 128, 131
Didion, Joan 402
Doniger, Wendy 211
Donker, Ad 44
Dorfman, Ariel *Death and the Maiden* 361
Dostoevsky, Fyodor 9, 10, 15, 30, 137, 143, 144, 145, 165, 187 n. 1, 202 n. 13, 224, 227–8, 255, 259, 260, 261, 262, 280, 295, 298, 299, 301, 302 n. 7, 305, 349, 350–4, 356 n. 27, 374, 376, 391, 392, 417, 425; *Crime and Punishment* 259
Demons (aka *The Devils*) 298, 350, 352; as *The Possessed* 22, 77, 144, 145, 146 n. 12, 418; *Notes from Underground* 77, n. 17, 298, 352–3; *The Brothers Karamazov* 202 n. 13, 224, 296, 296 381; *The Idiot* 352–3, 381
Dovey, Ceridwen 208, 312
Dovey, Lindiwe 416
Dovey, Teresa 98 n. 1, 339
Dreyfus, Alfred 379
Driver, C. J. (Jonty) 56–7, 379
Driver, Dorothy 20, 23; (ed). *A Book of Friends* 379
D'Souza, Tony 149–50
Dutch (language) 24, 64 n.2, 72, 133, 165, 312, 365, 426, 428, 429, 431

INDEX

Dyer, Geoff 212
dystopia(n) 7, 103, 272

Eckstein, Barbara 91
Eldridge, Richard 230
Eliot, T. S. 18, 55, 56, 58, 68, 159, 160, 162, 165 n. 2, 268, 305, 318, 322, 323, 411
Emants, Marcellus *A Posthumous Confession* (translated by J. M. Coetzee) 428
England/United Kingdom 7, 63, 75, 83, 93, 103, 118, 119, 162, 213, 323, 359, 377, 381. *See also* London
English (language and literature) 16–17, 33, 43, 44, 47, 72, 75, 81–2, 121, 161, 164, 185–6, 210, 224, 225, 230 n. 11, 239, 272, 310, 312, 319, 333, 343, 360, 365, 366, 375, 378, 397, 399, 427–31
Enwezor, Okwui 402
Erasmus, Desiderius 22, 163, 172, 173, 295
ethics 36, 85, 92, 121, 142–3, 153, 170, 211, 224, 226, 262, 323, 360, 373, 376–7, 402, 418, 425–6
Ezer, Ehud Ben 338

farm(s), farming 18, 20, 81, 103, 107, 108, 147, 153, 161, 225, 246–8, 296–8, 299, 300, 306, 363, 38. *See also* plaasroman and Voëlfontein
Farrant, Mark 420
Farrant, Mark, Kai Easton and Hermann Wittenberg, eds. *J. M. Coetzee and the Archive: Fiction, Theory, and Autobiography* 5
Faulkner, William 429
film, *see* cinema
First (Nation) Peoples 377, 379. *See also* Aboriginal Consciousness
Flanery, Patrick 7, 381
Flaubert, Gustave 210, 309
Ford, Ford Madox 33, 207, 268, 276, 322; *Youth* 295
Forster, E. M. 199, 202 n. 9
Foucault, Michel 93
France 174, 210, 237, 300
French (language) 153, 185, 196, 210, 319, 429, 430
Freud, Sigmund 9, 69, 87, 279, 327, 328, 329, 331
Fuentes, Carlos 359
Fugard, Athol 149

Gallagher, Catherine 202
Gallagher, Susan van Zanten 91, 133, 202
Gallope, Michael 412

Gamzu, Yossi 339–40
Garber, Marjorie 211
Gardam, Jane 122
Gass, William 81
German (language) 16, 223–4, 262, 319, 328, 329, 427, 430
Germany/Germans 11, 162, 165, 181, 196, 211, 213 n 3, 237, 300, 300–1, 317, 327, 363, 408
Ghosh, Amitav 72, 108
Giliomee, Hermann 17
Ginslov, Jeanette 419
Girard, René *Violence and the Sacred* 76
Glass, Philip 420
Glazer-Ta'asa, Miriam 338
Godard, Jean-Luc 319; *Alphaville* 272
Godwin, David 48
Goethe, Wolfgang von 209, 328, 330, 381
Goldblatt, David 400
Goldman, Per Francisco 364
Goldsworthy, Kerryn 378
González, Pedro 285
Gordimer, Nadine 5, 9, 12, 21, 22, 87, 105, 106, 127, 131, 148, 160, 162–4, 177 n. 32, 208, 210, 212, 249, 300, 310–12, 339, 345 n. 44, 349, 355; *Burger's Daughter*, *July's People* 338
Gothic (American) 7, 127–8, 129–30, 131, 132, 399
Graham, Lucy Valerie 77 n. 16, 149, 188 n. 30, 246, 344 n. 8, 393 n. 6
Grass, Gunther 328
Griem, Julika 38–9
Grondahl, Paul 121
Guerra, Ciro 416
Guttman, Amy 49

Hampton, Christopher 420
Hänsel, Marion 416
Haresnape, Geoffrey 56
Harry Ransom Center, University of Texas 4, 15, 16, 93, 300, 321
Harvey, Anthony 416
Hawthorne, Nathaniel 7; *The Scarlet Letter* 73, 83, 130, 210, 412
Hayes, Patrick 123 n. 6, 182, 186, 280, 299, 301
Hayes, Patrick, and Jan Wilm *Beyond the Ancient Quarrel: Literature, Philosophy, and J. M. Coetzee* 5
Head, Dominic 71, 106, 188 n. 19
Hegel, Georg 85, 297; Hegelian 256
Heidegger, Martin 196, 198–9
Heine, Heinrich 22
Heller, Agnes 277

Herbert, Zbigniew 55, 328, 398, 402
Herzog, Werner *Aguirre* 67
Hofmannsthal, Hugo von 173, 322, 323
Hoffman, Michael 427
Hofmeyr, Isobel 364
Hölderlin, Friedrich 10, 64, 209, 217, 327, 328, 332
Holocaust, the 209, 212, 260, 320, 339–40, 344 n. 38, 373, 427
Hope, Christopher 349
Howarth, R. G. 56, 57, 59
Huggan, Graham, and Stephen Watson, eds. *Critical Perspectives on J. M. Coetzee* 4–5, 12
Hughes, Ted 67, 332
humour 171, 174, 212, 275–83, 308

IBM (International Business Machines) 19, 267–70
ICT (International Computers) 19, 270
Iddiols, Katy 187 n. 7
illusionism (and anti-illusionism) 169–72
Innig, Howard 268
Israel 337–48; and apartheid allegory 337–43
Italian(s) 153, 171, 236

Jacobs, Steve 416
James, Henry 83, 210, 268, 309
Jameson, Fredric 69, 93, 94
Jankélévich, Vladimir 408
Jensma, Wopko 44, 46
Jews/Jewish 207, 213, 257, 327, 328, 332, 339–40, 341, 428
Jiminez, Ramón 211
Jolley, Elizabeth 121–2
Joyce, James 7, 68, 138, 145 n. 4, 175; *Ulysses* 137, 170, 322
Jubber, Philippa, *see* Coetzee
Judaeo-Christian(ity) 412
justice (concept) 92, 104, 105, 168, 197, 263, 321, 361

Kafka, Franz 9, 24, 106, 165, 171, 173, 177 n. 51, 222, 262, 301, 305, 319, 320–1, 327, 328, 329–30, 331–4, 381
Kahn, Herman 70, 76; *Can We Win in Vietnam?* 74
Kannemeyer, J. C. 17, 30, 35, 36–7, 38, 45, 49, 64, 71, 82; *J. M. Coetzee: A Life in Writing* 4, 36, 78 n. 23
Karoo, the 17, 20, 81, 95, 103, 249, 258, 307, 308–9, 363, 391, 416
Kaul, Aashish 379
Kelly, Michelle 410
Kenneally, Thomas 379
Kentridge, William 400–1

Khoi/Khoikhoi/Khoisan (people and Language) 45, 86, 124 n. 9, 308
Kirkwood, Mike 45, 46, 48, 49
Klaaste, Aggrey, 148–9
Klein, Melanie 214
Kleist, Heinrich von 10, 295, 302, 330–1, 419–20; *Michael Kohlhaas* 321
Knausgård, Karl Ove *My Struggle* 236
Kok (aka Coque), Martin 56, 57
Kossew, Sue 35, 99, 99 n. 14
Kossew, Sue, and Melinda Harvey, eds. *Reading Coetzee's Women* 5
Krige, Uys 36, 56
Kurtz, Arabella 30, 212, 213–17, 392
Kusek, Robert 397–8
Kuyper, Abraham n. 12; Kuyperism 286, 290

La Guma, Alex 82, 86, 87, 349
Lanchester, John 197
Latin America 359–72
Latour, Bruno 106, 107
Lawrence, D. H. *Lady Chatterley's Lover* 163
Leavis, F. R. 82
Lee, Hermione 24, 34
Lens, Nicholas 420
Lessing, Doris 162
Levi-Strauss, Claude 87
Levin, Bernard 91, 317
Levin, Hanoch 338
Levin, Harry 317
Lewis, C. S. *Mere Christianity* 237; *Chronicles of Narnia* 238
Lewis, Desiree 109
Lighton, Reginald 96
linguistics 72, 94, 160, 161, 213, 209, 222, 356 n. 16
Llosa, Mario Vargas 359
London 18–19, 29, 33, 49, 71, 93, 115–16, 117, 122, 159, 170, 268, 270, 377, 378, 398, 429
Lukács, György 199
Luther, Martin 172, 173; Lutheran 163, 237

Malkovich, John 416
Mandela, Nelson 18, 145, 149
Mandelstam, Osip 163, 353
Marais, Eugene 214
Mardorossian, Carine 149
Mariás, Javier *A Heart so White* 425
Márquez, Gabriel García 213–15; *Memories of My Melancholy Whores* 211; *The General in his Labyrinth* 381
Mars-Jones, Adam 24
Martial (poet) 59

INDEX

Marx, Karl 214, 331; Marxism 43, 67, 69; Marxism-Leninism 354
mathematics 18, 72, 160, 200, 228, 267–8, 272, 273 n. 32, 288, 328
Matthews, James 44
Mbao, Wamuwi 207
McCarthy, Cormack 11
McDonald, Peter D. 21, 22, 23, 44, 96, 149
McKinnon, Katherine 164
McLuhan, Marshall 268
Mee, Arthur *Children's Encyclopaedia* 18, 290 n. 10
Mehigan, Tim, ed. *A Companion to the Works of J. M. Coetzee* 5
Melamed, Arianna 340
Melville, Herman 84, 320; *Moby Dick* 83
Memmi, Albert 95
Menges, Chris 416
metafiction(al) 8, 105, 106, 115, 116, 123, 127, 161, 171, 174, 181, 211, 222, 249, 256, 297, 333, 339, 373, 415
Miller, Arthur 426; *The Misfits* 211
Miller, J. Hillis 425–6
Miller, Tyrus 75
Millin, Sarah Gertrude 162, 305, 306
Milner, Marius *On Not Being Able To Paint* 229
modernism 56, 68, 296, 317–19, 322–3
Moffat, Nicola 246
Monticelli, Anna Maria 416
Monticelli, Daniele 106
Morrison, Toni 127–8, 130, 131, 132, 134 n. 39
Moses, Benjamin 343
Moses, Michael Valdez 172
Motherwell, Robert 39; *Elegy for the Spanish Republic* 397
mourning 7, 138, 248
Mulisch, Harry 165
Murnane, Gerald 378
Murphet, Julian 172, 188 n. 25, 420
Murray, Les 378
Musa, Omar 379
music 11, 57, 198, 227, 238, 252, 258, 272, 277, 278, 301, 327, 420, 407–14. See also Bach; Beethoven; Webern.
Musil, Robert 10, 208, 222, 318, 328–9, 417

Nabokov, Vladimir 322
Naidoo, Kareesha 419
Naipaul, V. S. 208; *Half a Life* 211
Naudé, Beyers 44
Nazis(m) 262, 344 n. 38
Ndebele, Njabulo 128
Némirovsky, Irène 208, 211

Neruda, Pablo 58, 359
Netherlands, the 170, 312, 432 n. 6
Neto, Agostinho 361
Newton, Isaac 389
Ngai, Sianne 10
Nichols, Mike 20
Nietzsche, Friedrich 85, 183
Nolan, Sidney 373
non-human/ non human, the 96, 108, 169, 183–4, 186–7, 203 n. 35, 203, 255–6, 307–8, 417. See also animals
Noteboom, Cees 165

Okwui, Enwezor 402
Oswald, Alice *Memorial* 382
Oz, Amos 165

paedophilia 140–2
painting 229, 278, 308, 377, 397, 399, 400
Palestine 337–47
Parks, Tim 31
Pascal, Blaise 85, 140
Pasolini, Pier Paolo *Gospel According to St Matthew* 319
Paton, Alan 37, 72, 305, 306; *Cry the Beloved Country* 100, 124 n. 11, 155 n. 23, 339; *Save the Beloved Country* 162
patriarch/ patriarchy/ patriarchal 131, 148, 164, 234, 245, 249, 251, 376, 390
Paz, Octavio 85–7; *Labyrinth of Solitude* 85
Pellow, Kenneth 175
PEN International 22, 132, 170, 213; South Africa 22; Sydney 379
Penguin Random House 49, 359
Penner, Dick 82
Pessoa, Fernando, 373
Philip, David 44
Photographs, photography 39, 44, 45, 172, 174, 320, 342, 379, 387–95, 398, 400, 404
Pierneef, J. H. 399, 400
Piero, Mike 185–6
Pippin, Robert 195, 196, 198, 229 n. 2, 322
plaasroman (farm novel) 18, 23, 129, 133, 147
Plato, 196, 262, 381; *Phaedo* 263; *The Republic* 234, 236, 285, 297, 301, 305–6, 307
Poe, Edgar Allan, 210
Poirier, Richard 76, 82
Pollinger, Murray 48
pornography 70–1, 77 n. 16, 164
possession (spirit) 7, 70, 77, 140
postmodernism 68, 317, 318
Poteat, Joshua *The Regret Histories* 378

Pound, Ezra 55, 56, 58, 222, 268, 398
Poyner, Jane 84–5; *J. M. Coetzee and the Idea of the Public Intellectual* 5
Pratt, Mary Louise 361
Princeton University Press 49
Pringle, Thomas, 161, 305
Profile Books 49
psychoanalysis 163, 216, 327. *See also* Freud; psychotherapy
psychotherapy 32, 69, 70, 74, 75, 213–15. *See also* Freud; psychoanalysis
Puchner, Martin 417
Pynchon, Thomas 402

race/racism 67, 72, 76, 87, 121, 123 n. 8, 128, 147, 148, 149, 249, 306, 337, 340, 342. *See also* Aboriginal Consciousness; Black Consciousness; slavery/slaves
Randall, Peter 44–5, 46, 47, 229
rape 21, 82, 83, 147, 148, 147–53, 164, 187, 211, 235, 236, 242, 245–6, 248, 256, 333, 378
Ravan Press 20, 21, 43, 44–50, 82, 93, 224, 229, 230 n. 11, 429
realism 7, 8, 49, 82, 106, 117, 120, 127, 129, 169–70, 172, 306, 309, 311, 318, 320, 329, 373–4, 375, 389–92, 418
refugee(s) 11, 287, 319, 340, 379, 381
reputation (Coetzee's) 3, 6, 12, 20, 24, 55, 71, 93, 160, 275, 281, 320, 364, 373, 425
Rhys, Jean 373, 378
Richard, Samuel 164; *Clarissa* 295
Rilke, Rainer Maria 10, 165, 222, 255, 257, 258, 259, 262, 318, 327, 328, 332–3, 426
Rose, Arthur 182
Rosenberg, Harold 398
Rosenthal, Tom 47, 201
Roth, Joseph 328, 329, 427
Roth, Philip 208, 215
Rousseau, Jean Jacques 15, 30, 85, 86, 177 n. 35, 298, 305, 349, 350, 352; *Confessions* 122, 350–1
Rowe, Josephine *Tarcutta Wake* 378
Rubens, Peter Paul *The Rape of the Sabine Women* 397
Rushdie, Salman 21–2, 165; *Imaginary Homelands* 431–2; *The Satanic Verses* 21–2
Russia/Russians, language and literature 10, 33, 137–46, 163, 164, 165, 323, 349–58, 391
Rutherford, Jennifer 192
Rylance, Mark 416

Said, Edward; *Orientalism* 93, 309
Samuelson, Meg 29, 364, 365
Sarlo, Beatriz 363
Schopenhauer, Arthur 278
Schreiner, Olive 9, 37, 161; *The Story of an African Farm* 154
Schulze, Leonard 45
Scott, Joanna 15–16
Sebald, W. G. 214, 328, 402
Secker & Warburg 20, 21, 46–8, 93, 96, 230 n. 11, 429
Segal, Erich 276
sex/sexuality 8, 33, 35, 61–2, 73, 141–2, 144, 193, 195, 211–12, 245–54, 276; inter-racial 21, 47, 81, 87
Shakespeare, William 58, 318, 380
Sharpe, Christina, 132
Sharpeville Massacre, the 18, 63, 397
Shaw, George Bernard 103, 361
silence 11, 67, 119, 152, 163, 214, 246, 248, 251, 332, 361–2, 374, 375. *See also* speech
Singer, Peter 211
Sisulu, Walter 18
slavery/slave(s) 85, 86, 118, 130, 154 n. 1, 251, 297–8, 360
Smit, Bartho *Christine* 310
Smith, Pauline 161, 305
Socrates 263, 285
Solzhenitsyn, Alexander 163–4, 353–4
Sontag, Susan 398
Sophocles 214
South African Broadcasting Corporation (SABC) 45
South African Human Rights Commission 23
South African Publications Control Board (SAPCB)/Directorate of Publications 21, 44, 46, 47, 93, 96
Soviet Union, *see* Russia
Soweto (Johannesburg townships) 20, 127, 172, 257, 260, 285, 319; Uprising 47, 94, 132, 134 n. 33
Spain 359, 365, 416
Spanish (language) 3, 16, 81, 85, 154, 194, 233–4, 359–60, 363, 365–6, 366 n. 3, 409, 430–1
speech 19, 48, 62, 118, 121, 195, 213, 223–4, 226, 252, 258, 429. *See also* silence
Spinoza, Benedictus de 85
Spivak, Gayatri 121, 148, 285, 299, 360
Stalin, Joseph 162, 163, 164, 353, 354
Stein, Gertrude 69
Stevens, Wallace 173, 175
Steyn, Jan 425–6
Stockenström, Wilma *The Expedition to the Baobab Tree* 309
Suzman, Helen 162
Svevo, Italo 322

INDEX

Swift, Jonathan 177 n. 75; *A Modest Proposal* 76–7, 289
Sylvester, David 397
Szymanski, Wojciech 398

Tal, Nitzam 339
television 7, 11, 127–9, 131, 133, 416
Texas, University of, Austin 19–20, 29, 33, 93, 268, 270, 295, 300, 420. *See also* Harry Ransom Humanities Research Center
theatre 174, 255, 333, 339, 419–20. *See also* Baxter Theatre
Thomas, Dylan 56
Thomas, Gladys 44
Tofighian, Omid 379
Tolstoy, Leo 10, 15, 36, 298, 349, 350–4, 356 n. 29; *The Kreuzer Sonata* 350
torture 20, 76, 91, 94, 96–8, 118, 256–7, 277, 281, 329–30, 378, 398
translation 49, 55, 165, 208, 209, 309–10, 328, 334–5, 415, 425–34
Truth and Reconciliation Commission (TRC) 23, 153, 154, 235, 340, 361
Tucker, Albert 377
Turgenev, Ivan 10, 163; *Fathers and Sons* 355
Twidle, Hedley 207

Uhlmann, Anthony 148, 149, 230 n. 7
United States of America 7, 16, 19–20, 23, 33, 45, 46–7, 49, 67, 73, 81, 128, 132, 160, 170, 214, 237, 267, 270, 322, 359, 365, 426
Universities, *see* Adelaide, Buffalo, Cape Town, Texas

Van den Heever, C. M. 161–2, 305–6
Van der Vlies, Andrew 22, 32, 43, 45, 47, 150, 154 n. 2, 185, 230 n. 11, 306, 328, 334 n. 9, 341–2
Van Niekerk, Marlene 312–13
vegetarianism/vegetarians 103–4, 106, 377, 401
Vietnam (and War) 19, 33, 45, 69, 70, 73, 74, 76, 78 n. 30, 164, 270, 309
Virgil (poet) 159; *Aeneid* 129, 159
Vital, Anthony 109

Vladislavić, Ivan 312
Voëlfontein (farm) 17, 307, 308
Volschenk, J. E. A. 399
Voltaire, François-Marie 185, 381
Vorster, John 163

Walkowitz, Rebecca 24, 360, 415, 430–1
Wallach, Yona 338
Walser, Robert 208, 209, 216, 328
Walsh, Rachel Ann 129, 132
Watson, Stephen 85, 95
Webern, Anton 397
Wehmeyer, Louisa 17
Wehmeyer, Piet 16
Weidmann, Brigette 429
Weil, Simone 237, 239
Weill, Kurt 339
White, Patrick 208, 322, 378
Wicomb, Zoë 312, 314 n. 25; *David's Story* 314 n. 35
Wilhelm, Cherry 85
Wilm, Jan 16, 36, 306, 418
Wiman, Christian 236, 237
Witbooi, Hendrik 208
Wittenberg, Hermann 49, 398, 417, 419
Wittgenstein, Ludwig 238, 408
Wood, James 407
Woods, James 182
Woolf, Virginia 378; *Mrs Dalloway* 378, 382
Wordsworth, William 164, 262
Wright, Derek 106
Wright, Laura 100, 170
Wright, Laura, Elleke Boehmer, and Jane Poyner, eds. *Approaches to Teaching Coetzee's* Disgrace *and Other Works* 5
Wright, Lucinda 106, 373

Yavin, Avraham 338

Zimbler, Jarad 48, 145 n. 8, 229 n. 2, 297; ed. *The Cambridge Companion to J. M. Coetzee* 5, 29
Zola, Émile 379